LIFE WITH THE ESQUIMAUX

LEIGHTON, BROS.

HALL ON HIS EXPLORING EXPEDITION.

LIFE WITH THE ESQUIMAUX

A NARRATIVE OF ARCTIC EXPERIENCE
IN SEARCH OF SURVIVORS OF
SIR JOHN FRANKLIN'S EXPEDITION

BY

CAPTAIN CHARLES FRANCIS HALL
OF THE WHALING BARQUE "GEORGE HENRY,"
FROM MAY 29, 1860, TO SEPTEMBER 13, 1862

WITH MAPS, COLOURED ILLUSTRATIONS,
AND ONE HUNDRED WOOD CUTS

CHARLES E. TUTTLE CO.: PUBLISHERS
Rutland, Vermont & Tokyo, Japan

Representatives
Continental Europe: BOXERBOOKS, INC., *Zurich*
British Isles: PRENTICE-HALL INTERNATIONAL, INC., *London*
Australasia: PAUL FLESCH & CO., PTY. LTD., *Melbourne*
Canada: M. G. HURTIG LTD., *Edmonton*

Published by the Charles E. Tuttle Company, Inc.
of Rutland, Vermont & Tokyo, Japan
with editorial offices at Suido 1-chome, 2–6
Bunkyo-ku, Tokyo, Japan

Library of Congress Catalog Card No. 70-87795

Standard Book No. 8048 0383-8

First Tuttle edition published 1970

PRINTED IN JAPAN

TABLE OF CONTENTS

CHAPTER I.

CHAPTER II.

CHAPTER III.

CHAPTER IV.

CHAPTER X.

CHAPTER XI.

CHAPTER XII.

CHAPTER XIII.

CHAPTER XIV.

CHAPTER XVIII.

CHAPTER XIX.

CHAPTER XX.

CHAPTER XXI.

CHAPTER XXII.

CHAPTER XXIII.

CHAPTER XXIV.

CHAPTER XXV.

CHAPTER XXXVI.

CHAPTER XXXVII.

INNUIT OR ESQUIMAUX CHARACTER, CUSTOMS, ETC.

LIST OF ILLUSTRATIONS

Drawn by CHARLES PARSONS, W. S. L. JEWETT, H. L. STEPHENS, GRANVILLE PERKINS, *and* S. EYTINGE, *after Sketches by the* AUTHOR, *Photographs, and from Implements and Clothing collected among the Esquimaux.*

COLOURED.

INTRODUCTION TO THE NEW EDITION

CHARLES FRANCIS HALL—high school dropout, blacksmith, engraver, stationer, journalist, incipient publisher, explorer and indefatigable enthusiast—conducted three strange and adventurous Arctic expeditions. Though these resulted in three books, probably none were actually written by him; they were, however, to a very large extent based on his extensive notes, diaries, and letters. Before he could embark on an envisaged fourth expedition, the fifty-year-old Hall mysteriously died in northern Greenland on November 8, 1871, leaving behind a widow, two children and countless pages of manuscript.

The mystery surrounding his death has been partially cleared during the late summer and the last few weeks of 1968 yet, at the same time, it has become more pronounced and puzzling. Hall himself suspected that he was poisoned and said so repeatedly after he drank a cup of coffee brought to him by the ship's steward; ". . . he was immediately taken very sick. He vomited a good deal, retching violently" and his left side was paralyzed. "An inquiry into the circumstances attending the death of Captain Hall was made after the return of the officers and crew of the *Polaris*" and in December 1873 the secretary of the U.S. Navy declared: "From the circumstances and symptoms detailed by [Dr. Emil Bessels of the U.S.S. *Polaris*], and comparing them with the medical testimony of all the witnesses, we are conclusively of the opinion that Captain Hall died from natural causes—viz., apoplexy—and that the treatment of the case by Dr. Bessels was the best practicable under the circumstances."

However, the mystery surrounding his death remained (there was some other evidence of his poisoning and of some strong ill-feeling existing on the *Polaris*). In 1938, Vilhjalmur Stefansson suggested that an autopsy could be performed since Hall's body was buried in permafrost. In 1967 the always ebullient Farley Mowat, never fearful that facts might interfere with his truths, simply declared that "there is not much doubt that he [Hall] was poisoned, probably with arsenic, by a dissident portion of his crew who neither shared his ambitions nor his belief in the adequacy of his new methods of coping with the defences of the Arctic." In 1968 both Stefansson and Mowat were proven right.

Dr. Chauncey C. Loomis, Jr. of the English Department at Dartmouth College, who at present is writing a biography of Hall, exhumed his body last summer. The initial autopsy— "performed [by Dr. Franklin Paddock] in the grave after the mummified body had been uncovered"—proved unsatisfactory, however, "samplings were taken from fingernails and hair to see if death could have been from arsenic poisoning." These samplings were subsequently sent to the Toronto Center for Forensic Sciences and examined there by Dr. A. K. Perkons. The tests on fingernails and hair revealed definite traces of arsenic and thus, exactly ninety-five years after the official declaration of the U.S. Navy, the scientific evidence of December 1968 points to only one conclusion: Hall *was* poisoned. Obviously, Dr. Loomis's biography of Hall will contain many answers to the questions opened up by this finding, including the "strong personal animosities aboard Hall's vessel" and that inevitably "in the closed atmosphere of a wintered-in ship, even mild dislike could be intensified to the point of violence." In this context it might be well to remember that on his second expedition Hall himself had, probably quite unnecessarily, killed a white man because he had thought that this man had endangered "his" expedition and its "success"!

Hall was indeed a very unusual man and in many ways his restless nature was the source of both his great strength and his conspicuous weakness. In addition to being of so restless a nature, he was as much a mystic as a fanatic and, at the same time, highly self-conscious of those traits as well as of his lack of education. Equally contradictory was his uncanny insight into the Eskimo mind and into natural phenomena, combined with his extreme intolerance and bigotry in relating them to his religious precepts and "calls."

For instance, he observes that "we Americans talk about 'freedom and independence,' but we are far behind these Northerners. While we are pleased with shadows, the dusky sons of an arctic clime enjoy the substance. They *will* do as they please, without anyone having the acknowledged right or power to say to them, Why do you do so?" A fine and noble thought indeed; but he then goes on and says with great sanctimoniousness: "The Esquimaux really deserve the attention of the philanthropist and Christian. Plant among them a colony of men and women having right-minded principles, and, after some patient toil, glorious fruits must follow." If Hall only knew the Arctic of today!

Yet in spite of these criticisms, his positive qualities—predominantly his enthusiasm and his perseverance—were outstanding. Most important of all was his belief and his proof that in order to survive in the Arctic one had to live as an Eskimo. A contemporary of his, Professor Silliman (what a wonderful name for a professor!) of Hartford, Connecticut, summed up Hall extremely well:

"Mr. Hall possesses much knowledge not found in books, the fruits of his own experience; the discoveries he made in the Polar Regions are regarded by geographers as of decided importance. Indeed, he did not himself realize that importance until since his return after more than two years' exile. No civilized man has, heretofore, been able to identify himself so completely with the Eskimos. Speaking their language and adopting their modes of life and of voyaging, he is enabled to reach with safety, and even with comfort, regions hitherto deemed inaccessible."

Life with the Esquimaux is precisely about that and had Sir John Franklin (for whom Hall had searched so strenuously in the first two expeditions) really lived according to these principles (as Hall assumed Franklin must have done), Franklin would hardly have become lost in the first place and Hall would never have needed to search for him! As it was, Franklin lived like a British officer and gentleman and he did get lost and not only Hall's but some thirty other expeditions were sent in search of him and his lost hundred and twenty men. And so it came that white men learned to live in the Arctic and with the Arctic, and much land that was unknown before became known and settled with philanthropists and Christians, and with "men and women having right-minded principles"! What has happened to this country is another story, somewhat less heroic than Hall's.

Hall's first book, by the way, appeared in two first editions with slightly different titles. *Life with the Esquimaux* was first published in England in 1864 by Sampson Low, Son, & Marston and was reprinted in 1865. The first American edition, published by Harper and Brothers in 1865 and reprinted in 1866, appeared under the title of *Arctic Researches and Life Among the Esquimaux* but is frequently referred to as Hall's *Arctic Researches*.

Hall's first journey covered the period of May 29, 1860, to September 13, 1862. His second voyage (on which he actually uncovered and secured a great deal of information on the lost Franklin party), lasted from June 30, 1864, to September 26, 1869; "but of this he left no narrative, becoming absorbed immediately on his return in preparing for his third voyage, that of the *Polaris*," during which his sudden death occurred on November 8, 1871, only slightly more than four months after his departure from New York. The second voyage was posthumously published by the U.S. government in 1879 as J. E. Nourse's *Narrative of the Second Polar Expedition Made by Charles F. Hall* (a definite misnomer, for his expedition dealt entirely with a renewed search for the lost Franklin party) and was based largely on Hall's journals, notes, letters and official dispatches. The third voyage, published three years earlier (1876) by the American government, became C. H. Davis's *Narrative of the U. S. Polar Expedition: U. S. Ship Polaris,*

Capt. Charles Francis Hall Commanding. Only part of this book is based on Hall's papers due to his early demise in November 1871.

While the last two books conspicuously indicate Hall's involvement as author, the first volume (with equal conspicuousness) deletes the name of William Parker Snow, its definite editor (if not ghost writer). This neglect led to a great deal of scandalous attacks and allegations by Snow, a somewhat cantankerous and ever paranoiac British adventurer, explorer, pamphleteer, author, editor and amanuensis who used his polemics to present himself as a victim of American persecution of British generosity and virtuousness (by the way, as an amanuensis, Snow transcribed the first two volumes of Macaulay's *History*).

From a fascinating article on Snow which appeared in *Polar Notes* No. VI, June 1966, I feel certain that Loomis's biography of Hall will contain a great deal of interesting material on the strained relations between these two strong-willed men. However, Snow was not the only detractor of Hall's considerable achievements. I fear that Hall has been the most neglected and underrated of all Arctic explorers and this reason alone might be sufficient for him to occupy a particularly soft spot in my heart. Arctic exploration and research is full of social and scientific snobbery and thus Hall's humble image as a self-educated, intuitive enthusiast provides a fascinating contrast with many of the more erudite and dignified explorers.

Still, there are many other exciting Arctic adventures waiting for republication. In the meantime publishers Tuttle in the U.S. and Hurtig in Canada are to be congratulated for embarking on such desirable ventures with Hall's first voyage.

University of Manitoba   GEORGE SWINTON
January 1969

PREFACE

BEFORE this book passes from the writer's hands into those of the reader, the author will be once more among the ice of the arctic regions. Though the last page of manuscript was written on the morning of his embarkation, the work itself has been no hasty one. He returned nearly two years ago from the expedition which he has endeavoured to describe. Almost every hour since then, which could be spared from the arrangements for his second expedition, has been devoted to the preparation of these volumes from his voluminous journal and notes taken on the spot.

Before dismissing the work, however, from his hands, he wishes to say a few words by way of explanation of certain matters connected with his explorations. The reader will perhaps wonder why so much importance was given to the discovery of the Frobisher relics. He answers, partly because of the interest which attached itself to the remains of men so long ago left in that waste land ; but partly, too, because the discovery of these remains, and the tracing of their history among the Esquimaux, confirmed, in a remarkable manner, his belief that these people retain among them, with great positiveness, the memory of important and strange incidents ; and as their traditions of Frobisher, when the author was able to get at them, were so clear, he is persuaded that among them may be sought, by one competent, with every chance of complete success, the sad history of Sir John Franklin's men.

To make himself competent for this more interesting and important research, the author patiently acquired the language and familiarized himself with the habits of the Esquimaux, and he now returns to their country able to speak with them, to live among them, and to support his life in the same manner that they do theirs; to migrate with them from place to place, and to traverse and patiently explore all the region in which it is reasonable to suppose Franklin's crew travelled and perished. The two intelligent Esquimaux, Ebierbing and Too-koolito, who accompanied the author on his return home, after remaining with him for two years, go back with him on this second voyage.

The author enters upon this undertaking with lively hopes of success; he will not, like most previous explorers, set his foot on shore for a few days or weeks, or, like others, journey among men whose language is unintelligible : but he will again live for two or three years among the Esquimaux, and gain their confidence, with the advantage of understanding the language, and of making all his wishes known to them.

The author cannot close without offering his thanks to the Artists for the beautiful and accurate drawings made by them, under his own eye, from his rough sketches ; and to the Engravers and Printers for their constant forbearance in the trouble he gave them, unaccustomed as he was to literary labours, yet anxious to obtain the utmost exactness in his narrative.

C. F. H.

June 30, 1864, *on board bark Monticello,*
bound for the Arctic Regions.

TOOKOOLITO, C. F. HALL, AND EBIERBING

LIFE WITH THE ESQUIMAUX.

INTRODUCTION.

As this book is to be a work of narrative and adventure, and not one of argument and discussion, I shall touch but very lightly upon those subjects which might lead to the latter, while I endeavour to give as much variety and as much fulness of detail as possible to the former.

That argument and discussion may arise from portions of what I advance is very probable ; but, if so, it will be better to enter upon such in another form than this. Readers very naturally expect to be entertained, as well as, perchance, instructed in what a voyager or traveller puts before them. Long, prosy dissertations are seldom wanted. All that most people require is a truthful report of personal doings in strange lands, and a faithful record of incidents, discoveries, and interesting events connected with them.

Such, then, is the task I have taken in hand, with the hope that a ready excuse will be granted for all those imperfections necessarily consequent upon the mode and manner of my carrying on the work in which I was engaged. I pledge myself as to the literal accuracy of what I state, and my readers will be able to see, as they move onward with me through my narrative, how difficult it was—alone, and with no other pair of hands, no other mind, no other thought, sense, or perception but my own—to record, day by day, the occurrences that came under my eye.

In addition to this, I had to make all the observations—scientific, geographical, and otherwise—by myself, and this, too, with a knowledge self-acquired, and with instruments so few, and most of them so imperfect, till rectified by myself, that my labours were increased many fold. Thus, in the following pages, let truth, variety of incident, and a faithful report of discovery and adventure be alone expected. Elegance of style and diction must not be sought for.

As it will be well to avoid, as much as possible, breaking in upon the thread of my narrative elsewhere, I here give some particulars as to the cause of my embarking on a voyage to the Arctic Seas.

It is well known that, for many years past, the whole civilized world has had its interest attracted toward the polar regions in consequence of the lamentable fate of the Franklin Expedition. The labours of Great Britain to discover what had become of her lost children, and the sums of money devoted to that purpose (no less than 2,000,000*l.* sterling), stand unparalleled in past history. Nor was America behindhand in the generous and humane work. That the missing navigators belonged not to her made no difference. The one general feeling was the same with reference to a desire for participating in the search after those who, having perilled themselves in devotion to science and the good of mankind, had become as brothers to us all. Hence the banner of Columbia floated to the breeze of an Arctic clime, side by side with England's proud flag, in the noble errand of humanity, for which a goodly fleet of some twenty vessels had been sent forth ! Of the many bright names already chronicled for their generous deeds in connexion with those arctic explorations, need I say that none stand more conspicuous than that of Henry Grinnell ? What he and others have done is so familiar to all men who know anything of this matter, that I need not recapitulate what has been so often told ; but I cannot let pass the mention of that one name here without expressing the warm emotions of my own heart. Henry Grinnell has been to me, as he has shown himself to all who were at work in the Franklin search, a true and noble friend. To him I feel more than ordinarily indebted. He not only helped me in my undertaking, but he has cheered me on, and spoken words of comfort and bright hope when my soul was often nearly overwhelmed. The memory of his generous kindness frequently sustained and helped to invigorate me anew, when wearied and exhausted in the wild regions I have lately been exploring. May every blessing, therefore, attend him and his, is my earnest and grateful prayer.

As to the search for Franklin and his brave comrades, who has not heard of its fruitless result ? Money and means expended without success ! Large ships and small ships, in magnificent expeditions, sent out vainly as to the recovery of those lost ! True, some discoveries were made, and certain relics and information brought to England by Dr. Rae in 1854, which gave a clue as to where the missing navigators could have been found; but not until Captain M'Clintock, of the British Navy, in the spring of 1859, visited Boothia and King William's Land, was anything for certain known. Then, at last, we were positively assured of the locality where these martyrs to science had been, when, as a discovered document proved, the ships were abandoned, and the majority of the crews had taken to the shore. This occurred in April, 1848, and 105 men, as we are told, under command of Captains Crozier and Fitzjames, landed at a given spot, with a view of making their escape, if possible, toward their native home. What became of them, except two skeletons found in a boat, and one other near the beach, has not yet been known. Supposition alone has induced the world to believe them all dead ; and, despite proof upon proof, from facts, experience, and sound logical reasoning to the contrary, the Government of England, and British naval officials, with some eminent exceptions, have discarded all idea of farther search, though the truth could now so easily be obtained, and the ground to explore so small and comparatively so easy of access !

I will not trouble the reader now with my reasons for making these statements, based, as they are, upon some years of careful study and examination of all that has been said and written upon the subject. Let me here briefly mention why I myself, with no previous experience, and no past history of my own to help me, took it up as I have done.

In one word, then, it seemed to me as if I had been *called*, if I may so speak, to try and do the work. My heart felt sore at the thought of so great a mystery in connexion with any of our fellow-creatures,—especially akin to ourselves,—yet remaining unsolved. Why could not their true fate be ascertained ? Why should not attempts be made, again and again, until the whole facts were properly known? Captain (now Sir F. L.) M'Clintock, in 1857-9, had gone forth once more to seek for some elucidation of this mystery, but still I felt that something more might yet be attempted toward co-operating with that brave officer. It was already known that his vessel, the *Fox*, had been caught in the ice and delayed a whole year. It was possible that she might still not be able to get through to her destination, and therefore I fancied the work could be more effectually done by an independent expedition proceeding in some other direction, afterward to join with M'Clintock, if need be, in his task. Accordingly, I conceived an idea that perhaps the British Government would lend, for a new American expedition, the arctic ship *Resolute*, which, having been abandoned in the ice, had drifted out, and was picked up in 1855 by Captain James Budington, of New London, who brought her to the States, where she was completely refitted at our national expense, and returned as a generous gift, in amity and good will, to England. I had heard that she was afterward dismantled, and laid up as a hulk in the River Medway, and I thought it possible she might now be loaned to us for another attempt to be made under the American flag. A printed petition to the British authorities was got up and signed by S. P. Chase, (then Governor of Ohio), U.S. Senator George Pugh, and Mayor Bishop, of Cincinnati ; but, before other names were attached to send it to England, M'Clintock returned with news of what he had discovered. What this was the civilized world is well acquainted with. He had obtained a few facts, but still left the matter very mysterious ! That it could have been otherwise was almost impossible by such a hurried and cursory examination of the ground as he made in spring, when the land is clothed in its winter's dress. Nor could he obtain much knowledge of the truth by a few casual interviews with detached parties of Esquimaux, through an interpreter who he himself says, " did not well understand them." No ; neither M'Clintock nor any other civilized person has yet been able to ascertain the facts. But, though no *civilized* persons knew the truth, it was clear to me that the Esquimaux were aware of it, only it required peculiar tact and much time to induce them to make it known. Moreover, I felt convinced that survivors might yet be found ; and again I said to myself, Since England has abandoned the field (I did not then know there were any fresh efforts in that country to renew the search), let *me*, an humble citizen of the United States, try to give to my country the glory of still continuing it, and perchance succeed in accomplishing the work. Accordingly, after mature consideration, I determined to make the effort. But how ? what were my means ? what the facilities for reaching the coveted goal of my ambition ? Cincinnati, where I then resided, was in a highly *civilized* part of the world, where ready transit from one place to another could be obtained; King William's Land, where I wanted to go, was in the *uncivilized* and distant regions of the frozen North ! What was I to do ? give it up ? Perhaps many would say, as some did say, " Yes, what have *you* to do with it ? why does it concern you ! Away with the idea ! " But not so ; my convictions were strong, and I could not resist the desire upon me. I determined, therefore, to try ; and, first of all, get what means were in my power, then find a way. Many before me had accomplished much in the world upon as slight a foundation as that of mine. What, then, was to hinder my making the attempt ? Courage and resolution were all that I needed ; and though some persons might not concur in the wisdom or prudence of my effort, still, as my mind was upon it, try it I would, and try it I did.

I need not enter upon all the many difficulties I encountered. These fall to the lot of every man who essays to try his hand at something new, and especially so if he starts on a path trodden without success before him. But difficulties sharpen the wit and strengthen the mind. The experience of my native land was before me in proof of what man could accomplish ; and I can now safely say that, though the obstacles in my way were many and great, I finally succeeded in overcoming them. How I surmounted those difficulties and started upon my voyage cannot be told at any length here. Suffice it that I began in Cincinnati by mentioning my hopes and wishes, and laying my plans before several of the leading men and other persons well known in that city. I also wrote a letter to Mr. George Peabody, of London, stating that, in the event of my not succeeding in any other way to reach the arctic regions, I would attempt it overland by the great Fish River. This, however, was only an idea formed in case I could not get a ship of my own, or a conveyance in one by the sea route.

On the 8th of February, 1860, I issued a circular, to which were attached upward of thirty signatures, and among them were the names of W. Dennison, Governor of Ohio ; of the mayor, R. M. Bishop ; of Miles Greenwood ; Senator Chase ; several other persons of note ; and Thomas Hickey, who was with Kane on the second Grinnell expedition. Mr. Hickey sent me a letter which, from its value as the opinion of one competent to judge, deserves notice. I here give an extract from it bearing upon my own ideas. He says :—

" During the residence of our party in the arctic regions, we experienced many severe trials ; but, I must say, the major part of them emanated from our mode of living. When we lived as Esquimaux, we immediately recovered and enjoyed our usual health. If Providence had so ordered it that we should not find our way back to civilization, but should cast our lot with Esquimaux, I have no doubt we would have lived perhaps quite as

long, and in quite as good health, as in the United States or
England. Had we lost our commander, I confidently believe
not one of our expedition would have returned. Our countrymen might have come to us, but we could not have come
to them. *White men can live where Esquimaux can,* and frequently *where* and *when* they cannot. This I know by experience. . . . .

"Little did I think, on returning to the United States with
my companions and beloved commander, that I would ever again
go to the north; but believing, on my soul, from a practical
life in the arctic regions, that you are right in entertaining the
opinion *that some of Sir John Franklin's men are yet to be found
living with the Esquimaux, and that they should be rescued and
restored to their country and friends,* I hereby cheerfully offer my
services, and volunteer as a member of the expedition you propose
to organize.

"For direct evidence of me, and my devotedness to this cause,
I would refer you to the written works of him whose memory
and name I almost worship—Dr. Kane."

This confirmation of my views was exceedingly gratifying,
but I had one sent to me which still more stamped upon my
mind the truth of what I had surmised in respect to the
Franklin Expedition. It was from Henry Grinnell, Esq., of
New York.

                              "New York, March 14, 1860.

"Mr. C. F. Hall.

"DEAR SIR,—Probably no one in this country is more desirous
of arriving at the truth relative to the fate of Sir John Franklin
and his party than myself. The fate of Franklin and some of
his officers and men is known by the record found on King
William's Land by Captain (now Sir F. L.) M'Clintock; but the
fate of 105 members of Franklin's Expedition, living on the
25th day of April, 1848, and many other matters important to
the history of that expedition, has yet to be determined.

"I believe some of the 105 may yet be found habitants among
the Esquimaux of Boothia, of Victoria, or Prince Albert Lands.
I farther believe that the graves of Franklin and some of his
officers and men, known to be dead, as well as the records of the
expedition and many important relics, will be found on King
William's Land, if search be made there in the months of July,
August and September.

"The course you propose to pursue is entirely a new and
important one, and I see not why, with the exercise of your

best judgment, you may not ultimately accomplish all that could be desired in satisfactorily determining many of the unsettled questions indicated above, as well as increasing our geographical knowledge of that portion of the arctic regions over which you propose to pass.

"You have my earnest wishes for the accomplishment of the noble object you have in view, and I will cheerfully contribute towards the requisite funds to carry it out.

"With great regard, I am your friend,

"HENRY GRINNELL."

After laying my plans before friends at Cincinnati, I at once started for the Eastern States, with a view of consulting men of experience in the arctic whale fishery, and also calling upon other persons to whom I had letters of introduction.

On the 14th of February I went to New London, where I had an opportunity of meeting many experienced whaling captains, among whom was Captain S. A. Brown, who was very warm and kind in reference to my plans. Captain Christopher Chappel, who had passed a winter in Northumberland Inlet, likewise gave me great hope and encouragement. So did Mr. Thomas W. Perkins, who allowed me access to the logs of various voyages made in the arctic regions by vessels belonging to the late firm of Perkins and Smith. But to Messrs. Williams and Haven, upon whom I called when at New London, I am especially indebted. In every possible way they tried to help me as to my plans; and they most liberally tendered me the well-known schooner *Rescue* (formerly of the first Grinnel Expedition) for $2,000.

I am also under great obligation to Mr. R. H. Chapel, of the same place, who then displayed—and has so ever since—an earnestness in everything connected with arctic research that commands my respect and esteem.

Other persons that I called upon in New London were Captains Sisson, Tyson, Quayle, and S. O. Budington, with whom I afterward embarked on my voyage. Captain Budington had brought to this country an intelligent Esquimaux, named Kudlago, whom I afterward fortunately secured to accompany me as an interpreter.

At Groton I called upon an individual named W. R. Sterry. He had been four voyages to the arctic regions, and spent three winters in Northumberland Inlet. I asked him, how long, at any one time, he had remained with the Esquimaux? His reply was, two months in the spring of 1855, thirty miles from the vessel, and with three families, consisting of about twenty individuals, living in three or four huts.

Sterry was able to give me a great deal of useful information, which all tended the more to confirm my views upon the subject of arctic exploration.

From New London I returned to New York, where the great kindness of Mr. Grinnell, and the friendly attention of several other well-known names, much encouraged me. Promises of assistance were made, and donations tendered toward my expedition. Here, by invitation, on March 8th, 1860, I attended an informal meeting of the American Geographical and Statistical Society, to explain my views and intentions. At the meeting I gave a brief statement of my ideas on the subject of Franklin's Expedition, and argued upon the great probability of some survivors yet being found. Soon after this, Messrs. Henry Grinnell, Miles Greenwood, and R. M. Bishop kindly became treasurers of the fund raising for my voyage, and it was now determined to adopt the following plan, which, I may here state, was the one I acted upon, so far as I could, throughout my whole undertaking. I give that plan as promulgated by me at the time. I said, " My object is to acquire personal knowledge of the language and life of the Esquimaux, with a view thereafter to visit the Lands of King William, Boothia, and Victoria; then endeavour, by personal investigation, to determine more satisfactorily the fate of the 105 companions of Sir John Franklin now known to have been living on the 25th day of April, 1848.

" I take with me an Esquimaux interpreter, and during my sojourn in the arctic regions shall employ a crew of natives for the boat accompanying me. With these natives I purpose starting from Northumberland Inlet, and proceeding up an arm of it that runs westward toward a lake not far from its extremity. This lake will be reached by crossing a small *portage*. I then shall traverse the ·lake to its western outlet, which by Esquimaux report, is a navigable river emptying into Fox Channel. On arriving at 'Fox's farthest' (lat. 66° 50′ N., long. 77° 50′ W.), I shall, if practicable, turn to the northward, proceeding on the east side of said channel to the Straits of 'Fury and Hecla,' thus uniting the discoveries of Fox in 1631 and Parry in 1821-3.

" On completing this work I shall cross the strait to Igloolik (lat. 59° 20′ N., long. 81° 53′ W.), and try to establish friendly relations with the community of Esquimaux known to congregate at that point. I will there and then decide, by the circumstances, whether to winter at Igloolik, return to Northumberland Inlet, or proceed southward on the east coast of Melville Peninsula to Winter Island, or to push my way directly westward across the Gulf to Boothia, to Victoria Harbour.

" During the winter and early spring, sledge-journeys will be undertaken with a view of acquiring a thorough knowledge of the country.

" When at Northumberland Inlet and other places, I shall carefully examine into the facilities for travelling, so as to decide upon the most practicable course to pursue in my efforts to satisfactorily and truthfully determine the history of the Franklin Expedition.

" To extend this undertaking to a favourable conclusion will require the assistance of my fellow-countrymen.

" This voyage is one I am about to make for the cause of humanity and science—for geographical discovery, and with the sole view of accomplishing good to mankind."

Shortly afterwards, Messrs. Williams and Haven, of New London, sent me the following most kind and generous proposal :—

" As a testimony of our personal regard, and the interest we feel in the proposed expedition, we will convey it and its required outfits, boats, sledges, provisions, etc., *free of charge*, in the barque *George Henry*, to Northumberland Inlet, and whenever desired, we will give the same free passage home in any of our ships."

This generous offer relieved my mind of a great difficulty, and most gratefully I accepted their kind proposition.

Having thus far succeeded in opening the way, I now gave directions for a suitable boat to be built.

Mr. G. W. Rogers, of New London, who had built the boats for the expeditions under De Haven, Kane, and Hartstene, was commissioned to build mine. Its dimensions were as follows : length, 28 feet ; beam, 7 feet ; depth, $29\frac{1}{2}$ inches ; and thickness of her planking, which was of cedar, seven-eighths of an ince. In form she was similar to a whale-boat, drawing only eight inches of water when loaded with stores and a crew of six persons. She had one mast, on which a jib and main-sail could be carried ; a heavy awning to shelter the crew at night or when at rest ; and the lockers for stores at each end were sufficiently large that a man could, if need be, comfortably sleep in either of them.   Five oars, and all other essentials, formed a portion of her equipment.   The sledge I took was made under my own eye in Cincinnati, as also a stock of pemmican.

I now returned to the West for the purpose of settling my affairs and preparing for departure.

The press gave a friendly notice of my intentions ; and a circular was issued by Mayor Bishop and Miles Greenwood, inviting my fellow-citizens to meet me at the Burnet House. This meeting took place on the 26th of April, and I was much gratified with its auspicious character.

Soon after this (on May 10th), I bade adieu to my home and friends—to all of human ties that I held dearest to my heart, and departed for New York.   Here I devoted the remaining time to various matters connected with my departure, constantly receiving advice and assistance from Mr. Grinnell.   Finally, on Saturday evening, May 26th, I left for New London to join the *George Henry.*   The funds for my expedition were, however, so low, that I found myself sadly deficient in many things that were almost absolutely necessary.   But, at the last moment, when this was known to Mr. Grinnell, he unhesitatingly supplied the deficiency.

On the 29th of May, accompanied by Mr. Grinnell and several citizens of New London, I stepped from the wharf, amid a crowd of friendly spectators, and entered the boat that was to convey me on board.   A few strokes of the oars, however, had only been made, when we returned at the voice of Mr. Haven hailing us.   It was to give me a present, in the shape of a little book called " The Daily Food," which, though small in size, was great in its real value, and which proved my solace and good companion in many a solitary and weary hour.

Once more bidding adieu to all on shore, the boat swiftly carried me to the ship, where preparation was being made for departure.   In a few moments more the steam-tug was alongside, and we were towed out to sea.   Then came the final moment of parting.   The last farewell had to be uttered—the one word that was to sever me for many months, perhaps years, from my country, my home, my friends !   Never shall I forget the emotions I experienced when the noble Grinnell came to take my hand and say, " Good-bye !   God bless you ! "   Hardly could I respond to his kind and earnest expressions towards me and on my behalf. With warm but trembling utterance, this truly great and good man spoke of the brave old navigators, and of those of our own times, who had often dared the perils of unknown seas, relying on their own stout hearts, it is true, but depending more on the aid and support of a SUPREME POWER. He bade me ever do the same, and commending me to that MIGHTY BEING, he once more, with moistened eye, said " Farewell ! " and hastily embarked on the tug that was to convey the visitors on shore.

The last link binding me to my own dear native land was now severed. The steamer cast off as we were passing Montauk Point, and then there arose one deafening shout from those on board, when three loud cheers were given for the name of Henry Grinnell ; and, as the echoes floated on the air, our good ship, now under sail, bore me rapidly away. Thus I left my country to try and accomplish that object upon which I had set my heart—namely, the solving of the yet unsettled mystery connected with the LOST FRANKLIN EXPEDITION.

CHAPTER I.

IT was on Tuesday, May 29th, 1860, that I departed from New
London, Conn., on my voyage in the barque *George Henry*.
We were accompanied by a tender, the *Amaret* schooner, for-
merly the far-famed *"Rescue"* of arctic celebrity—a name that
I intend to retain in speaking of her throughout my narrative.

The officers and crews of these two vessels numbered in all
twenty-nine persons; my expedition consisted of Kudlago and
myself, thus making a total of thirty-one souls leaving New
London.

As I shall have frequent occasion to mention some of the
ship's company by name, I here give a list of them and their
rating on board.

List of Officers and Crew.

S. O. Budington . .	Captain.	A. S. Bradley	Seaman.
Frank Rogers . .	1st Officer.	J. B. Neil	,,
A. J. Gardiner . .	2d ,,	J. Buckley	,,
Reuben Lamb . .	3d ,,	S. Willson	,,
Robert Smith . .	4th ,,	W. B. Russell . . .	,,
C. Keeney . . .	Boat-steerer.	J. Gray	,,
E. W. Morgan . .	,,	W. Stokes	,,
A. Bailey . . .	,,	W. Conley	,,
W. F. Roberts . .	,,	W. Ellard	,,
W. R. Sterry . .	{ Blacksmith and Cooper.	M. Silva	,,
		W. Johnson	,,
J. R. Hudson . .	Steward.	J. Bruce	,,
Geo. Beckwith . .	Seaman.	J. Antonio	,,
R. A. Comstock . .	,,	F. Silva	,,
H. Smith . . .	,,	J. Brown	,,

My outfit for this voyage, and for this whole of my expedition, consisted of—

The boat, already described; 1 sledge; ½ ton of pemmican; 200 lbs. Borden's meat biscuit; 20 lbs. "Cincinnati cracklings"—*pork scraps;* 1 lb. preserved quince; 1 lb. preserved peaches; 250 lbs. powder; a quantity of ball, shot, and percussion caps; 1 rifle; 6 double-barrelled guns, covers, and extra fittings, one Colt's revolver complete; glass beads, a quantity of needles, etc. for presents to the natives; 2 dozen pocket-knives and choppers; some tin-ware, 1 axe, 2 picks, files, etc.; a good supply of tobacco and pipes; wearing apparel for self, and red shirts for presents; a supply of stationery and journal books, etc.; 1 common watch; 1 opera-glass; 1 spy-glass; 1 common sextant and 1 pocket sextant; 1 artificial horizon, with extra glass and mercury; 1 azimuth compass; 1 common compass; 2 pocket compasses; 3 ordinary thermometers and two self-registering ones. Some navigation books and several arctic works, with my Bible and a few other volumes, formed my library.

This list, with a few sundries, constituted all the means and material I had to carry out the great undertaking my mind had led me to embark in. How far I accomplished aught commensurate with the ideas I had formed, let the sequel show; but, even had I wholly failed, assuredly it would have been excusable under such circumstances.

With regard to myself personally, now that the excitement of preparation was over, and I had time to think more and more of my task, a reaction took place, which produced that depression of mind always to be found in similar cases. This was soon increased by the horrible sensation of sea-sickness which I experienced for several days after our departure. What my feelings were may be judged by the following extracts from an irregular diary, the only work I could at that time perform. Writing on the fifth day out, I find myself saying,

" More miserable days than these past few have been to me it would be difficult to imagine. And why? Because of sickness—sea sickness. And what *is* sea-sickness? Can any one tell unless they have experienced it? I imagine not; nor, perhaps, can many describe it who have come under its infliction. I know that *I* cannot well do so. I have felt myself swung, tumbled, jammed, knocked, struck, rocked, turned, skewed, slewed, warped, pitched forward and backward, tossed up and down, down and up, this way and that way, round and round, crossways and kit-a-cornered, in every possible manner. On the ocean, fresh from civilized life, this may be called *sea-sickness,* but elsewhere I should term it next to a torturous death! No more terrible experience can a man have of life upon the broad waters than his first few days at sea when thus attacked."

Again, at a later date I find, " A miserable time I have had of it—ill nearly since we left; and now, as I write. my head is like a mountain of solid rock. Sea-sickness is really too bad, especially after eating, or trying to eat, a good dinner."

An ancient philosopher, on reviewing his work at the end of each day, and finding no special good acquired or accomplished, used to write down in his diary, " *Perdidi diem* "—I have lost a day. Alas for me, I had to repeat that in *my* journal for twelve days ! It is true that several times I recorded the temperature of the air and sea, the state of the barometer, and made various other observations whenever the weather would permit, but, nevertheless, so powerless did I feel for mental or bodily work, that at the end of each day I felt compelled to enter down as a sad but truthful fact, " *Perdidi diem.*" At length I quite recovered, and on the 9th of June, for the first time since leaving port, I felt as a man should feel, once more strong and capable of any exertion. I soon began to classify my labours, devoting so many hours to reading, to study, to writing, exercise, reflection, and sleep. As my buoyancy of spirits arose, and I watched the good ship bounding on her way over the sparkling waters, everything seemed full of life and animation. The Giver of all good was supreme upon the blue ocean as He was upon the shore. Even the " Mother Carey's chickens "—the little stormy petrels—sportively played about, no doubt happy in their way, as they danced up and down, slightly dipping the tips of their wings in the uneven waves, and then hieing away to absent mates, that they might be brought to greet the passing ship.

About a week after our departure, the cry was raised, " There she blows ! there she blows !" and, hurrying on deck, I for the first time saw at a distance the blowing of whales. What this " blowing " was like may be described by asking if the reader has ever seen the smoke produced by the firing of an old-fashioned flint-lock ? If so, then he may understand the appearance of the *blow* of a whale—a flash in the pan, and all is over. I watched with eager interest this school of " fin-backs," numbering some twenty-five or thirty whales—a rare sight to see so many together. But they are not generally attacked, as they are difficult to capture, and yield but little oil.

A day or two after this, a cry of " Porpoises !" brought all hands on deck ; and here a circumstance occurred, which, though trivial in itself, well serves to illustrate the unartificial character of one of the ship's company, the William Sterry previously mentioned. It is related in my journal as follows :—

" Directly the porpoises were seen, Sterry, who has a genial heart and strong arm, took his position by the martingale, or, as a Dane would call it, 'Dolphin Striker,' which is under the bowsprit. Harpoon in hand, there stood Sterry, prepared for a whale or aught else, ready for his blow. Now *Sterry* was *Sterry* —Sterry the cooper—Sterry the ship's carpenter—Sterry the ship's blacksmith—Sterry the millwright—Sterry the genius— the *immortal* Sterry, who could eat more pork and beans, and drink more whiskey out of a two-quart pantry pitcher, without distinguishing its smell and taste from that of pure cold water, than any other *gentleman* hailing from his native place of Groton. *There* indeed was Sterry, seemingly hanging between the heavens and the sea, his feet dangling on a tow line, and his hands grasping the martingale back-rope. While I stood watching him, his eyes appeared to roll in fire as they pierced the blue deep, especially so when he struck his head against the 'bobstay-chains' in turning to look for the contrast between the porpoises beneath him and the jibboom above. And here I may add that Sterry was a great philosopher on 'contrasts,' *pros* and *cons*; *positives* and *negatives* were with him the only 'hanimals that have souls worth saving. Well, there stood Sterry preparing to 'pucker,' and *pucker* he did. A strange sound, which arrested my attention, stole out of his mouth. Startled, I listened attentively, and found him actually *whistling for the porpoises !* But no porpoise seemed to listen to his charm. Often did he poise his harpoon as his intended victim glided swiftly through the waters beneath him, but as often did he have to drop it again. At length the porpoises retired, and Sterry had to give up his game.

"When the attempt was over, I asked Captain B. if Sterry's whistling really did any good, and the reply was, as I expected, 'No, none whatever.' Sterry at the time was within hearing, and immediately said, 'I guess-it-didn't-do-much-of-any-harm-any-how-captain;' and then, turning to me, added, 'Captain Hall' (so he always called me), 'I tell you what it is, Before you have been up North a great while, you'll find you've got to whistle as many whistles as there are species of *h*animals, birds, and fishes, or you can never get on up there; you can never capture such things unless you do whistle.'

"'But,' said I, 'please to tell me, Mr. Sterry, what do you do when you see a *whale ?* ' 'Oh, then we always *holler*,' was his quaint reply."

I have mentioned this anecdote as characteristic of the man. He was frequently the life and soul of our party, and often I shall have occasion to allude to him.

On the 12th of June we passed through a fleet of codfishing schooners on the Banks of Newfoundland. Hundreds of boats were out, with a man in each, rapidly appearing and disappearing to our view as the fog, which was very thick, lifted, or as we neared them.

The next day preparation was made, and a close look-out kept for icebergs, the thermometer having fallen rapidly; but none were seen. Two whales, however, caused some interest in our vessel, and especially to myself. They were moving leisurely along in the same direction as the ship, and nearly under the bows. Every thirty seconds or so they came up to blow, and then sank beneath the water, leaving only a few feet above their backs. I saw them distinctly for several minutes, without cessation, thus propelling their vast bulk through the great deep. It was a most novel sight to me to see these two whales simultaneously gliding side by side, and even with the ship. Had they been a pair of naiads harnessed to the car of Neptune, they could not have been more uniform in their movements. They came up together, " blowed " together, and descended together.

Meantime two boats were lowered, with a chosen crew, to give chase. Swiftly they shot toward their prey; but the whales immediately altered their course, the boats following after them. For an hour was the chase continued; but, in spite of all efforts, the whales escaped, and our disappointed comrades returned.

For several days after this, nothing of note occurred worth narrating. A delicate snowbird lighted on the rigging, and, according to nautical ideas, was the augury of good luck. Other marine birds and porpoises were seen, but there was little to relieve the monotony of our life except when the winds increased to a gale. Then, indeed, I found a change that in one respect I could admire. To myself, who had never before been upon the vast ocean, it was truly magnificent to behold the mighty workings of the great deep! On one occasion, which I well remember, the sea appeared in "white caps," the bounding billows playing with us all day in fantastic gambols, while the ship plunged fearfully down into a deep abyss; then, like a thing of life, would she leap skyward, as a mad wave struck the bow in all its fury, burying it beneath the sheet of spray, which flew far and wide in its impotent wrath. But the *George Henry* heeded it not. Like a lion shaking the dews of heaven from his mane, so did our good ship appear, bathed in crystal drops, but still driving on and on majestically. Rarely did I enjoy myself more than when these storms encountered us. It seemed to me as if no one could, to the fullest extent, appreciate the beauty, the grandeur, the greatness of God's creation but in experiencing a storm at sea. Watching it as I did, firmly wedged against the mast, with my arm encircling a cluster of ropes, I could keep my place, notwithstanding the vessel now and then would be on her beam-ends, or some fearful wave, overleaping the bulwarks, seek to take me away. And as I stood there, I could study Nature and Nature's God. As far as the eye could carry me, say for seven miles in every direction, making an area of over one hundred and fifty square miles, the ocean was dancing as if wild with joy. One moment it would seem as if a universal effort was being made by the waters to kiss the clouds; in the next, diving low, low down, as if to hide their laugh over the daring deed; then, as if to signify their unwillingness of my being so cool a spectator, the ship would be borne high up in their snowy arms, and all at once plunged quickly down into the bosom of the sea, covering myself and the decks with tons of briny water.

On the 19th of June we were in lat. 51° 18′ N. long. 49° 12′ W. and here I give a few extracts from my diary to show my ideas and feelings at the time.

" This day saw several of the large-sized whales, *Balœna Physalis,* called ' sulphur bottoms' by the whalers. It is indeed the *king of fishes,* though this term applies to the whale family in general ; but, being a very difficult kind to capture, whalers seldom venture in their chase. Less quiet and tranquil in its movements than the *Mysticetus,* or Greenland whale, it becomes furious when wounded, and renders an approach to it dangerous. Its flight, when struck by the harpoon, is exceedingly rapid, and is so long sustained that it is very difficult—generally impossible —to tire it out. The game is not worth the cost and risk, for the blubber and bone of the *Physalis* are indifferent in quality and quantity. I had a fine view of these monsters of the deep, as they came within pistol-shot of the vessel. It was a grand sight to me to see a fish (is a whale a fish?) 100 feet long propelling itself quietly forward through the water as though it were but an humble mountain trout.

" *June 20th,* lat. 53° 9′, long. 51° 16′.—A good run, with a fair breeze since yesterday. Approaching the north axis of the earth ! Ay, nearing the goal of my fondest wishes. Everything relating to the arctic zone is deeply interesting to me. I love the snows, the ices, icebergs, the fauna, and the flora of the North! I love the circling sun, the long day, the arctic night, when the soul can commune with God in silent and reverential awe! I am on a mission of love. I feel to be in the performance of a duty I owe to mankind—myself—God! Thus feeling, I am strong at heart, full of faith, ready to do or die in the cause I have espoused.

"This evening the sun set about ten minutes to nine o'clock, but it was quite light at ten o'clock.

"*Thursday, June 21st.*—This morning, a few minutes after eight o'clock, I went upon deck to take my usual exercise. I noticed or felt a perceptible change in the temperature of the air. I looked at the thermometer and saw that it was falling. I tried the sea-water, and found that much colder also, being only two degrees above freezing point. I immediately concluded that we were near icebergs, and mentioned it to Captain B. also to Sterry; but, though the latter had been on several voyages to the arctic regions, and had spent four winters there, he doubted my ideas about it, especially when I ventured to predict we should see them within three hours. He said 'we should not,' and even laid a wager upon it; but at twelve o'clock the icebergs were really seen, and many of the old salts on board at once set me down as well up in arctic knowledge.

"Directly the announcement was made I went on deck, and there, far away to the west, had my first view of an iceberg. By the aid of a good glass, presented by M'Allister and Brothers, of Philadelphia, the grandeur of this icy mountain of the deep was brought before me. Brief, however, was the glance I had. The motion of the vessel was such that I could not at first keep the iceberg within the field of the glass. But perhaps it was well I did not see all its splendour and magnificence at once. For years I had longed to see an iceberg, and, even in the distant view I then had, all my conceptions of its grandeur were more than realized. When first seen it was perhaps ten miles off, and appeared about 130 feet high, judging from a calculation made. As, toward evening, we approached, it appeared a mountain of alabaster resting calmly upon the bosom of the dark blue sea. Behind it was the setting sun just dipping its nether limb in the waters, while its upper reached some thick, heavy clouds extending half around the horizon, bathing them in a flood of crimson! Close by, and peering out from a break in the sky, were Venus and the new moon, making a scene of sublimity and beauty fit for a poet's pen or the pencil of an artist.

Not before ten o'clock P.M. were we alongside this magnificent pile of ice, and then, as it were, I had an opportunity of shaking hands with the first iceberg I had ever seen. It is said that lovers like darkness better than light, and the hour named would seem to indicate that darkness was upon the face of the deep when I and my 'idol' met. But not so; light abounded : not that of noonday, but that of early eve, when the sun had withdrawn his glowing face. Then it was we met. Iceberg was silent ; I too was silent. I stood in the presence of God's work. Its fashioning was that of the Great Architect! He who hath builded such monuments, and cast them forth upon the waters of the sea, is God, and there can be none other!"

After this, numerous icebergs were seen, one of which we passed within a stone's throw. At a distance it had appeared of a pyramidal form, but on coming close its outline wholly changed. This I find to be a characteristic of almost all views—of none more strikingly so than that of an iceberg. "Distance lends enchantment to the view," so goes the old saw, and, to a certain extent, this is true.

But, on another occasion, I had a more minute inspection of one of these icy monsters of the deep. A large solitary berg at one time was not far from us, and, as the weather permitted, a boat was sent in charge of the mate that I might have the opportunity of examining it.

On arriving near, it was found of irregular form at the base, with several " tongues " or spreading pieces below the water. With some difficulty I got on to it at a sloping part, and began to mount toward the summit. Several pinnacles, ravines, gorges, and deep cavities were displayed as I ascended ; but decay was already making rapid progress, and evidently not long would elapse before the whole mass must fall to pieces. I succeeded, however, in reaching the top without danger, using a boat-hook as a sort of alpenstock to aid me.

Here resting awhile, and drinking in the ocean scene around, with our ship on the blue waters awaiting us, I then descended.

On the way down I unfortunately trod on the rusty part of the boat-hook, and having my boots off for surer footing, received a rather bad wound, which confined me to a couch for some days.

Our progress towards Greenland was so tantalizingly slow, owing to calms and head winds, that a fourth Sunday passed over us while still at a considerable distance from Holsteinborg, Greenland, the port of rendezvous of the *George Henry* and *Rescue.*

Of these Sundays at sea it gives me pleasure to speak in favourable terms as to their observance on board. The crew exhibited most excellent demeanour; and as the *George Henry* had a small but carefully-selected library in the cabin, furnished by the house of Williams and Haven (owners of the vessel), good books were occasionally distributed by the captain among officers and men, much to their satisfaction, and, no doubt, advantage.

ASCENT OF AN ICEBERG.

Again referring to my Journal:

"June 26th, at midnight, I witnessed a scene never to be forgotten. I found the whole north illuminated—not by the aurora borealis—but by the reflection of the sun's rays. The northern sky presented the appearance of a sunset perhaps twenty minutes over. I could hardly believe my eyes and my position as to the points of the compass for some time. It did not seem that the morning sun could thus early be approaching in the east, nor did it seem that the brightening before me was either *east or west*. But I soon found the cause that so attracted my attention was the *northern sun!* I was indeed delighted; for, though familiar with the theory of our planetary system, yet I had little thought of the beauty and variety of sun scenes presented to the view of man between the latitudes of Cincinnati and that of $58\frac{1}{2}°$, where we then were.

"Early in the morning, the captain came to my berth, and called me, saying that a sail was in sight, and that he was holding up for her. I was on deck in an instant with spy-glass in hand. All the men were on the alert, and every eye strained to discover what vessel it was. Our own colours were soon run up, and they were answered by the unknown showing the Danish flag. This immediately enlightened us, and we at once knew that the stranger was one of the government vessels of Denmark annually visiting Greenland. We laid-to for her, and, when she came near, ascertained her name to be the *Mariane*, from Copenhagen, bound to Disco. Our captain then sang out, ' What's your longitude ? ' Whereupon the lusty old Dane hung over the brig's side a ponderous ebony board, upon which was chalked in white ' 49° 20″.' Thus holding it a moment, we saw him turn his head broadside to us, and encircle his massive ear by his trumpet-shaped hand, as if to say, ' Now let us have yours.' In stentorian voice, the answer was ' 53° 30′.' If a forty-pounder had been shot from the *George Henry*, the old Scandinavian commander could not have jumped higher than on this announcement. Then giving our ship to the glorious breeze that was dancing to do us service, away she bounded on her course. As long as we could see the *Mariane* of Copen-hagen—a vessel bearing the royal F. R., wreathed by laurel branches, and crested by the imperial crown—she was still following in our wake."

It may be as well here to mention that this *Mariane* was the identical vessel in which Dr. Kane and his party, after their memorable escape on the second Grinnell Expedition, took passage from Upernavik, intending to proceed home in her *via* England. But, on touching at Goodhavn, Captain Hartstene, in the Relief Squadron, arrived in time to receive them, and thus prevented a longer voyage in the Danish brig.

"*Friday, June* 29*th*. During the night a smart breeze sprung up from the N.N.W. which now continues, doing us much service in putting us to the north. There is rain, and it is chilly ; but what of this to a determined soul ? Oh, to be strong from the circumstances ; to be excited from the powers of the mind ; to be inspired, as it were, by the Divine Spirit, that I may continue to the end of life in my studies of Nature and her laws ! May I be strong in the day of battle ; may I not forget that I am a child of Deity—a humble instrument created for work !

"*Saturday, June* 30*th*.—In a conversation with Captain B.

and his first officer, Mr. Rogers, this morning, I learned their views of the scurvy. They both understand the cause, the nature of it, and its cure. The former said he had gained his knowledge from dearly acquired experience. This is truly a fact, for in 1855, while in command of the *Georgiana*, on a whaling voyage, he lost thirteen of his men by scurvy. But, said he, ' I am not afraid of losing any more men by scurvy while I have command over them. Whenever there are appearances of it aboard, I will have every pork and beef barrel—salt provision of every kind—headed up at once, and every man shall live upon bread and *fresh* provision, such as whale, walrus, seal, deer, bear, ptarmigan, duck, &c. &c.'"

Mr. Rogers stated that in 1856, he went on a whaling voyage to the South Sea, and that during the year scurvy broke out among the crew. Nine were seriously affected, and one died of it, all from eating salt provisions. Said he, " Those who had it seemed *determined to die*, for, against all reasoning and advice, they would have salt pork in preference to fresh game, such as ducks, eggs, &c. which they had in abundance."

It may be here stated as a fact that the person who has the scurvy desires just that kind of food which he should not have, and, as a general rule, the same person affected will go almost any length to obtain it, notwithstanding he is well aware that death must follow in this contumacious course.

I now approach a subject that, even at this present time, in dwelling upon it, affects me greatly. I allude to the death of Kudlago, which occurred on Sunday morning, the 1st of July. Hitherto I have said but little concerning him, owing to an intention of confining my remarks to what I should have to narrate here.

I have mentioned in the Introduction that he had been brought to the United States in the previous autumn, and when I first saw him he appeared to be, what I always found him, a remarkably modest and unassuming man. From what I was then informed, he was quick to learn, and always endeavoured to do as other people did. He never expressed surprise at anything. He looked upon the works of civilization with interest, but never with wonder. The first time he saw a locomotive no words escaped his lips, nor did he exhibit any signs but what were consistent with the idea of his having seen the same a thousand times before. One day, while riding in the cars toward New York, a boy passed through, distributing circulars, giving one to Kudlago. He took it, looking attentively to see what

others might do, and then, as they did, so, to all appearance, did
he ! Others held the circulars up before them and read.   Kudlago held his up before his eyes and appeared to read.   Though
he could not read a word, yet he looked learned.   Solomon may
have been wiser, but surely not *sharper* than Kudlago.

KUDLAGO.

On.securing his services as my interpreter, I was in hopes that
he would long remain with me ; but, though apparently in good
health on leaving New London, the fogs we encountered when
crossing the Banks of Newfoundland gave him a severe cold,
and, though every attention was paid to him, he was evidently
failing very fast.   One day we shot an eider-duck, and lowered
a boat to get it, purposely that Kudlago might have a generous
meal in his accustomed way.   The bird was skinned and carried
to the poor sick Esquimaux, who dissected it at once, eating
only the heart and liver, *both raw.* He seemed to relish it
greatly, but could eat no more.   As he expressed a desire to be
on deck, a tent was erected there, that he might enjoy the sunshine and the air.   But nothing availed to save him.   The following day he was again taken below, and never again left his
berth alive.   He died about half-past four on Sunday morning.
His last words were, " *Teik-ko se-ko ? teik-ko se-ko ?* "—Do you
see ice ? do you see ice ? His prayer was that he might arrive

BURIAL OF KUDLAGO.

home, and once more look upon his native land—its mountains, its snows, its ice—and upon his wife and little ones; he would then ask no more of earth. We had sighted the Labrador coast on our way, and after that we sailed several days without seeing ice. Kudlago kept incessantly asking if we saw the ice, thinking, if so, we must be near to his home; but, poor fellow, he was still far away when his final moments came. He died in lat. 63° N. when near the coast of Greenland, and about 300 miles from his native place.

Suitable preparations were soon made for his burial in the sea, and as I had always thought a "burial at sea" must be a scene of great interest, the one I now witnessed for the first time most strongly impressed itself upon me. Never did I participate more devoutly in what then seemed to me the most solemn scene of my life. There before us was the "sheeted dead," lying amidships on the gangway board, all in readiness for burial. The whole ship's company, save a solitary man at the wheel, had assembled in sorrowful silence around our departed friend, to pay the last respect we could to him. By the request of Captain B. who was bound by strong ties of friendship to Kudlago, I had consented to take an active part in the services. I therefore proceeded to make such remarks as were deemed proper for the occasion. These were succeeded by my reading portions of appropriate exhortations from the "Masonic Manual," after which I read a prayer from the same excellent work. In this all seemed deeply, solemnly interested.

During these services the breezes of heaven were wafting us on—silently, yet speedily to the north. At a given signal from the captain, who was standing on my right, the man at the helm luffed the ship into the wind and deadened her headway. William Sterry and Robert Smith now stepped to the gangway, and holding firmly the plank on which was the shrouded dead— a short pause, and down sank the mortal part of Kudlago, the noble Esquimaux, into the deep grave—the abyss of the ocean! Oh what a scene! How solemn in its grandeur and its surroundings! The Sabbath morning; a cloudless sky; the sun shining in all its glory; the cold, dark blue ocean, its heaving bosom whitened over, here and there, with high pinnacled bergs; the lofty peaks of "Greenland's icy mountains" peering down from a distance in the east—these were some of the impressive features in the scene attending the burial of Kudlago at sea.

An hour after the *George Henry* had been given to the leading wind, I turned my eyes back to the ocean grave of Kudlago—a snow-white monument of mountain size, and of God's own fashioning, was over it !

KUDLAGO'S MONUMENT.

The next event of any importance to record was the celebration of our glorious FOURTH OF JULY, At that time we were in Davis's Straits, near a place called *Sukkertoppen*, in Greenland, under all sail for Holsteinborg, and we had been in great hopes to have arrived during the day, but contrary winds and calms prevented us. As it was, we did the best we could, and tried to prove ourselves, as we knew all of us to be, true sons of our country.

The day, commencing at the turn of the midnight hour, was ushered in by cheers and firing of guns. Pistols, guns, blunderbusses, were in readiness for the word that should make the mountains of old Greenland echo back our thunderings for FREEDOM AND OUR NATIVE LAND !

As the hour approached, several of us were stationed at various places, ready to discharge the weapons in our hands at command. Twelve o'clock came, and the Fourth of July, 1860, was upon us. "One! two!! three!!! Fire!!!!" was the signal; and never did the *George Henry* quiver more under the peal of deep-throated guns, in a noble cause, than on that occasion. After this the jubilee was continued by firing, and cheers on cheers. The national colours were run up (for it was now broad daylight) and saluted. At noon another salute was given, and again twelve hours afterward, when the next midnight proclaimed that another anniversary of American independence had again departed.

But we had other causes of rejoicing on this especial day. At five in the evening we had arrived at a point on the coast of Greenland which was very much like the neighbourhood of Holsteinborg. The bold mountain peaks were so thickly enveloped in clouds that it was impossible to determine the exact locality. The sea also was covered with fog; hence it was wisely determined to run off the land for the night and lie-to. This was done, and as we were upon good codfish banks, lines were put over to catch some. We were very successful. Before twelve o'clock three lines had drawn in full 800 lbs. of halibut and codfish, the latter largely predominating. I myself caught four cod weighing in all 100 lbs. One halibut weighed no less than 125 lbs. and two others fifty pounds each! I was astonished at the sight of every cod drawn in. Such gormandizers had they been—preying upon the smaller ones of their kind—that their stomachs were distended to the utmost limit of expansion.

The next day, July 5th, we once more stood in toward the land, but it still continued foggy, and we were unable to get near till about 4 P.M. having just before again sighted the *Mariane*. At that time two Esquimaux were seen coming at full speed toward us. In a few moments more they were alongside, and hoisted—kyacks and all—into the ship. Their names were "Samson" and "Ephraim," each 5 feet 6½ inches in height, with small hands, small feet, and pleasing features, except that both had some of their front teeth gone. These men had brought an abundance of salmon, caplins, sea-birds, &c. and eagerly began to trade with us. Speedily we were on the most friendly terms, and, as they were retained to pilot us in, merry-making was the order of the day. On entering the cabin to supper their conduct was most orderly, and when it was over they said, in good English, "Thank you."

That night I had not long retired to rest before the captain came and told me it was calm, and a good opportunity for halibut and codfish. I was quickly dressed and on deck with line in hand. Two or three minutes more, and a halibut weighing about 225 lbs. was fast to my line, fifty fathoms deep, and in another two minutes I had the fish up in the sun's rays with harpoon stuck through him. In one hour a ton weight of codfish and halibut was taken by the use of only three lines. Sometimes, as I was informed, halibut have been caught weighing 500 lbs. each, and measuring eight feet in length. The Esquimaux in Greenland use the transparent membrane of the stomach of this fish instead of plates of glass.

During the night our two faithful Esquimaux kept on deck, watching the almost obscured mountains, that they might guide us aright. Their clothing was quite wet from exposure to the high seas that prevailed when they came to us, but they sat themselves down on deck, and there watched, coughed, and quivered. I thought, at the time, it were better if they could be prevailed upon to adopt the custom of our seamen—always on the move when out in the open air; but I understood they look upon our walking to and fro as foolishness—a great amount of hard work, with much expenditure of tanned skins (shoe-leather) and muscle all for naught!

For about an hour, one of the Esquimaux made his way up into a whale-boat and went to sleep. On waking, he seemed quite thankful for the luxury of sleeping, though in the open air, his bed, for several days past, having been on the soft side of a boat, on the rocks of an island forty miles distant from Holsteinborg. He and his companion had been there engaged in hunting ducks, &c. when they discovered the *George Henry*. They were very ragged, and Captain B. presented each with some new garments, which made them truly thankful. Some of the articles were new pants, and each man immediately put on a pair. Samson's was a fair fit—that is to say, they were tight as a drum upon him; but Ephraim's! the waist would not meet within six inches. This, however, was all the same to him. He drew a long—very long breath; so long, indeed, that I could not but think him like a whale, breathing once in ten minutes, or, if occasion required it, once in an hour! Then, following this, Ephraim ceased for a moment to breathe at all, while he nimbly plied his fingers, and rapidly filled each button-hole with its respective button. Pants were now on and completely adjusted —*buttoned!* but as every living thing must have air or die, and as whales, when coming up to breathe, make the regions round about ring with the force with which they respire and inspire, so even an Esquimaux has to take in fresh draughts of oxygen, or he ceases to exist. Now Ephraim had, in buttoning his pants, suspended respiration for some time longer than nature was capable of sustaining. Accordingly, Nature resumed her functions; and, in the act of giving a full respiration, Ephraim's pants burst, the buttons flying all over the deck ! Civilization buttons and New London-made pants could not stand against the sudden distention of an Esquimaux's bowels after being once so unnaturally contracted. Here the saying of old Horace would be useful : *Naturam expelles furca tamen usque recurret*—You may turn Nature out of doors with violence, but she will return ; and he might have continued—though the violence be an Esquimaux's bowels much contracted by a pair of New London-made pants of the nineteenth century !

I will now again quote from my Journal :

" *Saturday, July 7th.*—After dancing around the harbour of Holsteinborg for many hours, we have at length made anchor within it.

" During the last two or three days a fog of remarkable character has troubled us in making harbour. All at once the whole heavens would be clear and bright ; in five minutes a thick fog would encircle us all around, closing from our view sunlight, the long ridge of Greenland mountains, the well-defined sea horizon, islands, and icebergs.

" Before coming to the North, I thought I was prepared to give a fair statement of the true theory of fogs. I now am satisfied that no one can give a satisfactory reason for the appearance and sudden disappearance—their reappearance and final dispersion, as I have witnessed them during the last four days.

" At five o'clock this morning a Danish pilot came on board, who understood fully his business, which is more than I can say of the two Esquimaux, Samson and Ephraim. Though they have shown great faithfulness, far beyond that of white men (as a general statement), yet I cannot award them great praise in navigating large ships in their own and neighbouring waters.

" Last night was a happy night for me. No sunset. The slow descending sun, just dipping its edge in the Northern Sea, then hesitating in its course, then slowly mounting again into high heaven, gladdening my whole soul near to uncontrollable joy !

" The incidents connected are worthy to be recorded. The evening (at least after ten o'clock) was fine ; sky as clear as a bell ; the air cool and invigorating.

" I found, by a hasty calculation, that we had made the

northing, which would allow us to see the sun continually when clear weather; that the sun would gladden our sight day after day without setting. I announced to all hands that the sun would not go down that night; that on such a moment it would commence to return—to rise again. This was a novelty to many of the ship's crew. I then made my calculations carefully as to time—the hour, minute, and second when the sun would arrive at its lowest meridian. This was necessary, that I might determine, as well as the circumstances would admit, the variation of the needle.

" Twelve o'clock, low meridian, midnight—I use this in distinction of high meridian, midday—was approaching. Every man, captain, and the ship's officers and crew, save the portion of watch off duty below and asleep, stood around me awaiting the anxious moment when the sun would cease its downward and commence its upward course.

" The *George Henry* was sweeping gently along, beating up northerly and easterly against the wind. From the larboard side we peered out upon the glorious scene. With my azimuth compass resting upon the bulwarks, my eye every other moment on it and the watch (the latter had just been placed in correspondence with the ship's chronometer below), I at length announced the wished-for moment—12 o'clock. Cheer—cheer upon cheer followed from the ship's company. Time passed on; the sun was slowly on its upward track. At first its motion was imperceptible; nevertheless, it was rising.

" I continued to watch the upward and onward progress of the sun. Its northern declination is now growing less and less, therefore the sun's presence here is less and less prolonged. Soon the arctic night will take the place of the arctic day, which is now fast clothing the mountains in green and flowers.

" Before we finally entered Holsteinborg Harbour, the *George Henry* beat up against the wind by tacking ship four or five times. At last the hour came when the position of the ship was pronounced by the Danish Esquimaux pilot—*Lars Kleijt* by name—to be good—very good. The morning was all that a high-bounding spirit could wish. I had turned in about two o'clock A.M. and was now greatly refreshed from a short sleep. When I arose the vessel was bending her beak toward the long-wished-for haven. Every one was on tiptoe with the joyousness of the present. An inquiry had passed back and forth why the natives did not come to meet us, as they were wont to meet American and English vessels. While yet far off, some one exclaimed, 'There they come!' Every eye was quickly turned that way. I saw them at a distance coming swiftly in their kyacks. Their number seemed legion. On they came. They meet us, and greet with smiles. The *George Henry* kept her course ; the kyacks followed in our wake. We looked forward ; others and others were coming, as if to welcome us to their bay and homes.

" As we neared the land, how eagerly I sought to catch every view that was within sight. My eyes wandered far back to the most distant mountain ; then I brought them quickly to those which seemed about to shake hands with me, piercing into their nooks and their time-worn rocks—now up their pinnacles, now down to their broad massive bases. I was happy.

" We saw the little Danish flag on the hill that stands as sentinel to the rock-ribbed bay. We passed on ; the western ridge, that runs far out into the sea, stole away the winds which were so gracefully carrying us to our chosen port, yet enough favoured us to go slowly. Soon Holsteinborg, in all its imperial greatness, met our eye. 'Tis true, Holsteinborg was not gaudily attired, as some kings' palaces are ; but there she was and *is*, sparkling in diamonds of pure water, radiating rainbows in continual sunlight. There she was and *is*, surrounded by walls more ancient than Jerusalem, or Thebes, or Babel's Tower—of God's creation—mountains that seem to prop up this arctic sky —mountains whose southern sides are now clothed in green and laughing flowers, and whose northern slopes rest beneath a bed of white.

" As we entered the harbour, our national colours, streamer, and ship's flag were raised, and the Governor of Holsteinborg responded by hoisting the Danish ensign. Then, at 10 A.M. of this day, the 7th of July, 1860, and the fortieth day from the port of New London, United States, we came to an anchor. Had it not been for head winds and calms, we might have made the passage in twenty-five to thirty days. Captain B. has made it in thirty-four ; he says it generally takes about thirty. As it is, we have reason to thank God for His care and protection over us in this voyage. Oh, may He continue His blessing ; may He be near unto me while in the prosecution of the great work before me ! With Thee, O God, I can accomplish much ; without Thee, what am I ?—nothing ! nothing ! !"

The *Rescue* schooner—our consort and tender—had not arrived. Her orders were to keep with us if possible ; but on the night of Thursday, 31st, the third day out, during the prevailing fogs and wind, we lost her. The rendezvous, however, was at this place, and we daily expected to see her.

CHAPTER II.

Land and visit the Governor—Brief History of Greenland—The Holsteinborg District—Esquimaux and European Population—Protection and Care of the Natives by the Danish Crown—Plagues of Greenland—Dinner at the Governor's—M'Clintock's Work—The Priest's Wife—Visit the Government Buildings—Arrival of the "Rescue"—Lars's Care for his Family—Dance on Shore—A Mountain Excursion—Action of Freezing Water in Crevices—Esquimaux Amusements—Schools and Printing.

IMMEDIATELY after we had dropped anchor, great excitement reigned on board. Some of us at once prepared for the shore, dressed in accordance with our home fashion of forty days ago, the captain and I intending to visit the governor. On landing, my heart leaped with joy as I touched the firm earth, and I could not help taking in my hands some of the rocky fragments on the beach, and saying, "Thank God, I am at last on arctic land, where I have so long wished to be! Greenland's mountains, I greet you!"

As Captain Budington had met the governor before, my introduction to him was easy. It was in the afternoon when our visit took place, and Governor Elberg received us with much kindly warmth. But the events that occurred during our stay were so various, and have been so minutely narrated in my private diary day by day, that I must try and introduce them as much together as I possibly can, first giving a brief sketch of what relates to Holsteinborg and its vicinity.

The early history of Greenland is generally well known, yet a brief *résumé* of it may not be uninteresting to the reader. In many respects it borders upon romance, as indeed all the old Scandinavian chronicles do, but well-attested facts state nearly as follows :—

About the middle of the tenth century, one Gunbiörn, an inhabitant of the previously settled Iceland, discovered land to the west, and, on returning, made a report of what he had seen. Soon afterward, in the year 983, a person known as "Eric the Red," was sentenced by the Icelanders to banishment for the crime of manslaughter, and he determined to visit the country

Gunbiörn had discovered. Sailing westward in a small vessel, he arrived at the new land, and coasted it toward the south; then turning a point now known as Cape Farewell, he came to an island, where he passed his first winter. He then remained three years exploring the coasts, and finally returned to Iceland, where he gave such a report of " Greenland," as he termed the new country, that it induced many of the colonists of both sexes to go back with him. Only some of these reached their destination, the rest turning back or perishing by the way. A colony was now formed, and communication kept up with Iceland, and even with Norway. Leif, the son of Eric, went to the latter place, and, by command of the king, was instructed in the Christian religion, whence he was afterward sent back, attended by a priest, who baptized Eric and all his followers.

In the year 1001, one of the colonists, named *Bjorn*, was accidentally driven in his ship to the southwest of Greenland, and discovered a new country covered with wood. On his return, Leif fitted out a vessel, and, with Bjorn as pilot, went in search of this new land. He found it as described, and termed it *Vinland*, which there can be no doubt must have been part of North America, about the latitude of 45°.

Meanwhile the colonists of Greenland increased in number and prosperity. In 1121 Arnold was elected the first bishop, and several churches were built. After this no less than seventeen bishops are known to have been elected from first to last, and the two settlements of East and West Greenland (into which the colonists had divided) numbered about three hundred villages. They had their little barques going from place to place along the western coast so high up as lat. 73°, and even, as is supposed from ancient records and from Runic inscriptions seen there, to the entrance of the present-named Wellington Channel.

For a long time after this the history of these colonists is involved in obscurity. Intercourse with Europe was obstructed about the beginning of the fifteenth century, and whether the colonists were cut off by hordes of the Esquimaux from the north or west, or were destroyed by a pestilence, is yet uncertain. There is, however, a document extant, discovered by Professor Mallet in the papal archives, which seems to warrant the idea of a hostile fleet " of wild heathen " having made a descent upon the colony, fell upon the people, " laid waste the country and its holy buildings with fire and sword, sparing nothing but the small parishes, and carrying captive the wretched inhabitants of both sexes." Nothing, however, has been certainly known of their fate. Only ruins of their churches and convents now remain.

At length, in 1576, Martin Frobisher visited Friesland, now known to be Greenland, on his voyage of discovery to the north-west, but brought to light no particulars concerning the original colonists. Afterward, in 1605, James Hall, an Englishman, under Admiral Lindenow, was sent by Denmark to rediscover them if possible. He succeeded in landing upon the west coast, and communicated with the natives, though nothing more resulted from his visit. Other voyagers touched upon its shores; but not until 1721, when that brave, and good, and truly Christian man, *Hans Egede*, conceived the project of himself going to Greenland, to spread religion among its natives, was anything permanently effected. Then Greenland soon came into notice, and, at various times, colonies and missionary establishments, under the Danish flag, were formed along its coasts. At present there are thirteen settlements, besides commercial and missionary stations. The most northern official settlement is Upernavik, in lat. 73° N. but there is a fishing establishment, called *Tessuisak*, some few miles still farther on. Holsteinborg is in lat. 66° 56' N., long. 53° 42' W. This latter place was, according to Crantz, the fifth colony begun in Greenland, and first settled in the year 1759. It is one of the most convenient places both for dwelling and trading.

Holsteinborg District begins at North Strömsfiord, and extends for about ninety-two English miles. Its breadth eastward from the sea is also about ninety-two miles. There are four fiords in the district, and the mountains upon it are high, though not so lofty as farther north. The only European who has penetrated far to the eastward through this district is *Kielsen*, in 1830. He found the land not so mountainous as toward the sea.

The harbour of Holsteinborg is good, and well landlocked. The spring tides are about 12 feet.

The buildings have, as I was told, the best appearance of any in Greenland. They may be thus enumerated:

The governor's house; priest's house; the church; the lieutenant governor's house; the dance-house; school-house; brewing house; the blacksmith's; two warehouses; one cooperage; one "try" house for oil; thirteen Esquimaux houses, Danish built; three turf houses for Esquimaux, and one dead-house, where deceased persons are placed for six days before burial. Graves are dug, even in winter, for burying. Thus the total number of buildings in Holsteinborg amounts to 29.

The population is as follows :

The inhabitants in Holsteinborg District proper number 197 ; in Kemortusük, 103 ; in Omanausük, 97 ; in Sarfangoak, 158 ; in Itiblik, 108—making a total of 663 souls.

In the town of Holsteinborg there are only ten Europeans, but throughout all Greenland in 1855 they numbered 250. At that date it was estimated there were 9,644 Esquimaux, three-fourths of whom were of Danish blood and the rest pure.

In the Holsteinborg District there are three small schooners, five small boats, and eleven whale-boats.

In 1859, which was considered a bad year, only one whale was captured, though sometimes ten and twelve have been caught in a single season. Of reindeer 300 were secured ; of seal-blubber, 5,000 lbs.; liver of sharks, 2,000 lbs.; blue fox-skins, 100 ; white fox-skins, 150 ; eider-down, before cleansing, 500 lbs. ; after cleansing, 100 lbs. ; and of stockfish—that is, dried codfish unsalted, 4,000 lbs.

I may state that during Governor Elberg's time, since 1850, there have been killed from 5,000 to 6,000 reindeer. Several years ago there were obtained in two years from the Esquimaux about fifty tons of reindeer horn, costing some two skillings, or one cent federal money, per pound ; 4,500 lbs. of it were sent home to Copenhagen, but it would not pay freight.

The governor also told me that "whenever the ships were obliged to take home to Copenhagen stone for ballast, they could sell it to no purpose, because it was complained of as rotten." This I found to be generally true. On several mountains I visited, stones exposed to the atmosphere were crumbling. On Mount Cunningham I had satisfactory proof of it. Small mounds of stone that have evidently crumbled off the larger mountains may be seen lying at the base. The winters are doing their levelling work, and doing it rapidly.

There are four midwives. Two have a good medical education, obtained in Copenhagen. They receive $70 (Danish) per year.[*]

* The Danish dollar at the time of writing (1860), was worth two shillings and threepence sterling. The following is the interpretation of the Danish of the six-skilling note :

   " No.——6 Sk[illings] C[ountry] m[oney].——2,450.
   "This order is good for Six Skillings Country Currency at the Commercial Towns in Greenland.   Copenhagen, 1856.
                                                        "B * * *

          "*Noted* [in the Registry of Records],
   "L * * * * * *"
One of these skillings is worth less than an English halfpenny.

								Danish.
The schoolmaster receives per annum			.	.	.	.	.	$ 125 00
Three other teachers, each	,,		.	.	.	.	.	100 00
Three	,,	,,	,,	.	.	.	.	25 00
Three	,,	,,	,,	.	.	.	.	10 00
Two	,,	,,	,,	.	.	.	.	6 00

One of these latter gets six dollars, and teaches his two children—the only two children of his district—to read and write!

Four women, who teach the children "A, B, C's," get each one dollar per year.

The men, sixteen in number, in the employ of government, get each forty to ninety dollars per year, besides provisions for themselves and families. Every fourteen days bread is baked for them.

In the town there are twenty-four stoves—only one to each house; and these stoves require 100 barrels of coal and five fathoms of wood.

There are reckoned to be 1,700 Esquimaux sealers in Greenland, 400 fishers, and one Esquimaux officer (a clerk), whose father was a Dane and the Governor of Lieveley—Goodhavn. In addition, there are of Esquimaux 17 foremen and boatsmen; 22 coopers and blacksmiths; 87 sailors; 15 pensioners, whose business is to look after goats, and who get half rations of beer, pork, meat, and butter, &c. but full rations of peas, barley, &c.

There are also 20 native catechists or missionaries.

The European missionaries and priests number 13 German and 11 Danish.

Of the first and second governors there are 31.

Three doctors visit each place one year. There are 36 European clerks; 7 boat-steerers; 28 coopers, carpenters, and blacksmiths; 19 sailors and cooks; and 8 pensioners.

The whole body of missionaries are paid per annum, in Danish money, $16,360; of which amount Government House gives $14,650, and the East India Missions, at the outside, $2,000. For schools and school-books the sum of $6,500 is appropriated.

I now proceed with my personal narrative.

Among the numerous visitors that greeted us on our arrival, I was astonished to find myriads of mosquitoes. Little did we expect so *warm* a reception in the *arctic regions.* Talk about mosquitoes in the States as being numerous and troublesome! Why, no man who has not visited the arctic shores in the months of July and August can have a good idea of these Liliputian elephants. In the States the very hum of a mosquito is enough to set any one upon his guard. How many a poor soul there has been kept in a state of torment all night by the presence of only two or three mosquitoes! But here, in the North, it is a common, every-hour affair to have *thousands* at one time around you, some buzzing, some drawing the very life-blood from face, hands, arms, and legs, until one is driven to a state approaching madness. Even the clothing worn in the States is no protection here against the huge proboscis with which each *lady* mosquito is armed.

On Monday, July 9th, a laughable circumstance occurred. It consisted in the fact that Esquimaux had managed to outwit Yankee, and thus it was:

Sterry—the sharp Sterry, who understands the Esquimaux language, had been assisting Smith, the third mate, in some "trade" with the natives. Samson, the pilot, was the man

GREENLAND CURRENCY.

who had come on board, with several others, to see what could be picked up. He was accosted by Smith, and asked if he had anything to trade; but the reply was that "all had gone." In fact, he had parted with everything of value in his possession, and that, too, for nominal prices in return. Smith, however, was not satisfied, and again pressed the Esquimaux. At length it occurred to Samson that he had money, with which he could purchase outright some tobacco. So he asked Smith if he had any to sell. Smith replied, "Yes; how much do you want?" Samson thereupon drew forth a Danish bill, marked "sex skilling"—a *shin plaster*—and said, "How much you sell for this?" Smith took the bill with avidity, and showed it to our acute, jocular, and ever good-humoured Sterry. A fac-simile of it is given on the preceding page. Sterry, seeing the "sex skilling" on the bill, thought it to be six shillings Yankee currency, and accordingly himself addressed the Esquimaux in native tongue. "How many *plugs* for this?" said he. "*Four*," answered Samson. Now this, if each understood the other, would have been clear, straightforward, and a bargain. But Sterry, though well talking Esquimaux on the west side of Davis's Straits, was not so proficient in it at Greenland, where there is a material difference. Accordingly, Samson's reply he took to mean four *pounds* of tobacco, which amounted to thirty-two plugs. This, even at the "six shillings" Yankee currency, was a pretty "steep price," for the tobacco was worth at least one dollar and sixty-eight cents. However, for certain reasons connected with an extreme thirst then raging throughout both Sterry and Smith, it was concluded to let the tobacco go that the money might be had. Smith, therefore, went to his chest and got what Samson wanted. As the plugs of tobacco were counted over to the Esquimaux, his eyes expanded with immense delight and astonishment. He hastened to his kyack with the "godsend," and hurried to the shore, the richest native man in Holsteinborg. Immediately he communicated to his friends the immense wealth that had befallen him from his "sex skillings;" how he had asked only *four* plugs of tobacco from the white man on board the ship, and he had got eightfold. It was enough. What California was to Americans, so was the barque *George Henry* now to the Esquimaux of Holsteinborg. Kyack after kyack came with its dignified Esquimaux, each loaded with a large complement of the fortune-making "sex skilling." Samson, who had so quickly got rich, was among the new-comers, eagerly seeking for more. But, alas for the hopes of men, especially when founded on bank-bills! A speculation had already commenced in town on the "skilling notes." They ran up above par to 300, 400, and, at one time, 800 per cent.! And when the Esquimaux, to some scores of persons, arrived on board, they found themselves partly ruined instead of being enriched. Our Sterry and Smith had discovered their mistake, and thus many an Esquimaux, who, like several white men, had invested his all in that sort of paper currency at high figures, found himself almost beggared. Directly Samson came on board, he was met by Smith at the gangway, and the following took place, to the dismay of the numerous new traders :

Taking the "cussed" bill from his pocket and handing it to Samson, Smith said, "No good ; too little money for four pounds tobacco." Samson, with honest face, looked Smith in the eye, and replied, "He be good ;" which really was true— good for its face, sex skilling, equivalent to about three cents federal coin. But Sterry, who had joined, now insisted, in as good "Husky" (Esquimaux) language as he could command, that "too little money for good deal tobacco," and he held up his finger of one hand, a thumb and all his fingers of the other. Samson now understood, and woefully but honestly said, "I go get tobacco and bring it back." Smith handed him the bill, but Samson at once told him to keep it until he should return. "No," said Smith, "take it along with you. I'll trust you. I see you're honest, and wish to do what is right. It's Sterry's fault," he added, afterwards, "or I should not have been caught so. But, if I never get my tobacco again, I don't care. I've learned a good lesson, and that is, not to deal in 'Husky' bank-stock. I'm now a Jackson man. D—n all banks except that of Newfoundland, where I hope yet to catch more cod on my way to and from these parts."

Need I say that the Esquimaux had to return on shore very crestfallen with their disappointment? Who would not have been, especially after investing in stocks, as many of them had done?

To finish the history of this affair, I may as well add here that, in a few days after this, "Samson," with all his family and his friends, left Holsteinborg for some other place. Smith therefore became minus four pounds of tobacco, and the "sex skilling" besides ! Thus the Esquimaux completely outwitted two of our smart Yankees, and, what is more, did it without the smallest intention of dishonesty at the time. Sterry always declared that he thought the "sex skilling" bill was six Yankee shillings, and both he and Smith acknowledged they were anxious to get some Greenland money to "splice the main brace." Ever afterwards they had frequent reminders from our ship's company of the joke.

Thursday, July 10th, was a most interesting day to me, on account of a visit paid by Captain Budington and myself to Governor Elberg. Leaving the ship, which was anchored half a mile from the landing, we were taken on shore by an Esquimaux boat rowed by natives, and arrived at Government House about 4 P.M. We found him busily engaged with his clerk in preparing an Annual Report for the King of Denmark; but he kindly welcomed us, and, putting aside his labours, escorted us into a private room. Here we soon entered into genial conversation; and a present from Captain Budington of sweet potatoes grown in Florida (never before seen by the governor), with a case of preserved quinces from me, much pleased him.

Hearing that I had on board a copy of M'Clintock's Voyage, he asked for a loan of it, and I let him have it soon afterward. Captain M'Clintock, in the account of his voyage, thus speaks of his visit to Holsteinborg in the latter end of April, 1858 :—

" We have been visited by the Danish residents—the chief trader or governor, the priest and two others. . . . I afterward visited the governor, and found his little wooden house as scrupulously clean and neat as the houses of the Danish residents in Greenland invariably are. The only ornaments about the room were portraits of his unfortunate wife and two children. They embarked at Copenhagen last year to rejoin him, and the ill-fated vessel has never since been heard of. . . . This is a grand Danish holiday; the inhabitants are all dressed in their Sunday clothes—at least all who have got a change of garment— and there is both morning and evening service in the small wooden church. . . . This is the only part of Greenland where earthquakes are felt. The governor told me of an unusually severe shock which occurred a winter or two ago. He was sitting in his room reading at the time, when he heard a loud noise like the discharge of a cannon. Immediately afterwards a tremulous motion was felt; some glasses upon the table began to dance about, and papers lying on the window-sill fell down. After a few seconds it ceased. He thinks the motion originated at the lake, as it was not felt by some people living beyond it, and that it passed from N.E. to S.W. . . . The mountain scenery is really charming. . . . The clergyman of Holsteinborg was born in this colony, and has succeeded his father in the priestly office; his wife is the only European female in the colony. Being told that fuel was extremely scarce in the Danish houses, and that the priest's wife was blue with the cold, I sent on shore a present of coals."

The governor invited us to visit the various buildings and the town. We first directed our steps to the general government store, where we saw almost as much variety as in a country store at home. There was a little of everything, with a good deal of malt, barley, peas, and dry bread, which will keep for years.

In a warehouse near the landing, I noticed large quantities of whale rope, butter, fish, and crackers enough for his whole population (numbering 700 souls) for two years. Everything was of the most substantial character, and stored in such a large quantity in case the vessel which is annually sent to the colonists from Denmark should be lost. There was also a large supply of deer-skins, seal-skins, water-proof clothing, &c. In a loft over the store I saw some swordblades, used for cutting blubber! Resolving swords into ploughshares is an old idea, but swords into blubber-cutters is something decidedly new.

While at the store a customer arrived—an Esquimaux. He wanted some *sugar* and *coffee*. This was served to him, and he paid for it by a Greenland bill of twenty-four skillings, equal to fourteen cents American.

We next visited the blacksmith's shop—a building that looks quite equal to a fine village dwelling-house. Inside was the machine-shop, with long rows of whale gear, harpoons, lances, &c. and three whale guns. Here I saw a cast-iron stove, which the governor said was the kind used by the natives. This stove was *filed* all over and polished ; the stove-pipe, twenty feet long, also of cast iron. Its price was equivalent to 3*l.* sterling. The blacksmith was a fine-looking, intelligent mechanic.

Our next visit was to the school-house. To enter it we had to stoop much. " He stoops to conquer," was an idea that entered my mind as I thought of the teacher who bends his head on entering that temple of knowledge. The teacher's business is *to bend.* " As the twig is bent, the tree's inclined." Intelligence and virtue will yet conquer ignorance and vice. Who would not stoop that such a cause—the cause of knowledge—might progress ?

On returning to the governor's house, we went into an upper room which overlooks Davis's Straits and the many islands around the entrance of the harbour. Here is the " apothecary's shop," the contents of which the governor himself dispenses as required among the sick natives. Shelves of stationery were also round the room ; and in a closet a quantity of eider-down, from which, in 1850, both Dr. Kane and Commodore De Haven had some for their beds. The keys of the government buildings —many of ponderous size—were also kept in a closet here.

After examining the several places of note, we sat down to an excellent supper of duck, salmon, trout, eider-duck's eggs, butter,

American cheese, some very rich goat's milk, white flour bread, Yankee-brewed rye liquors, and good tea. A Danish custom of shaking hands on rising from table followed. We then went out for a walk, and to call on the lieutenant-governor. This gentleman was very kind and urbane in his demeanour. He brought forth numerous specimens of Greenland rocks and of fossil fish—capelin *(Mallotus villosus)*—called by the Greenlanders "angmarset," by the Danes "sild," and by the English "capelin." This fish is about six inches long, of a bluish-brown colour on the back, and silver-white on the belly. The fossils were found about 100 miles up a fiord, the entrance to which is close by here. Though they are of great value, the lieutenant-governor most generously presented the whole to me.

At his house I saw some very good snow-shoes, such as are used in Norway. They are about *six feet* long by five inches wide, and covered with sealskin. They are made of a flat, thin piece of board, bent up at its fore part. This is the kind of snow-shoe Parry bought at Hammerfest, in Norway, when on his North Pole voyage in 1827. He afterwards used them for runners, on which he placed his two boats to be drawn over the ice.

We spent the evening in the governor's house, where a pleasant party was assembled, among whom were the priest's wife, Mrs. *Kjer*, and another lady, *Feoken Bülou*, daughter of the governor of the district of Goodhaab. The priest himself was absent on a journey. During conversation I related how M'Clintock found the paper belonging to Sir John Franklin's Expedition, and deep interest was evinced by all in the subject. The governor read from M'Clintock's work that portion relating to his visit here, and which I have already transcribed. When the part was translated which referred to the priest's wife being " blue with the cold," it caused immense merriment, none enjoying the joke more than the lady herself. The whole scene, indeed, was such as I cannot readily forget. The Esquimaux servants, in their costume, were around, M'Clintock's book in the governor's hand, while the chart and fac-simile of the Franklin record lay open before him.

After tea the ladies commenced knitting some lace, and during the evening Madam Kjer presented me with a mustard-ladle and two salt-shovels, all of ivory walrus tusk, made by an Esquimaux *with only a knife !* They were of excellent workmanship, and I valued them greatly. I had previously offered the ladies two pin and needle cushions, which they had kindly accepted.

During a conversation with the governor this day he informed me that the whole of Greenland belongs to the King of Denmark as his royal prerogative, and is the only dependency that is controlled exclusively by him. Much fault is found with this by the people of Denmark—much written in the papers. Those who are for the king retaining this right contend that otherwise the poor Esquimaux would at once become debased, and lose all the great influences that are now at work for their benefit. Throwing open the ports of Greenland would be followed by vessels of every country visiting the natives, and purchasing their skins, oil, and bone for liquor! The Esquimaux of Greenland will dispose of their all to obtain spirituous drinks, and the governor said that not for anything would he sell them a glass of liquor.

After bidding the party a cordial good-night, we returned to the beach at half-past ten, and found one of our boats ready to take us off. It contained Sterry (red as a beet), Smith, Rogers, and five or six others of the crew, who had been at a dance given by the mother-in-law of the lieutenant-governor. They had all enjoyed themselves amazingly.

The following day, Wednesday, July 11th, fogs prevailed. Hardly a mosquito had been seen since Sunday; and to me it was a singular fact, that a warm sunny day will bring myriads around you within the arctic circle, when, if it be at all foggy, none are to be seen. The bites of these annoying little insects remained for days, and my whole body was covered with merciless wounds inflicted by them.

In the afternoon an "oomiak," or *woman's boat*, came alongside, rowed by Esquimaux girls. There were in the boat two mothers, with their babies, and ten young women. They had been out gathering fuel,* and called upon us on their way back.

The accompanying illustration of an Esquimaux woman and child is a fac-simile of a wood-cut drawn and engraved by a Greenlander named Aaron, living near Goodhaab, who has received no better education than the generality of his countrymen.

About 2 P.M. of this day our consort, the *Rescue*, hove in sight, and, as the wind was almost gone, boats were sent to help her in. I went in one of the boats, pulling an oar, and, after rowing a distance of some miles, got on board the schooner. By that time it was calm, and the stillness of evening had approached. Another boat, containing Smith, and the noble, good-hearted

* A dwarf shrub—Andromeda tetragona.

GREENLAND WOMAN AND CHILD.
[Fac-simile of a wood-cut executed by an Esquimaux.]

Esquimaux pilot, called *Lars Kleijt*, had joined us, and there we were, in real whaling fashion, towing the new arrival into harbour. Four boats of beautiful form and finish—two white, with blue gunwales, and two green—were in a line ahead of the *Rescue*, pulling her along, while the merry voices of our men resounded upon the still waters, and were echoed back from the bold mountains in answering glee. It was a pretty sight as witnessed from the schooner's deck, and one to be often remembered.

"Otto," a pure-blooded Esquimaux, stood at the wheel to steer us in, and all hands besides, except the cook, were in the boats.

At midnight we came to an anchor within a couple of stones' throw of Government House.

Both *Otto* and *Lars Kleijt* were reckoned such good men and ice pilots that every confidence was placed in them. I asked the latter, "What for"—meaning how much—"you go to West land (King William's Land) with me?" His answer was, "My mother old man—she get no dinner—my little ones die!"

Captain Walker, of a Scotch whaler, last year tried to get "Lars" to go with him, and offered to make him second mate; but *Lars* said, "Me no go for all the world. My family!" A noble fellow this *Lars*. But, poor man! he was then much distressed, owing to the loss of his wife, who had died a few weeks previous to our visit. He himself appeared very sick, and my sincere wish was that so good a husband, son, and parent might be spared for his little ones and the mother he so greatly loved.

Otto loved his *grog*. He and Lars went out fishing. On return, coming aboard, he most earnestly asked for a glass of spirits, "to keep salt-water out of poor Esquimaux!"

In the evening of the following day, myself, the captain, mate, Lamb, and most of the crew, went on shore to a grand dance given by the Esquimaux girls to the white-men visitors. Sterry, our genial Sterry, was in his element. He had a most capital faculty for gaining the affections of the fair sex, and proved himself excellent on the variations. He had a continual crowd of the good-looking around him. We had an old sea-captain (an Esquimaux), Ironface, as a fiddler, perched up in the window, with pipe in his mouth, and merry, right merry did all of us become. Several dances, in excellent order, were performed, and many of our company went through their waltzing with Esquimaux partners in capital style. Everything was done in the most kindly and agreeable manner; and when the party broke up, it left upon the mind of each of us a feeling of the most friendly nature.

The first Sunday at Holsteinborg I determined to ascend the mountain on the north side of the harbour, and there worship in the great temple of the world's Creator. In the morning, accompanied by Sterry, we began the ascent, with a fine clear sky above, and the glorious sun shining warmly upon us. But, ere we had got far, swarms of mosquitoes came around. Fortunately, I had long hair on my head, and my beard and mustache were also of great length. Sterry, however, had to cover his face with a handkerchief having two little holes for look-outs.

As we went on, streams of pure and sparkling cold water came dancing down the mountain side, and at these we several times quenched our thirst. Thus steep after steep we mounted, but at what cost! The sun's rays poured hot upon our backs, and both of us soon had to doff our coats, leaving the mosquitoes to persecute us at will. All we could do was to push on quickly, to see if we could get into a higher region where these torments did not abound. But our bodies soon became weary; and the steepness of the way was such that one false step would have proved fatal to us; yet we were not without some relief. Patches of broad-leaved sorrel on the mountain side refreshed us greatly as we rested, and beds of moss, covered with smiling flowers, served as our temporary couch.

In about two hours we gained the summit, both of us covered with mosquitoes, and driven almost to madness by their stings. In vain we tried everything that mind could think of to get rid of them. Nothing availed. We were doomed by these merciless invaders, and our very life's blood was copiously drawn forth to supply their gluttonous desires.

On the other side of the mountain we saw a beautiful little lake; and upon standing by its side, it was found to be clear as crystal, mirroring forth the lofty peaks above us. On its north shore was a low shingly beach, that had been thrown up by the winds coming in this, the only direction they could cross the water. This lake was fed by various small streams that were leaping down from the snowy mountains, and, if it had got no other name, I termed it " William Sterry " Lake. We walked along it, and saw numerous salmon, small trout (three of which we caught with our hands), and many skulls and horns of deer.

It was now dinner time, and our appetite was well sharpened by the exercise we had enjoyed. Accordingly, a fire was lit whereby to cook the fish, though at first I was greatly puzzled how we were to get material for a fire; but Sterry, who had been so much in this arctic region, well knew its resources. Where all looked barren to me, he soon found moss and some low brushwood, like running hemlock. It is a tough shrub, with small leaves and white blossoms, which produce black berries with red sweet juice. Dwarf willow, heather, and small undergrowth wood of various descriptions are intermixed. The dead wood, the leaves, stalks, and limbs of preceding years, are thickly interspersed with the growing portions of this fuel, and it was with it that Sterry so quickly made a fire. A result followed, however, that we little expected. The abundance of such fuel around caused the fire to spread rapidly, and as a strong breeze was now blowing, it soon got beyond our control. Sterry, however, very calmly said, "Never mind; let it burn. Of what use is this to anybody, hemmed in here by these mountains?" So I very quietly made myself content, and sat down to the primitive meal—a carpet of heather for our table, and huge precipices yawning close by, with high broken mountains, that pierced the sky, grimly looking down upon us.

There is philosophy in everything, especially in eating. The world eats too much. Learn to live—to live as we ought. A little food well eaten is better for anyone than much badly eaten. Our pleasures have a higher relish when properly used. Thus we thoroughly enjoyed our food, and, after a short nap, started on the return journey.

As we passed along, I noticed several large rocks, thousands of tons in weight, that had evidently fallen from the tops of two lofty mountains, the detached portions corresponding in shape to the parts vacated. Everywhere was seen the effects of the freezing of the water that percolates into the crevices. The tremendous workings of Nature in these mountains of Greenland during the arctic winter often result in what many of the inhabitants think to be earthquakes, when, in fact, the freezing of water is alone the cause! In descending, we encountered several little clear babbling brooks, innumerable flowers, and shrub-fuel in abundance. Peat was also plentiful. Fox holes in numbers were seen, and a natural canal, with an embankment, in appearance much like the levee at New Orleans.

On arriving at the beach, which was a quarter of a mile long, we found it as smooth and inviting as that of Cape May. The limit of this beach was next to an abrupt bank with millions of broken shells upon it, and covered with driftwood ten feet above high-water mark. One piece was twelve feet long. Here, from a boat that took us off, we heard that the town of Holsteinborg was much alarmed about the fire up in the mountain, and, from what I afterward gathered in an explanation I had with the governor, when I apologized for our thoughtlessness, it was evident that the Esquimaux dreaded the loss of what they considered their best *fields*—not woods—of fuel. Fortunately, the fire went out in about an hour after its discovery by the people.

It was on this Sunday afternoon that I heard of a curious custom here. The dance-house is regularly opened after 4 P.M. The people go to church in the morning and afternoon, then they consider Sunday to cease, and amusement begins. I went to the dance-house, where I found the governor, his lieutenant, Miss Bülou, and Mrs. Kjer. Miss Bülou and the lieutenant-governor danced, but the governor has not for years, and the priest and his wife never. Sometimes 150 persons are crowded into this dance-house.

I asked the governor when the Sabbath began. He replied, " On Saturday evening, and ends Sunday at 4 P.M." I farther inquired if the Esquimaux were at liberty to work after that hour on Sundays. He said, " No, certainly not." " Then how is it the government dance-house is opened for balls at that time ? " said I. " Oh, that is not *work !* " responded the good Governor Elberg.

Referring to the amusements of these native Greenlanders, I am led to speak of a great festival that occurs here on the Danish king's birthday, and is general, on the same day, throughout all the settlements. His Danish majesty supplies the good cheer, and Europeans as well as Esquimaux join in the festivity. It is a most enlivening scene, as the accompanying sketch will show. The original of this picture, which I have in my possession, was drawn by a Greenlander, and Mrs. Kjer, who gave it to me, said it was an admirable representation of the great festal day.

On another occasion I visited the church one Sunday morning, when the school-teacher—a native Esquimaux—preached exceedingly well, and I must say that the general attention given would do credit to people anywhere. The preacher played an organ, and went through the whole services in a most praiseworthy manner. Indeed, I was much struck with the great advance made by the native inhabitants of Holsteinborg in Christian and general educational knowledge. Their school is well attended, and reading and writing are carried on admirably.

Very few persons here at home have any true conception of the great advance made in education by these Greenland Esqui-

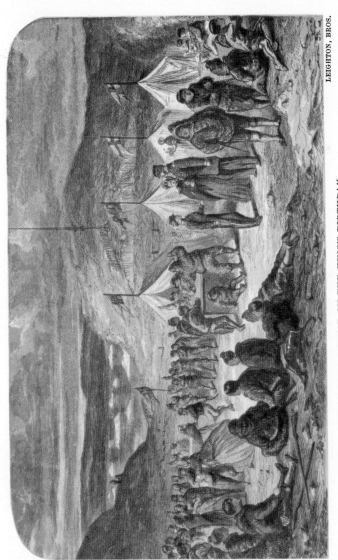

LEIGHTON, BROS.

GREENLAND FESTIVAL ON THE KING'S BIRTHDAY.

maux. It has often astonished me when listening to the apt and ready way in which even children would pronounce some of their extraordinarily long words, some of those words consisting of no less than fifty letters !

The following is one of their long words, but not the longest :—

Piniagagssakardluarungnaerângat.

In all the trials made on one occasion in the cabin, by both male and female—by old and young—by all, I found none but could read, and read well.

I was surprised to see the rapidity—the full, clear enunciation of every syllable, with which they read ; and one little Esquimaux boy seemed to exceed the rest, though all did well.

Perhaps I cannot give my readers a better idea of this than reprinting a small portion of a child's First Primer, beginning at the alphabet, and giving the sound of each letter. The explanation was carefully made to me by Miss Bülou.

The Greenland Esquimaux alphabet consists of twenty-four letters, as follows :—

A, B, D, E, F, G, H, I, J, K, K', L, M, N, O, P, R, S, T, U, V, Y, Æ, O.

The sound of each letter only varies from what we give to the same in the following :—

G is *ke* ; H, *ho* ; I, *e* ; J, *yoge* ; K, *qu* ; K', *qu* ; R, *er* ; U, *oo* ; Y, *oe-i*.

The following is the Lord's Prayer in Esquimaux :—

" Atâtarput k'illangmêtottina ! Ak'kit usfornariille ! Nâlægâvêt tikkiudle ! Pekkosfæt k'illangmifut nunnamisâak ta imãikille ! Tunnisfigut udlome pikfavtinnik ! Pisfaräunatta akkêtforavta, pisfængillavuttäak akkêtfortivut ! Usfernartomut pisfitfaräunatta, ajortomidle annãutigut ! Nâlægãunerogavit pirfarfõunerudluttidlo usfornarnerudluttidlo isfok'angittomut. Amen."

The minister Kjer has been at work translating " Robinson Crusoe" into Esquimaux, that copies might be printed and distributed among his people in Greenland. In his library there is an Esquimaux Bible, and everything is done to make the natives of Holsteinborg good and happy. Dr. Rink has also issued some useful story-books in Esquimaux, one of which books, and also a copy of the doctor's famous work, the governor kindly gave me.

Dr. Rink is so well known by repute among scientific men and others, that I need hardly say much about him. Unfortunately, he was absent at my visit, but I wrote to him about the object of my undertaking, and expressed my regret at not having had the pleasure of an interview.*

The following are a few interesting particulars I obtained from Governor Elberg concerning this eminent man :—

At the time I visited Holsteinborg he had been inspector of South Greenland eight years ; two years also governor of Julianna-haab. He is a tall man, and a clever student. He was employed by government to survey Greenland, and received during the time 500 Danish dollars per annum, besides found in everything. The government supplied all the boats, men, and provisions.

Dr. Rink's wife was 17 years of age when he married her. She was the daughter of Governor Müller, who in 1850 was succeeded by Governor Elberg over the Holsteinborg District. Mrs. Rink was born at Frederick's Haab, and she likes Greenland so well for her home that she would be sorry to leave it.

---

* The following is a copy of the letter I sent to Dr. Rink, and, as it explains some matters that belong to my movements after this date, I here append it :

"HOLSTEINBORG, Greenland, July 24th, 1860.
"On board the barque George Henry.

    " Dr. H. RINK

" DEAR SIR,—Though unacquainted personally, yet I claim to know you, in common with my countrymen, from your works, as a man devoted to the increase of knowledge among men, especially that knowledge pertaining to geography and science.

" On my arrival here, July 7th, it was with sorrow that I learned from Governor Elberg that you had departed. The pleasure and profit, intellectually, of meeting one so experienced in and devoted to the regions of the North would have been incalculable.

" I am on my way to King William's Land, <i>viâ</i> Frobisher Strait, Fox Channel, Fury and Hecla Strait, Gulf of Boothia, and Boothia. On the peninsula of Boothia and King William's Land I expect to spend the next three years, devoting myself mainly to the object of continuing and completing the history of the Franklin Expedition.

" I am satisfied that Frobisher Strait can be navigated, though no vessel has yet penetrated through its entire length. Fox Channel, on the east side, has never been navigated beyond latitude 66° 50' N. <i>Fox's Farthest</i>, and Parry's discovery near the east entrance of <i>Fury and Hecla</i> Strait, should be connected by other discoveries. I am hoping to complete this chain of discoveries this year.

" Since my arrival here in Greenland—17 days ago—I have received the most kindly and hospitable attention from Governor Elberg, the knowledge of which will be gratifying to my countrymen under whose auspices I am making this voyage.

" Governor Elberg has presented me with a copy of your work upon South Greenland. This is another valuable acquisition to the geographic and scientific world.

" Believe me, sir, Humani nihil alienum,
" Respectfully,   C. F. HALL."

CHAPTER III.

OUR consort, the *Rescue*, having rejoined us, it was determined by Captain Budington to depart for his whaling-ground on west side Davis's Straits directly all the necessary preparations about the ship were completed for navigating among the ice. Meanwhile I availed myself of the spare time to frequently visit the shore, and take rambles in the neighbourhood. But, though I find many things in my journal that might be worth mentioning at this period, yet there is so much to be said elsewhere, when I arrive on the actual field of my labours, that I must now hurriedly go over what more occurred at Holsteinborg.

I here make a few extracts from my journal:—

"*July* 13*th*.—This afternoon Governor Elberg, with his lieutenant and wife, visited us, and were welcomed to the best of our power. I had promised the governor to show him a collection of Arctic charts brought with me, and also the British Parliamentary Reports of the Searching Expeditions, and the works of Kane, Franklin, Parry, &c. He was greatly interested, making many inquiries that I took pleasure in answering. A map of the United States much attracted his attention, and he asked several questions as to our home progress, and the rise of new cities, inventions, &c. Street-railroads were quite new to him, he never having heard of such in the Old Country.

"He inquired very much about Mr. Grinnell, whose name is as familiar in Greenland as it is in the United States and Europe.

"At our tea the governor partook of two dishes which he then tasted for the first time in Greenland, viz. fresh lobsters and cranberry preserves. He pronounced them 'very good.' American

cheese—with which he keeps himself well supplied—he also
likes much.

" After an interchange of friendly gifts—that from the governor
being an Esquimaux suit of water-proof sealskin—our visitors
took their departure, and were rowed on shore by girls, two of
them very neatly attired in their native costume.

" This day, in presence of Captain Budington and Lars Kleijt,
I have had a prolonged conversation with Adam Beck, an Esqui-
maux who acted as interpreter for Sir John Ross in 1850-1.
Lars can talk much more fluently the English language than
Adam Beck. The latter said :—

" ' Captain Phillips ' (who was with Sir John Ross) ' speak :
Adam Beck, plenty lie." Beck then paused a moment and
added, " Sir John Ross very good man—plenty pray—plenty
eat—Carl Petersen no speak Husky (Esquimaux) quick—not
good Husky speak—small speak Husky ! " '

" Adam farther continued, and said, ' he spoke with the
Esquimaux at Cape York. They told him two ships had been
seen there ; that there were plenty of officers and men—much
butter and much bread—ships go all to pieces—all die. Adam
Beck speak to Petersen, *lie !* Petersen speak Adam Beck, *lie !*
Carl Petersen plenty lie—*d—d lie !* '

" Both Captain B. and myself are satisfied that Adam Beck
told to Sir John Ross exactly what York-Cape Esquimaux told
to him. It seems that Commander Phillips and Carl Petersen
repeatedly told Beck that he was a liar, and otherwise abused
this now almost wreck of a man ! The treatment Adam Beck
received from Sir John Ross is remembered kindly to this day.
Poor Beck was the instrument of communicating fabrications of
Cape York Esquimaux, and for this English historians have
written him down as the author, when it is not probable that he
was, taking all the circumstances into consideration. The stigma
cast upon him burns to his very heart's core to this day. Even
here his name is blackened by the public notoriety given him
abroad as the man who fabricated falsehoods relative to the
destruction of two ships near Cape Dudley Digges, and the
violent deaths of the officers and men supposed to refer to Sir
John Franklin's Expedition.

" Who of us that has not done an act worthy to be so
generally condemned could stand up against this tide ? Not
one in a thousand would do it ! Adam Beck is of the 999.
He lives on the ' don't care principle.' He has lost all self-
respect, for all shun him. I pity him from the bottom of my

heart. Would that cheering words like those Sir John Ross was wont to utter when living could be whispered in his ear. Adam Beck is wretched—poor. He has an old, rickety, leaky boat, that some one has abandoned. That is all he has in this world, save the old skins on his back that once warmly covered him. I will strive to show him the respect due as a human being. Though he be an outcast, I know there is in his breast a chord that will vibrate to *kindness and humanity.*

"*Saturday, July* 14*th.*—This afternoon I started out for the mountains accompanied by Adam Beck. I had with me, swinging from my shoulders, my sextant and my glass, and in my pockets, tape-line, geological hammer, chisel, and other traps.

"After some distance we came to a river that it was necessary to cross, but for three miles we could find no practicable ford. At length I determined to strip and wade over, carrying my clothes and effects on my head. The water was intensely cold, and two winds met exactly in my passage, yet the scene was extraordinarily beautiful! The golden sand under my feet —the diamond-shaped waves caused by the angular breezes— the arctic sun pouring down its bright, warm rays from just above the peaks of Greenland's mountains, and reflected from the sparkling waters around me, will never be forgotten.

" On landing, I replaced my clothes and trudged along, gathering many beauteous flowers by the way. Up, up the mountain —steep following steep—away we went, leaving piles of stones —three stones in each (I said in my thoughts, ' Faith, Hope, and Charity ')—to mark the way on our downward path, for our route was heretofore unknown by the native or the European population. At length we came to the top of all save the last mountain, which was covered with snow. Here we found the steepness to be such that for a moment I hesitated ; but, determined to try and ascend yet higher, I made the attempt. Adam looked up and shook his head, actually falling to the ground, saying he ' would not, *could not* accompany me for the whole world !' Therefore I had to go alone.

" The peak I was about to climb had the name of 'Woman's Hood,' and I started on my way up it with great caution, erecting piles of ' Faith, Hope, and Charity ' at intervals, to guide me back. Every now and then I was obliged to desist. The sun in the northwest was pouring on my back compound rays, in addition to the dazzling glare reflected from the sea. The exertion made was immense. Frequently I had to dig out cracks between the rocks for both fingers and toes to hold on by. I dared not look around. I was unable to do anything but go on. At length I reached a lofty peak, and to my dismay beheld another beyond it, with a precipice between! For a moment I hung to the rock upon which I stood. I closed my eyes. I gradually opened them, with shaded hands. I gazed upon the awful depths below; then, glancing round, I saw one of Nature's grand and mighty scenes. Mountains upon mountains, with great breaks between, burst on my view. On one side, the lake, river, and valley below, with Davis's Straits in the distance; on the other, peak upon peak, to some five hundred, towering upward to the skies. Mount Cunningham, as the highest was called, was evidently inaccessible, and to attempt it would have been foolhardy. I therefore ended my journey here, erected a pile of stones, and then marking my name, began the descent.

" I found Adam Beck anxiously waiting me, and, in due course, together we reached the town, where I procured a boat and got safely on board, well tired, but satisfied with my journey."

Adam informed me that his children had no food, and though I had paid him well, and did for him all in my power, yet that could not help him much. The next day he, his wife, two children, and an infant at her back, went out in their rickety canoe to try and catch fish for "poor picaninnies."

The following is a fac-simile of Adam Beck's writing, when I asked him to put down his name and date of birth, which he did, adding the name of Sir John Ross.

There is no C in the Greenland-Esquimaux alphabet, as already explained, and this accounts for its omission in the above.

On the 16th of July we endeavoured to return the many kindnesses shown us by the good people of Holsteinborg by inviting them to a ball. The lieutenant-governor and lady, the schoolmaster and his wife, with their infant child at her back, and most all the town, were there. Never did the *George Henry* and her crew look happier, gayer, or present a more varied scene. With warm hearts, honest faces, and a ready mood for the fullest mirth of the hour, did we enter upon the festive day.

The vessel was decorated for the occasion, and it would amuse many friends and readers at home were I able to give at length

DANCE ON BOARD THE GEORGE HENRY.

all that occurred. In this merry dance the Esquimaux did their very best, and our bold sailor-boys showed themselves not a whit behind. Even Captain B. Mate Rogers, and—myself! had to join in the dizzy whirl. As for myself, I was positively forced into it. In a jocular yet impressive manner, one and all insisted upon my treading on " the light fantastic toe." My hands were placed in those of two Esquimaux ladies, when I was fairly dragged into the dance ; and dance I did ! Yes, I *danced*,—

that is, I went through certain motions which in courtesy to me were called dancing; but what would the belles of my own country have said of it? I blush to think. However, it so happened that nobody was hurt, except a few of the Holsteinborg maidens, upon whose feet I had rather clumsily trod, and who afterward went away limping, with a remark, "That man may be a good dancer" (I never danced before in all my life), "but he's very heavy and far-reaching on his pedals!" As for the dancing, let me honestly confess that I felt the better for it. I am sure that many evils in my nature then found a way out at my feet.

After the ball on deck, we succeeded in getting up some singing below in the cabin. Among the Esquimaux, the schoolmaster—who is really a capital fellow—was the leader, and his singing was truly excellent. There was, however, this singularity in it—many of the songs were to church tunes! On our side, we had the national airs, "Hail Columbia," "Star-spangled Banner," &c. which were vociferously cheered. While the latter was sung, I raised the silk emblem of our beloved country that was given me by a dear one at home to erect over Franklin's grave. The schoolmaster, finding in "Ross's Second Voyage" some Esquimaux verses, first read and then sang them most admirably.

During the whole evening unbounded happiness reigned on board. Several presents were made, especially to the schoolmaster's wife, who received them with much modesty and pleasure. At length the party broke up, when our visitors departed for the shore in their numerous kyacks and family boats.

On the 18th of July occurred the sun's eclipse. The view in Holsteinborg Harbour was fine, though a part of the time it was obscured by clouds. The Esquimaux were generally out looking at it with pieces of glass dipped in water!

A singular fact in connexion with this eclipse was told me by Mate Rogers. He said that "during it he and his party could catch no fish, though before and after it there was abundance obtained!"

In the afternoon it began to blow a gale, and at the time nearly all hands were away on some duty or other. Mate Rogers and men were catching cod in Davis's Straits, and only Captain B. myself, and the young seaman, John Brown, were on board. The vessel began to drag her anchor, and, though we contrived to drop another, yet we were within a stone's throw of the rocky coast before she again held on. The three of us worked for our lives. John Brown put forth the strength of a giant, and myself and the captain did the same. Meantime our crew on shore had hastened off in a boat, and the governor had, in the midst of the gale, kindly sent another boat, with his superintendent and men, to our assistance. These enabled us to make all secure on board ; but our anxiety now was no longer for the ship, but for Mate Rogers and those with him out seaward in Davis's Straits. It seemed impossible that any small craft could survive in such a storm. *Our* chances had been doubtful, even in a good harbour ; what, then, had we reason to expect for the fate of those in a boat outside ? We felt dismayed, and eagerly were our glances bent in the direction our poor comrades had taken in the morning. Every glass was in requisition to catch a sight of them, but only the mountain waves dashing against the rock-ribbed coast, and sending their spray full fifty feet in the air, met our view. At last Captain B. who was aloft, cried out, " There they come ! there they come ! " and sure enough, we now saw them at a distance, struggling bravely, perseveringly, desperately, amid the roar and fierce turmoil of the wild sea threatening to ingulf them. Presently they emerge from the confused mass of waters, and we behold them more distinctly. Oh, how they seem to strain each nerve ! How desperate their all but Herculean efforts to try and save themselves ! One moment they appear to be lost ; the next we notice them again struggling on as determinedly as ever. " Pull pull, for dear life's sake, my good men ! " was the involuntary cry of each on board ; and right bravely did they pull. On they came, thrown about and driven about in the very maddest of revengeful sport that Ocean and Wild Storm could devise. At length they near the ship. A few strokes more—a well-directed movement of the steering-oar, and our beaten and exhausted comrades are alongside ! Hurrah ! thank God, we have them safe on board !

It appeared that the gale had overtaken them suddenly, and at first they attempted to land upon an island, but this the breakers would not admit. There was no alternative, therefore, but to make for the ship as best they could. In doing so, a heavy sea struck the boat, overwhelming it and them. But now was the time for trial of the will and arm of man against winds and waves. Brave souls were in that boat, and Mate Rogers proved himself fully equal to the occasion. The boat was cleared, and stern, bold hearts defiantly pulled her onward to the ship, which they finally reached, utterly worn out by their fearful exertions. Now that they were safe, all their power was gone. A child could have overpowered the whole together. Wet, cold, and enfeebled—their case required immediate attention. Dry clothing, warm drinks, and stimulants were at once supplied ; and thus, with careful treatment, they soon recovered.

At 10 P.M. the gale had died away to a calm, and we all retired to sleep, completely exhausted with our bodily and mental labours of the past few hours.

About this time I enjoyed a rare sight. One of the Esquimaux turned summersets *in the water seated in his kyack* ! Over

ESQUIMAUX FEAT—A SUMMERSET.

and over he and his kyack went, till we cried "Enough !" and yet *he wet only his hands and face* ! This is a feat performed only by a few. It requires great skill and strength to do it. *One miss* in the stroke of the oar as they pass from the centre (when their head and body are under water) to the surface might terminate fatally. No one will attempt this feat, however, unless a companion in his kyack is near. The next feat I witnessed was for an Esquimaux to run his kyack, while seated in it, over another. Getting some distance off, he strikes briskly and pushes forward. In an instant he is over, having struck the upturned peak of his own kyack nearly amidships, and at right angles, of the other. These feats were rewarded by a few plugs of tobacco.

The day after the gale we had a mishap on board that threatened to prove serious, and, as it was, it detained us some days longer in Holsteinborg. Our anchors fouled, and, in trying to get one of them, the windlass gear broke.

At this time our deck was crowded by the crews of both vessels, and Esquimaux men, women, and children, besides some dogs I had purchased for my future sledge travelling. These together presented a remarkably stirring picture, while the howling of the dogs, the sailors singing in chorus as they pulled on the ropes, with the varied voices of Americans, Esquimaux, French, Danish, and Dutch, made a confusion of tongues somewhat akin to Babel.

By noon all attempts to get the anchor, now the windlass was defective, proved vain. It was therefore decided to call upon the governor and ask him for his blacksmith to aid our Sterry in repairing the gear. Permission was instantly granted ; but the injury done was of such a nature as to require days to make it good. The following day, however, we succeeded in hoisting up our faithful anchor, and it was then determined, as soon as the windlass was ready, to sail for the west or opposite side of Davis's Straits.

While pulling on the ropes side by side with Esquimaux, I was strongly reminded of the opinion many civilized persons have of their savage and cruel nature. Why, instead of that, they are glorious good fellows. As for eating a man up, they would sooner let a hungry man eat them out of all, without saying a word, unless it was, " Welcome, stranger ! as long as I have, you shall share with me." This is just their nature. The time I was at Holsteinborg I saw much of the inhabitants, and my opinion as to their honesty, good-nature, good-will, and genuine hospitality is strong and unmixed. They possess these virtues to an eminent degree. The vices so prominent and prevalent in more civilized communities are all but unknown here. The test they were put to on board the *George Henry* was enough to satisfy any man that they are honest. Numbers of Esquimaux, of all ages and of both sexes, were almost constantly on board, yet not the slightest thing was missed by any of us. We never thought it necessary to "keep an eye" on this or that, though their desire for any of our trinkets was ever so great. Wherever we placed an article, there we found it.

Among other incidents well remembered of my stay at Holsteinborg, I must not forget the *garden* attached to Governor Elberg's house. He was very proud of this garden, though there was but little in it. One evening he took me there. The radishes and turnips looked flourishing, but they were diminutive in the extreme. Those I tasted were good. I relished them exceedingly, tops and all.

I have mentioned purchasing here some dogs for sledge-work. They were six in number, and the governor kindly gave me his experience in selecting the best animals. I bought the six for about Danish ten dollars, equivalent to a pound sterling. As these dogs will be frequently alluded to in my narrative, I here append a list of their Greenland names : 1. *Kingo ;* 2. *Barbekark ;* 3. *Ei*—pronounced *Ee;* 4. *Me-lak-tor*—the leader ; 5. *Me-rok ;* 6. *Me-lâk,* or *Ki-o-koo-lik,* afterward called *Flora.*

For their food I purchased over two bushels of little dried fish ("capelins") for an English shilling.

At length the repairs of our windlass were complete, and on Tuesday, July 24th, a fair wind gave notice we were about to take our departure. Two pilots—*Otto* and *Lars*—came on board, and as some of our men had gone ashore, the colours were hoisted for their return. All was excitement. My letters for home had to be finished, and my last farewell uttered to kind friends.

As I wrote in the cabin below, there was at my side a beautiful bouquet of arctic *flowers* in great variety, sent me by several of the Holsteinborg young ladies ; and I could not but feel, as I then expressed my letter, astonished at the profuseness of Nature's productions in that part of the world.

Having finished my letters all but a few concluding lines, I was soon in a boat rowed by Esquimaux, and carried to the landing-place at the foot of a hill leading to the town.

As we neared the shore all the inhabitants—including dogs and goats as well as Esquimaux and Danes—covered the place. On the beach were the *George Henry's* men just about to leave, having paid their farewell visit to the warm-hearted people. Hearty cheers from the boat as it pushed off signified most clearly that not in words alone, but from the very soul, was meant "Farewell, good friends ; we thank you for your kindness, and will remember you for ever !" To this the Greenlanders responded by similar cheers, and I am sure with similar feelings. Indeed, the parting exhibited several scenes worthy of notice. Almost every evening during our stay in the harbour, our "boys" had been invited to dances with the Esquimaux. Acquaintance ripened as interviews increased. Friendships became firmly established, and, in some cases, love finally ruled supreme. On this parting I saw more than one pair of eyes moistened. I say it to no one's discredit. Many eyes of our people also were darkened as the gloom of separation came upon them.

I hastened up to the governor's house with my letters. He and his deputy met me, and I was heartily pressed to enter. Every one knew of our early departure, and numerous boats full of Esquimaux were seen hastening to the vessel. But my own feelings at the time will be better expressed by the following extract from my private journal.

" Seated in the office-room, I added a few words to my correspondence home—to my dear ones, and to my noble friend, Henry Grinnell. I then sealed up my letters and gave them to the governor, who kindly offered himself to carry the packet to Godhaab, which place he soon intended to visit, and from whence a government vessel was to sail for Copenhagen in September. I was then invited down into the room where I had spent many pleasant hours with Governor Elberg. There I found awaiting the three parting glasses—one for me, one for the governor, and one for the lieutenant-governor. Each had some good saying to utter. Blessings must and will follow to us all if kindly prayers can avail. With all my heart I thanked the governor for his great and increasing kindness to me while within his harbour; ay, more, I thanked him for his hospitality, which was overwhelming.

" My time was short. The lieutenant-governor took me to his domicile. Then I hastened to the priest's, to bid Mrs. Kjer and Miss Bülou farewell. I then found the governor had ordered his boat to take me on board, he and the lieutenant-governor intending to accompany me. The ladies walked down to the landing with us, where I expressed a hope to have the pleasure of again seeing them after three or four years' time in the United States. I especially promised that the lady who sometimes here is 'blue with cold' should never be so while there. A warm —a last shake of the hand, and I bid them an affectionate adieu. I was then carried away, amid the sorrowing hearts of many. * * *

" On the 7th day of this month I rejoiced when I first put my foot where I was now bidding farewell in tears. Then I rejoiced that God had brought me in safety, that I might put my foot upon Arctic ground. Not a soul did I know in the whole North. In seventeen days I was acquainted with all Holsteinborg. I now leave with it regret. I sorrow at parting from so noble a people! * * *

"Kyacks in large numbers danced around us as we made our way to the ship. I remarked to the governor that with all the progress in ship and boat building of civilization, we had nothing in way of rowing with which we could equal the speed of a kyack. This is so. One Esquimaux with his kyack can outstrip any man or men among our people—or any other of the enlightened world—in rowing.

"When we got on board they were heaving up the anchor, and had nearly succeeded in getting under way, when, to the general consternation, our windlass broke again in a second place. Here was a dilemma. What to do was for a moment doubtful. To delay longer would be almost giving up the voyage; to go to sea thus would be unwise. One remedy alone was open to us. Sterry declared he could manage it if we had the screw-plate and certain gear in the blacksmith's shop that had been used in the repairs before. It was left to me to broach the subject to the governor, and after a consultation with him he generously granted what was desired. A boat was sent off for the articles, and upon its return sail was made on the ships. A last leave-taking in the cabin took place, and finally the governor, his officials, and all the good people of Holsteinborg left us under repeated cheers. A few minutes later, and *Otto* and *Lars*, the two noble pilots, also departed, and we were once more alone to ourselves, the *Rescue* following us.

"After our friends had gone I watched with long and eager gaze the receding mountains, especially the one I had ascended on July 14th. It was midnight, and the northern sky flooded in crimson light—the east and the west tinged in mellower hue—the long ridge of mountains, reaching far south, and far north sharply cutting their contour upon the sky, formed a glorious picture to the eye! The mountains looked black as Erebus in contrast with the red and glowing clouds that were behind, so that only a profile could be taken of them. As they faded in the distance, so was shut out the very spot where Holsteinborg lay; but not so was effaced the memory of it and its generous inhabitants while life exists within me!"

CHAPTER IV.

THE first day or two after our departure, I had a repetition of
my old complaint, sea-sickness. Here the dogs managed better
than I. *They* could walk the deck; *I* was unable. Perhaps
four props to my two considerably helped them. But the first
night out we had a terrible shaking. Davis's Strait was more
like the broad ocean, and certainly as boisterous. If this Strait
and Baffin's Bay were, as I suggest, called " Davis and Baffin's
Sea," then could its billows roll high as the heavens, deep as the
lowest depths, without our once thinking of their assuming to
be what they are not.

During the night, " things in general" got capsized. I would
not like to swear that the *George Henry* turned a " summerset,"
but, on my honour, I can say that when I retired to my berth,
an India-rubber cup, lashed firmly on my writing-table, and
holding a beautiful Greenland bouquet in water, was the next
morning emptied of its contents, and every flower and drop of
water scattered far and near, though the cup remained in its
position! Three half-reams of paper, that had been placed
securely over my bunk, and had there rested quietly all the
previous part of the voyage from New London, were found
scattered over an area of say seventy-five feet. One hetero-
geneous mass presented itself to all eyes in the morning. Medicine chest and contents — guns and ammunition — my arctic
library and the library of the *George Henry*—geological and
ornithological, cetaceous and floral specimens—sailors' chests—
magnetic and astronomical instruments—pens, ink, and paper,
charts and maps, &c. besides two human beings—the captain
and myself—wrapped in deep slumber by their side. But soon
out of all this chaotic mass we produced harmony again. Things
got into their places; and I, by degrees, mastered my sickness,
and was the man once more.

On July 27th we had a heavy snow-storm, and soon afterward the land on the west side of Davis's Straits were seen, the mountains covered with snow; but, owing to frequent fog (sometimes it seemed to *rain* fog) and unsettled weather, we could not near the *George Henry's* destination, which was now changed to a place more south of Northumberland Inlet. We came across but little ice, except *bergs*, and frequently expressed much surprise at it. The icebergs, however, were numerous, and many of them deeply interesting—one especially so, from its vast height and odd shape. I say "odd," though that applies in all bergs, for no two are alike, nor does any one seem long to retain its same appearance and position. The following is a sketch of one I called the Belted Iceberg; but ice movements

BELTED ICEBERG.

are as mysterious almost as the magnetic pole. The captain told me that he had known two vessels to be beset near each other in the ice, and in a few days, though the same ice was around each vessel, yet they would be many miles apart! Bergs have been known to approach and recede from each other in as beautiful and stately a manner as the partners in the old-fashioned, courtly dances of years gone by.

Of the various bergs I particularly noticed, a few descriptive words may here be said. The first view of one that attracted my attention looked as if an old castle was before me. The ruins of a lofty dome about to fall, and a portion of an arched roof already tumbling down, were conspicuous. Then, in a short time, this changed to a picture of an elephant with two large circular towers on his back, and Corinthian spires springing out boldly from the broken mountains of alabaster on which he had placed his feet. The third view, when at a greater dis-

GOTHIC ICEBERG.

tance, made it like a light-house on the top of piled-up rocks, white as the driven snow. It took no great stretch of fancy to finish the similitude when the sun to-day, for nearly the first time during a week, burst forth in all its splendour, bathing with its flood of golden fire this towering iceberg light-house !

Another berg I could not help calling the Gothic iceberg. The side facing me had a row of complete arches of the true Gothic order, and running its whole length were mouldings, smooth projections of solid ice, rivalling in the beauty of all their parts anything I ever saw. The architecture, frieze, and cornice of each column supporting the arches above were as chaste and accurately represented as the most imaginative genius could conceive. Here and there I saw matchless perfection displayed in the curvature of lines about some of its ornamental parts. Springing out from a rude recess, away up in its vast height, I saw a delicate scroll, which was quite in keeping with Hogarth's "Line of Beauty."

As I was gazing upon one of the many bergs we passed, it overturned, and burst into a thousand fragments!

Relative to the formation of these icebergs, Sterry—upon whose authority alone I mention it, and who is entitled to his own theory upon the subject—told me that, at a place between two mountains in Northumberland Sound, he once counted something like a hundred strata of ice that had been deposited, one layer each year. They were of various thicknesses, each course marked by a deposit of sediment like dirt. He did not complete counting the number of layers, as the height would not admit of his doing so.

On our way across Davis's Strait, not far from Cape Mercy, we passed the spot where, in 1856, the English discovery-ship *Resolute* had been found by the very vessel I was now on, the *George Henry*.

I have just been describing the beauty of icebergs as seen in our way across; let me now attempt to picture some of those gorgeous sunsets and phenomena of Nature we witnessed. I extract from my diary at the time :—

"*July 28th.*—This evening the whole horizon has presented a most beautiful sight. A zone of rich mellow purple, with matchless tints darting upward to the height of some thirty degrees, met the eye. Then all at once, as the sun disappeared, the purple was replaced by a deep blue. As to the 'tints' of which I write, I am at a loss to describe them. Take a thousand rainbows—stretch them around the horizon—intermix them—entwine them—spin and twist them together, and you have the appearance of those tints crowning that zone, first of purple, then of blue.

"*July 31st.*—Strange sights to-night. Looking through my marine glass to the north-east, when the sun was about three degrees above the horizon, I was astonished at the view before me. Mountains, islands, icebergs, and the sea were in one vast confusion. From the sun northerly to the south-east, wherever I turned my glass, confusion worse than things confounded met my sight. A little reflection, however, brought me to a realisation of the fact. The extraordinary appearance of everything at and beyond the horizon was from 'refraction,' so called.

"We speak of this and that 'looming up' at home, but little did I think what it signified until this night. Mountains far distant—mountains whose true position was considerably below the horizon — were now considerably above it, and icebergs dangling from their tops! This *refraction?* It was *Nature turned inside out! Nature turned topsy-turvy!!* NATURE ON A SPREE!!! Yes, Nature on a spree!

"As I went forward I was met by many of the crew (those now on their first voyage to these regions), who called my attention to some icebergs ahead. A few moments before, I had noticed these bergs as mere pigmies. Now the pigmies had become giants! 'Nature on a spree' had given to mere snowballs on the horizon all the beauty and symmetery of 'Bunker's Hill Monument,' running high up, in alabaster columns, to prop the azure sky!

DISTORTED MOON.

"Soon the moon came rolling up; and what a *phase* or face it showed, with its woefully distorted countenance! I took my Nautical Almanac for the year (1860), and there found, 'August 1st,' the sign for FULL MOON! The large round circle stared me in the face. There could be no mistake. A moon as 'big and round as a cart-wheel'—as we boys used to say— should be the aspect of fair Luna in the heavens this night. But here was the rising moon 'up to time,' yet where was the *full moon?* The moon as it ought to be was a moon somewhere else, not here; for, as it ascended above the horizon, its lower limb was like a crushed hat, then as a drunkard's face—fiery red, and swollen out to its utmost limit of expansion! Sketching as it then appeared, the preceding may give the idea, so unnatural was the goddess as she arose from her ocean bed to-night. But this, however, did not last long. A few moments sufficed to carry her upward in her regal course, and a short time afterward, as I looked again, I found

> " ' How calmly gliding through the dark blue sky,
>   The midnight moon descends.'

"*August 6th.*—Going on deck this morning, found Nature again on a spree. I have been observing its working for two hours. I will record some of its phenomena.

" When I first observed the unnatural appearance of the bergs, sea, and islands towards the south-west, the morning sun was ten degrees high, and shining brightly. The barometer then stood 29·35 inches, the thermometer 41°, wind blowing moderately from south-west. Looking to windward, I saw the *top* of a distant berg ; then all at once a snow-white spot, not larger than a pin's head, appeared in the clouds hanging directly over the berg. In few seconds it enlarged to the size of an Egyptian pyramid inverted. At every roll of the vessel this resplendently white pyramid seemed to descend and kiss the sea, and then as often ascended again to its celestial throne.

" *Dioptrics,* the science of refracted light, may satisfactorily account for all this, but I very much doubt it. Some land that was seventy-five miles distant, and the top of it only barely seen in an ordinary way, had its rocky base brought full in view. The whole length of this land in sight was the very symbol of distortion. Pendent from an even line that stretches along the heavens was a ridge of mountains. 'Life hangs upon a little thread,' but what think you of mountains hanging upon a thread ? In my fancy I said, If Fate had decreed one of the sisters to cut that thread while I witnessed the singular spectacle, what convulsions upon the land and the sea about us might not have followed ? But Nature had an admirable way of taking down these rock giants hanging between the heavens and the earth. Arch after arch was at length made in wondrous grandeur from that rugged and distorted atmospheric land ; and if ever a man's eye rested upon the sublime, in an act of God's creative power, it was when He arcuated the heavens with such a line of stupendous mountains ! Between these several mountain arches in the sky were hung icebergs, also inverted, moving silently and majestically about as the sea-currents drifted those along of which they were the images. In addition to all this there was a wall of water, so it appeared, far beyond the usual horizon. This wall seemed alive with merry dancers of the most fantastic figures that the imagination could conceive, and its perpendicular columns were ever playfully changing. Oh, how exquisitely beautiful was this God-made living wall! A thousand youthful forms of the fairest outline seemed to be dancing to and fro, their white arms intertwined—bodies incessantly varying, intermixing, falling, rising, jumping, skipping, hopping, whirling, waltzing, resting and again rushing to the mazy dance—never tired—ever playful—ever light and airy, graceful and soft to the eye. Who could view such wondrous scenes of divine enchantment and not exclaim, 'O Lord, how manifold are Thy works! In wisdom hast Thou made them all; the earth is full of Thy riches!'

"*August 8th.*—The sunrise this morning was fine. Long before the sun came to the horizon the clouds were all a-glow! They were in long, narrow belts, one overtopping another, the lower edges of all visible and pendent, reflecting the crimson of the sun's rays. To attempt to paint the beauty, the glory of this scene, either by *my* pen or by the pencil of any mortal artist, seemed to me like a sacrilege."

* * * * * *

Our progress towards the harbour we wished to reach was very slow. At length, on July 30th, we were within three miles of " Sanderson Tower," on the west side of entrance to Northumberland Inlet; but as it was late, and the wind unfavourable, we had to go seaward for the night. The following day head winds and calms still retarded us, and we were now also anxious for our consort, the *Rescue*, she having parted from us a short time previously. The place we wanted to reach was called by the Esquimaux Ookoolear, now named by me Cornelius Grinnell Bay, the anchorage being in about latitude 63° 20' N. For several days we had been struggling against strong breezes, and on the 2d of August we had only about six miles more southing to make ; but a very thick fog again came on, and once more we had to stand off to sea.

On the 4th we were not far from Ookoolear, and occasionally hopes arose that we might reach an anchorage before night. But it was not so. A dozen times was the ship headed for our harbour, and as often were we baffled by the fog. Sometimes it would disperse, leaving the heavens bright and warm ; then would our gallant barque be swiftly plowing the deep towards the wished-for haven. Suddenly the fog again descended, enveloping us in the gloom of night, so that we could not see a quarter of a mile in any direction, and then once more would the vessel's course have to be arrested. So it continued all day, and toward evening the annoyance was increased by a heavy gale. Of course there was no alternative but to run off the land to sea, and accordingly it was done.

The next day, when the weather moderated, we made sail back toward our harbour, and at 8 P.M. we were near the same position as on the 4th, still more than thirty miles distant from where we had to go. Fogs then encircled us, and thus we were till the following day, when more clear weather appearing, *Ookoolear* was seen, and ahead of us were observed " Sterry's Tower," " Rogers's Island," and " Sarah's Island."

As we were standing in to the land, the *Rescue*, under good sail, was discovered away near the mountains.

At this time a circumstance occurred that startled myself and all on board beyond measure. I will relate it from my journal as I find it recorded at the time.

" *Tuesday, August 7th.*—After dinner I had gone and perched myself up in one of the whale-boats hanging over the ship's side, for the purpose of viewing the mountain scenery as we passed along, and also sketching. I had my marine glass with me, and during an interval when the fog—which now and again settled upon us—disappeared, I swept the horizon all round. As I looked easterly, my eye caught a strange black sail. Directing the captain and mate's attention to it, they examined, but could not make out what it was. At length we decided that it was a whale-boat with dark-coloured sails, and approaching us. Nearer and nearer it came, though yet far off ; for when I had first seen it, refraction had made the small sails loom up higher even than those of a 300-ton vessel. By this time every one on board was anxiously looking to the strange boat, wondering what it was, coming from a direction seaward. After watching it more than an hour, we noticed that the sail was taken down, and soon afterward we lost sight of the boat entirely. In vain our glasses were pointed in the direction she was last seen. Nothing could be observed of her, and many began to think we had been deceived by refraction ; but at length the captain exclaimed, ' I can now see the boat, though a mere speck. I should not wonder if it is one of my own left here on the last voyage, and manned by the Esquimaux.' I looked long and attentively. At last I saw the flash of oars following each stroke, as the dazzling rays of a western sun fell upon the uplifted blades. I could see nothing else but these oars, and to me it seemed as if the rowers were pulling quickly—desperately. The excitement now became great among us, especially as the distance decreased between the boat and the ship. Captain B. thought it was an Esquimaux crew, and Mr. Rogers said the men were white.

"As they neared, it struck me that the rowers—now to be seen more clearly—might be some shipwrecked mariners pulling for dear life; and to ascertain this, the ship was deadened in her way. In a few moments more the strange boat was near enough to make her crew out for white men, nine in number; and directly they got alongside, a question was put by Captain B. as to who they were. The steersman promptly answered, 'Crew from the *Ansell Gibbs*, of New Bedford.' In reply to another question, he said, 'We are from the north, and bound to the south.' This was enough to satisfy us that they were runaways.

"In a few minutes a variety of questions was put as to the number of ships, the whaling, &c. in Northumberland Inlet, where we conjectured the *Ansell Gibbs* to be; and then the inquiry was made of them, 'You are runaways, are you not?' The response immediately was, 'Yes, we are!' They then told us that they had left *Kingaite*, in Northumberland Sound, on Saturday, August 2d, at 11 P.M. and had thus run the distance, 250 miles to where we met them, in less than three days. The reason they gave for deserting their ship was because of 'bad treatment on board,' and 'not having enough to eat.' They explained about this, and added much more, which may or may not be true. At all events, they made up their minds to start *for the United States* on the first chance, and this they did by taking a whale-boat, two tubs of whale-line, three harpoons and as many lances, a 'conjuror'—that is, a portable cooking apparatus—two guns and ammunition, a small quantity of provisions, a few blankets, and other trifling things; and this to go a voyage over a tempestuous sea, part of it often full of ice, and along an iron-bound coast, for a distance of say 1,500 miles! However, there they were so far. One instrument—a compass—only for navigation; no sextant or quadrant; no one in the boat capable of taking observations had they possessed instruments; and without food enough to carry them on. The chief of this rash crew was John Giles, 'a boat-steerer,' which means, in whaling parlance, one who has charge of the boat and crew when out whaling. Only two of the company had ever been to sea before, and those two had been on whaling voyages to 'Desolation' Island in the South Seas. They were all young men—Americans belonging to various places in the Eastern States.

"When Captain B. had asked several questions, the chief of these unfortunate men modestly supplicated for some food, as they were all very hungry. This was immediately responded to by the captain saying 'Come and eat;' but at first they hesitated, fearing they might be arrested. But hunger prevailed, and, making secure their boat, they entered the ship, and fell to upon the salt junk and biscuit like hungry wolves. Never

MY LAST SIGHT OF THE RUNAWAYS.

before did I see men eat with such avidity and relish. To them it was a feast, having had only half a biscuit each and one small duck among the whole number during the past day.

"I found that nothing would alter their purpose as to proceeding on their desperate voyage. They meant to strike for York Factory in Hudson's Bay; but on my showing them a chart and the course to Resolution Island, thence across Hudson's Strait to Labrador, this latter course was decided upon, with the hope that fishermen might pick them up.

"The captain kindly gave them some beef and pork, powder and shot, and a chart. To this I also added some ammunition and caps.

"They remained with us about two hours, and then, after deciding to go on, instead of landing for the night (perhaps they were still fearful of being captured), they got into their boat, and with many thanks to us, started on their perilous voyage. I watched them long as they passed away from us bending to their oars. It was 9 P.M. when they departed. The moon was shining brightly in the east—the alabaster mountains of ice were scattered about upon the darkening waters—the craggy rocks sharply cut their black profiles against the distant sky, and the winds were gently but coldly blowing in sad harmony with the occasion. As they vanished from my view I said to myself, 'Will the civilized world ever see these desperate men again? It is next to a miracle if so. And yet what lesson do they teach me? If these nine men can undertake such a voyage, and under such circumstances, with so little preparation, why should not I, having far better means, be able to accomplish mine?' 'For themselves,' I added, 'God be with them! I know not how just or unjust their cause may be, but I do know that human life is now at stake, and my sympathy goes with them.'"

Before I pass from this strange occurrence, it will be better to give the sequel of their history, so far as yet known, through three of the wretched crew who reached Indian Harbour, Labrador. The following particulars I gleaned at St. John's, Newfoundland, on my way home in the fall of 1862.

It seems that a Captain Nathan Norman, who does business in Labrador, and is also a magistrate, encountered the survivors of this boat's crew, and, hearing their tale, demanded from them a statement in writing; whereupon one of them, Sullivan by name, drew up an account, the original of which is in my possession. It was given to me by Mr. Robert Winton, editor and proprietor of the St. John's *Daily News*, through Mr. C. O. Leach, United States consul at that place. The following is a *verbatim* copy of Sullivan's written statement, made in the fall of 1861:—

"My name is John F. Sullivan. I left my home in South Hadley Falls, Mass. about the 1st of March, 1860, for Boston. I remained in Boston until the 20th of the same month. I applied at different offices for a chance to ship; being a stranger in the place, and a green hand, I found it very difficult to get a berth to suit me. At last I got a little discouraged, and that day signed my name at No. 172, Commercial Street, Boston, and left for New Bedford, Mass. Next morning, I shipped to go aboard of the ship

Daniel Webster, then laying at New Bedford, but to sail the same day on a whaling cruise to Davis's Straits, to be gone 18 months.

"I left New Bedford in the *Daniel Webster* on the 21st March, 1860. There were forty of us in the crew, all told. We had very rough weather for many days after leaving, which caused many of us to be sea-sick; I suffered from it about three weeks; after that time I began to recruit. There was nothing happened of any consequence worth mentioning until we passed Cape Farewell, about the last of May. After that we had quite a hard time, working the ship through the ice; occasionally, however, we made out to get her through, and came to anchor, July 6, 1860.

"We spoke many vessels going in. I will name some of them: the *Hannibal*, of New London; the *Black Eagle* and *Antelope*, of New Bedford; the *Ansell Gibbs*, of Fair Haven; the *Pioneer*, of New London. These vessels were anchored very close to one another in the harbour; the crews were at liberty sometimes to pay visits to each other; each one would tell how he was treated, several complained of very bad treatment, especially the crew of the *Ansell Gibbs*; they were planning some way of running away for a long time, but they found no opportunity till the 4th of August.

"My shipmate, whose name was Warren Dutton, was aboard that day, and heard a little of the conversation, and he joined in with them, and said he would go, and perhaps one or two more of his crew. He immediately came aboard and informed me; and he pictured everything out so nice, that I finally consented to go with him. We had no great reason for leaving our vessel; we could not complain of very bad treatment aboard; all we could complain of was that we were very badly fitted out for such a climate; and, after we arrived there, hearing of so many men that died there the last winter of scurvy, we were afraid to remain there, for fear that we might get it. We thought that by running away, also, we would be all right, but we were sadly mistaken.

"After it was agreed upon to leave, each one was busy making preparations for a start. I, with my shipmate, packed what few things we thought would be necessary into a travelling-bag which belonged to me; we then crept into the hold, and filled a small bag and a pair of drawers with hard bread, and waited for an opportunity to hide it on deck, unknown to the watch. After we succeeded in that, we made a signal to the other crew that we were ready. It being boats' crew watches aboard the *Ansell Gibbs*, they every one of them left; they found no difficulty in lowering away the boat, which after they did so they lowered themselves easily into her, and soon paddled under our bows; we then dropped our traps into her, and, taking with us two guns and a little ammunition, got into her, and soon pulled around a small point out of sight of the vessels. The names of the crew that left the *Ansell Gibbs* are as follows: John Giles, boat-steerer; John Martin, Hiram J. Davis, Williard Hawkins, Thomas Colwell, Joseph Fisher, and Samuel J. Fisher.

"At 11 o'clock at night, on the 4th of August, we left the vessels in Cumberland Straits, latitude 65° 59', about five miles from Penny's Harbour. Although it being a little foggy, with a fair wind we stood across the Straits. When about half way across we dumped overboard a tub of towline to lighten the boat some. We had nothing but a small boat-compass to guide us; we had no opportunity of getting a chart before we left, and not much of anything else.

"We made the other side of the Straits by morning; then, by taking the spy-glass, we thought we could perceive a sail in chase of us, but we soon lost sight of her. The other crew were depending mostly on us for bread, as my shipmate informed them that we had a better chance to get it out of the hold; their bread lay close to the cabin; so, what bread they had, with ours, would not exceed more than twenty pounds. We all saw that the bread would not last long, so each one desired to be put on allowance of one biscuit a day to each man. We hoped, by the time that was gone, to reach some place where we could find help. We made a very good run the first three days, sleeping at night in the boat; on the fourth day out we fell in with the barque *George Henry*, Captain Budington, of New London. He asked us aboard; the boat-steerer acted as spokesman. The captain told us we were very foolish to leave the vessels to undertake so long a trip. I believe he would have taken us all if we wished to stay; but as we had left a whaler, we did not like to go on board another, as he was also going to remain there through the winter; so we were determined to push along, as we had been foolish enough to start in the first place. However, before we left, he gave us a small bag of bread, a piece of salt pork and some ammunition; also a chart. We then bade him good-by, and set off again. That night we made a 'lee,' found some moss, and made a fire; before we ran in we shot a small duck, which made a good stew for all hands. Two days after this we shot a white bear; he was in the water when we shot him, and there being a heavy sea on at the time, we could get no more than his hind quarters in; them we skinned—the rest we could not save. That night we managed between us to cook it, as we were divided into watches, two in each watch; by doing so, we could watch the boat and keep her with the tide. We kept on in this way, always tracking the shore, and at night going ashore to lay on the rocks, with our boat's sail over us for shelter.

" We had very rough weather in crossing the Straits. We were on Resolution Island four days, waiting for a fair wind; we got it at last, but so strong that it came very near swamping our little boat many times through the night. It kept two of us bailing water out all the time, and we were glad to reach the land, after being in the boat thirty hours, wet to the skin. What bear's meat and bread we had was most gone by this time; there was nothing left but a few crumbs in the bottom of the bag. There was nine parts made of the crumbs; then they were caked off, each man taking his share.

" On the 16th of August we made Cape Chidleigh; on the 20th we divided the last crumbs; after that we picked up what we could find to eat. We found a few berries and mushrooms; we suffered very much from the cold, very seldom having a dry rag upon us.

" We continued on in this condition until the 3d of September, when, to add to our misfortune, Williard Hawkins and Hiram J. Davis (who we called 'the doctor') ran away from us that night, and took with them everything that was of any use to us; they even took the boat's compass, and left us in a miserable condition, with our boat broadside on the beach. It being their watch, they made out to get off. We thought it was useless to make chase after them, so we let them go. It then commenced to rain, and there was a heavy sea rolling in, and, weak as we were, we found some difficulty in shoving the boat off. However, after a hard tug, we succeeded, and then pulled out some ways; we then up sail; it was not up long before it blew so strong that it carried away the mast. We then ran in under a jib, and made a lee. About half an hour after we landed my shipmate died of starvation. The evening he died, Samuel Fisher proposed to eat him ; he took his knife and cut a piece off the thigh, and held it over the fire until it was cooked. Then, next morning, each one followed his example ; after that the meat was taken off the bones, and each man took a share. We stopped here three days. We then made a start ; but the wind being ahead, we were obliged to put back. Here we stopped two more days. During that time the bones were broken up small, and boiled in a pot or kettle we had ; also the skull was broken open, the brains taken out, and cooked. We then got a fair wind, but as we got around a point, we had the wind very fresh off shore ; we could hardly manage the boat ; at last we drove on to an island some ways out to sea ; we got the boat under the lee of it ; but the same night we had a large hole stove into her. Being unable to haul her up, we were obliged to remain here eight days : it was on this island they tried to murder me.

"The third day we stopped here, I was out as usual picking berries, or anything I could find to eat. Coming in, I chanced to pick up a mushroom. I brought it in with me ; also an armful of wood to keep. While kneeling down to cook the mushroom, I received a heavy blow of a club from Joseph Fisher, and before I could get to my feet I got three more blows. I then managed to get to my feet, when Samuel Fisher got hold of my right arm ; then Joseph Fisher struck me three more blows on the arm. I somehow got away from them, and, being half crazy, I did not know what to do. They made for me again ; I kept begging of them, for God's sake, to spare my life, but they would not listen to my cries. They said they wanted some meat, and were bound to kill me. I had nothing I could defend myself with but a small knife ; this I held in my hand until they approached me. Samuel Fisher was the first to come toward me ; he had a large dirk-knife in his hand ; his cousin was coming from another direction with a club and a stone. Samuel came on and grasped me by the shoulder, and had his knife raised to stab me. I then raised my knife, and stabbed him in the throat ; he immediately fell, and I then made a step for Joe ; he dropped his club, and then went where the rest was. I then stooped down to see if Samuel was dead ; he was still alive. I did not know what to do. At this time I began to cry ; after a little while the rest told me to come up ; they would see there was nothing more done to me. I received four deep cuts on the head ; one of the fellows dressed them for me, and washed the blood off my face. Next day Samuel Fisher died ; his cousin was the first one to cut him up ; his body was used up the same as my unfortunate shipmate's.

"After a while we managed to repair the boat, and left this island. We ran in where we thought was main land, but it proved to be an island. here we left the boat, and proceeded on foot, walking about one mile a day ; at last we reached the other side of the island in four days ; then put back again to the boat. It took us four days to get back again. When we got there, we found the boat was stove very bad since we left her. We tried to get around the island in her, but she sunk when we got into her ; we then left her, and went back again to the other side of the island, to remain there until we would die or be picked up. We ate our boots, belts, and sheaths, and a number of bear-skin and seal-skin articles we had with us. To add to our misery, it commenced to rain, and kept up for three days ; it then began to snow. In this miserable condition we were picked up by a boat's crew of Esquimaux on the 29th of September, and brought to Okoke on the 3d of October. The missionaries did all that lay in their power to help us along, and provided us with food and clothing, then sent us on to Nain, where we met 'the doctor,' who was picked up three days before we were. He reported that his companion died, and told many false stories after he was picked up.

"The missionaries of Nain helped us on to Hopedale; from there we were sent on to Kibokok, where two of us remained through the winter. One stopped with a planter, named John Lane, between Nain and Hopedale; the doctor stopped with John Walker until March, when he left for Indian Harbour; the remaining two, Joseph Fisher and Thomas Colwell, also stopped with planters around Indian Harbour. Mr. Bell, the agent at Kibokok, kept two of us until we could find an opportunity of leaving the coast. We left his place about the 10th of July, and came to Macovie, waiting a chance to get off.

"Captain Duntan has been kind enough to give me a passage; my companion was taken by Captain Hamilton, of the *Wild Rover*. We have had a very pleasant passage so far, and I hope it will continue so.

"Sir, I hope you may make it out; it is very poor writing, and was written in haste. JOHN F. SULLIVAN."

In addition to the above, Mr. Leach kindly furnished me with the following information in a letter dated Feb. 25th, 1863:—

"Mr. Kenneth M'Lea, jun., merchant of Newfoundland, informs me that he has had letters from the missionary settlements on the coast of Labrador, in which they say these men conducted themselves 'shamefully.' Instead of feeling grateful for the hospitality they received, they demanded to be supported with the privilege of doing as they pleased. I understand one of them still remained at Labrador. No doubt the rest have shipped under assumed names, feeling ashamed to return to their native country."

Soon after the boat, with its desperate crew, had left us, we were passing one of the channels leading to the long-sought bay. This bay is a very fine sheet of water, and is protected by "Sarah's" Island at the entrance. Its length is about fifty miles, and its width six miles. On entering it by the south channel we were becalmed, and the boats were set to work towing us in; but, though we were up all night, next morning saw us still at some ten miles distance from our harbour. At this time a perfect flotilla of boats was discovered approaching us. They were six whaleboats, fully manned, five belonging to a ship called the *Black Eagle*, Captain Allen, and one to the *Rescue*. As soon as they arrived, quietly greeting us, they wheeled in line ahead of our own boats, and aided in towing us in. An interesting scene it was before and around us: eight boats in line, pulling the ship onward, with brawny arms at the oars, and merry voices pouring forth the sailor's songs as mea-

sured and uniform strokes gave even time to the movement ;
the still waters of the deep bay, the perpendicular rocks by our
side, and the craggy mountains overhanging our heads, their
peaks reaching up as if to kiss the clouds !

At noon, August 8th, 1860, we reached our anchorage, and at
length were secure in the harbour we had so long been seeking.
The *Rescue* had anchored before us.

ICEBERG AND KI-A.

CHAPTER V.

PREVIOUS to our anchoring, Captain Allen, Mates Lamb and
Gardiner, joined us on deck, bringing with them an Esquimaux
named *Ugarng*, and others of his people. Several women were
also on board, dressed in the peculiar costume of the West Land
natives ; but not until we had dropped anchor could I do more
than give a passing glance at these strange-looking figures. The
excitement consequent upon arriving in a new place was naturally
great on my mind. The land around me—its inhabitants, its
rugged hills, its mountain tops covered with snow, all belonged
to that especial part of the northern regions connected with the
ultimate field of my labours. When, however, the vessel was
made stationary, and the greatest excitement had abated, I could
better examine our visitors, and never shall I forget the first
impression they made upon me.

It has been said by a writer, now deceased, when referring to
the Esquimaux, in an arctic book he was reviewing, that they
are "singular composite beings—a link between Saxons and
seals—hybrids, putting the seals' bodies into their own, and then
encasing their skins in the seals, thus walking to and fro, a
compound formation. A transverse section would discover
them to be stratified like a rolly-polly pudding, only, instead of
jam and paste, if their layers were noted on a perpendicular
scale, they would range after this fashion : first of all, seal—
then biped—seal in the centre with biped—and seal again at
the bottom. Yet, singular enough, these savages are cheerful,
and really seem to have great capacity for enjoyment. Though
in the coldest and most comfortless dens of the earth, they are

ever on the grin, whatever befalls them. When they see a white man and his knick-knacks, they grin. They grin when they rub their noses with snow, when they blow their fingers, when they lubricate their hides inside and out with the fat of the seal. Truly, then, as Sterne says, ' Providence, thou art merciful ! ' "

The above description must speak for itself ; but, without endorsing more than its reference to the good humour of the Esquimaux, I must say that, whatever they may be physically and socially, they are undoubtedly a kind-hearted, hospitable, and well-disposed race of beings. On my first meeting with them, at the time I am writing of, in Grinnell Bay, I was much struck by their peculiar dress and good-natured features. The women especially attracted my attention, and I could not but think of old Grimes—" that good old man "—in his long-tailed coat. The difference, however, in the coats of these Esquimaux women and that of old Grimes is that they do not button down *before*. In truth, there is no button about these arctic coats. They have a long, neatly-worked flap behind, with a baby-pouch on the shoulders, and are slipped over the head like a frock. But a full description of their dress will be given in a chapter devoted entirely to the manners and customs of these singular people.

Among the visitors on board when we anchored were a few who will frequently figure in my narrative. *Ugarng*, who has been already named, was a very prominent character, and it seems to me well to give some account of him and his family, especially as the history of most of all the Innuits I met is so full of strange adventure, and so indicative of their peculiar customs, that it cannot fail to be interesting. The particulars were gathered only at intervals long after my first acquaintance with the parties.

At the time of which I write there lived in the neighbourhood of my explorations a very aged and singular woman called Oo-ki-jox-y Ni-noo. This patriarchal dame was born on an island named An-nan-ne-toon, situated on the north side of Hudson's Strait, and when I first saw her I believe she could not have been less than one hundred years old. She was an important personage among her people, and, as the reader will find, proved of much service to me from the knowledge she had of Innuit traditions.

Now this woman had been married to a man called *Pier-koo-ne-me-loon*, who had also, at the same time, a second wife, Poor-loong-wong, sister of Ookijoxy Ninoo. By the second wife he had three children, with whom we have nothing to do. But by the former he had eight sons and daughters, and at length died in a good old age, leaving his other wife to survive all her own children except the Ugarng already named.

The progeny of this old woman was as follows:

1st. A daughter, that died at its birth, owing to an accidental fall previously received by its mother while playing ball in the spring.

2d. A daughter, *Tou-yer-nŭd-loon,* who grew up to womanhood, a large, strong woman. She married a *Pim-ma-in,* or chief, who was considered a very smart Innuit. After many years she had by him two children, and at the birth of the latter she died. The infant was then allowed to die, because, as was told me, " it was impossible to take care of it;" and two or three days afterward the husband also died. With regard to this woman, it was considered among the Innuits impossible to tell which looked oldest, her mother or herself.

3d. A daughter, called *Noo-ker-pier-ung,* who was born not far from Newton's Fiord, in Frobisher Bay. She married a man named *Oo-yung,* and these were the parents of *E-bier-bing,* a person who will often appear as a very important character in my narrative. The mother died about 1852.

4th. A son, *New-wer-kier-ung,* who married, first, a cousin of Ebierbing's wife, the intelligent Tookoolito, by which cousin he had a boy; secondly, a woman called *E-ker-too-kong* ("Polly," as we named her), by whom he had many children, who all grew very fast and fat, but died young. He died before his wife, and she then married a fine, bold, and—to white persons as well as his own people—most kindly disposed, humane man, christened by us "Bob,"—his Innuit name, *King-wat-che-ung.* The wife was a half-sister to another good but afflicted man, called Pauloo-yer, or, as I have always styled him from his loss of sight, "Blind George." Of him I will speak presently.

The fifth child of the old woman was *Ugarng,* whom I shall bring forward in a moment.

The sixth was a daughter, *An-ner-surng,* who married *Mik-e-lung.* They had two or three children, but one of them, *E-ter-loong,* a little boy, cross-eyed, was almost always by his grandmother's side, and was evidently regarded by her as a pet.

The seventh child was also a daughter, *Kood-loo-toon,* who

---

* " *Pim-ma-in,*" a term used in former times among the Innuits for the principal man (or chief) among them. It is now obsolete, as there are no chiefs or rulers among them. Every man is now on an equality one with another.

married a brother of one "Chummy" (a man that visited the States in 1861-2). By him she had two children; one died young, and the other is now living and married.

The eighth and last child was another daughter, *Oo-yar-ou-ye-urg*, who married and had two children, a boy and girl. The latter was named Oo-kood-lear, and I was well acquainted with her.

These were the children and grandchildren of old Oo-ki-jox-y-ni-noo. Now let me turn to the account of *Ugarng*.

This man was born at or near Newton's Fiord, in Frobisher Bay, and was about 50 or 55 years old. From his early days he displayed great qualities as a daring and successful hunter. Many of his well-attested exploits border on the incredible, so marvellous did they seem. Not a few, possibly, I shall be able to relate farther on. Perhaps, however, not among the least of them may be considered the fact that he had no less than *thirteen* wives; and, at the period I formed his acquaintance, had three living with him. His first wife, *Ak-chur-e-you*, he left, long before she died, because she bore him no children; his second, *Oo-soo-kong*, gave him a son and daughter; both, with herself, dead. The third wife was alive, but left at *Padley*. Afterward she had two children by another man. The fourth also had two children by another man; the fifth hung herself after giving him a daughter, now 14 years old. The sixth—still alive, and related to Tookoolito—had no children; the seventh was *Kun-ni-u*, whom I shall frequently name. She likewise had no children up to the time of my last seeing her; the eighth was *Kou-nung*, who had two children by another man—the children now grown up and married. The ninth was *Kok-kong*, or *Pun-nie*, his present second wife, but with no children; the tenth was *Ak-chuk-er-zhun*, who, however, left him and went to live with *Kooperneung* ("Charley"), a man I often afterward employed. The eleventh wife of Ugarng was *Nik-u-jar* ("Polly"), by whom he had a child called *Menoun*, about three years old when I last saw it. *Nikujar* died while I was up there. She had been the wife of *Blind George*, already mentioned, but left him a few years after he became blind.

Ugarng was a remarkably intelligent man and a very good mechanic. He had several excellent traits of character, besides some not at all commendable.

In 1854-5 he was on a visit to the States, and among his reminiscences of that visit he said about New York, "G— d— ! too much horse—too much house—too much white people. Women? ah! women great many—good!"

I now bring forward another man, already mentioned, Pau-loo-yer, or "Blind George." Of his parentage there is but little known, even by himself, except that his mother hung herself. He was born about 1819, and when young the Innuits took care of him. He grew up and became one of the first Esquimaux of his place. He was an excellent pilot, greatly attached to Americans, and very desirous of learning their language. He married the Nikujar already spoken of, and by her had three children. The first was born in the spring of——, and had black spots covered with hair on its body. It died before six months old.

In 1852-3 he became blind through an epidemic that took off very many of the natives. His second child also died; and the third, born in 1856, was an interesting girl called *Koo-koo-yer.*

Nikujar continued with her poor blind husband for five years after his affliction, and they were always attentive and kind to each other. But, as he was unable to work, she accepted the offer of Ugarng to become his principal or *family*, that is, household wife. She took with her the little girl *Koo-koo-yer*, and Ugarng became partial to it, and as he was a bold, successful hunter, generally contrived to provide for all his household, and even many more, without stint. "George," though greatly attached to his child, knew it was for her advantage to be with her mother, and thus allowed her to go, though occasionally seeking for her company with him.

I shall frequently speak of this afflicted Innuit in my narrative, and therefore have mentioned these particulars.

Another person to be referred to here is Kok-er-jab-in, the widow of Kudlago. She was born at Kar-mo-wong, on the north side of Hudson's Straits, probably about the year 1814. She had had three husbands, the first being a tall, stout man, called *Koo-choo-ar-chu* ("Samson"), by whom she had one son, *Ning-u-ar-ping.* But this husband she left because he added another woman to his household. Her second husband was An-you-kar-ping, a fine, powerful man. He was lost by the upsetting of his ki-a.* When the ki-a was found it was broken into fragments, and it is thought by the Innuits that he had attacked a hooded seal, which, in return, ferociously attacked and destroyed him and his boat. By this husband she had one son, often mentioned in my journal as "Captain." Her third husband was Kudlago, who had also been previously married to a woman

* The Greenland term for a boat or canoe containing one man is *Ky-ack,* but among the Innuits I was acquainted with *Ki-a* is the word, and such I henceforth use.

named *Ne-ve-chad-loo*, by whom two daughters, *Kok-er-zhun* and *Kim-mi-loo*, were born to him. The first of these was a pretty young woman, aged twenty-three, and married to *Shi-mer-ar-chu* (" Johnny Bull "), who was always exceedingly jealous of her. Kimmiloo was an interesting girl of about sixteen years old. By Kokerjabin no children were born. She and her third husband did not get on happily together. On one occasion this woman was nearly dead from a severe dropsical complaint. The angeko was then called in, and his wife's brother undertook to perform an operation for her cure. This he did in the following manner : Ebierbing held Kokerjabin while the operator, with a sort of lancet having a blade three inches long, stabbed her quickly and forcibly in the abdomen. Water poured forth copiously, and soon after this she recovered.

At the time of my first arrival among these Innuits, several of them were in different places hunting and fishing ; but I afterward became so well acquainted with them, and was on such familiar terms, that they and others I shall introduce seemed almost of my own family.

But I will now proceed with my own personal narrative.

In the afternoon, accompanied by Sterry, Gardiner, and Lamb, I went on shore. There I visited several of the natives in their *tupics*—summer skin-tents.

The *honesty* of this people is remarkable. I noticed on the beach coal, wood, four tubs of whale-line, tar, oil-casks, mincing machine, coils of rope, trying kettles, harpoons, lances, &c. all left here since the previous fall, and yet as safe as on board the ship ! Another trait of their character, however, is not at all commendable. One of the first things attracting my attention, close to the tents, was the skeleton of an Innuit, or Esquimaux woman, just as she had died some three years before ! She had been sick, and was left to take care of herself. The remains of her tent—her skin bedding, her stone lamp, and other domestic articles, were still by her side. This inattention to the sick and dead is a custom of the Esquimaux, and, in another place, I shall again refer to it.

When I returned on board, Kudlago's wife had just arrived. She had heard on shore of her husband's death, and at once, with her son (the daughter not arriving till next day), hastened to the ship. Sorrowfully, and with tears in her eyes, did the poor Esquimaux widow, Kokerjabin, enter our cabin. As she looked at us, and then at the chest where Kudlago had kept his things, and which Captain Budington now opened, the tears flowed faster and faster, showing that Nature is as much susceptible of all the softer feelings among these children of the North as with us in the warmer South. But her grief could hardly be controlled when the treasures Kudlago had gathered in the States for her and his little girl were exhibited. She sat herself down upon the chest, and pensively bent her head in deep, unfeigned sorrow ; then, after a time, she left the cabin with her son.

The following day I again went on shore for an excursion up the mountains, " Captain," a lad about fifteen years of age, accompanying me. My dogs had been landed immediately upon our arrival, and now greeted me with much joy. Poor creatures, how they liked once more to bury their shaggy, panting bodies beneath the snow ! They skip, they run, they come and look, as if grateful, in my eye, and then bound away again in the wildest exuberance of animal spirits.

I have before mentioned some particulars of these dogs, and I now relate an anecdote concerning them during our passage across from Greenland.

One day, in feeding the dogs, I called the whole of them around me, and gave to each in turn a *capelin*, or small dried fish. To do this fairly, I used to make all the dogs encircle me until every one had received ten of the capelins apiece. Now *Barbekark*, a very young and shrewd dog, took it into his head that he would play a white man's trick. So, every time he received his fish, he would back square out, move a distance of two or three dogs, and force himself in line again, thus receiving double the share of any other dog. But this joke of Barbekark's bespoke too much of the game many men play upon their fellowbeings, and, as I noticed it, I determined to check his doggish propensities ; still, the cunning, and the singular way in which he evidently watched me, induced a moment's pause in my intentions. Each dog thankfully took *his* capelin as his turn came round, but Barbekark, finding his share came twice as often as his companions', appeared to shake his tail twice as thankfully as the others. A twinkle in his eyes, as they caught mine, seemed to say, " Keep dark ; these ignorant fellows don't know the game I'm playing. I am confounded hungry." Seeing my face smiling at his trick, he now commenced making another change, thus getting *three* portions to each of the others' one. This was enough, and it was now time for me to reverse the order of Barbekark's game, by playing a trick upon him. Accordingly, every time I came to him he got no fish ; and although he changed his position rapidly three times, yet he got nothing. Then, if ever there was a picture of disappointed plans—of envy at others' fortune, and sorrow at a sad misfortune—it was to be found on that dog's countenance as he watched his companions receiving their allowance. Finding he could not succeed by any change of his position, he withdrew from the circle to where I was, and came to me, crowding his way between my legs, and looked up in my face as if to say, "I have been a very bad dog. Forgive me, and Barbekark will cheat his brother dogs no more. Please, sir, give me my share of capelins." I went the rounds three times more, and let him have the fish, as he had shown himself so sagacious, and so much like a repentant prodigal dog!

This dog Barbekark afterward again made himself remarkably noticed, as I shall have occasion to relate. He shared all my labours with me, and was here as my companion in the States, until he died a few months back.

I now return to an account of my excursion on shore.

The day was bright and lovely when I ascended the mountain. Beautiful *crimson* snow lay about by the side of large patches of the purer white, and as I travelled on, my heart felt as light and buoyant as the air I breathed. The scenery was grand and enchanting. Two or three lakes were passed, one of them half a mile long by the same in width, with its waters at a temperature of 38°, and as clear as crystal, so that the bottom could be distinctly seen. It had deep snow-banks all around it, and yet, to my surprise, mosquitoes were floating on and over its surface, breeding by myriads. Some beautiful falls were situated here, walled in by huge mountains and their fragments. Many of these were enormous rocks, apparently capable of being easily set in motion by a man's power with a crowbar, so delicately were they poised upon each other. The frozen waters of winter have been doing wondrous work in throwing down these mountains. If water can find a crack in rocks, they are sure to be broken asunder.

The inventions of men give them easy power to split rocks that are massive and hard. This is done by drilling holes and entering steel wedges, which are acted upon by slight blows. Another way is to drill deep into the rock and charge with gunpowder. But God has *His* way of splitting rocks! He uses the little snow and rain-drops. They find their way into every recess. Crevices are at length filled with solid ice. They are enlarged; chasms now yawn; another winter, and down from their rude heights the cliffs fall, making the earth to quake in her career!

There were many, very many rocks that would be cast from their places, high up the mountains, on the next spring. A person can hardly conceive the quantity of rock that is lifted from its base every season by the freezing of water.

Never can I forget the visit I made on this excursion to the stream that runs wildly down the mountain's side, between the first and second lakelets, near *Kow-tug-ju-a*—Clark's Harbour.

For one-third of a mile the stream was covered with a huge pile of snow. I crossed to the upper part of this with my Esquimaux boy, and went down to the stream itself to slake my thirst. I kneeled and drank of the sparkling waters. As I looked round before rising, what did I see ? a cave of alabaster ! snow-arches, numberless and incomparable ! At a point where several arches commenced to spring were pendant finely-formed icicles, from which poured perpendicularly to the earth, unbroken streams of water, having the appearance of inverted columns of crystal supporting the arches. The number of these columns was great. Away, far away, down the cave, through which the stream passed, all was dark—dark as Cimmerian darkness.

From this I turned my eyes upward. Overhanging my head were pinnacled mountains 1,000 feet above me. Far as the eye could see they extended. On my still bended knees, I thanked God that I lived to behold how manifold and wonderful was the world's creation. None but God and that untutored Esquimaux saw me there, amid the roar of that mountain waterfall, offering up this, my heart's prayer !

While there I gave the dogs some dinner (capelins), and then had my own along with the Esquimaux. A good appetite made me relish the sea-biscuit and Cincinnati pork, and then, after resting a while, I began the return journey. I had ascended to a height of about 1,500 feet above the sea, and two miles from the beach, making a collection of various geological and other specimens ; but these latter I unfortunately lost. On my way down, a good snow-slide, for about a quarter of a mile, on an angle of 50°, carried me swiftly on, and, in due time, I got back to the tents, where a score of Esquimaux at once kindly greeted me. Away from all the rest, seated alone among the rocks, I saw *Kudlago's* widow, weeping for the loss she had sustained. Her son at once went and tried to console her, but she would not be comforted, and her grief was allowed to have vent unrestrained.

The next day we had for dinner salmon, venison, and bear-meat ! It was then I took my first lesson in eating the latter.

I found it passable, with a taste somewhat akin to lamp-oil, but yet, on the whole, good.

A few days afterward I made another excursion; and as I passed on my way up the mountain steeps, flowers greeted me at every step I took, lifting their beautiful faces from behind the gray old rocks over which I was passing. At length I reached a height beyond which I could mount no farther. Under the friendly shelter of a projecting cliff, I sat myself down amid the most luxurious bed of sorrel that I ever saw. I made a good feast upon it, and in ten minutes I could have gathered a bushel, it was so plentiful.

While here I had a look around. What a magnificent picture was before me! The bold mountains across the bay,

PIPE SKETCH—CLARK'S HARBOUR.

with higher snow-capped ones behind them; the waterfall of 500 feet; the *George Henry*, the *Rescue*, and *Black Eagle*, lying at anchor beneath the shadow of those mountains, and the Esquimaux village low at my feet, was an admirable subject for a sketch.

I seized my pencil, but paper I had left behind. Still I was not to be balked. I had a new clay pipe in my mouth. I took this pipe and inspected the bowl. A little fancy line ran down its centre opposite the stem. This line would serve to represent the dashing, foaming waterfall before me; the plain surface on each side would do for the sketch. This I made; and such as it then was is here presented to the reader, even as I hoped I might be able to do, under the title of the "Pipe Sketch."

After this I gathered a bouquet of flowers, some geological specimens, and returned.

On my way I again met Kudlago's widow and another Esquimaux woman. As we passed a place where some tents had formerly stood, *Kokerjabin* called my attention, with tears in her eyes, to the spot where her husband had his tent when he bade her adieu on his visit to the States in 1859. She lifted up a portion of the back-bone of a whale which was bleaching near by, and said it was of one Kudlago had killed. Her tone, her manner as she spoke, was truly affecting, and I have no doubt she felt deeply the loss she had sustained.

On August 11th, among the Esquimaux arrivals was Kudlago's idol—a pretty little girl. She looked sad for the loss of her dear father. But how her eyes sparkled in the afternoon when several things were produced that her father had carefully gathered for her! The account of her first arrival I find in my journal as follows:—

"Kimmiloo has just been Americanized. Captain B——'s good wife had made and sent to her a pretty red dress—a neck-tie, mittens, belt, &c.

"Mr. Rogers and I, at a suggestion from me, thought it best to commence the change of nationality with soap and water. The process was slow, that of arriving to the beautiful little girl, whom we at length found, though deeply imbedded layer after layer in dirt. Then came the task of making her toilet. With a *very coarse comb* I commenced to disentangle her hair. She had but little that was long, the back part from behind her ears having been cut short off on account of severe pains in her head. How patiently she submitted to worse than the curry-comb process I had to use! This was the first time in her life that a comb had been put to her head. Her hair was filled with moss, seal, and reindeer hairs, and many other things—too numerous to call them all by name. Poor thing! yet she was fat and beautiful—the very picture of health. Her cheeks were as red as the blown rose. Nature's vermilion was upon them.

"A full hour was I before getting that child's hair so that I could draw the coarse end of a coarse comb through it! At last that job was completed. Her little fingers quickly braided a tag of hair on each side of her head. Then I gave her two brass rings (which is the fashion among the Esquimaux women) through which to draw the hair. The skin trowsers and coat were thrown off, and the red dress put on."

Many Esquimaux now visited us, and from them I tried to obtain all the information I could as to my intended journey toward King William's Land. I also discussed the question with Captain Allen, of the *Black Eagle*, who I soon found well capable and willing to advise me. It was, however, too late in the season to attempt *commencing* the journey then, and this all of those with whom I conversed, Esquimaux and white men, told me. I had therefore to wait, and meanwhile make myself well accustomed to the sort of life I should have to endure while actually prosecuting my undertaking.

A day or two afterward I was showing Kimmiloo, Ookoodlear, and Shookok (pretty little Esquimaux girls) the pictorial illustrations in a number of the Family Bible, when "Blind George" came on board. When I asked him his name, he said, in Esquimaux, "George—poor blind George, as Americans call me."

"What is your Innuit name?" said I. "Paulooyer," was the response; and then immediately added, "What is yours?" I told him, and after repeating it several times till he had pronounced it correctly, he was satisfied. I explained that the prefix "Mr." to the "Hall," which I had casually given, was an address applied to men; whereupon, soon afterward meeting the steward and blacksmith, and hearing them called by those terms, he at once said, "Mr. Steward—Mr. Blacksmith." I tried to explain the difference to him, and it was not long before he understood me. He was quick to perceive mistakes, and, when he saw an error of his own, had a hearty laugh over it. He made all his clothes—sealskins; and the way he threaded his needle was most amusing and singular. He took the eye end of a needle between his teeth, bringing the needle into proper position, and then placed it on his tongue near the end. He next brought the end of his thread toward the eye of his needle, and, after several trials, the thread was finally drawn through the eye by his very sensitive tongue. He then grasped with his lips and teeth the end of the thread, and thus the needle was threaded! I have seen "Blind George" thus thread his needle, time and again, in ten seconds!

Wishing to test his quality as a tailor, I gave him one of my coats to mend in the sleeve. It was full of rents, but to only one did I call his attention. I left him at his work; and being myself afterward busy at something else, I had forgotten him.

When I again went to him where he was generally seated in the main cabin, he had *every break* mended, and all his work *well done*.

I took out my little magnet and put it into his hands. He passed it through and through his fingers, and then I placed the *armature* upon it. This was a mystery to him. The Esquimaux exclamations that escaped his lips were numerous and amusing. I then took the armature and gave him a sewing needle, bringing it and the magnet together. This was also wondrous to him. It was many minutes before he became satisfied it was really so. He would pull one end of the needle off the magnet, and when he let go it would fly back. The approach of an armature to a magnet, both in his hands, also greatly surprised him. As they came near and he *felt* the attractive power, he instantly threw them aside, and it was some time before I could get him to make another trial. Still more careful was he the second time. The contact was at last made, and made quick as lightning, but just as quick did he drop the two. Finding, however, that he was not injured, and that the little girls were enjoying a hearty laugh at his expense—they having before tried it—he at last succeeded. I next tried him with a pair of needles, desiring him to bring the magnet near them. He did so, but at the cost of my time and patience, as I had to pick them up from all parts of the cabin. On discovering that the needles had sprung from his hand, he acted as if smitten by a thunder-bolt, throwing needles, magnet, and all helter-skelter away ! and still more, he at once declared I was an *An-ge-ko !*

At this time Ugarng was often on board the ship, and one day I was much amused at his vain attempts to pick up some mercury which I had out upon a sheet of white paper. The metal assumed a globular shape, and looked precisely like shot made of tin. Now the mercury thus presented to his view seemed to be quite beyond his comprehension. Generally, an Esquimaux is stoical under all circumstances, no matter how startling they may be, but here was something that completely upset his equanimity. After nearly half an hour's attempt to understand the lively substance before him, and to grasp it, he gave up, and also lost his temper. He burst out in some broken words, like oaths he had heard on board ship, declaring the d—l was in it, and nothing else.

A short time after our arrival at this anchorage I had a narrow escape of my life. It was most providential, and afforded me an assurance that the Almighty had protected me. In the afternoon I went down seaward for the purpose of examining some rocks. I had with me my revolver, pencil, and portfolio. The stratification of these rocks was very remarkable, and for several rods I saw a quartz vein running as straight as a line N.N.W. and S.S.E. Its dip was 60°, and in thickness one and a half to two inches. Everywhere around, the fallen ruins of mountains stared me in the face. I was perfectly astonished at the rapidity with which huge rocks had evidently been rent to pieces. I also saw, standing by themselves, square pillars of stone, the strata of which were completely separated, so that I could take them off one by one, as leaves of paper. Some were an inch, half an inch, two inches, and others six inches thick. Anxious to obtain some specimens, I was engaged, with my knife, digging out some quartz and gold-like metal, slightly bedded in a fresh-broken rock before me, when, as I leaned forward, the revolver fell from my belt, and instantly exploded close to my hand and face! For the moment I thought myself dangerously wounded, so great was the pain I experienced in my hand and forehead; but the next instant I ascertained that the ball had just cleared me, merely forcing the powder into my hand, forehead, and round my right eye. It was a narrow escape, and a warning thereafter to be more careful how I left the hammer of any gun or pistol I had about me.

The rocks about here were indeed very remarkable. One pile consisted entirely of mica, quartz, and feldspar; and the nearest approach I can give to its appearance is to let the imagination conceive that the feldspar was in a state like putty, and worked up into various uncouth figures, the spaces between each filled up with mica and quartz. Then would there be an appearance similar to what I observed on these rocks, only that ages and ages should be added to cut out deeply the mica and quartz, leaving the pure quartz veins almost unaffected.

On the 14th of August the brig *Georgiana*, belonging to the same owners as the *George Henry*, arrived from some other whaling ground. Thus four vessels were now near each other, the *Black Eagle, Georgiana, Rescue*, and our own; and a very sociable and agreeable time was spent, during leisure hours, in visiting each other. But none of us were unnecessarily idle. Preparations had to be made for the coming winter, and for whale-fishing while the season yet lasted. The *Black Eagle* and *Georgiana* had their own plans, but that of the *George Henry* was to visit another and smaller bay on the south side of this inlet.

Meanwhile Captain Budington had erected a stone and turf house for the benefit of his boats' crews, when, as was intended, some of the men should be stationed there "to fish." The roof was made from timber, with canvas well coated with tar over all.

On the 16th we sailed for Nu-gum-mi-uke, the intended winter quarters of the *George Henry* and *Rescue*. As we left the bay, we passed several prominent places, and among them Sterry's Tower. The following is a sketch of it :—

STERRY'S TOWER.

The next day, in company with many of the natives, we arrived at Nu-gum-mi-uke (a bay which I named after Cyrus W. Field, one of the promoters of my expedition). The harbour we entered was hard to find, but it was thought to be perfectly safe. Soon afterward the ship and her crew made ready for whaling ; but for myself, I determined upon mixing unreservedly with the natives, and for this purpose tried to secure

Ugarng as a guide and companion. I presented him with a beautiful ivory-handled knife. He was much pleased with it, and said, in his own tongue, *kuoy-en-na-mik* (I thank you).

Ugarng's wives were really good-looking, and capital workers, chewing more seal, reindeer, and walrus skins for boots and mittens than any other women of the country. This chewing process will be described at another time ; but I may here observe that it is one of the principal modes of making the skins pliable, and changing them into any desired form. It is a labour always performed by females, never by men. The Innuit women also washed clothes, and soon became so proficient that they could do them as well as the Americans. One morning I gave my clothes to be washed by a woman called *Nukertou*, and by the evening she returned the articles to me completed and in good order. Ugarng gave me an excellent pair of native boots, made by one of his wives, and, in return, I presented her with some brass rings, which the women greatly prize for doing up the hair.

Wishing to visit some of the innumerable islands that lay scattered about the bay, and also to place my dogs on some place best suited for them, where the remains of a whale were found, I took three Esquimaux boys and little Kimmiloo in the boat with me to pull. I accomplished my errand, and, on the return, much enjoyed the sight of my crew, including the girl (all fresh types of the Iron race of the North), smoking with pipe in their mouth, and, at the same time, pulling heartily at the oars !

On Monday, August 20th, after tea, the captain, myself, Smith, Sterry, Morgan, and Bailey took a boat, and went out a ducking. The wind was blowing fresh from the north-west, therefore we beat to windward. On the way we killed five ducks—a sport that was exciting enough, though not remunerative, five or six shots having to be expended in killing one duck. While tacking, I lost my venerable hat—the one I punctured with a pike when raising it high in the air on top of the first iceberg I visited.

On the 21st of August, at 7 A.M. the *Rescue* was got under way for the purpose of taking a party of us over to an inlet on the opposite side of Field Bay. It was intended by the captain to examine this and other places to see their availability for fishing depôts, and I gladly took the opportunity of accompanying him.

While heaving up anchor, an incident occurred that served well to illustrate the character of the Innuit *Ugarng*. His third wife, *Kun-ni-u*, with the captain and myself, were at the windless brake, and it was quite an amusing sight to behold us. Presently we had to stop for a moment, and, on commencing again, *Kunniu* could not quickly lay hold ; whereupon her husband, who was standing by, looking on with a sort of dignity, as if he were lord of all he surveyed, at once ordered her to go ahead ; and when she grasped the brake, he turned and strutted about the deck in quite an independent manner.

Two boats had to tow us out of the harbour, owing to there being no wind, and we passed through a channel between two small islands that was probably never navigated before. One man went aloft to con the way, and I stood on the bow to watch for rocks under water. Several I saw far down—some at five and ten fathoms deep, and looking white and yawning ; but they were harmless, even had they been much nearer the surface, for the *Rescue* only drew eight feet water.

At 8 A.M. a light breeze filled the sails, and, taking up our boats, away we went across the waters of the bay. A course nearly due south was steered, somewhat westerly of Bear Sound, and in due time we approached the opposite shores, where some wild and rocky, but magnificent scenery was presented to our view. At 2 P.M. we turned into one of three or four entrances that led, by a safe channel, into a long and beautiful bay. On either side of us were towering mountains, one especially of a bold and lofty character, with its peak looking down majestically into the waters below.

The breeze had now somewhat freshened from the N.E. and was sending us along full five knots an hour. Great was the excitement ; most exhilarating the whole scene. We were in waters quite new to us, and approaching Frobisher *Straits*—then, at least, so believed by me. Our lady-Esquimaux pilot, Kunniu, guided us safely on, but care was also needed ; Morgan, therefore, went aloft to look out, and I again took my place on the bowsprit end. Occasionally a huge white old rock peered up its head, as if to ask, Who were we that thus disturbed the usual quietude of the place, and unsettled the peace that had reigned during the world's age ? But no interruption to our progress was made. We went on and on, creating the most joyous emotions in my breast as we proceeded. My heart leaped within me as the vessel bounded forward.

I had taken my glass in hand and cast my eye to the southwest. There I could see the extent of the bay was limited by a very low coast, but beyond it were the high, bold mountains of

Meta Incognita, across the olden " Straits "—so termed — of Martin Frobisher. Though in the blue melting distance, and some fifty miles off, yet they seemed like giants close by. Then, too, the lofty hills of rock on either side of us, with the sun-glade, like a pathway of dazzling gold, ahead, made the picture beautiful and exciting in the extreme. It was my first visit and approach to the scenes of Frobisher's discoveries, and well might I be excused for the joyousness of my heart on the occasion.

At length the schooner carried us to the termination of the bay, and in a few moments more we had safely anchored in a good spot, having four and a half fathoms' depth at low water.

CHAPTER VI.

IT was half-past four o'clock, August 21st, when we dropped anchor in this beautiful inlet, which I name after Richard H. Chappell, of New London, Connecticut. We then had a hurried tea, and immediately afterward took a boat and went on shore. Our party consisted of the captain, Mates Gardiner and Lamb, Morgan and Bailey, besides myself. Four Esquimaux—two of them being Ugarng and his wife Kunniu—also accompanied us.

On getting ashore we found that the neck of land dividing the waters just left from those of Frobisher " Straits " was less than a mile in breadth, and so low that, except in one part where a ridge of rocks occurred, it could not be more than a few feet above the sea, and possibly covered at high tides. Portions of this isthmus were sandy, and the rest full of stones, rocks, and several specimens of shale, many of which I eagerly collected. On one plat of sand we observed some foot-tracks, which Ugarng stated to be of reindeer, though such an opinion seemed to me ridiculous from the appearance before us, and so the event proved on the following day, when we encountered some Esquimaux who had been here.

On arriving at the ridge of rocks, which I call " Morgan's Hill," and which overlooked the whole locality around, I paused a moment to gaze upon the scene before my eye. There, facing me, was the celebrated " Strait "—so called—of Frobisher, and beyond it in the distance *Meta Incognita* *—thus named by Queen Elizabeth, but termed *Kingaite* by the Esquimaux. Two

---

* " *Meta Incognita* " embraced both sides of " Frobisher Straits," and, in fact, was meant to include the whole of his discoveries.

FROBISHER BAY—META INCOGNITA AND GRINNELL GLACIER.

hundred and eighty-two years previously, in that very month of August, the great English navigator, then on his third voyage, was sailing on the waters now within my view, and, after many perils from storms, fogs, and floating ice, he and part of his original fleet (which consisted of fifteen vessels) assembled in " Countess of Warwick's Sound," which I supposed to be not far off. As I gazed, how I longed to be exploring it, then hopefully anticipating it would prove the highway to my ultimate destination, King William's Land! But such was not to be. Disappointment is the lot of all men. Mine afterward proved great ; and yet I have reason to be thankful for what I afterward accomplished.

I looked long and earnestly. The land on the opposite side of the "Straits" was clear before me, though at a distance of some forty miles, and it appeared as if a long line of ice or snow topped a considerable portion of it. I hastened from the place whereon I stood, and walked to the beach, where the waters of the so-called Frobisher Strait washed the shores. There, with spy-glass, I again carefully examined the opposite land. The same appearance presented itself. But not till some months afterward, when exploring up the " Straits," did I have positive proof that what I now saw was really an enormous and magnificent glacier, which, when I visited it, I called after the name of Henry Grinnell.

Continuing with my glass to trace the land westerly, it seemed to me that the mountains in that direction united with the land on which I stood, and if so, no " strait " existed. But, as refraction at first was going on, I fancied that I might be deceived. A longer look, however, made me still feel doubtful ;* and while I stood charmed and spell-bound by the picture before me, a crowd of strange thoughts filled my soul as I reflected upon my own position there, and remembered the history of those early voyages made by Frobisher and his companions. But I had not much time to ponder. The party was awaiting me, and I had to return.

On my way back I found many other specimens of fossils, a quantity of which I secured ; and as I was well-loaded, Kunniu, Ugarng's wife, offered to assist me in carrying them. The hood of her long-tailed coat was widely opened to receive my load. Some fifty pounds' weight of rock specimens, &c. were placed in

* A week later, as will be seen, six intelligent Esquimaux positively assured me that this was a bay, and not a "strait."

this convenient receptacle, now answering the purpose of a geologist's saddle-bag; another time, an Esquimaux lady's bonnet or pouch; and, next, a baby-house! One of the limestones, on being broken in two, exposed to view an imbedded mineral the size and shape of a duck-shot. I tried to cut it with my knife, but it was hard as steel; and no effect was made upon it except by scraping off the oxyd, which then left displayed something like bright iron. Unfortunately, I afterward lost this specimen by dropping it in the ship's hold.

We got on board the *Rescue* about nine o'clock, and had a very pleasant evening in the cabin. The next morning we were again on our way toward the *George Henry*. As we passed out of the bay, taking another channel, it fell calm, and two boats' crews were ordered ahead to tow. There was a strong tide running, and right in the channel some rocks were seen just below water. It was too late to alter the schooner's course, and, though every effort was made to get clear, yet we should have been left upon those rocks had it not been for the swell of the sea and a good pull at the oars carrying us *right over them!*

In the afternoon, while still towing, three ki-as, followed by oo-mi-ens (family boats of the natives) filled with women and men, approached. On the present occasion, a highly intelligent Innuit, Koojesse by name, was boat-steerer of one, while his family and other Esquimaux, with all of their connexions, their tents, cooking utensils, &c. accompanied him. As soon as they reached the *Rescue*, all came on board, Koojesse having with him one of the finest Esquimaux dogs I had seen. More dogs, deer-skins, walrus heads and tusks, with abundance of game, such as ducks, &c., were with the party.

Among the number now arrived was *Kudlago's* eldest daughter, *Kokerzhun*, a truly fair and beautiful young woman, already married to a young man called *Shi-mer-ar-chu*, otherwise Johnny Bull. She came alongside full of hope and happiness, expecting to hear of, and perhaps to meet, her father. Both herself and *Tunukderlien*, the wife of *Koojesse*, delayed approaching until they had made a change of dress, and then, when ready, on deck they came. But, alas! how sad was the blow she had to receive! Seeing *Kunniu*, Ugarng's wife, whom she knew, the question was put to her, "*Nou-ti-ma wong-a a-tă-tá?*"—Where is my father? and when Kunniu, in a calm but kindly way, communicated the painful news, it was as if a thunderbolt had riven her heart! That face, a moment before beaming with hope and happiness at the thought of meeting her father, was instantly changed to an expression of deep woe ! Tears coursed down her cheeks, and, though the usual calm dignity of Esquimaux nature forbade outcries or noisy lamentation, yet it was evident she most acutely felt the sudden calamity. Her Esquimaux friends, and all who knew her father, sympathized greatly with her, as indeed did we Americans. Everything in our power was done to alleviate her distress, but it was long before she got over the shock.

In one of the oomiens there were no less than eighteen women and children, an old " patriarch" named *Ar-tark-pa-ru*, who was crippled in both nether limbs, but blessed with the heaviest beard and mustache yet seen among his people—ten dogs, tents, reindeer skins in immense number, venison, seal-blubber, ducks, walrus heads and tusks, hunting instruments, and, in truth, all the worldly goods of some seven families !

Having made fast the oomiens astern, taken the kias on board, hoisted the old man up by a rope, and allowed all the rest to mount as best they could, we soon had our decks crowded with about thirty good-humoured natives of all ages and sizes, and of both sexes.

It was not long, however, before the female portion were put to work in skinning some of the ducks. While doing so I sat beside them, and eagerly watched their operations. They asked me for my knife, and were delighted with the excellent one I lent them. Taking a duck, and drawing the knife once round the outer joint of each wing and the head, they seized the cut part with their teeth, and stripped the fowl entire ! The ducks were very fat, and most of it adhered to the skin. This caused these daughters of the North to rejoice with each other on the feast of fat skins that awaited them on completing their work ! After all the ducks had been skinned, they were delivered to the cook as fresh provision for the ship's company. It was understood that for preparing these ducks the native women were to have the skins as pay, and this was considered ample. A short time afterward I saw mothers, fathers, sons, and daughters in bed on deck, with their duck-skins in hand, peeling off the " luxurious " fat with their teeth, each now and then giving a peculiar kind of grunt in great satisfaction ! " In bed " among the Esquimaux is to repose *in puris naturalibus* between reindeer skins with the hair on. Being well enveloped in these heat-retaining skins, they proceeded to eat themselves to sleep !

Most of the female portion of those on board had each a really beautiful ornament upon their head, bent like a bow, and extending from points just forward and below the ears up over the top of the head. At the apex it was one inch wide, tapering down to half an inch at the extremities, and it looked and glistened in the bright sun like burnished gold. There were two fastenings to this ornament—a string of variously-coloured beads going under the chin as a bonnet-tie, also one passing down behind the ears at the back of the neck and head. It struck me that this was not only a beautiful ornament to the Esquimaux women, but would also be to ladies at home.

Before Artarkparu came on board he was very anxious to make well secure some drift timber he had found. One piece was a ship's deck-plank, probably a part of the English whaling vessel *Traveller*, wrecked in Bear Sound in 1858. This vessel was about 500 tons, and was lost by getting upon the rocks, when, the tide leaving her high and dry, she rested amidships upon a craggy point, and so broke her back. Her anchors, oil tanks, and 150 fathoms of chain were said to be still lying there.

In the evening I conversed with Kokerzhun about her father's death. She was deeply interested at the many particulars I mentioned, and I was surprised to find her so intelligent and comparatively accomplished. She was, withal, really handsome, but retiring and ladylike. She understood several words of the English language, and was very solicitous of acquiring more knowledge of it. She and her husband were invited for the night into the cabin, where Mate Gardiner gave them up his berth, and, my wrappers answering for coverlets, they were soon asleep. The next morning we arrived at our anchorage, and I soon returned to my quarters on board the *George Henry*.

That evening I landed for a walk, and about half a mile from the beach I found a white man's grave—a mound of sand—at the head of which was an inscription cut upon a raised wood tablet, and reading literally as follows :—

DIED,

ON THE 31ST JULY, 1857,

WILLIAM JAMES, AGED 28 YEARS,

SEAMAN, P. H. D., ON BOARD THE

S. SHIP INNUIT, OF P. H. D.,

J. H. SÜTTER,

COMMANDER.

Dreary was the scene around that solitary grave, the last resting-place of one who was taken away in the prime of life, far from home and all who were dear to him. At the end of each line was rudely engraved a willow branch, a substitute for the cypress, which, in all ages, and in all parts of the civilized world, served as a memorial of the dead.

Strangely enough, after an hour's walk I came across another grave, but this time that of an Esquimaux. The grave was simply a steep ledge of rocks on one side, and on the other long stones set up on end. Within this were the bones and skull of the deceased man. At the head was a pile of rude stone covering the utensils that belonged to him when living. Through the openings I saw a powder-flask, a little tin tea-kettle suspended over a blubber lamp, the knives which he was wont to use, and other trifles, all placed in perfect order. Beside this pile were his seal, walrus, and whaling instruments. The grave was without cover, that he might freely roam over the mountains and freely traverse the seas to that world whither he had gone. The grave was situated on an eminence or bluff overlooking the bay, islands, and scenery far and near. As I stood by this grave the setting sun was crimsoning the whole heavens, picturing to my mind the glory that follows death to those that deserve it.

After-inquiries that I made enabled me to ascertain the name of the deceased, which I found to be one Al-lo-kee, a man celebrated in his day as a great hunter, persevering sealer, and daring whaler.

On Friday, August 24th, Koojesse made me an excellent chart of Nu-gum-mi-uke, Northumberland Inlet, Bear Sound, and lands adjacent—especially of the so-called Frobisher Strait. He signified his willingness to accompany me next season on my intended expedition, but declined to venture this year.

Trade to-day commenced with the natives for whalebone and walrus tusks. Several polar bear skins had already been bartered.

On Saturday, 25th of August (1860), had a very interesting, and, to me, important conversation with the intelligent *Koojesse*, *Ugarng*, and his wife *Kunniu*. The three of them were great travellers, both the former having been in the United States, and the latter was born at the "King's Cape" of Luke Fox, discovered by that navigator in 1631. She had been to the *Meta Incognita* of Frobisher, and all along the north coast of that land, which, by her account (as clearly explained to me), was connected with the opposite shores, thus making Frobisher "Strait" an *inlet* or *bay*. *Koojesse* and *Ugarng* had also visited the land referred to, and each of them declared that there was no other water communication to what we call Fox's Channel except through the Hudson's Straits. This I was very desirous of knowing more about; and at my request Koojesse finished drawing his chart of the coasts, bays, and islands from Northumberland Inlet to Resolution Island, and both sides of the so-called Frobisher Strait to its head. The original of this chart is now in my possession, and it has always astonished me for its remarkable skill and general accuracy of detail. A *fac-simile* of most of it is shown on the opposite page, reduced to one-twelfth of its original size.

The charts that I possessed of this locality were such as our geographers at that time believed to be correct, and I pointed out to Koojesse the places about which I desired information. I showed him the route I proposed taking when I got up to about longitude 72°, in what I had supposed to be Frobisher Strait, but he and the others stopped me by saying, *"argi! argi!"* (No! no!) They then took hold of my hand, moving it around till it connected with "Meta Incognita;" then following south-easterly the north coast of this land till arriving at the channel leading into Hudson's Strait, about longitude 66° W., and, turning round, went thence up Hudson's Strait continuously on to "King's Cape." Of course the names which we place upon our charts are unknown to the Esquimaux, and, consequently, I have endeavoured in this work, where possible, to give both together.

The knowledge that the Esquimaux possess of the geography of their country is truly wonderful. There is not a part of the coast but what they can well delineate, when once it has been visited by them, or information concerning it obtained from others. Their memory is remarkably good, and their intellectual powers, in all relating to their native land, its inhabitants, its coasts, and interior parts, is of a surprisingly high order. In what they related to me concerning Frobisher Strait there could be no doubt, and at once I felt convinced that no passage existed in that direction. However, this I determined to personally examine at the earliest opportunity. Meanwhile I tried all in my power to persuade *Koojesse* to go with me, without delay, to King William's Land, but in vain. Earlier in the season he would have gone; now it was too late. I had, therefore, no alternative but to wait until the following spring.

At midnight there was a fine display of the aurora borealis, or rather aurora australis, for the direction in which the lights appeared was *south*, not north of us. The barometer stood at 30·05; thermometer, 32°; wind, moderate N.W. and the sky "clear as a bell." I took on deck two delicate compasses to

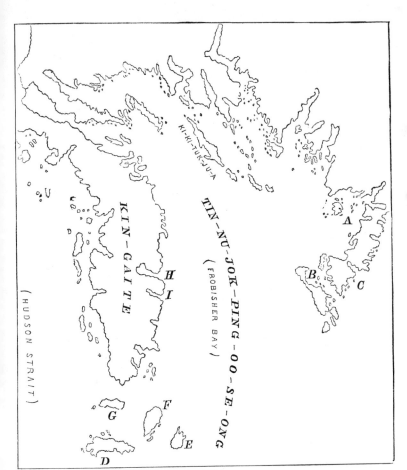

KI-KI-TUK-JU-A

KIN–GAITE

TIN–NU–JOK–PING–OO–SE–ONG

(FROBISHER BAY)

(HUDSON STRAIT)

A

B

C

H

I

F

G

E

D

ESQUIMAUX CHART

Nº 1
DRAWN BY
Koo jes se
— AT —
RESCUE HARBOR,
1860 for
C.F. HALL

observe if they would be affected by the lights, but they were not in the least. The display was really beautiful; the streams darting up like lightning, and passing the zenith. Some banks of light were so thick that the stars behind were obscured, even those of the first magnitude.

The following day we had a visit from *Artarkparu*, who, I find, is brother to Allokee, the man whose grave I had noticed. *Artarkparu* had a single brass button, as an ornament, pendent from his skin coat. The device on it was a bee with expanded wings, and the motto, "*Vive ut vivas.*"

A young man Esquimaux, whom we called *Napoleon*, from a resemblance in features to Bonaparte, used to visit us daily, dressed in a blue military coat minus the tail (which had been completely torn off), and with a row of big brass buttons running over each shoulder and down in front. The device on these buttons was three cannon on carriages, with a crown for the crest.

Another comical sight was a fat Esquimaux woman who appeared among us dressed in an old calico curtain put on over her seal-skin suit. The number of natives now visiting us was very great, but it was made a rule that all except a privileged few should leave the ship at 8 P.M. During the day much trade was carried on in bartering for skins, walrus tusks, &c. One pair of tusks measured full twenty-six inches in length. The skull of the walrus is very firm and thick. No rifle-ball would have the least effect on it. I have specimens that will show this.

Decidedly the Esquimaux are a happy people. As they crowded our decks, I one day noticed about a dozen women seated and busily engaged at their work. Two were mending one of the boat's sails. Some were chewing *ook-gook* (large seal) skins for soles of *kum-ings* (native boots), others sewing; while one was tending a cross baby. This little fellow, by-the-bye, was generally as good-humoured as the rest, but a piece of raw seal-blubber had disordered him, and hence his troublesome manner. It is rare to find an Esquimaux child but what is very quiet, and only on extraordinary occasions will they raise any cries. One Esquimaux lady, whose husband was as dark as half the negroes of the States, had a very pretty semi-*white* baby, looking true American all over!

On the 29th of August I thought it advisable to try my expedition boat, with a view to preparing her for the trip to King William's Land. Accordingly, she was brought in from where

she was anchored near the ship, and Captain B. myself, a
Smith entered her for a sail. She was found to answer adr
rably, and proved herself of high merit in model and capabilities.
Later in the day I again went away in her with Smith and two
men. We pushed outside into the bay. A fresh easterly breeze
was blowing, and this gave the boat a good test. Two of the
ship's boats were also out under sail, but we passed them at such
a rapid rate that it surprised every one. Truly glad was I to
find my boat so good, and little did I then imagine she was so
soon to be lost.

On the 30th of August I went in an Esquimaux boat, with
some of the natives, to convey across the bay, Annawa, his wife,
their infant, and a son, besides the widow of old Allokee, toward
their home, which was at the head of an inlet opening into Frobisher Strait. Koojesse was of the party, which was comprised
of fifteen persons.

We left the ship at 9 A.M. and when about two-thirds of
the way we landed in a bight of a large island. Here I saw
an old Esquimaux settlement, and I should think there must
have been no less than fifty huts formerly erected there within
a space of 500 feet of where I stood. The Esquimaux do not
make their winter habitations now as in the years when the
huts I allude to were built, the remains of which were before
me. During the last few years Esquimaux live almost entirely
in *igloos*—"snow houses"—through the winter season. Formerly they built up an earth embankment, or a wall of stone
about five feet high, and over this laid skeleton bones of the
whale on spars of drift-wood, then on top of that placed skins
of the seal or walrus. Many of the ancient embankments where
we landed had the largest of whale skeleton bones placed "cob-
house" style, and so incorporated with the earth as to keep the
whole firmly and enduringly together. The entrances were serpentine tunnels under ground, with side walls, and roofed with
slabs of stone. To pass through them one is obliged to go on
"all-fours."

I noticed here a dog-sledge, such as the Esquimaux use in
their winter excursions. It was ten feet in length, the runners
of one and a half inch plank, and shod with the jaw-bone of
the whale. The width was thirty inches, and the cross-bars
fastened by strings of whalebone.

Allokee's widow had wintered here, and she at once bent her
steps to the spot where she had formerly halted, and took from
the ground a large pewter plate that had been left there. I

asked her where she had obtained the plate, and her reply was "English"—thus probably obtained from one of the whalers. The use she made of this piece of ware was as a receptacle for needles, knives, beads, reindeer sinew for sewing, &c.

After staying here a short time we again started, and arrived at our destination about one o'clock. There the Esquimaux family left us, intending to foot it for about two days over mountains, through valleys, and across rivers before arriving at their home. But not only had they to walk that distance, they had to carry a heavy pack on their shoulders ; and I was appalled when I saw the load each one took, especially on such a journey, without the least particle of food with them.

Our return was made without difficulty, and I got on board much pleased with the excursion.

On the 3d of September we were visited by an old gray-haired Esquimaux woman called "*Pe-ta-to.*" In talking with her she declared that her children had numbered twenty-five, but all were dead except two. She explained this by throwing out both hands, fingers and thumbs widely spread, *twice*, and *one* hand *thrice*, thus making twenty-five. At the time I could not help doubting her, but she was afterward confirmed by other evidence.

Of this kind old woman I shall have more to say farther on, but at the time of her first visit she greatly interested me by her intelligence and excellent memory. *Kunniu*, Ugarng's third wife, also proved herself far more gifted than I should have supposed. Her husband wished me to have her as my own, and then she could go with me to King's Cape, where she was born ; and she herself frequently explained that I could not go the way I wanted by boat, owing to land all around the Frobisher waters ; but, as I was unable to start that season, I had to decline the offer.

Some of the amusing tricks played by these Esquimaux women are especially deserving notice. The variety of games performed by a string tied at the ends, similar to a "cat's cradle," &c. completely throws into the shade our adepts at home. I never before witnessed such a number of intricate ways in which a simple string could be used. One arrangement represented a deer ; another a whale ; a third the walrus ; a fourth the seal ; and so on without end.

This *Kunniu* was a first-rate woman in all relating to work, whether in boat or on shore. She was an excellent pilot, and could pull an oar with any of our men. One day a whale was captured by the *George Henry's* crew at the lower part of the bay, and it was necessary for all aid to be rendered in towing the monster alongside our ship. The natives gave every assistance, and I also went with a boat, rowed by *Kunniu* and three others, to help. But I found they were doing well without us, and accordingly returned. On our way back a strong north-wester was blowing, and it was becoming very difficult to cross the channel. A heavy sea prevailed, and the tide was strong, causing a commotion in the waters anything but pleasant. In the boat was that Esquimaux woman I have mentioned as possessing the semi-white child, and never did mother more dote upon a babe than she upon this. Her care and solicitude for its preservation were truly affecting. It lay in the bow of the boat as she pulled and pulled, seemingly with the strength of six men, and every now and then she would look at it with a tender glance, while renewed force was placed upon her oar. Mother? Yes, she was a true mother; and *Kunniu* evidently must have been the same, for she pulled like a giantess. How they watched to see if we progressed! How they turned their eyes to the sleeping babe, as a wave would occasionally mount up and top its white crest clear over our heads!

At length we were able to get the boat under the lee of an island, and so make more headway in smoother water; and finally, after some very severe labour, we got on board.

As for the whale, during the afternoon it was brought alongside, and a most interesting sight it was to see the seven boats towing this "king of fishes" toward the ship. I was reminded by it of the way in which old Rome celebrated her "triumphs" over great kings and kingdoms. We of the white race were proud of our victory over such a monster of the deep, and they of the darker skin were rejoiced at having aided in the capture of what would very soon give them an immense quantity of "black skin" and "krang" for food.

The skin of the *Mysticetus* (Greenland whale) is a great treat to the Esquimaux, who eat it raw; and even before the whale was brought to the ship, some of the skin, about twenty square feet, had, by permission, been consumed by hungry natives. The "black skin" is three-fourths of an inch thick, and looks like India-rubber. It is good eating in its raw state even for a white man, as I know from experience; but when boiled and soused in vinegar it is most excellent.

I afterward saw the natives cutting up the *krang* (meat) of the whale * into such huge slices as their wives could carry ; and as they worked, so did they keep eating. Boat-load after boat-load of this did they send over to the village, where several deposits were made upon islands in the vicinity. All day long were they eating ; and, thought I, " What monstrous stomachs must these Esquimaux have ! " Yet I do not think, on the whole, they eat more than white men. But the quantity taken in one day— enough to last for several days—is what astonishes me ! They are, in truth, a peculiar people. " God hath made of one blood all nations of men to dwell on the whole face of the earth, and hath determined the times before appointed, and the bounds of their habitations." Take the Esquimaux away from the arctic regions—from the shores of the northern seas, and they would soon cease from the face of the earth. The bounds of their habitations are fixed by the Eternal, and no one can change them. Thus these people live.

My opinion is, that the Esquimaux practice of eating their food raw is a good one—at least for the better preservation of their health. To one educated otherwise, as we whites are, the Esquimaux custom of feasting on uncooked meats is highly repulsive ; but eating meats raw or cooked is entirely a matter of education. " As the twig is bent, the tree's inclined," is an old saw as applicable to the common mind of a people in regard to the food they eat as to anything else. When I saw the natives actually feasting on the raw flesh of the whale, I thought to myself, " Why cannot I do the same ? " and the response to my question came rushing through my brain, independent of prejudice, " Because of my education—because of the customs of my people from time immemorial."

As I stood upon the rocky shore observing the busy natives at work carving the monster before me, my eye caught a group around one of the *vertebræ*, from which they were slicing and eating thin pieces of ligament that looked white and delicious as the breast of a turkey ! At once I made up my mind to join in partaking of the inviting (?) viands actually smoking in my sight. Taking from the hands of Ugarng his seal-knife, I peeled off a delicate slice of this spinal ligament, closed my eyes, and cried out " Turkey ! " But it would not go down so easy. Not because the stomach had posted up its sentinel to say " no whale can come down here ! " but because it was tougher than

---

* The blood of this whale, a short time after its death, was rising 100 Fahrenheit. Forty-eight hours after, its krang was still quite warm.

any bull beef of Christendom ! For half an hour I tried to masticate it, and then found it was even tougher than when I began. At length I discovered I had been making a mistake in the way to eat it. The Esquimaux custom is to get as vast a piece into their distended mouths as they can cram, and then, boa constrictor-like, first lubricate it over, and so swallow it quite whole! "When you are in Rome, do as the Romans do." Therefore I tried the Esquimaux plan and succeeded, but that one trial was sufficient at the time.

A day or two afterward I again went on shore to where a portion of the whale's carcass remained.

The natives were so careful of the prize that numerous piles of stones, covering deposits of krang and blubber, were seen on the islands around. This would seem to bespeak a *provident* instead of an improvident trait in their character ; but I am inclined to think that the former is more the exception than the rule.

One old woman kindly came to me and offered a generous slice of the "*whale gum*" she was feasting on. Reaching out my hand, with one stroke of her "ood-loo" (a woman's knife—an instrument like a mincing-knife) she severed the white, fibrous strip as quick as thought. It cut as old cheese. Its taste was like unripe chestnuts, and its appearance like cocoa-nut meat. But I cannot say this experiment left me a very great admirer of whale's gum, though, if the struggle was for life, and its preservation depended on the act, I would undoubtedly eat whale's gum until I got something better to my liking.

On September 5th, while taking a walk on *Look-out* Island, half a mile south of the ship, I discovered a large piece of what I supposed to be iron mineral, weighing nineteen pounds, and " in shape and appearance resembling a round loaf of burned bread." Circumstances afterward furnished me with many interesting particulars of this piece of iron, and ultimately I ascertained it to be an undoubted relic of Frobisher's Expedition.

CHAPTER VII.

Boat Incident—Life hanging on a Shoe-string—Courage of Esquimaux Boys
—Arrival of the "Georgiana"—Author's Sickness and Recovery—Attention
of the Natives—A fearful Gale—The "Rescue" and the Expedition Boat
wrecked—The "Georgiana" on Shore—The "George Henry" in great
Danger.

THE incidents connected with my every-day life for some time at this period, though never without novelty to myself, would, I fear, seem to present a sameness of character if too often brought forward in the disjointed form in which they occurred. I will, therefore, occasionally throw together several matters that refer to the same subject, though scattered over the next two or three weeks.

Of these not the least interesting to me were the native habits and customs as displayed in their beautiful villages. I was never tired viewing them, and at every opportunity was on shore among their tupics—summer tents.

At other times I would make an excursion to some of the many islands around the ship, for the purpose of exercise and collecting specimens. I took one or more of the natives with me generally, and, on a certain occasion, the following incident occurred :—

In the morning of September 8th, I went over in a boat to an island. I had with me a little "one-eyed" Esquimaux companion, and, after about three hours' ramble, we returned to the landing only to find the boat entirely out of our reach. The tide had risen so much that approach to it was quite out of the question. The fastening of the boat was to a rock now far out, and beneath the waters! Here was a dilemma. What was I to do? The dashing waves threatened every moment to surge away the boat ; and if that went, and we were left upon that solitary, barren island for a night, the probability was we should both suffer greatly. There was no other way of getting off but by the boat, and the tide was still fast rising. For a time I was puzzled what to do. But, as "necessity is the mother of invention," I at length bethought me of a plan. If I had a line long enough to allow of a stone attached to it being thrown into the boat, all would probably be right. But I had no line. What then could I do? Presently an idea struck me. The telescope-case, containing a spy-glass (which swung to my side), had a long leathern strap. My marine glass was also pendent from my neck by a piece of green curtain-cord. The native boots on my feet were made fast by strong thongs of sealskin. Quickly these were tied together and made into a line some twenty feet long. To this a moderately heavy stone was attached, and with a good throw I managed to cast it into the boat. With a steady, gentle pull, the boat was once more within reach, and my Esquimaux companion and myself able to rejoin the living world!

It is said that " our lives often hang upon a brittle thread! " True, indeed. Certainly it was something like it in the present case, and I believe there can be no impropriety in saying that mine and my little Esquimaux's depended for once upon a strong shoestring!

Another boat adventure may be here worth narrating. About a month after the previous occurrence I went on " Look-out " Island to spend the day making observations, &c. Two young Esquimaux accompanied me; but, though the place where I landed was only about half a mile south of the ship, we were some time getting there, and on arrival I found, from the high breakers ashore, it would be better to send the boat back. The troubled sea was such that in a little time the boat, if left there, would have been pounded to pieces. I wrote a note to the ship, asking for one of the working-boats to call for me at evening. As the two boys went off in the boat, no small anxiety was caused by witnessing the difficulty and delay they experienced in reaching the ship. And no wonder. The boat they had to manage was twenty-eight feet long and six feet beam, and this to take across a channel where the sea is often very considerable. However, the tide helped them, and in time they got alongside.

In the evening one of our whale-boats came for me under charge of Mr. Rogers, who also found much difficulty in approaching any place where I could get on board. He neared a rock upon which I stepped, but instantly found myself slipping. I had in hand and about my person sextants, artificial horizon, nautical and surveying books, tape measurer, &c. &c., and there I was, poised upon the edge of a precipitous rock, fixed in deep water, with furious surf around it! I felt alarmed, more, perhaps for my instruments than myself, for the former would be lost, while I might readily be saved. All of the boat's crew were anxiously bending their eyes upon me as I kept slipping, and for a moment unable to help myself. But, thanks to my Esquimaux boots, which had been well "chewed" by the native women, I was able, by a great effort, to press my feet and toes upon the ice-covered rock, until *Keeney*, the "boat-header," managed to spring on shore to my assistance, and in another moment I was in the boat. Thus I was saved on this occasion simply by the flexibility of Esquimaux boots !

One Sunday after dinner I took the dingey, a small boat belonging to the ship, and, accompanied by four Esquimaux boys, directed it to the foot of the mountains north of our harbour. The mountains are God's temples ; to them I like to bend my steps on Sundays.

" God, that made the world and all things therein, seeing that He is Lord of heaven and earth, dwelleth not in temples made with hands."

I used, therefore, to say, "To what place shall I go where I can better worship my God than on the mountains? How can I so well learn his power as looking upon and contemplating His mighty works ?"

After leaving the boat in a safe little harbour, we began our upward tramp, and I was much interested in a pile of rock which seemed nearly undermined by old Father Time. The remaining stone was feldspar ; that which had been eaten out —a stratum of five feet thick—was composed of mica and a small proportion of quartz. The distance excavated in some places could not have been less than three or four fathoms ! At first it seemed decidedly venturesome to go under this rock shed ; but, on witnessing the firmness of the feldspar, its immense height, length, and breadth, it restored my confidence.

I greatly enjoyed my walk, and returned on board without mishap by the evening.

On the 10th of September we were visited by some new-comers—an Esquimaux called *Tes-su-win*, and his family and boat's crew. They had left *Ookoolear*—Cornelius Grinnell Bay— on the previous day bringing a letter from Captain Allen, of the *Black Eagle*, which vessel was still where we had left her on the 16th of August, when sailing for this place. The number in Tessuwin's boat was eleven, including four females. He had with him his wife, *Neu-er-ar-ping*, and a sister's child called *Og-big*, meaning whale. Tessuwin and his wife had both been to Fox Channel from Kemmisuite, in Northumberland Inlet, and the information they gave me concerning those parts, and all around the Frobisher waters, was very interesting, fully confirming the other reports. Tessuwin had often seen, and, with many others, visited in his kia the Hudson's Bay Company's ships, as they passed up Hudson's Strait. He said that very few Innuits now dwelt on *Kingaite* (Meta Incognita), and nearly all the native inhabitants were fast dying off.

Soon after Tessuwin's arrival another boat from Captain Tyson's ship, then at the same place as the *Black Eagle*, came on board, and after a stay of two days returned, taking back several of the natives, among whom was Kookoodlear, the young wife of one of the *George Henry's* hired Esquimaux crew. Tessuwin left us on the 15th, he having engaged himself and family to Captain Allen for the whaling season.

A few days after this, on the 18th, we were much surprised at the sight of a vessel coming up the bay, and soon afterward we ascertained she was the *Georgiana*, Captain Tyson. It was evening when she neared, passing on the opposite side of some small islands that inclosed us in our harbour. As she was going along about three or four knots an hour, suddenly I perceived her upon a rock, and in another moment her bow was raised some four feet higher than the stern. All was then confusion. A boat was seen to take a line out, but the increasing darkness prevented much being observed, and I felt great anxiety as to her fate. Fortunately, the tide was on the flood, and in less than an hour I had the satisfaction of seeing her again free. In ten minutes more she dropped anchor about two cable lengths from us.

The following days an interchange of visits took place, and new life was diffused by the friendly spirit of emulation created by the two ships' companies in whaling. One day, when the boats were out, it was seen by those of us who had remained on board that a whale had been captured, but at first we could not tell which ship's company were the victors. By-and-by it was ascertained to be the *George Henry's*, and I here mention it to relate an instance of generous feeling on the part of Captain Tyson.

When Smith, who was the lucky captor, had fastened to the whale, and was looking for means to secure his prize, Captain Tyson, in his boat, came up, and, without a word, proceeded to lance the huge monster so as to render him incapable of further resistance. Directly this was done, Tyson left, to go cruising for others; nor did he once make any proposition in reference to a claim for a share, as customary among whalers. His act was most friendly, especially so where whaling has so much to create strife.

About this time I was very sick—indeed, had been quite prostrated for several days by severe rheumatic pains. The cause originated with myself in consequence of needless exposure. I had experienced no material illness before since leaving home; and I believed, even as I now believe, that what Governor Elberg, of Holsteinborg, said to me about the healthy condition of all who reside in the arctic regions, as compared with other parts of the world, was true. But I had neglected even the commonest precautions during wet, cold, and fogs, and thus I now suffered. I allude to it for the purpose of showing the great sympathy evinced for me by the Esquimaux whenever they came on board. In moving about near my cabin they would walk on tiptoe, as though instructed in our customs at home; and on one occasion, two little girls, *Ookoodlear* and a companion, were so careful lest they should disturb me, that they would hardly turn over the leaves of an illustrated atlas that had been placed before them for their amusement.

This sickness of mine continued, with intermissions, for several days; but eventually I triumphed over it, and was able to move about again as I had been accustomed to. During my sickness various dishes were prepared for me from game that was captured, but I well remember the joy I felt on eating a portion of a reindeer's tongue, brought on board by some of the Esquimaux after a successful hunt. The previous day all hands had been eating (and relishing it too) some soused "black skin" of the whale, and I had freely taken of my share, but the satisfaction was nothing compared to that produced by the reindeer tongue. Nevertheless, I still assert that the black skin is good, either raw or cooked; and when prepared as pigs' feet usually are, it is luxurious.

At this time the *George Henry* was feeding and employing in the whaling service thirteen Esquimaux—that is, two boats' crews and one over. They got three meals a day in the cabin. The ration to each was one sea-biscuit, a mug of coffee, and a slice of salt junk. Besides this, they were furnished with all the pipes, tobacco, clothing, guns, and ammunition they wanted. In return, they generally went out cruising for whales just when they pleased, came back when they pleased, and did as they pleased. If one or several took an idea to go off deer-hunting, or for any other object, away he or they would go. They *would* be independent in the fullest sense of the word, and restraint was what they could not brook.

We Americans talk about "freedom and independence," but we are far behind these Northerners. While we are pleased with shadows, the dusky sons of an arctic clime enjoy the substance. They *will* do as they please, without any one having the acknowledged right or power to say to them, "Why do you so?"

I could say much, very much upon this subject, but perhaps it may be considered out of place, I therefore leave it for another opportunity. Still, I must make one remark. The Esquimaux really deserve the attention of the philanthropist and Christian. Plant among them a colony of men and women having right-minded principles, and, after some patient toil, glorious fruits must follow. I cannot realize the fact that here is a people having much of nobleness and even *greatness* in their composition, yet unvisited and apparently uncared-for by the missionary world. Nothing, however, could be done toward their good until a course is adopted similar to that pursued by the King of Denmark with Greenland. It is a painful, but too evident fact, that the Esquimaux on the west of Davis's Straits are woefully debased, and fallen from their original virtues—though possessing many still—owing to the visits of reckless white men on their coasts. In Greenland the case is different. There, under the Danish king's control, Christian colonies, churches, schools, store-houses, and stores of every needful variety, are to be found interspersed from Cape Farewell to Upernavik, and the inhabitants comfortable and happy. Priests and catechists, schoolmasters and schoolmistresses, are educated to their several posts, and are well paid for their services from his majesty's coffers. Danes emigrate to the land, marry and intermarry with the Esquimaux. Knowledge and virtue, industry and prosperity are the results. And, notwithstanding the expenses for the support of all this, including the salaries of inspectors, governors, and several scores of employés, yet the net proceeds of this apparently desolate land exceed ten thousand dollars, federal money, per annum! This is well for Greenland. Paying for all her imports; paying the expenses of some ten ships annually from and to Copenhagen; paying all the other expenses named, including missionaries, and yet realizing an annual return of net profit for the King of Denmark of ten thousand dollars! How many nations of this modern day do better?

And, with this fact before us, why shall not the same occur (adopting the same plan) in the land of the Esquimaux on the west side of Davis's Straits? Let my countrymen look to it whenever the first opportunity arrives.

On the 27th day of September (1860) there broke upon us that fearful gale which caused the loss of my expedition boat and the far-famed *Rescue*, drove the *Georgiana* on shore, and came near proving the destruction of the *George Henry* and all on board. As it was of so serious a character, I will here give the particulars in detail.

Wednesday, the 26th, commenced with light winds from the N.E. At noon it began to snow, with an increasing breeze. At 1 P.M. all the boats came on board from their cruising-ground, and preparations were made for bad weather. The wind now rapidly increased to a gale, and at 8 P.M. the second anchor was let go, with all the cable given that could be allowed without letting the *George Henry* get too near the rocky island astern of us. The schooner *Rescue*, at this time, was about fifty fathoms distant on our starboard bow, and the brig *Georgiana* a little more easterly. At 9 P.M. the gale was still increasing, and a heavy sea rising. At this time the deck watch came in the cabin and reported that the *Rescue* was dragging her anchors, and as we looked upon her dark form through the thick darkness of the night, it seemed, as she kept moving by, that her destruction was inevitable and immediate. But, when abeam of us, she held on, though pitching and surging heavily. The *Georgiana* was seen but faintly, and it appeared as if she, too, was in great danger.

At 11 P.M. it was blowing a perfect hurricane, with thick snow, and just then we could perceive the brig driving astern toward the island. She had, as we afterwards learned, broken her small anchor, and dragged her large one. On she went, driving heavily, amid the wild stir of the elements, and the awful darkness of that snow-storm night—on and on, with nothing to save her, until presently we could see she had struck upon the island leeward of us, where, after "worrying" her anchor round a point of land, she got into some slightly smooth water, and there continued pounding her larboard side on the rocks. The crew now left her and went on to the island, expecting every moment that she would part her remaining chain, and so be driven out into the bay, where there would be no possible chance of saving their lives.

Meanwhile, we ourselves were momentarily expecting destruction. It did not seem possible that our anchors could hold. Wind, and storm, and a raging sea appeared to be combined against us. Thirty souls, besides near a score of natives, were on board, and all preparing for the moment when it was probable the *George Henry* would be adrift on the rocks. But thanks to Providence and our good anchors, we did not stir, though at no time very far from the rocks. Every now and then I was on deck, not to hear the howling winds, for the whole cabin below resounded with their roar, but to gaze upon the terrible scene. And what a scene ! It was truly awful. Never before had I seen its like—never had I pictured to my imagination the reality of such a night. As I tried to steady myself by holding fast to some fixed rope, my eyes were spell-bound by the fearful sight before me. There behind was the brig pounding away upon the rocks ; and here, closer to us, was our consort, the schooner, plunging and chafing at her anchors as if mad at the restraint put upon her, and insanely desirous of letting go her hold to rush upon the shore. Ever and anon would she throw her bows low down, taking up the briny sea, and then, swiftly surging to and fro, spring fearfully on her chains. On the rocky, desolate island astern, the moving figures of those belonging to the brig could be discerned, evidently doing their best to keep warm in that bitter night. Through the rigging of our ship came the howling wind and the driving snow, while the fierce waves played and leaped about in the wildest fury. Yes, it was indeed a fearful sight, especially as it was increased in horror by the dread uncertainty of our own and our consort's continued safety.

At length these our fears were in part fulfilled. Toward morning the hurricane became stronger. Every blast seemed as if about to tear us from our hold, and then lift us into the air and hurl us upon the rocks for destruction. Presently our eyes caught sight of the *Rescue* in a moment dashing before the storm toward the dreaded shore. She had parted chain, and, with one bound, went hopelessly broadside on, amid the breakers at her lee. Thump ! thump ! crash ! crash ! away the tottering masts ! the ropes, the bulwarks, the all of what was once the noble-looking, beautiful, and renowned schooner *Rescue !* In and among the rocks, with their jagged tops tearing her to pieces, and the boiling surges driving over her decks, as the snow-storm poured its heavy drift around, even as if it were a wondrous funeral shroud, so did the doomed craft meet its fate.

So, too, was my expedition boat torn from its moorings, and, sharing the *Rescue's* sad end, doomed me also to a wreck of disappointment in the hopes I had cherished concerning her. And all this we saw as, with startled gaze and anxious thought, we stood on deck, powerless to save, and equally powerless to avert our own doom, if it should come.

The night passed on. The morning light slowly and cheerlessly pierced through the increasing thickness of falling snow as it flew past us on the driving wind. Dimly at first, then more distinctly, but still in dread spectre-like form, loomed up the rugged island scene, with its wrecks and desolation. Figures all but indistinct were moving about, and the two ships were pounding upon the rocks, tearing at their anchors as if in the most convulsive death-throes. The *Rescue* was on her broadside, with her bow easterly, and evidently breaking up. The *Georgiana*. being in a more sheltered spot, appeared to be less hurt. But it was necessary to do something, if possible, to release the men from their position on shore, and get them on board of us, for we seemed now likely to hold on. Accordingly, the moment a lull in the wind took place, which was at 9 A.M. of the 27th, a whaleboat was carefully lowered and passed astern. Into it two brave hearts, Mate Rogers and a seaman, stepped, with a view of venturing through the boiling waves and surf to try and assist their wrecked comrades. Cautiously the boat was allowed to drift off toward the island, a strong and good line of great length attached to it from the ship. Skilfully was it guided over the seas and through the breakers. Mate Rogers and his bold companion well and nobly did their work. In a few moments the boat was under the *Rescue's* projecting bowsprit, and speedily, though requiring exceeding care, Captain Tyson, his crew, and those who had been on board of the schooner, got into her. A short time more, and all were standing safely on the *George Henry's* deck.

At noon both the stranded ships were pounding very heavily on the rocks, and jumping their anchors in such a manner as to cause the two vessels to move their position more round the island, though in opposite directions. Thus it continued throughout all of the 27th, the wind increasing rather than the contrary. But on the following morning the gale abated, and at nine o'clock a party of our people managed to get on shore. We found the larboard side of the *Rescue* badly stove, but the *Georgiana*, by being in a much less exposed place, was perfectly tight, and comparatively uninjured. Her crew soon afterward took possession of her again, and ultimately she was got off the rocks, and once more anchored in deep water.

As for the *Rescue*, after a careful examination, it was found

WRECK OF THE RESCUE AND EXPEDITION BOAT.

she was too far damaged to be repaired with any means at our command. Accordingly, it was determined to totally abandon her; and this was put in execution the following day by clearing her hold of all the contents, and saving whatever was valuable of her material.

I went on shore to examine what remained of the schooner, and also to look after my expedition boat. I found my boat totally wrecked, nothing remaining but the stern-post fast to a three-inch cable. It appeared that during a part of the gale she had been driven high up on the rocks, and though the *Georgiana's* crew endeavoured to save her by additional fastenings, her fate was sealed. The tempestuous elements would not allow her to escape, and she was broken to pieces in the fury of the storm.

I need not say how much I grieved at the loss of my boat. To me it was irreparable, and for a time I was nearly overcome by the blow; but I reasoned that all things were for the best in the hands of a good Providence, and I therefore bent submissively to His will.

The natives who had been on board of the *Georgiana* were on the island when I landed. They had found the sail of my boat, and turned it to account as a shelter, and now were as happy and merry as though nothing unusual had occurred.

The *Rescue*, when I examined her, was high and dry on the rocks with her bottom stove in. I mounted her side (her decks were inclining to the shore at an angle of 45°); I entered her cabin, and looked into her hold, and again descended outside, going under and around her. Then as I gazed at her battered hull, grieving at the end she had come to, what a number of interesting associations crowded upon my mind. She had been of the " United States' Grinnell Expedition " in search of Sir John Franklin in 1850–1, being the consort of the *Advance*, in which latter vessel Dr. Kane afterward made that memorable voyage (the second Grinnell Expedition) in search of Franklin in 1853–5. The *Rescue's* quondam consort, after having given forth freely of its planks and timbers for the preservation and warmth of Dr. Kane and his party, was finally given up to the ices of the North which unrelentingly grasped it. The *Advance* was abandoned Sunday, May 20th, 1855, in Rensselaer Harbour, lat. 78° 37′ N. and long. 70° 40′ W. Five years, four months, and seven days after this occurred the total wreck of the *Rescue*, in a harbour named after her, situated in lat. 62° 52′ N. and long. 64° 44′ W. nearly due south of her former consort.

After well examining the *Rescue*, I went to the wreck of Koojesse's whale-boat, lying on the windward side of the island. This boat had been fast to the schooner's stern, and, of course, went on the rocks at the same time. She had originally belonged to Kudlago, having been given to him in 1858. When Kudlago left for the States in 1859, he gave the boat to Koojesse to use until his return.*

I may add here, that an oomien (woman's or family boat) belonging to the natives went adrift during the storm and became a total wreck. A boat of this kind is of great value to the Esquimaux, and, when lost, is to them something akin to the loss of a first-class ship to us at home.

I must now say a few words concerning myself. Even in the midst of the howling tempest, when our own safety on board the *George Henry* was a matter of doubt, my thoughts kept turning to what I should do, now that my expedition boat was lost. But it did not take me long to consider. I was determined that, God willing, nothing should daunt me ; I would persevere if there was the smallest chance to proceed. If one plan failed—if one disaster came, then another plan should be tried, and the disaster remedied to the best of my power. Thus, without delay, and while yet the hurricane blasts made the ship tremble beneath us, as the captain and I stood on her deck, I asked him if one of the ship's boats could be spared me to prosecute my voyage to King William's Land, now that my own little craft was wrecked. His reply, after some consideration, was favourable ; but, when the time approached for my departure, it was found the one that alone could be spared to me was frail, rotten, and not seaworthy.

On the 1st of October the *Georgiana*, having made good her defects so far as she could, left the harbour under all sail, for Northumberland Inlet to winter. By her I forwarded letters to friends at home, should she meet, as was expected, with whalers returning to England.

---

* Before I close this account of the *Rescue's* wreck and the loss of my expedition boat, with the escape of the *George Henry*, it may be interesting to mention that this latter vessel did not live through another voyage after her return to the States in 1862. She was wrecked on the 16th day of July, 1863, on one of the lower Savage Islands in Hudson's Strait, about 100 miles farther south than Rescue Harbour.

CHAPTER VIII.

FOR several days now our life was of a very monotonous description, except so far as varied by the visits of Esquimaux, who were frequently on board performing different avocations more or less useful to us. Scrubbing the cabin floor, sewing and dressing sealskins, were some of the occupations that engrossed their time. Occasionally the younger members were ready pupils under my hand in trying to learn whatever I could teach them of civilized education.

But at this time the phenomena of Nature frequently gave me intense delight. The aurora, in all its glorious brilliancy, shone forth on several nights, and often did I linger on deck gazing upon it, with my soul entranced by the sight. It is impossible for me to give a just and full description of the immeasurable beauty and grandeur of such a scene. All I can attempt to do is to put before the reader my thoughts and sensations at the several times, as recorded in my journal.

November 23, 1860.—A few places at six o'clock this evening where the cerulean sky and stars can be seen. While standing on deck near the bow of the vessel, viewing Mars in its meridian passage at this place, all at once a bright, beautiful beam of aurora shot up midway between the star and the moon. The moon—some 39° or 40° east of Mars—was shining brightly, but above and below it were *cirri cumuli* clouds. Between the planets all was clear. The aurora beams increased rapidly. They were of prismatic colours to-night, pea-green predominating. Oh that I could pen or pencil the beauty of this display ! The kind of clouds which I have named are the most distant of any. The aurora, as it frequently ascended high in the heavens, plainly painted its golden rays upon the face of the clouds, thus proving it was at play *between* me and them. *Blind George*, the Esquimaux, was standing by my side. I told him what was going on in the heavens. I said the moon was shining, and the aurora showing off finely at the time. He wished me to place him in position that his face might be upturned toward what I saw and so

THE AURORA, NOV. 23, 1860.

admired. This I joyfully did. *Joyfully*, do I say? No, no! For, as *Paulooyer* (Blind George) asked me, I saw that he was possessed of an uncontrollable yearning, seeming to me like that of a pinioned eagle, to soar away to the regions of the stars. He sought to tear away the curtains which God, in His own dispensation, had seen fit to place before his eyes, that he might again see the handiwork of Him who made the stars, the world, and all that is therein.

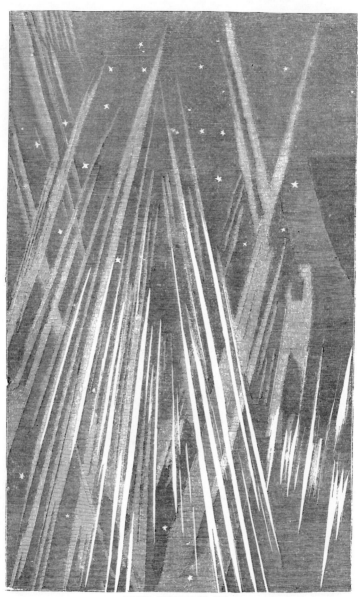

AURORA, DECEMBER 17, 1860.

Again, on another morning, December 17th, at six o'clock, I write, "The heavens are beaming with aurora. The appearance of this phenomenon is quite changed from what it has been. Now the aurora shoots up in beams scattered over the whole canopy, all tending to meet at zenith. How multitudinous are the scenes presented in one hour by the aurora! This morning the changes are very rapid and magnificent. Casting the eye in one direction, I view the instantaneous flash of the aurora shooting up and spreading out its beautiful rays, gliding this way, then returning, swinging to and fro like the pendulum of a mighty clock. I cast my eyes to another point; there instantaneous changes are going on. I close my eyes for a moment; the scene has changed for another of seemingly greater beauty. In truth, if one were to catch the glowing heavens at each instant now passing, his varied views would number thousands in one hour. Who but God could conceive such infinite scenes of glory? Who but God execute them, painting the heavens in such gorgeous display?"

At another time the aurora presented a *new phase*, rays shooting athwart the south-western sky parallel with the horizon.

Later still, March 11th, I write : " It seemeth to me as if the very doors of heaven have been opened to-night, so mighty, and beauteous, and marvellous were the waves of golden light that a few moments ago swept across the ' azure deep,' breaking forth anon into floods of wondrous glory. God made His wonderful works to-night to be remembered. I have witnessed many displays of the aurora since making anchorage in this harbour, a great many of them of surpassing magnificence, yet what I beheld this night crowns them all. I could never have anticipated the realization of such a scene !

" I was not alone enjoying it. Captain Budington and Mate Gardiner were with me, and we all looked on in wondrous yet delighted awe.

" The day had been fine, with a moderate wind from the north-west. When the sun went down behind the ridge of mountains limiting the bay, a perfect calm followed, with a sky absolutely cloudless. At 4 P.M. there had been seen one solitary and peculiar cloud hanging in the heavens to the north about 15° above the horizon. This cloud was a deep dark blue, looking much like the capital letter S. This at last disappeared, and the night set in, still beautiful and mild, with myriads of stars shining with apparently greater brilliancy than ever.

"I had gone on deck several times to look at the beauteous scene, and at nine o'clock was below in my cabin going to bed, when the captain hailed me with the words, ' *Come above, Hall, at once !* THE WORLD IS ON FIRE !'

"I knew his meaning, and, quick as thought, I redressed myself, scrambled over several sleeping Innuits close to my berth, and rushed to the companion stairs. In another moment I reached the deck, and as the cabin door swung open, a dazzling, overpowering light, as if the world was really a-blaze under the agency of some gorgeously-coloured fires, burst upon my startled senses ! How can I describe it ? Again I say, no mortal hand can truthfully do so. Let me, however, in feeble, broken words, put down my thoughts at the time, and try to give some faint idea of what I saw.

"My first thought was, ' Among the gods there is none like unto Thee, O Lord ; neither are there any works like unto Thy works !' Then I tried to picture the scene before me. Piles of golden light and rainbow light, scattered along the azure vault, extended from behind the western horizon to the zenith ; thence down to the eastern, within a belt of space 20° in width, were the fountains of beams, like fire-threads, that shot with the rapidity of lightning hither and thither, upward and athwart the great pathway indicated. No sun, no moon, yet the heavens were a glorious sight, flooded with light. Even ordinary print could have been easily read on deck.

"Flooded with rivers of light. Yes, flooded with light ; and such light ! Light all but inconceivable. The golden hues predominated ; but, in rapid succession, prismatic colours leaped forth.

"We *looked*, we SAW, and TREMBLED ; for, even as we gazed, the whole belt of aurora began to be alive with flashes. Then each pile or bank of light became myriads ; some now dropping down the great pathway or belt, others springing up, others leaping with lightning flash from one side, while more as quickly passed into the vacated space ; some, twisting themselves into folds, entwining with others like enormous serpents, and all these movements as quick as the eye could follow. It seemed as if there was a struggle with these heavenly lights to reach and occupy the dome above our heads. Then the whole arch above became *crowded*. Down, down it came ; nearer and nearer it approached us. Sheets of golden flame, coruscating while leaping from the auroral belt, seemed as if met in their course by some mighty agency that turned them into the colours of the rainbow, each of the seven primary, 3° in width, sheeted out of 21°; the prismatic bows at right angles with the belt.

"While the auroral fires seemed to be descending upon us, one of our number could not help exclaiming,

"'Hark! hark! such a display! almost as if a warfare was going on among the beauteous lights above—so palpable—so near—seems impossible without noise.'

"But no noise accompanied this wondrous display. All was silence.

"After we had again descended into our cabin, so strong was the impression of awe left upon us that the captain said to me,

"'Well, during the last eleven years I have spent mostly in these northern regions, I have never seen anything of the aurora to approach the glorious vivid display just witnessed. And, to tell you *the truth*, Friend Hall, *I do not care to see the like ever again.*'"

That this display was more than ordinarily grand was evidenced by the testimony of the Innuits, particularly Tookoolito, who, when she came on board a few days afterwards, stated that she had been much struck by its remarkable brilliancy, and that "it had exceeded in beauty and magnificence all displays ever before witnessed by her." I would here make the remark that the *finest* displays of the aurora only last a few moments. Though it may be playing all night, yet it is only now and then that its grandest displays are made. As if marshalling forces, gathering strength, compounding material, it continues on in its silent workings. At length it begins its trembling throes; beauty anon shoots out here and there, when all at once the aurora *flashes* into living hosts of *powdered* coruscating rainbows, belting the heavenly dome with such gorgeous grandeur sometimes that mortals tremble to behold!

On October 13th we had an unexpected arrival. A *steamer* and a sailing vessel were observed coming up from sea, and in the evening both vessels anchored on the opposite side of Field Bay. In a short time we ascertained that the strangers were well-known English whalers, being no less than the famous Captain Parker, of the *True-love*, and his son, commanding the steam-ship *Lady Celia*. They had come from Cornelius Grinnell Bay in less than a day, leaving Captain Allen, of the *Black Eagle* there. Intelligence of our schooner's wreck had reached them at that place a few days after it had occurred, an Esquimaux and his wife having travelled by land and carried the news.

Directly there was an opportunity I paid a visit to the new-comers, starting from our ship early in the morning. Ugarng's boat and crew took me there. The party consisted of himself, his wife Nikujar and child, Kokerjabin (Kudlago's widow), Sterry, and myself, besides other Esquimaux.

When we were one mile from *Look-out* Island the sun was lifting his bright face from the sea. The whole ridge of mountains, running south-easterly to " Hall's " ISLAND of Frobisher, was in plain sight, covered with white, and as we approached them, no opening into the harbour where the vessels were sup-

NIKUJAR, THE BOAT-STEERER AND PILOT.

posed to lie, could be seen. But *Nikujar* being a capital pilot, knowing every channel and inlet within two hundred miles of our anchorage, the steering-oar was given to her; and there, seated upon the logger-head, with her pretty infant in its hood behind her neck, she steered us correctly to the spot.

With a few good strokes of the oars, we soon entered the snug little cove where the Parkers had taken shelter. In a moment or two after passing the steamer we were standing on the deck of the *True-love*, most kindly welcomed by Captain Parker, senior, and shortly afterward by his son, who came on board. I there found "Blind George," who immediately recognised my voice, calling me by name, and saying, "How do you, Mitter Hall?" and then, without waiting for reply, adding, "Pretty well, I tank you!"

I was, indeed, right glad to again meet this noble, but afflicted Esquimaux. The four times I had seen him at Grinnell Bay caused him to be much impressed upon my memory, and now, strangely enough, here he was, and actually in presence of Nikujar, who was his former wife, before Ugarng took her away and made her his. Ugarng, however, *could* support the woman, and poor blind George could not ; hence the latter had to submit, and be content with an occasional visit of their only child, as an idol which he cherished even more than his own life.

Captain Parker soon took me into his cabin, and had an excellent breakfast spread on the table. After this, conversation turned upon many subjects of a most interesting nature. He had brought his ship, guided by an Esquimaux pilot—Ebierbing—from Niountelik, in Northumberland Inlet, to Grinnell Bay, through a channel 128 miles long, and not above one to two miles broad, behind a line of islands facing the sea. The steamer towed the sailing ship, as no vessel of their size could pass up or down such a channel unless with a fair wind. In the channel the flood tide runs south, while elsewhere it runs north. Captain Parker said the scenery was most magnificent, and there was plenty of salmon, deer, and other game. Altogether it was a trip, as he expressed it, that I would have been delighted with.

Among the many incidents related to me by Captain Parker, one or two may be worth recording here. He said that in 1833-4 he had been down Prince Regent's Inlet as far as Cape Kater, in company with the *Isabella*, Captain Humphreys, who rescued Sir John Ross and his companions after their four years' abode in an icy home. Parker had seen Ross's boats while on their way to escape, but supposing them to be the *Isabella's*, took no especial notice. In Regent's Inlet, he said, there were hundreds of whales between Cape York and Cape Kater. He had caught five off Cape Kater, and twenty-three more between there and Cape York. Seals, narwhals, white whales, and the walrus, were also in great abundance.

He likewise described to me, in a most graphic manner, the terrible storm of 1830 in Baffin's Bay, when twenty-two vessels were wrecked, and yet his own ship escaped without the slightest damage. One thousand men had to make good their retreat upon the ice toward the Danish settlements, some 600 miles distant, and all arrived safely with the exception of two, who died from the effects of spirituous liquors they injudiciously drank.

Captain Parker, at the time I saw him was sixty-nine years of age, and good, to all appearance, for half a score more in the arctic regions. He had been navigating those northern seas (whaling) for forty-five years, with an interval of about five years, when he rested. He commenced in 1815, and was a commander in 1820. He had never lost a ship. On the present voyage *neither vessel had a chronometer.* They depended upon dead reckoning for their longitude.

There was a doctor on board, quite a young man, and apparently of merit. He had been one year in Springfield, Ohio.

The *True-love* is well known in arctic history as connected with the late searching expeditions. In 1849 she landed some coals at Cape Hay, in Lancaster Sound, as requested by Lady Franklin, who sent them out, that fuel might be deposited at every likely spot where her husband and his companions might possibly visit. This remarkable vessel is 100 years old, and was built in Philadelphia.

I explained to Captain Parker all about my plans, and he expressed himself much interested in them, promising to let me have a boat I desired, as an additional one to that I should get from the *George Henry,* and which would be needed to carry my stores.

On Captain Parker's invitation I remained to dinner, and then, after a most agreeable visit, returned to the *George Henry.*

In a few days after this both the Parkers suddenly went to sea—as we supposed, driven out of their anchorage by a gale that had been blowing, and, owing to this, I did not receive the boat promised me, nor were we able to send home the letters that had been prepared.

It was about this time I was visited by two Esquimaux, man and wife, who will henceforth often appear in my narrative, and who, together with a child afterward born to them, accompanied me to the States. The man's name was Ebierbing—otherwise called by us " Joe "—his wife's Tookoolito, or " Hannah."

I was informed that this couple had been taken to England in 1853, and presented to Her Majesty Queen Victoria, and that the female was a remarkably intelligent, and what might be called an accomplished woman. They had remained nearly two years in Great Britain, and were everywhere well received. I heard, moreover, that she was the sister of *Toto* and *Ee-noo-loo-a-pik*, both celebrated in their country as great travellers and intelligent men, and the latter well known in England from his visit there in 1839, and from a memoir of him published by Surgeon Macdonald, of the ill-fated Franklin Expedition. Ebierbing was a good pilot for this coast, and had brought Captain Parker's ship through the channels, as already narrated. At the time of the gale, when my boat and the *Rescue* were wrecked, he was up in Northumberland Inlet, and also lost a boat of his own.

When I visited Captain Parker, "Joe" was not on board, nor did I know much of him until the above particulars were furnished to me. I was, therefore, naturally anxious to see this couple, and looked forward to our meeting with much hope that it would prove not only pleasing, but useful in many ways. The first interview I had is recorded in my journal as follows :—

"*November 2d*, 1860.—While intently occupied in my cabin, writing, I heard a soft, sweet voice say, 'Good morning, sir.' The *tone* in which it was spoken—musical, lively, and varied—instantly told me that a lady of refinement was there greeting me. I was astonished. Could I be dreaming? No! I was wide awake, and writing. But, had a thunder-clap sounded on my ear, though it was snowing at the time, I could not have been more surprised than I was at the sound of that voice. I raised my head : a lady was indeed before me, and extending an ungloved hand.

"Of course, my welcome to such an unexpected visitor in these regions was as befitting as my astonished faculties for the moment could make it. The doorway in which she stood leads from the main cabin into my private room. Directly over this entrance was the skylight, admitting a flood of light, and thus revealed to me *crinoline*, heavy flounces, an attenuated toga, and an immensely expanded 'kiss-me-quick' bonnet, but the features I could not at first make out.

"'Coming events cast their shadows before them.' Ladies are events casting *umbra and penumbra* along wherever their pathway be, thus bespeaking glory about them constantly. Knowing the philosophy of all this even before leaving the States, I immediately tried to do honour to my unknown visitor. But, on turning her face, who should it be but a *lady* Esquimaux ! Whence, thought I, came this civilization refinement ? But, in a moment more, I was made acquainted with my visitor. She was the Tookolito I had so much desired to see, and directly I conversed with her, she showed herself to be quite an accomplished person. She spoke my own language fluently, and there, seated at my right in the main cabin, I had a long and interesting conversation with her. Ebierbing, her husband—a fine, and also intelligent-looking man—was introduced to me, and, though not speaking English so well as his wife, yet I could talk with him tolerably well. From them I gleaned many interesting particulars of their visit to England, and I was gratified to hear that they had actually dined with Prince Albert, who treated them very kindly, and with much consideration.

" Ebierbing, in speaking of the Queen, said he liked her very much, and she was quite ' pretty.' He also said that Prince Albert was a ' very kind, good man, and he should never forget him.' "

The following conversation, as copied from my journal, written at the time, will show the sentiments of Tookoolito on civilized life :—

I asked her how she would like to live in England. She replied, " I would like very well, I thank you."

" Would you like to go to America with me ? " said I.

" I would indeed, sir," was the ready reply.

In reference to the Queen of England, she said,

" I visited her, and liked the appearance of Her Majesty, and everything about the palace. Fine place, I assure you, sir."

Tookoolito was suffering with a cold, and I noticed that whenever she coughed, she threw her face on one side and held her hand before her lips, the same as any lady of good manners would. Her costume was that of civilization, being a dress with heavy flounces, an elegant toga made of young tuktoo fur deeply fringed, and a bonnet of the style invented on the principle " cover the head by a rosette on its back ! "

As Tookoolito continued speaking, I could not help admiring the exceeding gracefulness and modesty of her demeanour. Simple and gentle in her way, there was a degree of calm intellectual power about her that more and more astonished me. I felt delighted beyond measure, because of the opportunity it gave me for becoming better acquainted with these people through her means, and I hoped to improve it toward the furtherance of the great object I had in view.

After a stay of some duration she went on shore, and the following day I visited her and her husband at their tent. She was then in native costume, and it seemed to me that this suited her even better than the other.

Some short time after this, I made an excursion by myself to the island on which was situated the Esquimaux "North Star" village.

The day became stormy after I had landed in one of the native boats, but I continued my walk, accompanied by the dogs, to a part of the island I wished to visit. On arriving there, I found a sort of natural *causeway*, formed of stones, leading to a smaller islet, and, crossing it, I continued examining the locality for for some time. At length the snowstorm increased so much as to compel my return, and I made my way back to the south side of the main island.

But now I could hardly see my way. The snow came down so thick that I was fain to take shelter under the lee of some rocks near me, and, while there, I examined my compass to ascertain if I was going right. To my astonishment, I found the course I had pursued was exactly the reverse of the right one. I looked again and again, and yet the needle pointed exactly opposite to what I had expected. What was I to do? retrace my steps? For a moment I hesitated; but at length moving on, I was about walking back as I had come, when, on looking at the compass again, I found it just the opposite of what it was before! Strange, thought I. Surely there must be local attraction in the rocks where I took shelter. But still it made me anxious, especially as the weather was becoming worse. Indeed, I felt it very possible I might be lost in the storm, and perhaps have to wander about all the coming night, or be frozen to death by remaining stationary, should the compass play me another trick; but at last, thanks to my faithful dogs, they actually guided me straight to the village, where I arrived without any mishap.

The one I entered was Ebierbing's. He himself had gone out, but Tookoolito welcomed me as usual, soon entering into lively and instructing conversation. Two native boys were there at the time, and Tookoolito herself was busy knitting socks for her husband! Yes, to my surprise, she was thus engaged, as if she had been in a civilized land and herself civilized, instead of being an Esquimaux in her own native wilds of ice and snow!

It was a strange contrast, the sight within that tent and the view without. The latter presented a picture of barrenness and storm; the former much that tended to the idea of warmth and home. Knitting stockings for her husband! How much of dear home was in that favourite domestic occupation! Then, too, her voice, her words and language, the latter in my own vernacular, were something more than common in that region. I have before said that she was peculiarly pleasing and refined in her style and manners; and now, while sheltering me beneath her hospitable roof, with the bright lamp before me, the lively prattle of the two boys came in strong contrast to the soft tones of her partly civilized tongue as my mind opened to receive all she uttered.

What she said, and what my impressions were at the time, will be found in the following extract from my journal:

"*November* 14*th*, 1860.—Tookoolito, after returning from England five years ago, where she and her *wing-a* (husband) spent twenty months, commenced diffusing her accomplishments in various ways, to wit, teaching the female portion of the nation, such as desired, to knit, and the various useful things practised by civilization. In all the places around Northumberland Inlet she has lived, and done what she could to improve her people. A singular fact relative to dressing her hair, keeping her face and hands cleanly, and wearing civilization dresses—others of her sex, in considerable numbers, follow these fashions imported by her. This shows to me what one person like Tookoolito could accomplish in the way of the introduction of schools and churches among this people. To give this woman an education in the States, and subsequent employment in connexion with several of our missionaries, would serve to advance a noble and good work. And yet I must state that, unless a working colony, or several of them, were established, co-operating in this work, and laws were made by the fundamental power that *should be as rigid* relative to whalers visiting the coasts, as those of Denmark to Greenland, all would be as nought.

"The working or trading colony would make its government, school, and church institutions self-supporting. Let the plan of Denmark for Greenland be followed. It is a good one, and works well.

"While in the tent, Tookoolito brought out the book I had given her, and desired to be instructed. She has got so far as to spell words of two letters, and pronounce most of them properly. Her progress is praiseworthy. At almost every step of advancement, she feels as elated as a triumphant hero in battle. She is far more anxious to learn to read and write than Ebierbing. I feel greater confidence (allowing it were possible to feel so) in the success of my mission since engaging these two natives.

They can talk with me in my own vernacular, are both smart, and will be useful each in the department they will be called upon to fill. Tookoolito will especially fill the place of an interpreter, having the capacity for it surpassing Karl Petersen, the Dane, who has been employed as Esquimaux interpreter by various expeditions in search of Sir John Franklin—1st, by Captain Penny, 1850-1; 2d, by Dr. Kane, 1853-5; 3d, by Captain (now Sir Leopold) M'Clintock, 1857-9.

"Tookoolito, I have no doubt, will readily accomplish the differences in language between the Innuits of Boothia and King William's Land, and that of her own people around Northumberland Inlet and Davis's Strait. The pronunciation of the same words by communities of Esquimaux living at considerable distances from each other, and having but little intercourse, is so different that it is with difficulty they are understood one by the other. I should judge, from the very great difference of the language as spoken by the Greenlanders and the natives on the west side of Davis's Strait, that Petersen was of little service to M'Clintock as an Esquimaux interpreter. This conclusion would be arrived at by any one reading the narrative of M'Clintock's interviews with the natives on King William's Land.

"The Greenlanders have a mixed language consisting of *Danish and Esquimaux*. . . . Even the intercourse of the whalers with the Esquimaux around Northumberland Inlet, has introduced among them many words that are now in constant use. Tookoolito informed me to-day that the words pickaninny, for infant; cooney, for wife; pussy, for seal; Husky, for Innuit; smoketute, for pipe, and many other words, are not Esquimaux, though in use among her people.

"I now complete the tupic interview. Before I was aware of it, Tookoolito had the 'tea-kettle' over the friendly fire-lamp, and the water boiling. She asked me if I drank tea. Imagine my surprise at this, the question coming from an Esquimaux in an Esquimaux tent! I replied, 'I do; but you have not tea here, have you?' Drawing her hand from a little tin box, she displayed it full of fine-flavoured black tea, saying, 'Do you like your tea strong?' Thinking to spare her the use of much of this precious article away up here, far from the land of civilization, I replied, 'I'll take it weak, if you please.' A cup of hot tea was soon before me—capital tea, and capitally made. Taking from my pocket a sea-biscuit which I had brought from the vessel for my dinner, I shared it with my hostess. Seeing she had but one cup, I induced her to share with me its contents.

There, amid the snows of the North, under an Esquimaux's hospitable tent, in company with Esquimaux, for the first time I shared with them in that soothing, cheering, invigorating emblem of civilization—T-E-A! Tookoolito says that she and her winga (husband) drink it nearly every night and morning. They acquired a taste for it in England, and have since obtained their annual supply from English and American whalers visiting Northumberland Inlet.

" By-the-bye, Tookoolito said to me during the entertainment just described, ' I feel very sorry to say that many of the whaling people are very bad, making the Innuits bad too ; they swear very much, and make our people swear. I wish they would not do so. *Americans swear a great deal—more and worse than the English.* I wish no one would swear. It is a very bad practice, I believe.'

" How think you, beloved countrymen, I felt with these hot coals on my head ? Oh that every swearing man, could have seen and heard that Esquimaux woman as she spoke thus ! Her words, her looks, her voice, her tears, are in my ears still. I confess, I blushed for this stain upon my country's honour—not only this, but for the wickedness diffused almost throughout the unenlightened world by the instrumentality of whalers hailing from civilized lands.

" This I am ready to admit, that some commanders, some officers, and some crews of whaling ships are as they should be, exemplary men—men who take pleasure in doing good wherever they are—who seek to extend the bounds of civilization, planting philanthropic and Christian institutions where darkness and ignorance had before reigned universal.

" Being now ready to return—three o'clock P.M.—Ebierbing kindly gathered a crew from among his friends to convey me aboard. Much seko (ice) had set into the cove, causing us great trouble and delay to get out. Once clear, a few strokes brought us alongside.

" 10 o'clock, night, thermometer 29°, barometer 29.525 ; wind south—fresh ; cloudy."

BONE SLEDGE-RUNNER.

CHAPTER IX.

Visit to Esquimaux Village—First Specimen of domestic Life among the Innuits—Female Tongues good Cleaners—The Angeko's Power—Mysteries of Innuit worship—Choice of Wives—Curious Guide Poles to Travellers —Charley's Independence of Angeko—Ship beset in the Ice—Sudden Movements of the Ice—Frozen in—A Bear-hunt—Visit the Tupic of Ebierbing—Scarcity of Innuit Food and Fuel—The Esquimaux Lamp— Patience and Perseverance of an Innuit Hunter—An Igloo.

At this time I frequently paid visits to the Esquimaux village, and one trip I find recorded in my journal as follows :—

"*October* 30.—After dinner a boat was sent from the ship to obtain some fresh water at the head of the bay, and I availed myself of the opportunity to go on shore. Smith had charge of the boat, and in less than an hour we arrived at a beautiful little harbour, two and a half miles distant northwesterly from the vessel. Here there was a complete Esquimaux village, and all the inhabitants, men, women, children, and dogs, rushed out to meet us. Our crew consisted of five white men, and each of them soon engaged a native to carry water to the boat, while he himself sought amusement among the tents. Smith and I walked on for about an eighth of a mile to the lakelet where the water was obtained, and put the Esquimaux fairly to work. We then returned, and called at one of the tents. Smith, being first, intended to pass in, but had no sooner lifted the folding door (pendent skins) and introduced his head, than he rapidly withdrew it again, exclaiming, 'Whew! By thunder, I'm not going in *there!* It's crowded, and smells horribly. How it looms up!' He then turned away, but I, having more induce- ments to bear the infliction, determined to pass in.

" Bowing down almost to a horizontal position, in went head, shoulders, body, and all. The next second I found myself butt up against a dozen Esquimaux, all lusty fellows, and crowded together in a heap, each armed with a knife! But there was no cause for alarm. The knives were not for any warlike or evil purpose. They were being used simply for cutting off strips of seal, to be shoved into the widely-extended mouths of the hungry people before me. Quite at the back of the tent I perceived my Esquimaux friend Koojesse seated between two pretty females, all three engaged in doing full justice to a dish of *smoking-hot seal-blood!* Seeing me, Koojesse at first seemed abashed; but, on my expressing a readiness to partake of any food they had to spare, one of the women immediately drew forth from the stew-pan about four inches of seal vertebræ, surrounded by good meat. I managed to eat the latter, and then determined to try the seal-blood. To my surprise, I found it excellent.

" On first receiving the dish containing this Esquimaux stew, I hesitated. It had gone the round several times, being replenished as occasion required; but its external appearance was not at all inviting. Probably it had never gone through the cleaning process, for it looked as though such were the case. But I screwed up courage to try it, and finally, when the dish came again to those by my side, I asked Koojesse, ' Pe-e-uke?' (Is it good?) '*Armelarng, armelarng*' (Yes, yes), was the reply.

" All eyes were fixed upon me as I prepared to join with them in drinking some of their favourite soup.

" Now the custom of the Esquimaux in drinking seal-blood is to take one long s-o-o-o-p—one mouthful, and then pass the dish on to the rest till the round is made. I followed suit, and, to my astonishment, found the mixture not only good, but really excellent. I could not have believed it was so far superior to what my previous notions had led me to expect.

" Seeing I was pleased with it, she who presided at the feast instantly made ready a pretty little cup, which was clean outside and in, or clean as an Esquimaux can make it, and filled it with the hot seal-blood. This I sipped down with as much satisfaction as any food I had eaten in my life; and, in return for the friendly act of my Innuit hostess, I gave her a highly-coloured cotton handkerchief. She was in ecstasies with it, and the whole company joined with her in expressions of kindness and goodwill toward me. Clearly I had ingratiated myself with one party of the natives here, and this I was determined to do in like manner elsewhere.

" Soon afterward I left them, and crawling out of their tent on all-fours, passed through the village toward the beach. On the way I heard a voice calling out ' Mitter Hall—Mitter Hall;' and, on turning round, perceived poor ' Blind George.' I went to him, and found that he was in great trouble. He tried to tell me all his grief, but with difficulty could he give utterance to his words. ' Ugarng,' said he, ' Ugarng home to-day? My pickaninny away go. Mitter Hall, speak-um, my pickaninny—speak-um, my pickaninny here.'

" The fact was that, as already stated, Ugarng had got his child, and the poor blind man wanted her to be with him for a while. I therefore spoke to Ugarng, and often afterward little Kookooyer was seen by her father's side.

" While in the village I called at another tent, and was treated to a liberal piece of ' black skin ' after it had been well cleansed of foreign substances by the free application of a lady's tongue ! "

On November 10th I again visited the shore, accompanying the water-boat. We found the lakelet frozen over, and that our ice-axe by mistake had been left on board. This would have proved a great annoyance to us, had not one of the Esquimaux (Charley) brought his seal-spear to our aid, and speedily opened a good-sized " well-hole." In helping to carry the water, I fell into line with the natives, joining them in their mirthfulness of heart as they went along. As we passed the tupics, every woman and child gave a joyous smile and kindly word to the stranger. It was on this occasion, after I had been about two hours on shore, that I noticed something unusual had occurred. An excited crowd of natives were rapidly gathering round a young man who appeared to be frantically addressing them. Whatever his object, I soon perceived that he contrived to greatly affect his hearers. One moment he made them like infuriated demons ; at another, they were melted to tears. *Now* they were clenching their fists, and gesticulating in a maddened way ; presently they were calm, and full of joyful repose. It was astonishing the hold he had over the people round him. So complete was this power, that a simple motion with the tip of his finger would be followed by demonstrative movements on the part of the audience. An Esquimaux might be quietly enjoying a smoke, when a word from the orator would bring the pipe from the smoker's mouth to the speaker's pouch, or into the man's own pocket, just as directed.

I soon ascertained that the orator was an *angeko*, or wizard-man, and that his name was *Ming-u-mai-lo*. Though young, he was very much credited by the whole population of that and the neighbouring village. As I approached, his eye soon caught mine, and immediately leaving his snow rostrum, he bounded like a deer toward me. With a face of innocence, and full of smiles, he grasped my hand and welcomed me to his magic home ; but, though returning the salutation in a friendly manner,

I could not so cordially evince pleasure at his acquaintance as I generally did with others. It appeared to me that he was one of those who lived upon the credulity and ignorance of his race, and this thought probably made itself perceptible on my features; at all events, in a moment or so he left me, and, throwing his arm round Ugarng's neck, he walked with him into a tent, whither they were soon followed by Charley and the rest of our hired water-carriers. Koojesse was of the number; and, while I was looking on, much surprised, loud and exciting words were heard from within. Presently Koojesse came out; and, upon my making inquiries, he told me, in a cautious manner, that the *angeko* was at work, as we should call it, exorcising and otherwise performing various spiritual exercises!

Fearing to be considered intrusive, I walked away toward the boat, Koojesse again taking up his water-bucket and continuing his work; but hardly had I reached the landing-place when down came Mingumailo with a proud and excited step. He took me by the arm and beckoned me to go with him. I did so, being desirous of witnessing some of the farther acts of this curious and important personage.

We walked arm in arm, toward what, though only a *tent*, I might well style his *temple*, for toward it several of his worshippers were bending their steps. As we passed along, Koojesse was seen in the distance with a bucket of water in each hand. In an instant, at one word, one motion of my companion, Koojesse, though otherwise a man of great intelligence and strong mind, left his water just where it was, and joined us. On approaching the tupic, Mingumailo ordered Koojesse to go in first, and then directed me to follow. I did so by falling upon my hands and knees, and, in this necessary posture, entered the abode of our Esquimaux prophet. The angeko followed, and immediately directed Koojesse to take a position on one side of the bed that was within, and me to be on the other side. Next to Koojesse was seated a pretty Esquimaux woman, one of the nulianas (wives) of the angeko, the other wife—for he had two —not then being at home.

Now commenced the solemn exercises of the peculiar worship of these people. Mingumailo sat facing us. He began by rapidly clapping his hands; so rapidly, indeed, that it was impossible to count the strokes. Then he accompanied this clapping by some metaphorical expressions beyond the power of ordinary intelligences to divine; and, indeed, no one but an *angeko* is considered capable of divining them. In fact, the word *angeko* signifies "*he is very great,*" and this is given as a reason why none but *angekos*—the really great—should understand. Of course, I demeaned myself accordingly, and was as quiet and serious a listener as any one there. Occasionally the *angeko* would cease his voice and the motion of his hands. Then all became still as death. Presently, with renewed vigour he would recommence his services, patting his hands—which were moved around during the operation—now in a circle, now before *my* face, now before Koojesse's. Another minute he would pat the chest on which he sat, first on one end, then on the other, next on this side, then on that, afterwards on the top, and so repeating all the operations again and again. Every now and then, with his eyes staring into the farthest recesses of the tent, he would become fixed as marble, and looking quite hideous.

At such times Koojesse was brought into active use. He was directed, as much by the angeko's signs as by the sudden and sharp words uttered, to fix his eyes upon this point of the tent, then that, but more particularly to where it was said by the wizard, "*Kudlago's spirit shook the skin coverings.*"

Poor Koojesse! I could not help pitying him, though myself hardly able to control the laughter reigning within me. There he sat, large drops of perspiration streaming from his nose (Esquimaux sweat profusely only *on the nose*), and as earnest as though life and soul were the issue. All at once came unusual efforts. The climax was at hand. A grand finale was to take place, and this was done with a sprinkling of clear words in Esquimaux, just enough for Koojesse and myself to understand. The angeko spirit spoke: "He was in want. The *kodluna* (*white man*) could relieve his wants. Would not the kodluna give the spirit one of the double-barrelled guns in his possession?"

This was enough. I saw through the scheme in a moment; but, though astounded at the impudence of the proposition, I betrayed nothing to show surprise. I merely turned to Koojesse, and quietly asked if that was really the angeko's meaning. The reply, in subdued tones, was "yes;" whereupon I farther asked him if this man would be very useful in my future explorations to King William's Land; and on being answered in the affirmative, I said aloud, "Well, if Angeko goes with me next season, he shall have a gun—one of my best." This made the wizard-man leap for joy; for he thought, as I afterward found, that I meant to give it him at once. He grasped my hands, he threw his arms about my n, cheek danced about the tent, and did many other extravagant things, which showed his gratification on making such a triumph of skill and strategy. He had, as he chose to believe (though I immediately explained, or tried to explain, that the gift was not intended for the moment), accomplished a great feat in charming a *kodluna* into giving him a gun as recognition of his magical power. So complete was his happiness, that he told me I should have the choice of his two wives, all his *tuktoo* skins (reindeer furs) that I might need, and sealskins for making boots, and other articles in abundance. That he had great riches of this description, probably obtained from his credulous worshippers, was evident from the rolls of beautiful skins I saw around me.

While the angeko was thus expressing himself, his second wife came in, and quietly took a position near the household lamp, which she began to renew with fresh seal-blubber. This gave Mingumailo the opportunity to again press the offer of one of his wives to me. He begged of me, there and then, to select either of them; but I soon gave him to understand I was already supplied with a wife at home.

This, however, neither satisfied his ideas about matrimony, nor, as it appeared, those of his wives; for both of them at once decked themselves out in all the smiles and blandishments that they possessed. I asked them if they really coincided in the offer their husband had made, and was immediately told that they gladly did. However, I was about again declining the offer, when the angeko suddenly made a sign to Koojesse, leaving me alone with the proffered wives. I uttered a few kind words to them, and, giving each a plug of tobacco with a friendly grasp of the hand, left the tupic and went toward the boat.

On my way, and just outside the angeko's tupic, I noticed an oar of a kia stuck upright in a drift of frozen snow. Upon it were suspended little packages done up in red woollen rags, differently and ingeniously arranged. On one side hung a portion of a well-dressed sealskin, beautifully variegated by particoloured patches sewed on it, as if for signs. I inquired of several Esquimaux the meaning of this, but none would inform me till I met Koojesse, who said it was for a guide to any Innuit stranger travelling that way, and who was thus welcomed, as well as directed what to do.

As soon as Koojesse had left the tent, he immediately set to work in completing the operation of filling our water-cask. He had been told by Captain B—— to find, fill, and send off another cask, left on shore during some stormy weather a few days back, and this he now did by directing nearly the whole inhabitants of the village to aid in the task. Every conceivable article possessed by the natives that would hold water, from a pint up to a gallon, was brought into requisition. Most of the articles were made of tin, supplied by the various whaling ships visiting Northumberland Inlet, but it would have puzzled a white man to detect any difference between their colour and a negro's. Some of the vessels, however, were made of *ookgook* skins, and were excellent affairs, water-tight, light, but strong, and in no danger of being broken or indented.

As soon as the one cask in our boat was full, we were ready for starting, when it was ascertained that Ugarng and Kunniu were absent. Seeking for them caused some slight delay, and, meanwhile, Angeko began his tricks again. By signs he first ordered one and then another of the Esquimaux to do this and do that, and, with a single exception, all obeyed. The exception was Kooperneung (Charley), who, standing in the boat's stern, was smoking a pipe. He was told by the angeko to put away his pipe; but Charley, with the same smiling face that he generally possessed, laughed loudly and heartily as he laid hold of his pipe, gave it a swing, and replaced it, smoking away as before. Evidently Charley was an Independent, though I imagined, from what I had seen of him before going to the wizard's tent, that his bravado now was more because he was under present civilized rule than from any real strength of mind in the matter.

The other natives pulling the boat were servilely obedient. At a signal from the angeko, who swung his arms on high, my Innuit crew tossed up their oars, and turned their attention to the shore. There we saw him surrounded by the villagers, and making signs for us to return.

Now Ugarng had on his neck a coloured kerchief, given him by some civilized hand. This was stated by the angeko to be a great encumbrance, and would be better off than on—in fact, would be better in his, the wizard's, possession, than the present holder's. Accordingly, with great reluctance, Ugarng unwound it from his neck and cast it on shore to his master. Mingumailo swung it proudly in the air, wound it around his waist, and expanded it between his outstretched hands, all the time making his way toward the village like a conqueror, followed by his people!

After this we were allowed to depart, and in due time I got on board.

"*November* 19*th*, 1860.—Last night the ice from the head of the bay set down upon the ship, completely closing us in. We are now cut off, for the present, from all the world. We cannot approach the land, nor can any one from the shore approach us. This will continue until the ice becomes solid enough to make a pathway upon it."

Such is the record in my journal under that date, and I transcribe it to note the day when we were *first* "beset."

The temperature at this time was + 5°, and the weather moderate and clear. In the day it was cloudy, but we had the sun shining upon us for a few moments, to show me how prettily its soft light could play with the crystal white of the ship's rigging. Again and again did I look upon the scene. It was truly beautiful! Hoar-frost crystals—piles upon piles of crystals standing out boldly to windward, six inches from the masts and rigging!

Two days afterward the ice had hardened sufficiently to form a good protection to the ship during a heavy gale that came on, and which probably would have driven us from our anchorage had we not been thus guarded. The next day, however, we had open water all around us, the ice having been broken and driven out to sea by a change of wind when the gale abated. But toward evening it again came in, though not strong enough to inclose us. Thus it continued setting in from seaward until, on the 23d, we were again fast bound and firmly fixed by a solid pack for the winter. To me the change seemed almost magical. At noon of Wednesday, 21st, we had been bedded in ice that seemed fast for the winter. At 6 P.M. of that day, in some places the ice began to give way. During the ensuing night all of it had left the harbour and bay.

Morning of the next day saw us clear. At 3 P.M. the wind being southerly, some pieces of ice were seen floating toward us from sea, but still we were free. This morning of the 23d, however, the harbour and bay, save a narrow channel of water, formed one complete mass of ice. Up to the extent of the bay, running N.N.W. full fifteen miles from its entrance, all was quite a solid pack, much of it five to seven feet thick, though in some parts only from one to three feet.

The temperature of the sea water at this time was 26°, and the air 18°; the barometer 29.55, and wind fresh from the west.

On this day, finding it impossible any longer to use the boats, they were dismantled for the season. Nearly nine months must elapse before they can be used again.

Sunday, the 25th of November, we had a heavy gale from the eastward, bringing with it a remarkably warm air (the thermometer 32°), and breaking up some of the ice in such a manner that one time we expected to be driven out to sea with it. We were, however, preserved by the pack in one portion remaining firm, and thus giving us a shelter, though not more than a hundred yards from where the disruption was taking place. On the 1st of December there was a great calm, lasting till the 4th; but finally, on the 6th of December, we were no longer under any doubt as to being well secured in the solid ice for the winter. In all directions, the harbour and bay were completely frozen over.

On November 24th I had my first sight of, and encounter with, a polar bear. I was engaged writing in my cabin, when a shout was heard on deck, "A bear! a bear!" and immediately relinquishing my pen for the rifle, I went up and joined a party who started in chase.

Sterry and the Esquimaux Ugarng had already gone off to the hunt, and I rapidly followed, accompanied by "Charley," while all the natives that had been on board, and several of the ship's crew, came after us. The bear took a direction near the island where my dogs had been placed, and the howling they made was truly terrible.

As Charley and I neared one of the outer islands, about half a mile from the ship, bang went the first gun. Then a second report, and soon afterward I could see the bear retreating across a channel to another island. He had received some severe wounds, for blood was pouring out on either side of him, crimsoning his white coat and the ice beneath. The channel was covered over with ice that appeared too frail for us to make passage upon. Down through this ice every now and then the bear would plunge. But soon returning to the same hole, he slid himself out of it upon the ice in a very sprawling, but to me interesting manner. Once out, he immediately rose upon his haunches, knocked his tormentors (the Esquimaux dogs) to the right and left with his fore-paws, and then ran on. But the dogs were again upon his track, surrounding and cutting off his retreat to the shore. Thus we were soon up with him, though keeping at a respectful distance from the wounded prey. Charley desiring to try his hand at my rifle, and knowing he was a good marksman, I allowed him to do so. He fired as the bear was again on his haunches engaged with the dogs. The shot took effect in his breast, and the brave beast fell kicking and tumbling; but, after a moment's

struggle, was once more on his feet again, flying away. Morgan,
of our ship, now tried his double-barrel, with three bullets in
each, but both barrels missed fire. Another shot was then fired,
and this time the bear tumbled over, as we all thought, *dead*. A
cheer from us followed; but hardly had our voices died away,
when the poor beast was again on his feet struggling to get off,
white men, Esquimaux, and dogs all after him. Once more a
heavy charge—this time from Morgan's gun—went into him,
striking his face and eyes, and down went Bruin "dead again."
One cheer was given, then another commenced, when, lo! as if
the noise had revived him, the brute, seemingly with as many

BEAR-HUNT—"TAPPING THE JUGULAR."

lives as a cat is said to have, went off again, running feebly, but
still with some remaining vigour. Spears were now thrown at
him by the natives, but these rebounded from his tough hide,
proving as harmless to him as tooth-picks.

Once more he was down. Then raising his head, and looking
round upon his foes, which numbered a full score without including the dogs, he seemed as if preparing for the last fight and
death-spring. It was a dangerous moment, and so all felt. But

now was the time for me to try my hand. Hitherto I had not fired. This, then, was the moment to do so. I stepped out, and placed the hair-trigger as it should be, and levelled my gun.

"Shoot at his head! give it him in the skull!" was the cry of those around; but I watched my opportunity, and, when he gave a certain downward throw of his head, fired, tapping the jugular vein. It was enough. One convulsive movement, as the blood oozed out from the keen cut made by my rifle ball, and the life of the polar bear was ended.

The next task was to get the carcass on board, and at first we intended to drag it there. A line of sufficient length was upon the ground, ready for placing round the bear's neck; but this was finally abandoned, as his weight (near that of an ox) would break through the treacherous ice around the island where we were. It was then decided that the Esquimaux should skin the animal on the spot, quarter it, and thus carry it piecemeal to the ship. Accordingly, we left them to the task, and had not long been back to our cabins when the prize arrived, the carcass still smoking hot, though the skin was already frozen stiff.

I should mention that, as soon as the bear was discovered, Ebierbing hastened after it with his dogs, which were regularly trained to keep bears in check until rifles and spears should arrive. The dogs which I had brought from Greenland never had been "educated" for bear fights, therefore they seemed to act upon the principle that "distance lends enchantment to the view" by getting upon the most distant and highest part of the island on which the bear was killed.

As regards the use made of our prize, I have only to say that we divided it with the Esquimaux, and had a capital dinner off a portion of our share. I liked it better than the best of beefsteaks.

A day or two after this bear-hunt I paid another visit to *North Star* village, accompanied by Ebierbing, who took me direct to his tupic. After passing on all-fours through the low snow-passage which he had made, leading to the interior, I found myself facing Tookoolito, seated near a lamp, and herself covered with skins, she having been taken sick on the last occasion of visiting our ship. Mittens, boots, stockings, and articles of clothing, all in a wet state, were on the "dry net" that always hangs over the lamp, but on this occasion the lamp was not performing its usual heat-giving functions. Owing to the backwardness of the cold season in freezing up the bay, the condition of the natives from want of blubber and food was in an alarming state. Many of them could have no friendly lamp to give light and heat.

The Esquimaux lamp is the "all in all" to these people. By it their igloo is lighted and kept warm; by it they melt ice or snow for their drink; and by it they dry their clothing, mittens, boots, stockings, &c. Without the *lamp*, Esquimaux could not live—not so much because of its warmth or use for cooking, but because it enables them to dry their skin clothing, melt ice for

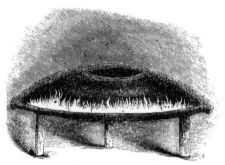

KOOD-LIN AND IK-KU-MER,
the Stone Lamp and Fire of the Esquimaux.

drink, and gives them light during the long arctic night of winter.

When I called upon Tookoolito the lamp was without oil, and could not give either sufficient light, heat, or drying power, hence the melancholy aspect of her otherwise happy abode. Ebierbing, however, intended very soon to make a sealing excursion, and obtain blubber at any risk.

When obliged, Esquimaux do not hesitate in undergoing the greatest privations to get food for their families. They will watch over a seal-hole for one hour or fifty, if need be, in the coldest weather, waiting for the seal to come up and breathe. *Kudlago* in this manner caught the first seeds of the complaint which carried him off. His family were starving; and after bearing the pain of seeing them suffer for a few days, he could endure it no longer. He went out in some of the worst and coldest weather known here, and exposed himself for nearly two days and nights continuously, patiently watching for a seal, which he eventually captured. Ebierbing now intended to do the same thing rather than allow his home to be wretched much longer.

I need hardly say that everything in my power was done for *Tookoolito*, as also for poor *Nukertou*, who was very sick.

From Tookoolito's I walked a little way on, and found two Esquimaux, " *Charley* " and " *Miner*," making an igloo, or snow-house. In a short time more it was finished, and I was quite surprised at its beauty. With the exception of a single stain upon its spotless snow at the apex or centre of the dome, it was one of the most chaste pieces of architecture I ever saw. The exceptional stain was, I am sorry to say, something emanating from civilization. It was the juice of tobacco! I seized the long snow-knife from the hands of one of the Esquimaux, and scraped away that which so marred the beauty of the whole, while the inmates looked on, and then applauded me when it was done.

About this time, and toward the end of November, I was much astonished at the changes in the temperature. On the 19th the thermometer, on this glorious fair and calm morning, was − 20°, barometer 30.175. Cold indeed; by thermometer, 52° below the freezing point. Yet so calm was the weather, that to my person it seemed no colder than at the commencement of the season, when the thermometer indicated 32° above 0. But let a smart breeze spring up coming from the N.W. then how like hot iron it will burn! The weather was such that, unless we soon had snow, the ice would freeze thick and solid throughout the regions. Snow upon the ice serves to keep it *warm*, the same as snow on the ground in the Northern States of America.

In my journal at this date I find as follows : " I have just been out walking and running, exposing myself, my face and hands, to the cold air. A light breeze prevailing from N.W. I am confident there is something yet to be discovered relative to air and cold. The human system is not such a *liar* as three excellent thermometers I have would make it, if I gave full credence to their story this morning. My three thermometers say 20° below zero, and yet far greater exposure now than at other times with a higher register of temperature, leads to no unpleasant results. I am aware moisture in the air makes a great difference as affecting the human system ; but a fact is a *fact*. The cold air from the same direction—equally charged with aqueous matter at different times—shows a difference of ten to twenty degrees in the thermometer; and yet the air at the lowest temperature affects the human system less than the highest.

EK-KE-LU-YUN,
The white-stone salmon-bait used by Esquimaux

CHAPTER X.

THE month of December came in, as I have previously said, with
a great calm of four days, and though the ice was then much
broken up, making a transit to the shore difficult, yet I contrived
to frequently land for exercise, and to see more of Innuit life.

One day, while walking near a channel between two islands,
I heard a very remarkable echo, of so striking a character that
an Innuit boy and three dogs, near at hand, could hear my voice
only through its reflected sound. The tide was out, leaving a
rock bluff on the opposite side of the channel, whence the sound
was reverberated. After giving utterance to my voice, in one
second of time the echo came back to me, thus making the
distance across 550 feet, as sound travels 1100 feet per second.

On December 8th, at noon, the thermometer was at zero,
and on the 9th, 15° below zero, or 47° below the freezing
point. Yet, strangely to me, the cold was not felt so much as I
should have supposed. The ice was solid around us, and our
good ship quite laid up in winter quarters. Now and then we
could hear some heavy and startling cracks, as if disruption was
about to take place ; but nothing of any note occurred to disturb
or to vary the usual monotonous life on board. Visits from the
Esquimaux were made daily, and often we had several sleeping
on the cabin floor and on sea-chests in impromptu beds made of
sails, thick wearing apparel, &c. and a curious picture it was
thus to see them. Frequently, accompanied by some of these
visitors, I went to their village and to the islands around us,
always being received by the natives in the most friendly
manner.

Once we had a stranger arrive who had formerly lived near
" King's Cape," at a place called by Esquimaux *Se-ko-se-lar*.*

* From various sketches drawn for me by Esquimaux, I concluded Se-ko-
se-lar to be a place on the north side of Hudson's Strait, near a large bay
as yet *undiscovered* by white men. This bay is somewhere between the

This man's name was *Koo-choo-ar-choo*, but known by us as
"Samson," from his great size and strength. He was large and
muscular, five feet six inches high, and weighing over 200 lbs.
He was famous, too, as a great hunter, and had even captured
whales by himself, with only the aid of a boy! When he visited
us, his pretty little daughter *Puk-e-ne-yer*, of about ten years
old, accompanied him, and I was much amused with the nimble
way in which she undid and then rebraided her hair. The use
of a comb she did not know until I gave her one and showed
her. As for the father, I found him very intelligent, and,

THE "GEORGE HENRY" IN WINTER QUARTERS.

through Tookoolito, who acted as my interpreter, he gave me
much geographical information.

Another of our visitors was *Puto*, the mother of a *white* child.
This woman had once been considered handsome, and even now
showed some signs of her former beauty. She was about 35

longitude 72° and 75° west, making far up, due north, and abounding in
seals, walrus, white whales, and the *Mysticeti*, or Greenland whales.

years old, and, though she had a hard time of it alone, supporting herself and child, yet she was generally cheerful, smart, kind, and industrious. On one of my visits to Tookoolito's igloo, *Puto* with her child was there, and I then witnessed the operation—very rarely performed—of washing a child's face. This was done by *licking* it all over, much as a dog would do the hand that had just contained a fresh beefsteak. She did this twice while in my presence, and the true colour of the child's face was then more clearly seen.

Owing to some cause or other which I could only surmise, *Puto* suffered more from various privations than the other women. She was often a week with hardly anything to eat, and, in consequence, her poor child was nearly starved. On the occasion I now refer to, after I had left the igloo and wandered about to other dwellings, I came across Charley and Ebierbing, just arrived with a sledge-load of frozen krang, whale-meat, for the dogs. *Puto* at the moment also came to the spot, and immediately asked for some. They gave her about twenty-five pounds of it ; and this she slung on her back, along with a pack of equal weight already there, besides the child !

Ye mothers of America ! what say you to taking an infant, besides an additional pack of fifty pounds on your back, and starting off on a tramp of several miles—such was the distance to Puto's home—with the thermometer 40° or 45° below the freezing point ?

On this visit I met a sister of Ebierbing, and also another woman, just taking up their quarters in the same place. In fact, it was a matter of mutual accommodation, for the purpose of creating more warmth within, and economizing light and fuel. They arrived, bringing their worldly goods, while I was talking to Tookoolito, and at once the new-comers proceeded to place their lamp on the opposite side to that of the mistress of the igloo. They first filled it abundantly with seal-blubber, then putting in large wicks of moss, soon brought forth a long even train of light and a glorious heat. The new-comers, it appeared, had managed to procure some of the precious seal-blubber so much needed.

At Ugarng's igloo, which I visited the same day, I there encountered several women and children congregated together. I was welcomed at once by Nikujar, " Polly," the *first* or family wife of Ugarng, and by *Punnie*, his *third* wife—No. 2 wife, *Kunniu*, being absent, though her lamp was bright and in full trim. Little Kookooyer (the child of blind George) was also there, and, with her fat cheeks, laughing eyes, and pleasant voice, greeted me as I entered.

"Polly," in speaking to me could only raise her voice to a whisper, for she was suffering from a pulmonic disease, and almost unable to utter a word without pain.

While waiting at this igloo, in came Puto and her child—Puto finding it necessary to re-arrange the pack at her back prior to a final start for the upper village. Her infant was given to little Kookooyer to hold ; but, as it was rather noisy, I thought to pacify the babe by taking it in my own hands, and, in doing so, tried to show them how civilized mothers carry and nurse their children. This, however, only produced a hearty laugh ; and I was made to understand that, in all the matters relating to the tending of infants—even in the very minutest, as there and then shown to me—the Innuit custom was the best.

I could here mention one or two facts, but it will be unnecessary more than to say that mothers here at home will comprehend all my meaning when I tell them that an Innuit infant is carried naked in the mother's hood, yet in close contact with the parent's skin. Thus every childish necessity is generally anticipated in good time by the ever-sensitive, watchful mother.

On the 18th December we heard of an arrival at the upper village from *Annawa*, the Esquimaux who, with his family, it may be remembered, went away on the 30th of the previous August. This Esquimaux was a brother of some of the most enterprising Innuits in the North. He lived almost the life of a hermit—that is, he resided with his small family in a distant part, away from other people, his abode being at an island called *Oo-pung-ne-wing*, in the Countess of Warwick's Sound, on the north side of Frobisher's Bay. It was his son who had now arrived, with a view of doing a little trade, if he could.

Many of the Esquimaux came to me, not only as ordinary visitors, and to see what they could get in the way of presents, but also to do some trading. At the same time, several of the younger ones gladly received instruction from myself in the civilized tongue. As regards trading with them, it was generally done for articles of use, reindeer-skin dresses especially being necessary for me for winter, and no one could be more expert or more tasteful than the Innuit women in making them.

On one of my visits to the upper village, a daughter-in-law of Artarkparu was just finishing off her winter coat with a long tail, the universal fashion there among the ladies. It was prettily ornamented (?) with federal coin of the United States—

old copper cents—eight in number, arranged in rows, and fixed as pendents to the tail.

On another occasion, when Kokerzhun came on board with her husband, she had on a beautiful *tuktoo* (reindeer) fur dress, having a skirt standing out hoop fashion! The variety of colours of the tuktoo was prettily arranged, and so well did she appear, that it was said by some of us that she would pass at home for a " Broadway belle."

So excellent were the dresses made for me by these Innuit women, that I did not hesitate paying tolerably liberal for them, particularly as they were rather scarce. I obtained a native jacket for a knife, two small skins for another knife and some powder, and a good deerskin for more powder, buckshot, and caps. Many of the natives had guns, obtained from the whalers of Northumberland Inlet, either by barter or as returns for services rendered. I could not, at that time, get all I desired in the way of Innuit apparel, though it was useless to attempt travelling in any other costume, as nothing but that could withstand the cold ; but from my first arrival I had been obtaining several articles, and thus I was now tolerably well supplied

" *December* 20th, 5.30 A.M. — Thermometer -- 5°, barometer 30.200. Wind *very light*, N.W. Yet there must be a storm prevailing not far from us, as a tremendous roar of waters and cracking of ice comes from the direction of Davis's Straits. The ice around the shore of this harbour is constantly ' singing,' indicating that a heavy sea is now affecting us even here . . . . 7 A.M. the wind went round to the N.E. when it commenced snowing ; thermometer 4°, barometer 30.100. At 10 P.M. we had the thermometer 14° above zero, barometer 30.050, wind N.E. blowing a gale, the ice breaking up in Field Bay, and also in our harbour.

" *Friday, December* 21st.—Thermometer 21° above zero, barometer 30.012. Wind light from east. The bay is nearly clear of ice. What little there is fastens up our harbour. The weather is too warm for the igloos ; they have commenced dripping. If the like continues, down will come snow-houses.

" *Saturday, December* 22d. — The thermometer is actually + 32½° ; barometer 30.100. Wind N.E. During the night considerable *rain* fell. The natives are in sad plight. There has been not exactly a *conflagration* in the Esquimaux village, but disruption, and a melting down. Nearly every igloo is in ruins, owing to the unexpected storm of rain. Some have fallen, others about to. The men Innuits are busily engaged in erecting outer walls, filling in snow between the old and the new. I visited nearly every habitation, and found the natives exclaiming, '*pe-ong-e-too!* pe-ong-e-too!'—bad! bad! '*Karg-toon*' —very hungry.

"At Ebierbing and Tookoolito's there was great distress. Their igloo was nearly destroyed. In the night the whole of the dome had fallen in, covering their bed, furs, dresses, &c. in wet snow. Ebierbing was busy in making a canvas tent over the ruins, while Tookoolito cleared out the snow from beneath. He was wet through, and had not a dry skin upon his back, having been out all the morning trying to save his igloo from the almost universal ruins around him.

"*Dec. 22d.*—Raining hard throughout this day, with occasional sleet and snow. Tookoolito visited the ship, and upon her return I let her have an umbrella, which, though *she* well knew the use of it, was really a novelty to others of her people, who considered it a 'walking tent.'

"The extraordinary mildness of the season has caused a most sad state of things among the natives. They cannot obtain their accustomed food by sealing, as the ice and cold weather alone give them the opportunity. Hence in many of the igloos I have seen great distress, and in some I noticed kelp (sea-weed) used for food.

"Whenever I visited the natives, such small quantities of food as I could spare from my own slender but necessary stock were taken to them, and on one occasion I gave Tookoolito a handful of pressed 'cracklings' which I had brought with me from Cincinnati. They were given me by a friend there for dog-food, and I can now record the fact that Cincinnati pressed 'cracklings' made as rich a soup as ever I had eaten."

The preceding extracts from my diary about the weather, and its effects upon the condition of things around me, will show that almost the very existence of these children of the icy North depends upon the seasons being uniform with the time of year. The high temperature we had experienced, however, did not long continue. A few days afterward, on the 30th of December, the thermometer was down to zero; and on the 5th of January it was sixty degrees below freezing point! The bay and harbour had again been coated over with solid ice, and parties of Innuits were out in all directions seal-hunting, but with such slight success that several of them departed for other quarters, where they hoped seals would be more abundant. Among these were Ugarng and his family. They started for Cornelius Grinnell Bay, but, before leaving, a few cakes of hard bread were given them, that the party might have something to fall back upon in case of success not following immediately.

It was not long, however, before Ugarng returned very sick. He left in the morning, and arrived at the ship about 4 P.M., thus making a rapid journey on his sledge of about forty miles. Two days afterward, having received extra aid and medicine, he once more started, and, as will be presently related, when I made an excursion to where he had gone, I found him busily engaged sealing.

Among the other incidents to be mentioned as occurring about this period of my narrative, I must not forget to say that Christmas and New Year's Day were celebrated by us in our winter quarters with all the honours it was in our power to show. A few of the natives were on board to dine on Christmas Day, and I took the opportunity to give Tookoolito a Bible that had been placed in my hands by the Young Men's Christian Union of Cincinnati, and which I thought could not be devoted to a better purpose. I inscribed upon it the following :—

"*Presented to Tookoolito, Tuesday, December 25th, 1860.*"
Her first act was to read the title, "Holy Bible," then to try and read some of its pages, which she still longs to understand.

The new year of 1861 was welcomed by me at its very earliest commencement, having been up throughout the night. The previous evening I had been paying visits on shore among the natives, and at 1 A.M. of the first day of January I was engaged in writing, in the midst of the sleeping forms of Esquimaux made warm and happy for the night in our main cabin. *Paulooyer* (Blind George) and his little girl, Kookooyer, were there, well wrapped up, and Kimmiloo, in my sleeping bag, was asleep on a sea-chest. Koojesse and his wife Tunukderlien were in my berth, and two other Esquimaux were on the cabin floor. Ebierbing and Tookoolito were on shore in their own igloo, and it was to them that, at half-past 5 A.M. I made my first New Year's "call." Various other "calls" were made, all with a view to some beneficial result, and, if possible, to do the poor people good in their then wretched state, and throughout the day sundry manifestations among our men were given, akin to those adopted at home.

On this day, January 1st, 1861, we had the thermometer —1°, barometer 29.20, and the weather calm, with light clouds. We did not, therefore, feel the cold as might have been expected, and thus our New Year's Day passed off most agreeably.

I have now to relate an occurrence that was as startling to me in its terrible yet solemn character as anything I had ever before known or heard of.

I have mentioned that another Esquimaux woman, called Nukertou, was found to be very sick, and I therefore determined to again call upon her, taking some medicine, and a little quince jelly that had been given me by loved ones at home.

I left the ship, and, after crossing some very broken and dangerous ice, which formed a sort of unstable and disjointed causeway, arrived at the village during the morning. I asked Tookoolito to accompany me, which she cheerfully did, and together we went to the tupic of Nukertou. She had been left alone in her sickness, all uncared for, as was customary, I regret to say, with the Esquimaux when any of them were helplessly ill.

The poor woman was very glad to see me, but she was so weak and suffered so much that she could hardly move. I gave her medicine, which soon relieved her, and for this I received many thanks ; but I thought her end near. I could see by her wasted form and utter prostration that she had not long to live. Perhaps, had she received such early attention from her own people as is shown among families in civilized life, she might have survived ; but from no one did she get this, and only by chance did her illness reach my ears.

I have before mentioned her kindly nature, ever ready to do anything she could for all of us on board without looking for fee or reward, and, so long as she had strength, she was to be seen at some friendly task ; but her absence was not particularly noticed, owing to the fact that Innuits are of a character so thoroughly independent that they come and go just as they please.

On the present occasion, Nukertou was living in an igloo occupied by *Shimerarchu* (Johnny Bull), with his wife, *Kokerzhun,* and her little sister, *Kimmiloo.* The latter came in while I was speaking to Nukertou, and when Tookoolito left, the girl showed much attention to her.

The sick woman lay on skins of the reindeer placed on the snow platform opposite the entrance of the igloo, and, though in the usual condition of Esquimaux when in bed, said she felt quite warm. The medicine, and perhaps the kindly words, had done her good. But some days afterward I found her snow bed had become unfit for sleeping upon. Some unusually high temperature of the weather for that time of the year, added to the heat—though not much—of her own body, had melted the snow couch, and she had sunk into a position of great uncomfort. Accordingly, one day (December 21), assisted by her friends, I made her a fresh bed by procuring blocks of drifted snow, crushing them finely as flakes, and making the same into a soft, smooth basis, upon which was placed the usual layer of the small dry shrub, and on top of that some reindeer skins. This, then, was the new bed for poor sick Nukertou, and for a time she seemed more comfortable. But neither the attentions of Tookoolito or myself availed. Gradually she declined ; and, though we administered to her such food as was necessary (all the Innuit people, at this period, being near a state of starvation, owing to a very bad season for seal-hunting again), her death rapidly approached.

On December 30th, I find the following in my journal concerning her :—

" Invited Tookoolito to go with me and make a call upon sick Nukertou. We found her as yesterday. I had a talk with her, Tookoolito acting as interpreter. What a scene for my memory ! There sat Kokerzhun before her fire-lamp, drinking in every word, as Tookoolito interpreted to sick Nukertou what I had requested to be said. Tookoolito went on talking to Nukertou all that I had taught her of God, Christ, heaven, the good, &c., and there she stood, weeping over the form of her whom we all love as a sister—the kind Nukertou.

" After this interesting interview Tookoolito and Kokerzhun proceeded to the vessel, while I went to the former's igloo, and obtained my spirits of camphor for the purpose of laving the temples of Nukertou. Here I remained, chafing the hot, tattoed brow of this afflicted but resigned Esquimaux—here I remained alone with her, whose spirit may soon be in the presence of God and angels."

The day but one afterward I paid my usual visit to Nukertou, and found that Shimerarchu was building a new igloo for her. Upon inquiry, I found that it was to be *her living tomb !* I was thunder-struck. A living tomb ! And so, Tookoolito said, according to custom, it must be ; and so it was.

On the 4th of January, 1861, Nukertou was removed to the new igloo. She was carried thither upon reindeer skins by four women, who took her in through an opening left for the purpose *at the back*, not by the usual entrance. Snow blocks were then procured, and the aperture well closed, while a woman stood by and gave instruction what to do. An ordinary entrance was then made, and, as soon as completed, I went into the igloo.

Nukertou was calm, resigned, and even thankful for the change. Of course she knew that it was to be her tomb; but she was a child of her people, and as she had now become a helpless burden to them, with only a few days more to live, it seemed to me that she took it as a matter of right and justice, and no one could object. Therefore she was thankful that her last moments were being so carefully seen to.

A new igloo of stainless snow, a well-made bed of the same material, where she could breathe her last, would make her few remaining hours happy. True, she would be alone—for such was the custom of the people—but she did not fear it. She was content, and appeared cheerfully resigned.

On the 8th of January she died; and as the incidents connected with her death were very striking, I will transcribe them from my journal as entered down at the time:—

"*Monday, January 7.*—This evening, fearing that Nukertou was wholly neglected, I went on shore about five o'clock. Of course it was then quite dark, with the thermometer 57° below the freezing point, and it was necessary for me to have a lantern in hand, besides some of the natives to guide me across the ice. On arriving at the igloo, Ebierbing and the others remained outside, while I, pushing aside the little snow door, drew myself through the low, narrow-tunnel entrance, which was just of size sufficient to admit my squeezed-up body, and neared the inner part. A strange and solemn stillness pervaded the place, only interrupted by the perceptible, but irregular and spasmodic breathings of the dying creature within. I raised myself up, looked toward her, and gently uttered her name. She answered not. A second call from me was alike unresponded to. I therefore went to her and felt her pulse. It still beat, but told me that she was dying. I cried out for Ebierbing and Koodloo (the latter a male cousin of Nukertou) to come in. They did so reluctantly, and at my suggestion the former went to inform Tookoolito of Nukertou's condition. A few moments found Tookoolito in the presence of the dying.

She remained here as long as was required, and returned to her igloo, leaving me and Koodloo with Nukertou. In one hour I left Koodloo alone in charge, and stepped over to Ebierbing's for a few moments. Upon my return to Nukertou's, what was my astonishment when I found the igloo sealed up—blocks of snow placed firmly in and around the entrance way. It seemed to tell me that she was dead. I had but a short time before learned it to be the usual custom among the Innuits, when one of their number is dying, for all to retire from the igloo or tupic, whichever it might be, and not return to it. But I thought after all, perhaps she is not dead. I threw back block after block of unspotted snow, till I made my way into the main igloo.

" Nukertou was not dead ! She breathed, and was much about the same as when I last saw her. I determined then to remain, doing what I could to smooth the pillow of the dying. The lamp was nearly out ; the cold was intense, the thermometer outside being 51° below the freezing point ; and though I had on the Esquimaux dress, it was with difficulty I could keep my blood from congealing. There I was, the lone, silent watcher of the dying Esquimaux, encircled within walls that were soon to become her tomb.

" About twelve, midnight, I heard footsteps approaching. Soon the sound as if the entrance was being closed up again. I thought, Can it be that I am to be imprisoned here, doomed to have this *my* living tomb ? I listened a while. I found it true that I was being shut up as though dead. Of course those who were doing this knew not I was there. At length I cried out ' Turbar ! turbar !' Stop ! stop ! At this, all was again silent as the grave for a moment. I then said, 'Ki-ete'—come in ; and in came the two who were performing the last sad act of respect to the dead. But what shall I say of their last act to the living ? The two proved to be *Koodloo* and a woman called *Koo-ou-le-arng*, or *Suzhi*, as we named her. Here they remained half an hour with me, then departed. I was again alone with the dying Esquimaux. Nearer and nearer drew her end. Coldness was creeping over her. Indeed, I found the cold taking hold of me. The native lamp, which serves for light and fire, had ceased from want of blubber or oil. There was only my lantern-lamp to give light, and the oil of this was kept fluid by the caloric of my encircling hands.

" During the day my fur stockings had become damp from perspiration, therefore my feet were nearly frozen. Every few minutes I was necessitated to jump and thrash myself—to do anything I could to keep my limbs from frostbites.

" How intently I watched each change in Nukertou ! One, two, three, four, five, six, seven did I slowly count in the inter- vals of her breathing, and these increasing to even double that number. At last I could count nineteen between her inspirations but her respirations were short and prolonged—irregular. At length Nukertou ceased to live. I exclaimed, 'She's dead! Receive back her spirit, I pray Thee, O God, for she is Thine.'

"I now left for another part of the island, to call her cousin Koodloo. He was asleep in an igloo, and, on awaking him, he accompanied me back. But I could find no one willing to lend a helping hand; no one would touch the dead. I therefore determined to lay the corpse out myself. Koodloo would do nothing but hold the lamp, and I had to perform the whole. I put her on a snow bed, crossed her hands upon her breast, closed her lips, and placed lumps of the pure snows of heaven upon

THE DYING ESQUIMAUX—NUKERTOU.

her lips, with a snow pillow under her head. This done, I then left for the ship, having first taken the precaution to seal up the igloo so as to prevent the dogs from eating up her remains.

"It was three in the morning when Nukertou died, and as I left her, so did her body remain, unvisited, uncared for, within that igloo tomb."

My journal continues: "It might as well be here stated what occurred in Nukertou's igloo on the arrival of my valuable and esteemed friend Tookoolito, when her husband informed her of the dying condition of Nukertou. To my mind the incident goes to show how strongly are fixed among any people *customs*, however absurd they may appear to others.

" Tookoolito, on arriving last evening, proceeded to examine Nukertou's condition—feeling her pulse, listening to her breathings, watching her every motion. Too true, indeed, did she find what I had said. Tookoolito gently spoke words that astonished me, because they came from one who is not only conversant with my vernacular, but with the belief and practices of civilization. She said Nukertou was dying, and that we must all retire at once ; that if we delayed till Nukertou's death, the skin dresses we had on would never do to be put on again.

" This was spoken with an *earnestness* that wanted no guarantee of her firm belief in what she said. Under the circumstances, I had no hesitancy as to my course then and there. I knew she had confidence in me ; that she knew I always treated her people as well as I could my own ; that she knew I never endeavoured to cast a slur or make light of any of the customs of her country. Therefore I said, 'Tookoolito, listen to *wong-a* (me) a moment. On Christmas day I gave you a good book —the Bible. That book is the Word of God. It tells you and me—everybody—to visit the sick, the afflicted, the widow, the helpless, the poor.'

" Kindly I proceeded, to the best of my poor ability, to show her wherein it was wrong thus to leave the sick—the dying. Her astonishment at what I said seemed as great to her as was mine at her recorded remark. During this important conversation, allusion was made as to working on tuktoo furs during the season of catching walrus. It is a fact that, when the Innuits begin to catch walrus, no work is done on reindeer skins ; therefore all winter clothing is made up before any attempts are made to get walrus. The reasons *why* will be stated some time hereafter.

" In my arguments with Tookoolito I told her it was not to be wondered at that she and her people believed many unreasonable things, when there had been no one to teach them better— no one to tell them of the Bible. I told her that some people of America and in England believed a great many ridiculous things, but that did not make them true ; told her that I only wished to do her good ; that whenever I could kindly show where they—her people—were doing wrong, I should do so ; that if she or her people could prove to me her or their ways were all the best, then I would be one to do as Innuits did. After this interview under the snow roof of the dying, I heard Tookoolito, in her igloo, earnestly engaged in telling her wing-a all that I had told her. They both seemed thankful for what I had said."

In connexion with the preceding account of Nukertou's death, and the Innui customs referring to it, I may here mention another occurrence somewhat similar, which took place about the same time.

There was a sick native, whom I visited on two or three occasions, named *Kooperarchu*, who suffered greatly from ulcers on the neck. His case was desperate, and no remedies we applied availed him. As his end approached, the *angeko* took possession of him altogether, and when I once tried to see the patient, all the natives assured me it would be useless while the angeko was there. But I determined to make the trial, and, as a great favour, was admitted by the dying man's family.

This time the angeko was a woman, and when I entered, her position was at the farther side of the igloo, with her back to me, but seated, cross-legged, under a pile of skins. At her side was the poor man, Kooperarchu, kneeling, and in a state of complete nudity, though snow and ice were above, beneath, and around him.

At first I was startled at this; but, remembering what great wonders have been and can be accomplished by a sick person's complete faith in his physician, I made no attempt at interference, except motioning for one of the brothers to place some covering over the patient's shoulders.

The angeko was constantly engaged in addressing some unknown spirit, doing it in as varied a way as could be well conceived. The whole family participated in the scene, placing themselves in position, responding, ejaculating, and doing whatever the angeko required; and all this with a solemnity that was particularly striking, so much so, indeed, that the exercises reminded me, in some respects, of what is known as a Methodist "love-feast."

When the exercises were through, the angeko turned round, appearing to notice me, and expressed surprise; but I soon mollified her rising anger by a slight present, which made her and the family very friendly.

Notwithstanding all the efforts made by this angeko, they availed nothing in arresting the rapid strides disease was making on this poor man's life. On the following day, myself being sick on board, I requested Tookoolito to see the patient, and took to him certain medicines I gave her. She did so then, and likewise on the next day, remaining half an hour with him. Soon after she had returned to her igloo, "Jack," a brother of Kooper-archu, called and said the sick man was dying. Immediately Tookoolito went back, and, feeling his pulse, found it almost gone. Kooperarchu felt himself dying, and said to her, as, in our language, she explained it to me, "I going to die—I cannot help it—I wish to die. My mother and father in *kood-le-par-mi-ung* (the Innuit heaven)—I go meet them—I must go—I cannot stop!" She asked him, "Go now?" He replied, "Yes." This was the last word he spoke. Thus Kooperarchu died.

Kooperarchu was buried soon after his death. His friends and relatives wrapped him in two tuktoo skins and carried him away. The frozen corpse was suspended across the shoulders of his brother by a strap placed under the arms and across the breast, as one would carry a gun. Tookoolito headed the funeral train, and a married sister of the deceased, with a younger brother, and a couple of dogs, besides some of the natives, followed him to the grave. This grave was but a little distance from the village, and merely consisted of a recess made in the snow, with the same material piled over the dead body.

* * * * * *

Three days after Kooperarchu's decease I was able to visit his family igloo. There I found his relations all sitting in a close group on the snow platform. They were bemoaning the loss of a brother and *excellent seal-hunter*. For three days from the death his family had thus to mourn, according to Innuit custom. At the end of that time they expected their lost brother would be in "kood-le-par-mi-ung," there for ever to enjoy its pleasures, feasting on reindeer meat, and wandering from star to star.

CHAPTER XI.

HAVING a great desire to try and do something in the way of exploring, and particularly to accustom myself to actual life among the Innuits, I at length determined to venture on an excursion by sledge and dogs to Cornelius Grinnell Bay, whither Ugarng had already gone. Accordingly, after due preparation, myself and party were ready on the 10th of January, 1861, and away we went.

The following account of the first day's journey is from my journal, as written every evening in an igloo—snow hut :—

"*Thursday, January 10th*, 1861.—Thermometer 30° below zero, or 62° below freezing point ! My company consists of self, Ebierbing, Tookoolito, and Koodloo, the cousin of the deceased Nukertou. By 4 A.M. I was up, and, with lantern in hand, went and called Ebierbing and his wife. They arose, and at once proceeded to gather up whatever things they would require during our stay. I then returned to the ship and packed up my own material. The outfit for this trip consisted, in provisions, of 1½ lb. preserved boiled mutton in cans, 3 lbs. raw salt pork, 15 cakes (4 lbs.) sea-bread, ¼ lb. pepper, 2 lbs. ground burnt coffee, 1 quart molasses, 1 quart corn-meal, and 3 lbs. Cincinnati cracklings for soup. Then, for bedding, 1 double wool blanket, 1 sleeping-bag, 1 cloak and 1 shawl for bed-covering. For clothing, besides my native dress upon me, I took 1 extra under-shirt, 1 woollen shirt, 2 pairs extra stockings, 1 pair extra pants, 2 towels, and 2 pairs mittens. My books were Bowditch's Navigator, Burrit's Geography and Atlas of the Heavens, Gillespie's Land Surveying, Nautical Almanac for 1861, a Bible, and ' Daily Food.' My instruments were, 1 telescope, 1 self-registering thermometer, 1 pocket sextant, 2 magnetic compasses, and 1 marine glass. I had also a rifle and ammunition, oil for lamp, and a hand-saw, besides paper, ink, pens, memorandum and journal book.

" At 10 A.M. we were in readiness—Ebierbing with the loaded sledge and team of dogs (five of his and five of my Greenlanders) —alongside the *George Henry*. Tookoolito was gaily dressed in new tuktoo skirt, tuktoo pants, jacket, &c. Bidding adieu to our friends on board, we then started, Tookoolito leading the way—tracking for the dogs—for about one mile to the shore, in a north-easterly direction. Thence our course was that which Ugarng had evidently taken the day before. Over hill and mountain, through vale and valley, away we went.* Sometimes, when on a descent, our speed was rapid. Now and then we all got on the sledge for a ride. My spirits were high, for this was my first sledge-travelling trip. Ebierbing managed the dogs admirably. Indeed, I should consider him a capital dog-driver. I think I never perspired so profusely as I have this day. Some of the events during our journey have been most amusing. Once we were descending a steep incline, all of the company holding on to the sledge, so as to prevent its too great speed downward, when, one of my feet breaking through the treacherous snow-crust, headlong I went, and, like a hoop, trundled to the bottom of the hill. Tookoolito hastened to my relief, and, seeing a frostbite on my face, she instantly applied her warm hand, the Innuit way, till all was right again. Another steep incline caused the sledge to descend so rapidly that at length it went over three or four of the dogs, who were unable to keep ahead of it, though running at great speed.

" By 3 P.M. we neared the frozen waters of the ocean, after passing over some very abrupt and rocky ground. On the margin of the sea the cliffs were almost perpendicular, and it was necessary to *lower* the sledge down to the ice below. Accordingly, the dogs were detached, and while Tookoolito, whip in hand, held on by their traces, which were from twenty to thirty feet long, we lowered the sledge. The tide, however, was out, and it caused some difficulty in getting on to the main ice. At length all was safely accomplished, and once more we started on our way, Tookoolito again leading. Then we proceeded for about five miles, when we came to an igloo out on the ice, which

* For route of this sledge-ship, see track on Chart. From Rescue Harbour, lat. 62° 52′ N. long. 64° 44′ W. over land to Tuk-e-lik-e-ta Bay; thence on the sea to Roger's Island, lat. 63° 12′ N. long. 64° 32′ W.

had evidently been erected and occupied the night before by Ugarng and his party. Here we should have stopped; but, as the igloo was too small for building a snow house, we encamped at 5 P.M."

Ebierbing and Koodloo at once commenced sawing out snow-blocks, while I carried them to a suitable spot for erecting the igloo, which took us one hour to make. And a right good one it was, as I soon found. The door sealed up, and the cheerful lamp in full blaze, with a hot supper preparing, made me feel remarkably comfortable, though in a house of snow, built so speedily upon the frozen surface of the treacherous ocean. I will here give this matter more in detail.

Soon as the igloo was completed, Tookoolito entered and commenced placing the stone lamp in its proper position. It was then trimmed, and soon a kettle of snow was over it making water for coffee and soup. She then proceeded to place several pieces of board we had brought with us on the snow platform where our beds were to be made. Upon these pieces was spread the canvas containing some of that small dry shrub I have already alluded to. Over this went the tuktoo skins, and thus our sleeping accommodations were complete.

I should mention that every article on the sledge is passed in through an opening at the back of the igloo, for the purpose of convenience. When all is thus within, then this opening is closed, and a proper entrance made on the side opposite the beds. The dogs are left outside.

The drying of whatever has been worn during the day, or whatever has become wet with perspiration, falls to the lot of the "igloo wife." She places the things on the *in-ne-tin* (a net over the fire-lamp), and through the night attends to the turning of them, as occasion requires. Her other duties consist in the repairing of such clothing as may be needed. Nothing is allowed to go one day without repair. Everything, where *care* is required, even to pipes and tobacco, is placed in the igloo wife's hands—in this case, Tookoolito's. These matters I particularly noticed on the occasion of *my first night* spent in an arctic igloo.

Presently our evening meal was ready. It consisted of Cincinnati crackling soup, a small piece of raw salt pork for each of us, half a biscuit, and coffee. Tookoolito proved herself an excellent cook; and I soon felt convinced that no party should think of travelling in these regions without an Innuit man and his wife, for the latter, above everything, is the "all in all," or at least the "better half."

After supper, myself and the two male Esquimaux had each a pipe, and then turned in, my position being between the hot-blooded Innuits Ebierbing and Koodloo.

I slept as well as I would ever wish, and on the following morning, about nine o'clock, after breakfast and repacking the sledge, we again started. Our proper course was due north, but, owing to hummocky ice, we could not follow it. In truth, sometimes we were obliged to make a retrograde movement to get out of " a fix " that we were occasionally in among icebergs and hammocks. Owing to this, we made but five miles direct toward our destination during the day.

It had been expected that we could reach Cornelius Grinnell Bay in one day from the vessel, but too many obstacles existed to allow it, and thus a second night came upon us while still upon the frozen sea. A storm was also gathering, and its darkness, with the howling wind, which had changed from off the land to right upon it, was foreboding. We were likewise much wearied with the day's labours, and it was some time after we stopped before a suitable place was found and our second igloo erected. At length, though long after dark, we were comfortably located, enjoying a hot supper beneath the snowy dome, the foundation of which rested on the frozen bosom of the mighty deep. But not too soon were we under shelter. The storm had burst in all its fury, and we could hear the wind roaring outside as we warmed ourselves within.

All night long the gale continued, and the next morning—the third of our journey—it was found impossible to go on. It was blowing a strong gale, and continued so all day, with snow in impenetrable thickness. We were therefore obliged to keep inside our shelter, wrapped in furs.

While thus detained, I took the opportunity to have my hair cut by Tookoolito. It had grown to a great length, even to my shoulders, and I now found it very inconvenient. My beard, whiskers, and moustache were also shorn nearly close to my face. In musquito time they were serviceable, but now they had become quite an evil, owing to the masses of ice that clung to them. Indeed, on the previous night I had to lose a portion of my whiskers. They had become so ice-locked that I could not well get my reindeer jacket off over my head, therefore I used my knife, and cut longer attachments to them.

I may here mention that, after this, when we vacated the snow-house, our dogs rushed in to devour whatever they could find, digestible or not, and my locks were a portion of what they seized. In went my discarded hair to fill up their empty stomachs! A few days later, I saw the very same hirsute material, just as clipped from my head, lining a step leading to another igloo, having passed through the labyrinthian way from a dog's mouth onward.

About 4 P.M. Ebierbing ventured outside to see how matters looked, but he soon returned with the astounding news that the ice was breaking, and water had appeared not more than ten rods

STORM-BOUND—ENCAMPMENT ON THE FLOE IN DAVIS'S STRAITS,
JANUARY 11TH AND 12TH, 1861.

south of us! I looked, and, to my dismay, found that a crack or opening extended east and west to the land, distant about three miles! The gale had evidently set the sea in heavy motion somewhere, and its convulsive throbs were now at work underneath the ice close to and around us. It still blew very hard, but as yet the wind was easterly, and so far good, because, if a nearer disruption took place, we should be forced toward the land, but if it changed to north or north-west, away to sea we must go and perish !

Seriously alarmed, we consulted as to what was best to do—whether at once to hasten shoreward, or remain in the igloo and stand the chance. On shore, nothing but rugged precipices and steep mountains presented themselves ; on the ice, we were in danger of our foundation giving way—that is, of being broken up, or else driven to sea. At length we decided to remain while the wind lasted in its present quarter, and, to guard as much as possible from any sudden movement taking us unawares, I kept within sight my delicately-poised needle, so that the slightest shifting of the ice on which we were encamped might be known.

In the evening the gale abated, and by 10 P.M. it was calm, but the heavy sea kept the ice creaking, screaming, and *thundering*, as it actually danced to and fro ! It was to me a new but fearful sight. When I retired to bed I laid down with strange thoughts in my mind, but with the conviction that the same protecting hand would watch over me there as elsewhere.

The night passed away without alarm, and in the morning Koodloo made an opening with a snow-knife through the dome of the igloo for peering out at the weather. He reported all clear and safe, and, after a hot breakfast, we packed and started, though under great difficulty and hazard.

The ice had given way, and was on the move in every direction. The snow was also very deep—sometimes above our knees—and moreover very treacherous. We could hardly get along ; and the poor dogs, which had been near starving since we had left the ship (Esquimaux dogs endure starvation, and yet work, amazingly), had to be assisted by us in pushing and hauling the sledge, while constant precaution was needed against falling through some snow-covered ice-track. Every now and then we came to openings made by the gale and heaving sea. Some of these were so wide that our sledge could hardly bridge them, and a *détour* would have to be made for a better spot. At other places we had to overcome obstructions caused by high rugged ice that had been thrown up when masses had been crushed together by the tremendous power of the late storm.

To guard against and extricate ourselves from these dangers, yet find a track amid the hummocks around, each of us by turns took the lead, and in this manner we proceeded on our way ; but it was evident we had hardly strength enough to persevere in reaching our destination that night. By 2 P.M. we were so exhausted that I deemed it best to make a halt, and use a little more of the slender stock of provisions I had with me, and which, owing to our being so much longer on the way than expected, had become very low. Each of us, therefore, had a slice of *raw* salt pork and a quarter of a biscuit. This, however trifling, gave renewed strength, and again we pushed forward, hauling, scrambling, tumbling, and struggling almost for our lives.

It was dark ere we got near the locality where our next encampment was to be made, and where, in fact, we intended to remain a while for the purpose of hunting and sealing, and myself exploring.

At length we caught sight of an igloo which afterward proved to be Ugarng's, and, as soon as we saw it, fresh efforts were made to get nearer, but we found our passage more and more obstructed by the broken, upturned ice. Often the sledge was carried onward by making it leap over these impediments, sometimes from one point of ice to another, and at others down and up among the broken pieces. Finally we succeeded in reaching the shore ice, which we found all safe and sound, and in a short time more we were alongside of Ugarng's igloo, encamped on the south-west side of Rogers's Island, overlooking Cornelius Grinnell Bay and the mountains surrounding it.

Immediately I ran into Ugarng's igloo, and obtained some water to drink, for I must mention that all day long we had been famishing on account of thirst. The material to make water had been abundant around us—beneath our feet, here, there, and everywhere—but not a drop could be obtained, owing to our fire-lamp and equipments not being in use. Thus it was most thankfully I received the warm-hearted welcome given me by Nikujar, family wife No. 1 of Ugarng, as she handed a cup of refreshing cold water. Then I remembered how, on one occasion at the ship, this same woman, with her infant, came and asked *me* for water, which I gladly gave to her, with something else. Now *she* gave it to me.

I should mention that, in winter, water is most precious to the natives. It is made only by melting snow or ice over the ikkumer (fire-lamp), which is an expensive heat and light when oil and blubber become scarce ; and in this case our materials for fuel were all expended.

While our own igloo was being erected, Ugarng and his second wife arrived from sealing, and, to the joy of all, brought with him a fine seal. He generously supplied us with what we wanted, and thus an excellent supper was added to cheerful light and genial warmth from the now well-fed lamp.

My fourth night in an igloo, on this journey, was spent more comfortably than the previous two had been, and on the following morning I rose greatly refreshed and strengthened. As I looked upon the expanse over which we had passed, I was startled to find the ice all gone out to sea. This was confirmed by a view shortly afterward obtained from the top of a mountain behind our igloos, and I felt truly grateful to HEAVEN for having so preserved us.

During the day I took a walk on shore, and the two Esquimaux went sealing. They returned at night with a fine prize, which made us an excellent feast; and, as my own stock of provisions was exhausted, except a trifle I reserved in case of sickness, this supply was most timely.

On the following day, January 15th, Ebierbing and Koodloo departed, with the sledge and dogs, on a hunting excursion, and I went away to examine the locality around. During my walk over the hills I came across numerous tracts of rabbits, and I also saw in the distance several prominent headlands that were familiar to me from noticing them when we first arrived here in the ship.

While rambling about, I fortunately preserved myself from a severe frostbite in the face by taking the precaution of carrying a small pocket mirror which belonged to Tookoolito. I had asked the loan of it, knowing how necessary it was, when one is alone in those regions, to have a detector of frostbites; and I found the use of a mirror in such a case equivalent to the companionship of another person.

That night I was alone with Tookoolito and Punnie; the latter Ugarng's third wife, she having come to our igloo to keep company with us until the husbands returned. It was very cold—the thermometer down to 57° below freezing point. Now my usual sleeping-place was between Ebierbing and Koodloo; but they being absent, I had to lay on the general bed, wrapped in my furs and blankets. During the early part of the night my feet were almost frozen. I tried all I could to keep them warm, but in vain. At last a smooth low voice reached my ear:

" Are you cold, Mr. Hall?"

I answered, " My feet are almost frozen. I cannot get them comfortable."

Quick as thought, Tookoolito, who was distant from me just the space occupied by little Punnie (that is, Punnie slept in the middle), got down to the foot of her bed; thence she made passage for her hands directly across my feet, seizing them and drawing them aslant to her side. My modesty, however, was quieted when she exclaimed, " Your feet are like ice, and must be warmed *Innuit* fashion ! "

Tookolito then resumed her place beneath her tuktoo furs, intermingling her hot feet with the ice-cold ones of mine. Soon the same musical voice said, " Do your feet feel better ? "

I responded, " They do, and many thanks to you."

She then said, " Well, keep them where they are. Good-night again, sir."

My feet now were not only glowing warm, but *hot* through the remainder of the night. When I awoke in the morning, as near as I could *guess,* there were no less than three pairs of warm feet all woven and interwoven, so that some difficulty was experienced to tell which were my own.

Ebierbing and Koodloo did not return until the next evening, bringing with them some black skin and krang—all the success attending them—which was obtained from a *caché* made the previous fall by the natives when our ship was in the bay. The black skin was compelled to be our food, as nothing better could be had ; and at supper I ate heartily of the *raw frozen whale hide.*

The following noon a very heavy snow-storm came on, and continued throughout the next and two following days, confining us almost entirely to the igloo, myself obliged to live on black skin, krang, and seal.

On Sunday, the 20th of January, ten days after leaving the ship, we found ourselves in a sad state from actual want of food. The weather continued so bad that it was impossible to procure any by hunting, and all we had hitherto obtained was now consumed, except a very small portion held in reserve. I had intended sending Koodloo back to the ship for supplies, but waited for more suitable weather. This morning, however, it was absolutely necessary an attempt should be made, and as Koodloo refused to go alone, I decided upon proceeding with him.

We expected to be obliged to make one night's encampment on the sea ice, now again, so far as we knew from that around us, compact, and we hoped to reach the ship on the following day. My only preparation was a sleeping bag and shawl, with a carpet sack of sundries, and half a pound of baked mutton, which I had carefully preserved to the present moment.

At 8 A.M. we were in readiness with a sledge and team of 12

dogs, most of them nearly starved.   Bidding adieu to Ebierbing and Tookoolito, Koodloo and I started on our journey.

At first, much hummocky ice impeded the way, but this we got through, and I anticipated a speedy trip.   I was, however, disappointed.   Soon, deep snow appeared ; and though we struggled for some miles due south, it was at length evident that to go on like that would be impossible.   Occasionally the sledge and dogs contrived to get forward pretty well, but often they were so buried as to be almost out of sight.   Koodloo seemed to think of giving it up, and I was so weak as to be hardly capable of dragging myself along.   While in this dilemma as to what we should do—go on, or return to the igloo—I perceived Ebierbing and Ugarng on their way toward us.

They had noticed my difficulty, and Ebierbing now came on snow-shoes to offer his services in going to the ship in my stead. I accepted the proposal, and he, with Koodloo, went forward, Ugarng going in another direction, seeking for seal-holes, while I, slowly and with difficulty, owing to my weakness, returned to the igloo.   I was a long time getting back, and when I arrived there was obliged to throw myself on the snow platform quite exhausted.

Toward evening, the weather then being fine, I walked on to a hill that overlooked the bay, and with my glass saw Ebierbing and Koodloo slowly wending their way along near where our second igloo had been erected, the former leading.   The night and the following day I was hardly able to move.   My weak state, owing to want of food—all my daily fare being a small piece of black or whale skin—had become very serious.

In the evening I went to Ugarng's.   He had just returned from sealing, having been out *two days and one night* over a seal-hole.   All the reward he had, however, for his patient exertions was the seal coming up and giving a puff; then away it went, leaving Ugarng a disapointed Innuit.   But he bore his disappoint-ment very philosophically.   He said, in his native tongue, " Away I go to morrow morning again !"

The next morning, which was very fine, Ugarng and Jack went out sealing again, while I visited several portions of the island. The following day Ugarng returned once more unsuccessful, though he had remained all night over the seal-hole.   This was very bad for the whole of us.   We could not now have even a fire-light until another seal was captured ; and when I called at Ugarng's, I found they were in the same condition.   Nikujar (Polly) was alone, except her infant and Kookooyer, their

daughter by George.   They were without light.   Her child was
restless, and she said the cause was hunger.   " Me got no milk—
meat all gone—blubber too—nothing to eat—no more light—no
heat—must wait till get seal."

While I waited, the second wife came in and said Ugarng was
still watching over a seal-hole.   Jack soon afterwards returned
without success.   Sad—very sad !   My own state was bad enough,
and I felt it severely ; but I could not bear to witness the wants
of the poor people around me, having no power to relieve them,
unless Ebierbing should soon come back with some provisions
from the ship.   All that I had to eat was my piece of black skin,
and this I relished.   Indeed, I could have eaten anything that
would have gone towards keeping up the caloric within me, and
make bone and flesh.

One night I asked Tookoolito if I might try the taste of
some blackened scraps that hung up.   I knew that she had
reserved these for the dogs, but nevertheless I had an uncontrollable longing for them.   I was very hungry.   Tookoolito
replied that she could not think of my eating them—the idea
made her almost sick ; therefore I did not urge the matter more ;
but soon afterward I saw they were gone, Punnie (Ugarng's
third wife) having taken them, and passed the whole into her
own stomach !

Ugarng came in late again unsuccessful, and Tookoolito gave
him a cup of tea, such as it was, for, owing to the absence of
proper light and fuel, it could not be well made.   Directly he
had it, off he went once more to try for seal.

The next morning Ebierbing had not returned, and we were
all at our wits' end to find something to eat.   At length Tookoolito made out to cut off some of the white from a piece of
black skin.   From it she "tried" out sufficient oil to use for
heating some snow-water, which, when warmed, was thickened
with Indian meal, a few handfuls having been found remaining
of the small quantity I had brought with me.   The quantity of
meal did not weigh above two ounces, yet it seemed to " *loom
up* " as it was incorporated in the tepid water, and the incident
strongly reminded me of the good woman and Elijah of Bible
history.   Tookoolito, with whom I shared the meal, thought
the " pudding " excellent, and so did I.   Indeed, I shall not
readily forget that breakfast, even—as I wrote at the time—
" if I live to enjoy a thousand more dainty ones in my native
home."

CHAPTER XII.

At this time, though I kept in general good health and spirits, I was fast losing flesh. But almost worse than want of food was the want of light and fuel. On several occasions, the only way I had to keep myself from freezing was by sitting in bed with plenty of tuktoo furs around me. The writing of my journal was done with the thermometer + 15° to less than 0, while outside it was from − 25° to − 52°. During the day I several times went up the hill to look for Ebierbing's reappearance from the vessel, but no signs of him met my eye, and the night of January 24th (fourteen days from the ship) saw us with our last ration of food, viz., a piece of "black skin" 1¼ inch wide, 2 inches long, and ¾ of an inch thick. It was under these very "agreeable" circumstances I went to sleep, hoping to dream of better things, even if I could not partake of them. "Better things" fortunately did arrive, and in a way that I *could* partake of them.

At midnight I heard footsteps within the passage-way to our igoo. Intuitively I knew it was Jack with ook-gook—seal-blubber. I sprang out of bed and drew back the snow-block door. There *was* Jack, his spear covered with pierced seal-blubber hanging in strips like string-dried apples. I had allowed my poor starving dog "Merok" to sleep within the igloo that night, and, directly I had opened the door, on his scenting the luscious fat, quicker than thought he gave one leap—a desperate one, as if the strength of a dozen well-fed animals were in him. In an instant I grappled with the dog, and made great efforts to save the precious material; but, though I actually thrust my hands into his mouth, and though Tookoolito and Punnie also battled with him, Merok conquered, and instantly devoured that portion he seized.

This misfortune, however, was not single. Before Jack could get his well-loaded spear and himself into the igloo, all the other dogs about the place were around him, fighting for a share of what was left. They succeeded in obtaining nearly all before we could drive them away, and thus the good portion intended for us from what Jack had procured was lost *to us*, but not to the dogs! Jack, who was of Ugarng's party, and had brought this as a present, returned to his own igloo, and left us disconsolate to ours. "Better things," therefore, in that case, were not for us; but, nevertheless, as I have said above, they did arrive, and that speedily.

Not before 9 A.M. did I again leave my tuktoo bed and go outside the igloo to look around. Naturally and longingly my first glance was in the direction whence I expected Ebierbing. In a moment my eyes caught something black upon the almost universal whiteness. I looked again and again. It moved, and immediately my heart leaped with joy as my tongue gave utterance in loud tones to Tookoolito within, "Ebierbing! Ebierbing! He is coming! he is coming!" The response was, "That is good;" and I—merely adding, "I go to meet him"—bounded away as fast as my enfeebled body would allow.

I soon found, however, that if progress was to be made toward him, I must do it by slow degrees and patient steps. "Black skin," in homœopathic quantities, daily taken for food, had but kept my stomach in sufficient action to support life. All the strength I now had was mostly from the beef-steaks of dear Ohio, eaten and moulded into human fat, muscle, and bones before leaving my native home. But this remaining strength was very, very small, and thus my efforts to get on soon nearly exhausted me.

After a great struggle through the deep snow, I at last got within hailing distance, and sang out to know if it was really Ebierbing, as the party I had seen was no longer advancing. No reply came to my question, and I immediately hastened my feeble steps to see the cause. A moment or two brought me near enough to be convinced. It *was* Ebierbing, with the sledge and dogs, but so exhausted with his labours that he had been obliged to throw himself down, completely overpowered. Soon I was by his side grasping his hand, and, with a grateful heart, thanking him for the really good deed he had performed in thus coming alone with the relief I saw before me.

In a short time the loaded sledge was examined, and I found a box of sundries sent from the ship, as also a very fine seal, caught that morning by Ebierbing himself. There was likewise a quantity of whale-meat, brought from Rescue Harbour for the use of our dogs.

Directly Ebierbing could renew his journey, we started together; but the dogs and both of us were hardly able to get the sledge along. Finally we reached the shore ice, and here we were so exhausted that not one inch farther could we drag the loaded sledge. Kunniu, wife of No. 2 of Ugarng, seeing our condition, hastened to give assistance, and with her strong arms and our small help, the sledge was soon placed high on the shore by the side of the igloos.

Ebierbing's first and most earnest call was for " water." This was supplied to him, and then we commenced storing our new supplies. The seal was taken into the igloo—the usual place for a captured seal—and the sledge, with its contents, was properly attended to. Of course the news of Ebierbing's arrival with a seal " spread like wildfire," and in our quiet little village, consisting of three igloos, all the inhabitants with exhausted stomachs—including my own—were prepared for wide distension.

The seal weighed, I should say, about 200 lbs. and was with young. According to Innuit custom, an immediate invitation was given by the successful hunter's family for every one to attend a " seal feast." This was speedily done, and our igloo was soon crowded. My station was on the dais, or bed-place, behind several Innuit women, but so that I could see over them and watch what was going on.

The first thing done was to consecrate the seal, the ceremony being to sprinkle water over it, when the stalwart host and his assistant proceeded to separate the " blanket "—that is, the blubber, with skin—from the solid meat and skeleton of the seal. The body was then opened and the blood *scooped* out. The blood is considered very precious, and forms an important item of the food largely consumed by Esquimaux. Next came the liver, which was cut into pieces and distributed all around, myself getting and eating a share. Of course *it was eaten raw*— for this was a raw-meat feast—its eating being accompanied by taking into the mouth at the same time a small portion of delicate white blubber, which answered the same as butter with bread. Then followed distributing the ribs of the seal for social picking. I joined in all this, doing as they did, and becoming quite an Innuit save in the *quantity* eaten. This I might challenge any *white man* to do.   No human stomach but an Innuit's could possibly hold what I saw these men and women devour.

Directly the " feast " was ended all the company dispersed. Tookoolito then sent around bountiful gifts of seal-blubber for firelamps ; also some seal meat and blood.   This is the usual custom among the Innuits, and, undoubtedly, is a virtue to be commended.   They share each other's successes, and bear each other's wants.   Generally, if it is found that one is short of provisions, it may be known that all are.   When one has a supply, all have.

After the feast and the gifts were over, we had leisure to attend to ourselves, and in what " great good humour " we were soon to be found !   Our lamps were all aglow and our hunger sated.   I then took up the letter sent me by Captain B., which added to my pleasure in its perusal.

It appeared, by what I read, that every one on board the ship, as also the natives in the two villages, had given us up for lost during the gale we encountered when encamped on the ice. From the long absence of all information about us, and the fact that the same gale had broken up the ice in Field Bay, it was concluded that we had been driven out to sea, and probably had perished.   Koodloo's wife never expected to see him again ; and old *Ookijoxy Ninoo*, the grandmother of Ebierbing, said she dreamt about him in such a way that his death was almost assured to her.

My information from the ship told me that the natives in both villages were still badly off, not having caught one seal since our departure.

I must now mention, briefly, how Ebierbing obtained the fine seal he brought with him.   On his way to the ship he discovered a seal-hole, but, being hurried for time, he merely erected a small pile of snow near at hand, and squirted tobacco-juice as a mark upon it.   On his return, he readily found the hole by this mark, and, though he felt the necessity of hastening on to our relief, and had received instructions from the captain to hurry forward, yet he determined to try for the prize by spending the night in attempting to gain it.   Accordingly, binding my shawl and various furs around his feet and legs, he took his position, spear in hand, over the seal-hole.   This hole was buried in two feet of snow, and had been first detected by the keen sagacity of one of the dogs with him.   Ebierbing, while watching, first thrust the spindle shank of the spear a score of times down through the snow, until he finally hit the small aperture leading

LEIGHTON, BROS.

SEALING IN THE WINTER.

through the ice. It was a dark night, and this made it the more difficult, for, in striking at a seal, it will not do to miss the exact spot where the animal comes to breathe—no, not by a quarter of an inch. But, to make sure of being right when aiming, Ebierbing put some dark tuktoo hair directly over it, and thus, after patiently watching the whole night long, he was rewarded in the early morning by hearing the seal *blow*. In a moment more he captured it by a well-directed aim of his spear.

The next morning, January 25th, the Innuits Ugarng, Ebierbing, and Jack all separated for some place where they hoped to get seals. I supplied them as liberally as I could with my provisions, and then myself remained behind to proceed with certain observations I daily made in reference to determining positions, and otherwise noting down particulars concerning the locality around me.

The rations sent me from the ship were examined and placed in safety from the dogs, but not from the truly honest Innuits, for such precaution was not needed ; and then I tried to go on with some work. But it was colder than we had yet experienced, the thermometer being that night (the seventeenth of my igloo life) 75° below the freezing point ! Remembering that our sealers were out on the ice, and, as they had said, would each be watching for a prize, I shuddered, fully expecting they must be frozen to death ; but what was my surprise and pleasure in the afternoon to see Jack and Ebierbing return, each with a seal—the one captured about midnight, the other early in the morning.

Ebierbing admitted that he had felt the cold very much while watching, and, though well wrapped in furs tied around him, could hardly prevent his feet from freezing. As to his nose, *that* did get touched by the frost, but he soon remedied it by smoking a Yankee clay pipe " loaded " with Virginia tobacco.

Ugarng returned in the evening unsuccessful.

Another " seal-feast" was of course made, and on this occasion I supped on seal soup, with about two yards of frozen seal's entrails (very good eating) as a finish to the affair.

These seal suppers I found to be most excellent. The seal-meat is cooked in a pan suspended for three or four hours over the fire-lamp. Generally it is boiled in water—half of it sea water—and blood ! When ready, it is served up by first giving to each person a piece of the meat. This is followed by a dish of smoking-hot soup, that is, the material in which the seal has been cooked ; and I challenge any one to find more palatable food in the world. It is ambrosia and nectar! Once tasted, the cry is sure to be "*More! more!*"

The seal-meat, I may state, is eaten by holding it in both hands, the fingers and the dental "mill" supplying the offices of both knife and fork. This mode of eating was known before such instruments were thought of. Among the Innuits generally, the following practice prevails : before the igloo wife hands any one a piece of meat, she "*soups*" it all over, that is, *sucks* out all the fluid from the meat that would probably otherwise drip out. Farthermore, if there be any foreign matter upon it, such as seal, dog, or reindeer hairs, she *licks* them all off with her pliant tongue.

On January 29th we had the cold so severe that the thermometer showed, during the night and in the morning, 82° below the freezing point! yet, strangely, I had experienced more severe sensations of cold when the temperature was at *zero* than at this low state. Still it was cold, and bitingly cold? How Ebierbing and the other men—who had again left on the previous evening—could keep to their watch during that cold night was to me marvellous; yet they did so; and when Ebierbing returned about 9 A.M. without success, he told me that he was unwearied in his watchfulness all through the dreary time. At midnight a seal had come to breathe, but he was not so ready or so smart—probably was too much frozen—as to strike in time, and therefore lost it.

Sometimes the wives accompany their husbands sealing, even in such weather.

Recording my own experience of igloo life at this time, I may here say that, having then spent twenty nights in a snow house, I enjoyed it exceedingly. *Now*, as I look back at the past, I find no reason to utter anything different. I was as happy as circumstances permitted, even though with Innuits only for my companions. Life has charms everywhere, and I must confess that Innuit life possesses those charms to a great degree for me.

On the 31st we had a stranger visit us—a boy called *Noo-ok-kong*—who arrived from a spot one mile west of where our first igloo had been erected. He had found us out, and stated that he left behind, at the stopping place, Mingumailo the angeko, with his two wives. They had started for that spot a short time preceding us, but now, having been a long while without food, he came to see if we could supply him. The lad had an abundance given him, and never before did I see such an amount of gorging as I did by that boy.

Next day Ugarng departed on a visit to the ship, and with sundry presents of seal-meat, &c. from Ebierbing to his aged grandmother and friends. I also sent a letter to Captain B., preferring to remain until I had completed all my observations. While taking some of these, however, I "burned" my fingers most sadly by laying hold of my brass pocket sextant with my bare hand. I say burned them, because the effect was precisely the same as if I had touched *red-hot* iron. The ends of my finger-nails were like burnt bone or horn; and the fleshy part of the tips of my fingers and thumbs were, in appearance and feeling, as if suddenly burnt by fire.

On the 3d of February we caught sight of some reindeer on the ice, making their way slowly in single file northward, and eventually coming within a quarter of a mile of our igloos. I had given my rifle to Ebierbing on the first sight of them, that he might try his skill in killing one; but, owing to the charge of powder being too small, he missed, and the reindeer, alarmed, darted off with the speed of the wind, much to our regret.

That night, about 12 o'clock, we were aroused by a call from some one evidently in distress. The cry came from the passage-way just without the igloo, and was at once responded to by Ebierbing telling the stranger to come in. He did so, and who should stand before us but Mingumailo the angeko! He spoke feebly, and said that he was very ill, thirsty and hungry; and that he, with his family, had had nothing to eat for nearly one month! Immediately a pile of frozen seal-meat was pointed out to him, with permission to eat some, and, quick as lightning, the famished man sprang to it like a starving bear. But how he did gorge! He swallowed enough, I thought, to have *killed* six white men, yet he took it without any apparent discomfort. Water was supplied to him, and of this he drank copiously—two quarts went down his camel stomach without drawing breath! Seeing his tremendous attack upon our precious pile of fresh provisions, I really felt alarmed lest he meant to demolish the whole, and leave us without. To feed a hungry man was well enough, and a ready act on the part of all of us; but then for him to have a stomach as huge and voracious as any polar boar, and try to fill that stomach from our limited supply of food, was more than we could reasonably stand. I grew impatient; but finally the angeko gave in. He really had no power to stow away one piece more. He was full to repletion; and, throwing himself flat on the igloo floor, he resigned himself to the heavy task Nature now had to perform in the process of digesting the monstrous heap he had taken within.

After a time the angeko told us that one of his wives had accompanied him, but had gone into another igloo. The other wife kept with them as far as she could, when he was obliged to leave her till means of relief could be found. He had built an igloo for her, and then hastened on to our snow village. In the morning Noo-ook-kong, the Innuit lad, went with some food to her, and soon afterward brought her in, thus making an addition of no less than four hungry mouths to aid in consuming our supplies. To add to our dilemma, Ugarng returned on the following day bringing with him *three* more fasting beings besides himself. They were his mother, Ookijoxy Ninoo, his nephew Eterloong, and his niece Ookoodlear, all related to Ebierbing.

Ugarng, however, brought for me additional supplies from the ship; but I saw quite clearly that, whatever I might feel inclined to do for my late companions in their need, it would never answer to begin supplying all strangers that arrived, particularly the angeko, who was lazy, and living upon the credulity of his people. Therefore I determined to stop this as speedily as possible. The angeko, however, left us in a day or two for another place, where he and his wives were afterward found, again starving.

News from the ship told me that all were well on board, and that the natives had caught *one* seal, the captor being Koodloo, who had remained there when Ebierbing went with him on the first trip back to the vessel.

Sterry, of the ship's company, had been for some time living at a place in Frobisher Bay, and had, with the natives, caught two walrus. Captain B. intended going thither the next month with some men, to see what could be done the coming season in the way of whaling.

After this arrival, the usual daily incidents of our life were unvaried for some time. Occasionally seals were obtained, principally by Ugarng and Ebierbing, and then a grand feast of raw food took place.

The improvidence and thoughtlessness of the Innuit people are remarkable. If they can live bountifully and joyously *to-day*, the *morrow* may take its chance. This was repeatedly shown in the conduct of one and all during my residence with them in the igloos. Not even Ebierbing and Tookoolito were exempt from this failing. They would eat, and let others eat up *all* they had one day, though they—and, I must add, *myself*—

starved the next. In addition to this want of due consideration concerning food for their own home, Tookoolito was generous in the extreme, always giving when asked, and trusting to what might happen afterward for replenishing the supply. Ugarng's numerous family, consisting of no less than seven individuals, made incessant demands upon her and Ebierbing, and also upon myself, whenever it could be done by cajolery, or—as I often thought would follow—by intimidation. My own stores I freely gave to an extent that I considered advisable, and no more; but I frequently pointed out to my Esquimaux friends the necessity of husbanding what they obtained by their persevering and arduous labours. It was, however, of no use. Eat, eat, give, give, let go and never mind, seemed the principle that guided them; and, consequently, in a short time starvation again stared the whole village in the face.

Ebierbing, however, was a most persevering and indefatigable sealer. During that season he caught more seals than any other man; and on one occasion, by the aid of my rifle, which I had loaned to him, he succeeded in bringing back four seals, after having taken six, but two were lost. This was on an excursion he took by way of Clark's Harbour to Allen's Island. Ugarng had gone with him, and built an igloo near a narrow channel kept open by swift tides, discovered at that place. The angeko, staying at Clark's Harbour, would not stir from there, having found a deposit, formerly made by us in the ship, of whale krang, and upon this he and his two wives were living—that is, so far as he allowed the poor women to share with him. When, however, Ebierbing was returning with his great prize, this lazy, worthless angeko must needs join him to share in the feast which followed. I need hardly say that my own feelings toward the man were not of the most peaceable; but I was alone, and even my two Innuit friends yielded to the sway of their angeko; hence I was powerless to avert aught such a man might instantly command to be done, had I offended him.

When Ebierbing returned with the four seals he merely stayed long enough for the feast, and was off again, with the understanding to look out for me, as I purposed following him. This I did on the 16th day of February, being the thirty-eighth of my departure from the ship, and of my living thus wholly among the Innuits. The Innuit Jack was my companion, and we arrived at Kowtukjua (Clark's Harbour) about 3 P.M.

This place was where we had anchored in the ship during the previous fall, and where I nearly lost my life by the accidental pistol-shot on the 13th of August. I examined the locality, and then, at 4 P.M. started for Allen's Island.

We arrived at Ugarng's igloo about 7 P.M. and were welcomed by Kunniu, Ugarng himself being out sealing. Here I stayed until the 18th, aiding them as far as I could, and curiously watching the various efforts made to sustain and enjoy life by these singular people of the North.

In a future chapter I shall dwell upon this more largely; but now I must only say that great success attended Ugarng's exertions, and when we all started for the igloo village it was with a good store of food upon our sledge. We arrived in the afternoon, and, after the usual feast, passed the evening in social conversation.

I had now been forty-two nights in an igloo, living with the natives most of the time on their food and according to their own customs. I therefore considered that I had gained some experience in the matter, and having made several observations for determining the locality of places, prepared for my return.

I bade adieu to my Innuit friends in the village, and on the 21st of February left what I then called " my Northern Home" for the ship. I was accompanied by Ebierbing, Ugarng, and Kunniu, and we had the sledge and dogs with us. The parting from Tookoolito was affecting. She evidently felt it; but the hope of herself and husband soon being with me again on my future excursions removed much of the disappointment she then felt at my going away. In fact, both she and Ebierbing were as children to me, and I felt toward them like what a parent would.

It was a fine day when we left the village at 7 A.M. and rapid progress was made. As we moved out into the bay, a glow of red light suffused the heavens at the eastern part of the horizon, and when we had made about four miles south the sun began to lift his glorious face, his darting rays kissing the peaks of the mountains around. Occasionally I looked back to the igloos where I had spent so many days—far from uncomfortable ones —among my Innuit friends; but soon they were out of sight, and my thoughts now turned wholly to the warm hearts that I hoped to meet on board that night.

At 9 A.M. we reached new ice, which started the sealers to try their hands once more for a prize. In ten minutes more Ebierbing had found a hole, and actually secured a seal! He hailed me to come, and, on reaching the spot, I was asked to pull the seal up while he enlarged the hole, that it might be drawn on to the ice. I did so ; and as the beautiful, eloquent eyes of the victim met my sight, I felt a sort of shudder come over me, for it seemed to say, " Why disturb me here ? I do no harm. Do not kill me ! " But the great sealer, Ebierbing, with his spear, had already enlarged the hole, and, hauling the prize higher up, speedily ended its life by a few well-directed thrusts midway between the seal's fore-flippers. Not a struggle did the victim make. Its end was as peaceful as that of a lamb.

Ugarng had been unsuccessful ; but the one prize of Ebierbing was something, and, after properly securing it to the sledge, away we went on our course again. At 10 A.M. we lunched on frozen seal, and our dinner was the same. We reached the land at 3 P.M. and crossed in two hours and forty-five minutes to Field Bay. A half hour's travelling upon the ice brought us to the ship, where I found all the crew ready to welcome me with outstretched hands, and, I am sure, kindly hearts. For a moment, on once more standing upon the ship's deck, I felt myself overpowered ; but, speedily recovering, I returned the congratulations offered, and, after seeing my companions were attended to, I descended to the cabin, where numerous comforts of civilization awaited me. A warm supper was most acceptable. I was much fatigued with my journey ; and, soon after a short conversation which followed, I gladly retired. Once more, then, did I enter my own little domicile, where I did not forget to return thanks to Him who had so preserved me in health and safety during that, my first experience of personal life among the native Innuit tribes of the icy North.

CHAPTER XIII.

MY first night (February 21st, 1861) on board the *George Henry*, after forty-three days away in an igloo, was a sleepless one ; not from any want of comfort, but in consequence of the super-abundance of it. From the pure atmosphere of a snow house to the warm, confined air of a small cabin, the change is great, and I felt it extremely while undergoing the resulting "sweat-ing" process.

The next morning I visited the crew to see how the men were, and was sorry to find one or two cases of scurvy among them. The legs of one man, from his knees down to his feet, were almost as black as coal tar. In reply to a question put to me, I said that forty-three days in an igloo among Innuits was, in my opinion, the best cure for them. I then went on shore with Captain B.

My dogs were all well, and right glad to see me. The wreck of the *Rescue* still existed, though much of its materials had been used for fuel and other useful purposes.

I found, astern of the *George Henry*, several igloos built upon the ice, though but few of the natives remained here. Nearly all the inhabitants of both villages had gone away to Frobisher Bay, where they hoped more success would attend their exertions to procure food. Indeed, I understood that not less than a hundred Innuits were located in one place, and doing well.

On the 24th of February Ebierbing returned to Grinnell Bay,

carrying with him many presents and articles of provisions for himself and wife, given by Captain B. and myself. Ugarng also went away well-loaded; and Koodloo and his family, Sharkey, with some of our dogs, and one or two other persons, likewise departed for the same place. Sharkey was to come back soon with the dogs, which were only loaned to him for the occasion. Koojesse, Johnny Bull, Kokerzhun, and all the natives that were about the ship on my arrival, or who came over soon afterward from Frobisher Bay, evinced their joy at my return in a way that much pleased me, and showed that I had a hold of no slight nature upon their affections.

Thus two or three days passed away while preparations were being made by the ship's company for their spring whaling, and by myself for another excursion, previous to making an effort toward proceeding on the main object of my voyage.

While thus occupied, an incident occurred that, when related, as here, from notes taken at the time and from facts well-attested, may perhaps, by some of my readers, be deemed almost incredible. But precisely as it took place, just so I narrate it.

About 9 A.M. of March 4th, the Innuit Charley, then on deck, reported reindeer in sight upon the ice. This immediately caused much excitement, and, from captain to cabin-boy, the cry ran through the ship, "Tuktoo! Tuktoo!" Of course we were now all but certain we should get a taste of north country venison, for there were numbers of us to give chase and insure a capture. Guns were charged, and a whole party were going off to the hunt, when it occurred to the more knowing ones that it would be wise to let Koojesse, who offered himself, proceed alone, taking with him only the rifle which I put in his hands. The wind, which was blowing from the north, placed the herd on the windward side of him, thus making his chance more favourable on account of the deer being unable so readily to "scent" the foe.

As Koojesse cautiously proceeded, we all watched him most eagerly. Fifteen minutes saw him "breasted" by a small island toward which the deer approached. When they were within rifle shot he fired, but evidently missed, for the game wheeled round and darted away.

Directly the report was heard, *Barbekark*, my Greenland dog, bounded off toward the battle-ground, followed by all the other dogs. This was annoying, as it threatened to put an end to any more firing at the game; and if they would have heeded us, we should have instantly recalled them. But it was now useless.

The dogs were in full chase, and fears were entertained that if they got too far away, some, if not all of them, would be lost. At length we saw Barbekark pursuing—not in the deer *tracks,* circuitous, flexuous, mazy in course, but—in a *direct* line, thus evincing a sagacity most remarkable. The other dogs, not taking the same course, soon fell behind.

On and on went Barbekark, straight for a spot which brought him close upon the deer. The latter immediately changed their course, and so did Barbekark, hot in pursuit after them. Thus it continued for nearly two hours; first this way, then that; now in a circle, then zigzag; now direct, then at right angles, among the numerous islands at the head of the bay.

For awhile nothing more was thought of the affair, save an expression of regret that the dogs would not be able to find their way home, so far had they been led by the enticing game.

A little before twelve, midday, Barbekark was seen coming back, and presently he came on board, with blood around his mouth and over his body. No importance was attached to this beyond supposing that he had come into collision with the deer; but as for killing one, the thought was not entertained for a moment. Those who had often wintered in the arctic regions said they had never known a dog to be of any use in hunting down deer, and therefore we concluded that our game was gone. But there was something in the conduct of Barbekark that induced a few of the men to think it possible he had been successful. He was fidgety, and restlessly bent upon drawing attention to the quarter where he had been chasing.

He kept whining, and going first to one and then another, as if asking them to do something he wanted. The captain even noticed him jumping about, and playing unusual pranks; running toward the gangway steps, then back again. This he did several times, but still no one gave him more than a passing notice. He went to Keeney and tried to enlist *his* attention, which at last he did so far as to make him come down to me (I was writing in my cabin at the time) and mention it; but I gave no heed, being so much occupied with my work. Perhaps had Barbekark found me, I should have comprehended his actions. As it was, he failed to convey his meaning to anybody. Presently one of the men, called " Spikes," went off to the wreck of the *Rescue,* and Barbekark immediately followed; but, seeing that Spikes went no farther, the dog bounded off to the northwest, and then Spikes concluded that it was really possible Barbekark had killed the deer. Accordingly, he returned on board, and a party of the ship's crew started to see about it, though the weather was very cold and inclement. They were away two hours; and when they came back, we could observe that each was carrying something like a heavy bundle on his head. Still we could not believe it possible that it was portions of the deer; and only when they came so near that the strange fact was perceptible could we credit our senses. One man, almost Hercules like, had the skin wrapped around him, another had half of the saddle, a third the other half, and the rest each some portion of the deer that we all had especially noticed. In a short time they were on board, and deposited their loads triumphantly on the scuttle-door leading to the cooking department below.

Every officer and man of the ship, all the Innuits and Innuit dogs, then congregated around the tempting pile of delicious fresh meat, the trophy, as it really proved, of my fine Greenland dog Barbekark. The universal astonishment was so great that hardly a man of us knew what to say. At length we heard the facts as follows :—

Our men had followed Barbekark's return tracks for about a mile from the vessel, in a direct line northward; thence westward some two miles farther to an island, where, to their surprise, they found Barbekark and the other Greenland dogs seated upon their haunches around the deer lying dead before them.

On examination, its throat was shown to be cut with Barbekark's teeth as effectually as if any white man or Innuit had done it with a knife. The windpipe and jugular vein had both been severed; more, a piece of each, with a part of the tongue, the skin and flesh covering the same, had actually been bitten out. The moment "Sam," one of the men in advance of the rest, approached, Barbekark jumped from his watchful position close by the head of his victim and ran to meet him, with manifestations of delight, wagging his tail and swinging his head about. At the same time he looked up into Sam's eyes as if saying, "I've done the best I could; I've killed the deer, eaten just *one* luscious mouthful, and lapped up some of the blood. I now give up what you see, merely asking for myself and these my companions, who have been faithfully guarding the prize, such portions as yourselves may disdain!"

The snow around the spot showed that a terrible fight had taken place before the deer gave up its life. Somehow during the struggle one of the deer's hind legs had got broken; and when our men arrived at the spot, several crows were there picking away at the carcass. But Barbekark and the crow family were always on good terms, and probably this was the reason why he did not drive them away, for sometimes they rested upon his back.

As soon as our men had reached the dead deer and found it ready for them, they skinned it, and then cut it in pieces for carrying

BARBEKARK KILLING THE REINDEER.

on board. They regretted that no harnesses were at hand, so that they might have had the dogs—Barbekark at the head as conqueror—drag the whole carcass to the ship. As soon as the prize was on board, it was fairly distributed among the ship's company fore and aft, and my brave dog was greeted with many a word of praise for his remarkable hunting feat !

In afterward dressing the deerskin, it was seen that the ball from my rifle, fired by Koojesse, had really taken effect. It was found in a piece of the flesh still adhering to the skin, at that part which covered the hip. The ball had gone through the skin, and was flattened by striking the bone. I have that ball, and keep it as a memento of this remarkable affair.

In referring to this incident a day or two afterward, Captain B—— said to the men, " Boys, who at home, think you, will believe that affair of Barbekark's and the deer-hunt, with what followed ?" The general reply was, " Not one in a thousand will believe it." " In fact," added the captain, " *I* can hardly believe it even now, though it was so." And thus may many others say ; yet the facts are precisely as I have related them, and they are evidence of the keen sagacity and almost human intelligence, allied to great bravery, of my faithful Greenland dog Barbekark.

On the 5th of March *Sharkey* returned from Cornelius Grinnell Bay. He was accompanied by one of the angeko's wives, and brought us information of all my Innuit friends, and also of *Nikujar's* death, which occurred about two or three days after I had left.

I have before mentioned that this woman, Nikujar, was the family wife No. 1 of Ugarng, and had formerly been the wife of Blind George. Indeed, until he became blind, she was to him a happy and loving partner, giving him the one child, *Kookooyer*, he now so much doted upon ; but when the curtains of an endless night were drawn over him, he lost her. She consented to become the wife of Ugarng, leaving the noble-hearted but now blind " eagle " to be alone.

By Ugarng, Nikujar had another child, *Me-noun*, but she was always wishing to have her first one, Kookooyer, with her. Thus it was that I so often saw the girl in Ugarng's home, instead of with her own father. Nikujar, however, did not get on quite so well as she had expected. Ugarng's second wife, Kunniu, seemed to be his favourite, probably on account of her being so serviceable to him in hunting and sealing ; and Nikujar had frequently to remain by herself, or with wife No. 3, to take care of their home. Disease also laid hold of her. She was sick when I first saw her, and consumption had sown the seeds of death in her frame. Gradually she wasted away, and during my sojourn at the igloo village it was evident to me she could not long survive. It was therefore no surprise when I heard of her decease. To Blind George, however, who was on board when the news arrived, the intelligence was a heavy blow. Notwithstanding her faithlessness, he had always retained his original love for the mother of their dear child ; and when he heard she was no more, he went and hid himself, that he might mourn without restraint. When I sought him out, I found he was giving way to almost uncontrollable grief, his eyes streaming with tears, and his lamentations loud and painful to hear. I tried to comfort him, and by soothing words direct his thoughts upward, where the best consolation is ever found.

At this time a very serious event occurred, the narrative of which I here transcribe from my diary :—

"Two of the *George Henry's* men, John Brown and James Bruce, both afflicted with scurvy, were sent to Oopungnewing, in Frobisher Bay, distant by sledge-route seventeen nautical miles, for the purpose of having them stay with the Innuits for awhile, living exclusively on fresh meat, walrus and seal. They accompanied, as there stated, the Innuit 'Bob' (King-what-che-ung), with whom Captain B—— made distinct arrangements to care for them, providing for all their necessities. This Innuit Bob has a noble soul, one that prompts him to *noble deeds*, continually outpouring in behalf of the poor, the friendless, the unfortunate, and the sick. He is the one to whom Captain B—— feels himself indebted for saving his life in the disastrous winter here of 1855--6, when he (Captain B——) lost thirteen of the crew of his vessel—the *Georgiana*—by scurvy.

"On Friday last, March 15th, by the journal (my MS. journal), it will also be seen that Koojesse and Charley (Koo-per-ne-ung), went over to the Innuit settlements at Frobisher Bay with the dogs and sledge, for the object of trafficking for walrus tusks and meat. It was expected that they would return by the evening of the same day, but the inclement weather that succeeded their starting out, the gale of the night and next day, prevented their return till twelve meridian of Saturday, at which hour they started.

"John Brown and James Bruce feeling so much relieved of their complaint, they prepared themselves to return with Koo-jesse and Charley. While the load of walrus skins, walrus meat, &c. was being lashed to the sledge by the two Innuits, Brown and Bruce started on together. They had not proceeded more than half a mile when Bruce proposed that they should return, delaying their journey to another day, as the wind was blowing strong and cold ; the indications of the weather being otherwise unpropitious. To this proposal Brown objected. Bruce declared they would be frozen before they could reach the vessel, and this being his honest conviction, he not only decided to go back to the igloo they had just left, but strenuously exerted himself to induce Brown to do likewise. The last words of this unfortunate young man to his companion (Bruce) were, ' I'm going on ; for, by G——, I'm determined to have my duff and apple-sauce * at to-morrow's dinner.'

"Bruce returned to Bob's igloo, taking from the sledge his sleeping blankets. Brown finally retraced his steps until he met the sledge party, which he joined, continuing his journey home-ward to the vessel. The sledge was heavily loaded, so that their progress was very slow. Having proceeded some seven miles, hummocky ice obliged Charley and Koojesse to leave the greater part of the load. To unload and make a deposit under piles of ice was a work of time. Brown was anxious to proceed without the delay requisite to make the *cache*. He made known his determination to proceed alone. The two Innuits, who foresaw the dangers to which Brown was about to expose himself, ad-vised that he should wait for them. All that these experienced, storm and cold proof men of the North could say in warning him, did not suffice to cool the ardent desire of Brown to join as early as possible his cheer companions at the *George Henry*.

"Seeing that Brown was about to take his departure, Koo-jesse and Charley persuaded him to take along one of the dogs, that it might guide him in the direct route to the ship. Koojesse disengaging the single trace from the *peto*,† the same was passed to Brown's hand. Thus he had a guide, a leader in harness, whose instinct was truer than that of any man, with all his boasted intelligence. But this dog Brown exchanged for a younger one unused to the route. With heart bounding with hopeful throbbings that he would soon be among his home com-panions—that he would soon be participating in the longed-for food of civilization (for which he had acquired a hundred-fold stronger desire than he ever had before, in the course of his brief stay among the Innuits, whose almost sole living is fresh animal food), Brown started on, travelling with vigorous step the rough ice-road before him. Long before the safe ice-covering had been made over the meat deposit, Brown was out of sight of Koojesse and Charley.

---

* Sunday is duff-day with the forward hands. "Duff" is a favourite dish with them, and also, I may say, with the officers and all in the steerage. The "apple-sauce" referred to in Brown's remark is explained by the fact that dried apples are incorporated in the "duff."

† The *short line* that connects all the draught lines or traces of the dogs to the runners of the sledge.

"A few minutes after twelve o'clock that night (Saturday) I retired. A little later, I heard first the cry of the dogs; then the loud, peculiar, and unmistakable voice of the Innuit dog-driver; and then the musical sledge, whose glassy bone shoeing rung to the music of the snows.

"Previous to my turning in, all hands had retired. No one was up to learn the news from Frobisher Bay settlements.

"The sledge was driven up alongside of the *George Henry*; the dogs were quickly unharnessed; the small portion of the original load was placed on deck, out of reach of the dogs, Charley departing for his igloo near the stern of the vessel; while Koojesse (whose winter quarters are with us) hastened in, divesting himself of his dress, and placing himself alongside of his warm sleeping *nuliana*, Tu-nuk-der-lien, who had retired hours before I did to the usual place of their tuktoo bed, close beside the door of my sleeping apartment. A few moments found the weary Innuit, my friend Koojesse, in the arms of sleep. The sleep of a tired Innuit is usually accompanied with loud nasal sounds.

"My lateness in retiring on Saturday night, my unquiet sleep, made me a later riser on the following glorious day of days—the Sabbath.

"Breakfast hour with us is eight o'clock. I was up and dressed only half an hour in advance. What was the first news that awaited me? That one of my 'Greenlanders' had been outrageously mutilated by some Innuit, who had cut clean off the animal's left ear. 'King-ok,' a fine dog, was the subject of this wicked act. King-ok's offence was biting harnesses. As I have said before in my journal, let a dog offend an Innuit, and woe be to the dog! Any instrument at hand is used in administering punishment. In this case a snow-knife was seized, and my noble dog King-ok became the terrible sufferer of an ungoverned passion.

"I had allowed my six dogs, in order to complete the team of twelve, to be used in making this Frobisher Bay trip for the advancement of the *George Henry's* interests. Captain B—— burned with laudable indignation on learning the sad condition of my dog. What astounded me, and every one of the ship's company, was the discovery of the fact that Koojesse was the Innuit who committed this brutal deed. His only excuse was that his companion Charley had first severed the ear of *his* dog, and *he* (Koojesse) thought he must do the same to my dog.

"But what of this—cruel and savage though these two acts

were—compared with the terrible story I am yet to relate?
Yesterday morning, after breakfast, I went upon deck, and there
met Ad Bailey, who said to me, standing by the gangway,
'Charley has just told me that the Frenchman, John Brown,
started from the igloos of Frobisher Bay with them (Koojesse
and Charley); that he, Brown, finally left them, and came on
ahead; that they saw nothing more of Brown; but, as they
passed from the land on to the ice of Field Bay, this side, saw
his tracks, and wished to know of Bailey what time Brown
arrived at the vessel.'

"Bailey had just ascertained from the hands forward, where
Brown belonged, that *he had not arrived!* At once, under a
painful apprehension of the real state of the case, I rushed down
into the cabin, made my way into the captain's room, where I
found him preparing for his usual deck-walk, and announced to
him the facts I had just learned, telling him of my immediate
readiness to go in search of him who I knew must be lost, suffering,
or—as I feared from the cold of the night (57° below the freezing
point)—*a dead man.* Captain B. instantly went forward, and
learned that what I had told him was too true—that Brown had
not arrived. Only a bundle of blankets and fresh walrus-meat
was there, just brought in by Charley, the same having been
placed on the sledge by Brown on the point of starting home.
Captain B. ordered Brown's ship companions to go in immediate
search. This was responded to cheerfully, of course. Captain
B. returned to the aft cabin, and told me that parties were getting
ready to move. As fast as I could, I made the exchange of
civilization dress for my Innuit costume. With my marine glass
and compass in hand, I made my way on deck. A company of
ten men met me there, prepared for the dangerous work before
us. The thought occurred to me that we should take along with
us one of the Innuits of the sledge party which came in on
Saturday night, either Koojesse or Charley. Seeing the former
on deck, I asked him to accompany us. He quickly joined in.
Our first work was to go to the spot where the tracks of poor
Brown were seen as reported.

"We set out at 8·20 A.M., taking a true W.N.W. course. Our
movements were rapid, impelled by the feeling that incited all
hearts with the hope we might be in time to save human life.
It was only occasionally that we walked—*we ran!* I felt, Oh
that we had wings, and could determine these anxious fears and
doubts in a few moments, instead of waiting the hours that it
will require to settle them! Koojesse and Sam, both great

travellers, were for pressing on with all their immediate strength.
I knew this would not do; that by this course they would not
only sacrifice their own important services for a long search,
which evidently it would be, but also those of all the other men.
I therefore repeatedly cautioned them to do only as they and all
of us could also do and hold out. But neither reason nor a
prudent foresight of the prolonged hours which would be required
in this painful service could stay them. One after another of our
company fell back. Ere we came within two miles of the track,
even Koojesse gave out. He was obliged to move with slow
steps from his over-exertion. The sequel will show the wisdom
of my advice, which was finally acknowledged by all, even Sam.
I may as well state here that, after proceeding three miles from
the vessel, I saw, away in the distance, objects that appeared
moving. I called attention to them. Then I first learned that
a party of five had preceded us in this search. Though they had
fifteen minutes' start of us, we were soon up with them.

" When we came within a quarter of a mile of the land, the
tracks of poor Brown were found by Koojesse, who had seen
the same but a few hours before. The distance made from the
ship was full six geographical or sea miles in one hour and forty-
two minutes, the party arriving at the tracks at 10·10 A.M. Only
four out of the ten accomplished this, myself of the number that
did. I could not be in the rear, injudicious as I knew to be the
over-exertion that we were making.

" Soon as we struck upon the almost obliterated footprints of
the lost one, our movements were even quickened. Yet the
tracks led, for more than a mile, in a direct course to the vessel,
and but a few steps southward of our way up. I have written,
a few lines preceding this, the words, 'the almost obliterated
footprints of the lost one.' By reference to my journal (MS.
journal) of last night, I see that I there noted the following
phenomenon, viz., 'Showers of snow while the heavens are clear.
Stars shining brightly.' At midnight, the time of my last visit
to the deck, I wrote this, though a previous record had been
made of the same phenomenon taking place as early as 9 P.M.

" ' Twelve, midnight, stars shining; all clear over the whole
expanse, yet snowing ! Thermometer — 12°.'

" This accounted for the filling up of the tracks. Besides, the
light wind of this morning had swept the beautiful fine snow-
crystals into them.

" We followed on hopefully, some of our number even saying,

' It may be we shall find John has arrived at the vessel ahead of us.' Oh that it had proved so!

" The course of Brown was so near ours outward that those who had fallen behind had but to turn a little southward to reach it. Hence those who were *last* became *first* in the search. The upper part of Field Bay is studded with islets. To one of these his footprints were directed. At length they turned around its southwestern side, where he met with hummocks that obstructed his course. Still farther south he bent his steps to get around them. Each of these turns had a tendency to throw him out of the true course to the ship, which at first he evidently had in mind.

" One of the men, finding a place among the ice to which Brown had turned in, actually exclaimed, ' Here he is!' But his outward steps were soon traced, so that this gleam was soon overshadowed.

" Getting out again in full view of the bay, Brown nearly regained his original course. Following this awhile, he again deviates. Now our hearts are cheered again, for he takes a proper course; another minute and we are sad—he diverges. After having taken a wrong course, which overwhelmed all with sorrow as we followed it for seven minutes, he suddenly turned northerly toward a magnificently-pinnacled iceberg that is ice-locked away up the bay. This we thought he had recognized, and that, on reaching it, he would then know where he should direct his steps. But, alas! too soon he turns in another—a wrong direction.

" His tracks by eleven o'clock A.M. showed that he was lost. Up to this hour it was evident to us that John had in mind nearly the proper direction in which the harbour of the vessel lay. It is true that now and then his tracks led in a direction that indicated doubt, but mainly otherwise. When John Brown first made Field Bay, passing from the land over which he had just come from Frobisher Bay, it must have been nine o'clock last night. He could have been but a little in advance of the sledge party he had left in Frobisher Bay. Hence it was not by daylight that he was struggling to reach the vessel; for, not being used to travelling alone, nor familiar with the route, and it being by night he was travelling, no wonder at his deviations, as indicated to us up to the hour I have named, to wit, eleven o'clock A.M. But at this hour I exclaimed, ' See! see! he who made those tracks was lost.' They were tortuous, zigzag, circular, this way and that—every way but the right way.

"At length John took a course S.S.W. leading him obliquely to the opposite side of the bay from where the vessel lay. How our hearts ached at this. Making, finally, a large circular sweep —having perhaps seen the dark, black, buttress-like mountains before him, which he must have known were not on the side of the bay he wished to make—he then took a S.S.E. course, which was the proper one, had he not been making the southing which he had. But this he did not long follow. Another and another bend in his steps, all leading him out of the way.

"I here state that, in following the tortuous tracks leading southwesterly, Sam Wilson and Morgan continued a direct course southeast. Soon the alarm was raised that Sam and Morgan had sighted the object of our search. We looked in that direction, and concluded they had, for they were under a full run. A piece of dark-coloured ice, raised up from the main, had, however, deceived them.

"On, on we followed the steps of the lost for miles, leading generally southeast.

"Some distance ahead of me and William Johnston were Morgan, Sam Wilson, and 'Fluker.' I felt that I was acting the judicious part, and therefore kept up a rapid walk—a gait that I could sustain for hours. Occasionally I cast my eyes back. Groups were still following after, some of them far behind. At 12 o'clock, I was pained to see that all in our rear had become exhausted, and were directing their steps toward the vessel. Out of twenty men in all who left the ship, but five of us now continued the search.

"I must confess that the race of the morning had seriously exhausted my strength. Nothing but the hope of saving human life could have induced me to take another step at twelve. By occasional rests, myself and my companion were reinvigorated. By this prudence, and that of avoiding farther over-exertion in running, we found that we were fast gaining upon the three ahead of us.

"Thirst—burning thirst continually harassed me. Seeing an iceberg at our right, we turned to it. Seating ourselves by it, with our knives we chipped off piece after piece, with which our thirst was partially allayed. The first piece which I put into my mouth froze it fast. Tongue, palate, and lips refused further service, until the ice became of freezing water temperature. The cause of this of course was that the ice contained a degree of coldness even far lower than the temperature of the air then around us. The air at twelve and one o'clock was only 42° below freezing point, while the berg was 60°—that is, 28° below zero. I took the precaution of holding succeeding pieces in my mittened hand until I raised their temperature to near freezing point, when I could with perfect safety introduce them to my parched tongue.

"By-the-bye, I found one serious obstacle to my stopping to rest. Cramps of a most excruciating character in the calves of my legs threatened to overpower me. After 1 o'clock P.M. I suffered less from them. This grievous affliction arose, undoubtedly, from the over-exertion upon our setting out.

"At 1 o'clock P.M. I and William Johnston saw the three ahead of us (Morgan, Sam, and Fluker) throw themselves flat on the ice. By this we knew they had become exhausted. Fifteen minutes later found us with them, and flat beside them. Oh, how glad I was to make my bed for awhile upon this bosom of the deep! how refreshed we all were by that prostration of our weary limbs! While we were resting, Sam exclaimed, 'Well, come, let us eat dinner;' these words being accompanied by the act of drawing out of his pocket two sea-biscuits. One of the other men drew out another. These three cakes of bread made us a feast, though weighing but three quarters of a pound total. The foresight that could make this provision should have kept in reserve the strength which the exigencies of our undertaking required.

"We were all invigorated by the repast, and by resting, though only for the space of fifteen minutes.

"At 1.30 P.M. we resumed our march. We were now on dangerous ice, near the mouth of Field Bay, the tracks of the lost one still leading us seaward. A heavy sea might take us beyond our power to return. Every one felt that if Brown continued the course in which we were then following him, he must have arrived at a point where he had been carried out to sea on some floe.

"Most of our little company felt that they could not go farther, so exhausted were they. Sam Wilson was the first of the five to declare he would not; *he said he could not* go farther, although he was one of the forward ones of the morning. Yet he did continue on with us until ten minutes past two P.M. They felt they had tried to perform their duty. This was a terrible blow to me. I felt that I could not give it up so, discouraging as was my condition. I resolved, that, so long as God should spare me strength, I would follow on and on; and knowing the risk, I did not feel that I could take the responsibility of persuading any one to accompany me. Up to this time the course of the tracks was tortuous—now sweeping almost in circles, now to southeast, now to the south, but mainly leading to the open sea, far to the east. I regretted much that some one of us had not thought to bring a snow-knife. With this simple instrument in hand, I would have taken the responsibility of inducing some one to continue on with me. With this we could have erected an igloo for the night, or any other time, if we should be overtaken by a gale or storm before our return. Fifteen minutes after two P.M. I left my companions, who had resolved to return, and proceeded on *alone*. I knew God would be with me in my work. I had not proceeded far before I was overtaken by William Johnston, who said, 'I have resolved that I will accompany you rather than return now. I do not feel that I have more than strength enough left than would enable me to return to the vessel; but I may feel better soon. John was my shipmate, and I loved him. I shall ever regret, perhaps, if I return now.'

"As we passed on together, we were soon encouraged by finding the tracks bending away from the direction of Davis's Straits. Our feelings of hope were soon increased almost to those of joy, for we found the main course of the tracks now led west, as if John had seen the mountains westward, and to them was attempting to make his way, and then follow them up to the point where he left the land. But how soon was this cup dashed from our hopeful lips! The steps of the lost soon circle around to the southeast, then east, carrying us back again. For fifteen minutes we followed a true course west. Hope lifted us up again, and quickened our steps. At last they turned, circling to the south; thence around all the points of the compass, crossing, for the first time, his own tracks. This occurred one hour after parting company with our men, whom we had left to return. Having followed his footprints around this circle of twenty rods radius, in less than three minutes another circle occurs. He now strikes due north. With bounding, almost happy hearts, we follow, for this course leads almost directly to the vessel. The channel of water leading to Bear Sound of Frobisher was only ten miles due south of us. This place, though of historical and geographical interest to me, was as naught in the work I was now performing.

"But how oft is man doomed to disappointment! The tracks turn again in a circle. Now they come in rapid succession. Round and round the bewildered, terror-stricken, and almost frozen one makes his way. Five circles, one interlocking another, does the lost man make; then strikes out, and continues two more—in all, twelve circles did John make within less than two miles.

"During our protracted search, I and my companion often threw ourselves flat upon the hard snow that covered the sea-ice. This gave us rest. At one of these resting-places I fell instantly into a sound sleep. Had I been alone, I know not what would have been the result; but Johnston roused me after considerable exertion, and we pressed on. Every now and then we came to places where the lost one had seated himself to rest. In all, we found eight such places. Just before the company parted, we came to a spot where John had made a hole down into the snow, evidently with the desire to get some of the most compact with which to quench his thirst. During this whole search we made frequent calls on ' John' by loud shouting.

"At four o'clock, while following the tracks, which were then tending northward, I thought I heard the cry of dogs. I threw back my hood, which is attached to the jacket in the Innuit way, and listened. I asked Johnston if he had heard anything. He answered nay; adding, he thought it only my imagination. I saw that my companion was getting exhausted. Here we were far from the vessel, the sun sinking lower and lower, and the cold increasing.

"Somehow I felt that, upon the return of the three who left us a little after two o'clock, the captain would send out a native with kummitie (sledge) and dogs, suitably provided to co-operate with me in keeping up the search. I regretted, indeed, that I had not sent word by Morgan for the captain to do this. It would be an easy matter to find us, as the tracks of the three would lead to ours, whence we could be traced.

"Fifteen minutes after 4 P.M. the tracks of John turned south. Johnston had said he would continue with me till we should reach the coast on the west side of Field Bay, if John's track should continue there. Now they turned from the vessel south. Here, for the first time, I solicited him to go with me as far as a point of land toward which we were headed. He acquiesced. Passing two miles south, a magnificent mountain of ice—an iceberg—stood a little way to the left. As we came in line with it—the berg bearing east—we found the footprints of John Brown squarely turned toward it. At any other time, how I should have enjoyed the sight before me—a pile of alabaster, pinnacled as no human mind could design or human art execute—here and there a covering of cream colour, the side facing the descending sun reflecting dazzling prismatic colours. To this, in the darkness of night, John had directed his steps. As we arrived at its base, we found that this berg was evidently grounded, the ice between it and the sea-ice being in fragments, from the rise and fall of the tides. We feared we might find that poor John had lost his life about this berg, for his tracks showed that he had ventured where no man by daylight would dare to put his foot. One place gave palpable evidence where he had followed around to the south side and there fallen in. But from this he had extricated himself, and continued around to the east side, where he again ventured. From appearances, I thought John in search of some place where he could be protected from the wind and cold, where he could sleep. He passed across the dangerous broken ice floating amid sea water on to a tongue of the berg. He walked along a little cove that was roofed by overhanging ice; he finds no safe place there. But where are his outward steps? For a while we thought it certain that John was either in some of the recesses of this vast berg, or had made a false step, and gone down into the deep. Passing northerly, I finally descried returning tracks. He had made a fearful, desperate leap from a shelving alcove to the main or sea-ice, and thence, after passing a few rods east, he turned again to his course south, which he had pursued before turning to the berg.

"It was now half-past 4 P.M. On we continued, though the steps of my companion were growing moderate. Down again we threw ourselves flat upon the ice. While we were thus resting listlessly, Johnston cried out, 'Hark! I do hear the dogs.' No sooner had he spoken this than the driver's cry came to our ears. We jumped up—looked away to the northeast. Thank God! Captain Budington has sent us help. New life was ours. Kummitie and dogs, and two co-helpers, are fast approaching. I cannot express the thankful joyfulness of heart I felt, even in the still doubtful issue of our search. Still on and on, to the south, we followed John's tracks. As I knew Johnston would soon be overtaken, I quickened my steps, and soon left him far behind. I turned a few minutes after, and who hailed me? My noble friend the captain himself. Now I felt sure we should not return till the fate of the lost man should be determined. Captain B. bid me make my way to the sledge, for he knew I must be very much fatigued. He required the Innuit Charley, the dog-driver, to take my place in tracking.

It was a relief to me and Johnston that we received this assistance just as we did.

"Captain B. had set out a little past two, immediately on seeing the return of the major part of the company of five. He had visited Look-out Island, and with his 'spy' had watched our movements. He directed his course to the returning party; followed their tracks, on meeting them, to the place where we parted, thence followed ours—which, of course, were the circuitous, serpentine, and angular one of 'the lost'—until, with his sharp eyes, he sighted us, when he struck a direct course. When Captain B. overtook me it wanted five minutes to 5 o'clock. A few moments brought us to a recess in the coast near the point which, according to Johnston's promise, was to terminate his farther search with me.

"John's tracks showed that he had endeavoured to make land. I left the sledge, and, with Charley, followed them up, while Captain B. and Johnston awaited our determination of the course John had finally taken. John, we found, had endeavoured to mount the shore, but the high, perpendicular walls of ice thrown up by the ever-changing tide would not admit of his accomplishing the undertaking.

"From behind these ice barriers the edges of sombre rocks peered through. Johnston was deceived thereby at one particular spot, and exclaimed, 'There he is! There! do you see?' pointing excitedly to the point indicated. For a few moments all eyes were strained; but sighting showed that John's tracks led easterly, and then south, around the spit of land, on the ice. Again we followed on for half a mile when we were led into a cove that was terminated by a high rock bluff. Here the ice became rough. Captain B. and myself were on the sledge, while Charley and Johnston kept directly upon the track. From the bottom or extreme line of the cove that made up to the base of the indicated bluff, sprung out another spit, which swept around a little way to the south, its southern side being limited by the channel* through which we passed last fall with the *Rescue*, up into the bay, where we made anchorage while we visited Frobisher Bay. As the tracks of the lost led up into this recess, Captain B. and myself thought that John had made his way up into it for the purpose of

---

* In this idea, at the time, I was mistaken. The channel (leading to Chapell Inlet) is full five miles more to the southward of French Head. *Vide* Chart.

passing directly across the neck of the peninsula instead of going around it.

"Charley and Johnston thought it best to continue on his track, while Captain B. and myself concluded to pass on with the dogs and kummitie till we should reach the place where John would probably make the ice on the other side. The distance around, we thought, could be but trifling. Before we had passed out of sight of the track followers, we heard the loud but mournful toned voice of the Innuit Charley. We checked the dogs, turned them back, and thence followed up. Our eyes were watching intensely each movement, each step of Charley. All at once he stopped, then threw up his arms and hands, letting them fall slowly, droopingly.

"It needed no other language than what we saw in the motions of this noble-hearted Innuit to tell us the terrible termination of this day's search.

"Charley and Johnston turned to meet Captain B. and myself. Said they, 'We've found him, and fear he is dead.' Neither had approached nearer than within half a dozen rods of him whom we had so long sought. I flew as fast as my limbs would carry me. A few moments found me grasping his arm. It was as cold and rigid as the mountains of ice around us!

"Deep silence reigned for awhile, as our little company of four stood around the frozen body of John Brown. There, in the midst of the little circle, lay the form of him who was lost.

"I had hoped to find the lost man—to have become a guide to him—to have given hope to the despairing—to have saved human life; and yet how thankful I felt that his fate had been truthfully determined.

"Evidently, from his tracks and the rigidness of his limbs, John had died some time in the morning. From the iceberg for a distance of two miles the footprints were quite fresh compared with the tracks we had seen leading to it. It is quite likely that in the covered shelving of the iceberg, whither he made his way so desperately, he spent some of his time in resting—perhaps sleeping. It was almost a sleep of death, for his tracks indicated feebleness—almost a blindness. Two rods before reaching the final spot of his death, we found where he had fallen down as he walked along, the disturbed snow showing that great effort had been made to regain his walking posture. The place where we found him also exhibited unmistakable

signs of a terrible struggle to raise himself up again ; but alas !
a foe as irresistible as iron had been fastening his fingers upon
him all the night long.   John had fought like a true soldier—
like a hero ; but he had to yield at last.   He died facing the
heavens, the left hand by his side, the right extended, and his
eyes directed upward, as if the last objects mirrored by them were

THE LOST FOUND—FROZEN DEAD.

the stars looking down upon him in his death struggles.   His
face bore evidence that his death was like sweet sleep.

"Every article of John's clothing was in its place—his hands
mittened—his head, ears, and nose protected as well as they
could be by a Russian cap—his feet shielded by native boots
and stockings, and his body well clothed in woollen garments,
over which was his sealskin jacket.

"Well, we found the lost, determined his terrible fate, and now what remained to be done ?

"We considered it imprudent for us to attempt to convey the remains back to the vessel; we thought it our duty to show all becoming respect for the dead, and equally our duty to guard well the living against the exposures that threatened us on our return, for it was now five o'clock P.M., and we were full ten miles by direct route from the ship.

"Captain B—— and myself concluded to make his grave ashore, at the base of a noble mountain bluff or headland, that would stand for ever as the monument of the deceased. But it was soon found that not a stone could be moved. We then decided to make his grave upon the ice, on the very spot where he died, covering his form with the unspotted ice and snow that lay in profusion around. This sad duty was performed with weeping hearts. When all was completed, with reverential awe of the God of the heavens and the earth, we bent over the grave of our friend, and shed the tears of mourning, tempered with the hope that 'now it is better with thy spirit !'

"With slow steps we moved from this toward the dogs and sledge, by which we were to travel for hours to our quarters. It was half-past five when we left the grave of John Brown. Our team of twelve dogs made rapid progress some of the way, while at times there seemed to be a 'hugging' of the sledge-shoes to the snow that made the draught very heavy. We had some earnest work to do to keep ourselves from freezing. Every now and then we took turns in jumping off and running. Captain B—— had unfortunately ventured out with a pair of civilization boots, having found his native ones too small. On the return passage he got Johnston to pull off one of his boots, as he found one foot freezing. This simple, quick act of pulling off the captain's boot (with unmittened hand), gave Johnston a pile of frozen fingers. Half a dozen times Johnston's nose was frozen, and as often I rubbed it into order. I took the precaution of keeping myself in active exercise by running along beside the sledge for more than half of the way home. The thermometer was down to 49° below the freezing point, with a fresh wind from the north-west. Thus we had severe battling to do to keep from becoming subjects of King Cold.

"Every now and then I threw myself flat on the sledge, there keeping myself well to the leeward of Captain B—— and the excellent dog-driver Charley. I then, with face upturned, could see the workings of the Almighty in the heavens above.

The aurora was spanning the blue vault, painting in beauteous colours that part of the sky which seemingly overhung the ever-to-be-remembered spot where we had bid adieu to the remains of our friend, John Brown.

"As we neared the vessel, groups of anxious friends came out to meet us. How they peered among our number—all four of us upon the sledge—to see if John Brown was among our company! None of us could speak. It was like a funeral train.

"I was sorry to find every one who had been out engaging actively in the search completely used up. The three from whom I parted a little after 2 P.M. did not get to the vessel until near six.

*   *   *   *   *

"The distance travelled was full fifty-one English miles, a feat at which I myself am surprised.

"On reaching the vessel about 9 o'clock at night, we found there had been an arrival of Innuits (seven in number) on two sledges, with dogs, from Frobisher Bay settlement. They brought along a portion of the walrus deposited by Charley and Koojesse on the other side of the land that lies between us and Frobisher Bay.

"They also brought the dog which the unfortunate Brown took with him as a guide. They met the dog out on Frobisher Bay, returning toward the igloos. It had on simply the harness without the draught-trace, which, to all appearance, had been cut with a knife close up to the harness. This dog is a young black one, and was not suitable as a guide. Had Brown taken either of the others (he had his choice), he would have been conducted safely to the vessel. But he felt sure he knew the way. How fatal that assurance proved to him!

"Bruce, the companion of Brown, arrived with the party of Innuits last evening (5 P.M.). When coming, he was pushing on ahead of the party, and saw, in the distance before him, a black creature which he took to be a *bear*. He turned upon his heel, and ran as fast as his legs would carry him back to the advancing sledge party, crying to them vociferously to '*ki-ete*' (hasten toward him), as a bear was after him. It proved to be the young, docile black dog of Captain B——'s, which John had taken as his guide to the vessel. The draught-string of ookgook skin, (large sealskin) had, without doubt, been used by John to fasten around his kum-ings (native boots), to keep them properly on his feet. We noticed, when we found him last evening, that his feet-gear had apparently just received the addition of new thongs. His tracks showed that his kum-ings had a tendency to slip down, and to make him slipshod.

"The natives brought the dog along with them. As they came across the land, when near Field Bay they found where this black dog had lain down to sleep, and found also that, as he rose, he walked round in circles, then struck westward, instead of the direction of the vessel. This certainly shows that the dog had not answered the purpose as guide to poor John.

"Had he listened to the advice of either Captain B. —— or his own companion, or to the warnings of the two Innuits, Charley and Koojesse, this sad end of his life which I now record would not have been made.

"His age, I understand, was eighteen, and his parents reside in France.

" ' Requiescat in pace.' "

PARHELIA, OR MOCK SUNS,
seen at Field Bay, March 14, 1861

CHAPTER XIV.

FOR several days after the search which was made for poor
Brown on the 17th of March, I was much troubled with boils,
the result of eating the ship's salt meats, which caused great
prostration, and rendered me unable to do anything but take a
few observations and register the weather. It was noticed by
every one that I had considerably decreased in weight; indeed,
my whole frame showed signs of hard usage, and that I was
getting emaciated; but, having a good constitution, I soon re-
cruited, and after a short period of rest, I was able to get about
my work again.

On the 20th of March several of our Innuit friends arrived
from various places where they had been hunting and sealing,
thus striving to find means of subsistence.

The Innuits are, as I have frequently said, most persevering
sealers, and will go, with their dogs, even in the very coldest of
weather, and under most dangerous circumstances, to hunt for
seal-holes. The sagacious dog, on snuffing the air and finding it
charged with seal odour, follows it to the windward till he leads
his master to the very spot where a seal has its hole. The man
then proceeds *prospecting* with his spear through one to three
feet depth of snow, until he finds the small opening in the ice
leading to the main seal-hole. The hole found, the long spindle
shank of the spear is withdrawn, carefully avoiding all distur-
bance of the snow. Then the sealer remains silently and patiently listening for a seal's "blow."

On hearing the second or third "puff," the spear is forcibly
struck through the snow to the seal-hole, the harpoon pene-

trating the *unseen* seal's head. The seal instantly dives, and runs out the full length, say six to ten fathoms, of the line that connects the harpoon to the harpooner. The seal's breathing-hole is then "unsnowed" and enlarged to the size of the main, when the prize is drawn forth.

AN ESQUIMAUX AND HIS SEAL DOG.

Thus seal-holes are found and seals captured during the long winters of the North.

Among the Innuits just referred to as now arrived were Ugarng, Ebierbing, and Tookoolito; and I was glad to find them well, though the latter two had suffered considerably since I had been with them.

Tookoolito informed me that a short time after my departure

from Cornelius Grinnell Bay, the Innuit "Jack," while out sealing, had nearly lost his life by falling through the ice into the swiftly-running tide. He only saved himself by catching his chin on to the edge of some firm ice just as the current was sweeping him under, but his gun, powder, and everything else belonging to him was carried away. She also told me that the angeko, whom I have formerly mentioned as being so lazy, had, with his two wives and this same "Jack," nearly perished by being driven out to sea on some ice that broke away. They had gone on a sealing excursion several miles up the coast, northerly and easterly of where I had spent my time during the trip of January and February. All at once the ice on which they were became detached, and away they drifted to sea. In a few days wind and tide set the floe back again, and thus they escaped a terrible death.

Ebierbing related to me several incidents of the fearful exposure of his friends, who had, at various times, been swept away from land on the sea-ice.

In the winter of 1859, the Innuit "*Samson*," and a party of fifteen others, were out walrus hunting on the ice in Frobisher Bay, when a gale came on, and drove the ice out to sea. Escape was impossible. On and on the ice moved. The despairing Innuits erected an igloo, and then awaited their fate. The cold was so terribly severe that most of the dogs perished. Two survived for some time, but had finally to be eaten as food. Thus for thirty days the Innuits continued, until at length the ice upon which they were floating united to some near the land, and they were enabled to reach an island in the bay. Thence they got upon the main shore, and returned to their families alive, but such skeletons in form that they were hardly recognizable by their friends. One of the party, from weakness, had fallen into the sea, but was taken out again, his garments immediately freezing hard upon him. The Innuits, *Sharkey*, *Kop-e-o*, whom I called "Dick," and most of those now at the lower village, were of this company.

Another incident mentioned to me was that a party of Innuits, a few years ago, went out on the sea-ice walrus hunting, and being driven away from land, were unable to reach it for *three months !* Fortunately for them, however, they did not suffer as the others had done. Walruses were caught, and thus they were enabled to exist.

Not a winter passes but similar occurrences take place among the Innuits. Indeed, during our stay in Rescue Harbour several persons were carried away on the ice, but in a day or two afterward succeeded in getting ashore again.

Numerous anecdotes of remarkable escapes were at different times related to me by the Innuits. One or two may be aptly brought forward here. The following was told me by Tookoolito.

In the spring of 1857, a company of Esquimaux, natives of Northumberland Inlet, were far out on the floe, by open water, for the purpose of whaling. A whale was at length seen moving leisurely along within striking distance, when the Esquimaux succeeded in making fast to it by four harpoons, each of which was fastened by a ten to fifteen fathom line of ookgook hide to a *drug* made of an uncut sealskin inflated like a life-preserver.

By some incautious act of one of the harpooners, one of his legs became entangled in the line, and quick as thought the whale dragged him down into the sea out of sight. His companions were horror-stricken, and for awhile all around was still as death. The whole party earnestly peered out upon the blue waters far and near, looking for the reappearance of their comrade. They paced to and fro ; when at last a shout came from one of their number—"The lost is found !"—which brought all to one spot.

The circumstance which led to this fortunate discovery was the sight simply of the finger-tips of one hand clinging to the top edge of the floe. The rescuers, on looking over the verge, found the almost dead man moving his lips, as if crying for aid, but his voice was gone ; not even a whisper responded to his most desperate struggles to articulate. Another minute, it was certain, would have sealed his fate—an ocean grave.

It seems that, on coming up from the "great deep," the unfortunate harpooner had attempted to draw himself on to the floe, but this he was too enfeebled to do. When this whale turned flukes, as it instantly did on being struck, it went down perpendicularly for soundings, as the Mysticetus (Greenland whale) generally does. Its great speed, and the resistance of the "drug," with that of the *drag* of the victim's body, caused such a strain upon the line that it parted. On this very fortunate moment the buoyant "drug" shot up like an arrow, bringing with it its precious freight—a living soul. A few weeks after, this same whale with the four harpoons fast to it, was found in drift ice dead. The Esquimaux state that whenever a harpoon penetrates to the flesh of the whale, it will surely die. Harpoons struck into the blubber, and remaining there, will not prove fatal; it is only so when it goes through the blubber into the "krang" (flesh).

Another incident, but of a most fatal character, occurred not many years ago in Field Bay. A party of Innuits were out in two oo-mi-ens (large skin boats) when a whale was struck. The line, in running out, whipped round a leg of the harpooner, *instantly tearing it from the body at the hip-joint !* The shock capsized the boat and all that were therein. The sea all around the victim became thick with *oug* (blood). A landing was early sought and effected, but the poor creature soon died.

The following sad accident was also related to me : Koo-ou-le-arng's wing-a (husband) was killed, when Ebierbing was a boy, at Kingaite, in Northumberland Inlet. He was out sealing near the base of the high land (Kingaite signifies high land), when an avalanche of snow came suddenly upon him, not only over-whelming him, but a large extent of ice, carrying it and him down, far down into the sea. Being missed, he was tracked to the fatal spot, but no other traces of him were ever discovered.

While on this subject I may as well relate one or two occur-rences narrated to me by whaling captains, which show that white men often do go through *seven* perils, and endure the same sort of life as the Esquimaux.

Captain Sisson, on one occasion, told me of a shipwreck that occurred in September, 1853, forty miles north of Cape East, in Kamtschatka. The crew were obliged to remain about eleven months on shore, living among the natives in a perfectly helpless condition, and without anything of value. Yet they were well treated, and soon acquired the habits of the natives, eating the same food, and living in the same manner; and finally, without the loss of a man, came away quite fat and healthy.

Again, another case may be mentioned as reported to me. In the fall of 1851, Captain Quayle, of the *M'Clelland*, whaler, from New London, entered a harbour in Northumberland Inlet, but, not meeting with success, it was proposed that some of the ship's company should winter there with a view to commence whaling in the spring, if that should be practicable. The first mate, now Captain S. O. Budington, and W. Sterry, with ten other volunteers, agreed to do so. Except the first officer, the whole were single young men.

The understanding was that the *M'Clelland* should return for them by the next July; and meanwhile provisions, two boats, and various other effects, were placed on shore for their use.

The twelve men now went to work to make preparation for

their stay. A house was built of stone, filling in the walls with turf and snow on the outside, making a total thickness of six feet. The roof was made of sealskins sewed together and placed on poles. For a window, which was in the roof, intestines of the whale answered well. The stove served for cooking and heating, and coal had been left for fuel; but this becoming exhausted by the end of December, an admirable substitute was found in some skeletons of whales, which were discovered frozen in the ice some thirty miles distant, and were transported to the house by means of dogs and sledges. The bone burned well, being full of oil, and it was easily cut up with an axe.

An incident connected with the transport of this bone is worthy of record. One day in February, a younger brother of Captain Quayle, with a companion, set out for the bone dépôt on a dog-sledge. On their return a furious snow-storm came on, and the dogs, as well as the men, lost their way. Darkness overtaking them, they determined to rest till morning under the lee of an island, but during the whole night it was a terrible battle for life. The only salvation for them was in pounding each other, wrestling, tumbling, kicking, &c. Occasionally the "death-sleep" would be found creeping over them, when all their strength and resolution were called into action in the manner just described. The next day they arrived in safety at the house.

The stock of provisions left with the party was exhausted before any ship arrived, but whale-meat, seals, venison, and ducks were found in abundance. The natives also were very kind, sharing with them whatever game they found. Thus they lived until September, 1852, when Captain Parker, in an English whaler, took them away.

On March 27th another man came near being frozen to death. Strangely enough, it was Bruce, the very companion of the unfortunate Brown!

It appeared that Bruce, who was still under attacks of scurvy, had again gone to the Innuit settlement at Oopungnewing, but one morning suddenly determined upon returning to the ship. Esquimaux "Bob," with whom he was staying, insisted upon his remaining that day, as the weather was too bad. But no; Bruce *would* go, and at once started off alone.

Seeing that the white man was apparently bent on his own destruction, or did not know what he was about, the noble-minded Esquimaux "Bob," being himself unable to leave, engaged an Innuit woman, whom we called *Bran New*, to accompany Bruce. The good creature readily did so, and by her means (as Bruce admitted) he was enabled to reach the vessel in safety.

Another circumstance occurred, which, though not very serious in results, might have proved so, had it not been for my dog Barbekark.

On the 28th March Mate Rogers started for the whaling dépôt in Frobisher Bay. He had with him sundry articles required for spring operations, and a sledge and dogs, driven by Koojesse. Among the dogs was my Greenlander, Barbekark.

They left at 6 A.M., the weather then moderate ; but at noon it was blowing a hard gale from the north-east, with thick-falling snow, which continued during the day.

At half-past nine in the evening one of the ship's officers, Mr. Lamb, going upon deck, heard the cry of dogs, and soon found that Mr. Rogers was returning. In a few moments, to our astonishment, for the gale was severe, he and Koojesse, with the sledge, arrived alongside, and soon afterward the mate was down in the cabin, but so completely overpowered by exhaustion that he could hardly speak. His face was the only spot, in appearance, human about him, and even this was covered with snow-wreaths pelted at him by the ruthless storm.

After sufficient time for restoration, he related the incidents of the past fifteen hours. It appears that, as they passed from Chapell Inlet to Field Bay, at about 1 o'clock P.M. it blew quite a gale, and the air was so filled with snow that they could hardly see the dogs before them. Here Koojesse advised that they should build an igloo, and remain in it until the end of the gale, but Mr. Rogers thought it better they should return home to Rescue Harbour, after resting a few minutes, and refreshing themselves with some snow-water. This, with some difficulty, they obtained, and at two they started back for the vessel.

At first they got on pretty well as far as Parker's Bay, keeping the ridge of mountains running south-east and north-west on their left, and within sight. On reaching Parker's Bay, they then struck across the ice toward the ship. This was almost fatal to them. Esquimaux dogs are often unmanageable when it is attempted to force them in the teeth of a storm, and so it proved now. The leader of the team, a dog belonging to the Innuit Charley, lost his way, and confused all the rest. The snow-storm was upon them in all its fury, and men, as well as dogs, were becoming blinded. Presently the leading dog directed the team towards some islands near the head of the bay ; but, on approaching them, it was seen that Barbekark was struggling to make a *different* route, and these islands convinced the two human minds that dog sagacity, when known to be true, was best when left to itself in such emergencies. Accordingly, Barbekark was allowed to have his own way, and in a short time he led them direct to the ship.

I asked Mr. Rogers what they had intended to do if the vessel could not be found. His reply was, that when it became dark, Koojesse had once proposed to stop for the night on the ice, and, to insure as much safety as possible, they were to throw themselves among the dogs, cover themselves with the two bearskins they had, and thus try to preserve life until daylight would help to show them where they were.

The end of this adventure was, that Koojesse remained so far blind for days that he could not see to do anything ; and Mr. Rogers's face, in its uncovered portions, had actually turned to a deep dark red, while the shielded parts were perfectly white, thus showing what contrasts these Northern storms can paint in one short day.

A lesson to be gathered from this, as I then thought, and still believe, is to allow the natives to do what they consider best in such times. They thoroughly understand the way to prepare for and withstand the warring elements of their own regions, and it is well for white men always to heed their advice, however unreasonable it may seem to be at the time.

On the 8th of April the cooking apparatus and other material were moved up from below, where they had been during the whole winter, and thus what we might call symptoms of spring (though there is no real *spring* in those regions) presented themselves.

About this time Koojesse made reference, in a vague way, to a certain matter which at first excited but little of my attention, and yet, in the sequel, it will be seen that it related to what was of the most important character. I had several conversations with this Esquimaux in the presence of Captain Budington, who, being more proficient at that time than myself in the Innuit vernacular, assisted me as interpreter.

This native spoke of a time long, long ago, when kod-lu-nas (white men) built a vessel on an island in the bay lower down (Frobisher Bay). Spoke also of brick ("*mik-e-oo-koo-loo oug,*" small red pieces), timber, chips, &c. as having been left there.

The idea of a vessel having been built in those regions seemed too improbable to be entertained for a moment. So unreasonable did the story appear of constructing a ship in such a perfectly woodless country, that I thought it a waste of time and paper to make a record of it; therefore what transpired in the first two or three interviews with Koojesse, in relation to this subject, is not in my original notes. Finally, in a few days, I began in my reflections to connect the Esquimaux report with the time when Martin Frobisher made his discoveries, and simultaneously commenced to make record of whatever was stated to be in subsequent interviews.

The commencement of said notes is under date of April 9th, 1861. I now extract them from my original journal, as made immediately after an interview with Koojesse on the P.M. of same date :—

" Among the traditions handed down from one generation to another, there is this : that many—very many years ago, some white men built a ship on one of the islands of Frobisher Bay, and went away.

" I think I can see through this in this way : Frobisher, in 1578, assembled a large part of his fleet in what he called ' Countess of Warwick Sound ' (said to be in that bay below us), when a council was held on the 1st of August, at which it was determined to send all persons and things on shore upon 'Countess of Warwick Island ! ' and on August 2d orders were proclaimed, by sound of trumpet, for the guidance of the company during their abode thereon. For reasons stated in the history, the company did not tarry here long, but departed for ' *Meta Incognita*,' and thence to England.

" Now, may not the fact of timbers, chips, &c. &c. having been found on one of the islands (within a day's journey of here) many years ago, prove that the said materials were of this Frobisher's company, and that hence the Innuit tradition ?

" In a few days I hope to be exploring Frobisher Bay. I may thereafter have something to add to the matter above referred to."—I now turn to other matters in my journal.

" *April 9th.*—As I write, the main cabin table of the ship is surrounded by natives playing *dominoes.* There are Ebierbing, Miner and his wife, Charley and his wife, Jim Crow with his wife.

" The gale of to-day has been terrific. One would have to contest sharply with the elements in order *to breathe,* if outside of the cabin for a moment. In the afternoon an alarm was raised that Sharkey's wife had fallen down the forecastle steps and was dying. It seems that in mounting the stairs leading therefrom with her semi-white child, she was taken with a fainting-fit, in which she fell. Though no bones were fractured, yet she was so severely injured that she has been in a critical condition ever since, and some of the time unconscious.

"*April* 10*th*.—This day Sterry left for Frobisher Bay settlement, to remain awhile among the natives. Parties are now very often going backward and forward, conveying ship's material to the intended whaling dépôt at Cape True.* In the evening there was another magnificent display of the aurora. At 9 o'clock a long line or arch, extending from the west to the east, began to rise from the horizon. I noticed a peculiarity of this night's display worthy of record. When the centre of the auroral arch had risen about three degrees above the horizon, a long line of narrow black clouds rested parallel with the base of the aurora. Slowly the arch mounted the heavens, the clouds all this time becoming less and less black, until they were finally exhausted. The clouds were as *dark* as ' thunder-clouds' when I first saw them. In half an hour the stars shone brightly where they had been. They seemed to follow upward as the arch lifted. When the arch became elevated 25°, other belts of aurora sprang into action, so that there was a sight worth the admiration of beings even superior to man !

" To-day I have purchased of the captain the chronometer that had belonged to the *Rescue*. I intend to make record of all the observations I take, leaving most of them to be worked up on my return home. Some undoubtedly will prove to be erroneous ; but I shall do what I can to make all my observations reliable. There is nothing that has weighed more heavily upon me than the want of a good time-piece. When I make my journey westward and northward to King William's Land, I shall require the chronometer. Indeed, I need it in my journey up Frobisher Bay this spring. I am anxious to perform work that shall redound to the credit of those who have so generously assisted me in my outfit for the voyage I am making here in the North. God giving me health and help in the prosecution of my work, I will do my duty as a geographer and a humanitarian.

"*April* 12*th*.—This morning is gloriously fine. I must do outdoor work to-day. I will off for a trip up Budington Mount, and from its peak take some angles and bearings of prominent places around and about the bay. * * * Just returned, and

* So named after Benjamin C. True, of Cincinnati, Ohio. *Cape True* is in lat. 62° 33′ N. long. 64° 55′ W.

a fine time I have had of it. It was, however, dangerous business going *up* the mountain's steep, icy, and hard, snow-covered sides, but it was even worse coming *down*. Any one who is experienced in mountain excursions, especially in these regions, must know that the latter is far more difficult than the former.

"When at the summit it was very interesting. I had an Innuit companion with me, and, while I took my observations, he slept on a bed of snow, and seemed as comfortable as any white man on a bed of down. As we descended, he made steps for us with a long, sharp stone which he had picked up for the purpose ; but even then we had to exercise great caution. A mishap might have endangered our lives, and also my instruments.

"To-night the aurora is beautiful as usual. Its rays shoot up somewhat more dome-like than before. It extends north-west around to the south, and thence to the east. How many are the times I am blessed with the sight of this phenomenon. Its changes are constantly going on. I never see it twice alike. Every moment the scene changes. In bright disorder, the heavens are almost nightly painted with the blaze of this incomparable, *incomprehensible* light. As its brightness oft is mirrored by my eyes and soul, I often feel that I am truly

" 'Arrayed in glory and enthroned in light.'

" *Eleven o'clock, night.*—A few minutes ago I came from deck. The aurora then spanned the heavens near to the zenith ; a few minutes later—I have just been on deck again—all is gone ; not a beam anywhere visible. The stars have it now all to themselves, Jupiter bearing the palm, as he outshines them all.

" *April* 15*th.*—Have had a long tramp to-day round the head of Field Bay, triangulating and making observations. Koojesse accompanied me for awhile, but the charms of sealing soon took him away, and some time afterward, when I was on a mountain peak, I saw him at a distance, by the aid of my glass, most unmercifully punishing his dog, probably because the poor animal could not find a seal igloo. The Innuits, when they do punish dogs, beat them cruelly.

" *April* 17*th.*—Yesterday I took my first lunar observation. I did it alone, expecting only to obtain an approximation to the true longitude of this place. To-day I have taken another, with assistants to measure altitudes at the same time.

" I have had equally unexpected success in making some of my own instruments. Being without a protractor, I made one, the other day, from a piece of copper which had formed a portion of the *Rescue's* sheathing; and this served a double purpose, being useful in my chart-work, and also remaining as a relic of the once memorable expedition schooner. Another instrument I had also to make, and succeeded in making though it occupied much time, namely, an artificial horizon. I constructed it with various contrivances of my own, and now I have both these instruments by me as pleasing mementos of my sojourn in these dreary regions, where no stores exist to supply me with articles so indispensable.

"*April 19th.*—To-day I was not a little amused to see the rig in which the laughing Innuit Sharkey appeared. A present was made him of a new wool shirt, edged all round, except the flaps, with scarlet—*bright flaming red.* He proudly strutted around among us white folk with this *on the outside* of all his other clothes, wearing it like a frock !

"*April 20th.*—To-day the snow embankment around the ship has been taken away, and the crew are busy putting the vessel in complete order for service. Paint and varnish are now freely used in the process of renovation.

"*April 21st.*—I am preparing to go over to-morrow to the Innuit settlement on Frobisher Bay, intending to explore around the waters mapped out by the geographers as Frobisher *Strait.* My wish is to chart the lands around that place within the next month, and even to do much more. Koojesse has promised to go over with me if the weather will permit.

"I have omitted to mention the 'spot' on the sun that I first saw on the 19th when taking observations. At the moment I thought it was a defect in my sextant glass, but afterward found it to be on the face of old Sol.

"*Twenty minutes before midnight.*—I have just returned from deck entranced by the fires that are burning in the heavens ! A *new play* to-night by the aurora—at least so to me. Going up, I saw that the moon was struggling to penetrate, with her borrowed light, the white clouds that enshrouded her. Looking around, I found the heavens covered with *petite* dancers clothed in white. My powers of description of this peculiar appearance and workings of the aurora at this time are inadequate. There is no colour in the aurora to-night; it is simply white, like the world beneath it.

"*Midnight.*—I have been on deck again. I am now satisfied that I have occasionally seen the aurora during this month in the daytime, when the sun was well up in its course and shining brightly."

CHAPTER XV.

On Monday morning, April 22d, 1861, at half-past 10 o'clock, I started on my trip—the first yet made by me into Frobisher Bay. My guide and companion was Koojesse ; and as we should have to cross a neck of land between the two bays, and thence travel on foot upon the ice, I could not carry much baggage. All, therefore, that I took was the following :—

My native tuktoo jacket, pants, and mittens, an extra pair of native boots and stockings, my charts and chart material, pro-tractor, dividers, parallel and plain rule, artificial horizon, with bottle of mercury, a pocket sextant, azimuth compass and tripod, marine glass, thermometer, besides beads and several plugs of tobacco, for presents to the natives. With these articles pen-dent to a strap passing over my shoulders, across my breast, and down my back, I departed.

Our course from the ship was westerly to the other side of Field Bay, where we struck the land, and met some of the natives with dogs and sledge, conveying walrus hide, meat, and blubber to the vessel. A couple more were also going thither to obtain eye-water for Sterry, who was at that time living with some of the people near the island called Oopungnewing. From Field Bay our track was over the mountain-pass much frequented by the natives. This pass, which I have named after Bayard Taylor, was, in some parts of it, very steep and fatiguing, but the scenery was grand and captivating.

Half-way on the route we stopped at a spring of delicious

water, and there had our dinner. Thence we continued to ascend until reaching the summit of the pass. We then commenced our descent by following a course between high rocks, along a path that was, in one or two places, very steep.

Presently, after passing through a magnificent gorge, we came on to a small inlet leading up from an arm of Countess of Warwick Sound. This we traversed for about an eighth of a mile, until, coming to an abrupt turn where a bold, bluff mountain was on either side, I caught sight of Frobisher Bay, and the mountains of Kingaite beyond. The view was, to me, quite exciting. The ice-covered bay, with the distant peaks of *Meta Incognita*, and the dark, abrupt cliffs at our side, seemed a glorious picture to one, like myself, beholding it for the first time.

The sun was now descending, but the moon's silvery rays would serve to guide us on, therefore we hastened forward, though the distance was yet some miles to travel. In a short time more we were traversing the snow-wreaths that covered the bay-ice, and, as we passed on, Koojesse pointed out a place at our right which he said was where the "white men a long time ago, had masted a ship;" but this seemed so improbable that I did not at that time believe him.

The island we were now going to was the one Annawa and his family went to at the time we escorted them part of the way the previous fall (see page 107), and we now intended to rest there for the night. But it was quite 9 p.m. before we arrived, and then some of the family were in bed. This, however, did not prevent our having a prompt and most friendly reception. The aged Annawa and all those with him quickly gave us food, and a prompt offer of hospitality for the night. They were all much rejoiced to see me, and, though there was no "spare bed," yet I was cordially invited to share theirs. Soon afterward, tired and sore with my long walk of near twenty miles over ice, mountain, and ice again, I retired to rest as best I could.

That night my sleep was a sound one, though I was tightly squeezed, the sleepers being numerous, and all in the same bed! There were nine of us, besides *the infant at the breast*— a boy 3½ feet in height, of portly dimensions!

The order of our sleeping was as follows: Key-e-zhune, the wife of Annawa, lay in her place by the ik-ku-mer or fire-light, with "infant" *Kok-uk-jun* between herself and her husband; then next to him was the child Oo-suk-jee; I lay alongside of the child, Koojesse next to me; then came Esh-ee-loo, with his wife Oonga, all of us facing upward. Then, with feet at our faces, were a young man Innuit, and the little girl Kimmiloo, who lives with Annawa.

The space in which the ten were compacted and interwoven was less than as many feet! Of course, I had to sleep in my day-dress, as no spare bed is kept in reserve for company, nor have they a tuktoo covering more than they need for the family; but I got along through the night after a fashion. It was, however, not very pleasant. Whenever I attempted to turn to relieve my aching bones, a little boy by my side roared like a young lion, awaking all the sleepers, and thus a confusion followed that would have deprived me of farther slumber but for my great fatigue. However, the night passed on, and early in the morning I slipped out as a snake from his *deciduous epidermis*, and prepared myself for a walk.

The igloo was built at the base of a mountain, and up this I ascended until, reaching its summit, I had a good view of the region around me. I was now where I had long hoped to be. Below, and encircling the island, was a field of ice, making an excellent footway for travel. To the south and the west were the open waters of Frobisher Bay, its surface dotted over with broken ice, which was quietly floating about. This however, just then, was vexatious, as it prevented me from making my intended sledge-journey to the westward. Resolution Island and *Meta Incognita* were also in sight (the former visible on the horizon, probably by refraction); and at my back the bold mountains seemed all but touching me, though some miles distant.

On the top of the mountain I found many small pieces of lime-stone, and, while collecting some of them, Annawa and two other Innuits joined me. They had come for the purpose of looking out to see if any seals or walrus were near; and when, through my glass, I discovered one, they were off immediately. Soon afterward I perceived them on the ice prepared for the hunt.

After staying on the summit nearly an hour, I descended, and found a substantial Innuit breakfast of walrus meat and soup ready for me. This breakfast had been prepared by Oonga, wife of Esheeloo, both of whom shared Annawa's igloo. This igloo of Annawa's was adorned on the exterior with a score of walrus skulls and tusks. The family had lived here, as I have already mentioned, for some time alone, but latterly their privacy had been invaded by some of the ship's company, and by several Innuits from the North Star and upper villages. Among these latter I recognized Miner, with his wife *Tweroong,* and Artarkparu, brother of Annawa. There was also *Puto,* the mother of that Anglo-Saxon child before referred to; and *Paulooyer* (Blind George), whom I noticed facing the sun, as

BLIND GEORGE AND HIS DAUGHTER.

was his way when it shines. He immediately recognized my voice, and gladly greeted me when I hailed him. These, and many more, were domiciled in some half-dozen igloos built near Annawa's; but there was also another village, called *Twer-puk-ju-a,* where several Innuits resided, and to this, after breakfast, I bent my way, taking Koojesse with me.

Before starting, I delivered everything I had, as was customary with the Innuits, into the hands of Nood-le-yong for safe keeping. We then started about nine o'clock, taking a course over the hilly centre of the island. Arriving at the top, I heard a sound filling the air as if something was sweeping by. It was like the rush of many waters, or the groaning of ice far away. I asked Koojesse what it was, and he replied Meituks (ducks). I thought it could not be possible, but was a whimsical reason given by Innuits for something they know exists, and yet cannot comprehend. I laughed, shrugged my shoulders, and then passed on.

We arrived at the other village after a walk of about three miles, and there I met Mr. Sterry, the *George Henry's* carpenter. He was suffering from snow-blindness, brought on by exposure upon the ice while out with a party of Innuits walrus hunting. He had obtained leave of absence from his duties on board, and was now living with the natives, "keeping house" (igloo) as though he was of the country.

Together we went on a hill to watch the movements of the Innuit *Miner*, who, with a gun, was sealing. We saw him working his way almost imperceptibly along in his kia through the openings in the ice toward his coveted prey, which rested quietly unconscious of his presence. As Miner approached, he kept up a loud, peculiar noise, a mixture of Innuit singing and bellowing, which seemed to work as a *charm* upon the seal. Every few moments he would lay down his gun and make a stroke or two with his long, double-bladed oar; then the seal, as if alarmed, would seem about to depart. As soon as the slightest motion indicative of this appeared, Miner would again seize his gun and aim, at the same time vehemently increasing the tones of his seal-song. The seal, thus again charmed, kept quiet, and Miner would once more take to his oars, thus endeavouring gradually to decrease the distance between them. So it occurred for several times, and evidently Miner had great hope of securing a good prize, but suddenly, and when the hunter was almost as near as he desired to be, the seal broke away from the " soothing voice of the charmer," raised its head, made a plunge, and, before Miner could fire, disappeared. Then came upon our ears, as we looked and listened, the loud, peculiar ejaculation of disappointment, *E-e-e-ŭk !* and no wonder, for the poor hunter lost by it about half a ton of fresh provisions. I, too, owing to the interest I felt, was also nigh having a loss, which, though not so important as his, was one which I did not then wish to experience. A meridional observation on the ice with my pocket sextant was secured only just in time to save it.

I continued my walk, and ascended a mountain close by, picking up fossil stones on its summit, and enjoying the view around me. Soon I was joined by the Innuits Kokerjabin (Kudlago's widow) and Neitch-ee-yong, both of whom were born on the shores of the great bay before us. Kokerjabin pointed out to me the place of her nativity, on the opposite side of the bay, called by her Kar-mo-wong, an inlet which makes its way up into the interior of Kingaite (Meta Incognita). She said that from a high point at the termination of that inlet she had often seen the *oomiens* of *kodlunas* (ships of the white men) pass up, and then, at a later time, down the waters which were on the other side of Kingaite. This made Kingaite to be merely a narrow tongue of land, the extreme of which, as Kokerjabin stated it to be, I could see bearing from me by azimuth compass 102°, or true bearing S. 16° W. Karmowong bore S. 51° W. true. I took several other observations and measurements the next and following days, for the purpose of mapping the locality and accurately placing upon record all that I might discover bearing upon Frobisher's expedition. My sleeping accommodations at night were with the natives in their igloo, and I partook of their food, eating even as they themselves did, and, I might add, thoroughly enjoying it.

Thus two days passed away, and on the third, which was April 25th, I again started for an extension of my trip.

It was about noon when I left, accompanied by Sterry, Kokerjabin, and her son " Captain." This youth of twelve years would insist upon taking with him a *toy* sledge, to which " Pink," a little dog of a few months old, was harnessed, and, as he made it a point to have the sledge, I was obliged to let it be taken with us.

Our first five miles was circuitous, though on a general course (true) of about W. N.W. From the breaking up and consequent absence of the sea-ice, which had occurred two days before my arrival, we were obliged to follow the shore-ice, walking on what Dr. Kane called the " *ice-foot*." Thus we were one moment this way, the next that, and sometimes walking on shore. This made it very difficult to get on, especially as the tide at that time rose and fell full thirty feet ; and, besides, the frequent change from ice to land was no easy work.

When we had gone about four miles, an old Innuit man was seen with his gun quietly seated on the rocks overlooking the bay and watching for seals. A few words of greeting were exchanged, and I then looked around the place. I noticed that here and there was quite a level spot of ground for these regions; and what more particularly attracted my attention was a complete natural breakwater of stones, evidently thrown up by the heavy seas. The side next the sea was sloping at an angle of 40°, and that facing the flat of land, which it protected, about 50°. The stones were of every variety of shape, though not much worn, and weighing from one to twenty-five pounds.

On this flat portion of land I perceived many signs of its having been the frequent resort of Innuits during the summer months—circles of stones for keeping down the skins which form their tents; bones of walrus and reindeer were also numerous. Here, too, I saw, to my surprise, ship's blocks, iron hoops two and a half inches wide, part of a coffee-pot, preserved meat canisters, an oaken bucket in good order, and several pieces of wood, all, as I afterward conjectured, formerly belonging to the "Traveller," an English whaling vessel, lost three years previous near "Bear Sound," about thirty miles nearer the sea.

It was at this place we lunched, and had the pleasure of finding abundance of water on the rocks to quench our thirst. Here, on a point of land called by the Innuits Evictoon, was a native monument such as they usually erect on prominent places.

As we were about to resume our march, two seals were discovered in the sun near some cracked ice. Immediately the old man started off to try his rusty gun upon them, at first stumbling hurriedly over some broken ice that intervened, and then proceeding very cautiously. When within forty rods he lay down upon his front, and kneed, footed, and bellied himself along, not unlike the movements of the seals he was after. But, as in Miner's case, a moment afterward his prey, taking the alarm, rose up, and with a plunge instantly disappeared. The old man jumped up, crying aloud *E-e-e-ŭk !* and walked on.

As we travelled forward the mountains of Kingaite loomed up in magnificent grandeur, and, on looking at them, something struck me as it had done when first viewing the place in August, 1860, that more than mere land existed there. It seemed as if a huge ice ridge ran along parallel with the coast, uniting mountain with mountain and peak with peak. Seeing how intent I was upon this, Kokerjabin readily answered my inquiry as to what it really was. In reply, she said "it was *solid ice*, and never had she known it to change its appearance, either in summer or fall."

This was enough.   I immediately concluded that there were glaciers over there, and certainly the one I then looked at appeared to be not less than fifteen to twenty miles long.   But, as I afterward visited the locality, I shall reserve farther mention of them till I come to another part of my narrative.

About dusk we reached the south point of the island Nouyarn,* where we had expected to find an Innuit village, the place of our intended visit.   But, to our disappointment and vexation, the settlement was not there.   Within two hundred fathoms of the shore we saw sledge-tracks leading from the land out into the bay, and thence northward and westward.   Here, also on the ice, we saw two double-barrelled guns standing up in the snow, and an Esquimaux lamp; but not a human being besides ourselves was there.   We knew not what to do.   Dark and cold, we should undoubtedly suffer much if unable to get shelter.   What *could* we do?   We might, for a while, follow the sledge-tracks, but not long, as the darkness was upon us.   Eight o'clock, and we had neither shelter, food, nor light.   Even to keep warmth in us for a moment, it was necessary to be in action, or the chances were we should freeze; and to remain so all night, we might perish.   Sterry proposed that we should return to the igloos we had left in the morning, but to this Kokerjabin and myself objected.   The best thing we could do, as I thought, was to follow the tracks, and, if not meeting with Innuits, build an igloo and make the best of it. This was agreed to, and again we started forward, Kokerjabin leading the way, which she did most admirably, guiding us here and there among numerous inlets, without once being in the wrong or confused.

The moon had now risen from her sea-bed, but looked as if guilty of some wicked act, being both horribly distorted and red in the face!   But the higher up she got, the better was her appearance, and the greater was her usefulness to us night-travellers.   At length, about half-past ten, and when we had gone some three miles farther, Kokerjabin brought us to a small island called *An-nu-ar-tung*, where she expected to find the Innuits.

We listened; we strained our eyes for an igloo light, but in vain; not a sound, not a glimmer of anything we had hoped for met our ears or our eyes.   Still, we determined to be thoroughly convinced, and accordingly tried to get on shore.

* Lat. 62° 55′ N. long. 65° 52′ W.

This, however, even in daylight, would have been a difficult task where there was so great a rise and fall in the tide as thirty feet, but at night we found it a terrible job. At last it was accomplished; and looking about for the igloos, and meeting with none, it was finally settled that we should have some supper before trying anything more.

Our stock of food consisted of a small piece of "salt-junk" and some few pieces of hard bread, all of which I had brought from the vessel with me; nevertheless, every mouthful we took was delicious to our hungry appetites. But the thirst! how could we quench it? We had nothing by which to make snow-water, and we had vainly searched the rocks around for some. Every particle was firmly locked up in the fingers of zero cold. "*Thirst*, most thirsty!" we had to say, and, in sooth, to remain thirsty.

The next thing we did was to build an igloo, where, at all events, something like shelter could be obtained, and warmth by clustering together. Four human stoves, besides as many heating, smoking tobacco-pipes, would help to make us passably comfortable; and so we found.

Kokerjabin, the master-mason, aided by Sterry, built the igloo out of a snow-bank which faced a ledge of rocks running lengthwise of the island—under the lee of which, fortunately, it was—while I and the Innuit boy went upon the higher part of the land seeking for water. The igloo completed, on lying down we found that it was too limited, and that we should be inconveniently and perhaps injuriously cramped; therefore a remedy must be found, and this was by cutting "pigeon-holes" in the snow-bank *for our feet*. This answered, and soon we were fast asleep, though upon a bed of snow, and at my back a snow-bank.

Toward morning I felt myself getting very cold, and, to warm us up, it was judged wise for all to smoke, which was done most agreeably. I then cut a doorway, and crawled out of the igloo on all-fours. The wind was fresh and piercing from the east, and, to get some circulation in our veins, Sterry and I made a run to the top of a hill. There we had a good look around, and then descended, but on arriving at the igloo we found Kokerjabin and her son gone. We therefore followed in their tracks, and soon overtook them on the highest point of the island. Presently Kokerjabin discovered, through the glass, some igloos on an island farther on. To these we immediately determined to bend our steps, more especially as Kokerjabin said she knew the island well, and had often resided there. It was called *Ak-koo-wie-shut-too-ping.** One hour's walk across the ice brought us close to it. Ice boulders, however, always between the sea-ice and the "ice-foot," gave us the usual trouble in getting on shore ; but, this over, we soon found ourselves, to my great joy, among familiar faces. The first I saw was Samson, who, taking me kindly by the hand, squeezed it, hugged it, *patted* it, and then led me into his igloo.

It was an early hour for them, and his family were still in bed, yet they all arose and heartily welcomed me. Food, and especially *water*, was plentifully put before me, and I need not say how gratefully I partook of both. Four large igloos were there, each occupied by two families. The bay being partially frozen over, the men were preparing to start on a grand sealing excursion toward Kingaite, which here seemed to be only about twenty-five miles off. Two of the women accompanied this party, and before they left I arranged with Samson to stay in his igloo until he returned. His wife was sick, and with her two daughters she remained to "keep house."

Samson and his party started about 8 A.M. on Thursday, April 25th, and at noon a snow-storm raged so furiously that some fears were entertained for their safety ; but they returned in the afternoon, having captured one fine seal. A feast, as usual, followed ; and here I noticed for the first time an Innuit custom of giving to the youngest child *the seal's eyes.* That night, while in bed, I received a rather unwelcome visitor in the following way.

It has been justly said that "knowledge is often *pursued* under difficulties," but in my case the knowledge I desired *came to me* instead of my seeking it.

I was desirous of making myself acquainted with the tides in that region, and took every opportunity to investigate the subject ; but, on the night in question, between seven and eight o'clock, *the tide came pouring into the igloo*, threatening destruction to all within it. The full moon, by Greenwich time, was, April 24th, 10h. 23m. and, consequently, the highest rise of the tide would here be some forty hours after. I had watched for it during some time, and finally retired to my tuktoo firs, little expecting it would show itself to me by my bedside in the way it did ; but such a proof was enough. From it I ascertained that the rise of tide at full and change was thirty feet. Fortunately, the tidal flow and abrupt inundation produced no serious

---

* In lat. 62° 56′ N. long. 65° 51′ W.

damage, though it gave work to the females of the igloo, who hurriedly secured the fur dresses and other valuables from the salt water.

It was strange to me to see them cleaning or currying the seal-skins. The mouth of the female currier served as a deposit for all the scrapings, and the tongue was kept in constant requisition to keep free the scraper, a dish being by to receive the contents of the mouth when full.

The scrapings of board, hands, &c., all went first to the mouth, then to the dish, and thence to the dogs !

The storm continued during the following day, and I remained where I was, studying more and more the habits of this strange people, and endeavouring to give some elementary instruction to the children.

Our breakfast and dinner were both excellent ; for the former, raw frozen walrus, of which I had a piece for my share of about five pounds, and at the latter, seal. The portion of this allotted to me and Sterry was the head. We complied with the Innuit custom. Sterry took a mouthful, then passed it to me, and when I had done the same it was returned to him, and so on. Of course *fingers* were all in all. No knives and forks are found among the Innuits ; fingers and teeth are more than their equivalent.

When the meat, skin, and hair were all despatched—even the eyes, except the balls, which were given to the youngest child of Samson—we " tapped " the brain. I was surprised at the amount of a seal's brain, and equally so at the deliciousness of them ! The skull was almost as thin as paper. Shoot a seal in the head and it dies. Shoot a walrus in the head, and the damage is *to the ball*, which immediately flattens, without effecting any injury whatever to the walrus.

Later in the day I attended another feast in the igloo of Kookin, who had invited his old mother, *Shel-lu-ar-ping*, and two other venerable dames, and I must say that if my friends at home could then have seen how like an Innuit I ate, they would have blushed for me.

First came a portion of seal's liver, raw and warm from its late existence in full life. This, with a slice of *ooksook* (blubber), was handed to each, and I made away with mine as quick as any of the old adepts. Then came ribs inclosed in tender meat, dripping with blood. How ambrosial to my palate ! Lastly came—what ? *Entrails*, which the old lady drew through her fingers yards in length. This was served to every one but me in pieces from two to three feet long. I saw at once that it was supposed I would not like to eat this *delicacy;* but, having partaken of it before, I signified my wish to do so now; for, be it remembered, *there is no part of a seal but is good.* I drew the ribbon-like food through my teeth Innuit fashion; finished it, and then asked for more. This immensely pleased the old dames. They were in ecstasies. It seemed as if they thought me the best of the group. They laughed—they bestowed upon me all the most pleasant epithets their language would permit. I was one of them—one of the honoured few!

Soon as this round of feasting was ended, one of the old lady Innuits drew my attention to her afflictions. She had a dreadful pain in her side and back, and had been badly troubled for weeks. Before I had time for thought, she drew off her long-tailed coat over her head, and sat there before me nude as Nature made her. The laughing face and the joyful, ringing voice of the old lady were now exchanged for expressions indicative of suffering and the need of sympathy. The whole party present were now absorbed in the subject before me. I put on as long and dignified a face as I could in this *trying* scene, and, as much was evidently expected from me, I was determined no disappointment should follow. Therefore I proceeded to manipulate the parts affected, or, rather *plowed* my fingers in the rich loam—*real estate* —that covered the ailing places. The result was that I gave notice that she should live on, eating as much fresh seal and walrus as she wanted, drinking water several times a day, and applying the same amount at the end of every ten days that she had shrank in that time to the *outside* of her body by the process of scrubbing, which I there and then practically explained to her and the others. I told her, moreover, that as the suk-e-neir (sun) was day by day getting higher and higher, she must keep herself warm and dry, and then, in *my* opinion, she would soon be quite relieved.

So caressingly did I finger the old lady's side during the delivery of my impromptu advice, that she declared I was the best angeko she had known, and positively she felt much better already. Placing on her coat, she then jumped up and ran away to her own igloo, as lively as a cricket.

During the time I was stopping in Samson's igloo I made every inquiry possible about the *tradition* concerning the ships entering the bay a long time ago; but I was unable, from my then slender knowledge of their language, to get intelligible answers. Therefore I had still to remain patient about it.

The following day, Saturday, April 27th, we commenced our return ; but it was cold and stormy, and, as I had left some of my fur dress at Annawa's, I sought to borrow reindeer trousers, mits, and socks there. These I readily obtained ; but the first-mentioned article being too small for my dimensions, one of the Innuit women slit them down with her *oodloo* till they did fit, after a fashion. But, on attempting to move, I was as if in a vice. I could not walk, I could not run, nor could I seat myself ; I could only *waddle* and tumble down ! On the ice in front of the igloos I tried to get on, but you, my reader, should have been there to have seen and enjoyed the sight I presented, and to have heard the ringing, side-splitting laughter of this generous-hearted and kind band of Innuits at the grotesque figure I cut in old Seko's skin-tight breeches. A sledge drawn by dogs had been loaned to us ; and upon this I threw myself ; but, long after our departure, on my looking back, I could see the merry lot still watching, and apparently enjoying the fun I had created.

Our sledge went fast, the dogs being good ones, with an excellent Innuit driver, Ning-u-ar-ping, the son of Samson and Kokerjabin On the smooth clear ice, which extended from Samson's village to where we had first halted on our way up, our progress was very rapid. As we passed the island where we had spent the night before meeting the Innuits, I saw our igloo still standing. A little farther on, I observed to the north a peculiar mark—the work of nature—by the west side of the entrance to Newton's Fiord, standing out boldly upon one of the mountains. On inquiry, I found it was considered by the natives as a remarkable spot, known to them from time immemorial. It was called *In-gee*. Whoever would know what this means, let him confidentially ask an Esquimaux man.

After some miles' travel we came to a dépôt of walrus flesh, made by Samson's people on a previous occasion ; and here, after loading from it, the sledge left us on its return.

Sterry and I, Kokerjabin and Captain, then walked on, and, after a tedious journey of about fifty miles—though *direct* only some twenty from the village—we arrived at *Twerpukjua* at 2 P.M. so thoroughly fatigued as to be right glad of the friendly beds immediately offered us.

Next morning I arose much refreshed, and took a walk on the neighbouring hill. The ice had before parted and left the bay almost free, but I was greatly astonished at the immense number of ducks I saw swimming about. For miles and miles around the waters were literally covered and black with them, making such a *thundering*, indescribable medley of sounds as quite startled me. Talk about the "absence of life" in these regions of ice and snow! Why, before my eyes were countless numbers of animated creatures, from the winged fowl of the sea to the seal and walrus!

What do all these creatures live upon? Why are they here? The waters must be alive with *other* innumerable creatures! Soon "great whales" will be here, and for what? Is there food for *them* here too?

At 9 A.M. I left Twerpukjua, and directed my way to Anna-wa's, at the island of Oopungnewing, where I arrived in due course, and was kindly welcomed as usual. Noodleyong was busy sewing skins together for making the summer tupic or tent, and Annawa, with other men, were out sealing. In the afternoon these latter returned, and we had the customary feast in the open air.

It was Sunday, and I could not help thoughtfully looking upon the scene before me. There was the snow village of pure white igloos, with their *wadlings* and *took-soos* embellished by trophies of the walrus hunts. A score of laughing, happy, untutored, uncivilized, and "unchristianized" sons and daughters of the North were around or near me. There was a group on my right commencing the feast; three women, that had been out gathering *kelp* (seaweed) as an article of food, coming up from the beach; Annawa and his sealing company drawing up their kias on the floe-ice seaward; open water near by covered with ducks: Blind George standing in front of Bob's igloo, facing and welcoming the sun's warm rays; a number of boys drawing another captured seal across the rugged ice lining the shore; and one young urchin with a brace of ducks newly shot. In the narrow distance were some icebergs and floating masses of ice, and behind, as well as far off, the bold mountains, which gave a grandeur to the view.

The next morning, April 29th, accompanied by Esheeloo and his wife Oonga, I started on foot for the ship in Rescue Harbour, a distance of about twenty miles.

Part of the way was over broken ice, and this made the journey both tedious and difficult. At noon we were at the foot of Bayard Taylor Pass leading to Field Bay, and after a lunch we walked on over the land, stopping a moment at the half-way station for a drink of delicious water, and arrived on the other side at 4 P.M.

IGLOOS OR SNOW-VILLAGE AT OOPUNGNEWING.

Field Bay had firm ice upon it, and over this we travelled as rapidly as we could, finally reaching the ship at 8 P.M. having been just twelve hours on the way.

OOD-LOO, OR WOMAN'S KNIFE.

The illustration one-third the size of the original.

In the hands of an Esquimaux woman, this simple instrument, made of bone and iron (the arc simply edged with iron), is equivalent to the knife, hatchet, scraper, and shear of civilization.

CHAPTER XVI.

DIRECTLY after my arrival on board, on April 29th, 1861, I had a good wash, which I stood much in need of. I then found that snow-blindness had come upon me. During the journey I had felt some difficulty in sighting the way, but did not experience any pain. Now, however, my face *burned* as if on fire, and my eyes were intolerably painful. My cheeks were much the colour of tanned hide, and all about my features gave unmistakable evidence of exposure to severe weather.

That night I again enjoyed the luxury of taking off my skin dress, which I had not been able to do for the previous eight days. But my snow-blindness, which is attended with most excruciating pain, allowed me little rest, and the next morning found me so bad that I could hardly do anything.

It was now the last day of April, and many symptoms of a change from winter to summer (the only real changes during the year in arctic climes) were observable. True, a heavy snow-storm was prevailing, but the weather was much milder than it had been, and the ice was beginning to yield. In the morning the ship was released from her ice-fetters, and had lifted herself up full two feet, showing how much lighter she had become through the consumption of stores since the period of freezing in.

On the 3d of May, which was a beautiful and warm day, Ebierbing and Tookoolito arrived, with all their effects, intending to stay with me until I was ready, as previously arranged, to leave for King William's Land. They were well, and had got through the interval since I had last seen them in the usual precarious manner, sometimes with, sometimes without success in sealing, so alternately with or without food.

The following morning we had another snow-storm, which continued with slight intermissions for several days.

On the 6th of May, Captain B., wishing the dogs to be well fed previous to being employed in transporting the whale-boats, stores, &c. over to the whaling dépôt at Cape True, asked several of the Innuits to take them over to Oopungnewing, where there was plenty of walrus skin and meat; but one and all refused. They said "the weather was too bad;" whereupon I volunteered to go with any Innuit that would accompany me; but, finally, the gale having abated, the Captain himself determined to go, taking with him two of the Esquimaux, who at last consented to accompany him.

There were twenty-five dogs, and these we had harnessed to a sledge by the Innuits Charley and Jim Crow, who were ready to start. The Captain went ahead, and I following with the sledge, soon overtook him, but not until I had seen a good specimen of dog-driving.

At the beginning it was slow work to get the dogs under way, but, once on the start, away they went, pell-mell together, and swiftly, over the fair white snow. It was amusing to see my Greenland dogs, with the others, weaving and knitting, braiding and banding their traces into knots and webs that apparently would defy human devices to unravel. One dog would leap over the backs of a dozen others; another dog, receiving the snap of the thirty-feet lash in the driver's hands, thinking it the work of his nearest neighbour, would seize him, as if to repay it by a ten-fold severer snap; then the rest would join in the fray, till all became involved in a regular dog-fight. It was a picture to see these twenty-five dogs flying almost with the speed of wind over the frozen surface of the deep snow. But, after joining the captain and resigning to him my place, it was not quite so pleasant for me to return. I had but light garments on, and the weather was still severe. However, the distance was not far, and I reached the ship without much difficulty.

Captain B., to my astonishment, returned on the following day at about 10 P.M. He had duly arrived at Oopungnewing; was hospitably received in Bob's igloo for the night; and, having supplied himself with a load of walrus meat—indeed, he might have had half a dozen loads, so abundant was the supply at that time—and preferring to return rather than stay where the igloos were about tumbling down, owing to the moist weather, he came back in the midst of the continuous storm.   The labour of getting over the Bayard Taylor Pass was very severe to him, especially at the steep ascent on the other side.   He could only make two or three steps before he was obliged to rest, each step carrying him thigh deep into the soft snow.

With the captain came "Bob" and his wife "Polly;" but this time Bob came in a *professional* capacity.   He was a doctor, or, rather, an angeko, and now came to visit the sick mother of *Sharkey.*

The following day I chanced to witness him engaged at the work.   I was walking among the ruined igloos, which, having fallen down, had been nearly all replaced by skin tents, when I heard the peculiar sound of *ankooting* close by.   It was near the tupic of *Ar-tung-ung*, mother of Sharkey; but I did not enter, for generally no one but the family is allowed to be present on such occasions; and, though one cannot help pitying the superstitious feeling that directs them to this, yet why should any of us make light of it?   They are earnest in the matter, and only follow the customs of their fathers for generations before them.   Possibly, however, it may yet be the honour of our country, through some Christian philanthropist, to bring them to a knowledge of the one true God.

The Innuit Bob was a man that every one of us highly esteemed.   I have before alluded to him in warm terms, and I will now mention a circumstance which belonged to the romantic incidents of his life.

In the winter of 1854-5, he and a companion, with some dogs attacked a large polar bear.   His companion's name was *Se-nik-too*—"Moose," as called by the whalers.   He afterward, in 1858, died at Allen's Island, leaving a widow—the Puto whom I have frequently named.

Moose fired at the bear, when it rushed toward them.   Bob stood his ground until he too had fired, and then immediately turned and ran; but the next moment the bear was upon him, and, seizing his left shoulder in its jaws, threw him high over its head, as if he had been a mere bag of feathers!   Bob fell about four fathoms off, and was getting up, when the bear again laid hold of him, this time by the leg, and gave him another toss. The dogs, however, now managed to keep the animal at bay; and Moose coming to Bob's aid, they bravely renewed the attack, until at length these courageous Innuits succeeded in conquering the brute. Unfortunately, they lost him after all their trouble, for the ice broke, and the tide swept their prize away.

I saw the scars of the wounds inflicted by this monster, Bob taking off his reindeer dress in the main cabin to gratify me. Captain B., said that the laceration was terrible, for he had seen it a few days after the occurrence, and administered such relief as was in his power. Bob was undoubtedly a powerful man, muscular, full breasted, of great nerve, and firm as iron. When he stripped I had a good opportunity to see this, and he allowed me to take the measurement of his body.*

On the 10th of May Ebierbing's grandmother, the aged *Ookijoxy Ninoo*, arrived with him from Cornelius Grinnell Bay, where he had been to fetch her to his home. I was anxious for a conversation with her, as she could give me much information, from native traditions and personal observation, about the Frobisher expeditions of 1576-8; but it was not until the next day that I had the opportunity.

Next morning I went on shore at Cooper's Island, a small island near the *George Henry* in Rescue Harbour, where Ebierbing, Tookoolito, and Ookijoxy Ninoo lived in tupics. Our conversation commenced by my leading the way, through Ebierbing, his wife acting as interpreter, which, aided by my own increasing knowledge of the language, enabled me to quite understand the old lady's narrative.

Ebierbing said that "he well recollected, when a boy, seeing, on an island near Oopungnewing, *oug* (something *red*, which I inferred, from his subsequent explanation, to mean *bricks*) and *coal*. At that time he knew not what those things were, but when he visited England in 1855, he there saw bricks, and understood their use for the first time. Coal he had seen on board an English whaler previous to that, but not until years after his noticing these things on the island. He said he used to play with these bricks, piling them up in rows and in various forms, as children often do, and also marked stones with them, and was delighted to see the red strokes. He also remembered Innuit women using the bricks, whenever they could be obtained, for polishing the brass ornaments worn on the

---

* King Watcheung's (Bob's) measurement was as follows:—38 inches around his body, over the breast; 42 inches around his shoulders, over the arm; 15 inches around his neck; 22 inches around his head; 5 feet 2 inches in height; 5 feet 3 inches from finger-tip to finger-tip; from forty to forty-five years of age.

head. Likewise he could well remember how some of his aged people told him that many—a great many years ago, ships came into the Bay *Tin-nu-jok-ping-oo-se-ong*" (Frobisher Bay). This was Ebierbing's statement. I now proceed to that of his grandmother. But, before doing this, let me describe the scene as it was at the time of my receiving the following important communication from her.

Her tupic was very small—only large enough to hold herself comfortably in a sitting or reclining posture—but I managed to

OLD OOKIJOXY NINOO NARRATING THE TRADITIONS OF HER PEOPLE.

squeeze in beside her, seating myself at her right side. Tookoolito was *outside* by the entrance, facing the old lady and myself.

The position of Ookijoxy Ninoo was usually a reclining one, she resting her elbows on the pillow-place of her bed, and her chin upon her hands. By her side was her little kood-lin (lamp), and in front of that was a small board, on which was a handful of baked beans given to her by some one from the ship, and also a few broken pieces of sea-bread which Tookoolito had saved for her. There was, besides, abundance of walrus blubber and skin for her to eat when hungry.

During the time I was in her tupic and listening to her words, a favourite grandchild of hers, E-ter-loong, was just outside, frequently crying for food. The old lady gave the child a part of the beans and biscuit; but his noise was a great interruption.

The weather was very cold—bitterly so; and I often requested Tookoolito to take my place inside, but she preferred my retaining "the seat of honour."

The following is the substance of her statements to me respecting the objects of my inquiry.

Placing before her the sketch-chart formerly drawn by Koo-jesse, and showing her Cornelius Grinnell Bay, Singeyer, Field Bay, tracing along down through Bear Sound to Cape True, thence to Oopungnewing, I asked her if she recognised those particular parts. Her reply was that she did; and immediately asked, "What is the name of the island where *Koochooarchu* was?" meaning the island where myself, with Sterry and Koker-jabin, visited Samson on the previous April 27th. I replied, "*Ak-koo-wie-shut-too-ping.*"

"That," said she, "is where I have spent much of my life—many of my best days. But the place where the kodlunas (white people) of the ships landed is called *Niountelik*, an island near Oopungnewing."

She then proceeded to say that upon Niountelik she had seen bricks, and coal, and pieces of timber of various sizes. She had also heard from old Innuits that, many years before, ships had landed there with a great number of people. She remembered, when a little girl, hearing Innuits tell about these people having killed several Innuits; also that farther down, or on Kingaite side, as the old lady spoke it, they took away two Innuit women, who never came back again.

I asked her if she knew how *many* ships had come there? Her reply was, They came every year; first two, then three, then am-a-su-ad-lo oo-moo-arch-chu-a (many—a great many ships). "Five Innuits were also killed by the kodlunas" (white people). Not feeling quite certain of the meaning of her answer, I repeated the question, How many ships came here? Tookoolito, on receiving the answer, gave it to me in this way: "She said 'they came every year,'" and then ceased from repeating more of the old woman's words. This puzzled me; I knew not what to make of it. I began to think that perhaps whaling ships had annually visited the great bay. But, after a few moments, I found Tookoolito had ceased speaking merely to consider the true interpretation of what the old lady had said into my vernacular. She continued by saying, "First two, then two or three, then many—very many vessels."

This was clear; and I immediately took up the only book I then had with me bearing upon the subject, "Barrow's Chronological History of Arctic Discovery," and, turning to the account of Frobisher's voyages, I read what had been given to the world by means of writing and printing, and compared it with what was now communicated to me by means of oral tradition. *Written* history tells me that Frobisher made three voyages to the arctic regions as follows:—

First voyage in 1576, with *two* vessels.

Second voyage in 1577, three vessels.

Third voyage in 1578, fifteen vessels.

Traditionary history informs me that a great many, many years ago the vessels of white men visited the bay (Frobisher's) three successive years:—

First, in *two* vessels.

Second, in three vessels.

Third, in many vessels.

But this is not all that traditionary history gave me on that day. *Written* history states that Frobisher lost *five* of his men on his first voyage when conveying a native on shore. *Oral* history told me that five white men were captured by Innuit people at the time of the appearance of the ships a great many years ago; that these men wintered on shore (whether one, two, three, or more winters, could not say); that they lived among the Innuits; that they afterward built an oomien (large boat), and put a mast into her, and had sails; that early in the season, before much water appeared, they endeavoured to depart; that, in the effort, some froze their hands; but that finally they succeeded in getting into open water, and away they went, which was the last seen or heard of them. This boat, as near as I could make out at the time, was built on the island that Frobisher and his company landed upon, viz. *Niountelik*.

I have here put down a part only of what I recorded in my

journal at the time, and, consequently, much of it will be found to have been the result of some slight mistake in what I then understood ; but, coupled with the previous statements of Koojesse, and the information which I afterward obtained, it will be seen that the main facts about Frobisher's Expedition are well supported by evidence.

The old lady further informed me that frequently, in her lifetime, she had seen wood, chips, coal, and bricks, and *large pieces of very heavy stone*, on the island of *Niountelik*.

This again puzzled me. What could " very heavy stone " mean ? I asked her " what *kind* of stone it was," and to this she replied, " It was *black*, and very heavy. No Innuits had ever seen such kind of stones before."

This at once led me to conclude that the heavy stones were *iron ;* and still more so when Tookoolito observed, " I think, from what the old lady says, these stones were very heavy, a *small* one being as much as an Innuit could lift. I think, perhaps," added she, "they were iron." " And so do I. By-and-by, I will see to it," was my reply.

The information thus obtained seemed so clearly to bear upon Frobisher's Expedition that I determined, as soon as I could, to visit *Niountelik*, and ascertain all about the matter. I thought to myself, if such facts concerning an expedition which had been made nearly three hundred years ago can be preserved by the natives, and evidence of those facts obtained, what may not be gleaned of Sir John Franklin's Expedition of *only sixteen years ago ?* The singular fate of La Perouse and his expedition was unknown to the civilized world for thirty-eight years, and then brought to light only by the exertions of one individual, Captain Dillon, an English master of a merchant ship ! Here, too, we have the first intimation of the fate of Frobisher's five men— after being shrouded in mystery for 285 years—all but determined by personal inquiry among the natives ! Why not, then, be able to ascertain from the same natives—that is, of the same Innuit race—all those particulars so interesting, and many of them so important to science, concerning the Lost Polar Expedition ? I was now convinced, more than I had ever been, that the whole mystery of their fate could have been, and may yet be easily determined with even the smallest well-directed aid. At all events, I felt that, while life and health should be spared me, I would devote myself to this undertaking.

Such was the current of my thoughts at the time I was in the old lady's *tupic* and listening to her words ; and, let me add, such are now my thoughts, and, so far as may be permitted, such are my intentions.

In continuation of my interview with the aged Innuit, I asked her why Innuits, as I had been informed, do not now live upon the land beyond Bear Sound, extending eastward between the waters of Frobisher Bay and Field Bay ?

To this, as interpreted, she said—

"A great many years ago, before I (Ookijoxy Ninoo) was born, the Innuits all around these bays were very many. The number of Innuits on *Ki-ki-tuk-ju-a* (*Lok's Land* of Frobisher) and the other islands in that direction was great ; but at one time they were nearly all out on the ice, when it separated from the land and took them out to sea. They never came back, nor did any Innuit ever hear of them again. Since then, Innuits never live there, nor ever visit the place."

As she spoke about this catastrophe she did so under evident feelings of constraint and horror ; and when I asked if *she* had ever visited it, her emphatic reply was, "*Never !* NEVER !"

This accounted to me for much apparent mystery which I had noticed respecting the region in question whenever I addressed any Innuit upon the subject. They could not—or would not—give me any information about it ; and when I once tried to get a company of natives to go there with me, all refused. Yet every year they make frequent passages, backward and forward through the channel *Is-se-hi-suk-ju-a* (called by Frobisher Bear Sound), dividing the " ill-fated land " from the main.

The old woman further added that the Innuits had lived on that land, as Innuits do live—that is, moving about wherever food can be had—both before and after the white men's ships came years ago ; but, since the great disaster occurred which swept so many of her people away, no Innuits would go there.

After eliciting all the information I then could from the old woman, I left her, with great astonishment at her powers of memory, and the remarkable way in which this strange people of the icy North, who have no written language, can correctly preserve history from one generation to another.

Nine generations had passed away since the visit of Frobisher, yet now, on the 11th of May, 1861, I received from an old woman, probably a hundred years old, statements which I could not otherwise than believe to be facts concerning him and his co-adventurers ! I was astonished, and also, in a measure, pleased, for it gave me stronger hopes than ever of my being able thereafter to obtain all the knowledge I required concerning the expedition of Franklin. Meanwhile I determined upon revisiting Oopungnewing, and going to Niountelik as soon as possible.

At this time all on board the *George Henry* were very busy in certain matters connected with the ship, such as refitting and preparing her for the time when she might proceed to other quarters for whaling operations. Boats on sledges, men and their apparel, sleeping-gear, and other necessary material, were daily sent off to the working dépôt at Cape True, in Frobisher Bay, so that on the 17th of May only three white men remained in the vessel.

I now decided to make a sledge exploring trip up the Bay of Frobisher, as I could not depart for King William's Land till about the 1st of August, the earliest practicable moment of being able to commence my journey by boat to that locality.

At this time Tookoolito was suddenly taken ill. It was on the evening of May 8th, when, as I was engaged upon my charts, Tookoolito aiding me in the Innuit names, I noticed she suddenly dropped her head, as I thought, to reflect upon something. But Sharkey's wife, who was sitting opposite, soon convinced me to the contrary by springing toward her. I saw what the matter was in a moment. Tookoolito had fainted ; and, when aided by such means as were in my power, she soon revived, but a general prostration, accompanied by terrible pains in the head, ensued. As it was necessary for her to have immediate rest, she was placed in my berth, and the little girl, Ookoodlear, sent to attend upon her.

Meanwhile I had another patient suddenly on my hands. Directly Tookoolito revived, *Mam-ma-yat-che-ung*, wife of Sharkey, was seized with bleeding at the lungs. The poor woman, like many of her people, especially those of her sex, was in a rapid decline, and, as I thought, had not long to live. She had gone upon deck, where I found her coughing and vomiting up blood most fearfully. The snow-wreath at the gangway was crimsoned as if a bear's jugular had been opened there. I at once gave her a glass of alum water, which checked it after she had bled for some twenty minutes. She then went down to my cabin, and attended upon Tookoolito until the return of Ebierbing, who was greatly affected at the condition of his wife.

Poor Tookoolito continued very sick for some days, but, with such care and relief as could be given to her, she ultimately got well enough to go about as usual. Perhaps the cause of her sickness was over-exertion in moving their tupic from one island to another the day previous. It had been heavy work for her, but she had to do it, for the custom among Innuits is to make the *women* perform all such domestic and ordinary labour.

Before leaving for my exploration of the Frobisher waters, I determined to examine the head of Field Bay, the bay where we were now at anchor. I commenced to work at 9 A.M. of the 20th of May. The Innuits Ebierbing and the angeko, with *Mam-ma-nar-ping*, one of the wives of the latter, were with me, though the two former only went part of the way, they leaving me to chase some reindeer, the tracks of which we found near the foot of Grinnell Mountain. I myself, with the woman as guide and attendant, continued the trip alone.

The travelling was very bad, in consequence of the snow having melted and formed several pools. Over these pools, which almost uniformly covered the sea-ice, was a thin coating of fresh-water ice, not uniformly of sufficient thickness and strength to bear our walking upon it; indeed, but a small portion of it was firm enough to hold us up. Whenever it gave way down we would go, ankle deep, and sometimes deeper. Then, too, the dazzling glare of the ice on the upper part of the bay caused additional care and labour in walking.

Every few rods we saw seals out on the ice, basking in the sun's rays.

At 4 P.M. we made land, and there stopped to rest and dine. I had abundance of hard bread and a large piece of salt pork, and at that season of the year there was plenty of fresh water to be obtained. Thus we were able to make a good repast, and, after a short stay, proceed on our journey.

Our way led us toward Alden Mountain;* and we had to go over an extensive plain, deeply covered with snow, which is at the head of Field Bay. Almost every half-dozen steps were sure to be succeeded by a downfall of no pleasant character, and it was severe to me, besides being injurious to my box chronometer slung at my side. Never did I experience more annoying travel. As we proceeded it became much worse. Every few steps, down, *down* we went, oftener waist-deep than otherwise. Sometimes the surface snow would appear firm, and then I had hope of all being right for our getting forward, but the next moment we were sinking to our hips in some treacherous

---

* A mountain at the extreme head of Field Bay, which I have named after Charles Alden, of Newburg, New York.

spot. Occasionally I would be making fair headway, when my Innuit guide would go down, and, while trying to help her up, the snow-crust would give way, and I then followed suit. It seemed as if it took three hours for us to make one mile.

After much struggling we arrived at a small rocky hill, and, ascending it, an extensive view was before me. On the west of us I could see a lakelet, long and narrow, that extended in a northerly direction to the base of Alden Mountain. This lakelet, on my way back, proved to be influenced in its waters by the sea for two or three days at the periods of high tides—full and change.

It was now 8 P.M. We were both much fatigued, and yet it would not do to remain. Not a blanket had we, nor any article that would serve to keep warmth in us during the night, which, however, was now daylight all through. The heavens were covered with portentous clouds, and many circumstances led me to conclude it most advisable to return; but I could hardly determine in what direction it would be best to go. There were the plains, but they were covered with the treacherous snow. As I reflected, a passage in the "Good Book" came to my mind: "Be angry, and sin not;" but, whether I sinned or not, God only is my judge. This, however, I must confess: that as I walked on that treacherous snow-crust, every now and then going down, *down, down,* my temper at length would fly up, *up, up,* making the scale-beam keep dancing for full three hours, until some fair walking gave ease to my weary limbs and quiet to my ruffled soul.

On a careful survey of the routes we could follow, I finally decided upon going to a low ridge which was farther west of us and free from snow. That ridge extended in a line running to the S.S.E. and lay in about the direction I wanted to go. To reach it we had to traverse along an abrupt sand bank bordering the lakelet already mentioned. We then came to a beautiful grassy plain quite destitute of snow, and over which it was a perfect luxury to travel. All my weariness and pain were quite forgotten in walking across this carpet of Nature. It was surrounded by rugged, sombre, rocky mountains, and consequently appeared to me like an *oasis* in the great desert. For nearly one year I had sighted nothing but rocks, rocks, rocks, here, there, and everywhere, piled into mountains of such varied and horrible shapes that they seemed as if created to strike *terror* into the heart of man; and now to fall thus unexpectedly upon a plain covered with grass, yielding so friendly and "down"-like to my aching feet, particularly under the circumstances described, was enough for me to express my great joy and admiration.

It is said that the name Greenland was given to that land by the Norwegians and Icelanders because it looked greener than Iceland. I could, therefore, on my trip across that grassy plain, fully appreciate *their* feelings on beholding a greener land than their own. Yet many a one going directly from the United States and visiting Greenland would from the bottom of his soul exclaim,

"*This* Greenland! Then, indeed, have I come into a Paradise, but into that of which Milton speaks :—

> " '. . . o'er the back side of the world far off,
> Into a limbo large and broad, since called
> *The Paradise of Fools.*' "

With reference to the plain I crossed over, Tookoolito afterward informed me that in 1860 a company of Innuits, herself and Ebierbing of the number, spent three weeks in passing over the land amid the mountains, and on other plains of great extent westward of Cornelius Grinnell Bay. Their trip was made for a reindeer hunt. On their way, and running north-west from the plain near what I have called Alden Mountain, was another plain, extending in every direction as far as the eye could reach. This convinced me that in general arctic navigators know but little about the interior of the northern country. Rarely anything but the coasts are seen and explored. On the trip I am now referring to I saw more level ground than since I left the United States. Nothing in Greenland that I saw could compare with it.

Tookoolito also informed me that reindeer visit those plains in great numbers. On their excursion they killed as many as they wanted; and so numerous were the deer that they might be compared to flocks of sheep. Much of the meat they had obtained during the hunt was left behind. The *fawns* were chased down by the Innuits and caught ; as she said, "their feet being dry, they could not run well. When the feet of tuktoo are wet, they can go much faster over the mountain rocks."

From information I afterward obtained, the plains here spoken of appeared to be well known to our friendly Innuits as a breeding-place for the deer; and the whole country between Frobisher Bay and *Niountelik* (a place in the north part of Northumberland Inlet) had been frequently traversed by several of the intelligent natives who visited us ; but, unless discreetly questioned, it is rare for an Esquimaux to say much of himself, his people, or his native land. It is only by degrees, and by a long association with them, that any one can elicit any material facts.

At half-past 10 P.M. we were on the top of another mountain. Here we had something more to eat; and then, proceeding to the sea-ice, directed our steps toward the vessel. The walk was one of great labour, yet not so trying to the *temper* as that of some previous portion of the day.

At three o'clock in the morning we arrived on board of the ship, completely exhausted with the fatiguing journey, made, during eighteen hours, over a distance of about twenty-five miles.

HEAD AND ANTLERS OF THE ARCTIC REINDEER.

CHAPTER XVII.

A successful Deer-hunt—Se-ko-se-lar Innuits—The Land Pass—Magnificent Scenery—Countess of Warwick Sound—Important Discovery—Relic of Frobisher's Expedition—Sledge-drive in a Snow-storm—Value of a Compass—Safe Arrival on Board—State of the Ice—The Whale Dépôt—Stranger Innuits arrive—Two boats af White Men land on the Coast——After-knowledge of the Truth—Loss of the English Store-ship "Kitty"—The Locality of Sekoselar—Tradition of Parry's Voyage—Old Innuits remember visiting him—Sekoselar Innuits dislike civilization Food—"Barbarous Stuff"—Physical Superiority of the Sekoselar Men.

THE following day, May 21st, 1861, Ebierbing and Mingumailo returned from their deer-hunt. They had been successful, having shot with a rifle of mine three deer, one of which was lost, and the other two were secured. It appeared that Ebierbing first shot one of a group of eight which they came across. It struggled and fell before he could approach the spot, but rose again and ran away. In a moment more, however, he managed to shoot another, and Mingumailo a third. Thus was secured to us several hundred pounds of fresh venison.

The deer were killed high up in the mountains, and the two hunters had to carry the carcases (portions at a time), a distance of two miles down to the sea-ice, where they made a cache by piling on heavy stones. What they could carry off to the ship they did, and all of us on board had an excellent feast.

About this time we heard that some Innuits had arrived at Samson's settlement from the "Sekoselar" mentioned in a note at page 153. The news made me still more anxious to proceed on my exploring trip, but various causes tended to prolong my delay, and, even when ready for the excursion, I was unable to proceed farther than a day's journey.

The Esquimaux are good as guides, as companions, as hunters and purveyors of food, but it is impossible to place any great dependence upon them in keeping faith as to time or one's wishes on a journey. They *will* do just as they please; and if aught is seen that may serve them for food, they will away in chase no matter how much delay is thereby occasioned in a white man's enterprise, or however great the loss and inconvenience. In my case, absolutely dependent upon them for aid in exploring, I could do nothing but exercise my patience to the fullest degree. Hence it was not until the 27th of May that I was able to start on another trip to the waters of Frobisher Bay.

At that season of the year, travelling over the ice and snow-covered land by *day* was almost impossible. The slush and the numerous pools of water upon the former rendered a passage not only very difficult, but often dangerous; and, upon the land, the fatigue occasioned was more than could be well endured. Night, therefore, was chosen for our journeys, unless occasion required us to continue on during the day.

Accordingly, at 10 P.M. of the 27th of May I started from the ship with dogs and sledge, after having my outfit well attended to by Tookoolito. She was unable to accompany her husband, who had joined my company. The rest of my companions were two Innuit men and two women, one of them being Punnie, and the other a beautiful young woman called An-nu-tik-er-tung, wife of Kus-se-e-ung. Myself and the two women led the way, and in about an hour arrived where the upper village had been during the winter. Here we stopped to collect various things belonging to the Innuits who were with me, and which they had left there when departing for Frobisher Bay. We also stopped at another spot not far off, and collected tent-poles, coverings, kia frames, buckets, skins, &c. making a very considerable addition to our already heavy load. It was an hour and a half past midnight when we again started, but our foot travel was now good, the best of the season, the ice being firm during the night.

During the walk I had an interesting conversation with Ebierbing, who, among other things, told me of the great price the Sekoselar Innuits were willing to give for any articles of iron. A small piece of good iron, suitable for a spear-head, would procure a seal or tuktoo jacket from them, and with a needle one could purchase a deerskin. The Sekoselar Innuits can only obtain iron occasionally, when a communication is had with natives living on the coast. They still use bone needles, bows, and arrows.

As we neared the land on the opposite side of Field Bay the sun was tipping the mountains with red. It was then nearly half-past 2 A.M. and I also noticed that clouds were hugging some of the high lands. This indicated a coming storm. At 3.45 A.M. we passed from the bay to the main land, and now it began to blow strongly from the south-west. I selected the lee side of some rocks and took several compass bearings, then proceeded on my way alone, the rest of my party, with the sledge, having gone on before. I overtook them at the summit of Bayard Taylor Pass, and then together we began the descent on the other side.

I have already spoken of this pass, but each time I traversed it I could not help being transfixed with wondering awe. Near its western termination each side is walled by bold, craggy mountains, and the scenery there is truly magnificent. Shortly after, when we reached the frozen waters of the bay, the dogs and sledge carried us along past scenery ever changing and remarkable. While crossing this, I judged it to be Frobisher's Countess of Warwick Sound.

Our course this time, owing to a wide gap in the ice, led us to the north of Oopungnewing, as we intended to make for the low point of land called Twerpukjua ; hence we passed the island at some little distance. Here, when nearest to it, Punnie left us to go to Annawa's settlement ; and after resting awhile, employing the time in sealing, we again proceeded. Niountelik Island we passed about a quarter of a mile off, and then, at 10 A.M. we arrived at Twerpukjua.

When approaching the shore-ice we met a party of Innuits with a sledge and team of dogs going to the vessel, having just come from the island where I had been April 25th and 26th, while staying with Samson. Among them were Johnny Bull, his wife Kokerzhun, and *New-wer-che*, one of the most enterprising and energetic Innuits with whom I was acquainted. They reported that the ice had broken up, and said it would be impossible for me to proceed on my journey by sledge. This I soon perceived to be the case. While consulting with them, I could see quite enough to convince me so. The wind was then blowing strong from the south. A heavy sea was at work tearing up the ice between Niountelik and Twerpukjua. To where we were, the distance from the raging, open sea was not two hundred fathoms.

It was a trial to me to give up this trip, yet I acted as I believe a wise man should, and accordingly determined to abandon the attempt and try it by boat. I therefore ordered our return ; but as I wished to examine the islands of Ooopungnewing and Niountelik, I proposed to Ebierbing that we should stay three or four days at Annawa's ; and, to prevent our being encumbered with so much baggage as I had brought for an extended trip, told him to make a transfer of it from our sledge to Johnny Bull's, who would take it back to the ship.

While this transfer was being made, my eye accidentally caught sight of a piece of *brick*, among sundry odds and ends of Innuit articles brought from the upper village at the head of Field Bay. While looking upon it, I called to mind the story I had heard from old Ookijoxy Ninoo about relics of this kind seen on Niountelik, and I at once asked Kusseeung and Arngmer-che-ung what it was. They replied, " Stone "—a stone that the old mother of the latter had given him a long time ago. I then asked from whence she got it, and both Innuits immediately pointed to the island Niountelik, which was less than half a mile from where we stood.

Ebierbing took this *bright- coloured brick* from my hand, looked at it, and said, " That is the same as I have seen on that island," pointing to Niountelik. He then added, " Many of my acquaintances up the inlet (meaning Northumberland) have pieces of the same kind that came from that island."

My feelings upon seeing the piece of brick, and hearing what was said about it, may be easily imagined. There, in my hand, was undoubtedly a relic of that expedition which had visited the place only eighty-six years after the discovery of America by Columbus, since which time it has remained unknown to the civilized world ! This relic, then, was more precious to me than *the gold* which Frobisher sought there under the direct patronage of Queen Elizabeth. Until now no proof had existed that Frobisher and his expedition ever visited the particular bay or " straits " bearing his name ; but, from all that I had gathered from the information given me by the natives, and from what I had now seen, a strong conviction rested on my mind that it was so, and doubt was at an end.

After stopping at Twerpukjua nearly three hours, I bade adieu to those of my Innuit friends who were going to Samson's, and proceeded toward Annawa's at Oopungnewing. Johnny Bull and his party took their way to the ship, Ebierbing accompanying me.

When near Oopungnewing, we saw Punnie coming to meet us, and soon she gave us the information that Annawa and the whole settlement had gone to Og-bier-seer-o-ping (Cape True), and now not a tupic remained. Here again was another disappointment. I had no tent with me, having left my own at the vessel, and it would not do to remain without shelter, as a gale was even then blowing, therefore we had no alternative but to return.

Accordingly, we rejoined Johnny Bull with his party, and were soon on our way, at a swift speed, over the ice, toward the land pass.

Our backs were nearly to the wind and snow, and therefore our trouble from this source was far less than if facing it.   The gale helped us greatly a part of the way back.   It drove the sledge sometimes faster than the dogs could go ; thus occasionally they were dragged along instead of their drawing us.   Besides this, the strong wind had closed the gap which we had been obliged to avoid in the morning, and we now traversed the ice as safely as though we were passing over a marbled floor.

Soon afterward we came to the glare ice of Lincoln Bay,* which is on this (the west) side of the Bayard Taylor Pass. Here the wind and snow played fantastic tricks with the sledge, dogs, and all our company.   We were in company with the other Innuits, but Joe, myself, and Johnny Bull were footing it while passing along this bay.   Had the wind been against us all would have been well, but it came quartering on our right hand and at our backs, and this caused numerous eddies and snow-wreaths.

We were ahead of the sledge, intending to jump upon it as it passed.   After resting a while, on it came ; and, watching the opportunity, Joe and Johnny were fortunately able to spring on, but I could not.   Just as I made my attempt, a terrific gust sent me whirling along for nearly a quarter of a mile over the glassy ice.   Then my feet caught upon a firm snow-wreath, and I stuck fast till I gathered my senses to look round and see where I was. It was snowing fast and furiously, and what with that coming down, and that thrown upward by the wind, every object three or four fathoms distant was hidden from sight.   Fortunately, the almost perpendicular side of a mountain that I had before noticed was within a distance that could be seen.   From this I struck a course leading up the bay to the land-route.   In a short time I had overtaken the party, which had been detained by one

---

* There are three important bays that make up from the ever memorable "Countess of Warwick Sound," which was discovered and so named by Frobisher nearly three centuries ago.   The geographical position of this sound, as well as the nature and extent of Frobisher "Strait" a (misnomer, for it is a bay), remained unknown to the civilized world from the days of Queen Elizabeth down to 1860-2, when I had the good fortune to re-discover, examine, and determine much relating to Frobisher's Expeditions of 1576, '7 and '8.

The three bays—*important* on account of their geographical and historical connexions—I have named,—1st. Lincoln Bay ; 2d. Victoria Bay ; and, 3d. Napoleon Bay.

of the dogs giving out. Casting it off, I took a seat upon the sledge, and away we went merrily toward the pass. As we drove along we were a curious sight to behold, for we resembled a *living* snow-bank.

We ascended the pass on foot, crossed the summit, descended on the other side, and again made the sea-ice of Field Bay. Here two more of our dogs gave out, and we cast them adrift, though they still followed us. We had nine remaining, and this made a good team.

We rested half an hour, then started again, the Innuits endeavouring to find their way, as usual, by the previous sledge-tracks; but we had to go this way and that way, in and out among the numerous islands covering the head of the bay, until finally all traces of our route were lost. Nevertheless, they would have found a course to the ship, though, perhaps, with some delay and difficulty, but I saved all this by using my compass, and thus directing them which way to go, and by 9 P.M. we were on board, having been absent only $22\frac{1}{2}$ hours.

The following day, May 29th, was the anniversary of our departure from home. My thoughts I find mentioned in my diary as follows:—

"One year ago to-day the *George Henry* sailed from New London. It seems to me a *short* year, though spent in regions that, to many civilized men, would be *repulsive*, and would appear unqualified *desolation*. Still, I like this country—not as a place in which to spend all my life, if it be one of four-score and ten years, but for *work* to be continued three or five years."

On the following day, as there appeared to be some indications of its turning out fine, I thought of taking a trip to a place called by the Innuits *Sing-ey-er*. Accordingly, I procured the services of Ebierbing and started; but in two hours afterward there came on thick weather, and every indication of a storm. We had, therefore, to abandon the journey and return. While we were out, however, and I was engaged taking observations, I heard a cry, "Mr. Hall!" I looked around, and saw Ebierbing, at a little distance off, crawling out of a hole in the ice into which he had fallen. I hastened to his assistance, but before my arrival he was out. and fortunately without any injury.

As I have before mentioned, it is risky travelling on the sea-ice at this season of the year, on account of pools of water just beneath a covering of snow. A traveller passing along over an apparently excellent route often finds himself unexpectedly floundering in water, and the cause of this danger may be explained in the following manner :—

I examined several of these " man-traps "—as they really prove to be—and found large leaves of seaweed within these holes in the ice. Any extraneous matter, such as this seaweed, stones, ashes, &c. put on the surface of the ice, absorbs the solar heat, and soon sinks down into the ice, forming a water-hole not only the size of the object itself, but encircling quite a space around. A driving storm may afterward cover the surface with snow, and thus make a perfect man-trap.

Soon after our return on board there was an arrival from Cape True, where the *George Henry's* officers and men were staying to prosecute whaling. I learned that they were all doing well in the way of fresh food, ducks, walrus, &c. being abundant.

On the second day of June a party of Sekoselar Innuits, six in number, came to the ship, and we soon became very friendly together. At first these natives said nothing very particular further than that they had visited the Hudson's Bay Company's ships while passing up and down; nor should I have obtained any other news had it not been elicited almost by accident. In fact, unless there be some motive to engage them in conversation with strangers, the Esquimaux are seldom communicative. It is as if the knowledge which they possess ought not to be given away unless for some especial reasons. The Innuits, as a race, are naturally reticent. They are often distant and reserved, and only by kindness, tact, and gradually leading up to a subject can any information be obtained from them. Thus it was not until the following day, when a letter arrived from Captain B. that I learned of these Esquimaux being acquainted with some facts concerning *white people dying at Sekoselar*. The captain had heard it so reported by other natives, and wrote to me that I might make some inquiries about it.

On the receipt of this letter I immediately sent for Ebierbing and Tookoolito to come on board and act as interpreters. I then invited the two Sekoselar men (by name Ook-goo-al-loo and Too-loo-ka-ah) into the cabin, and opened a conversation, in which both participated. Tookoolito was the principal speaker, and she interpreted very well my own questions and their answers. That her interpretation was correct, and equally so their information, has, since my return home, been proved by facts, which at that time I was unacquainted with. Indeed, I then misapplied the story, firmly believing it to bear upon the lost Franklin Expedition. What that story was may be seen in the following substance of all which was related to me through Tookoolito :—

The Sekoselar Innuits said that " no kodlunas (whites) had ever been to or ever died at Sekoselar, but two years previous to this time two kodluna boats, with many oars (meaning many oarsmen), arrived at a place farther down (at *Karmowong**)— so they, the Sekoselars, had heard—and there stopped awhile ; how long, whether one or two days, was not known. That these kodlunas had plenty guns, plenty powder, plenty shot, plenty balls, and plenty small casks of provision. They had many tuktoo skins (reindeer furs) to wrap around their bodies and their feet.

" To make their boats not so deep in the water, the kodlunas (whites) took out *amasuadlo* (a great many) balls and placed them on a rock. The Innuits at that place, and in the vicinity where the kodlunas landed, thought the balls were soft stones. They supposed the whites had come from ships that had been lost or wrecked in the ice.

" When these whites left the land they went farther down toward the big sea.

" The whites had arrived at Karmowong in the fall of the year, one day when the weather was very bad, wind blowing very hard, and snowing fast. It was very cold too.

" The Karmowong Innuits thought the whites had obtained their tuktoo furs of the Sekoselar men. The skins had on the winter coat of the tuktoo. None of the kodlunas died there. They all went away in boats, and the Innuits never saw or heard of them more."

From further questions that I put, and which were readily answered, I concluded in my own mind that the kodlunas must have been at Karmowong in the fall of 1858, and the way the Sekoselar Innuits heard of it was by a native man who had seen the whites and the two boats.

Now, upon receiving this information, I at length came to the conclusion that it referred to some of Franklin's lost crews. Two boats of white men going toward the great sea, and apparently subsisting upon Innuit food, with reindeer skins for wrappers, and other such material, would seem to indicate that

---

* I think *Karmowong* to be the islands called by Baffin " Middle Savage Islands," north side of Hudson's Strait. Indeed, it may also include quite an extensive bay in that neighbourhood, which the Esquimaux sketched for me as being there.

a few of the long-lost voyagers had at last made their way from King William's Land and Boothia toward the goal of their ultimate deliverance. The experience I had already gained of Esquimaux life proved to me what white men could endure under the exigency of circumstances. There was myself—not reduced to any such absolute necessity as the poor English voyagers undoubtedly must have been—yet capable of sustaining and even of enjoying life among the natives. How much more so, then, the unfortunate men of Franklin's wrecked ships? To me the matter seemed conclusive, although I could not give implicit confidence to what I had heard until personally testing the truth by examination.

On my return home, however, I find that the whole story must have had reference to the loss of a British vessel called the *Kitty*, which was crushed in the ice of Hudson's Strait in the fall of 1859, and the crew obliged to escape by two boats. Some of the particulars of their history remarkably coincide with the information given to me by the Sekoselar Innuits, as may be seen in the Appendix.

Another instance of the faithful preservation of traditions among the Innuits, and also of the accuracy of their reports when communicated freely, is to be found in the following additional information given to me by the Sekoselar natives.

In seeking to obtain the truth concerning the two boats and white men, I induced Ookgooalloo to sketch me his "country" on paper. He did so, and by that sketch I was convinced that Sekoselar was not the King's Cape of Fox, as I had at one time supposed, but lies east of it, extending along the coast on the north side of Hudson's Strait about two degrees; say from longitude 75° west to longitude 73° west. This, then, would fill the blank on Parry's chart of that locality, and give to it, as the Innuit showed me, a deep bay, flanked by lowlands, with a narrow isthmus between the waters of this bay and the head of Frobisher Bay, thus shown so to be, instead of a "strait."

The sketch which was drawn by Ookgooalloo extended from above Fox's farthest down to King's Cape, and thence along the north shore of Hudson's Strait to North Bay, where the upper Savage Islands are situated. "North Bluff" is adjoining that bay, and is called by Innuits Ki-uk-tuk-ju-a, and King's Cape, Noo-ook-ju-a. When the Sekoselar party left home in the previous year, 1860, they travelled, as Innuits generally do, *very slow*. In the fall they arrived at the head waters of Fro-

bisher Inlet, and Ookgooalloo marked upon his sketch the
track they pursued from Sekoselar to the place where they commenced the land route across the isthmus. The head waters
of Frobisher Bay they called See-see-ark-ju-a, and into it ran,
according to his account (which I afterward found true), a river
of fresh water, sometimes very large, and containing salmon in
abundance. During the winter of 1860-1 this party of natives
made their way down the bay till they came across " Samson "
and his people, at the place which I had visited a short time
previous.

Ookgooalloo then told me " that ships did not come in sight
at Sekoselar, nor at Noo-ook-ju-a ; but his father, Koo-ook-jum,
had said that many years ago *two* ships came close to Noo-ook-
ju-a (King's Cape) and Sekoselar, and that he, Koo-ook-jum,
with many other Innuits, went out to the ships in kias and
oomiens, and went on board."

Now these two ships could be no other than Parry's, in his
expedition of 1821–23, and consequently it was full forty years
since the occurrence now mentioned took place. Parry's account
is as follows :

"*July* 31*st*, 1821.—Latitude 64° 01′, longitude 75° 49′ west.
In the afternoon Captain Lyon discovered and made the signal
for an Esquimaux oomiak coming off from shore under sail,
accompanied by eight canoes. We tacked to meet them, and
lay to half an hour for the purpose of adding to our stock of
oil. In this boat were sixteen persons, of which number two
only were men, an old and a young one, and the rest women
and children. In the features, dress, and implements of these
people we saw nothing different from those of the Esquimaux
last described (those of the Savage Islands), but they were
better behaved than the others, with whom our ships (meaning
the Hudson's Bay Company's ships) have had more frequent
intercourse."

Again, under date of August 1st, Parry continues :—

" We beat to the westward, between Nottingham Island and
the north shore (King's Cape), the distance between which is
about four leagues, and the latter fringed with numerous islands.
In the course of the morning several canoes and one oomiak
came off from the main land, containing about twenty persons,
more than half of whom were women and children. They
brought a little oil, some skin dresses, and tusks of the walrus,
which they were desirous of exchanging for any trifle we chose
to give them."

In this account we see a complete verification of the statement made by Ookgooalloo as to his father's visit to the only ships known to have been near his own "country." And I the more particularly allude to it because of many other reports given to me concerning the past, all of which, in my opinion, have received equal confirmation.

The natives from Sekoselar were not partial to civilized food, especially Ookgooalloo and his wife Pittikzhe, for they had not tasted any before. We gave each of them a mug of coffee and some sea-biscuit. They tasted it—spit it out—tried it again and again, and finally the man contrived to "worry" it down; but the woman gave it up, declaring, in her own Innuit way, that "such *stuff* was not fit to eat." Though repeatedly urged to participate in the regular meals served to the Esquimaux on board, Pittikzhe positively declined tasting any more "such *barbarous* food."

I found that the Innuits of Sekoselar had a very peculiar way of speaking—that is, with a slow, drawling tone. Their words are "long drawn out." The natives in our locality made fun of this, and it still more convinced me that there is a considerable variance between the dialects of different bands of the Esquimaux. Another thing I noticed was the physical superiority of these men over those living around Field Bay, and along the coasts visited by whaling ships. Whether all of the Sekoselar people were equal to those whom I saw I am unable to say, but "Samson," who was also a native of that district, showed, as I have before said, to similar advantage when compared with the Innuits in our vicinity.

After making these men and women several presents, for which they expressed much gratitude, they departed at 5 P.M. on their return to Samson's tupic, then near *Evictoon*, about one day's journey N.W. of Oopungnewing.

CHAPTER XVIII.

Journey to the Unknown, or "Dreaded Land"—Sylvia Island—Lupton Channel—Jones's Tower—A Butterfly—Cape Daly—Hummocky Ice—Ancient Piles of Stones—Discover a new Channel—Dr. Kane's Channel—Immense number of Seals—Extensive View—Davis's Straits—Resolution Island, and high Land to the North—Sudden appearance of a Steamship—Mount Warwick—Return Journey—Mode of making Traces and Walrus Lines—Note-book lost—Its Recovery—Ancient Dwellings of Innuits—Rapid Journey back to the Ship—Dangerous Travelling—Ice breaking up—Safe Arrival on Board—Means of sustaining Life in these Regions.

On Wednesday, the 5th day of June, 1861, a day or two after the departure of the Sekoselar Innuits, I prepared myself for another trip, intending this time to visit what the Innuits term the "Dreaded Land," which comprises all the islands eastward of Bear's Sound and Lupton Channel, between Frobisher Bay and Field Bay. As was necessary, I left on board the ship some instructions how to find me and my companions in case the ice, which was becoming very precarious, should break up, and leave us on some of the islands, unable to get away. My intention was to fall back upon the land should the ice break up, and then, if we had to be sought, it would be necessary to look for us somewhere between Hall's Island and Bear Sound.*

On the 5th of June, at about three o'clock in the afternoon, in company with Ebierbing and Koodloo, I left Rescue Harbour, and set out for the "Dreaded Land." Our sledge was drawn by six dogs, just half the number that such a journey required. Our progress was slow ; for, besides the want of a sufficient team, we saw many seals, the ice being dotted over with them, and the Innuits consumed much time in making their peculiar, cautious approaches (elsewhere described), which are always necessary in order to take these animals. Koodloo is a good sealer. Having

---

* Hall's Island, lat. 62° 33′ N. long. 64° 60′ W. and Bear Sound, lat. 62° 31′ N. long, 64° 50′ W. were so named by Frobisher ; the former after Christopher Hall, master of the *Gabriel*, of the expedition of 1576 ; the latter after James Bear, master of the *Michael*, one of the expedition ships of 1577.

selected his game, he succeeded in crawling up to within thirteen fathoms of the seal, and shot him in the head. In five minutes we who were on the sledge arrived at the spot where our prize lay by his hole, when a general dog-fight took place.

The weight of fresh meat thus obtained being no less than 200 pounds, we found ourselves in the predicament of the man who bought the elephant. What should we do with our seal? Finally, we fastened it behind our sledge, dragged it to a convenient place, and cut it up; took with us a part of the meat and blubber for present use, and deposited the remainder *en cache*— that is, we buried it under snow by the side of a hummock, and tarried awhile to have a raw seal-feast.

In the evening, after our repast, we resumed our journey, proceeding at first in the direction of Dillon Mountain,* at the east end of "Lok's Land,"† but changed our course at ten o'clock on account of hummocks, and now proceeded due south toward Lupton Channel.‡ Some time after midnight we made our first encampment on the ice, and lay down to repose upon a couch of snow.

At 10·30 A.M. of June 6th we resumed our journey, and soon after observed a seal upon the ice; but, as we were to windward, it scented us, and down it went. We were still among hummocks, and enveloped in fog. Before noon the fog lifted, and we found ourselves in sight of land near Lupton Channel. We stopped a while opposite the entrance to this channel for a seal which was discovered ahead. But seal, land, mountains, and clouds became closed in by thick fog; a snow-storm came on from the W.N.W. and it soon blew a gale.

This weather compelling us to hold over, we all left the sledge

---

* This prominent and peaked mountain I have named in honour of a warm friend of arctic explorations, J. D. Dillon, of London, England. It is in lat. 60° 32′ N. and long. 64° 12′ W.

† The land which I think I have identified as the one so named by Frobisher in honour of Michael Lok, one of the earliest, warmest, and most liberal supporters of his (Frobisher's) expeditions of 1576, '7, and '8. "Lok's Land" is an island on the east side of Bear Sound and Lupton Channel, and extends easterly eighteen nautical miles; its width is twelve. It is called by the natives *Ki-ki-tuk-ju-a*, which means Long Island. The centre of "Lok's Land" is in lat. 62° 29′ N. long. 64° 28′ W. (See Chart.)

‡ I have named the channel uniting the waters of Field Bay to Bear Sound after James Lupton, of Cincinnati, Ohio, one to whom the Young Men's Mercantile Association of said city owes a debt of gratitude for his great and untiring service in its behalf.

Lupton Channel (its north termination) is in lat. 62° 35′ N. and long. 64° 38′ W.

and dogs, and went a few rods on to the land, to prospect for a suitable spot for an encampment. We found one by the side of a mountain of rock. Here we broke up a beam—a part of our sledge—for fuel to prepare our coffee. We ought, for this purpose, to have taken with us more of the *ooksook* of the seal taken the day previous; but we expected to have captured another by

VIEW FROM THE TOP OF SYLVIA ISLAND.

that time. We saw two in the morning, but they were shy, and went down. Had it not been for the hummocks, we should have pursued our course towards Hall's Island; but it requires weather in which one can see more than five fathoms ahead to travel safely over such ice.

The land on which we here encamped is an island about a quarter of a mile long, which I have named Sylvia,* at the east

* After the daughter of Henry Grinnell. Sylvia Island is in lat. 62° 35½' N. long. 64° 36' W.

side of the entrance to Lupton Channel. When on the highest part of it, about 500 feet above the sea, I drew the opposite sketch.

Here before me, looking southerly, was the open water of Lupton Channel, which, as my native attendants informed me, *never freezes over*, in consequence of the swiftly running tides. Yonder, leading south-easterly around the bold front of Lok's Land, is Bear Sound ; there, farther south, the low islands ; and, showing darkly over these, the open water of Frobisher Bay, and away in the blue distance the huge mountains of Kingaite (*Meta Incognita*) ; while there, on the right, and on the left, and behind me, all was solid ice.

On Friday, June 7th, having slept soundly on the rock, we breakfasted on raw seal, and, with the aid of more fuel (another cross-bar) from our sledge, made some hot coffee, which indeed is a great luxury at any time to an arctic traveller. Not long after, Ebierbing started on ahead, while Koodloo struck tupic, harnessed the dogs, and packed the kummitie, and I triangulated and made observations for time, latitude, &c.   With beautiful weather and a cloudless sky, Koodloo and myself left Sylvia Island, though not before half-past 1 P.M. and travelled on the ice along the coast toward a noble-looking mountain not far off. The dogs *flew*, for they scented and sighted seals in the bay. At 3 o'clock P.M. we arrived at the base of Jones's Tower,* the mountain just alluded to.

A short time after this I began to ascend Jones's Tower, the mountain which I especially observed for the first time some months before, when entering Field Bay.

At the top of the tower I took several observations, and then attempted to descend on the opposite side to that by which I had climbed up. But I found here, as I had before, that going down a precipitous mountain is much worse than going up it. I could not manage it by the new route, and therefore had to reascend in order to take the other.

From the summit of this mountain the view was extensive, yet I could not thence discern Frobisher Bay, although, as I then thought, it was not more than from five to seven miles off.   I here found a butterfly just bursting its prison walls. The wind at the time was so strong as almost to defy my power of holding on.   The place looked like a huge tower rather than a mountain ;

* A mountain I have named after George T. Jones, superintendent of the Cincinnati branch of the American Bank Note Company. Jones's Tower is in lat. 62° 33′ N. long. 64° 34′ W. (See Chart.)

and on one side of it there was, as it were, a broad highway, leading spirally to within fifty feet of the apex. From this elevation a hundred icebergs were in view. On the way down I found some skeleton bones of a whale, about 300 feet above the sea-ice; and also tufts of grass and some reindeer moss. At the base I found Koodloo and Ebierbing with more seals which they had killed, and a fire made of the small shrub*before mentioned.

In the evening we encamped here, close to Robinson's Bay;† a beautiful sheet of water on the east side of the tower. Here we erected our tupic, such as we could make, and the United States' flag floated from its top. Our appearance at that time may be conceived from the following sketch.

ENCAMPMENT AT THE FOOT OF JONES'S TOWER.

Next morning, having a cloudless sky and a gentle breeze (which afterward, however, increased to a strong gale), we pursued our way. In a short time we captured another fine seal, which was deposited *en cache* to be available on our return. As we proceeded, scenes of increasing beauty met my eye. The shore of the " dreaded land " presented many features of interest to me, for it was all new, and especially attractive from its asso-

* *Andromeda tetragona*, a plant of the heath tribe that abounds throughout the arctic regions.
† This Bay I named after Samuel Robinson, of Cincinnati, Ohio.

ciations with the expeditions of Martin Frobisher. On the left were several channels of open water. Before and around me were several icebergs frozen in the pack—one berg in particular being very magnificent in appearance, and resembling a Gothic church.

We had now advanced about six miles from Jones's Tower, and had reached Cape Daly,* when the rugged character of the ice hindered our farther progress with the sledge. Koodloo and I therefore walked ahead inland about half a mile to "prospect," and, arriving upon an eminence at the opposite side of the cape, we thence saw that we might have better travelling by rounding it and reaching the other side. Accordingly, we returned to the sledge and refreshed ourselves with a feast of raw seal.

The wind greatly increasing in violence made travelling still more arduous, but we were determined to persevere, and so we rounded the cape, but with great difficulty, owing to hummocky ice and deep, soft snow. Cape Daly is the termination of a neck of land distinguished by a remarkable gap in its ridge.

Resuming our proper course, we hurried forward toward another cape—Cape Hayes†—the most northerly point of Hudson's Island.‡ There we again prospected, and found it would be impossible to proceed farther with the sledge on account of the hummocky ice in our way.

Hall's Island at this time was less than two miles distant; but to reach it by our present course, on the northern side of Hudson's Island, was an utter impossibility, in consequence of the indescribably rugged ice with which M'Clintock Channel§ was firmly packed.

While examining Cape Hayes we came to circles of stones, evidently placed there many years ago by the Innuits that formerly inhabited this now forsaken land; but beyond this,

* Named in honour of Judge Charles P. Daly, of New York City. Cape Daly is in lat. 62° 35′ N. long. 64° 21′ W.

† I have named this cape after I. I. Hayes, surgeon of the second Grinnell expedition. Cape Hayes is a low point of land, flanked by a high ridge of rugged rocks, and is the north extreme of Hudson's Island.

‡ Hudson's Island, so called in honour of Frederick Hudson, of New York, a strong friend of arctic explorations. The centre of this island is in lat. 62° 34′ N. long. 64° 8′ W. Its length is about three miles, extending north and south; width, two miles.

§ The channel between Hall's Island of Frobisher and Hudson's Island (*vide* Chart) I have denominated M'Clintock Channel, after Captain (now Sir Leopold) M'Clintock, commander of the yacht *Fox* in search of Sir John Franklin in 1857-9.

nothing worthy of note was to be seen. We therefore returned to the sledge, and thence back about a quarter of a mile to a bight flanked by high mountains.

While Koodloo and Ebierbing were here erecting a tent, I ascended one of these mountains, and thence discovered to the south-west, between Lok's Land and Hudson's Island, a channel that no white man (unless of Frobisher's expedition) ever saw before—a channel that probably no Innuit of any late generation had ever visited. The next day, June 9th, we pursued our journey down through Dr. Kane's Channel,* which connects Frobisher Bay with Field Bay; the extreme land, which I especially desired to visit, lying from five to seven miles to the east of the lower or southern termination of said channel. The sledge went swiftly, bounding from snow-wreath to snow-wreath, but I managed to pencil down my notes as we rode along.

Never did I see a more interesting sight than that now presented. Wherever my eye turned, seals appeared in great numbers on the ice by their holes; and, as may be supposed from what I have previously said of the Innuit character, it was quite hopeless to expect that my companions, or the dogs, would attend to my wishes in getting forward. No; a "seal-hunt" was inevitable; and away we went at the rate of ten miles an hour, bounding like deer over the smooth ice, and were quickly among the animals, dealing death around. It was the work of but a few moments; and the very notes from which I now write were recorded as I sat by a seal-hole, the water of which was crimsoned with blood, some of which still marks the age before me. Around me was a scene of death. Our captured seals were now so many that my Innuit companions did not know what to do with them. They appeared almost crazy with joy, at least so far as they are capable of showing signs of extravagant delight in matters of this kind.

Ebierbing said that, "although they had all dreaded this land, it *was* a good land, and now he was not sorry he had come. There was plenty land—plenty water—plenty seal—and nobody there!"

In addition to the numerous seals, we soon afterward came across polar bear-tracks, and could see where Bruin had torn up the sea-ice in his path. But just then we would not stop for anything except for Ninoo. It was "onward" with us now. The way was clear, the day fine, and good prospects before us

---

* Thus named in memory of Dr. Kane, the arctic explorer. This channel divides Hudson's Island from Lok's Land.

for getting around to "Hall's Island" of Frobisher, to the extreme eastern limit of all that land toward the great sea. Therefore I urged my companions on, though it was with some difficulty I could persuade Koodloo to accompany us. He had been uncomfortable from the moment we had trodden upon a portion of the "dreaded land," and now that we were going round it by the "big waters," which had carried off so many of his people, he was in a state of great agitation. But I succeeded in persuading him to stay with us, especially as I promised to return as soon as I had visited the extreme land.

As we opened out to the south, and arrived where we had expected to see the entrance of Frobisher Bay frozen and solid like Field Bay, which we had just left, my astonishment was great to see, at a short distance from us, open water, with numerous icebergs drifting, and a heavy sea rolling in, and beating on the edge of the floe.

About noon we stopped to allow Koodloo to make up to a seal that he was desirous of obtaining, and I was as deeply interested as ever in the way in which he contrived to get so near his intended prey. While the seal would be taking his "cat-nap" (a sleep of ten to fifteen seconds), Koodloo made his approach by hitches, propelling himself along, recumbent on his side, by one foot, till he got close up, say within twelve fathoms of it. During the seal's *watchful* moments it seemed to be charmed by the peculiar talk, and by the scratching noise made by the sealer. But the animal proved too shy; the charm was broken, and down through its hole in the ice it plunged; and away we went again, our course leading us close by the side of the expanse of open water, in and upon which were numerous seals and ducks, giving evidence of animal life here in abundance. The seals were frequently hunted; and although it did not aid our progress, yet it served to relieve the tedium, and give excitement to our journey.

We now neared the land; and when within half a mile of "Hall's smaller island" of Frobisher, I went on by myself, leaving Ebierbing to occupy himself among the seals.

On my walk I saw numerous bear-tracks, and such other evidences around me that I could not help exclaiming, "This outcast region is indeed one of plenty instead of barrenness!"

In a few moments I was on the top of the highest elevation of "Hall's smaller island," and from it took several compass bearings as I viewed the scene around. But I was unable to stay long; and intending to revisit the spot, I soon went back to the sledge.

During my absence two seals had been killed ; but unnecessarily, for it was impossible to carry more than their skins and livers with us. Still, wherever a seal was observed, the two Innuits would away after it. This seriously delayed us, and it was near midnight before we got back to our previous night's encampment on the northern side of Hudson's Island, where we again rested.

The next day, Monday, June 10th, we once more passed through Dr. Kane's Channel, and at 8·47 P.M. reached the middle of the south shore of Hall's Island. Here we encamped by a little cove on this shore, near the west end of the channel which runs on the north side of the small island which I ascended the day previous. Ebierbing went to seek fuel, which he found on the shore of our little bay in the shape of drift-wood. Koodloo and he then prepared our food, while I was off to ascend the mountain that flanked the place of our encampment. On the top of this mountain I found an Innuit monument which evidently had been erected centuries before, for it was black with the moss of ages.

The "monument" was a very long stone stuck up between two larger ones, and the whole made firm by other stones wedged in, and in a way peculiarly Innuitish.

The view from the summit was fine. Meta Incognita, Cornelius Grinnell Bay, Field Bay, Davis's Straits, and Frobisher Bay, were all in sight. Inshore of me there was a beautiful lakelet a mile long and half a mile wide, surrounded by several hills of rugged rock, that contrasted strangely with its smooth and uniform white.

After spending a short time upon the summit, I began my descent, when, as I turned toward the north, what was my great astonishment and joy to perceive a vessel—a steamer—with English colours, close to the land ! There was the black hull, the smoke-stack, and everything about her seemed plainly visible. In a moment I was back to the summit for a more distinct view, and saw her tack ship again and again, presenting first one side of her hull and then the other, as she worked up and down the open "lead" (a narrow channel of water in the ice), close by the shore.

What my thoughts were I leave the reader to judge. I was all but overpowered with joy. I should now hear news of my native home—perhaps of dear friends. I should again mingle with the inner world of civilization, and hear tidings of what was going on in the ever-changing theatre of active and social life at home. I should probably know who had been elected President of the United States, and how my own country progressed in national weal.* This and much more I should learn if I made speed and could get on board before this stranger vessel moved too far away.

Accordingly, I rapidly descended to the encampment, and told Ebierbing and Koodloo what I had seen. Not a moment was lost in getting ready for a walk across the land to the other side. Loaded guns were taken for the purpose of firing a signal, that the vessel might send us a boat ; and away we went, hurrying along as fast as the rugged surface of the ground would permit.

How beautiful was the picture fancy painted in my mind while we were thus hurrying across the island from its south to its north shore. How eagerly I wished we were there, and ready to push off on the ice, if need be, to visit the stranger. What surprise, too, I thought within myself, would be occasioned by our coming from the " dreaded land," especially seeing me, a civilized man, alone with the natives.

But all my pleasant visions and romantic fancies were suddenly and rudely dispelled when we reached the other side, and stood upon a spot near the north shore. No ship—no vessel was there ! Had she disappeared? No. The object upon which I had gazed with such a transport of feeling was indeed there before me, as I had seen it from above ; but what was my disappointment—my utter amazement and chagrin, when I found that the supposed steamer was only a remarkably-shaped portion of the mountain's side ! Never before had I been so completely deceived ; and perhaps, had I had my perspective glass with me, I might have detected the mistake while upon the mountain-top. Yet even now, after the illusion was dispelled, I was astonished at the similitude which nature had here pourtrayed of a steam vessel. The black of that projecting rock, with the white snow apparently standing out apart from the mountain-side to which it belonged, made up a figure so completely like that of a ship, and my change of position at every few steps so magically represented the appearance of repeated tacking, that only the close inspection which I was now making could convince me of the illusion. But it was now dispelled. It was almost cruel, if I might use such a term, to be aroused from my late dream of

* Little did I then dream that my country had been plunged into a cruel civil war !

expected joy to the reality of so great a disappointment. However, so it was; and if anything would have relieved my vexation, it was the blank look of astonishment depicted on the features of my two companions on ascertaining the truth. Strange to say, by the time we had arrived at the spot where the best view of it could be obtained, it looked no more like a vessel than a cow! One glance, and we turned away—I in disgust.

Our journey back was anything but agreeable; but we took it leisurely, and at half-past 1 A.M. of the 11th arrived at our encampment.

In speaking to Ebierbing about the reasons for the Innuits deserting a place which we now had evidence to show was abounding with animal life, he told me that the dread of it could not be removed. It had left upon the minds of all Innuits an impression of horror which descended from parent to child, and was likely to last for a long time. Even he himself would not have come now but for much persuasion and the influence of the civilized white man over the dark races, besides his strong personal attachment to me. As for Koodioo, he had been induced by the example and persuasions of Ebierbing more than by any favourable feelings on his own part. After he had arrived here, it was plain to me he regretted it; and possibly, in his inner soul, "the mysterious ship" may have added to his superstitious feelings concerning the place.

While returning from this trip across Hall's Island, Ebierbing related to me the following anecdote, prefacing it by the simple remark that the breaking away of the sea-ice, and carrying off one or more Innuits is not a rare occurrence. Once two of his people were driven out of Cornelius Grinnell Bay while on the ice sealing. The ice finally brought up against Lady Franklin's Island,* twenty-five miles from the mainland, upon which island the forlorn Innuits landed. Here they lived for several months on ducks, walrus, bears, and seals, which they found there in abundance. They did not make their appearance for months, and were given up as lost. But, to the surprise of every one, they ultimately returned, having effected their escape by means of "floats" made of the skins of seals which they had killed. I may here mention that also, in returning on the before-described vexatious walk, we noticed a wall of stone—moss-covered stone—at the outlet of the lakelet, which was made, as

---

* Named by me in honour of Lady Franklin. Lady Franklin Island is in lat. 62' 55' 30'' N. long. 63° 30' W.

Ebierbing said, by his people that had lived a great many years before, for a hiding-place, to enable them to kill tuktoo as they followed along their path, which was close by. Numerous old bones of this animal we saw by this wall.

On the 11th of June, at noon, I put on a rock a delicately-balanced compass needle, the north pole of which stood on zero. At 12 midnight it was one degree west of zero. At 3·30 A.M. of the 12th it was one degree east of zero point; but more about this in its proper place.

On the same day, the 11th, half a mile north-west, on the top of the mountain in the rear of our camp, I took bearings of various prominent places; and while taking the angle of an island five miles distant to the south, Ebierbing and Koodloo with me, the former, looking around with the glass, suddenly exclaimed, "Ninoo! Ninoo!" pointing, at the same time, in the direction of the very island I was sighting. In an instant Koodloo rushed off to harness up the dogs, and I after him, Ebierbing remaining behind for a moment to watch the bear's movements. Presently I decided upon returning to continue my work and let both the Innuits go in chase. Reascending to the spot I had left, I continued to the northward and westward till I had ascended a still higher mountain, *the table-topped "Mount Warwick" of Frobisher.*

There I remained for hours, with changes of the atmosphere so tantalizing that it vexed me greatly. One moment there was a beautiful sky, the next everything was enveloped in thick fog. So it continued, calm as a summer's day at home, not a cloud in the sky as the fog lifted, the sun shining brightly for a moment, and anon darkened by impenetrable vapour. I was greatly disappointed. I had fixed a capital point by sun to take my angles of various mountains, bays, headlands, &c. but, in consequence of the state of the weather, was obliged to leave my work incomplete.

In descending to a lower point, I distinctly saw *Meta Incognita*, the fog having dispersed in that direction. Also Resolution Island, which bore S. 12° W. (true).

I returned to the camp shortly after, but Ebierbing and Koodloo had not yet returned.

While waiting for the two Innuits, I gathered some fuel, kindled a fire, and filled the tea-kettle to make coffee. Presently I heard the crack of my rifle, and concluded that another seal was killed, little imagining what had actually occurred. But near midnight, when Ebierbing and Koodloo arrived, they told me that not only one of the largest-sized seals (ookgook) was killed, but also the bear. I could hardly believe them. A bear? It was too much to believe. I could readily conceive that they had succeeded with seals, but that they had captured the bear, and without the smallest signs of any struggle, was almost incredible. I could not, therefore, help laughing at Ebierbing as he persisted in the statement; and I said to him, "You are making game of *me*." On the instant he replied, "Come to the sledge (which was only a short distance off) and see." There, true enough, was Ninoo's skin, with portions of the meat; and now we had beef in abundance. The ookgook had been left on the ice, at the edge of the floe by the open water.

Ebierbing told me that they went over to the mountain island where he had first espied the bear, and saw the brute lying down. On their approach he sprung up and darted away. Three of the dogs were immediately let loose by cutting the traces with which they were harnessed to the sledge. After these three had started, the remaining dogs were cast adrift, and soon overtook the others, and assisted in bringing the bear to bay. They barked, bit, struggled, and fought bravely, the bear doing his best to defend himself. Now and then Ninoo would start to run, but the dogs were quickly fast to his stern, turning him round more rapidly than the rudder does a ship under a nine-knot breeze.

The dog and bear fight continued for half an hour, when Ebierbing, getting as favourable an opportunity as he desired, sent the messenger of death to Ninoo's heart.

The bear was very fat, as all polar bears in the neighbourhood of the "deserted land" must be, in consequence of the immense number of seals there. His stomach was filled to its utmost capacity, and, Innuit-like, the two men took care of every portion that was serviceable.

The bear was immediately skinned, and the best portions of the carcass brought away. The rest was left to feast other animals than man. On returning from this bear-hunt, Ebierbing shot the ookgook which he referred to.

Our feast that night was uncommonly good. Some of the fat, with portions of the lean, was well cooked; and when we lay down to rest, I would not wager that our stomachs were not as widely distended as had been that of the defunct Ninoo.

I may here mention that the bear's bladder was inflated and hung up to the pole of our tupic, and, according to Innuit customs, should remain there three days.

Early in the morning of Wednesday, the 12th of June, I was up, and ready for a proposed trip. It had been decided to set out this day on our return to the ship, but I could not think of leaving this interesting region without visiting the utmost extreme of land—the "North Foreland" of Frobisher. Leaving my two companions asleep, I walked off alone. The snow was deep

NORTH FORELAND OF FROBISHER.

and soft, making my travelling laborious. When about half-way, I ascended a hill that overlooks the channel between "Hall's Island" and "Hall's smaller Island." The channel was free from ice save near its west end, close by the little bay of our encampment, and presented an animated picture of life, for seals and aquatic birds in great variety were sporting there. But as only a brief time remained for this journey, I was obliged to hasten on. At length, after a laborious walk, I reached "North Foreland," the goal of my ambition in this pleasant trip.

Here the view was as enchanting as it was extensive. The sea around, as far as the eye could reach, was open; yet much ice, in the various forms of "sconce" pieces, floes, and bergs, was drifting about.

"North Foreland" presented a bold front. As I looked down from its heights (an elevation of several hundred feet), the sea was "playing fantastic tricks," its mighty waves dashing in quick succession against the rocky rampart by which I was shielded, leaping upward as if to meet and greet me, saying, "White man, we saw your namesake here nearly three hundred years ago; *where is he now?*"

Nearly south of North Foreland are three islets, the nearest one-fourth of a mile off shore. The largest is a quarter of a mile long, and is distinguished by a prominent rock that looks like a huge bee-hive, with smaller ones on each side of it. The others are quite small, being respectively about seventy and a hundred and forty fathoms in length. In every direction about here I saw recent traces of reindeer and rabbits, also circles of stones, and other signs of Innuits having lived here long ago.

The following are some of the measurements which I made while on this morning walk: The width of North Foreland (which is the eastern extremity of Hall's Island), measuring it a short distance back from the cliff, is about a quarter of a mile. Hall's Island extends a mile farther eastward than "Hall's smaller island." The latter is eight-tenths of a mile in length.

After spending an hour at this interesting spot, taking bearings of distant objects, and observing the general appearance of the locality, I reluctantly retraced my steps to our encampment, a distance of two miles, where I found on the sledge everything in readiness for our departure.

At 9·19 A.M. we set out on our return to Rescue Harbour. When out on the sea-ice, we stopped by the edge of the floe, next the open water, at the carcass of the ookgook killed by Ebierbing the day before. In the dilemma which followed as to what we should do with it, I proposed that it should be carried to land and buried under heavy stones, supposing that Captain B., then at Cape True with his men, might send a boat's crew round by Frobisher Bay, which was all open water, and get the blubber, and perhaps the meat, and also some of our deposited seals. But Ebierbing assured me that it mattered not what might be the size or the weight of the stones covering it, Ninoo would find out the deposit and rip it up. It was finally concluded to save only the skin. To effect this, they girdled the animal's body, cutting the skin transversely in widths of about five or six inches, and then slipped it off in cylinders, each of which was to be afterward cut spirally, making a long strip of skin, which is of great value for walrus and seal lines, and dog-traces. This ookgook was an object of more than common interest. Though so easily despatched—the rifle ball, on penetrating his skull, causing instant death—yet, as Ebierbing pointed out, it bore numerous marks of wounds received in a conflict with a polar bear. It had had a struggle with its mighty foe, and had escaped.

We did not get ready to proceed on our journey until 12 A.M. We then crossed the floe at the south side of Hudson's Island, taking the same route we had travelled three times before. When we were nearly through Kane's Channel, and while I was examining its shores, having occasions to make some record, I opened the covers of my note-book, and found, to my consternation, that its contents were gone! I knew not what to do. I felt that, if they should not be recovered, most of what were to me the important notes that I had taken on this trip would be useless, owing to the break in my narrative which the loss of these would occasion. My hope of recovering them was indeed slight, for my record had been kept on a few small oblong leaves of paper, slightly stitched together, which the wind might speedily scatter away. Still, I determined to go back and search for them, Ebierbing agreeing to accompany me.

We made our way back over rugged ice and snow by following our own tracks; but the wind, then from the south-east, blew at right angles, and made it less likely that we should succeed. Ebierbing went ahead, a little on one side, and I kept straight on the course by which we had come. Thus we retraced our steps for some three miles, when, to my great joy, I heard Ebierbing shout, " *Ni-ne-va-ha ! Ni-ne-va-ha !* "—I have found it ! I have found it ! And, sure enough, there, in his hands, I saw my little note-book, which he had just picked up.

The distance we had traversed was three and a half miles, so that, in returning to the spot from which we had set out, we had walked full seven miles. This, however, was not of much account in comparison with the value of my note-book.

I had directed Koodloo to proceed with the sledge ; but before we had reached him a furious gale from the north-east broke upon us, accompanied with much snow. This threatened an end to our day's travel, and I therefore determined to encamp as soon as possible.

We traced Koodloo by the sledge-tracks down Allen Young's Bay,* near some sheltering land, and there found him, on the lee side of the sledge, flat on the snow, asleep ! yes, sound asleep, and covered with drift, while the gale was beating around, and roaring almost with a voice of thunder. So thick and fast did the snow come down that we could not see a dozen yards before us. Yet here did Koodloo—as most Innuits can—sleep away as undisturbed by the storm as if in his tent. Here a great danger threatened us. This gale might break up the ice ; and if so, and we were encamped on an island, escape would be impossible, for we had no boat. The wind was so furious that we could hardly stand erect, and already it was tearing up the ice in all directions about the main bay. It was an awkward position, and one that I had anticipated. But it was necessary immediately to prepare some shelter, and accordingly we selected a spot on a point of low land, north of and near Dillon Mountain, where Innuits evidently had erected their tupics very many years before. Bones of seal and walrus, fragments of wood, and circles of stones, showed the dwelling-places of Esquimaux who had lived there before the land became abhorred.

The erection of our tent was a matter of great difficulty. One of us had to stand up before the blast to break its force, another to erect the tupic, and the third to try to make it stand. Placing the covering over the tent-poles was a toil especially arduous. The wind seemed to press with a force of tons. Flap, flap went the canvas, beating us about, and giving us such bruises that several times I thought it impossible to get through with the task. But at length it was accomplished. All the crevices were filled with moss, so as to render the admission of fine snow nearly impossible ; and thus, in the teeth of a remarkably heavy gale, we finally succeeded in getting as much shelter as could be expected under such circumstances. The next day, June 13th, the gale continued with unabated fury to 11 A.M. Most of the time during this storm we had to keep

* Named in honour of Captain Allen W. Young, second in command under M'Clintock, in search of Sir John Franklin in 1857-9. Allen Young's Bay is in lat. 62° 33′ N. long. 64° 14′ W. its east side bounded by Dillon Mountain.

inside the tent; and whenever we did venture out, it was necessary to use great care, lest the force of the wind should throw us down. That the tent stood was a marvel. But stand it did, and gave us shelter until Friday the 14th, about 12 meridian, when we resumed our homeward route.

Our journey was comparatively rapid. We arrived at Sylvia Island at 10 P.M. without any obstacle save in rounding Cape Daly, though the seaward ice was anything but safe; and after

HOMEWARD BOUND—ICE BREAKING UP.

resting and partaking of coffee prepared with a tent-pole for fuel, we made a direct course for the ship. Now came the danger. Everywhere the ice was cracked, or moving, or gone! We carefully pursued our way, literally with fear and trembling. Not for one moment was our footing safe. The thick-ribbed ice was broken into every conceivable form and size, and nothing but the absolute necessity of avoiding detention on the islands would have induced us to venture on the treacherous footing; but it was our only hope under heaven—our only means of escape—and upon it, and across it, we pursued our way.

To add to the dangers of our situation, a thick mist soon settled upon us; and there we were, three men, the dogs, and sledge, on the broken ice, in the middle of a bay wide open to the sea. Even the Innuits were more than usually alarmed, and finally became so confused that they wandered out of the proper course ; and it was only through my insisting that my compass was the best guide that, after going three miles out of our way, we at last arrived safely on board the ship at 10·37 A.M. on Saturday, the 15th of June.

Thankful was I that we met with no serious accident ; and this was the more extraordinary considering our rate of travelling (we were only twenty hours coming from near Dr. Kane's Channel) and the dangerous character of the ice over which we had come.

As an instance of what can be accomplished in securing the means of sustaining life in the arctic regions, I will here give a few particulars bearing upon the subject, and belonging to this particular journey.

We set out with—

20 sea biscuits, weight	5 lbs.
Salt-junk ,, ...	5 ,,
Coffee and pepper, say	1 ,,
Total provisions for the three . . .	11 lbs.
Powder	1 lb.
Balls, in number	30.

1 rifle, 1 gun, 2 seal spears, with lines and harpoons.

We were away ten days, and in that time obtained—

1 polar bear, equal to	1000 lbs.
1 ookgook (largest sized seal)	1500
9 seals	1800
Making a total of	4300 lbs.

—that is, over two tons of fresh meat, besides skins for clothing, and oil for fuel and light.

Most of the meat and blubber we deposited *en cache*, and the ookgook we left on the ice ; but we were obliged to abandon all, excepting a very little blubber, and the small proportion of meat which was consumed by ourselves and the dogs. The skins we saved.

CHAPTER XIX.

On my return, June 15th, 1861, I found Innuit visitors at the ship. The only two men left on board were quite well. I was also much pleased to see that all my own apparel had been put in order, and such as needed it washed by Tookoolito, who had occasionally visited the vessel during my absence, and had thus thoughtfully provided for my comfort.

The following few days I devoted wholly to resting and pre-paring for my long-desired voyage to King William's Land, which I intended to make as soon as I could obtain the means of prosecuting it, and the ice would permit.

On the 17th another heavy gale burst upon us, which con-tinued until the 20th. It blew hard, but there was no danger just now to the ship, for Rescue Harbour was still paved over with thick, solid ice ; yet she trembled through her whole frame, and her masts quivered like reeds. In the outer bay, seaward, the ice was broken into innumerable fragments. On account of the storm, the natives on board, who had come from Cape True, could not return, and those on shore I perceived to be suffering from a general wreck of their habitations. Hardly a tupic was standing. The gale had razed them to the ground.

My late companions, Ebierbing and Koodloo, set out on the 20th sealing, and returned the following day, having secured eight seals, weighing in all about 1,400 pounds. This would have supplied them with food for a long time had they provident habits.

At this time news came by Koojesse from the whaling depôt at Cape True, in Frobisher Bay. All the officers and crew stationed there were well, though still unsuccessful.

As Koojesse was to return as soon as possible, I determined to go with him, and accordingly we set out on the following evening, June 21st.

At 7 P.M. we left the ship, with sledge and a team of eight dogs, including my faithful Barbekark. Our load was light, and we went along over the uncertain ice at three miles an hour. We had a thick fog all the way in crossing Field Bay, and Koojesse, though a capital guide, was evidently taking a wrong course after leaving Rescue Harbour, until I showed him by my compass how we ought to go. By that means we got into the old sledge tracks, marking the course to and fro, and were even with French Head * in two and a half hours from the ship.

On the passage we saw many seals out on the ice, but did not succeed in killing any, though Koojesse made several attempts. . . . At 7·43 P.M. Rescue Harbour time, the dog Merok (brother dog of the notable Barbekark), a good sealer, saw a seal which he had scented some moments previous. Away he darted as fast as his now inspirited companion dogs would allow him. Koojesse at once saw what was up, and set up a peculiar, continued loud cry, in which I joined. The flying dogs, with kummitie, and our noise, so alarmed poor seal that it knew not what to do. The seal had his head over his hole, yet high raised, looking at the motley sight, and listening to the pandemonian sounds, which frightened it near unto death. On we went ; but when the dogs were within a few paces only, the seal regained his senses, and down he went just in time to save his—blubber ! Koojesse said that young seals are often captured by such procedure as this, but seldom old ones.

On arriving near the base of French Head, a little the other side of it, we turned toward Chapell Inlet, intending to cross over the isthmus at its head. The channel by which we had first entered this inlet in the *Rescue* (August 21st, 1860) was now full of hummocks ; we therefore crossed over a neck of land

---

* " French Head " is a prominent headland, south side of Field Bay, and so named to commemorate the death of the Frenchman, which occurred near its base, as related in Chapter XIII. French Head is in lat. 62° 44′ 30″ N. long. 64° 45′ W.

INNUIT STRATEGY TO CAPTURE A SEAL.

perhaps half a mile wide, covered with submerged ice. The floating qualities of the sledge as well as of the load, including ourselves, made our passage by water rapid, though not very comfortable.

We crossed this " pass "—used frequently by the Innuits and the ship's crew in going to and from Cape True—and entered the inlet. Here I found many portions of the ice covered with the melted snows, and in some places the sledge sank deep in the water, much to the annoyance of the dogs as well as to ourselves.

On the way Koojesse again had "talk" with some more seals which we saw, and it was with great interest I watched him. He lay down on one side, and crawled by hitches or jerks toward his victim ; then, as the seal raised its head, Koojesse would stop, and commence pawing with his right hand and foot while he uttered his " seal talk." On this the seal would feel a charm, raise and shake its flippers both " fore and aft," and roll over on its side and back, as if perfectly delighted, after which it would drop its head to sleep ; then Koojesse would hitch, hitch along, till the seal's head would pop up again, which usually occurred every few moments. But Koojesse approached too near, and this broke the charm, allowing the seal to escape, and leaving the disappointed sealer to cry, " *E-e-e-ŭk !* "

The great trouble with the Innuits in this mode of sealing is that they often endeavour to get too near—say within five or seven fathoms—so as to make sure of their aim with a gun or spear, and this alarms their prey.

During our progress up the inlet I observed a very small newly-made igloo, and asked Koojesse what it meant. " *Wich-ou, wich-ou* " (wait, wait), said he in reply, and in a few moments we came alongside. The next instant Koojesse had jumped off the sledge, and with a grab through the snow, drew forth by one of its hind flippers a fine seal that he had killed when on his way up to the vessel.

As we proceeded up the inlet, gradually the low land at its head appeared, and at two in the morning of the 22d we had reached it. From here we turned westward, following the sinu-osities of the coast for two miles, when we struck across the narrow strip of land dividing Chapell Inlet from Frobisher Bay. A few minutes sufficed to find us slowly working along the badly-broken shore-ice ; on that side, the bay itself being wholly free, except a few bergs. Occasionally the dogs went *pell-mell* down, and over the steep broken ice ; then the sledge would butt against a perpendicular hummock, sending us forward, very much like a stone out of a sling; but we got along without serious mishap, and arrived at Cape True at half-past two in the morning.

As my eye first caught sight of the whale depôt I was quite astonished. I had formed no conception of its being such a busy-looking place. There were numerous and thickly-crowded habitations, white men and Innuit tents, mills (*toy* wind-mills, and a liberty-pole, holding high to the breeze an extemporized emblem of our country! People were already up and about, and every pinnacled rock had some person upon it to witness our approach. The dogs soon landed us on the rocks which formed the "public square" of the town, and quickly, from one and all, I received a hearty welcome. It seemed almost like home again to behold so many friendly and familiar faces. Several Innuits were here, most of whom I well knew, and they were delighted to see me.

Immediately on my arrival I was invited by the captain and officers into their quarters, and had an excellent breakfast put before me. Of course one of the first inquiries was about my trip to and return from the "dreaded land." This I soon answered by giving an account of what I had done, and then, my morning meal ended, I took a walk along the beach. Everywhere I found fragments of limestone in abundance, and my pockets were soon filled with specimens, which I brought home.

One object of my visit to the whale depôt was to see about preparing for my departure to King William's Land, and to consult Captain B. respecting it. The boat promised me had to be made ready, and therefore I at once entered upon the subject with him.

The Captain said that he had been out in this bay (Frobisher) several times since coming over, and that he had been much impressed with the subject of my making my trip or voyage this summer, as expected, in a whale-boat. He thought it his duty to open the matter to me at once, announcing the conclusion he had come to, painful to him and to me. The boat which I had had made in the States, especially designed and made for my expedition to King William's Land, was a suitable one for me, but a whale-boat was unfit. He continued to say that I had not any more of an outfit, provision, &c. than I should take, but that, with the crew necessary, I could not possibly carry more than a very small proportion of what I had. He found that with the boat's crew, and the three line-tubs each boat had, no additional weight could be added to navigate in such waters as he knew I would be obliged to go in, in getting to the point of my destination.

This, of course, was a serious matter with me. If the loss of my expedition boat, which was well planned and strongly made, had really taken from me the proper, the only judicious means of carrying out my purpose of going to King William's Land, then I must delay—I must lose one year in returning home, and prepare again for the voyage that I am still determined to make, *God willing.*

Among the Innuits staying at the whale depôt was the woman *Puto,* mother of the semi-white child. This poor woman was very badly off, her husband being dead, and she had but scant means of providing for herself and offspring. Seeing her sad condition, I gave her several trinkets, and, in addition, a box of 100 percussion caps. This latter present caused her to weep for joy. She knew not how enough to thank me. With them she could trade among her people for many conveniences she wanted. Anything in the way of ammunition is thought more of by the Innuits than almost any other articles that could be named.

At this time the weather was fine, and the view of Kingaite, with its miles and miles of mountain wall, its glaciers, and its snows, was grand indeed. More than ever was I desirous of exploring that coast; and I thought that, even if nothing else could be done, I might possibly examine some of the places made famous by Frobisher's voyages in 1576, '7, and '8. "Bear Sound" was but a short distance to the eastward, and the second day after my arrival at the whale depôt, I took with me "Captain" (Kokerjabin's youngest son), and walked toward it. But he proved only a hindrance to me. I had to go full fifteen miles to reach a point of land not more than two and a half miles in a direct line. I was obliged to make for the head of Chapell Inlet by first wading through some soft, wet snow, that covered shore-ice and the land on my way. Then I had to make a long circuit around some stones and rocks, and afterward ascend hill after hill, going through valleys full of snow soft and deep enough to cover my whole body. But wherever I went, small pieces of limestone were in abundance, even to the very mountain-tops.

At length I arrived at my destination on the west side of Bear Sound. There—beside those waters, on whose shores

Frobisher and his men had laboured for the mineral wealth which he believed he had found there—I had my noon repast, my Innuit companion sharing it with me. Resting awhile, I forgot my youthful attendant, while contemplating the scene around me. Presently I rose to return, and missed "Captain." I called; no reply. Where had he gone? There was a steep precipice close by, and I became alarmed lest he had fallen over it. I therefore instantly sought for him, and after some moments found his tracks. He had left me without a word, intending to go by a more direct, but, as I thought, dangerous course to the depôt. I followed him, and we returned together, arriving at the tents much fatigued.

While I was stopping at Cape True the boats frequently went to get fuel from the scattered remains of the *Traveller* before mentioned. The shore was strewed with portions of the wreck, which would serve for many years for fuel for ships' companies occupied as the *George Henry's* was at the whaling depôt.

The crew of the *George Henry* were at that time living "in clover." They had plenty of ducks, duck-eggs, seal, walrus, &c. and whenever they wanted a supply they had only to go and take what Nature here so plentifully furnished. On one of these occasions (June 24th) I accompanied a party that went "duck-egging." It consisted of two whale-boats, manned by whites and Innuits, under command of Charles Keeney and A. Bailey. I went with the latter, leaving the whale depôt early in the morning, and striking right across a little bight to the west entrance of Bear Sound.

On entering this sound I was surprised at the velocity and singular movements of the tides. As we advanced the tide was ebbing, and running swiftly up toward Field Bay. But when we had reached Ellis Island,* the movement of the tidal waters appeared to be reversed, and they were throwing themselves furiously about. Eddies, and whirlpools, and mill-races were there running and whirling around in the wildest and most fantastic way, carrying on their foaming surface small bergs, "sconce" pieces, and ice fragments of all shapes, in utter disregard of each other. When the tide turned, these masses came whirling back, as if madly bent on heaping destruction where-

---

* A prominent, bold rock island, west side of Bear Sound, about one-sixth of a mile in diameter, three miles from Field Bay, and named after John W. Ellis, of Cincinnati, Ohio. "Ellis Island" is in lat. 62° 32' N. long. 64° 45' W.

ever they could. This scene in Bear Sound was singularly grand
and striking.

As to egging and duck-hunting, I can say no more about it
now. The ducks were very numerous, flying over our heads in
every direction. They were in the water drifting with the
swiftly-running tide, on the ice, and on nearly every one of the
numerous islands we passed. Wherever we saw a great many
upon or around an island, we visited it for eggs.

SCALING AN ICE COLLAR IN BEAR SOUND.

The first island we pulled to was one in the midst of a
sweeping, driving tide, so that it seemed to defy all human
exertions to approach it; yet, after "a long pull, a strong pull,
and a pull altogether," we conquered. The boat was taken round
to the opposite side of the island from that where the tide struck
it, and though the water rolled and tumbled as if mad, we
managed by a plan of our own to get upon the top of the magnificent "ice-collar" that engirdled the island.

This was the first time in my life that I saw eider-ducks' nests, and consequently the first occasion in which I aided in abstracting the large, luscious eggs. In ten minutes four of us gathered six dozen, and at another island, in twenty minutes, sixteen dozen and five. The eggs taken are replaced by fresh ones, as the ducks lay every two or three days. Many ducks were shot, but, owing to the swift tide, only a few were obtained. The rest were swept away.

In speaking of the "ice-collars" surrounding the islands, I may mention that if they had been simply perpendicular the difficulty in mounting them would not have been so great; but they projected over from ten to thirty feet, and when the tide had fallen some twenty-four feet it was no slight task to surmount them. We managed it in some cases by extending two of our long oars from the boat to the top, thus forming a substitute for a ladder.

Many of the islands in Bear Sound were locked together by natural ice-bridges, several of these being arched in a most remarkable manner.

We approached to within three miles of Sylvia Island, the same on which I and my Innuit companions had encamped on our late journey to the "dreaded land," and I could not but view it in a most friendly way when I remembered how its warm, dry rocks gave us a good bed and protection from the storms.

Our excursion lasted some hours, and we returned to the tupics, both boats well laden with eggs. The total acquisition of our two boats' crews was one hundred dozen eggs, and five ducks. An eider-duck egg is nearly twice the size of a hen's.

At this time Captain B. was absent with two boats a short distance up the bay, "prospecting" for whales. He returned on the 28th of June, during a fierce storm of wind and rain, and he informed me that the trip back was made under most unfavourable circumstances. The previous night had been passed on an island above Evictoon, the only shelter obtained from the storm being that which their boats' sails afforded when put up as a tent. His own crew suffered greatly from the cold; but the Innuits with him, not finding sufficient room inside the tent, went out and lay down under the lee of some projecting rocks! *They* rested and slept well, while the *white men* could hardly keep themselves, as they said, from being frozen.

On the evening of Friday, the 28th of June, having spent seven days at Cape True, I purposed starting back the next day for the vessel. An extract from my journal of that date I will here introduce :—

"To-morrow I accompany Captain B. back to the *George Henry*. He goes with the expectation of remaining there until the vessel is liberated, when he intends to return to this bay, and cruise around awhile, and if unsuccessful, to return to Field Bay, or proceed to Cornelius Grinnell Bay. Two boats' crews are to follow in a few days, while two remain here (Frobisher Bay) for a little while, to continue cruising for whales."

Here follows another entry in my journal, made just before leaving the whaling depôt :—

"*Saturday, June 29th*, 1861.—I soon start for home—that is, set out for the vessel. Captain B. and I are to have one sledge for ourselves and our traps, and will have Koojesse for dog-driver. Charley, the good-hearted Innuit, is to take another team along, to convey the clothes of two of the *George Henry's* men—one the carpenter, a Portuguese, and young Smith, who are to go along.

"Puto and Miner's wife have been mending my *kum-ings* (native boots) this morning, that I may go dry-shod to the vessel, as we anticipate watery travelling."

At 8 A.M. of the 29th we left Cape True, and at 6 P.M. arrived at French Head. As we passed "French Head," where poor John Brown had met his death a little over three months previous, we had a look at the spot. Lo! there were his remains just as we had left them, except that the foxes or bears had eaten part of his skin clothing. His corpse was untouched! As for the monument we had erected over him, *that* had melted away, and soon the ice beneath his body would melt away also, and lower him into his ocean grave.

The journey back to the ship was very difficult. In many places pools of water and broken ice led to the apprehension that no passage would be found; and nearly the whole way we had to walk almost knee-deep through slush and water covering the sea-ice. But at length, about midnight, we arrived on board, and soon threw ourselves down to rest, after a most fatiguing journey of sixteen hours.

Four days later was the Fourth of July, when eighty-five years ago the Declaration of American Independence was made. Soon after nine the previous night all turned in, agreeing to be on deck a few minutes before twelve, midnight. Sleep stole so heavily upon us, that it was 1 o'clock A.M. when Morgan came to my berth and called me. A few moments sufficed to find a company, armed and equipped as the law (the *George Henry's*) directs, ready for action. Some of the company were, as they leaped from their blankets, in stocking-feet and drawers. Nevertheless, they had willing hands and patriotic hearts, wide mouths and deep-toned throats, therefore they *"passed muster."* The signal was given by me, and then followed cheer upon cheer. The ensign was hoisted, while we saluted it with a round of cheers and sulphurous fire.

After a capital dinner, an old cast-away gun, that had been lying about the deck, was filled to the brim with powder, the charge hammered down, and the barrel plugged to the muzzle. The stock had been ripped off in the morning by the Innuits, leaving only the barrel. It was now taken far out on the ice, placed on a pure white bed, and fired. One grand explosion filled the air, and the old gun was shattered into innumerable fragments, some flying over the vessel, others mounting high into the air, and one piece going as far as Cooper's Island, a quarter of a mile off, where it was afterward picked up.

Such was our celebration of Independence Day, 1861. The same afternoon I visited Cooper's Island, and, with chisel and hammer, dug out some of the " black ore," such as was discovered by Frobisher's expedition of 1578, with which many of his ships were laden. This ore attracts and repels the magnetic needle about like iron. It is very heavy.

On the 6th of July I went to Whale Island for the purpose of looking seaward, that I might see the state of the ice and consider the probability of the ship becoming free. It was only about six miles to the open water—the sea. Good prospect, therefore, of soon being entirely free, All the ice, except that around the ship, where islands blocked up the passages, had drifted away, and hope rose strong within us that we should soon be able to make sail from Rescue Harbour, where the vessel had lain so long.

Another island (*Look-out* Island) I found wholly destitute of snow, and vegetation was quite luxuriant upon it. Grasses and flowers looked truly beautiful when contrasted with the bay and snow-covered mountains around.

On the 7th of July we were visited by the first *musquitoes* of the season ; and, from the torment they gave me, I was strongly reminded of my sufferings at Holsteinborg the previous year, and also had a taste of what would probably come.

Another arrival this day was Ugarng and his wives. He was loaded with the spoils of a successful reindeer hunt, and, in addition, had killed a *white* whale in Cornelius Grinnell Bay. He and several more Innuits went off to the whale depôt to see what prospects existed there for hunting or fishing, but he did not remain long. Upon his return he determined to revisit the place he had lately left.

Ugarng had great influence among his people, and I have often thought he was not a man to be wholly trusted. Indeed, I sometimes felt that nothing ever done for him would cause a grateful return. He was a bold, successful, and experienced hunter, and, as such, was frequently engaged by the whalers he encountered; but little dependence could be placed upon him. The strongest agreement would be instantly set at nought whenever he saw anything more likely to conduce to his own interest.

In the present case Ugarng was using all his powers of persuasion to induce every Innuit to leave our locality and go with him. What his real motive was I cannot say; but it is probable that now, when there was abundance to be had by hunting and sealing, he—who disliked the restraints of civilization—wanted to go farther away, and to take along all his friends, relatives, and acquaintances, so as to be perfectly and absolutely free. He tried every means to induce Ebierbing and Tookoolito to go with him, and for a time there was some hesitation on their part about it; but their attachment to me prevailed, and neither of them would consent to go. A general migration, however, did take place. Many of the Innuits accompanied Ugarng; and I afterward heard that several others, as Annawa, Artarkparu, and all belonging and known to them, went away about the same time from the whaling depôt (where a few of the ships' crews still remained to look for whales), taking their course up Frobisher Bay.

Ugarng's party consisted of his two wives, Kunniu and Punnie; infant, Me-noun; nephew, Eterloong; and his aged mother, Ookijoxy Ninoo, besides Johnny Bull and his wife Kokerzhun, Bob and his wife Polly, Blind George and his daughter Kookooyer, and, lastly, E-tu the *wifeless*.

About the time of leave-taking an incident occurred that especially deserves to be recorded. There was an Innuit young man named *E-tu*, who had lately joined the natives from some other place. This Etu I had noticed as somewhat singular in his ways, and remarkable in his appearance. He was much under the protection or rule of Ugarng, and seemed to be his willing follower.

Now Ugarng wanted little Ookoodlear (cousin of Ebierbing and niece of Ugarng) to marry this Etu, but she unhesitatingly expressed her dislike to the proposal.

On the day of Ugarng and his company's departure, I was on shore to bid them all farewell.

I went into Ebierbing's tupic, and there found Tookoolito busy in attending to her friend Kokerzhun's departure. These two women were strong friends, and the separation for what would probably be a long time was evidently painful; but I saw some one else also much affected. Little Ookoodlear was weeping as if her heart would break, and, on inquiry, I ascertained it was because Ugarng wanted to take her away and marry her to Etu. So great was her dislike to the young man, that nothing but force would make her his wife.

Ebierbing, seeing the wretchedness of her mind on the subject, went, in company with Koodloo, to Etu, and told him that the girl was yet too young to marry, and that, moreover, she did not like him. This explanation had some effect, and Ookoodlear was allowed to remain behind, on Ebierbing declaring that he and his wife would be her protectors.

I heard a most extraordinary account of this Etu. It seems that, in consequence of something that happened to his mother before he was born, the poor infant came into the world marked over with snow-white spots and black spots, just like a *kou-oo-lik*, a large, spotted kind of seal. The father, looking upon this spotted child as a monster—a living curse in his family— determined to get rid of him, and accordingly conveyed the boy to *Ki-ki-tuk-ju-a*, *i.e.* Long Island, called by me Brevoort Island,* the southern point of which is Cape Murchison.† This island was quite destitute of means of subsistence, and, to appearance, the poor boy was left to perish of starvation. Strange to say, however, Etu lived on. He succeeded in catching partridges *with his hands*, an act never before or since known to have been done by Innuits. Thus the summer passed on, and winter approached. Still he lived, subsisting upon whatsoever he could find in the shape of food, a wild hermit-boy, on a solitary, almost

* So named after J. Carson Brevoort, of Brooklyn, New York. This is a very long and prominent island south of the cape, on the west side of the entrance to Northumberland Inlet; its southern cape— Cape Murchison —is nearly on a parallel with the north entrance to Cornelius Grinnell Bay.

† Named after Sir Roderick I. Murchison, of London, England. Cape Murchison, the south extreme of Brevoort Island, is in lat. 63° 13′ N. long. 63° 55′ W.

unapproachable island, far from his fellow-beings. Release came to him in the following manner :—

One day a party of Innuits visited the island, and, to their astonishment, saw this young child standing upon a rock looking at them. He was like a statue, and they, knowing the place to be uninhabited, could hardly tell what to think of it. At length they went towards him, and he, seeing them kindly disposed, at once rushed into their arms, and was thus saved from the cruel death intended for him by his inhuman father.

Since then he had grown to manhood, being, when I saw him, about twenty-five years old. He had had *three* wives, none of which remained to him. The first was accidentally drowned ; the second was taken away by her mother ; and the third—her fate I never learned. His intended fourth, Ookoodlear, who was only about thirteen years old, escaped in the way I have mentioned.

Etu's fortune was a hard one. Few liked him. He seemed to be *tabooed* from his youth, and as if always destined to be an outcast, because Nature had put marks upon his body, making him to differ from others of his kind. Whether it was the knowledge of this isolation that made him a lazy and indifferent hunter, I cannot say ; but certain it is, such was the character he had, and it redounds to the credit of Ugarng that he gave the poor fellow the hand of friendship in the way he did.

On Wednesday morning, the 17th of July, 1861, we were delighted to find that our ship had broken from her eight months' imprisonment during the past night, and now swung to her chains in the tidal waters of Rescue Harbour. But it was only in a pool she was free. Ice still intervened between our anchorage and the main bay, and we could do nothing but wait yet longer with whatever patience we could command. I myself was getting quite impatient. Time was passing on, and no chance yet offered for my going away on one or other of my intended explorations. What could I do? I was, at times, as if crazy; and only a walk on some island, where I could examine and survey, or a visit to my Innuit friends, helped to soothe me. But the reader will feel little interest in all this; I will therefore pass on to some other incidents of my voyage.

Ebierbing had been out one day with dogs and sledge where the ice was still firm, when suddenly a seal was noticed ahead. In an instant the dogs were off toward the prey, drawing the sledge after them at a marvellous rate. The seal for a moment acted as if frightened, and kept on the ice a second or two too long, for just as he plunged, " *Smile,*" the noblest-looking, best leader, seal, and bear dog I ever saw, caught him by the tail and flippers. The seal struggled violently, and so did dog *Smile,* making the sledge to caper about merrily; but in a moment more the other dogs laid hold, and aided in dragging the seal out of his hole on to the ice, when *Smile* took it wholly in charge. The prize was secured this time wholly by the dogs.

On the 18th we had an excellent supper of *fresh* fish, caught by the Innuits with spears and hooks among the ice cracks ; and almost daily something fresh was added to our food.

At this time most of the ship's crew were again at the whaling depôt, cruising in every direction for whales. Indeed, Mate Rogers and some of the men had been left there to keep a look-out when the captain came away, to see about getting the vessel round, and frequent communication had, as usual, been maintained.

DOG "SMILE" CAPTURES A SEAL.

On the 23d it was necessary to send a supply of sundries to the company there, and a boat's crew were despatched, I accompanying them.

As the ice still hung together between the ship and open water in the bay, the boat was lashed upon a sledge drawn by dogs, my favourite Barbekark being one, and away we started, arriving at the sea-edge of the ice in about two hours' time. There we launched the boat, and were soon bounding along upon the sparkling waves toward Lupton Channel. Many seals were seen bobbing their heads above water ; and, as we entered among the islands within the channel, ducks were to be seen in every direction, some flying, some in the water, and some on the islands. They were in such numbers that, when above us, they almost darkened the air. Nearly all were *king* ducks (males), their mates being engaged in domestic affairs at home—sitting—while the "lords of the house" were gathering food for them.

In passing through the channel and Bear Sound the tide was favourable, and swept us along with great rapidity. Occasionally we were in a mill-race of waters, and it required much care to navigate the boat.

At a quarter past 4 P.M. we reached the whaling depôt, distant about thirty miles, having been eleven hours coming from the ship.

We found the officers and men all well and in good condition. They had lived on ducks, duck-eggs, seal, walrus, and venison, which they had in abundance, but they were much disheartened at their poor success in whaling. Not a whale had been caught since the past fall. Walrus in any numbers could be obtained, and many had been secured for their skins and tusks; but the main object of the voyage had as yet been a failure.

With reference to the walrus, Mr. Rogers told me that one day, when out cruising for whales, he went, with two boats and crews, half way across Frobisher Bay, and then came to an iceberg one hundred feet above the sea, and, mounting it, with a spy-glass, took a look all around. Whales there were none; but walrus— "Why," to use his figurative but expressive words, "there were millions out on the pieces of ice, drifting with the tide—walrus in every direction—millions on millions."

On their way back, Mr. Lamb, in charge of the second boat, had a fight with some walrus in the following manner. Approaching a piece of ice on which some of these creatures were basking, he attacked one of them, whereupon all the rest immediately rushed toward the boat, and vigorously set upon him and his crew. For a time it seemed necessary to fly for safety; but all hands resisted the attack, and would have got off very well, but that one of the walrus herd pierced the boat's side with his tusks, and made the invaders retreat to repair damages. Mr. Lamb had to drag his boat upon an ice-floe near by, and stuff in oakum to stop a serious leak thus caused. Finally he succeeded, though with some difficulty, in getting back, and thus ended his encounter with a shoal of walrus.

With reference to Frobisher Bay, I may here mention that, in taking a look with my glass from "Flag-staff Hill," adjoining this whaling depôt, and sweeping around from the south-east extreme of Meta Incognita toward the land I recently visited (the *dreaded land*), I was astonished to see, just on the horizon, what appeared to be islands stretching nearly across. One of the Innuits (Sharkey) told me that he had been to those islands, and that his people sometimes made a passage across the entrance of the bay by starting on the Kingaite side, and then striking from one island to the other, by way of *Too-jar-choo-ar* (Resolution Island), until able to make the distance (avoiding the dreaded district) to the place where we then were—Cape True. Years ago reindeer were very numerous on those islands, but at last the moss failed and they all died. Their horns and bones are to be found scattered all over the place. Polar bears are plentiful there.

I was sorry to find several of my Innuit friends at this place very sick from the complaint that was introduced to their race when first brought into contact with civilization, viz. consumption. Sharkey's wife was rapidly declining. Her bleeding at the lungs had left her white as the driven snow, and poor as fleshless bones could be.

The following incident will serve to show how fond some of the Innuits are of *sweets*, as well as of fat or blubber.

Mr. Rogers was carrying along over the rocks a jug of " las-as-ses," as the Innuits pronounce *molasses*. All at once the bottom of the jug dropped out, and the contents splashed down, his hand flying up as if an electric shock from a strongly-charged battery had been given him. Quick as it was noised about, the spot sweetened over with the " lasasses " was not unlike a sugar hogshead near a bee-hive on a warm sunny day. The Innuits, men, women, and children, crowded round it to lick up the sweet mixture !

After arranging all matters that the Captain had asked my attention to, and enjoying a good rest in one of the officers' tents, we started on our way back to the ship, taking with us several saddles of venison, half a dozen brace of ducks, and other good things for those on board.

When about half way through Bear Sound, the commotion and roar of the waters was such as no person who has not witnessed the like could form an adequate idea of. Small icebergs were swept along, roundabout, this way and that way, at a speed of full eight knots an hour. On one side piles of ice were carried swiftly to the south, and on the other side ice was sweeping in the contrary direction. The turmoil and confusion seemed almost demoniac. At length the surging ceased for awhile, and then it began again, everything to appearance being in readiness for a race up toward Lupton Channel. And so it continued, obliging us to ply the long steering-oar briskly to keep the boat in its course, as we were borne along with the rapid tide.

When we got out of the Channel a fresh breeze helped us onward until we came near "French Head," when it failed. Here all the ice had disappeared and gone down the bay, thus, at last, carrying to the great sea the mortal remains of poor John

FRENCH HEAD.

Brown, there soon depositing them to rest quietly beneath the waters that link together people of all nations of the earth. He now lies buried in the world's great grave-yard. Nature, however, marks the spot where he must have fought valiantly the last battle of life. The bluff stands out boldly to view whenever any one may be navigating in or near Field Bay. "*French Head*" is a monument as enduring as the everlasting mountains.

At 4 P.M. we reached the ice-floe, and there re-lashed the boat upon a sledge sent forward ready for our arrival. The ice was very much worse than it had been the previous morning, and we fell through it in many places. Finally we reached the ship at 8 P.M. greatly fatigued with the laborious exertions we had made.

At this time the *heat* was almost overpowering. On the 25th of July, at 2 P.M. the mercury stood at 95° in the sun, and no work could be done except when we were clad in the lightest garments. What a contrast to the period only a few weeks past, when my reindeer furs were needed.

The day after my return to the ship I visited the tupics on shore, and took sundry articles of my apparel for Tookoolito and the other women to put in order for me, as they generally did. On the way I had far more difficulty than I anticipated. Two of the sailors had brought me in a boat as far as the broken ice would permit, and then I proceeded toward the shore by moving from one piece of ice to another. But it soon became evident that there was much dangerous work ahead. The ice around the shores and about the harbour and bay was now disappearing like dew before the morning sun. I was indeed surprised to find the changes that had taken place within one day. Several wide chasms between boulders of shore-ice had to be crossed, and my leaps were often made with more or less danger of getting a downfall into the briny deep. Now and then I was obliged to throw my pack in advance, and then go back for a good run, so as to make my flying leap sure to carry me over the yawning gulf. For a full hour did I work thus to accomplish a distance of perhaps twenty rods. Now I would be upon a small piece of ice, pushing along as though it were a boat. Soon as I reached another piece I would have to run on to it; thence to another, leaping cracks and channels that would certainly have made my hair stand on end at an earlier period of my life. At length I reached the last piece between myself and the shore. It was divided from the beach by a breach of some considerable distance; but there was no alternative; leap it I must. Therefore I first threw my pack ashore, which went into a pool of water on the rocks, and then, with a good run, made a great spring, which fortunately just carried me on to *terra firma*.

Many of these occurrences are common enough in the life of an arctic voyager; but I mention this one as a passing incident, and to show what was the state of the ice around our ship at the time we were all so desirous of moving her.

In the evening I got on board again without much difficulty, as a boat came for me to firm ice, which I had gained.

The following morning, July 27th, all the ice about the vessel had nearly gone, though there was still some heavy pieces intervening between us and the outer bay. But what especially causes me to remember this day was the sudden disappearance of the wrecked *Rescue*. On looking toward Cooper's Island, where her hull had remained for so many months, we were surprised to find it gone. The waters had floated it away, and, for a moment, we fancied nothing more of the famous schooner

THE GHOST OF THE "RESCUE."

would again be seen, unless away toward or on the great sea. But shortly afterward, on visiting Whale Island, close by, we saw that the *Rescue* had drifted off with the tide, and had got into the narrow channel of open water that then surrounded the island.

The *Rescue* was doomed to wander about "like a ghost"—as some of the men said—for days. By the alternate ebb and flow of the tide, she was carried seaward, to be brought back to her old place, then to be carried out again. Then back again she came, dancing from place to place, like the ever-changing ice-sconces surrounding her. She made the circuit of another island south-east of Cooper's, and again came near to us ; and so in and out, dancing here and moving there, the poor *Rescue* played about us, until at length her very presence seemed to cause a superstitious dread. This was especially so when another day, and yet an-other, passed on, and still our vessel could not be moved away.

As an illustration of this superstitious feeling among the seamen, it may be mentioned that the want of success attending the *George Henry* in whaling was attributed to the circumstance of bringing the *Rescue* with them as a tender. Some said she had never been anything but a drawback since first built, and that she had nearly caused the loss of numbers of lives ; now she seemed to hang about them as an omen of ill luck—*as a ghost !*

At 8 P.M. of the 27th of July the breeze freshened up strongly from W. and W.N.W. Soon the ice yet in the vicinity of the vessel began to move, and in heavy patches came toward the ship. All the crew had retired to rest, except the captain and myself, but the men were quickly called up to ward off the threatened danger. On came the ice, directly toward the ship. A portion struck the cable, and strained it till the metal tinkled like steel. Fortunately, a projecting point of Cooper's Island partly arrested the entire floe of ice, and thus broke the shock ; yet the strain upon the ship's cable was intense. Men were ordered to get over the bow on to the floe with chisels and other implements, to cut away that portion pressing upon the chains, which was done after some hard work. But we fully believed the ship was dragging her anchor, and at this precise moment, lo ! the immortal *Rescue* was seen, like the ghost in Hamlet, emerging from the mist, and moving on from near Cooper's Island straight to the very spot where she had been at anchor when overtaken by the hurricane which had wrecked her. The instant she was discovered, an exclamation burst from the crew that the very acme of bad-luck seemed to have reached them ! They never could do anything until that curse was out of sight ! Indeed, some of the expressions used about her were much stronger, and certainly, to others less interested in the *Rescue* than myself, her appearance so often, and apparently in such mystic form, was enough to cause annoyance, if not actual superstitious dread.

All through that night great vigilance was needed in guarding the vessel, for the ice pressed tremendously upon her, and in the morning men were again at work cutting the floe. Finally they succeeded in separating a part that strained most upon the cable, and thus we escaped the greatest danger.

On July 28th, in the morning, I went over to Whale Island and brought Tookoolito on board, to continue the work begun some time previous of getting up a vocabulary of the Innuit of these regions for collation with Parry's, compiled on his second voyage up Hudson's Straits. Tookoolito was very serviceable in this. She gave me valuable explanations of words, and also expeditiously interpreted into her own tongue portions of the "Progressive Reader" which I had previously presented to her.

At this time the men that had remained at the whaling depôt were summoned on board the ship, and on the evening of the 28th it was reported that some of them were coming. I went on deck, and asked one of the sailors, whom we called "Spikes," who was then on watch, where they were. He replied, He didn't exactly know, but thought they might be that way—pointing to an island south-east of us—for he heard voices in that direction. I listened, and then gave a shout. But my first idea was that Spikes had been mistaken, as the echoes of Innuit voices on Whale Island were often heard. Soon, however, I was satisfied. An answering shout from white men came back to mine. A boat, therefore, was soon manned by Smith, myself, Spikes, Bill, and young Smith, and away we went in the direction whence the sound had come.

We made a quick passage down the harbour as far as open water permitted ; then we struck into broken ice, where our progress became slower. But, by the good steering of the elder Smith, we still pushed on, oftener using the ice for our oars to rest against than water. We passed the "Ghost," which was now floating with the tide ; and her bow—or so much of it as was above water—became a resisting medium on which the starboard oars of our boat found hold in several heavy pulls.

Presently we came to a desolate island, and on it we found Morgan, Bailey, Keeney, and Ebierbing, who had come from a point some three miles below, and made their way there by trudging over ice, ferrying across spaces of water on drifting ice, wading, &c. This party was but a small portion of the one that left the whaling depôt in the morning for the ship. The remainder had stopped for the night at a point below, where, owing to the ice, the boats they had with them could not be taken farther.

Morgan and his company, however, felt determined to try and reach the ship that night, but had run great risks in so doing. The ice between the islands below was all in a disruptured state, and only by great daring did they succeed in getting to the place where we found them. In making across several channels their only way was to find a fragment of floating ice, place themselves upon it, and paddle over by a small piece of board which they found. We succeeded in getting this party to the vessel; and, finally, Mates Rogers, Gardiner, and Lamb, each with his boat and crew, also arrived, though not without great difficulty on account of the ice which they encountered on their way. And thus the whole ship's company were safe on board.

The information given me by Mr. Rogers I found very interesting. It was as follows:

On the day I left the whaling depôt, Rogers—who, with an Innuit crew, had gone up Frobisher Bay—arrived at the native settlement beyond Evictoon. Here they found Samson, Ook-goo-al-loo, their families, and the old lady Innuits, whom I met the previous April. For some time Rogers did not recognise Samson, though well acquainted with him, for he was completely changed in appearance, and not much more than a mere skeleton. He was informed that, some weeks before, a little pimple made its appearance near Samson's left breast. It received a scratch. Inflammation followed, and this had increased so much that his very vitals were being eaten out. The sight was horrible! No Innuit of Rogers' crew dared behold it. Nothing was done, or could then be done, to alleviate the poor fellow's distress or arrest the progress of his disease, which was evidently, as Rogers thought, a cancer. It was neglected, and the dirt, tuktoo hair, &c. that were allowed to accumulate within it, irritated the sore and hastened its progress.

Ookgooalloo was also confined to his tupic, unable to sit up, and spitting blood. And the other Innuits seemed to be all starving, only one man being in a condition to go out and hunt for food. On the following morning Rogers started for an island a little farther up, and arrived there at 11 A.M. While there he visited a place in which, he was informed by the natives, a good harbour could be found; and he saw that such was the case for small vessels, but not for the *George Henry*, as only eight feet water, and this over black sandy bottom, could be found. He remained an hour there, and then struck a course direct down the bay for the whaling depôt. The wind, however, came against him with so great force that he was obliged to make for Samson's settlement, and remain there for that night. Next morning he again set out, and on the way his Innuit crew killed many ducks, which they ate *raw*. Rogers was offered some, but he said to me, " I could not go *that*." He arrived at the whaling depôt, at Cape True, about 11 P.M. on the 26th, and finally returned to the ship as already stated.

The return of the *George Henry's* crew on board, and the breaking up of the ice, were the signal for the ship's departure to another place, to try anew the chances of whaling ; but with all relating to such work, except where it is connected with my own personal labours, I have nothing to do. My task was that of research, exploration, and discovery, and not to aid in the capture of whales, albeit that, in itself, was an exciting and adventurous occupation. I had come to the North for another and, to me, a more glorious purpose. When, therefore, the time approached for the vessel to move away, the hour had also come for me to leave her and take up my abode with the natives, as I had originally proposed. What my plans and intentions were, as noted and recorded at the time, I will now proceed to show.

It was now the 28th of July, 1861. In two or three days the vessel was to leave Rescue Harbour to cruise for whales. I intended, therefore, to make a boat voyage to explore the so-called " Frobisher Strait," which had been proved to me, by Innuit testimony,* in the fall of 1850, while in Rescue Harbour, to be a bay. The course I purposed to pursue was down and across Field Bay to Lupton Channel and Bear Sound, and thence along the northern coast of the misnamed " strait " to its termination, and thence, if possible, down Kingaite (*Meta Incognita*) side ; then crossing over to " North Foreland," and returning to Field Bay by way of the south side of the " dreaded land," and thence through Bear Sound and Lupton Channel. The boat which I now had was not as good by any means as I should have wished, but I was obliged to make it answer. My crew were to be all Innuits. I had arranged for Ebierbing and Tookoolito, Koodloo and Jennie his wife, and probably Jennie, sister of Ebierbing, to be of the party, with Suzhi also, who was likely to be exceedingly useful, in consequence of her great strength, notwithstanding her weight, which was not less than 200 pounds. I expected to be gone two months, at the end of which time, if the vessel should still be hereabouts, I would again rejoin her to return to the States. I earnestly hoped to succeed in accomplishing all this. God willing, I was resolved it should be done.

* See page 104 and the Sketch Chart page 105.

The vessel was expected to sail on the 30th. I therefore gathered up some of the things I designed taking with me on my boat voyage, and carried them on shore to Ebierbing's tupic.

On Tuesday, the 30th, A.M. preparations were made to weigh anchor. The time had come for me to leave. I placed such other things as I required in the old, rotten, leaky, and ice-beaten whale-boat with which I was to make my voyage to the head of Frobisher Bay. I also compared my chronometer with the *George Henry's*; my two assistants, Jennie and little Ookoodlear, were in the boat to pull me on shore, and now nothing remained but to take leave of captain, officers, and crew.

It was done. The farewell was uttered. The *George Henry* was under sail, and I set out on my way to Whale Island, to commence life in earnest among the Esquimaux. I took up my abode in the tupic of Ebierbing and Tookoolito, other natives, relatives of theirs, being with us and near by.

As I walked about—the only white man among them—my position seemed, and in reality was, strange. At last alone; the ship gone; all of my own people, my own blood, my own language, departed; and now, by myself, to do whatever work I could. Well, this was what I designed. I would not despond. It was good. Freedom dwells in the North—freedom to live as one pleases, act as one pleases, and go where and when one pleases; so I determined to look brightly forward, placing all my dependence on God.

I watched the ship's progress. She got along but slowly. There was a light wind from the south-east against her. It was tack, tack, all the day long. Every now and then I ascended a hill on the island to look at her. It was past meridian before she got down as low as Parker's Bay.* By evening she had reached French Head, but late in the P.M. had drifted back, evidently with the tide, to Parker's Bay. White clouds now capped the high land about there, which was the precursor of a storm.

During the day, Sharkey, E-e-u-ar-ping (the latter the youngest son of Artarkparu), and a boat's crew of those Innuits remaining at Rescue Harbour, started off to French Head. Koodloo also, in my boat, with Suzhi and Ookoodlear, with the children, went among the islands ducking, but obtained only two ducks. Wishing to manufacture some balls of the lead which I had with me for my rifle and Koodloo's gun, the thought came into my

* Named after Captain John Parker, of Hull, England. Parker's Bay makes westward from Field Bay, and is in lat. 62° 48′ N. and long. 64° 55′ W.

head that the hull of the *Rescue* had still some hard coal in her, and that, by taking advantage of the low tide, I could obtain it ; therefore I and Koodloo, with Suzhi, went in the boat to the "ghost." The tide was still ebbing when we got alongside, but, on examination, it was found that the water inside of her was too deep to *fish* for coal. We therefore started elsewhere to fish for something else, or try for seal. We drew up to the point of an island to gratify the Innuits in killing some little birds about the size of our robins at home, but here called by the natives *sik-yar-ung.* They were too small game for the expense of powder, therefore Koodloo tried to kill them by throwing stones, but failed, though they were by no means shy. We then rowed off to look for seals. Presently we saw one. My rifle was instantly raised, but just as I pulled the trigger a little boy in the boat lifted himself up and unsettled my aim. The seal went off, much to our vexation, as we had nothing on shore to eat except the two ducks. We again saw the seal, but were unable to kill it ; therefore we returned to the "ghost," and this time were able to enter her hull. After some trouble I succeeded in procuring about two and a half buckets of hard coal, and having had an old stove placed in my boat when I left the ship to leave on Whale Island, the present acquisition made it very serviceable.

In the evening Sharkey and ten more Innuits returned without any success in procuring food. Thus we had a large company now here, and nothing to eat except the two ducks. True, I had a barrel of sea-bread, about twenty pounds of salt pork, a ninety-pound can of pemmican, ten pounds of coffee, two gallons of molasses, one pound of tea, and half a pound of pepper, all of which excepting the pemmican I procured at the ship by exchange. But this stock was for my Frobisher Bay expedition, not for consumption here. Unfortunately, my right-hand man Ebierbing was now very sick, but I was in hopes I should bring him round again in two or three days. I had taken from the vessel my case of medicines, and with these I hoped to do him some good. I took one more look at the ship. There she was, still endeavouring to get out of the bay, but with no wind to help her. I thought she would, perhaps, be out of sight before the morning. Farewell, then, I said in my heart, gallant ship, and may good luck attend you. Good-night to all. I then retired to my Innuit bed, among my honest, kind-hearted Innuit friends.

On Wednesday, July 31st, hardly awake, and still on my sleeping-couch, I heard an exclamation of surprise from Too-koolito, who had gone outside the tupic. The wind was blowing

a gale, with rain. Tookoolito's cry was, "Ship coming back!"
Up I got, and, on rushing to the skin door-way, true enough,
there was the *George Henry* nearly up the bay. I watched her.
She advanced still higher up, and presently dropped anchor north-
west of us, some two or three miles off. The return of the *George
Henry* was wise, for the gale had become furious, and, had she
continued on, it might have driven her on shore lower down the
bay. Once more, then, the ship and her company were near
me. Little had I expected this when looking at her the evening
before.

I may here as well relate something very curious, which I have
recorded under this date as having occurred during the previous
night. Ebierbing was very ill, and both his wife and his aunt
were alarmed. The latter went out at midnight, and brought in
Jennie, wife of Koodloo, who is a female angeko, to practise on
the sufferer. She took her position at once, sitting, Innuit
fashion, in a corner of the tupic, facing from us, and proceeded
with her incantations, while deep seriousness fell on all around.
As she went on, ejaculatory expressions of approbation were
occasionally uttered by the persons present, as also by the
patient. Presently Ebierbing became more calm, his pains seemed
to decrease, and finally he fell asleep, and actually slept well!
This is strange, most " passing strange ;" yet it is a fact that the
ankooting does seemingly benefit the patient, acting as a charm.
The mind being diverted from all thought of the clay house to
something above which the *soul* aspires to reach, makes one for-
getful that there is anything like pain in his or her system.

This people, knowing that I did not make fun of them or
taunt them for believing as they do, had confidence in me,
therefore I was a privileged one in their midst when ankooting
was going on. It is against their customs to have any but the
family present, but hitherto I have always had access to their
meetings.

Let Christians plant a colony among the western Innuits, as
has been done in Greenland, and *in time* this people will become
converts to Christianity, for that is the only true religion ; and
the truth when properly presented to honest minds, will be
received with open hearts.

Jennie is not only a good angeko professionally, but also of
pleasing features, and would pass for handsome with many judges
of beauty.

On the 1st of August the weather still continued bad, with
rain and mist. I was obliged to open my case of pemmican, and

in doing so, found under the top a card, incased in tin, reading thus : " George Schlee, Cincinnati, Ohio. Farewell !" Though, I am unacquainted with the person whom this name represents, yet this told me that some one in the employ of H. W. Stephenson, of Cincinnati—the maker and sealer up of my pemmican cans —had kind thoughts and good wishes for me, though a stranger to him. " Farewell " is a word of rich import from well-known friends, but from a stranger, whose soul may be beating in unison for the same noble cause to which one devotes his life, the word becomes almost sacred to the life and heart of the adventurer.

The next day Ebierbing still continued very sick. Several of the natives took a boat and went up to the ship ; and I heard that she was to remain in the bay, seeking a secure harbour higher up. Later in the day I saw her under sail, but the fog soon closed her from my view.

An extract from my journal of this date (Friday, August 2d) runs thus :—

" This morning for breakfast cold rock pemmican. It goes better this way than when made into soup. The two families already mentioned as members of the expedition trip I purpose to make seemed to like it. A very little of this solid, rich food satisfies one's appetite. This article is eaten, not because it tastes good, for it does not, *but to live.* It is almost like eating tallow candles. One must have a sharp appetite to eat pemmican in the usual way it is prepared. In the manufacture of mine I used the best of beef and beef suet in the place of what is generally used, to wit, beef and hog's fat. The composition consists of an equal weight of beef (dried and granulated) and beef suet, which are incorporated while the latter is hot, and then put up in tin cans and hermetically sealed. Thus made and put up, it will keep good for years. One pound of my pemmican is equivalent to two and a half pounds of fresh beef-steak. Four pounds of fresh beef, on being dried, is reduced to a pound."

At 2·30 P.M. I went up to make my call on Captain B. in his new harbour, two and a half miles off, taking with me Koodloo and other Innuits as my boat's crew. We soon arrived, and after the first greeting between us, I mentioned my desire to take Koojesse with me instead of Ebierbing, who was too sick to go on my Frobisher Bay trip. The arrangement was made, so far as concerned the Captain (he having pre-engaged Koojesse's services), and, after a short stay on board, I departed.

There was some difficulty in getting back to my Innuit home, owing to both wind and tide being against me, and, when the island was reached, my boat could not be hauled up on account of low water. I was therefore obliged to keep on the watch nearly all night, to guard against the danger of losing her.

The night was a stormy one; the rain, at times, descending in torrents, and the wind blowing furiously. Every now and then I enveloped myself in an oil-suit, and went down to watch the condition of the boat. The tide would soon be up so far as to enable us to draw her on the beach; so, thinking that all was right, I laid myself down to rest.

About 2 A.M. of the 3d, however, I was aroused by invalid Ebierbing, who said that, from the noise, the sea was beating on shore. Immediately I went down to the boat, and, finding it in a precarious condition, called up all the natives, and with their aid at once had her dragged above reach of the sea. This done, I again retired to my couch, and slept soundly till the musical voice of Angeko Jennie once more aroused me. Looking round, I saw she was renewing her professional practice over her patient. Tookoolito and Suzhi were seriously, I may say *solemnly* engaged in the exercises, enthusiastically making their responses to Jennie's ejaculations. The effect upon the suffering patient, Ebierbing, was, as before, quite beneficial.

On Sunday, the 4th of August, while in the tupic, I learned something that surprised me. On the previous day myself and some Innuits had gone ducking and sealing without any success. Now I was told that our ill luck was on account of our working during Ebierbing's sickness, as all of the natives, including intelligent Tookoolito, sincerely believe. They consider that it is wrong to work when one of their number is sick, and especially to work on skins that are intended to *keep out water;* for instance, it is wrong to work making kum-ings (outside or water-proof boots) and covering for boats.

The way I happened to find this out was as follows: I had arranged for Koodloo to make a sealskin covering for Ebierbing's kia, and to put it on. This morning, as nothing else could be done on account of the bad weather, I asked Tookoolito if Koodloo could not proceed with it. To my astonishment, she replied that " Innuits could not do such work at the present time." Her answer seemed to me so strange that I made farther inquiries of her, when she told me that " if they worked on the skins for the kia, Ebierbing would never get well; he would die. The '*first Innuits*' adhered to this custom, and they must too. All their people believe this, and could not help it. Many

Innuits had died because of the working on skins for kias and kum-ings while one of their number about them was sick at the time." She added, " The reason why Koodloo could not shoot anything yesterday, though close by some ducks, was because wrong was done in working while Ebierbing lay sick."

" But," said I to Tookoolito, as I was engaged chafing Ebierbing's side and back, and applying liniment, " what are you doing now but working."

She replied, holding up her hands full of needles that were flying swiftly in knitting, " *This is not work.*"

Her answer nearly made me laugh aloud ; but I repressed the feeling, and quietly accepted her definition of what was or was not work. I was also told that during Ebierbing's sickness the angeko must do no work on any account.

We were now living on pemmican and coffee. I dealt out enough bread for Ebierbing, as he was sick, but there was no supply for any of us yet. Sunday night was a stormy one, with the wind from the northeast blowing almost a gale. Everything was in a wet state, outside and in, except bedding and clothing. A flood of water occupied half of the tupic.

It would astonish most people at home to see how comfortably I lived with the Innuits, like one of themselves. While I jotted down notes, or more fully wrote out notes previously made, Suzhi chanted some Innuit tune, and Ebierbing and Tookoolito enjoyed what among civilized white folks would be a " tea-table chat." We lived also, at times, on pemmican and kelp, a sea-weed gathered by the Innuits when the tide is out. These people are not *exclusively* flesh-eaters, for in the summertime they occasionally gather and eat a few berries and leaves of stunted wild plants that grow sparsely in these regions. Both summer and winter they collect kelp, and eat it, but only as a sort of luxury, except in cases of great scarcity of food, and then they fall back upon this resource. I have acquired a taste for this sea-weed, and eat it as they do, raw or boiled, in which latter state it is more tender.

The stormy weather continued some days, and no work could be done. On Tuesday, August 6th, the wind blew a gale, with rain. On Wednesday we had a little better weather, and I went over to the ship again to see the Captain. I hoped to set out on my trip up Frobisher Bay within a day or two. On Wednesday evening, during ebb tide, the " ghost " of the *Rescue* drifted out of the harbour into the bay, and went seaward. I thought this was probably the last we should see of her. On the same evening I communicated to Ebierbing and Tookoolito my intended immediate departure, and informed them that I had made arrangements with the captain for their removal nearer the ship, so that Ebierbing might receive some better attention. They were sorrowful at my leaving, but hoped to see me again before many weeks.

I then requested Ebierbing to assist me in persuading Koodloo and his nuliana " Jennie " to accompany me, which would just complete my now proposed crew. I soon found that both Ebierbing and Tookoolito were very loth to have the angeko (Jennie) leave while Ebierbing was sick. I therefore gave her up, accepting Koodloo's offer to go without her.

On Thursday morning, the 8th of August, I found that Ebierbing had slept better than for several nights past. At 9 A.M., while Koodloo was on the top of our island (Whale Island), he cried down to Tookoolito, who was making our morning coffee, under the lee of some rocks, that a boat was coming from the ship. I ran up, and was delighted to find it so, for I knew by this that the proposals I had made to the Innuits Koojesse and Charley, whom, with their wives, I wanted for my crew, had been accepted ; and yet I was pained, as I thought of the necessity of leaving behind my faithful friends Ebierbing and Tookoolito. I hastened back, took my cup of coffee and dish of lump pemmican, and breakfasted.

Well, the boat arrived, and brought me a note from the captain. I told Ebierbing that we could now remove him and his effects ; that Captain B. had kindly responded to my request, and sent down for him, and that so good an opportunity ought not to be lost. He was willing to do as I advised ; but Koodloo was slow to move. Meanwhile almost a gale had sprung up in the east, rendering it inexpedient to venture to take Ebierbing to the ship in his weak state. As it was necessary to visit the ship prior to my final departure on the proposed voyage, I left Ebierbing and Tookoolito with the assurance that I would call again the next day, and that they would be removed as soon as Ebierbing could bear it and the weather should permit. We arrived on board just at noon. Shortly after, Koojesse and Charley came aboard from the Innuit village near the ship, when I soon found that they were fearful I wished to prolong my stay at the head of Frobisher Bay until the cold weather, and, if so, they were not disposed to go. I therefore explained to them that I should probably return in about a month, or, at furthest, in less than two months. They were then quite satisfied, and agreed to accompany me. My-journal of this day, August 8th, 1861, concludes thus :—

"As I meet Koojesse and Kooperneung (Charley), I find them in capital spirits. At tea their wives Tu-nuk-der-lien and Ak-chuk-er-zhun are aboard, and appear in good new dresses, and hair dressed in 'States' fashion.' Converse with them of the voyage we are about to make to '*wes-see-poke*' (far-off land). I am highly elated, my crew so far excellent. The captain advised me to take Ebierbing's aunt, Koo-ou-le-arng (Suzhi), making, with Koodloo, a crew of six—five at the oars and one boat-steerer, leaving me free to be constantly on the look-out. The only objection to Suzhi is that she is very heavy, weighing not less than 200 pounds—the very heaviest Innuit of the country.

"All arrangements are now made to start from the vessel early to-morrow morning. Breakfast is ordered to be in readi-ness at 5 A.M. The Innuits are to strike their tupics, and have them in the boat, and be alongside at that hour. The weather is now good, and to-night gives every indication of a fair day to-morrow. May it prove so. I have taken out of the ship's 'run' a can (ninety pounds) of pemmican, and one cask of 'Borden's' meat-biscuit (about one hundred pounds), brought with me from home. These I shall carry along in the boat, being the most condensed form of valuable provisions. Not that I expect these will be the only provisions I shall have, for there is reason to suppose we shall acquire much in going up Frobisher Bay in the way of ducks, seals, and reindeer, the latter when we arrive at the head of Frobisher Bay.

"At a late hour I turn in, to rise early, that we may be off to reap the benefit of a fair tide not only in going down to, but proceeding through, Lupton Channel. An ebb tide will favour us much in getting to the channel, and the flood in getting through it."

CHAPTER XXI

"*Friday, August 9th,* 1861.—I was up in good season, and
got everything in readiness ; then started off in a boat a company
of young Innuits—'trundle-bed Innuits,' as the captain called
them—who slept aboard the *George Henry* last night, to call up
Koojesse, and Kooperneung, and their nulianas (wives).

"Breakfast was ready at the appointed moment, and the
Innuits of my company ready for it. This despatched, my bag
and baggage were placed snugly in the boat, along with the
already well-packed assortment such as Innuits have. As usual
in starting off, I compared chronometers. . . . .

"All in readiness and aboard, we start, purposing to stop at
Whale Island for Koodloo, Koo-ou-le-arng (Suzhi), and my
things, as well as to bid my Innuit children, Ebierbing and
Tookoolito, good-bye. All hands were on deck to witness our
departure. As the boat was pushed out into fair water for a
'white-ash breeze,' standing with steering oar in my hand, I
asked Captain B. if—'in the name of God and the Continental
Congress'—I should take possession of the country I was about
to visit and explore, planting the American flag upon it.

"He answering affirmatively, I then bade him and all adieu,
expressing the hope that when I returned I should find every
cask of the *George Henry* overflowing with oil, and all her decks
filled high with bone.

"We started from the vessel at 6·14 A.M. and arrived at
Whale Island at 7. I found the Innuits, my friends Ebierbing
and Tookoolito, expecting me. They seem to regret they

cannot accompany me on this trip. I was glad to find Ebierbing improving. Having spent a few moments with them, I
told them that, to make out my crew, I must have Koo-ou-le-
arng, Ebierbing's aunt, if they could spare her. In ten minutes
she was ready for the journey of two months. I called on Koodloo, who made all haste in preparing to accompany me. Jennie,
Koodloo's wife, as I have said, could not be spared, as Ebierbing
and Tookoolito thought her indispensable in her profession as an
angeko for the former while he is sick.

"As we (Koodloo and I) had not succeeded in getting anything of consequence in the way of fresh provisions for Ebierbing
and Tookoolito during my stay upon Whale Island, I left them
the remainder of the can of pemmican on hand, also a small
portion of the bread, coffee, and tea of the allotment to me for my
Frobisher Bay trip. Captain B. is to send a boat from the
George Henry for these Innuits, also for Koodloo's wife and
children, to remove them to the place where the other Innuits
are, near the present position of the vessel."

*   *   *   *   *   *

It was 8 A.M. when we left Whale Island, Rescue Harbour,
under sail. My company consisted of Koojesse and his wife
Tu-nuk-der-lien (" Belle "), Koo-per-ne-ung (" Charley "), and
his wife Ak-chuk-er-zhun (" Susy "), Koodloo, and the widow
Koo-ou-le-arng (" Suzhi"). They were all in excellent spirits as
well as myself. In about forty minutes a boat came alongside
manned with Innuits, who were on their way across the bay for
a tuktoo hunt.

From the ship to Whale Island, and also from Whale Island
out into the bay, we encountered much ice that the wind and
tide had driven in from Davis's Straits. Between Parker's Bay
and French Head we made an island which I found to be entirely
of rock, without a particle of vegetation or of soil. An impenetrable fog had surrounded us nearly all the afternoon, and the
boat compass was in constant use until toward evening, when
the fog began to lift. Charley shot a seal at a long distance
with my rifle. We now had a raw seal feast. As we approached
Lupton Channel—which it was doubtful if we could get through,
on account of the quantity of ice—we passed a berg, which
Tunukderlien ascended. At 6·44 P.M. we reached the entrance
of Lupton Channel, and found a strong tide running into Field
Bay, whirling, foaming, roaring, and boiling like a caldron. As
we laboured on, at our right were the iron cliffs of Bache's

PASSING THROUGH LUPTON CHANNEL.

Peninsula,* and conspicuous among them was a bold rock terminating like a chimney-top. On the left lay Lok's Land, the "much-dreaded land" of the Innuits; and looking forward down the channel, we saw the bold front of Ellis Island. By dint of hard pulling we at last got through the channel, but I had to give up all idea of reaching Cape True that night, as had been my intention and hope. We therefore stopped at 8 A.M. in a small cove on the southeast side of Bache's Peninsula, and opposite to Ellis Island, and there made our first encampment.† Ducks were abundant, and the Innuits shot several. We found wood plentiful, from the wreck of the *Traveller*. We were closely packed this first night out, in our large tupic, after a glorious supper of seal, ducks, and coffee.

Here we found relics of former Innuit encampments, circles of stones, bones of seal, walrus, &c. We saw a white whale making its way up the channel.

Next morning, Saturday, August 10th, 1861, at 8 A.M. we proceeded on the voyage. In passing down through Bear Sound, soon after leaving, I witnessed a novel proceeding on the part of my companions. It consisted in drowning some of the ducks that played about us in large numbers. This cruel method of obtaining game was used to save shot and powder, and the manner of accomplishing it is as follows :—

A flock of ducks was seen swimming some distance ahead of us. As we approached, most of them flapped their wings and flew away, but the rest dived below the surface of the water. One of them was selected for the subject of Innuit amusement, thus : whenever it popped its head out of water, the natives made a great noise, accompanied with every conceivable motion, throwing about their hands and arms to frighten the bird down again. On its reappearance, wherever it showed itself, the boat was steered by Koojesse toward it. Then the same noise and frantic gestures were repeated, and continued without intermission, so as to allow not one moment's breathing-time to the terrified duck. Koodloo stood on the bow of the boat, pointing out the course taken by the duck, which could be easily traced in the clear waters below, and on the instant of the sign being given, Koojesse most expertly turned the boat in the direction indicated. In seven minutes the duck gave up the chase. It

* I have named this peninsula after A. D. Bache, Superintendent of the United States Coast Survey. It is bounded by Field Bay, Lupton Channel, Bear Sound, and Chapell Inlet.

† First encampment in lat. 62° 33′ N. long. 64° 43′ W.

came to the surface utterly exhausted, and was easily captured by Koodloo, who hauled it in with his hand.

The joyous feelings displayed by the Innuits over this capture, which was to them a source of amusement, was hardly less than if they had killed a *Ninoo*. The rocks and hills bordering on Bear Sound resounded with their joyous shouts and boisterous laughter. Echo sent back their merry voices, until I myself, though vexed at any delays that might retard us, could not help joining in the hilarity of the scene.

This way of securing ducks was continued for some time, and ended with what was to me an affecting trait of nature, always touching to the heart. One of the ducks caught was a mother, with its young still unfledged. The parent was dying, and the fledgling, at each gasp of its mother, would place its beak in contact with that of its parent, as if soliciting food, and then crouch beneath the old duck's wings to nestle there. Again and again was this done, as if trying all its power to attract the watchful attention of its mother ; but it was soon left alone, and Tunukderlien then took care of it.

So much time had been consumed in drowning ducks and in sealing that the tide was now against us, forcing us to hold over a while ; therefore we landed on Lefferts Island,* which is in the midst of Bear Sound. Here I took a walk back upon the island while the Innuits were feasting on ducks and seal. At meridian I took observations for latitude, and soon after we again started, making our way down on the west side of the sound. The ducks we now saw were innumerable ; the water and air were black with them.

On arriving at Cape True, the old whaling depôt, we rested awhile, and I examined the now deserted place. Of course no white man's tent or Innuit tupics were to be seen, but several fragments denoted what had existed there.

Frobisher Bay had no ice upon its waters except a few bergs, and not a ripple disturbed its glassy surface. This compelled us to use the oars for some time after leaving this place, and what with the many stoppages made for game by my Innuit companions, and a fog that afterward settled upon us, it was a tedious passage to our second encampment, which was at Cape Cracroft,†

---

* So named by me after Marshal Lefferts, of New York City. This island is the largest in Bear Sound.

†This cape, at the south-east side of the entrance to the Countess of Warwick's Sound (of Frobisher), I name after Miss Cracroft, niece of Lady Franklin. It is in lat. 62° 41′ 30″ N. long. 65° 07′ W.

a point of land connected by a narrow neck with Blunt's Peninsula,* instead of at Niountelik, as we had expected.

We passed the night as the previous one, and the next morning again proceeded direct for Oopungnewing Island. The same kind of tantalizing but exciting chase after ducks delayed us considerably, until when about two miles from Oopungnewing. Koojesse was steering, when, suddenly taking up my spy-glass, and directing it to some islets near Oopungnewing, he cried out, "Ninoo! Ninoo!" This was enough to make each of the boat's crew spring into new life, for of all game that they delight in *Ninoo* is the chief. They started ahead with fresh vigour, the women pulling hard, but as noiselessly as they could, and the men loading their guns ready for the attack. I relieved Koojesse at the steering-oar.

When we first saw Ninoo we were about two miles distant from him, and I could perceive this "lion of the North" lying down, apparently asleep; but when within half a mile Ninoo saw us, raised himself upon his haunches, looked around, then fixedly at us, and off he started. Immediately the men began to make some most hideous noises, which arrested Ninoo in his course, and caused him to turn round. This was what we wanted, to gain time in the chase which had now begun. But Ninoo was not so easily entrapped. His stay was only for a moment. Off he went again, flying over the island, and quickly disappearing. Then, with a strong pull, and a firm, steady one, the boat was sent swiftly along. Presently a point of the islet where we had seen Ninoo was rounded, and again we beheld him far ahead of us, swimming direct for Oopungnewing. This encouraged the Innuits. They renewed their shouts without intermission. Every now and then the object of our pursuit would wheel his huge form around, and take a look at his pursuers; and now the chase became very exciting. We were gaining on him. Ninoo saw this, and therefore tried to baffle us. He suddenly changed his course, and went out directly for the middle of the bay. In an instant we did the same, the old crazy boat bounding forward as swiftly as our oarsmen could propel it in the heavy sea that then prevailed. But we could not gain upon him. He seemed to know that his life was in jeopardy, and on he went without any more stopping when he heard a noise. The "voice of the charmer" no longer had charms nor

* The land bounded by Bayard Taylor Pass, Field Bay, Chapell Inlet, and Frobisher Bay, I have named after Edward and George W. Blunt, of New York City.

aught else for him.   He had to make all speed away ; and this
he did at about four miles per hour, striking out more and more
into the open bay.   Once he so changed his course that by some
dexterous movement of ours we succeeded in cutting across his
wake, and this gave us an opportunity to fire.   We did so, but
only the ball of Koojesse's gun took effect.   Ninoo was struck
in the head, but the poor brute at first merely shook himself and
turned his course from down the bay in a contrary direction.

WOUNDED NINOO TOWS HIS OWN CARCASS FOR

The shot, however, had told.   In a moment or two we could see
that Ninoo was getting enraged.   Every now and then he would
take a look at us and shake his head.   This made the Innuits
very cautious about lessening the distance between him and the
boat.   Again we fired.   One or more shots took effect.   Ninoo's
white coat was crimsoned with blood about his head, and he was
getting desperate.   His movements were erratic, but we finally
drove him in the direction of Oopungnewing, our policy being

to make him tow his own carcass as near the land as would be safe to prevent his escape, and then to end his life. This was accomplished when within about one eighth of a mile from the island. The last shot was fired, and Ninoo instantly dropped his head without making another motion.

We now pulled to him. He was quite dead, and we at once took him in tow by fastening a walrus thong around his lower jaw, its huge tusks effectually serving to keep the noose from slipping off. Thus we towed our prize along, until, reaching the land, we hauled him on shore, and made our third encampment upon the southwest side of Oopungnewing Island.*

During the chase I had a narrow escape from losing my life. Koojesse was seated on the locker at the boat's stern, with gun cocked and levelled at Ninoo, when, just as he was about to pull the trigger, I, intent upon the bear, suddenly rose, right in a line with his aim. It was but a second of time that saved me. Koojesse had just time to drop his gun, as frightened as man could be at the danger in which I had unknowingly placed myself.

While we were firing at the bear, Tunukderlien and another of the women, for some reason unknown to me at the time, lay down in the boat completely covered with tuktoo skins.

As soon as we landed I went to the top of the island to make observations and look around, but the vast swarms of musquitoes attacked me with such violence that I was almost desperate. After catching a few sights for time (longitude) and a solar bearing, and taking a round of angles, I beat a hasty retreat. So tormented was I that I thought I had lost as much blood during the time I was up there as the Ninoo we killed.

Musquitoes are fond of white men's blood. They can smell it a long way off, I am sure, for they came in swarms from every direction, and made me the centre-point of their bill presentations. When I got back to the encampment I must have looked very hideous, for my hands and face were blotched all over.

I found the Innuits had skinned Ninoo, and were feasting on its delicious meat—beef-like, bright red, and juicy. I made a hasty meal, and, without further delay, prepared to gratify my now cherished and eager desire to penetrate the mysteries hanging over the Frobisher expeditions. I now copy from my journal :—

* Oo-pung-ne-wing is near the west side of Countess of Warwick's Sound, and is one mile and a half long, and one mile wide. It is like all the land of that country—rugged rocks and mountains. This island is in lat. 62° 46′ 30″ N. long. 65° 17′ W.

"*Sunday, August* 11*th*, 1861.   *   *   *   *

*   *   *   *   I soon made up a company to go with me to Niountelik. It consisted of the women of the crew, Koo-ou-le-arng, Tu-nuk-der-lien, and Ak-chuk-er-zhun. Of course I was boat-steerer. It was near 6 P.M. Rescue Harbour time, before we got under way. As we rounded the northwest point of Oopungnewing Island, a fresh breeze from the northeast met us. Before making half a mile it increased to almost a moderate gale, making progress difficult for us. By turning the boat off the course I desired to pursue we were able to make better headway, being under the lee of the island Niountelik. Before getting across the channel between Oopungnewing and Niountelik, I began to think, as my crew was so small, I should be obliged to turn back. Indeed, the wind began to blow so furiously that I had thoughts that we might be blown out into the Bay of Frobisher, which often has all the characteristics of an open sea; but, being shielded by the island, we coasted along the base of the bluffs on the southern side of Niountelik till we arrived at a small bight well protected from all wind. Into this I directed the boat, which greatly relieved us from the dangers through which we had just passed. This bight is partly surrounded with a high, steep sand-bank, most of it, however, by bluff rocks. I did not consider it safe to leave the boat without a party to care for it, as there was a heavy sea from the south, therefore I requested Tunukderlien and Akchukerzhun to remain by or in it till I and Koo-ou-le-arng (whom I wished to accompany me as guide, as she had often visited the island in her young days) could make a search over the place and return. Climbing the steep bank, though a feat not easily accomplished, was soon performed. When up we directed our steps along a narrow, smooth, grassy, slightly inclined plain, hemmed in by rough old rocks. Thence we turned to the left, mounting the rocks leading to the highest part of the island. We kept our eyes fixed on the ground over which we made our footsteps, anxiously searching for fragments of brick, which I thought must somewhere be found on Niountelik. I had understood Koo-ou-le-arng to say that she had seen brick on this island, therefore every few minutes I said to her, '*Nou-ti-ma brick ?*' (where is brick?) To make her understand '*brick,*' I took up a small stone spotted over with a peculiar red moss, calling her attention to the *red;* and then, taking off her head ornament—'*kar-oong*'* (a rounded, polished piece of brass in the form of a

* For the way this ornament is worn, see head of Nikujar, page 130.

semicircle, fitted to and worn on the head by the Innuit women as an adornment), I made motions as if polishing it, for I knew, from information I had gained from time to time, that Innuits had procured pieces of brick on or somewhere in the neighbourhood of the island on which we were, and used them specially for brightening their ornaments, to wit, hair-rings (*toong-le-lê-une*), finger-rings (*nuk-guer-ming*), and kar-oongs.

" Koo-ou-le-arng knew by my description what I desired to find, but did not seem to recollect where she had seen brick : though, from her expressions and conduct, I was satisfied she had seen *mi-e-oo-koo-loo* (small) pieces somewhere in the vicinity. Gaining the top of the island, we made search there for relics, but found none. I looked specially for some signs of a stone monument, which I conceived Frobisher might in his day (if he visited this island) have erected, this being the highest point of the whole island. But none whatever could I find. Thence we directed our way down on the west side to a small grassy slope, not far from the termination of the island. Here we made careful search, but without finding anything that I so ardently wished. Thence we commenced to make a circuit of the island, moving along as near the coast as the bluff rocks would permit, keeping the main island at our right—that is, continuing northwest, then around to the north, thence northeast and east. At the northwest end of the island we found abundance of evidence that Innuits had made Niountelik a stopping-place. There we saw the usual circles of stones, always to be seen where Innuits have had their tupics (summer tents). We saw seal, walrus, tuktoo (reindeer), meituk (duck), and various other bones in abundance, some moss-aged, and some nearly fresh, of not more than two or three years' exposure. Here we found also pieces of wood, some with the ends charred, small pieces of tuktoo skins, and one relic of civilization—a piece of an old calico dress ! This did not excite me as a matter extraordinary, as I knew that the whalers now visit every year the inlet at the north, called ' Northumberland Inlet ' (the ' Cumberland Straits ' of Davis), and distribute freely among the Innuits various articles of civilization, especially cast-off calico dresses that they have brought from the States or from England, which are highly prized by the Innuit women. It is rare to find, at the present day, a native family that does not possess something of the kind.

" We continued on around the island, finding, every few fathoms in our progress, numerous Innuit relics. At length we arrived at a plain that extended back a considerable distance from the coast. Here we recognised, at our right, about sixty rods distant, the point to which we first directed our steps on reaching the high bank after leaving the boat.

" I was several fathoms in advance of Koo-ou-le-arng, hastening on, being desirous to make as extended a search as the brief remaining daylight would allow, when, lifting my eyes from the ground near me, I discovered, a considerable distance ahead, an object of unusual appearance. But a second look satisfied me that what I saw were simply stones scattered about and covered with black moss. I continued my course, keeping as near the coast as possible. I was now nearing the spot where I had first descried the black object. It again met my view; and my original thought on first seeing it resumed at once the ascendancy in my mind. I hastened to the spot. 'Great God! Thou hast rewarded me in my search!' was the sentiment that came overwhelmingly into my thankful soul. On casting my eyes all around, seeing and feeling the character ('moss-aged,' for some of the pieces I saw had pellicles of black moss on them) of the relics before and under me, I felt as—I cannot tell what my feelings were. What I saw before me was the *sea-coal* of Frobisher's expedition of 1578, left here near three centuries ago !

" Koo-ou-le-arng, seeing that I had discovered something that made me joyous (even unto dancing), came running with all her might. Though she and other Innuits have known all about this coal being here (as I find by what she and Koojesse inform me to-night), yet not a word* had ever been communicated to me about it. I had, by perseverance, gained information during the year of brick and heavy stones (the latter, of course, I thought to mean iron), but nothing of coals.* As soon as Koo-ou-le-arng came up, I held out my hand to her, which was full of coal, asking '*Kis-su ?*' (What is this?) She answered, '*Innuit kook-um.*' By this I took it that the Innuits *have* sometimes used it in cooking. Said I, '*Innuit, ikkumer e-a-u ?*' (Did the Innuits ever use this for a fire to cook with?) '*Armelarng*' (Yes) was the instant response. I then asked, '*Noutima ?*' meaning, 'Where did these coals come from ?' Koo-ou-le-arng's response was, '*Kodlunarn oomiarkchua kiete amasuadlo echar.*' (A great many years ago, white men with big ship came here).

---

* When I wrote the original, of which the above is a verbatim copy, I had forgotten the mention of coal in the communication made to me by old Ookijoxy Ninoo, recorded on the 11th of the previous May. See page 248.

This answer made me still more joyous.   From what I find on
my return to Oopungnewing, Koo-ou-le-arng has communicated
to her Innuit friends some of my conduct while on that coal-pile.
She said that I acted just like an angeko, and that I had done

THE DISCOVERY OF FROBISHER RELICS NEARLY THREE HUNDRED YEARS OLD, SUNDAY,
AUGUST 11TH, 1861.

one thing an Innuit could not do—that I had danced, and
laughed, and made a complete somerset on the coal !
    " And why did I feel so happy ?   Because of the discovery I
have made to-day of what is a confirmation of the testimony—
oral history—I had acquired by great perseverance from the

Innuits, that a great many years ago—many generations ago—*kodlunarn oomiarkchua* (white men with big ship) came into this bay (Tin-nu-jok-ping-oo-se-ong); because of the chain that I felt was now complete, that determined this to be the bay that Frobisher discovered in 1576, and revisited consecutively in the years 1577 and 1578, and that Niountelik,* the island of my visitation to-day, was the identical one on which Frobisher landed with the object of establishing winter quarters for the colony of a hundred men that he brought here in his last voyage, to wit, in 1578!

"The account which Frobisher gave of his discovery was so indefinite that the civilized world has remained in doubt for nearly three hundred years of its locality. Even to this day geographers know not its location. Some one has made a guess, and approximated to the fact—simply approximated. In a few days I trust I shall return, either confirming it to be a 'strait,' as it is called, or with the full conviction that this water is a bay, which I believe it to be, from what the Innuits have told me.

"I now resume the incidents of this day. A few minutes after Koo-ou-le-arng's arrival at the coal-heap, I proceeded to investigate more searchingly into the probable time it had been there, and all other matters pertaining to it.

"I first dug down in the centre to ascertain its depth; found it to be one foot in the thickest part, and thinning off to an edge at a distance of five to ten feet from the centre. On walking around, I found that the winds, mostly those from the northeast, north, and northwest, had scattered the coal (chiefly small pieces) over a great extent of ground. In fact, wind from the opposite points would carry such coal as it could lick up, into the water of 'Countess of Warwick's Sound,' as Frobisher denominated the water at the northwest, north, northeast, east, and southeast of Niountelik, for the coal deposit is close by the bank bordering the sound.

"To satisfy myself fully that this coal must have been where it lies for a great many years, I dug around and beneath the clods of thickly-matted grass—around and beneath stunted willows and 'crowberry' shrubs—around and beneath mosses. Wherever I made these excavations I found coal. Many places overgrown with grass I examined, digging down a depth of several inches, and overturning sods exhibiting coal at the

* This conclusion was too hasty, as I discovered on my return from the head of Frobisher Bay, when I visited Kodlunarn Island.

base, then a layer of sand and coal, then another layer of two or three inches of sand, overtopped by interlocked roots, whence extended thrifty grass. The roots of the stunted willows, half an inch in diameter at the base of the trunk, pierced down into sand, and thence into coal! On examination of many pieces of coal, bedded—some in grass, some in sand, and some in moss—the upper side, exposed to the air, I found to be covered with pellicles of black moss, such as one finds upon the rocks of ages.

"I am convinced, from what I have seen to-day, that this coal has lain there for centuries. If it was placed there by Frobisher (and I have no doubt that it was), then the time of its deposit was but eighty-five years after the discovery of America by Columbus.

"We continued our search for other relics. I desired very much to find even the smallest fragment of brick; but the shades of night prevented a thorough search; therefore, filling my pockets with the sable relics, which drew a hearty laugh from Koo-ou-le-arng, I reluctantly turned from this deeply interesting place, and led the way across the island to the boat. We found everything all right, and ready for a quick sail to our third encampment, Oopungnewing. Getting out of our boat harbour, the wind filled our sails (it was still blowing hard), and away we bounded. Now and then a gust came that almost threw our craft on her beam-ends. While Koo-ou-le-arng steered, I held on to the sheets, ready to 'douse,' or let go, on the instant of any sudden or violent blast. Several times during our passage free play was given to the sail; but in good time, and safely, and with a thankful heart, on my part at least, for the discovery I this evening have made, we arrived back.

"Koojesse, Kooperneung, and Koodloo had an excellent hot supper ready for us on our arrival. There, upon the clean, tide-washed rocks of Oopungnewing, the cerulean dome, pierced with star points, for our canopy, we made a feast on sweet, juicy fresh 'beef'—*Ninoo*. Incomparable is the relish with which I have partaken to-night of the polar bear-meat, with its two-inch coating of fat, white as the driven snow.

"The fresh meat of Ninoo, with which we have been blessed to-day, exceeds 800 pounds. Every one of my company participates in my joy in making the discovery I have to-day.

"A heavy sea has been rolling in all day from the south. We have had a hard tug to-night drawing up the boat above the reach of the tide.

"Now we have a Ninoo, of course the Innuits will inflate the bladder, and attach it, with several peculiar charms, to a staff, which must be kept in a prominent position—in the boat while we are voyaging, and on the tupic while encamped. In accordance with Innuit custom, it must be thus exposed for three days and three nights.

"We leave a considerable portion of the Ninoo here on deposit against our return. The bear's length was eight feet ; it was not of the largest size ; its condition was fine, very fat, and its meat as tender and palatable as any beefsteak I ever ate. The liver of the polar bear is never eaten by the Innuits. Of course they know the general effect of eating this part to be as if one were poisoned. They say it makes them feel very sick, especially in the head, the hair dropping off, and the skin peeling from their faces and bodies. They do not allow the dogs to eat it, because it makes them also sick, and causes all their hair to come off. They either bury the liver or cast it into the sea. Even after this precaution, dogs sometimes succeed in getting hold of it, and it really poisons them."

CHAPTER XXII.

THE following day, Monday, August 12th, 1861, Suzhi and
myself remaining at Oopungnewing, the rest of my company set
out in the boat for the main land on a tuktoo hunt. My time
was occupied in taking observations, writing, and examining
the island, while Suzhi was busily engaged in dressing sealskins
for jackets, and "milling" old native boots—that is, making
the soles soft and pliant by *chewing* them.

During the day I heard some extraordinary noises, like the
rumblings of an earthquake. I had noticed the same on our
way from Cape Cracroft, but now the sound was so loud that I
could not help asking Suzhi if she knew what it was. She
replied that it came from the Kingaite side of the waters ; and,
from what I afterward learned, it must have been caused by
large masses of ice — icebergs— from Grinnell Glacier falling
into the sea. The distance traversed by the thundering sound
thus occasioned was about forty miles. At other times, while
in this bay, I have felt the earth tremble from the same cause.

In the evening Suzhi and I took a walk round to the north
side of the island. We had not gone far when she asked me, in
her native tongue, "Do you see walrus?" pointing to a long
white line running up the mountain's side. I looked, and at
first supposed it to be a vein of quartz running up among the
dark, moss-covered rocks ; but, on closer inspection, I found it
to consist of over a hundred walrus jawbones, placed in line
about two feet apart. Some parts of each were white as the
snows of Kingaite, but a considerable portion was covered with

thick black moss. What this singular arrangement meant I had yet to learn,

We next came to a spot situated by the margin of a grass-plot, completely covered with bleached bones of seals, walrus, whales, and tuktoo. Ask an Innuit to what animal this and that bone belonged, as you pick them up, and he or she will

SUZHI'S BOOT "MILLING."

tell you at once, the people being in reality good natural anatomists.

We passed on half a mile, and reached a point of high land, which looked out toward Niountelik, but could see none of our party returning. It was then ten o'clock; the night was fine, and a few stars were visible, but it was not yet late enough in the season to bring out the host there is above. Koojesse and his party returned about midnight, but wholly unsuccessful, though they had seen eight tuktoo. This, however, was not of serious importance, as we then had an abundance of provision.

We resumed our voyage on the morning of the 13th. Twice before leaving the island I again heard the loud thunderings already alluded to, and felt the vibrations of the very earth itself. What could this be? Was there a volcano on the Kingaite side, or were its mountains of ice falling from their precipitous heights?

It took a long time to strike tupics, and get everything into the boat and in order. Last of all Suzhi brought aboard the Ninoo's bladder and the charms, and placed them at the bow of the boat, mounted on a stick. Without them I strongly doubt whether the Innuits would have considered it safe to go on. Our course at first led toward Sarah G.'s Cape* (Twer-puk-ju-a), the way by which I went when making a hurried visit four months previous. Strangely enough, as it now seems to me, and no doubt to my readers also, I felt as safe and contented as though I were with civilized men instead of being alone among the wild, independent natives of that frozen land. I even did not hesitate to depend upon them occasionally for some of the work I wanted done in the way of delineating the coasts as we passed along. Koojesse—the really gifted Esquimaux—now and then acted as my assistant draughtsman, his sketches, however, being afterwards carefully examined by me. While I sat in the boat's stern steering—a position which allowed me to have good views of the land—he sat before me actually laying down most correctly upon paper the coast-line along which we sailed, and with which he, as well as Suzhi and Tunukderlien, was perfectly familiar. There was not a channel, cape, island, or bay, which he did not know perfectly, having visited them again and again.

One unacquainted with a new country would often make great mistakes by charting nearly everything as main land, where portions of it might be islands, failing also to give proper depths of inlet coast, unless he had time to visit every locality. On my present trip up the bay I had not that time, and therefore I reserved—to be made, if possible, on my return—a closer examination of places now draughted down under my eyes. During all this voyage, however, I kept up a constant record of dis-

* This cape at the west entrance to the Countess of Warwick's Sound (of Frobisher), I have named after Mrs. Henry Grinnell. Sarah G.'s Cape is two miles northwest of Oopungnewing, and is in lat. 62° 74′ 30″ N. long. 65° 20′ W.

tances run and courses steered, and made as frequent landings for taking observations for latitude, longitude, variations of the compass, &c. as the circumstances would admit.

Between Oo-mer-nung Island and Iron Island—the former in Wiswell Inlet* and the latter near Peter Force Sound †—a heavy sea prevailed, rolling in from the northwest, and it was astonishing to see my heavily-laden boat ride so well over the dashing, heaving, irregular waters that came upon us.

Iron Island is an interesting place, and I gave it the name because of the resemblance of its rocks to oxydized iron. Innuit monumental marks, made of the huge bones of the whale, were upon the island. Here also, on our landing, was found an excellent piece of timber—live oak—which probably belonged to the wrecked *Traveller*, already alluded to. It was dry, and so large and heavy that one of the Innuits could only just carry it. We took it away in the boat to use for fuel ; and on sawing off a portion, I found it as sound as it had ever been.

The place where we determined to make our next or fourth encampment was called by the natives *Toong-wine* ; this I named Jones's Cape,‡ and here we expected to find a settlement of Innuits. Before we reached it a breeze sprung up and helped us on. A snug little harbour appeared ahead, and an Esquimaux was observed on an eminence near the shore, eagerly watching us. As we drew near, all the inhabitants appeared to be out on the rocks to await our arrival ; and when we landed, such as were able cheerfully assisted in getting up our tents and in other work. Most of those I now saw were familiar faces. They belonged to the party which I had visited the previous April farther up the bay. But Samson was now away on a tuktoo hunt. He had recovered from his illness already mentioned ; the report of it brought us was doubtless exaggerated, being founded on an incorrect idea of the disease. The old ladies whom I then met— Shelluarping, mother of Kookin, and two of her friends—who were so pleased at my eating with them in the genuine Innuit

* This inlet I name after William Wiswell, of Cincinnati, Ohio. It is on the north side of Frobisher Bay, extending north twelve miles from Oomernung, a small high island on the east side of the entrance of the inlet, in lat. 62° 50′ N. long. 65° 26′ W.

† A beautiful sheet of water, mostly surrounded by rugged mountains, and thus named by me after Peter Force, of Washington, D.C. The entrance to this sound is in lat. 62° 55′ N. long. 65° 48′ W.

‡ So named after John D. Jones, of Cincinnati, Ohio. Jones's Cape is in lat. 62° 55′ 30″ N. long. 65° 45′ W.

style, were here, and gave me a hearty welcome. Ookgooalloo was sick, and I therefore visited him as soon as I could. I was guided to his tupic by his groans; but when I entered and asked the name of the sufferer before me, I was surprised to learn that it was my old friend, so sadly changed. Sickness seemed unusually prevalent; indeed, the only three men of the place were so feeble that not one of them could go out hunting or sealing.

INNUIT MONUMENT AT TOONG-WINE—JONES'S CAPE.

At this spot were some remarkable monuments of stone, one being in the form of a cross, and about six feet high.

In the evening, being in want of oil for my lamp, I went to Koojesse's tupic to obtain some. There I beheld a scene for a picture:

Koodloo and Charley made search, found seal-blubber, brought it in, and passed it to Suzhi, who was in tuktoo, as I may say—that is, a-bed. Of course, like all Innuits when in bed, she was entirely nude; but she immediately rose on her elbows, and proceeded to bite off pieces of blubber, chewing them, sucking the oil out, then spirting it into a little cone-like dish, made by inverting the bottom of my broken tin lamp. In this way she obtained with her dental "mill," in less than two minutes, oil enough to fill two larged-size lamps. Koodloo and Kooperneung were standing up in the tupic at the time. I was seated with Akchukerzhun at my right, on tuktoo, by Suzhi's head, waiting for my lamp, while Koojesse and his partner, Tunukderlien, were at my left, wrapped in Innuit slumbers. It was a novel scene, that of Koo-ou-le-arng's operations in grinding blubber for oil; in particular, the incidental exhibition of what Burns describes as

"Twa drifted heaps, sae fair to see,"

exaggerated in size, as is the case with most Innuit women, struck me forcibly. The whole scene, though so strange to me, was taken by the Innuits as an every-day affair, and quite a matter of course.

The Innuits certainly show peculiar skill in thus expressing oil without allowing a particle of moisture to come in contact with it. It may be doubted that such a thing is possible, but so it is. My replenished lamp burned brightly, allowing me to write up my diary with great facility.

Jones's Cape was really one of the finest places I had seen in the North, not excepting even Greenland. Force's Sound is nearly surrounded by magnificent mountains, and is sheltered from winds and heavy seas by a number of islands. There is an excellent entrance for ships, and the harbours, I thought, might rival any in the civilized world. If a colony should ever be planted in those regions for the purpose of Christianizing the people, Jones's Cape presents many of the advantages desired.

On the following morning, August 14th, I took Koojesse and ascended a mountain in the rear of our encampment. The view was very extensive, and I could plainly see more than fifty miles of Kingaite coast, the nearest point being distant some thirty miles. On my way I observed a considerable quantity of the stone I had noticed upon Iron Island, and I also saw many small pieces of limestone on the very summit, about a thousand feet above the level of the sea.

I remained at Cape Jones until noon for the purpose of obtaining a meridian observation. While making this I was amused to see the astonishment depicted in the countenances of the Innuits of the settlement around me—as far, at least, as they ever do exhibit unusual interest in any subject.

At 12·30 P.M. we again set out on our expedition, directing our course westerly across the east arm of the bay. The natives assembled in large numbers to bid us *ter-bou-e-tie*, which may be rendered thus : " Good-bye, our friends. May you fare well." We rowed for about half an hour, when, finding the sea too heavy for our frail boat, we hoisted sail and steered direct to the middle of the island—Nou-yarn. At about 2·30 P.M. we stopped at a point of the island, and Koodloo went ashore, shortly returning with a shoulder-load of live oak for fuel, which was clearly part of the *Traveller* wreck.

From Jones's Cape we had a hard and tedious passage across the mouth of the sound, consuming two and a half hours in making good three miles. The wind freshened to a strong breeze, and for an hour we were in the " suds." Every few minutes a " white-cap " was sent with all its force into our boat, thoroughly wetting us and everything. Tunukderlien was kept constantly baling, and Kooperneung tucked his nuliana under the folds of his oil jacket to keep her from the overleaping waves. The sheet was not made fast, but was kept in the hands of some of the lady crew, ready at any moment for the word—Let go !

The passage was by no means free from danger ; but God rules the waves, and He brought us safely over. A light shower of rain soon came, accompanied by the glorious bow of good promise, which presented a vivid contrast with the dark moss covering of the rocky mountains forming the background of the picture. At about 3 P.M. we reached Brewster's Point,* the southeastern extreme of Barrow's Peninsula,† where we made our fifth encampment.

That night, looking with my spyglass over the snow mountains of Kingaite, I saw what I at first thought to be the fires of a volcano. After consultation with Koojesse and Kooperneung, I concluded it to be the light of the declining moon reflected from the snow. The effect was strikingly peculiar, the light being red, but in form like a comet's tail.

The next day, August 15th, a head wind condemned the boat's crew to a hard pull ; and, as they made slow progress, I

* I named this point after A. Brewster, of Norwich, Connecticut. It is on the west side at the entrance to Peter Force Sound, nearly on a parallel with the place of fourth encampment, and is in lat. 62° 55′ N. long. 5° 51′ W.
† Named by me after John Barrow, of London, England. It is bounded by Newton's Fiord, Peter Force Sound, Frobisher Bay, and Hamlen's Bay. (*Vide* Chart.)

took my compass and tripod, and walked along the southern coast of Barrow's Peninsula, directing Koojesse to come for me when I should signal him. Charley likewise had gone ahead with his gun to hunt tuktoo. The boat kept close in shore until we came to Hamlen's Bay,* which had to be crossed. Here I embarked with Charley, and with a fair breeze we sped across at the rate of about five miles an hour. On the west side of the entrance to this bay were some islands, between which and the main land was a channel ; and, in order to get to the northward and westward (which, being the general trend of the coast thus far, I had reason to suppose to be probably its direction to the head of the bay), we must pass through this channel. We should have done so without delay but that the ebb of the tide had left it dry. Not being aware of this, I told Koojesse to go on. With a twinkle in his eye, he said, "Well, you tell 'em so—we try." Accordingly we went on until, rounding an island that was at the mouth of the channel which is called by the Innuits *Tin-ne-took-ke-yarn* (Low-tide Land), I saw we were on the verge of dry land. A rise and fall of twenty-five feet in the tide made that impassable at low water which six hours before was a deep channel.

Koojesse, on seeing my surprise, looked at me with such a merry laugh that I could not rebuke him had I been so inclined. We turned the boat round, and formed our sixth encampment upon Blanchard's Island.†

In the early part of this day, while yet close to Brewster's Point, and while walking on the beach, I met with remains of many Innuit habitations of former days, when they used to build them of earth and stone. Bones of the whale, and of all other animals that principally serve the Innuits for subsistence, lay there in abundance, many of them very old, their age probably numbering hundreds of years. One shoulder-blade of a whale measured five feet along its arc, and four feet radius. Whale-ribs, also, were scattered here and there, one of them being eight feet in length. I also noticed there several graves, but nothing, not even a bone, within them. An old drift oil-cask was also there, sawn in two ; one half was standing full of

---

* Named after S. L. Hamlen, of Cincinnati, Ohio. This bay runs up almost due north, and is five miles across at its mouth. The centre of its entrance is in lat. 62° 58′ N. long. 66° 10′ W.

† So named after George S. Blanchard, of Cincinnati, Ohio. Our sixth encampment was in lat. 62° 58′ N. and long. 69° 17′ W.

water, the other half was lying down.   I gathered up the oak staves and heads for fuel.

Next morning, Friday, August 16th, when I awoke, I found the tide ebbing fast, and it was therefore necessary to get under way at once.   In a quarter of an hour we had everything on board, and set out for the desperate work of running the "mill-race" of waters pouring over the rocks, whose tops were then near the surface.   If we could not succeed in the attempt, we must either wait until next tide, or make a long *détour* outward around several islands.

It was an exciting operation.   Koojesse stood on the bread-cask that was at the bow of the boat, so that he might indicate the right passage among the rocks.   Occasionally we touched some of them, but a motion of the boat-hook in his hand generally led us right.   There was a fine breeze helping us, and we also kept our oars at work.   Indeed, it required all the power we could muster to carry us along against so fierce a tide.   At one time, thump, thump, we came upon the rocks at full speed, fairly arrested in our progress, and experiencing much difficulty in moving forward again.   But, favoured by the breeze, we at last got through this channel, and soon stopped at an island to take our much-needed breakfast.   That despatched, we again pushed on, keeping along the coast.   The land was low, with iron-looking mountains in the background.   But some spots showed signs of verdure, and altogether, the day being fine, the scene was charming.

By evening we had arrived at Tongue Cape, on the east side of the entrance to Waddell Bay,* and there made our seventh encampment.   The whole of the next day was spent by the male Innuits in hunting tuktoo, and by the women in sewing skins and attending to other domestic matters.   As usual, I was occupied with my observations.

On Sunday, August 18th, we left our seventh encampment and proceeded along the coast.   As we neared Opera-Glass Cape, a point of land on the west side of Waddell Bay, round which we had to pass, a kia was observed approaching; and in a short time, to my great surprise, the old Innuit Artarkparu was alongside of us.

This man was the father of Koojesse's wife, and therefore the meeting was additionally pleasant.   He was, as may be recol-

* Named after William Coventry H. Waddell, of New York City.   Its east side (Tongue Cape) is in lat. 63° 11′ 30″, and long. 66° 48′ W.

lected, an invalid, having lost the free use of his lower limbs by a disease in his thighs; yet he was rarely idle, every day going out sealing, ducking, or hunting for walrus and tuktoo. In the winter he moved about by means of sledge and dogs, and no Innuit was ever more patient or more successful than

INNUIT SUMMER VILLAGE.

he. Artarkparu had come out from a village not far off, and to that place we directed the boat. We found four tupics erected there, and many familiar faces soon greeted me. Annawa was among them, and also Shevikoo and Esheeloo. The females were busily occupied in sewing skins—some of which were in an offensive condition—for making a kia. A small space was allotted to them for this purpose, and it was particularly interesting to watch their proceedings. The kia covering was hung over a pole resting on the rooks, everything being kept in a wet state while the women worked, using large braided thread of white-whale sinews. As I stood gazing upon the scene before me, Annawa's big boy was actually *standing* by his mother and nursing at the breast, she all the time continuing her work, while old Artarkparu hobbled about in the foreground by the aid of a staff in each hand.

Venison and seal-meat were hung to dry on strings stretched along the ridge of each tupic, as shown in the opposite engraving, and provisions were clearly abundant. In the tupic of Artarkparu, Koojesse and Tunukderlien were at home feasting on raw venison, and with them I was invited to partake of the old man's hospitality. Before returning to the boat I also received, as a present, a pocketful of dried tuktoo meat, given me by Annawa.

After a short stay and friendly adieu, we again departed on our way; but just then I thought it possible that old Artarkparu might be able to give me some information. Accordingly I turned back, and, through the aid of Koojesse as interpreter, entered into a conversation with him. We seated ourselves by his side, and the first question I put to him was, had he ever seen coal, brick, or iron on any of the land near Oopungnewing? He immediately answered in the affirmative. He had seen *coal* and *brick* a great many times on an island which he called *Niountelik*.

He first saw them when he was a boy.

He had also seen heavy pieces of iron on the point of Oopungnewing, next to Niountelik.

"No iron there now, somebody having carried it off."

"Bricks and coals were at Niountelik."

I then asked him, "How many years ago was it when the Innuits first saw these things?"

His reply was, "Am-a-su-ad-lo" (a great, *great* many). His father, when a boy, had seen them there all the same. Had heard his father often talk about them.

"Some of the pieces of iron were very heavy, so that it was as much as the strongest Innuit could do to lift them."

"Had often made trials of strength, in competition with other Innuits, in lifting. It was quite a practice with the young men to see who was the strongest in lifting the '*heavy stone*'" (Innuits so call the iron).

"On the point of another island near by, an oo-mi-ark-chu-a (ship) was once built by kodlunas (white men) a great many, many years ago—so the Innuits of a great many years ago had said."

VIEW AT CAPE STEVENS AND WARD'S INLET

I took from the boat a little bag which contained some of the coal that I had gathered up with my own hands at Niountelik, and asked him if it was like that he had seen.

He said " All the same."

I then asked him " where it came from."

His reply was, " He supposed from England, for he had seen the same kind on English whaling vessels in Northumberland Inlet."

This information I obtained from the old man ; and I could not help noticing how closely it corresponded with that given to me by Ookijoxy Ninoo some months before.

The whole interview was particularly interesting. I felt as if suddenly taken back into ages that were past ; and my heart truly rejoiced as I sat upon the rock and listened to what the old man said of these undoubted Frobisher relics.

After this interview with Artarkparu, we started at 2·45 P.M. along the coast, closely examining its features, and noting down everything of importance which we saw. The land was bold and high, with much of the iron-rust look about it. Scarcely any vegetation was perceptible. Numerous islands bordered the coast ; and, as I looked across the outer waters, it seemed as if a complete chain stretched across the bay to Kingaite.

On reaching the spot which we selected for our eighth encampment—Cape Stevens*—I left my crew to unload the boat and erect tupics, while I ascended a mountain that flanked us. On the top I found numerous shells and fossils, some of which I brought away. On descending I took the opposite or north-east side, next a bight that made up into the land. This side of the mountain was almost perpendicular. The winter forces of the North had thrown down to the base a mass of stone, which enabled me to pass upon a kind of causeway to the foot of another mount toward the tupics. There I could not help pausing and glancing around in wondering awe. Overhead was hanging the whole side of a mountain, ready, as it seemed, at any moment, and by the snap of one's finger, to fall ! I felt as if obliged to take light and gentle steps. I breathed softly ; and, as I looked and looked again, I praised God for all his mighty works.

I ought to say that, on a better view of this mountain I

---

* Named by me after John A. Stevens, Jun., of New York City. Cape Stevens is in lat. 63 21′ N. and long. 67° 10′ W.

perceived on its perpendicular side large caverns, with huge projecting rocks hanging directly over them.

I returned to the tupics; and that night, as I lay on my back by our camp-fire, viewing the glorious heavens, I beheld the aurora in all its wondrous beauty. In the vicinity of the moon, where the aurora was dancing and racing to and fro, it was strangely grand. But the most remarkable phenomenon of the kind I ever witnessed was the peculiar movement of the clouds overhead. For some length of time they moved by "hitches," passing with the wind slowly, and then stopping for a few seconds. I called the attention of the Innuits to it, and they noticed this as something they had never seen before. It seemed as if the clouds were battling with an unseen enemy, but that the former had the greater power, and forced their way by steps along the vault above. These clouds were white, and of the kind classified as cumulus. I thought it a very strange matter, and, according to my idea, the aurora had something to do with it.

TUNUKDERLIEN (wife of Koojesse).

CHAPTER XXIII.

On the following morning, Monday, August 19th, 1861, we
were in readiness to leave our eighth encampment, and pursue
our journey. Starting at 10·15, we crossed the mouth of a deep
bay, across which, and about ten miles up from our course, lies
a long island, called by the natives Ki-ki-tuk-ju-a. Koojesse
informed me that he had been to that " long island," and that
the bay extended a considerable distance beyond. The shores of
this bay I found to trend about N.N.W. Koojesse also said that
it was one day's journey to the head of it from the island. From
this, and other data which he furnished, I concluded, and so
recorded it in my journal at the time, that the bay is from twenty
to twenty-five miles in extent.*

Unfortunately for my desire to get on, a number of seals were
seen, and my crew were soon engaged in pursuit. This delayed
us some time ; and when another similar stoppage took place, I
felt that it was hopeless to think of going far that day, and
accordingly landed, while the Innuits followed what they supposed to be seals, but which, as will shortly be seen, were quite
another sort of game.

---

* I effected a complete exploration of this bay and the island named on
a sledge-journey which I made in the spring of 1862. This, however, will
come in its proper place in the sequel of my narrative.

I walked among gigantic old rocks, well marked by the hand of Time, and then wandered away up the mountains. There I came across an Innuit grave. It was simply a number of stones piled up in such a way as to leave just room enough for the dead body without a stone touching it. All the stones were covered with the moss of generations. During my walk a storm of wind and rain came on, and compelled me to take shelter under the lee of a friendly ridge of rocks. There I could watch Koojesse and his company in the boat advancing toward what was thought an ookgook and many smaller seals. All at once what had seemed to be the ookgook commenced moving, and so likewise did the smaller seals. A slight turn of the supposed game suddenly gave to all a different appearance. I then perceived a boat, with black gunwales, filled with Innuit men, women, and children, and also kias on each side of the boat. Seeing this Koojesse pulled in for me, and we started together for the strangers. A short time, however, proved them to be friends. The large boat contained " Miner," his wife Tweroong, To-loo-ka-ah, his wife *Koo-muk* (louse), the woman Puto, and several others whom I knew. They were spending the summer up there deer-hunting, and had been very successful. Soon after joining them we all disembarked in a snug little harbour, and erected our tents in company on Rae's Point,* which is close by an island called by the natives *No-ook-too-ad-loo*.

The rain was pouring down when we landed, and the bustle that followed reminded me of similar activity on the steamboat piers at home. As fast as things were taken out of the boats, such as had to be kept dry were placed under the shelving of rocks until the tupics were up. Then, our encampment formed, all parties had leisure to greet each other, which we did most warmly.

Tweroong was very ill, and appeared to me not far from her death. Her uniform kindness to me wherever I had met her made her condition a source of sadness to me. I could only express my sympathy, and furnish her with a few civilized comforts. She was the mother of Kooperneung, one of my crew, by her first husband, then deceased.

A great feast was made that evening upon the rocks. A captured ookgook was dissected by four carvers, who proved

---

* Named by the author after Dr. John Rae, the well-known English arctic explorer. Rae's Point, place of our ninth encampment, is in lat. 63° 22′ N. long. 67° 33′ W.

themselves, as all Innuits are, skilful anatomists. Indeed, as I have before said, there is not a bone or fragment of a bone picked up but the Innuits can tell to what animal it belonged. In the evening I also took a walk about the neighbourhood, and was astonished to see such an abundance of reindeer moss. The ground near our tents was literally white with it, and I noticed many tuktoo tracks.

Our stay at this encampment continued over the next day, and I took the opportunity of questioning Tweroong, who was said to know much about the traditions of her people, as to any knowledge she might possess concerning the coal, brick, and iron at Niountelik. Koojesse was my interpreter, and through him I gained the following information :—

Tweroong had frequently seen the coal there, and likewise heavy pieces of stone (iron) on an island close by. She had often heard the oldest Innuits speak of them. The coal and other things were there long before she was born. She had seen Innuits with pieces of brick that came from there. The pieces of brick were used for brightening the women's hair-rings and the brass ornaments worn on their heads.

She said old Innuits related that *very many* years ago a boat, or small ship, was built by a few white men on a little island near Niountelik.

I showed her the coal I had brought with me from Niountelik, and she recognised it directly as some like that she had seen.

Owing to the condition of my own boat, I was anxious to have the company of another craft in my voyage up the bay. I accordingly effected an arrangement with the Innuit " Miner " and his party to keep along with me ; and on the following day, August 21st, at 9 A.M. we all set out from the encampment to pursue our journey.

While Koojesse and my crew were loading the boat, I ascended a mountain close by, and, after as good a look around as the foggy weather would allow, I began to descend by another path. But I soon found that the way I had chosen was impracticable. The mountain-side was one vast rock, roof-like, and too steep for human feet. Finally, after a long, hard tug down hill, up hill, and along craggy rocks, I gained the beach, and hailed the boat, which took me on board after a walk of two miles.

We made what speed we could to the westward and northward, having to use the oars, the wind being right ahead. In an hour's time we came to an island, where the other boat was stopping awhile. Here I saw "Jack," the angeko, performing the ceremony of ankooting over poor sick Tweroong. The woman was reclining on some tuktoo furs in the boat's bow, while Jack was seated on the tide-wet rocks, making loud exclamations on her behalf. It is very strange what faith these people place in such incantations. I never saw the ceremony otherwise than devoutly attended to. I then took my usual exploring walk upon the island, seeing the bones of a huge whale, portions of which were covered with moss, and the rest bleached to a pure white, but all as heavy as stone.

When we again started, the sight of the two boats and two kias pulling side by side was particularly interesting. There were fourteen souls on board the other boat, men, women, and children, the women pulling at the oars ; in each of the two kias was also an Innuit man. The raven hair of the females hanging loosely about the head and face—the flashing ornaments of brass on their heads—their native dress—their methodical rock to and fro as they propelled the boat along, formed, indeed, a striking picture. All were abreast, the two boats and the two kias, and pulling in friendly competition. "Miner" had a flag of checked red, white, and black at the bow of his boat, and the ensign of the United States was streaming to the breeze at the bow of mine.

Our progress during the day was not very great, owing to the frequent stoppages of my Innuit crew. Let me be ever so anxious to get on, or to do anything in the way of making observations, if a seal popped up his head, or anything appeared in the shape of game, away they would go in chase, utterly regardless of my wants or wishes. They mean no ill ; but the Innuits are like eagles—untameable.

Before reaching our tenth encampment * that night, which was similar to the previous one, we passed numerous small bergs, left high and dry on the rocks near the coast by the low spring-tide, as seen in the following engraving.

On the following morning, August 22d, we again set out, making our way among numerous islands, and along land exhibiting luxuriant verdure. Miner's boat and company proceeded on up the bay, while Charley and I were set ashore on the north side of the island "Frobisher's Farthest," leaving

* In lat. 63° 32′ N. long, 67° 51′ W. by a small cove one mile north of the *important* island I have named "FROBISHER'S FARTHEST," called by the Innuits Ki-ki-tuk-ju-a.

instructions with the rest of the crew that we would make our way in two or three hours northerly and westerly to the upper end of the island, where we would get aboard. The place where

ICEBERGS ON THE ROCKS—GREAT FALL OF TIDE.

we landed was very steep, and the ascent was laborious. I had belted to my side my five-pound chronometer, and also a pocket sextant. In my hand I carried a compass tripod and azimuth compass. Charley had his double-barrelled gun, ready for rabbits or any other game.

After getting to the summit the view was very extensive. To the N.W. the appearance was as if the bay continued on between two headlands, one the termination of the ridge of mountains on the Kingaite, *Meta Incognita* side, and the other the termination of the ridge running on the north side of Frobisher Bay. The coast of Kingaite was in full view, from the " Great Gateway " * down to the " President's Seat," † a distance of one hundred nautical miles. A line of islands—their number legion—shoot down from " Frobisher's Farthest " to the Kingaite coast.

At noon and afterward the weather was exceedingly beautiful, and the water as smooth as a mirror. Kingaite side was showing itself in varying tints of blue, its even mountain range covered with snow, throwing a distinct shadow across the surface of the bay. The sun was warm, and yet casting a subdued light on all around. The rocks and mountains upon our right were bare, and of a red hue, while far to the southeast were the eternal snows of the Grinnell glacier.

We encamped, ‡ as before, among the friendly Innuits who had accompanied us, and on the next morning (August 23d), at an early hour, I went by myself for a walk among the hills. Mountains near the coast on that side of the bay had disappeared, the land being comparatively low and covered with verdure. I was delighted to find this such a beautiful country ; the waters of the bay were teeming with animal life, and I thought that here was indeed the place to found a colony, if any one should ever renew the attempt in which Frobisher failed.

Before I came back from my walk I perceived the camp-fires sending up their clouds of smoke, and I was soon after partaking of a hearty breakfast, cooked and served in Innuit fashion. Abundance was now the rule. Seals and blubber were so plentiful that quantities were left behind at our encampment. Even whole seals, with the exception of the skins, were frequently abandoned. Thus these children of the icy North

* The opening between the two headlands alluded to above, which are about ten miles to the north-west of the head of the Bay Frobisher, I named the " GREAT GATEWAY."

† The most cónspicuous mountain on the coast of Frobisher Bay I named President's Seat, after the chief executive officer of the United States Government. President's Seat is in lat. 62° 09′ N. long. 66° 43′ W.

‡ Our eleventh encampment was in lat. 63° 38′ N. long. 68° 10′ W.

live—one day starving, and the next having so much food that they care not to carry it away.

We started at 10 A.M. and passed in sight of more low land, some of which was covered with grass. Seals and ducks were so numerous that it was almost an incessant hunt—more from habit, on the part of the natives, than from necessity. The signs of reindeer being in the neighbourhood were such that the males of my boat's crew landed to seek them. Some of the Innuits of the other boat had done the same, and frequent reports of fire-arms gave evidence that the game was in view. Presently Koojesse returned, having killed one of the largest of the deer, and after some trouble we got some portions of it on board—saddle, skin, hoofs, horns, and skull. My boat soon after carried at her bow not only the American flag, but also the noble antlers of the deer. I felt at home, with the flag of my country as my companion and inspiring theme.

Early in the day, before the shooting of the reindeer, I heard what seemed to be the roar of a cataract, and perceived that we must be approaching some large river. Presently I was astonished by Suzhi saying to me, "*Tar-ri-o nar-me*" (this is not sea-water). She then took a tin cup, reached over the boat's side, dipped up some of the water, and gave it to me, after first drinking some herself, to show me that it was good. I drank, and found it quite fresh. It was clear that the river was of considerable size, or it could not throw out such a volume of fresh water to a considerable distance from its mouth against a tide coming in.

After a while we came to an estuary where the waters were alive with salmon. My Innuit crew were in ecstasies, and I too was greatly rejoiced.

On a point of land at the mouth of this fine river we pitched our tents,* and away went the men for another hunt. They were out all night, and on the next morning, August 24th, returned with two more deer. This, with what had been shot on the previous day, made our list of game four reindeer, besides several seals and sea-birds. We might have had more, but the Innuits were now indifferent to everything but the larger sort.

While at this, our twelfth encampment, there was quite an excitement occasioned among the Innuits by chasing a "rat."

---

* Our twelfth encampment was in lat. 63° 43′ 30″, long. 68° 25′. It was on the west side of Sylvia Grinnell River, on a narrow strip of land called *Tu-nu-zhoon*, the south extreme of which is *Ag-le-e-toon*, which I named Tyler Davidson Point, after Tyler Davidson, of Cincinnati, Ohio.

ENTERING OF SYLVIA GRINNELL RIVER, HEAD OF FROBISHER BAY.

There they were, when I went out of my tent, with clubs and stones, ready for battle with the little animal. But lo! in a few moments the rat proved to be a leming—an arctic mouse. It was hunted out of its hiding-place and speedily killed. Shortly after another one was seen, chased, and killed in like manner. Both of them had very fine fur, and two of the Innuit women skinned the pretty little animals for me. I asked Tweroong if her people ever ate such creatures? With a very wry face, she replied in broken English, "*Smalley*" (little, or seldom).

While we stayed here, Tweroong employed herself in my tupic drawing, with remarkable skill, a rough outline of Frobisher Bay, Resolution Island, and other islands about it, and the north shore of Hudson's Strait. Too-loo-ka-ah also sketched the coast above and below Sekoselar. Every half minute he would punch me with a pencil I had given him, so that I might pay attention to the Innuit names of places. As soon as he had sketched an island, bay, or cape, he would stop, and wait until I had correctly written down the name. At first he was very loth to make the attempt at drawing a map, but the inducement I held out—some tobacco—succeeded, and, for the first time in his life, he put pencil to paper. His sketch was really good, and I have preserved it, together with Tweroong's, to the present time.

The whole of this day, August 24th, and the following day, were passed at the same encampment. All the Innuit men went out hunting, and killed an abundance of game, now valued not for food, of which there was plenty, but for the skins, of which there was very soon quite a large stock on hand. The women were employed in dressing these skins,* and in such other work as always fell to their lot. I was engaged in my observations and in making notes. The weather was delightful, and the scenery around fine. But as I am now writing of that period when I was able to determine the question as to Frobisher "Strait" or Bay, I copy my diary as written on the spot.

"*August 25th*, 1861, 3·30 A.M.—Another and another is added to the number of beautiful days we've had since starting on this expedition. Can it be that such fine weather is here generally prevailing, while bad weather everywhere else north is the ruling characteristic?

---

* The skins of the reindeer killed in August and September are valued above others, for the reason that winter dresses can be made only of them. At the time mentioned they are covered with long, thick, and firmly-set hair.

"This certainly is a fact, that here, at the head of Frobisher Bay, a milder climate prevails than at Field Bay and elsewhere, or the luxuriant vegetation that is around here could not be. The grass plain, the grass-clothed hills, are abundant proof of this. I never saw in the States, unless the exception be of the prairies of the West, more luxuriant grasses on uncultivated lands than are here around, under me. There is no mistake in this statement, that pasture-land here, for stock, cannot be excelled by any anywhere, unless it be cultivated, or found, as already excepted, in the great West.*

"How is it with the land animals here? They are fat—'fat as butter.' The paunch of the reindeer killed by Koojesse was filled to its utmost capacity with grasses, mosses, and leaves of the various plants that abound here. The animal was very fat, his rump lined with toodnoo (reindeer tallow), which goes much better with me than butter. Superior indeed is it, as sweet, golden butter is to lard. The venison is very tender, almost falling to pieces as you attempt to lift a steak by its edge. So it is with all the tuktoo that have as yet been killed here. Rabbits are in fine condition. Not only are they so now, but they must be nearly in as good order here in winter, for God hath given them the means to make their way through the garb of white, with which he clothes the earth here, for their subsistence.

"Koodloo returned this morning with the skins and toodnoo of three reindeer, which he has killed since his leaving the boat on Friday noon. In all, our party of hunters have killed eleven reindeer, but very little of the venison has been saved—simply the skins and toodnoo. . . . . . This afternoon the wife of Jack has been ankooting sick Tweroong. The sun set to-night fine. I never saw more beautiful days and nights than here—the sky with all the mellow tints that a poet could conceive. The moon and aurora now make the nights glorious.

"*Monday, August 26th.*—This morning not a cloud to be seen. Puto visited me, the kodluna infant at her back. I made her some little presents—pipe, beads, file, and knife, and a small piece of one of the adjuncts of civilization—soap. Somehow I thought it possible that I had made an error of one day in

---

* To a person going to the arctic regions direct from the pasture-land of the Middle States, this passage of my diary would naturally seem too strong ; but when one has been for a year continually among ice, snow, and rugged rocks, as was the case with me, the sight of a grassy plain and green-clad hills could hardly fail to startle him into enthusiastic expression.

keeping run of the days of the month, but the lunar and solar distances of yesterday have satisfied me that I was correct. I started on a walk up the hills. I came to an Innuit monument, and many relics of former inhabitants—three earth excavations, made when the Innuits built their houses in the ground. I now see a company of eight wolves across the river, howling and running around the rocks—howling just like the Innuit dogs. Now beside a noble river. Its waters are pure as crystal. From this river I have taken a draught on eating by its banks American cheese and American bread. The American flag floats *flauntingly* over it as the music of its waters seems to be ' Yankee Doodle.' I see not why this river should not have an American name. Its waters are an emblem of purity. I know of no fitter name to bestow upon it than that of the daughter of my generous, esteemed friend, Henry Grinnell. I therefore, with the flag of my country in one hand, my other in the limpid stream, denominate it 'Sylvia Grinnell River.'

"For the first half mile from the sea proper it runs quietly. The next quarter of a mile it falls perhaps fifteen feet, running violently over rocks. The next mile up it is on a level; then come falls again of ten feet in one fifth of a mile; and thence (up again) its course is meandering through low level land. From the appearance of its banks, there are times when the stream is five times the site of the present. Probably in July this annually occurs. The banks are of boulders the first two miles up; thence, in some cases, boulders and grass. Two miles up from where it enters the sea, on the east side, is the neck of a plain, which grows wider and wider as it extends back. It looks from the point where I am as if it were of scores and scores of acres. Thence, on the east side, as far as I can see, there is a ridge of mountains. On the west side of the river, a plain of a quarter to half a mile wide. This is a great salmon river, and so known in this country among the Innuits. At our encampment I picked up the vertebræ of a salmon, the same measuring twenty-one inches, and a piece of the tail gone at that.

"On returning from my ramble this afternoon up Sylvia Grinnell River, saw the wolves again on the other side. They have been howling and barking—Innuit dog-like—all day. I hear them now filling the air with their noise, making a pandemonium of this beautiful place. I now await the return of Koojesse, Kooperneung, and Koodloo, when I hope to have them accompany me with the boat into every bay and to every island in these head-waters of the heretofore called 'Frobisher Strait.'

"The hunting-party has not yet returned; possibly it may continue absent a week. When these Innuits go out in this way they make no preparations, carry no tupic or extra clothing with them. The nights now are indeed cold; near and at the middle of the day, and for four hours after, the sun is hot. This afternoon I started with my coat on, but, getting to the top of the hill, I took it off and left it.

"*August 27th.*— A splendid sun and a calm air this day. To-morrow I hope to be off, even if Koojesse and party are not back, looking here and there, and taking notes of the country; I can *man* a boat with the Innuit *ladies* here if I can do no better. Puto came in with her infant on her back, and in her hand a dish of luscious berries that she had picked this afternoon, presenting the same to me. Of course I gave her some needles and a plug of tobacco in return. The berries are of various kinds, among which are blueberries—called by the Innuits *Ki-o-tung-nung*—and *puong-nung*, a small round black berry that has the appearance, but not the taste, of the blueberry.

"This evening, while in the tupic doing up my writing for the day, I was visited by several of the Innuits, among whom were Suzhi and Ninguarping, both well acquainted with this part of the country. I tried to get the former, when she first called, to sketch me Kingaite side of Frobisher Bay, as well as the coast about here; but she, never having used the pencil, felt reluctant to attempt its use, so she called loudly for Ninguarping, who soon came running with all haste to answer to her call. She told him what I wanted, and that he must assist her. I gave him paper and pencil, and he proceeded, giving me very good ideas of the Kingaite side.

"The night is glorious! The sun left the sky in crimson, purple, and all the varied shades that go to make up one of God's beautiful pictures in these regions. The moon now walks up the starry course in majesty and beauty, and the aurora dances in the southern sky.

"*Wednesday, August 28th.*—Another day of beautiful, glorious weather. Jack called on me early this morning, presenting me with two reindeer tongues. Last evening I received another bountiful present from an Innuit of ripe poung-nung. They taste very much like wild cherries. But what carries me nearest home is the blueberry, it is so like in looks and taste what we have. Ninguarping and Jack brought me in this afternoon a present of two fine salmon, each measuring twenty inches in length. The Innuits call large salmon *Ek-er-loo ;* small salmon, *Ek-er-loo-ung.* Salmon are caught by the Innuits with a hook affixed upon a stick, which answers for a handle. They are also caught by spearing them with a peculiar instrument which the Innuits manufacture for themselves.*

"On the return of the party, the seal which Kooperneung shot coming in was made the subject of a feast. He (Kooperneung) went around and invited all the men Innuits here, who soon came, each with seal-knife in hand. They squatted round the seal, and opened him up. A huge piece of toodnoo (tuktoo tallow) in one hand and seal liver in the other, I did justice to the same and to myself. The Innuits and myself through, the ladies took our places. They are now feasting on the abundance left. Seal is the standing dish of provision among the Innuits. *They never tire of it ;* while for tuktoo, Ninoo, ducks, salmon, &c. they soon find all relish gone.

"Too-loo-ka-ah shot his deer with Koojesse's gun. He usually uses only bow and arrows, the same being in universal use among the Innuits on the north side of Hudson's Strait. This evening I got Toolookaah to try his skill in using these instruments—bow and arrow—in making a mark of my felt hat one hundred feet off. The arrow shot from his bow with almost the speed of a rifle-ball. The aim was a trifle under. He missed 'felt,' and lost his arrow, which is no small matter. Its force buried it in the ground, covered by the luxuriant grass, and all our long search proved unsuccessful. The arrow is made with great pains, pointed with iron, spear-shaped."

---

* There is a third method of catching salmon much practised : a kind of trap, called *tin-ne-je-ving* (ebb-tide fish trap), is made by inclosing a small space with a low wall, which is covered at high tide and dry at low water. The salmon go into the pen over the wall, but are left by the receding tide till it is too low to return the same way, and they thus become an easy prey.

CHAPTER XXIV.

It was on Thursday morning, August 29th, 1861, when we made preparations to leave our twelfth encampment to cross over to the westward to Kingaite, along the head of the Bay of Frobisher. Before I proceed with my narrative, let me bring forward an extract from my journal written the evening previous :—

" Indeed we are in a land and by waters of plenty. I am constantly overwhelmed with presents of the very best of choice eating—tuktoo tongues, toodnoo, venison, ducks, seals, and salmon. Kooperneung this moment (8 P.M.) comes in, saying that Koojesse is near by. *Now for the trip across the head of Frobisher Bay to Kingaite side. . . .* 8·30 P.M. Koojesse has just arrived ; brought four tuktoo skins, showing that he has killed as many reindeer. What a pity that such excellent meat as venison should be abandoned ! He has seen nothing of Koodloo, who still remains out. The weather continues fine, and indications are every way favourable of its continuance."

Thursday morning Koodloo had not returned from his prolonged tuktoo hunt. Arrangements having been previously made with him that, in case he returned and found us gone, he should make his way over the land terminating Frobisher Bay to Kingaite, where he would find us, we decided to strike tupics, pack boats, and push on. At 10·30 A.M. the two boats and two kias were under way, our course nearly due west, to a point of land called by the natives *Kou-mark-bing*—named by me Peale Point*—that shoots down abruptly some three miles from the most northerly extreme of Frobisher Bay.

We soon passed an indentation in the coast of about three miles, at the head of which was a grassy plain, a little inclined from the water's edge to the hills that flank it, and extending back for about a mile. As we approached Peale Point I found it fringed with many islets, and, on arriving there, landed for making meridional observations. Peale Point consists of rugged rocks, which, though not of great height, are yet considerably more elevated than any part of the land at the head proper of Frobisher Bay. Here we found on the sandy beach large and remarkable time-worn boulders, nearly white, and numerous tuktoo tracks. I noticed, also, the usual signs of Innuit encampments, such as circles of stones, bones of various animals, &c. On reaching the lower group of islands near the cape, Koojesse, who was in his kia, came alongside. I asked him, "*Nou-ti-ma?*" —where now? He pointed toward a long island out of our regular course across the bay. I told him I wished and expected to go direct to the opposite side from our last encampment—to go to *Ag-goun*, the west side of the head of the bay. He replied that we could not get there, as the tide would be too low for the boat before arriving. I thought differently, and said I wished to go there and spend a day or two. He, however, seemed not disposed to please me, and remarked that I could see the whole head of the bay from the point where he desired to go. I answered that this would not do; *I must go where I wanted to.* If he wished to visit the point named, well and good; he might go there and spend the night, but on the morrow I must have him and the others proceed with me in the direction I wished. He agreed to this, though evidently considering it useless, so long as I could see the termination of the bay.

According to my original purpose, I thought it well to attempt to go back by the Kingaite side, that is, opposite to my upward route. At all events I would endeavour to get as far as the island Kikitukjua, Gabriel's Island† of Frobisher which is not far from the locality where "Samson" and his people were located during my visit to them in the previous winter. It is true that I had intended to revisit the coast on that side; but still enough had

* Named after Washington Peale, of New York City. It is in lat. 63° 43′ 30″ N. long. 68° 33′ W.

† The centre of Gabriel's Island is in lat. 62° 51′ N. long. 66° 22′ W. (*Vide* Chart).

been done, with sufficient accuracy, for the civilized world to gain
a knowledge of the general situation of Frobisher Bay.   At least,
the opinion that these waters are a strait ought not any longer to
be entertained.

LANDING FOR THE NIGHT'S ENCAMPMENT.

At 4 P.M. having made a distance of six miles from Peale's
Point on a course S. 40° W. true, we entered a channel, with
Kingaite on our right and Bishop's Island* at our left.   The
coast on each side was steep, but in many places covered with
grass and the usual vegetation to be found here in the North.
The entrance to this channel was about half a mile wide ; but,
on making a quarter of a mile, it brought us into a harbour that
appeared to be a fine one, not less than two and a half miles in

* Thus named after R. M. Bishop, of Cincinnati, Ohio.   The centre of
this island, which bounds the north and eastern side of the harbour of the
thirteenth encampment, is in lat. 63° 37′ N. long. 68° 35′ W.

diameter. Thence we passed on a course nearly south to the west side of the harbour, where we landed, and there made our thirteenth encampment* on Kingaite.

Throughout this day, on approaching the islands or main land, I noticed that the water seemed very shallow, and it was certain that no large-sized ships could attempt to reach the head of Frobisher Bay with any degree of safety.

Before arriving at the place of our encampment, I saw the tupics of our other Innuit friends and the curling smoke of their fires. As I landed Koodloo greeted us. He had just come in from his hunt, having shot and secured skins and toodnoo of four deer. This made *thirteen* that my three men had killed within four days. On making up to our intended encampment, all hands commenced unloading the boat, the females, as was customary, acting as pack-horses in conveying everything up the

RAISING THE AMERICAN FLAG.

steep rocks beyond reach of the tide; then they selected a convenient spot and erected the tupics.

A few moments after our arrival, with the " stars and stripes" of my country in one hand and my spyglass in the other, I made my way to the crest of a high hill in the rear of our encampment. Before starting, the sun was down—to us ; but, as I reached the summit, his glorious rays burst upon me. And how glad was my heart as I planted the flag of America upon that mountain-top,

* Our thirteenth encampment was in lat. 63° 36' N. long. 68° 43' W.

and beheld it fluttering to the breezes of heaven in the sun's light.

How soul-inspiring was the scene before me as, drinking in the sweets presented to my eyes, I wended my way from one mountain-top to another. It was night when I got back to our encampment, and I was immediately greeted with two welcome presents of *blueberries*. Tweroong brought hers in a gold-banded *china* saucer. And a most strange sight it was, here amid the gray old rocks, and among this iron people, to see such an emblem of civilization as a *tea-saucer*. It was brim full of ripe, luscious berries, which were then very abundant.

As I descended from the mountains I saw that the white clouds were kissing their tops. I knew this was an omen of bad weather. A thick fog soon settled, and this, on the following day, August 30th, turned into cold and wet, confining me the whole time to our tent. During the day Puto was in our tupic cutting out a jacket for Kooperneung's wife. The skins were of a kind of seals called by the natives *kus-se-gear*, which has softer hair than some other species, and visits salt and fresh water alike. These skins being beautifully mottled and glossy, make fine-looking dresses, and are much prized by the Innuits. Koomuk, wife of Toolookaah, both of Sekoselar, brought me a huge reindeer tongue. In return I gave her some beads, which greatly delighted her. Tweroong was there at the time, and I asked her what she had done with the beads I had recently presented her. Her reply was that she had given them to the angeko for his services in her sickness. As she was a truly generous, kind-hearted woman, I selected a few more and gave them to her, and in returning the remainder to a little tin case, in which I kept my journal, observation books, and a few other precious things, my eye rested on the Bible. I took it out and held it up before the women, saying, "This talks to me about *Kood-le-par-mi-ung* (heaven)."

If a flash of lightning had come down into the tupic with all its blaze it could not have had a more sudden effect than what I said and showed to them. At first they looked affrighted, but the next instant smiles of great joy appeared upon their countenances. I never shall forget that moment. Tweroong was sitting by my side on some furs spread upon the ground, making a sketch for me of the coast on the north side of Hudson's Strait, while Koomuk was lying on the grass by the tent door, with her head inside, facing us. On the instant that I said the Bible talked to me of heaven they both sprang up, apparently banishing all thought of everything else from their minds, and expressed a wish that I should *talk* to them about what it said to me. My imperfect knowledge of their language, however, precluded me from telling them much that it did say. Neither could I do more, when Tweroong asked me if it talked about *Ad-le-par-me-un*, pointing down, than to answer in the affirmative, bringing forth more surprise from them. I need hardly say how much I longed to possess the power of communicating to them the truthful beauties of our Christian faith ; of dwelling upon its heavenly Founder, and of telling them of God. Perchance the day may yet come when these people shall no longer be without some one who can do so.

On Saturday, August 31st, the weather was thick and foggy. In the morning I had a good wash with snow—not snow of this season, however. What its age was I know not ; perhaps it belonged to many winters ago ; but, notwithstanding, it was fresh and white, and it gave me clean, cool hands and face, which is a luxury in the North as well as in any other place. By the side of this friendly snow-drift was abundant vegetation, green and fruitful, and blueberries all around. I picked some with rather cold, stiff fingers, and made a capital feast. I had not found any place where there was a greater variety of vegetable growth within the same space. In a little spot, not over four feet square, one could count more than fifty different kinds of vegetation. Mosses, grasses, berry-bushes, flowers, willows, and many other plants, could be enumerated as abounding in that little plot. But all these were quite diminutive ; for instance, the blueberry-bushes were only from an inch to two inches in height.

On this day I made arrangements with Miner and Koojesse for the whole company in the boats and kias to return by the Kingaite side. It was agreed that we should proceed first to *Aggoun*—the Innuit name of the west side of the head of Frobisher Bay—and thence return and follow down the coast of Kingaite. The chief reason for my making such an arrangement was that, by having *two* boats, should a mishap occur to one, the other would be our " *Rescue.*"

We started from our thirteenth encampment in the afternoon, leaving behind two of the Innuit tents erect, and some sundries, to be called for on our return from Aggoun. Our course was direct for the northwest end of Bishop's Island, upon which I landed. From its top the whole head of Frobisher Bay, from Sylvia Grinnell River, north-east side, to Aggoun, west side, was in view. It is fourteen nautical miles across. The termination is not by deep bays or fiords, but by slight indentations, the greatest not exceeding three miles. Bishop's Island was well covered with vegetation, especially with reindeer moss, the ground, in many parts, being quite carpeted with it.

As we descended the hill-side leading to the boat, I found the women busily engaged with their cups in blueberry picking, pulling them now and then by the handful, the berries were so large and abundant. Before long the party came on board, bringing with them quarts of the luscious fruit, with which they entertained us very agreeably, the whole scene carrying me back at once among the friends of my youth.

Innuits will always be Innuits. When we left our thirteenth encampment, one of them had gone off with his kia to an island to hunt some tuktoo, which had been seen two hours before. A part of the company had been left with the other boat to await the return of the deer-hunter, while the rest of us went on slowly, stopping at Bishop's Island, as above related. We had but just re-embarked, when Koojesse, looking through his spyglass back toward the encampment, announced that the other party had a tuktoo in the water—a live tuktoo! This fired every Innuit; all the powers of reason could not keep them from going to see the fun; and so about we went, and in a moment they were all pulling back as for dear life. The sequel was more amusing and satisfactory to me than to my Innuits. When they came near enough to see their *live tuktoo*, it turned out to be only a *goose !*

After sundry other vexatious delays of a similar nature we were fairly under way, and the scene was for a time pretty indeed. The boats were alongside of each other. The Innuit women were at the oars. In the jacket-hood of Puto was her child, the constant, measured rock of the body in pulling the oar being equal for sleep-giving to any patent Yankee cradle ever invented. The gilt head-bands of the ladies glittered and flashed, and the whole picture was peculiar and charming.

At about 6 P.M. we stopped for our fourteenth encampment,* the fog shutting us out from all view except of the coast on our left. The place where we encamped was on the Kingaite side of Frobisher Bay, at the base of a long straight bank of sand and shingle, from thirty-five to forty feet high, the top being a grassy slope which extended back some three hundred fathoms to the mountains.

* Our fourteenth encampment was in lat. 63° 41′ N. long. 68° 48′ W.

"*September 1st*, 1861.—A day of trials and discovery. At last I am where I have long desired to be. *From my own vision, 'Frobisher's Strait' is a myth.* It only exists in the minds of the civilized world—*not in fact.*

"I find this side still more interesting than the other. Here, at the west extreme, are far more extensive plains of grassy land than elsewhere. Koojesse has this moment passed to my hands what I think will prove to be rare geological specimens—fossils."

But let me give the day's occurrences in a methodical form; for I wrote the above, and much more, in my diary while sitting on the rocks that are at the head of Frobisher Bay, after several hours' severe labour.

The morning commenced thick and foggy, with occasional glimpses of finer weather. I ascended to the plain in the rear of the fourteenth encampment, at the top of the sand and shingle bank, and saw much vegetation, with numerous signs of reindeer in the neighbourhood. Then I examined wherever I could; but my view was very limited, as numerous islands bounded the vision toward the bay. At low water frequent shoals are exposed, and even to navigate our boats thus far we had been obliged to wait for the tide at half flood.

When I desired to get under way, I found that Koojesse, without saying one word to me about it, had gone out on the mountain tuktoo hunting. Kooperneung had also taken Miner's kia, and had set out in advance after seals. Thus was I perpetually annoyed by the freaks and vagaries of this free and independent people. At last, however, at 1 P.M. we left our encampment and proceeded up the west side of the bay, toward its extreme head, called by the Innuits *Aggoun.*

I had a boat's crew of women; for Koodloo, who had frequently proved himself a lazy dog, sat in the bow with his oar peaked, leisurely reclining on his thwart. Having gone for some time in a northwesterly direction, I turned the boat toward the shore (Kingaite side), intending to land and visit a remarkable ridge of what seemed to be sand, stretching a mile or so along the coast. Before getting near the shore, though, I could see that the water was becoming very shallow, the bottom being of fine sand, and the boat soon grounded. As I could not make a landing, I concluded to push on, for I felt sure that we were very near the termination of Frobisher Bay. I reckoned without my host, however, in thinking to get on without trouble. The Innuits of my boat looked back to the craft of

" Miner," and declared that the latter was making an encampment about a mile behind. I found the crew bent on going thither, but I was determined this should not be. I asked Suzhi, " *Noutima Aggoun ?* "—where is Aggoun? She pointed to where Miner was. I knew this to be but a trick to get me back. I felt that I could manage women at least, and cried out *A -choot !* — pull ahead — returning a decided negative to their prayers to go back. With some difficulty I brought them to their working senses.

Finally we reached the estuary of a river—Jordan's River,* as I have named it—and, after crossing it, landed on its eastern side. We were then obliged to wade quite a distance to the shore proper through mud that was nearly knee deep. On a small grass-plat of Hazard's Banks,† we made our fifteenth encampment.

Leaving the Innuits to unload the boat, I started off on a tramp of discovery, and continued my course up the river, which at first ran in a northwest direction, and then, for a short distance, more northerly. As I walked along, charmed with the prospect before me, I came across a skull, which I took up for the purpose of ascertaining from the Innuits to what animal it belonged. I afterwards found that it was that of a white whale. I saw around me, as I advanced, that vegetation was abundant, and signs of animal life were very numerous. As I rounded a rocky eminence by the river side, at a distance of a mile from where I had left the boat, a beautiful cascade, at the head of tide-water, was before me, and at its base a little sheet of water nearly covered with Brent geese.

From this point an extensive and picturesque scene burst upon my view. Before me were long and wide plains, meadows of grass, smoothly-sloping hills, and a range of mountains beyond, which, parting in one particular spot, formed, as it were, a natural gateway, that might almost lead, in fancy, to some fairy land beyond. At my left, across the river, was a ridge of white, which I afterward named Silliman's Fossil Mount,‡ and behind it the unbroken front of a line of mountains

---

* Named after Daniel B. Jordan, of Cincinnati, Ohio.

† The land on the east side of the estuary of Jordan's River I have named after Charles S. Hazard, of New York City. Hazard's Banks are in lat. 63° 46′ N. long. 68° 52′ W.

‡ Thus named after Benjamin Silliman, Jr. of New Haven, Conn. This fossil mount is on the west side of the termination of Frobisher Bay. It is in lat. 63° 44′, long. 68° 56′.

extending northwesterly to the opening which I have called the Great Gateway. On the other, or northern side, the mountains continued from this singular opening on by Frobisher Bay to the locality around Field Bay, far to the southwest and eastward. Flocks of little chirping birds greeted me at every turn, and nowyers and ducks were in numbers before my eye. Words cannot express my delight, in view of this scene, as I stood by the waterfall, beholding its white spray, and the clear, limpid stream of the river.

The fall is about twenty-five feet in three or four rods, and at no place over four feet descent at once. The river is not so large as the Sylvia Grinnell, and yet, though the season is evidently a dry one, much water flows along, and at certain portions of the year this stream must discharge a large quantity. The banks in some places are of fine sand, and in others, farther up, of ledges of rocks that are from fifty to sixty feet high. I wandered about for two hours and then returned to our camp.

Miner's boat was out at the time, but I soon saw it approaching at great speed, its crew shouting lustily. In a moment I perceived the cause of their excitement. A white whale was swiftly making its way through the waters toward the main bay. The Innuits were after it, and their shouting voices made the neighbourhood ring again; but it escaped, and the boat came to our encampment, the occupants in no good humour. One of the men, Charley, clearly proved this. His wife was helping to unload the boat, and had to walk through deep mud with a heavy load upon her shoulder. Suddenly, for some unknown cause, Charley, with great force, threw his seal-hook directly at her. It caught in her jacket. Turning round, she *calmly* took it out, and then walked on again. It was a cruel act of the man, but these Innuits always summarily punish their wives for any real or imaginary offence. They seize the first thing at hand—a stone, knife, hatchet, or spear—and throw it at the offending woman, just as they would at their dogs.

Two of our party were still absent. Koojesse, however, made his appearance on the opposite side of the river, and it was necessary to send the kia to fetch him off. Now a kia has but one hole in its covering, for the person who uses it; therefore, if a second person is to be carried anywhere, he or she must take a position directly behind the other occupant, lying flat on the face, perfectly straight and still. It was in this manner that Koojesse, and afterward Toolookaah, were brought off.

I had another walk up to the falls, and again the scene appeared to me as one of the most beautiful I had ever beheld. I felt like those old Icelanders who visited the regions west of them, and, because of more verdure seen than in their own country, exclaimed, " This is Greenland ! " In the present case, my feeling was that no more appropriate name could be given to the district before me than " Greenwood's Land," in honour of Miles Greenwood, of Cincinnati, Ohio. I think no one, not even an English geographer, will question my right to name this land. At the head of Frobisher Bay—now positively determined to be such, and no longer a " strait "—exists this beautiful and fertile district, and I considered the name of Greenwood to be especially appropriate.

On the morning of September 2d, after breakfast, reindeer were seen on the plain across the river, and immediate chase was given by some of our hunters. Two were speedily captured, and all hands soon began the task of skinning the animals and preparing food. While the people were thus occupied, I started, accompanied by Tunukderlien and Toolookaah, for an excursion inland toward the Great Gateway. We arrived at a place opposite the falls, and there, seated on the green carpet of nature, the woman commenced sewing, while I occupied myself with my journal. Koojesse, who was to go with me, shortly arrived, crossing the river to us by fearful leaps from rock to rock over the rushing stream. Soon after, Toolookaah—who had gone across the river to a feast at the place where the reindeer were killed—rejoined us, and we again proceeded on our exploring trip ; but in a short time rain fell, and we had to take shelter under a huge boulder rock, distant from the tupics six miles. Finally, as a heavy storm set in, spoiling my excursion for the day, we returned to the encampment. During our journey a white owl was seen ; also partridges and other wild game. Several rare specimens of fossils were also picked up, and in every direction I found abundant evidence of a region fertile to the explorer.

The two reindeer shot this morning were mother and young. The latter was fired at first. The parent then hastened to her offspring, and this enabled the shrewd Innuits to kill the doe. It is the general custom among this people, in chasing the deer, to kill the fawn first ; then it is rare indeed that the mother is not also secured.

For some time past I had been suffering from painful boils, and the morning of September 3d, found me quite ill, and confined to my fur bed inside the tupic. I felt no inclination to eat until the kind-hearted Tweroong came in, with her pretty china tea-saucer full of golden salmon, smoking hot. The very sight of it made me better. It was delicious, and seemed to fairly melt in my mouth. It did me much good, and I could not help thinking of my present situation as contrasted with that of other civilized men. There, alone, among a people termed " unenlightened, savages, and degraded beings "—away by myself in a newly-discovered region, that is, in a district previously untrodden by my own white race—confined by sickness within a shelter that scarcely protects from rain and wind—everything dripping wet—suffering from the pain of my body, and having no person to procure me what I might want, I am unexpectedly visited by a woman of the land, bearing in her hand a beautiful emblem of civilization filled with the most dainty dish—boiled salmon—fresh from the river I had just discovered. Truly woman—a good woman—is an angel wherever she is. The vision of Tweroong will long live in my memory. God bless the kind-hearted Innuit for her thoughtfulness, and her care of the white-man stranger in her own wonderful land.

During the day Koojesse was using in his soup some pepper which I had brought with me as a condiment. Koomuk desired to taste it, and Koojesse at once gratified her wish. He sifted some into her open hand, and she immediately lapped it up in one dose. The next moment all the contortions, grimaces, jumping, and spitting that could be imagined followed. The woman seemed as if struck with sudden madness, and, when once more calm, declared that nothing should ever induce her to put such vile stuff in her mouth again. An hour later, Toolookaah, Koomuk's *wing-a* (husband), was served in a similar way. He came into the tent, and, seeing that something from my well-seasoned dish was still left, he desired to have it. What he thus coveted was merely salt and pepper, articles to him unknown. He, thinking it to be a delicacy of the white man's, licked it all up in quick time. The result may be imagined. Though myself sick, I could not control my laughter, in which " Miner" and the other Innuits joined on beholding the poor man's terror and dismay, added to the most comical contortions of his countenance. In Koomuk's case she had only pepper, but Toolookaah had a double dose—pepper and salt— and he suffered accordingly.

The next day, September 4th, I was still confined to my tent by sickness. The abscess on my shoulder had become so painful that every remedy in my power to apply was resorted to. At length a salve formed of reindeer tallow gave me some relief. During this time every kind of attention was paid to me by the Innuit women, especially Tweroong, who frequently brought various cooked dishes to tempt my poor appetite.

A very high tide occurred on the morning of September 5th. The weather was pleasanter, but many signs were manifest which urged me to return to the ship. The Kingaite mountains were topped with white, and the cold was sensibly felt in the night-time; but my sick state still prevented me from moving out on any land excursion, as I wished. The same morning "Miner," with his wife and crew, left for the place of our thirteenth encampment.

I here bring forward a few extracts from my journal :—

"*Thursday, September 5th.*—. . . To-morrow we leave our fifteenth encampment for the place of the thirteenth. There I shall find my good-souled Innuit friend, Tweroong, who will prepare me something good. I do not like to leave here till I have done more work; but I must go, sick as I am.

"The weather now indicates a favourable change. The evening is pleasant. I pray God to bless me with restored health.

"This evening, at high tide, I and Koojesse were going to take the boat and ferry the river, that I might visit the remarkable phenomenon of these regions—the Sand Mount; but I have sent for him to come to my tupic, saying I could not go—was not able, indeed.

"The snow that fell last night, and which whitened the mountains of Kingaite this morning, has disappeared during the day.

"*Friday, September 6th.*—Another terrible night of struggle with pains. When shall I be well again? The fine weather of to-day has been of some benefit. God be praised.

"This morning, at an early hour, I was up. I might as well have been up all night; for, though down on a soft tuktoo bed, and dry, yet I could get no sweet sleep.

"When the tide was up sufficient to set the boat afloat, I got Koojesse and Koodloo to ferry me across the river, that I might visit the peculiar sight which had been constantly staring me in my face during my five days' stop at the fifteenth encampment. I visited that phenomenon; I mounted it, and went around it also. It is a mount of marine fossils in limestone, half a mile long, and over a hundred feet high. It presents something of the appearance given in the engraving below, the long line of Kingaite mountains behind stretching away to the Gateway northwest.

. . . "The débris of the fossils begins at or near the top of the mount, falling at such an angle as broken stone from a mountain always makes—an inclination of about 40°. Above the talus, or heap of broken stones, is a mass of fossils in limestone, strata-like. A smaller mount* of the same character is

SILLIMAN'S FOSSIL MOUNT.

close by, but all in débris. It seems to have been divided from the main by the rushing down of waters from the mountains behind. A small stream comes down the mountains, passes along, and finally makes its way out between the two fossil

* The small mount referred to is not represented in the illustration, but is to the right, or northwest of the main one.

mounts. This is also indicated in the course of the stream, as an acre or more of the plain is covered several feet in depth with the washed-down débris of fossils. I picked up several specimens, and have them with me. The top of Silliman's Fossil Mount is covered with boulders and grass. Even when close to the small mount it looks like sand, but on examination it is fine broken limestone and fossils.

"Having spent two hours on and around this interesting mount, I made my way over the plain of grass between said mount and the river, and cried to those at the fifteenth encampment. Soon Koodloo, with two of the lady portion of the crew, put out after me. I had my arms and pockets full of specimens, and a hard, weak, weary time did I have of it.

"I had thought to cut in stone, somewhere near the fifteenth encampment, my name, or something to indicate my visit here (to the head of the Bay of Frobisher), but I had not the tools to do it with. This thought occurred to me on the idea that some of civilization who may yet make a voyage here might have this proof that I had preceded him or them.

"But the description of the river, the falls, the fossil mount, the miles of exposed bottom at low tide, will answer as well. What better proof do I want?

"When we got back to the encampment the tide had begun to fall. This indicated that, if we would get away to-day, we must make haste. The tupics I found all struck, and everything ready for departure. I made the observations which commence this day's record, and then we were ready for our homeward voyage by way of Kingaite side. What deep regrets thus to depart from this interesting land that I have denominated Greenwood's Land!"

CHAPTER XXV.

Departure from Greenwood's Land—Numerous Rocks—Furious Tides—
Narrow Escape—Preservation Island—Beginning of Winter—Ice Form-
ing—Visit the principal Islands at Head of the Bay—Koojesse a
skilful Boatman—Nearly wrecked—Saved by the Rising Tide—Departure
Homeward—The Kingaite Coast—Boisterous Weather—Detained on a
Rugged Island—Difficulties with the Innuit Crew—Freedom and In-
dependence—Land.

MY desire was to have continued here much longer, and thoroughly
to have examined the vicinity of the natural " Gateway," already
mentioned ; but my companions were urgent to go, and I was
obliged to yield. Accordingly, on the morning of September
6th, 1861, our tupics were struck, and we set out on the return
journey.

It was 9·37 A.M. when we left our fifteenth encampment, and
at ten o'clock we landed Koojesse and Koodloo on the opposite
side of the estuary. They were desirous of going on another
tuktoo hunt across the mountains, and were to rejoin us at the
place where our thirteenth encampment had been made, the
point to which we were now bound. There were thus left in
the boat with me only the three women of my crew, and I was
not free from anxiety till we had passed a point of land which
I called the " Little Peak," and which was by the water's edge,
surrounded by dangerous shoals. Then I supposed we had got
over the critical portion of our way.

When abreast of the fourteenth encampment, and near a small
island about one mile from that station, I found we were being
carried along by the ebbing tide at a rapid rate, but I then
apprehended no danger. Suzhi, who was experienced in boating,
joyously called my attention to the swiftness of our progress,
saying, with a sweeping motion of her hand, " *pe-e-uke !*" (good.)
But soon this feeling of pleasure was destroyed. It was not five
minutes after Suzhi's exclamation when we were all struggling
for dear life.

The island we were approaching was small, and it seemed to
us that it mattered little on which side of it we should pass.

On standing up, however, and looking ahead, this opinion was changed. I saw that rocks began to peer out in the channel between the island and the mainland, and we therefore steered for the other channel. But all at once, and only half a mile ahead, rocks appeared above water right in our course. This led us quickly to look over the boat's side, to see if we could see the bottom. To our dismay, jagged rocks showed themselves almost within reach of our hands, the boat meanwhile being carried along at a mill-race speed by a fierce rushing tide. It was enough to make one feel how feeble a creature man is at such a time. The Innuits were terribly alarmed at the sight ahead and under us. The rocks showed how fearfully fast we were going. On smooth water the speed is not so perceptible : but where objects, and especially dangerous objects, are visible ahead, around, and under you, such swift motion is not only seen, but felt. So it was then with us. Immediate action, however, was necessary ; and seeing what I thought to be an eddy not far off, I at once turned the boat's head in that direction.

By the time we reached this eddy we had been swept down some distance, and in order to clear the threatened danger from the rapids ahead, I reversed our course, and tried to pull back. The tide was now falling rapidly, and we rowed for our lives ; but all we could do was to hold our own. Our greatest exertions could not advance us one step away from the danger. Every moment I looked over the boat's side to see how far we might hope to escape the rocks ; and it was truly awful as I caught sight of what was beneath us. The tide was rushing as if in the maddest fury. We could not clear ourselves. Our strength was fast failing, and if the boat were allowed for a moment to sweep with the tide, we should be lost. No chance seemed possible unless we could make the island itself. But how to reach it was the question. The tide rushed along its side as fiercely as where we then were, with a noise which could be heard in all directions. Still, we had no alternative.

Placing the boat's head in such an oblique direction as to make allowance for the current, we pulled toward a bight of the island, where there seemed to be smoother water. The next moment, however, the boat was whirled round, stem for stern, in such a manner as to take all power out of our hands. Then again we thought ourselves lost ; but the very movement which thus terrified us really threw us into such a position that a few strong pulls sent the boat within that island cove, where all was still as a summer lake. "Heaven be praised !" said I ; and there was occasion for gratitude, for not ten minutes after nearly all the rocks in the course we had made were above water. Soon after getting on shore, the boat was left high and dry by the receding tide, and in another hour we could see the bottom of the bay for miles, one mass of boulder and shingle. The different islands could now be visited by walking to them dry-shod. No ship, and hardly a boat, except with much care, could venture up the side of the bay. It was only by watching, and taking advantage of the tide, that even our small boat could be navigated to the head of Frobisher Bay.

A DESPERATE PULL.

I may here mention the singular action of the tides. While on our way hither I had heard the roar of waters, as if a heavy surf were beating on the shore, and I several times asked Suzhi what it meant. Her reply was " *Tar-ri-o,*" meaning " the sea ;" but as no severe storm had raged sufficiently to cause such an uproar of the waters, I replied, " *Tarrioke na-me. Koong !*"— not the sea ; it is the river. Thereupon she appealed to her companions, both of whom confirmed her statement, saying it was the sea. When we were upon the island I was convinced that they were right. The sea—that is, the waters of the bay— came rushing up on the flood tide, and went out with the ebb in the impetuous manner already described. It will be recollected that I doubted Koojesse's judgment on the day we left our twelfth encampment, and crossed with a view of proceeding to Aggoun. He objected to making the attempt, asserting that there would be difficulty in doing it, owing to the shallow water and the tides. I now knew that he was right, and I well understood why the Innuits dreaded the trip, and held back. In commemoration of our providential escape, I called this place "Preservation Island."

We remained on that island six hours, and at 6 P.M. resumed our trip. I found that the tide was quite eight feet higher when we left than when we put in to our place of refuge. How it could be so, and still be rushing past the island with such velocity that little headway could be made against it, I cannot explain. When the tide turned from ebb to flood we could see it coming in afar off. Its roar was like that of the sea raging in a storm. On it came with great volume and velocity. A person situated midway between some of the islands about there when a flood tide is commencing would have to run at full five miles an hour to escape being overwhelmed. The flood tide, indeed, seemed even swifter than the ebb. How long and anxiously I stood on Preservation Island, watching that incoming of the mighty waters! How I gazed at the boiling and the seething waters, the whirlpools—waterfalls—mill-races made by the tide as it rushed along! The sun was fast sinking behind the mountains of Kingaite, and the air was becoming cold. I once thought we should have to stay there for the night, but it was evident that such a course would be our destruction, as the island would undoubtedly be submerged at high water. Waiting, therefore, would not do; and, accordingly, we pushed off at the time I have mentioned.

My continued illness made me almost incapable of exertion; yet it was necessary to work, and to work hard. I steered the boat, and also aided Tunukderlien at the oar nearest me. I had constantly to keep a good look-out ahead for shoals. These, however, were foam-crested, showing where danger was to be avoided. And thus on we went, pulling rapidly down to the point of destination under difficulties that few can understand. Darkness coming on, our bark a frail boat, our crew Innuit women, and myself almost incapacitated by illness, it is easier to imagine than describe my feelings while we were thus making the passage from the head of Frobisher Bay to the place where our whole party had to encamp.

Suzhi was so powerful at her oar that she often pulled the boat half round, and I had to guard against this by my twenty-two feet steering-oar. But all were earnest in the endeavour to reach a good landing before the tide again turned ; for if we should not accomplish this, nothing, in all human probability, could save us.

At length we arrived in safety at the place of our thirteenth encampment, the point we desired to reach, and where we now made our sixteenth encampment. Here most of the company were awaiting our arrival.

On the 7th of September I kept myself quiet ; indeed, I was obliged to do so. The abscess on my shoulder was so painful that I could not stir without difficulty. I thought of the many obstacles I had encountered in the prosecution of my discoveries, but consoled myself with the reflection that, at all events, something had been done since my leaving the United States. Overwhelmed with disappointment at not being able to proceed on my voyage to King William's Land, I yet had some gratification in the knowledge that my present voyage had not been wholly lost. I had, at least, established a geographical fact, that " Frobisher Strait " is nothing but a *bay*. While I was reclining on my couch suffering severe pain, I said to myself, Perhaps the kind friends at home, who have helped me in my exertions, may consider that, under all the circumstances, I have not thrown away my time and labour, and may still give me their friendship and support. If so, I shall be well repaid.

This day " Miner " and his crew departed for the purpose of hunting more game and securing furs for the winter. The males of my party—much to my annoyance—had left me two days before, on the chase.

On the next day, September 8th, I felt that winter had indeed begun. Ice formed at night, and a severe snow-storm that morning set in. We were still detained by Koojesse and his comrades, who continued absent ; and for two days I was confined to my tent, with only occasional walks in the vicinity. On the 10th of September I went over the mountains westward to make a survey, as far as possible, of the whole of this locality. On my route I met Koojesse and Koodloo, just returning from their four days' hunt. Koojesse was so much fatigued that he could hardly speak. Both of them had packs of skins upon their backs, which they soon threw off, and then sat down to rest. Their first call was for tobacco, but, much to their disappointment, I had none with me. Poor fellows ! they had been without a " smoke " or a " chew " for two days, and were suffering much from the want of it.

I found that Koojesse had the skins of four tuktoo, and

Koodloo of three.   For these seven skins they had been four
days and three nights out, ascending mountains, wading rivers,
sleeping out in snow-storms, their garments wet, with no spare
ones to put on, and exposed to every change and privation.
These Innuits do indeed toil for their winter clothing.   I asked
Koojesse how they managed in such stormy weather as we had
experienced, and with the nights so dark.   He replied that
when each had killed one or two deer, they were all right.
They stacked their guns, or, if near rocks, selected a suitable
spot for a temporary tupic, made of the skins with the hair-side
in.   They then wrapped themselves in a tuktoo skin, and so slept
warm and soundly.   Helping them with their burdens as far as
my weak state would permit, I continued on my trip of observation and discovery, while the two Innuits returned to the
encampment, where, much to their vexation, they learned from
the woman that a bear had been seen close by.   My walk alone,
of six miles or more, resulted in my making the discovery of the
two streams which flow into the Bay of the Two Rivers.

That night another severe snow-storm came on from the
south-east, and toward noon of the 11th the wind shifted to the
north-west.   The weather then moderated, and I set out in the
boat, accompanied by Koojesse and Koodloo, for the purpose of
visiting the islands inclosing a kind of harbour, on the shores of
which we were encamped.   The wind was blowing strong in our
favour, and we therefore made sail, intending to keep under
canvas the whole way.   We had only one oar available, the rest
having been used as frames for the tupics.   As we sailed along,
how exhilarating was the scene!   The boat seemed to fly, so
buoyantly it sped on its way.   Koojesse steered, and well did
he guide us between rocks and sand-pits in our course.   Bounding over the crested waves, and lifting itself clear of everything
but spray, our frail bark soon carried us to the point I wished to
reach.   It was on the east side of the harbour, on Bishop's
Island, that I landed with Koojesse, while Koodloo remained in
the boat to keep it from grounding, as the tide was already on
the turn, and going out swiftly.

Our steps were rapid as we went over the banks of snow, up
one hill, and then across a valley, and thence up to the crest of
another hill—Mount Observation, as I called it—whence I
could obtain a good view.   Here I took several observations, as
fast as I well could, noting them down at the time.   The view
from this point was extensive.   It included the whole coast
that terminates Frobisher Bay.   I embraced that as the last

opportunity I should have of linking together, by the use of my survey instruments, many important places in that locality. Some of the observations I there made for relative geographical positions include the following points : the Great Gateway ; Hazard's Banks, place of fifteenth encampment ; Peale Point ; place of twelfth encampment, by Sylvia Grinnell River ; place of fourteenth encampment ; place of thirteenth and sixteenth encampments ; island " Frobisher's Farthest ; " and a long line of coast down on the Kingaite side.

Having accomplished my purpose, we then quickly returned to the boat. Again we made sail ; but hardly had we started, when, in an instant, we were aground. Out jumped Koojesse, who, with two or three good " *heaves*," cleared the shore, and once more away we went. But soon—ahead, here, there, everywhere—shoals appeared. Koojesse, however, now showed himself to possess much of the daring and fearlessness of a skilful sailor. He was the wild spirit guiding us safely through many dangers. His skill, however, could not save us from a peril into which we now ran, and out of which we escaped only by the care of a merciful Providence. The tide proved too strong for us, and we found ourselves, near nightfall, driven on a small rocky island of the harbour by our sixteenth encampment. We at length made our slow and tedious way in the midst of a strong gale, among dangerous shoals and threatening waves. At times, driven out of our course by the force of the wind, we would lose all the ground we had gained, finding ourselves really farther from home than when we started ; and at last we were on the point of giving up in despair of reaching our encampment that night, when the tide turned. Even with this favouring us, we sped along in imminent peril ; and now, while I write, the thought of that moment comes to me with a thrill of excitement. As we flew over a rocky bottom that almost kissed our keel, I exchanged looks with my companions that expressed more than words could have said ; and as now and then our boat would ride with a shock upon some boulder in its course, all hands would work with a silent energy which spoke volumes regarding the critical posture of our affairs. Our satisfaction and my gratitude may be imagined when we at last reached the spot we called home, and found hot coffee, besides all the comforts of Innuit life, awaiting us at the hands of Suzhi.

Thursday, September 12th, was the thirty-fifth day from the ship, and the seventh at the sixteenth encampment. On that morning I determined no longer to delay, but at once to return to the *George Henry* (if she had not sailed), going down by the Kingaite side of Frobisher Bay. Accordingly, at 10 A.M. we all started on our homeward journey. The tide at starting was just sufficient to float us over the rocks, and we had a breeze to help us, but the weather was unfavourable. In some places we could see a snow-storm raging, and every sign of winter was now perceptible. Our trip that day was along the Kingaite coast, and after a few hours' sail we reached an island I have named Tweroong,* on which Miner's party had encamped, where we also pitched our tents for the night, making our seventeenth encampment.

The next day (September 13th) we were confined to our tents on a small rocky island by a heavy gale and a furious sea ; but on the 14th the weather became more moderate, and we resumed our boat-voyage, crossing over from the island to Cape Rammelsberg,† on the Kingaite side, that I might examine it.

While we were there, a fine-looking tuktoo was discovered lying on one of the little plains. Kooperneung at once went off with his double-barrelled gun to secure it. I could see the royal antlers of the noble animal as it quietly reposed, unconscious of its fate. As Kooperneung approached it scented a foe, started up, and away it went at full speed ; but too late. One report— another. The tuktoo was a prize, having rushed on its fate in fleeing towards a rocky pass where the cunning Innuit had secreted himself.

We made our eighteenth encampment about four or five miles from this place, at Cape Caldwell, ‡ and on the morning of September 15th proceeded on our way. I may here observe, that few of those who read this book can have any conception of the many difficulties I had to encounter in my task. Innuits are Innuits, and such they ever will be. They are independent of every other human being, and will never brook control, no matter what engagements they enter into. At this particular time of which I am writing—and, indeed, during all my work at the head of Frobisher Bay, and on my way thither and back —I was completely at the mercy of Koojesse and his companions. He especially would do just as he pleased ; and if I attempted

* After the noble-hearted Innuit woman Tweroong. This island, place of our seventeenth encampment, is in lat. 63° 28′ N. long. 68° 21′ W.

† Named after Frederick Rammelsberg, of Cincinnati, Ohio. This cape is in lat. 63° 21′ 30″ N. long. 68° 20′ W.

‡ I have named this cape after John D. Caldwell, of Cincinnati, Ohio. It is in lat. 63° 23′ 30″ N. long. 68° 17′ W.

to show opposition or express a determination to do as *I* might wish, ominous looks and sharp words met me. Several times I felt obliged to submit, for I knew my life was wholly in their hands.

When Koojesse, who steered the boat, was directing our course away from the Kingaite side, and when I requested him to remain where I wished to make an examination, he curtly and even savagely repiied, " You stop ; I go." I was forced to smother my anger, and submit to the mortification of being obliged to yield before these untamed children of the icy north. Reflection has, however, convinced me that I can hardly blame them, as I then felt inclined. They are born free as their native wilds ; they have no one to control or check them ; they roam about as they will ; and, while they have to find subsistence as best they can, it would be almost too much to expect any subservience from them to a stranger, especially when he is alone. They are in so many points naturally noble in their character, and I have received so much kindness at their hands, that it would be unjust to make their obstinate self-will, when on excursions with me, a cause of great complaint. I mention the matter, however, to show that I was unable to accomplish as much as I wished, owing to this very cause.

CHAPTER XXVI.

Land on an Island—Leave Kingaite Coast for the North Side of the Bay of Frobisher.— Extraordinary Scenes — Singular Customs— Drinking Deer's Blood —More Ankooting—Mystical Songs —" Fool's Gold"— Parting with old Too-loo-ka-ah—Arrival at Niountelik —Proceed to Kodlunarn, or " White Man's" Island—Important Discoveries— —Ship's Trench—Ruins of Stone Houses—Coal and Tile—Return to Niountelik and Encamp—Cruise in " Countess of Warwick Sound"— Arrive at Tikkoon—Discovery of a heavy Piece of Iron—Passage across the Sound—Proceed up Victoria Bay—Precipitous Mountains— Ekkele- zhun—A fine and secure Harbour—Discovery of several Tons of Coal and Flint-stones—Return to Niountelik.

On the 15th of August, 1861, we started from our eighteenth encampment at 6·15 A.M. wind light from the west, and cloudy. Both boats and two kias under way. " Miner " has just shot a nowyer on the wing from his kia. First pop, down it comes. We are on the rocks first thing ; "bad beginning, good ending." Under oars ; the fifth oar cannot be used on account of the over-loaded boat. Another Job's comforter on my shoulder, the sinister. Geese flying to the southward. Little girl Shoo-kok (whalebone) on board our boat. 8·45 A.M. land on a small island to bale the old leaky boat. This moment I ask Koojesse which way now, the many islands ahead making it doubtful which is the better course. He points across the bay to the other or north side. I suspected this was the way he was direct- ing the boat. He acts the devil with me. My work on this, the Kingaite side, is ended. I said to him I cannot do the work I wanted to. . . .

At 9 A.M. we were crossing toward a long, high island that trends in the same direction as Kikitukjua (Frobisher's Far- thest). The head of Frobisher Bay not seen now, the sea or water of the bay to the north-west being the horizon. A remarkable sand or fossil mountain island, by Kingaite side, two miles off at our right, bearing W.N.W. by compass ; I could not determine its true character with the glass. A line of islands now seen that runs across Frobisher Bay from Frobisher's Farthest to Kingaite side. The trend I will determine soon, and make a record of it.

The snow-squall continued but four minutes. Very cloudy. Sun shining occasionally on the mountains each side of Frobisher Bay. . . . Stop at meridian on an island after passing through a channel, the island of the group running from Frobisher's Farthest to Kingaite, and here ascended a high hill to triangulate.

. . . As we came up the channel between the islands that lie across the Bay of Frobisher, we found the tide (which was ebbing) to run very swiftly. Made no headway for full half an hour, though under sail and oars. Through this channel the ebbing tide was running toward the head of Frobisher Bay—a curious feature, but accounted for by the position of the islands each side the channel.

After spending half an hour on the island, we directed our course for the north side of the bay, which we made in one hour; thence we coasted along toward Rae's Point, where we arrived at 3·15 P.M. and made our nineteenth encampment at the place of our ninth.

During the evening the Innuits fired many salutes, and there was clearly some demonstration making, though I could not tell whether it was to invite the good spirits or to repel the bad, of whose presence thereabouts I suppose the angeko had told them.

It would seem from the shouts of men, women, and children, and the reports of the guns, as if the 4th of July had come again. Jack's wife kept up a kind of shouting and howling till past midnight. After she had continued it for over two hours, with a voice that made the mountains about ring, Jack joined her, he being an angeko. At midnight there was a round of guns. Charley was in the same tupic as myself, having been asleep until the firing aroused him. He sprang up, and was but a moment in getting ready to join his people. Soon Jack, with his howling wife, came down from the hill where they were, and marched around, keeping up the same hideous noises—so loud and broken, that only throats of brass, and cracked ones too, could equal them. It was a miserable, sleepless night for me—in Bedlam, and racked with pains.

A remarkable feature of the mountains of Kingaite is that they are covered with snow, while those on the opposite side of the bay, near the coast, are wholly destitute of it. On arriving at the latter from Kingaite I at once felt the great difference of temperature, it being much warmer.

I may here mention, as another illustration of the peculiar customs of the Innuits, that when they kill a reindeer, after skinning it, they proceed to cut off bits of different parts of the animal, and bury them under a sod, moss, stone, or whatever happens to be at the exact spot where the deer was shot. On two occasions I noticed this. Once they cut off a piece of the paunch, then a bit of the nose, next a portion of the meat, skin, and fat, burying these portions together, as just described. I asked one of them if such a custom was always practised by the Innuits when they killed tuktoo, and the answer, given in a very serious tone, was that it had always been so.

On the previous day, when Charley killed the deer at our eighteenth encampment, I noticed that, on its being skinned, there was a greenish appearance about the legs and lower parts of the body. This made me remark to Koojesse that I thought the tuktoo must have been sick. He said "no;" but that the peculiar look was from the deer's having been swimming much of late in the cold water of the bay, during his passage from point to point.

The following day, September 16th, we resumed our voyage, but could not get far, owing to severe stormy weather, which compelled us to make our twentieth encampment on Mary's Island,* on the west side, and at the entrance of the inlet which I crossed on the morning of August 19th (*vide* page 347). Here we were detained two days, and I was now so enfeebled by sickness that it was difficult for me even to write. The Innuit women, particularly Tweroong, were very attentive to me, but the men seemed to consider my sufferings as of little importance. Their demoniac yells, during a continuation of the same kind of exorcisms already described, were truly frightful, and to one sick as I was all but maddening.

Fortunately, the next morning, September 18th, we were again under way on the homeward trip. A fair wind sent us rapidly along, and we passed our late encampments, as also many other places familiar to me from our visits when coming up. At one place—west side Waddell Bay—Koojesse and the other Innuits landed to go in chase of some deer seen in the distance. We slowly followed in the boat, and came to a cove on the coast, where we saw them with a prize in hand. This deer—which made up the number thirty-nine now killed by my three hunters

---

* So named by me, after one of the daughters of Augustus H. Ward, of New York City. Mary's Island is in lat. 63° 22′ N. long. 67° 38′ W.

—was a very fine one, and in a short time we were all feasting on portions of its meat. When this deer was opened, old Too-lookaah, with his broad hand, scooped up the warm blood and drank it, to the quantity of nearly two quarts. I joined in the eating, and partook of some toodnoo and marrow, the latter blood-warm, from the mashed bones of the tuktoo's legs. The most delicious part of the deer is the toodnoo or fat which is on the rump, and it is this part the Innuits first seek. After our feast, we packed up the remains and again started, arriving about dark at the place of our twenty-first encampment, on the south side of Tongue Cape—the same cape where we had our seventh.

The following day, September 19th, we made good progress downward, with nothing particular to note except the following incident :—

Jack's wife, who was on board pulling at an oar, was suddenly taken with what I at first supposed to be a fit. She broke out into the wild singing which I have already spoken of as per-taining to the practice of ankooting. The scene at that moment in the boat was a strange one ; Jack was steering, Annuarping sat close wedged by my side, Ninguarping was between Suzhi and the angeko*tress*, holding the little dog *Neitch-uk*, two women were pulling at the oars, Koodloo sat upon a huge pile of skins at the bow, and the little boy reclined where best he could. They all started into immediate action the moment Jack's wife began her mystical song. As she sent forth her unmelodious voice—her lips sounding like so many fire-crackers on a Fourth of July festival at home—one and then another of the Innuits took up a responsive chorus to her incantation. As she sang in this wild and singular strain, her arms worked stronger at the oar, and she seemed as if suddenly possessed of a demoniac strength. There was a startling vehemence about her ; and when the others joined in chorus, it was as though unearthly visitants had taken possession of them all. All night, when we again encamped, the strange ceremonies were continued. Jack took up the preaching—if it can be so termed—while the women sang, and the men loudly responded to their angeko. Thus it continued till a late hour, and, with intermissions, through the two following days. They seemed to regard it as a duty, somewhat as we hold sacred certain observances on set occasions.

September 20th and 21st were but a repetition of preceding days, presenting difficulties in getting the male Innuits to work as I wished, forcing me to submit in almost everything. Per-haps, had I been in robust health, I could have managed them better, but I was too sick and feeble to contend. Once, when Koojesse acted in direct opposition to my desires, I turned upon him, and in sharp tones insisted on his doing as I wished about the boat. I spoke firmly, and with a show of determination. It had some good effect. He steered in the direction I wanted to go, and was as friendly afterward as though no hard words had passed between us. All this time the other Innuits continued at the oars, apparently as indifferent as though nothing was occurring; but I must confess that I myself did not feel quite easy in my mind as to the possible consequences.

On the 20th we had a few minutes of excitement, which occurred thus : Miner's party had made a landing before my boat could get up, and I shortly afterward saw Tweroong sitting upon the tide-washed rocks in such a position that I thought she must be searching for some lost article. By the time we effected our landing, every Innuit of the other party was gathered round her in great commotion, some of them trying to break off pieces of the rocks about. I asked Koojesse what all that hubbub meant. He said Tweroong had found *gold !* This word started me at once. I threw my cloak from my shoulders and leaped over the bow, landing on a sand-beach, knee-deep in sea-water. I was followed by my whole crew, for I had communicated the *yellow fever* to them, and, bounding from rock to rock, we arrived at the desired spot. A huge, heavy "yellow boy" was soon in my hand. *Gold, gold,* indeed, was now in the list of my discoveries ! Ought I not to be satisfied, after all my trials and perplexities ? But, on the first touch of my knife, I found that I had only *fool's gold*, and I brought away but small specimens of this precious metal.

A short distance from Gold Cove we made our twenty-third encampment, on the south side of Jones's Cape, not far from the fourth encampment. At this place old Toolookaah and his wife left our party. He intended to remain at that spot until his son, who was with Samson up an inlet near by, should return. I made him a present of matches and tobacco, and gave his wife two papers of needles. In parting with him I said, " Toolookaah, I may not see you again. Soon I shall go to my own country— America ; but I hope by-and-by to meet you in *Kood-le-par-me-ung* (heaven)." A tear started in his eye and trickled down his iron face as we pressed hands and said the final word, " *Ter-bou-e-tie !*" (farewell.)

Our twenty-fourth encampment was made on an island called Oo-mer-nung, at the entrance of Wiswell's Inlet, and on the following day, at 10 A.M. we were again under way for Niountelik, then only a few miles off.

After landing upon Niountelik, and taking an observation of the sun at the spot where I first discovered the coal, we proceeded toward an island, on which, according to Innuit tradition, the *kodlunas* built a small ship *amasuadlo* (a great many) years ago. The heavens were cloudless, there was a fine breeze from the northwest, and the boat bounded along

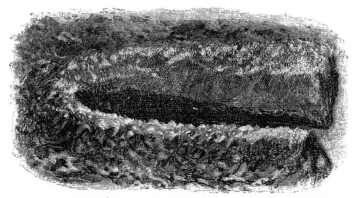

ONE OF FROBISHER'S GOLD MINES, CALLED BY THE NATIVES SHIP'S TRENCH.

rapidly toward the island. Around us was high land, white with its winter dress, and beneath, an immense forest of sea vegetation, over which we sailed. We soon reached the shore, and I immediately landed to examine the place as well as the short time at my disposal would permit.

I soon came across an excavation, which was probably the commencement of a mine dug by Frobisher, though the Innuits, judging only from what they saw, called it a reservoir for fresh water, a quantity of which collected in it at certain seasons. This excavation was at some distance from the ruins of the stone houses, and was eighty-eight feet long and six feet deep.

On the shore of the north side of the island I found also an excavation which I called a ship's trench, for the Innuits said that was where a ship had been built by the white men. It had been dug out of stone, which was of such a nature as to yield to the persevering use of pickaxe, sledge-hammer, and the crow-bar. The bottom of the trench, which was one hundred and ten feet in length, was an inclined plane, running from the surface of the ground to a depth of twenty-five feet at the water's edge.

On the top of the island I found the ruins of a house, which had been built of stone, cemented together with lime and sand. The foundation still remained, and was of "lyme and stone." It was about twelve feet in diameter, and every portion of it was covered with aged moss. From appearances, some of the stones had been turned over, as if done by Innuits seeking treasure.

A few feet east of this house was a sort of stone breastwork, such as the natives erect for shelter when hunting, and also a pile of stones, which might have been made, as I thought, by Frobisher's men, to cover some memorial left by them when trying to escape in their ship.

Much of the island was covered with shingle, and this, on the north side, was so compact, and of such even surface, that it reminded me of the small cobble-stone pavements in cities.

I collected as many relics from these ruins as we could possibly carry, and, with Koojesse, returned to the boat. On our way he said to me,

"The men who built the ship, and started with it, all died —*died with the cold.*"

I asked him how he knew this; and he replied that "all the old Innuits said so."

This agreed precisely with what old Ookijoxy Ninoo told me the previous winter in the oral history she then communicated to me, and I felt convinced that all the evidences before me could refer to no other than Frobisher's expedition, and the men left behind by that explorer. She said that the five men built a ship, and found so much ice that they could not proceed, and finally all froze to death.

This island is generally called "*Kod-lu-narn*," because *white men* lived on it, and built stone houses, and also a ship. The ship was built for the object of escaping from this region. In the previous winter, while passing on our way from the ship to Oopungnewing—an island three miles southwest from Kodlu-narn—Koojesse had pointed out this latter island, and said that white men once built a ship there. I gave little heed to his statement at the time, because I knew that to build a ship such materials were required as the regions thereabout were quite destitute of. But when I heard the history of Ookijoxy

Ninoo, I saw at once the probability there was that Koojesse was right.

From what I saw that day, I was fully convinced that many, very many years ago, men of civilization did live upon the island called by the Innuits *Kodlunarn*, and that they did build a vessel—probably a schooner—there.

The evidence was contained in the following objects which I saw around me, viz. —

Coal; flint-stone; fragments of tile, glass, and pottery; an excavation which I have called an abandoned mine; a trench made by the shore on an inclined plane, such as is used in building a ship on the stocks; the ruins of three stone houses, one of which was twelve feet in diameter, with palpable evidence of its having been erected on a foundation of stone cemented together with lime and sand; and some chips of wood which I found on digging at the base of the ship's trench.

Upon this evidence, then—coupled with Esquimaux tradition, as given to me by several persons apart from each other, and at different times—I founded my opinions respecting Frobisher's expedition, as I have already stated them.

It was night before we left the island, darkness alone ending the search. We had to row back, the native crew pulling cheerfully as we bounded along. The lights of the tupics on Niountelik were my beacon ahead, and above were the glorious stars in all their beauty, while the silvery moon was rising from behind the mountains of Tikkoon. The time seemed long since all had appeared so fair to me as then; and when we arrived at the tents, I went to my rest truly thankful at having been permitted to accomplish what I had that day been enabled to do.

The following morning, September 23d, I continued my researches in this interesting sound, leaving Niountelik at 8 A.M. There was a strong head wind, but my crew were good at the oars, and away we went merrily toward the mainland beyond Kodlunarn. As we passed across the bay, my heart was greatly elated at the thought of what I was then accomplishing. A glance at the red, white, and blue cheered me onward in the work of ripping up the mysteries of three centuries. That symbol was my constant, cheering, helping companion night and day.

In about an hour we arrived at the cape of land called Tikkoon, and, upon landing, I proceeded to a small plain about a quarter of a mile from the cape. The Innuits went on before me, I having my compass and tripod in hand to take bearings.

All at once my attention was drawn to the extreme of the plain, facing Kodlunarn, by the beach, where I saw *Koo-ter-e-nier* (Miner) calling by shouts to the other Innuits and myself, holding up his arms and hands. The Innuits started on a run, and so did I, for I was sure something of interest had been found. Arriving at the spot, what was before me ? A relic of three centuries ! Iron—time-eaten, with ragged teeth !

This iron, weighing from fifteen to twenty pounds, was on the top of a granite rock, just within reach of high tide at full and change of moon. The iron stain from this specimen was in the rock ; otherwise its top was cleanly washed.

This was just what I wanted to find—some of the *heavy stone* which the venerable Innuit woman, Ookijoxy Ninoo, had told me about the previous winter.

The Innuit circles of stones at Tikkoon, indicating this to be a place for the summer residences of the Innuits, were very numerous. I know not where I have seen more numerous signs of Innuits than on the plain a little distant from the cape. Between the plain and the extremity of the cape the usual rough old rocks are the nature of the land. The north side is flanked by high, bold mountains, a bay extending back for a mile or so on the west side. On the east side extends the bay, one branch of which leads toward Field Bay. The plain extends across the cape from one bay to the other, the distance being less than one-eighth of a mile. The " heavy stone " was found at the coast edge facing *Kodlunarn*, which island is about half a mile off. Bones of ducks, tuktoo, walrus, and whale were numerous all around. Some were very old, being nearly overgrown with grass and moss. I doubt not, two or three centuries old were some of these remains.

On leaving Tikkoon the wind was strong from the northeast, and it soon increased to a gale. Kooterenier (Miner) was my boat-steerer, and well he performed his task in passing several dangerous places where heavy gusts came rushing down the ravines or over the abrupt mountains. Our boat shipped much water, the mad waves frequently flying over us. Once a sharp gust caught us while under sail, and instantly sent the boat onward toward a dangerous reef of rocks on our lee. In a moment sail was down, oars out, and all hands pulling strong and rapidly to clear the danger. Fortunately, a few moments of hard work carried us free, and we soon after reached Cape *Ood-loo-ong* and landed.

Here I took a few compass bearings, and walked about to

examine the spot. Many relics of Innuits were seen here. After remaining there an hour we again started, and proceeded up Victoria Bay, keeping well inshore for smoother water. The

BOAT IN A STORM.

scenery was magnificent. Stupendous cliffs rose up almost perpendicular from the water's edge, and mountains towered high above me, the sides of some crumbling as if from age and the work of winter's freezing power. One precipitous mountain, about half way up the bay, had the whole side of it torn from summit to base, and cast down.

As we approached this mountain my eye caught sight of a cave. I landed to examine it, and the moment I set foot on shore I was struck with amazement at the huge rocks, high up and overhanging my head, seemingly ready to totter and fall. The cave was one of those made by the action of ice in winter and the sea in summer. The ice had rent the rocks and fastened upon them ; the sun, with its heat, and the wind, with its power, then went to work, tearing up the frozen masses of ice, and forcing out the rocks, thus leaving the mountain partly disembowelled, as I found it. By measurement, the cave was fifty feet long, by a width of ten feet, and a height of fifteen to twenty feet at the entrance. The strata of rocks were perpendicular. The sides, however, were not as rough and jagged as were the roof and base. Icicles, long, numerous, and large, hung from the top, giving an air of enchantment to the scene.

Returning to the boat, we resumed our hard labour at the oars, the wind being right ahead. We had not proceeded far before Koojesse sighted a seal floating a little distance off on our right. He instantly prepared for a shot, and stood up in the bow of the boat ready to fire. In another moment, and within twenty-five feet of the seal, crack went the rifle. A floundering commenced, the boat was in an instant alongside of the prey, and Koojesse laid hold of his prize with both hands, the other Innuits immediately aiding him. I shall not soon forget that scene. A line was thrown around the seal's flippers, but the animal was still alive, and struggled so much that all the power we had could hardly get it into the boat. As it was drawn up, the dying seal glanced around and upon us with its plaintive eyes, and its innocent-looking face seemed to plead for mercy, as though it were human. I actually felt a shudder creeping over me as it looked at us ; but, on the instant, —a knife in the hands of Kooperneung was buried deep in it. Another struggle, and the poor seal lay dead. Koojesse told me that occasionally, on a windy day, seals will thus float upon the surface of the water for the sake of having the wind blow on their backs.

A little later we landed at Ek-ke-le-zhun, a point of interest and importance to me. This place is a tongue of land which juts out nearly half across the bay, and serves to form above it one of the safest and finest harbours I ever saw. The scenery around is grand and impressive, and I saw enough to convince me that it is a most desirable spot for a vessel to anchor in.

While the Innuits were feasting on the seal I took a walk upon the shore. All the land above high-water mark was covered with snow; but, looking attentively on the ground, to my delight I discovered a small, thin lamina of coal. On the day we left Oopungnewing (August 13th), on our voyage up Frobisher Bay, Koojesse told me that he knew of a place not far off, up a bay, where there was a great deal more of the coal such as I had found at Niountelik. My experience, now narrated, shows both that Koojesse was honest in his statement, and also—which is a point of great importance—that the Esquimaux traditionary history, extending back for centuries, is wonderfully accurate.

Imbedded in the rocks I also found some heavy black substances, larger and more numerous than any I had before seen. These I concluded might be the " stone like to seacoal" described by Frobisher in the account of his voyages. I secured some specimens, which I brought home with me.

But I was not content with the hasty examination thus made. After returning to the boat and lunching on raw seal, I renewed my search, in company with Koojesse and Kooperneung. Soon, by digging under the snow, coal was found in considerable quantities, and also a little pile of flintstones similar to those discovered in the coal at Niountelik, and in the cement of the stone-house ruins at Kodlunarn.

My feelings were so buoyant and excited at this discovery, and the proof it furnished to my mind that Frobisher had been there, that I could hardly contain myself. But my excitement was considerably increased when Miner, from the top of the highest part of the tongue of land, raised a shout and said he had found more. We rushed toward him, and lo! more and more was indeed found. There was a large space clear of snow, and covered with coal to the amount, I thought, of some five tons. I was perfectly astounded. But I could not lose time. I therefore at once commenced an inspection of the heap, and soon found a large chip imbedded in the coal. This chip, my companion declared, was never the work of an Innuit knife. It had the appearance of having been chopped out of a large piece of oak timber with an axe. I dug down fifteen inches into the coal before coming to any earth. The Innuits willingly assisted me, and, as at Niountelik and Kodlunarn, everything they found was apparently passed to me. I discovered, however, that they pocketed some of the best specimens of the flint-stones, and I had eventually to resort to diplomacy in order to recover them.

Leaving the main pile, I dug in other places through the snow, and found coal extending over a wide area. There could be no doubt that a large deposit was made here, and I could arrive at no other conclusion—from the evidences of the age of the coal, in the mosses and other signs upon it—than that this was done by Frobisher. I filled a keg with specimens of the coal, the moss, and the lichens, to bring home, and just as I then packed it, so it appeared when opened in the presence of many persons after my return.

Night was now fast approaching, and I could stay no longer. The Innuits had descended to the boat before I could tear myself away from the interesting spot; and long after we left, and while we were running rapidly out of the bay under a favouring breeze, did I keep my gaze fixed and my thoughts centred upon it.

Our course back was directly across Countess of Warwick's Sound to Niountelik. The wind was strong and in our favour, so that we made rapid progress, and in good time reached the island. But the surf was too high for landing on the weather-side. Accordingly, we went round into the same bight where I landed on the memorable day of my first discovering the coal here.

It was dark when we arrived, and there was much difficulty in getting everything up the abrupt bank flanking the place of landing. My own labour was severe, especially in my then weak state. Many were the struggles I made to carry up safely the chronometer and other important articles. Two hours were occupied in doing this, and in getting up the boat above high water; but at length all was accomplished, and we arrived at the tupics at a late hour, wearied beyond measure with our exertions.

This time no hot coffee or tea awaited me, as heretofore, when Suzhi attended to the matter. My supper was ice-water and molasses, with bread soaked in it, and some dried venison—a poor diet to a cold and enfeebled system.

CHAPTER XXVII.

On Tuesday, September 24th, 1861, a snow-storm from the north-east was upon us. This delighted me, for it made a stay of another day necessary, impatient as the Innuits were to get back to the ship. After breakfast, enveloped in my cloak, I sauntered out, determining to give Niountelik a good look. I first proceeded through snow and furious wind to the opposite side of the island, but found nothing worthy of note in my walk there. On my way back, however, by the beach east of the tupics, I found several pieces of coal in the sand, and up a gully much more, with some flint-stone. A little farther on I suddenly encountered another deposit of coal, No. 2 of Niountelik, on the bank, by a cove with a sandy beach, a short distance east of where I had found the first deposit some months before.

At this moment the Innuits came round with the boats, and landed in the cove; and the idea immediately struck me that this was the identical landing-place of Frobisher in 1578. The coal-bed was within thirty feet of high-water mark. Its depth, in the thickest part, was six inches. It was nearly overgrown with grasses, shrubs, and mosses; and some of it was washed down into the sand and shingle of the beach. The flint-stones were numerous, and of the same character as in the two other lots found. Having made a very thorough examination here, I looked elsewhere over the island. Relics of Innuits were in all directions, but especially on the eastern slope; and some small pieces of drift-wood, overgrown with grass, were met with and secured. After going to the camp for a seal-spear, I succeeded—

by dint of great exertion and perseverance, digging through the frozen ground—in obtaining several good specimens of the coal interlocked with moss, grass, and shrubs.

The weather was not propitious on the morning of September 25th, but the Innuits were anxious to get away, and I had to submit. While the boat was being prepared, I went to the highest part of the island and took some bearings by compass, and carried with me, on my return to the boat, more coal and other relics to take home. Miner and his crew were not ready, owing to some of their dogs being missing; but I hurried off, hoping to induce my companions to stop once more at Kodlunarn on the way.

This I was fortunately able to do. I concluded an arrangement with them to stay there for a short time, for which favour I had to give to Koojesse five boxes of percussion caps, Koodloo two, and Charley two. I could not leave this locality without, if possible, making another examination of the "White Man's Island." Moreover, I wanted additional relics from the stone house ; and, also, to take some measurements and bearings. Accordingly, after leaving Niountelik, our course was taken direct to Kodlunarn Island, where we landed at the same place as before, and I at once began to examine this interesting locality. I made a very close and minute inspection, taking measurements of distances, so as to be quite sure of the data from which my deductions could be drawn. Rough outline sketches were also made on the spot, and everything was done to insure correctness in my notes and observations. The plan of the island, which is incorporated in the chart accompanying this work, will better serve to convey the general facts to the reader than the most laboured description with the pen.

The result of this, my second examination of Kodlunarn, brought to light new facts in connexion with the past. A piece of iron, semi-spherical in shape, weighing twenty pounds, was discovered under the stone that had been excavated for the "ship's way," and many other small pieces were also found at the head of the trench. Fragments of tile were found all over the island, and numerous other relics, indicating that civilized men had visited the place very many years ago.

The large piece of iron was found in the following manner : Koojesse and I had been examining the "ship's trench," to see how high up in it the tide at full and change rose, and then, leaving him to search for relics, I ascended the eastern bank, and walked along it to the bluff facing the sea. As I looked down to the base of the tongue on which I stood, I saw, wedged in between two rocks, what appeared to be a stick of timber, about two feet long and six inches square, very old in appearance. I called to Koojesse, and directed him to examine it, as, from where I stood, it was some twenty-five feet perpendicular to the bottom; he hastened down and around, and, on arriving at the supposed relic of wood, said it was a stone. I was surprised and disappointed, and then proceeded with my occupation of pacing off the trench. In half a minute, I heard Koojesse shout "*Shev eye-un !*" (iron.) I turned round, and saw that he had boldly mounted the steep bank beneath me, using the sharp rocks as stepping-stones, and had his hand resting on a piece of rusty iron just protruding from the débris of stone that had been dug out of the trench, and thrown up, making a bank. Koojesse continued shouting "Iron ! big iron ! Can't stir him ! "

ONE OF FROBISHER'S GOLD "PROOFS."
(An Iron relic of 1578.)

I was soon on the spot, though at considerable risk, and trying to disengage the iron, but I could not move it. After digging around it, however, a few strong pulls started it. The rust of three centuries had firmly cemented it to the sand and stones in which it had lain.

The piece of iron* was of the same character as that found at Tikkoon, less than one mile from Kodlunarn, and also as that obtained on "Look-out" Island, Field Bay; and the origin of it, as well as its significance, may be gathered from the following facts :—

Of the one hundred men sent out from England with Frobisher in 1578, the majority were "miners," sent for the express purpose of digging for the rich ore of which Frobisher had carried specimens home on his return from his second voyage, and which was supposed to be very valuable. The miners made "proofs," as they are called, in various parts of the regions discovered by him. Some of these "proofs" are doubtless what I found, and they furnish clear evidence, in connection with other circum-

---

* The same, together with a case of some of the other Frobisher relics which I discovered and brought home, I sent to the British government early in the year 1863, through the Royal Geographical Society of London.

stances noted in the course of this narrative, that I was, when at Kodlunarn, on the precise spot of Frobisher's "Countess of Warwick's Mine."

Delighted with my discoveries, and gathering up as many relics as I could carry, placing them in my old stockings, mittens, hat, and everything that would hold them securely, I labelled each article, and rejoined the boat, immediately afterward departing on our way for "home."

FROBISHER RELICS IN MY OLD STOCKINGS.

That night we reached the termination of the high land below *Sharko*, and encamped* till the next morning.

Our passage on September 26th was made with some difficulty, owing to the heavy sea that prevailed. A moderate gale, or even a fresh breeze from certain directions, causes a dangerous sea for boats running between Countess of Warwick's Sound and Bear Sound, a fact we proved by personal experience. On arriving at the old whaling depôt, Cape True, I landed and went to Flagstaff Hill. There was still enough remaining to show where the ship's company had lived so long: the tattered remnants of a flag, some boards, a dismantled table, an old cooking-stove, with broken-down walls around it, oil-casks covered with sods, some rope and ice-gear, with the usual indications of Innuit tent life, met my view; but it was solitary as compared with the life and animation displayed when I was there only a few months

* Our twenty-sixth encampment was in lat. 62° 38' N. long. 65° 02' W.

before. Slowly I turned my steps away from this place, where I had spent so many happy hours; and I could not help saying to myself, "Shall I ever again behold it? God only knows!"

We stopped at Cape True nearly an hour, and then pursued our way through Bear Sound. On arriving at the next place of encampment, the last before reaching the harbour where I had left the ship, the Innuits informed me that it was called *Shar-toe-wik-toe*, from a natural breakwater of thin or plate stone, the native word meaning "thin flat stone." It is on a tongue of land nearly surrounded by water, on the west side of Lupton Channel, within a mile of Field Bay, and has a beautiful little boat-harbour. A few moments after landing, some of the Innuits found the remains of recent encampments of their people. On examination, we discovered that several tupics had been there, and it was concluded that Annawa, Artarkparu, and other families had made this their resting-place on the way from where we had met them up Frobisher Bay to Field Bay. At this place I found some deposits of seal and walrus, evidently freshly made by the party preceding us; and here I noticed an instance of honesty and good faith which deserves mention :—

These deposits were beneath piles of stone, with a stick running up obliquely from each, so that if the ground should be covered with snow, the place might be easily found. The Innuits with me noticed all this, and saw the meat thus deposited, yet *not one would touch a morsel of it*. They knew it belonged to others, and therefore it was sacred in their eyes, unless in cases of actual extremity.

From the present (27th and last) encampment our first one on the outward trip was not far distant—about a mile off—and on the opposite side of the channel was Lok's Land, the "dreaded land." I made some inquiries about it, but not one of my companions could give me any information, though only about a mile distant. They never had been there, and, as they said, "never would."

On the morning of Friday, September 27th, I mentally arranged a plan for getting from my Innuits all the flint-stone relics they had pocketed when making my researches in the coal deposits found at Niountelik and up Victoria Bay. I began my operations by feasting all my crew. I got Koojesse to make an abundant soup of pemmican and meat-biscuit for them all. After they had eaten this I gave to each a dish of hot coffee and handfuls of sea-biscuit. I was particularly conversational and cheerful with all; carried hot coffee and bread to " Miner " and his wife, and gave bread also to such others of his company as I knew to possess the relics I sought. Then I told Koojesse that, if he had any of the "flint-stones," I would give him some boxes of percussion caps when I got to the vessel if he would give them all to me. I told him, moreover, that I wanted him to assist me in inducing all the others to do the same, promising on my part to give Kooperneung and Koodloo the same reward I offered him, and to give to the nulianas of himself and Kooperneung, and to Suzhi, beads for all they had. My strategy worked like a charm; the relics came in by scores, each bringing me a quantity that surprised me, for I had not thought my company so largely deceitful. When I had obtained from my immediate crew all they held, I took Koojesse with me to "Miner's" company, and made an important addition to my stock there. The Innuits had secreted these flint-stones for their own use in "striking fire."

We soon after started on our way, and made good progress up Field Bay, arriving near Parker's Bay toward evening. There we heard the report of fire-arms from the shore, and saw tupics near the beach. My party immediately responded, and desired that we should land; but as we were now only about seven miles from the spot where I expected to find the ship, I refused permission. The usual opposition and sulky demeanour then followed. The men would not work, and the women, though willing, had to do as their masters told them. Night was approaching, and the cold was becoming severe; still, I felt it would be much better to go on and ascertain if the ship were really there than to encamp for another night. Accordingly, I tried every argument and persuasion to induce Koojesse and the others to persevere, finally succeeding after much sulkiness on their part.

And now I was full of excitement as we neared the place where we expected to find the ship; but darkness came over us before we got across the bay, and I became very anxious for our safety among the shoals, of which there were many about. Happily we escaped serious peril, and on reaching the point of land to be rounded before entering the harbour, danger was lost in the general excitement. We looked eagerly and often for a sight of the ship. Presently a dark mass loomed up before us. A few more strokes of the oars, and all doubt was removed. The *George Henry* was in sight!

As soon as the vessel was seen, my Innuit crew, unable to repress their joy, fired their guns and sent forth loud shouts and cheers, in which I could not help joining, overjoyed to find the ship not yet departed. The watch on deck was at first in doubt what to make of the noise, but a second thought told him that I had returned with my party, and, giving a shout in reply, he rushed to inform Captain Budington of our approach.

In a few minutes more I was alongside, and saw the captain, with all hands, ready to greet me. Quickly I ascended the ship's side, and was receiving the captain's warm grasp, and the hearty welcome of all around me. I found that every one on board and most of the Innuits around had given us up, concluding that we were lost. It was supposed that our boat could never stand the trip for so long a time, so that when we returned in safety it was almost as if the dead had come to life. A hot supper was at once prepared for the whole party of us, and, meanwhile, numerous questions and answers passed. My first question was, " How many whales secured ? " and I was surprised to receive the reply, " Not one."

Until near midnight Captain Budington and· myself prolonged our talk in the little after-cabin, and then, when I did retire, it was impossible to sleep, owing to the great change from the free, cool air of the tupics to that of the stove-heated ship. Fifty days and forty-nine nights I had been without any fire to warm me save that which burns within the human system. For many days before getting back to the ship the mountain streams had been fast bound in chains of ice, yet, as a general rule, and excepting the time during my recent sickness, I had always slept well. Now, however, I could not sleep, and was restless and disturbed through the whole night.

OO-MI-EN, OR WOMEN'S BOAT.

CHAPTER XXVIII.

On the following morning, Saturday, September 28th, 1861, at an early hour, I was on deck, finding every one astir, getting ready for the customary cruise after whales. The ship's company generally started at daybreak to try their luck, and they were sadly disappointed with the result hitherto. On inquiry, I found that some of my Innuit friends were still in the neighbourhood, and, after breakfast, I went on shore to visit them. I may here state that, on my return, I found the vessel at the same anchorage—in George Henry's Harbour*—as it was when I left it on August 9th.

The first call I wished to make was at Ebierbing's tupic, which was pointed out to me at no great distance. I entered without "ringing," and found "Jennie"—Koodloo's wife—there to welcome me, as she did with unmistakable pleasure. On inquiring for Tookoolito and Ebierbing—whom I considered almost as adopted children—I found that I had entered the wrong tent, Ebierbing's tupic being next door, and thither I soon made my way.

As I entered the tupic of Ebierbing I caught a mere glimpse of a woman's face, which I had hardly time to recognise as belonging to Tookoolito. She gave me one look, and then the face I beheld was buried in her hands trembling with excitement. It was, indeed, Tookoolito, overwhelmed with tears on seeing me again. The tears sprang to my eyes also as I saw this

---

* Thus named after the barque *George Henry*. This harbour is in lat. 62° 53′ N. long. 64° 48′ 15″ W. and is at the south extreme of the longest island of Field Bay, not far from the termination of said bay.

evidence of strong attachment. It was some time before the silence of the tupic was broken by voices. She and her husband, in common with all the other Innuits and white men, had never expected to see me again. She had often ascended a hill, near by and overlooking the bay, to search the horizon for my returning boat, but had as often come down disappointed.

In the midst of our talk I was startled by the plaintive cry of an infant, and, turning back a corner of the ample tuktoo furs with which Tookoolito was wrapped, I found a boy only twenty-four days of age, her only child!

Tookoolito told me she had been very ill, and had nearly died during her confinement. I was about to leave the tupic, having spent a very pleasant hour with my friend, when she drew toward her a bag, from which she took two pair of nether garments—*kod-lings*—which she had made for me before her sickness. One pair was made of *kus-se-gear* (black sealskin and fur), a beautiful mottled material; the other pair was of the common seal, made in the Innuit fashion, the former being made in the style of civilization. She also gave me three specimens of her netting or crochet-work, made especially for me to take home to America. They were table mats, and beautiful specimens of a skilful hand. But I had not yet reached the depths of her generosity; she next presented to me a pair of sealskin socks, and a pair of meituk socks (made of the skins of eider ducks with the feathers on), saying, at the same time, that she had the material at hand, and would soon have ready for me a pair of winter boots—*kumings*.

I told her she was doing too much for me. "Nay, nay," was her response, "I cannot do half so much as I ought for one who has been so kind to us." As I was leaving the tupic she said, "I was so glad when I heard last night that you had got back in safety that I could not sleep; I lay thinking of it all the night. I feel very happy now. My *winga* thought you lost too; and now he also is happy."

In the afternoon old Artarkparu visited me. He had arrived, with his company, from up Frobisher Bay a little before my return, and I now gladly conversed with him, through Koojesse as interpreter, about the pieces of iron I had obtained at *Tikkoon* and *Kodlunarn*. I asked him if he had ever seen them before, and he replied, "No, not those, *but one much larger*." He then made a circular motion with his hand over and around the piece of iron I had placed on the table, and, according to this, that which he had seen must have been five times as large. He added to this remark that a very strong Innuit could just lift it, and there were very few who were able to do so. This piece of metal was, as he explained, on the southwest side of Oopungnewing Island, just above high-water mark. He had seen it six years before, but not since. The metal was "soft" and "smooth," not "hard," like the pieces I had before me.

Ebierbing, visiting me that day in our little after-cabin, was conversing with me, and speaking of his sickness and recovery —of the critical state in which his nuliana lay for several days succeeding the birth of their child—of the loss of his very valuable seal and sledge dog "Smile," and another of his dogs. He said further, "We thankful that still live and able to work. Lose our dogs; sick and unable to go tuktooing; no tuktoo skins for winter; never mind; we alive and together; got fine boy, and are happy." I thought this was indeed akin to Christian philosophy, deserving respect and admiration.

Annawa and his wife Nood-loo-yong visited me on the morning of September 30th, and I showed them the relics I had obtained. They at once recognised them as coming from the places I had examined. These people had spent most of their days round the waters of Frobisher Bay, and especially on the islands Oopungnewing and Niountelik. The portion of brick which I had found the previous winter, when transferring my things from one sledge to the other, opposite Niountelik, was unknown to them in so large a form; but they had often seen smaller pieces, and also coal, in each of the places where I had discovered it. They had likewise found "heavy stone," such as I showed them, at *Kus-se-gear-ark-ju-a*, a cape half a mile N.N.W. of Kodlunarn.

I asked them where these things came from, and the reply was, "Kodlunas brought them." I immediately said, "Did you see those kodlunas?" Their answer, with eyes wide open and countenances expressing surprise, was, "*Ar-gi! ar-gi!*" meaning No! no!

"How, then," said I, "do you know that kodlunas brought them?"

Their response was, "All the old Innuits said so. The first Innuits who saw the white men were all dead, *many, a great many* years ago."

The more I searched into this subject the more I found it to be well known, as a traditionary fact, that white men—*kodlunas*—once lived on the island then and since called by the Innuits *Kodlunarn;* that these men had built a ship there; had launched it, and started away for their homes ; but that, before they got out of the bay, hands and feet were frozen, and finally the whole of them perished of cold. Ebierbing's statement to me was as follows :—

Recollects hearing his father tell of these white men, and how they built a ship. The kodlunas had brought brick, coal, and " heavy stone," and left them on Niountelik and at other places about there. His father did not see them, but the *first* Innuits, who saw them, told other Innuits so. and so it continued to his day. Old Innuits tell young Innuits ; and when *they* get to be old, they in turn tell it to the young. " When our baby boy," said he, " gets old enough, we tell him all about you, and about all those kodlunas who brought brick, iron, and coal to where you have been, and of the kodlunas who built a ship on Kodlunarn Island. When boy gets to be an old Innuit he tell it to other Innuits, and so all Innuits will know what we now know."

Thus, by the simple unadorned statement of Ebierbing may be known how it is that oral history is preserved among the Innuit people of the North.

On the day following this conversation, several old Innuits arrived from different places ; among them were Ugarng, with his two wives and child; " Bob," his wife " Polly," and children ; " Johnny Bull " and Kokerzhun, and Blind George, with his darling girl Kookooyer. Ugarng had left his mother, old Ookijoxy Ninoo, at Cornelius Grinnell Bay, so that I was unable to obtain from her any additional information concerning the relics I had found ; but the others all confirmed the story already given to me about the white men, and what they had left behind.

The testimony of Blind George was particularly interesting from the circumstances under which he gave it. Being unable to see, he by signs and motions mapped out the position of various places in Countess of Warwick's Sound, where these things had been noticed by him before losing his sight. Placing his hand on his own person, he said, " Oopungnewing ; " then placing it on a corner of a sea-chest in the main-cabin, where we were, he continued, " Niountelik ; " then pointing with his finger to a spot on the table, he said, " *Twer-puk-ju-a*," to another, " Kodlunarn," to another " Tikkoon." Before he could place all to satisfy him, he went back and repeated his steps frequently, at last accomplishing the geographical feat satisfactorily to himself and quite to my gratification. He also identified

the specimen of "heavy stone" I placed in his lap by lifting
it up and touching his lips to it ; he felt its indentations and
roughness, weighed it in his hand, and said "all same" as
he once saw at Kodlunarn. He then, without any leading
questions, described the trenches made by the white men ; and
his testimony was confirmed by Tweroong, who also added that
old Innuits said the ship was built from wood left on the island
for an *igloo*—a word applied not only to their own snow-houses,
but to the dwellings of civilized men generally.

The information thus obtained, though satisfactory, still made
me desirous for more ; and as at that time the number of Innuits
in the neighbourhood could not have been less than a hundred,
I thought it an excellent opportunity for procuring what I
sought. Accordingly, I went to some of their tupics, and
getting Tookoolito to be my interpreter, asked a number of
questions, the answers to which perfectly satisfied me with
regard to the main facts concerning Frobisher's expedition and
the fate of his men.

The result of all the information thus obtained convinced me,
however, of the necessity for another and longer examination of
the locality possessing so much interest as regarded this subject.
Therefore I again prepared for another trip, and on Monday,
October 7th, at 11 A.M. I once more started for the Countess of
Warwick's Sound. My boat's crew consisted of Ebierbing, as
boat-steerer and interpreter, " Suzhi," "John Bull," Kokerzhun,
Annawa, Ou-le-kier, and Shevikoo, thus having only one (Suzhi)
of my previous party with me.

As this trip, owing to the very severe weather, was nearly a
failure, I need only give such particulars of it as may prove
generally interesting to the reader. The wind was strong when
we started, and every dash of water upon our boat froze as it
touched the side. Sometimes the gusts were so heavy that great
care was needed lest we should be capsized ; but we managed
to cross the bay and reach land on the other side without
mishap. Here, for a time, we had better weather, but the wind
soon became adverse, and when we got near to French Head it
was deemed advisable to encamp for the night.

We stopped at a bight, or indentation of the land, close to
the place where we used to cross over to Chapell Inlet, and there,
in searching for drift-wood, I came across a piece of my lost
expedition boat. The women attended to our encampment,
consisting of two tents, one formed of my boat's covering, the
other of boats' sails ; five persons were in one and three in the

other. Thus we passed the first night, and early next morning, October 8th, again started.

The weather was very discouraging; the wind was right against us, and occasionally it snowed heavily. A mile or so after leaving our encampment a perfect storm came upon us, and I saw that Ebierbing and the rest felt most unwilling to go on. Indeed, I myself now feared it would be impossible to prosecute our voyage. The delay had been such that every day now brought the severity of winter fast upon us; still, I determined to persevere as long as we could, feeling that if the ship departed soon for home I should have no opportunity for examining farther into the Frobisher expedition.

The wind soon increased to a gale, bringing the snow furiously into our faces; the waves ran high, every crest leaping the boat's side, and almost burying it in the trough of the sea. Our condition was becoming dangerous, and so thought my Innuit companions, as they frequently glanced at me to learn my intentions. It was soon evident to me that all my hopes of getting forward were likely to be disappointed. The season was too far advanced for boat excursions; snow-storms, cold and windy weather, met me each day. My companions, wiser than myself, plainly intimated that it would not do to persevere: they would go on if I determined to do so, but they knew their own coasts, their native waters, and their seasons better than myself; and I felt that, much as I wished to accomplish another examination of the islands where relics could be obtained before the *George Henry* sailed, I should be unable to do so without running a risk that would be considered foolhardy.

Our encampment that night was at a place where, as we soon perceived, some Innuits had lately rested. Traces of their abode and deposits of provisions were found, and, upon inquiry, I discovered that one of my crew, Shevikoo, was of the party that had rested here. This explained why he so readily opened the deposits, and took from the store of walrus and other meat what he wanted.

The gale now increased almost to a hurricane. I had encountered nothing so severe since the memorable one of the past year, when my boat was destroyed and the *Rescue* wrecked. We could only with the greatest difficulty keep our tents from blowing away; we frequently had to secure them afresh by additional weights of stones at their base, and my readers may conceive better than I can describe the position I was in during my detention on that desolate coast.

During this trip I had opportunities for much talk with the Innuits concerning the Frobisher expedition, and also concerning some of their own traditions and superstitions. Concerning the "dreaded land," Annawa said :—

"Years ago many Innuits were carried away on the ice and never came back again. Then Innuits would not live there for a long time. Finally they began to go there again in great numbers, when once more they were all lost, but *how* no Innuit could tell. At last, hearing nothing from the people who had gone there, a boat's crew of Innuits went to ascertain their fate. They arrived in the region they sought, but the very first night they could not sleep, owing to a terrible noise, all the same as if *Nu-na*—the land—cracked, shook, and broke. There was no sea, no wind, no ice; *se-lar*—sky—fine, weather good, yet the dreadful noise continued. However, the searching party went on shore to examine; they looked around, and they went all over the land, but not one of their people could be found. All were gone! Some mysterious fate had overtaken them. This frightened the new visitors; they knew not what to make of it. Then, too, the dreadful noises continued; each night their sleep was troubled by a repetition of the direful sounds. The earth cracked and rumbled, and seemed as if breaking up in all directions. It was enough! Without farther delay, the visitors took to their boat and left the *dreaded land*. Since then no Innuits will live there." Annawa said the last catastrophe happened when he was a boy; the first was a long time before he was born.

On Wednesday, October 9th, though within a mile of Lupton Channel, I determined upon returning to the ship; it was all but impossible to proceed. But here again were other disappointments; the wind changed, a heavy storm set in right against us, and, after accomplishing a short distance, we had once more to encamp, this time close to "French Head."

My trip thus far had been anything but pleasant. In the boat I was so cramped, and wet with the spray, that I could hardly move. When I landed my limbs almost refused their several functions, and it was necessary for me to have a good walk before I could restore proper circulation. It was a comfort to have such a walk, a greater comfort to be within the tupic, and a still greater to have, after a time, hot coffee placed before me by the ready hands of Suzhi.

The next morning, October 10th, we renewed our boat-voyage back to the ship. On the way a deer was seen, and my crew immediately landed to secure it. This was done without much difficulty, guns having been brought into good use for the purpose. The animal was a fine one, and very soon made a great feast for all of us. It was quickly skinned, and the raw food greedily eaten. I partook of some of it, and especially of the marrow of the legs, the bones having been broken by pounding them with a stone. "Johnny Bull" took the head, broke open the skull, and feasted on the brains. Suzhi now and then thrust her fingers down into the paunch, drawing forth portions of the contents, and eating them with much relish. While waiting at this place I took a walk along the beach, and found a ship's beam high and dry on the rocks. It was of oak, twenty-seven feet long, and eighteen by twelve inches square. Spikes that had once helped to hold fast the ship's deck, and the bolts running through at each end, were much eaten with rust. It probably belonged to the *Traveller*.

When we again started it was with difficulty that any progress could be made, owing to the head wind; but at last, toward evening, we neared the locality of the ship. At that time another boat under sail was observed, and we soon found it to be manned wholly by Innuits. It was a pretty sight, that boat, with no load save its light crew, sailing in the strong wind, with a heavy sea prevailing. The masts and sails were bent over, almost touching the waves, and yet she bounded forward, beautifully rising over the waters, and dashing along like a white whale in alarm. As soon as the boat neared us, we learned that during my absence the crew of the *George Henry* had captured two whales, and this news was soon afterward fully confirmed when I saw the huge carcasses alongside of the ship.

On board, Captain B. and his crew were busy and joyous over the work. A friendly word was hastily given, and I went below. I regretted to learn that a man had been seriously injured, nearly losing his life by a blow from one of the captured whales. The boat in which this man was had run with a six-knot breeze right on the whale in an oblique direction, its bow actually mounting the monster's back near its tail. At that moment the "boat-header"—Morgan—threw, with all the force of a bold, expert man, two harpoons in quick succession. The whale, feeling the concussion of the boat and the sharp wounds of the irons in his back, desperately and fiercely struck his flukes about, right and left, with the force of a thousand-horse engine. The sea became white under its maddened fury. Occasionally the tip of one of his flukes was raised high above the boat's side, as if about to deal instant destruction to all, and once a blow came heavily down. Morgan saved himself by jumping on one side ; but the nearest man was struck and knocked down senseless. The boat's mast was lifted from the step, and the sail thrown in the water, but, fortunately, the boat itself escaped destruction. The huge monster expended most of his power in lashing the water, and then " sounded," that is, dived into the depths below. On returning to the surface he was met by lances, which caused the usual spouting of blood, and then followed the death-stroke, which made the whale a prize to the daring seamen who attacked it.

CHAPTER XXIX.

THE events that followed my return to the ship on Thursday, October 10th, 1861, were similar to those that I have already related. We all naturally wished to get away and proceed on the voyage home; ice had begun to form, and we felt that the time was now come for our departure, if we meant to leave that year. Thus a few days passed on, during which several of our friends, the Innuits, who had been at different places hunting and sealing, returned. Among them were Ugarng, Artarkparu, and Annawa. Each of these, on my questioning them, spoke of the particular relic on Oopungnewing I had been so anxious to obtain from the moment when Artarkparu told me of it, as recorded in the previous chapter; and upon requesting them to do so, they each made from wood a model of the article, working at different times, and without the least consultation among themselves.

Suzhi, at my request, made a pencil sketch of its shape—at least, as near as she could. She evidently never took a pencil in her hand before. Ugarng, who is quite experienced in map sketching, marked out its shape on the same leaf as Suzhi's sketch. This had some correspondence to the delineation of the one Artarkparu made some days since.

I got Ugarng to cut out with his knife its representation in wood. When he finished it I held it out, asking " *Kis-su ?* "— that is, What was the heavy iron at Oopungnewing formerly used for? His answer was an intelligible one, and one that determines the nature of this important relic beyond all question. As an anvil! such as were made in former times, without a horn. This Innuit had been to the States (*vide* page 82), and while there he visited various manufacturing establishments, being naturally of a mechanical turn of mind. His answer to my question was, holding the index finger of his left hand on the little carved block as I held it up, with his other hand angled into fist and raised above finger to represent hammer, he said, "*All the same as blacksmith.*" This expression, in connexion with his pertinent symbolizing, settles the matter satisfactorily to my mind that this relic of Frobisher on Oopungnewing is an anvil.

UGARNG'S WOOD MODEL OF THE
IRON RELIC.

ARTARKPARU'S WOOD MODEL OF THE
IRON RELIC.

Another wood model,[*] of great similarity to the above two, was executed on the 15th of October by Annawa.

When Ugarng saw the relic, or "heavy stone," it was "red with rust;" and Artarkparu informed me that it had been carried to Oopungnewing from Kodlunarn many years ago by

KOO-OU-LE-ARNG'S TOODNOO MODEL OF
THE IRON RELIC.

Innuits on a sledge. Annawa, in speaking of it, said "it was something that did not grow there," and each one confirmed the others' testimony, though examined apart and at different times. Suzhi also made a rude model of it by chewing some toodnoo and then fashioning it into the shape opposite. Thus everything seemed to confirm me in the belief that the article pro-

bably yet to be found on Oopungnewing was an anvil formerly belonging to Frobisher's expedition; hence my desire was great to induce some of the natives to go for it, hoping they might return before the ship sailed. But I found no one who cared to undertake the task.

* This model I sent to the English government with many of the Frobisher relics which I discovered and obtained in the Countess of Warwick's Sound.

It was the intention of Captain Budington to leave the country on the 20th October, and the minds of all had been made up accordingly. I was anxious to go, before sailing, to a high point near Bayard Taylor Pass, where I could complete my operations pertaining to the trigonometrical survey I had commenced. With this design I set out on the morning of October 17th for an excursion thither, and I now copy from my diary a portion of the record made on the evening of that day and on subsequent days :—

"*October* 17*th*, 10 P.M.—At present it is thought that *we are ice-prisoned in Field Bay for the winter !* Solid '*pack*' in Davis's Strait has been seen to-day. How true it is that we know not what a day may bring forth !

"A few hours ago we were anticipating the short time that remained before the *George Henry's* sails were to be given to the wind, and we to be away to our loved ones at home ; but *now* we are thinking of preparations for *sustaining life* in these regions of ice and snow. I must make as enduring as ink and paper will allow the incidents of this day. I begin with my trip across to the west side of the bay, to the highest mountain-top between Field Bay and the Bay of Frobisher.

"Early this morning the four boats, with the *George Henry's* crew, started off to cruise for whales. I set to work engaging a crew of the best Innuits among those who had just come aboard to accompany me across the bay, and a few minutes sufficed for this. Those selected were Ebierbing, Shevikoo, 'Jim Crow,' 'Miner,' *Oo-ming-mung, At-tou-se-ark-chune.*

"After making up the west side of the island, near which the vessel is anchored, and which forms the north and northwest side of the harbour, I was surprised to find much ice. Indeed, early this morning there was no ice in the harbour, but at the time we left it had formed so thick that it was with great difficulty that the boat could be pulled through it. Finding the ice too heavy to make progress, and apparently much thicker ahead of us, we concluded to turn our course and strike southwest, using the wind, which was favourable to the latter course. Sail being made, away we sped at a capital rate, occasionally plowing through 'sludge,'* that served greatly to deaden our speed.

"At about eleven o'clock we reached the land where the winter passage is made in going to Frobisher Bay. A few minutes were spent here in deciding which of the party should accompany me

* Just as the ice begins to make, sometimes the sea-water, to a considerable depth, becomes so cold that it is thick like porridge—so thick, indeed, that a boat might as well be pulled through a lake of tar as through "sludge."

in my tramp to the mountain-top. All but one seemed reluctant to undertake it; the *one* I shall always remember, as he seemed rather anxious than otherwise to be my attendant; it was Shevikoo, an Innuit that I like more the more I see of him. The rest of the crew were to remain with the boat, taking it, if they chose, to hunt duck and seal.

"Shevikoo and I started. The first quarter of a mile was over a plain of fresh-water ice that had been formed by springs bubbling up and spreading their waters about. This passed, we commenced our ascent of the rugged hill that lay between us and the mountain proper that I desired to visit. A few minutes' walk up this incline decided what kind of work we had before us for the next two or three hours. I started from the boat with my tuktoo jacket and trousers on. Climbing rough rocks covered with soft, treacherous snow created a *boiling* heat; I therefore divested myself of the said clothing, reserving only my civilization dress.

"Resuming our walk—or rather our leaping, plunging, and tumbling, for this was the nature of our motions during the five hours we were absent from the boat—our progress up was slow —slow indeed, for the way was really rugged, though not so in appearance. Had there been no snow we could have got along very well, but as it was, the travelling was *terrible*. This may be believed when I state that nearly the whole distance is covered with sharp and boulder rocks—rocks upon rocks—and over these a covering of snow that made all look fair, but, on attempting to make passage over it, down through soft snow we went till our feet rested on stones, which sometimes proved firm and sometimes proved man-traps. Now and then we sunk thigh deep, our feet dropping into chinks, and becoming quite firmly wedged therein. As we wound our zig-zag way up the steep mountain, I was expecting every moment that my volunteer companion would refuse to go farther, but in this I was happily mistaken. He was a match for me.

"I was rejoiced to find, as we drew near the top, that the snow became sufficiently hard to bear us up, thus enabling us to make better progress. The summit was finally reached, and a moment's look around was sufficient to repay me for all the efforts I had made to gain that point. Field Bay, Davis's Strait, Frobisher Bay, and Kingaite were within sight. I was surprised at the height we had evidently gained. Lady Franklin Island, out in Davis's Strait, Monumental Island, and the islands of the extreme land between Frobisher Bay and Field Bay, which I visited last winter, loomed up as I had never seen them before at so great a distance from them, showing that the high land on which I was was high indeed.

FIELD BAY AND DAVIS'S STRAIT FROM THE HEIGHT OF BAYARD TAYLOR PASS.

"I took the spy-glass, and proceeded to make a prolonged observation. I first directed the glass toward the vessel, which was at a distance of seven miles; I then directed it to Davis's Strait. This I saw was filled with a heavy *pack*. I swept with the instrument along down said strait to the extremity of Hall's Island. No black water—nought but *pack, pack*, met my view! I was somewhat surprised at this, but thought that perhaps to the captain this would be but a familiar, every-year affair. The sequel to this will be soon written.

"I asked my Innuit attendant to take the glass and '*tak-koo seko*'—look at the sea-ice. When Shevikoo had viewed it carefully, I asked him, '*Seko amasuit?*'—Do you see much ice? He replied, '*Noud-loo—noud-loo!*'—Yes—yes. From the deep, slow tones of his voice, as he answered me, I understood that he too was surprised at the sight. I wondered how a vessel was to get out of Field Bay; but the next instant I thought, 'Well, now, Captain B. will find some way, of course, which my inexperienced self cannot discover, by which the *George Henry* can be put through that pack.' My thoughts were also of

Captain Parker and his son, who had, each with a vessel, left about this time last year and proceeded home,

"I took another prolonged look, before I left, at Davis's Strait. Monumental Island was white, and its sides presented no black rock peering out; and the same was true of Lady Franklin Island. The pack appeared very rough; much pinnacled ice was among it, and it was especially to be seen around the first island of the extreme land next Davis's Strait. As far as the eye could reach by the aid of the most excellent glass, up and down the strait, no open water met my view. I then turned to Kingaite. Miles on miles of mountain there were before me. A long line of black cloud stretched from the extreme south to the extreme northwest, just enveloping the tops of most of the Kingaite ridge. I was disappointed in not getting a sight of Oopungnewing and Niountelik; the ridge of another mountain, distant two miles, ran in such a direction as to hide them, but a small island near Oopungnewing was in sight. The termination of the grass plain, Kus-se-gear-ark-ju-a, opposite and near Niountelik, was within view. The little bay on the Frobisher Bay side, making up to within one mile of Field Bay, was nearly down beneath us.

"On climbing this mountain my clothing became saturated with perspiration. On making the top the wind was blowing cuttingly cold, thus serving to chill me too hastily for comfort or for long endurance. Before I finished the observations I made up there, I came near freezing my fingers, and the time was long, after leaving that exposed position, before I could bring them back to their natural warmth. The stinging pains I endured in those fingers, while the restoration was going on, seemed almost unbearable.

"We remained forty-five minutes on this mountain-top. Had it not been for the lateness of the hour, I should have proceeded two miles farther; this distance would have led me to the ridge which limited my view, shutting out from sight the interesting places named. This ridge is by the entrance to the little bay, or, more properly, the harbour making up nearest Field Bay.

"Taking a last look at the scenery around, we started down the mountain. Our steps were rapid. I had the misfortune to get one severe fall. As we were descending the steepest part, my right foot caught between two stones that were deep beneath a snow covering, and the swift rate at which I was going threw me headlong while I was fast in the rocks. I recovered myself and extricated my foot, though not until the cramp had seized my leg and tied knots in it. I cried lustily to Shevikoo, who was ten rods ahead. He did not hear me at first, but the second call brought him to. I managed to get the knots rubbed out of my leg before he reached me, though it was some time before I could proceed. The time of our descent was not a quarter of that consumed in going up. When within a mile of the boat, I saw the remainder of my crew awaiting our return, and we reached the boat at 4 P.M. having been five hours absent from it.

" We started at once for the vessel, making slow progress at first on account of the ice. At length we reached open water, raised sail, and sped along. As we approached the harbour we found that the ice had become so thick that it was only by hard pulling, and hard drives of the oars into it, that we got to the ship. As soon as I was aboard, I asked the captain if his men had another whale. He replied that as yet he did not know, but the indications were, as his boats were not in, that they had. He was in fine spirits. But, alas! how soon were they changed to the very depth of grief!

" Shevikoo was the first one of the crew up the side of the vessel. As soon as he got aboard he said they had seen much ice down at the entrance of the bay. The captain asked me if I had seen any heavy ice—*pack*—in Davis's Strait. I told him that I had, and proceeded to give him as truthful an account of it as I could. I was astonished at the effect it produced upon him. Then it was that I first began to realize the overwhelming importance, the momentous character of that pack. On getting through my description, telling him that I not only took repeated careful looks of it through his glass, but had required Shevikoo to do the same, the captain, with fevered brow, responded, ' *Our fate is sealed! Another winter here! We are already imprisoned!*'

" This was now the theme, the all-important subject of thought of every one who heard the explanation of how it was that all hope of returning to the States this season was now cut off. Captain B. no longer felt able to rejoice at the capture of another whale. To and fro he paced the cabin—now on deck—another moment back again.

" At eight o'clock the four boats came in announcing the fact that another whale had been secured. At any other time this intelligence would have been received by the captain with a joyful heart, but now he was occupied in thinking what he was to do under the present dismal circumstances. When the boats came in and were placed in position on their cranes, the captain broke to the officers the subject that now before all others pressed upon him. During the evening he proceeded to state that, from various circumstances during the year, he had been thinking there might be something of the kind, to wit, pack-ice, coming down Davis's Strait. He said, 'Last winter hung on late ; there has been no summer ; the year has been an unusually cold one ; the water of the bay has been almóst of sea-ice temperature, while now the first cold snap turns it at once to porridge, and then into solid ice. All these results are from the heavy pack that has probably been coming down Davis's Strait nearly all the season.'

" To take the pack at this season of the year, continued the captain, would be the very height of foolhardiness. In the spring the whalers do not hesitate to do it, for then constant daylight, and warm, thawing weather are expected. But now everything is freezing up. Long, dark nights are upon us, and the *George Henry* is not such a vessel as one should think of venturing with her into dangerous places. It is so far fortunate said he to me, that you made the trip you did. What would have been our condition had you not seen and reported this ? As soon as possible I should have been on our way ; I should have weighed anchors and raised sail at the first fair wind. But in what kind of a situation should we soon have found ourselves? In the pack, *without the power to retreat !*

" *Friday, October* 18*th*, 1861. This morning, the first and all-important matter of our being obliged to winter here absorbs our attention. It is the general subject of conversation fore and aft. The captain started off at 7 A.M. taking with him his principal officers, for the purpose of making a survey from Budington Mountain * of the pack in Davis's Strait. At 9·15 A.M. he returned, reporting that Rescue Harbour was so solidly frozen that he could not get through it, and was obliged to make for another point this side. At last he made a landing, and proceeded to an eminence this side ; but it was not such a view as he desired to make, though he saw enough to satisfy him that it would only be running a terrible risk to attempt getting out this season.

" *October* 20*th*, 1861.—This morning the ice in the harbour was firm. As soon as I went on deck, long before the sun was

* So named by me. This mount, 500 feet high, is in lat. 62° 53′ N. long. 64° 42′ W. ; is three miles due east of the George Henry Harbour, and a ilttle over one mile north-east of the centre of Rescue Harbour.

up, I made my way down the ship's side upon it. The pack outside the bay, and the new ice now nearly covering it, have us imprisoned. For nine months to come *we are ice-bound !* Some of the men still think we shall get out, but I do not think the captain has the remotest idea that we can.

" Now (1 P.M.) the thermometer is at 13°, the sun shining brightly, the sky cloudless. For three days now, had there been a clear way before us, we could not have got out, for there has not been wind enough to fill the sails.

" . . . . . *Monday, October 21st,* 1861.—The ice this morning I find by measurement to be four inches thick. During the night it was nearly calm, and the thermometer ranged from 9° to 10°. Notwithstanding the dubious circumstances by which we have been surrounded for the past few days, we have all had more or less hope of still arriving at our homes this winter ; but, *dreaded as it is,* we have to bring our hearts to submit to this dispensation of Providence. The *George Henry* is fated to be ice-bound here for full nine months to come. The 20th of October, instead of finding us on our way as purposed, with hearts swelling with joyous anticipations of a quick passage home, and of soon meeting with our loved ones, finds us engaged in planning for subsistence during an imprisonment of nine months in these frozen regions. What a change ! what disappointment ! and yet who shall say it has not been wisely ordered. ' Man proposes—God disposes ; ' cheerfully, then, we should submit to our lot.

*   *   *   *   *   *   *

" *Friday, October 25th,* 1861.—This morning, to all appearance, our winter's fate is sealed. The ice is now seven inches thick, and is rapidly increasing. It is now twelve o'clock, noon, the sun shining brightly, the wind blowing strong from the northwest, and the thermometer only one degree above zero.

" After breakfast Captain B. sent out three Innuits to go to Budington Mountain and see the position of the pack. They returned at half-past four ; their report *removes the hope* of all those who were still looking to get out of our imprisonment this season. The Innuits state that seaward it is all ice ; the bay is all ice except the small opening to be seen from the ship's deck. The lower and entrance part of the bay is filled with *pack;* in Davis's Strait nothing is to be seen but *pack—* ' all white, no black.' The effect produced by this upon some of the *George Henry's* men was very painful.

" Feelings of disappointment—sad disappointment—steal over

me now and then at our not being able to proceed according to our plans ; but I confidently believe *it is all for the best.*"

It was upon the captain that the care and anxiety principally fell. He had to plan and arrange for his ship's company during another nine or ten months, and there was but a scanty supply of provisions and fuel to do it with. As to the latter want, that could be met in various ways. The jawbones of three whales recently captured would serve for a long time ; one of these was sawed, chopped, and split for use. The bone is very porous, and filled with oil ; the heat from it is great. One cord of bone must be equivalent to four cords of live oak. There was also some timber of the wrecked whaler down the bay.

As regarded food, we had to husband our stores very carefully. On Sunday, October 27th, a new order of things commenced, and instead of three meals a day we had only two. Bread or flour was the most nourishing food then on board, with the exception of beans, which were to be served out twice a week. There was salt junk and salt pork, but eating either was felt to be almost worse than being without. Thus we soon found it best to fall back upon our Innuit food, and it would have amused many persons at home to have seen our messes at our daily meals. Some, too, would have wondered how we could eat such stuff ; but certainly that surprise would cease when they were told we must eat it in order to live. I do not think it can be said that any of us ate "black skin" (whale skin) and other Innuit food because we really liked it. Some wise person has said that man should not live to eat, but *eat to live.* We were of the latter class, hence the necessity for relishing whatever came in our way.

I may here mention an incident that occurred about this time which shows the simplicity of the Innuit character in matters connected with money. Of course *money*, as we have it, is to them unknown. One day "John Bull" came to buy a new one-dollar shirt, handing *two* American cents as payment. Ugarng, in like manner, tried to buy a violin to which he had taken a fancy. The violin belonged to Bailey, one of the steerage hands, and Ugarng, calling him aside, whispered in his ear, "Viddle, viddle—wonga—piletay—money," and then slipped into Bailey's hand what he supposed to be a generous sum, *one cent* of the latest coinage. But Bailey could not trade for that, and Ugarng went away without his "viddle."

I conclude this chapter with an extract from my diary of October 30th :—

" The *George Henry* is short of provisions for the time she is now obliged to remain here. I have already signified to Captain B. what I know will, under the circumstances, meet the approbation of the contributors to the expenses of my outfit in the way of provision, ammunition, &c. I have told him that whatever I have that will contribute to the sustenance of his ship's company the present winter, the same is at his command. I have nine cans of pemmican, of about one hundred pounds each, remaining of the twelve and a half which I had when I left the States. I have also one and a half casks of Borden's meat biscuit. The pemmican and meat biscuit are of the most excellent quality, and equivalent to fully 3,200 pounds of fresh beefsteak. Of these articles, as also of ammunition, I have already spoken to Captain B., saying that they were ready to supply his and the ship's company's necessities."

I BEGIN this chapter with the sketch from my diary of a sad scene which passed under my observation :—

" *October* 28*th*, 1861.—This morning, or during the night, ' *Mam-ma-yat-che-ung*,' ' Mary,' the wife of ' Sharkey,' died. This Innuit woman has long been an invalid. Her disease was consumption, one that is carrying off more Innuits than all other diseases together. Some months ago it was thought she could not survive long ; the Innuits gave her up, I may add, *as one dead*. Her *wing-a*—husband—Sharkey, though all his previous conduct was kind to her, gave her up as dead. A tupic was made, and into it Mary was removed ; *it was her living tomb !* Sharkey took to himself another wife. For weeks and weeks Mary lived helpless and almost starving. Occasionally some few of the Innuits would carry this dying woman morsels of seal, duck, or walrus. Of course, all that was valuable or convenient for Mary's comfort was taken away when the Innuits carried her to the ' house of her death,' for it is their custom to leave everything in the tupic or igloo where one of their number dies as unfit to be touched ever after. Mary must have died during the night, for when Suzhi called this morning at the tupic with cooked meituk—duck—sent her by Tookoolito, no answer was made, and, on looking in, Suzhi *saw that she was dead*. Innuit custom will not permit one of that people to enter the place of the dead under such circumstances. One of the Innuits came over to the vessel and announced the death of Mary, the captain with one of the ship's men, went over to bury her. The captain looked in, and saw enough to chill one's heart's blood. The corpse met his view with head erect, and eyes staring at him with the overpowering glare of death ! The tupic became her winding-sheet, and stones were piled over her —her only monument."

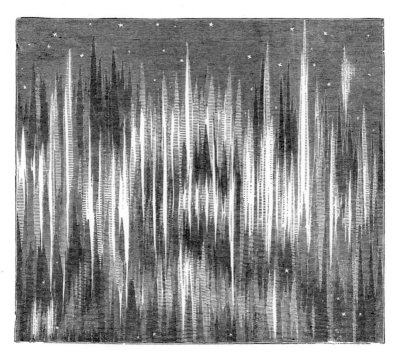

AURORA, AS SEEN FROM FIELD BAY NOVEMBER 2, 1861.

On November 2d, at 6 P.M. there was another magnificent display of the aurora. From east to west—south of us—was a beautiful arch of living gold. The eastern base rested, to all appearance, on the high land, as did also the western, and the centre of the arch was 10° above the horizon south.

The wind was blowing strong, and the aurora truly appeared as possessing life. It danced to and fro from one extreme to the other. Its colours rivalled the rainbow, the pea-green predominating over the other hues. At the east a bank of golden rays shot up far above all the rest. The stars were obscured as the "merrie dancers" swept along in piles of coruscations. The arch continued to recede, falling lower and lower ; the reverse is the usual course of the aurora, as far as my observation has extended. Not a cloud could be seen.

At 7·30 P.M. the aurora was lifting its *arches* zenithward ; there were now two reaching from east to west, and for some portion of the way there were *three*. The wind was blowing almost a gale, the thermometer being 6° above zero. The stronger the breeze, the more beautiful was the aurora, the brisker its racings and dancings, and the more glowing its colours.

I accompany this description and illustration with a picture of a still more remarkable display which occurred on the evening of October 13th, 1860, one feature connected with which was a meteor of great brilliancy ; it shot from a point in the heavens near Cassiopeia, crossing Ursa Minor, and losing itself among the folds of Draco. It was followed by a trail of light twenty degrees in length.

On November 4th I visited Ebierbing and Tookoolito. During my stay the latter informed me that she had to make calls the next day in all the tupics, and perhaps at the ship. On my asking the reason, she answered that her infant would be two months old, and that it was the custom—the first Innuits having done so—for the mother to call at every tupic of the village at the end of the period mentioned. During these two months Tookoolito had not been into any tupic except her own. She added that, in accordance with custom, she should cast away all the clothing she then had on, and should never touch it again.

Some time after I was informed that the grave of Nukertou had been visited by Innuits, according to another of their singular customs. They took down small pieces of tuktoo skin with the fur on, and of toodnoo. When there, they stood around her grave, upon which they placed the articles they had brought. Then one of them stepped up, took a piece of the tuktoo, cut a slice and ate it, at the same time cutting off another slice and placing it under a stone by the grave. Then the knife was passed from one hand to the other, both hands being thrown behind the person. This form of shifting the implement was continued for perhaps a minute, the motions being accompanied by *constant talk with the dead*. Then a piece of tuktoo fur and some toodnoo were placed under the stone, with an exclamation signifying, " Here, Nukertou, is something to eat

AURORA AND METEOR OF OCTOBER 13, 1860.

and something to keep you warm." Each of the Innuits also went through the same forms.

I was told by Tookoolito that this strange custom was invariably practised among the Innuits. But they never visit the grave of a departed friend until some months after death, and even then only when all the surviving members of the family have removed to another place. Whenever they return to the vicinity of their kindred's grave, a visit is made to it with the *best* of food as presents to the departed one. Neither seal, Ninoo, nor walrus, however, is taken.

At the time of this visit but little remained of Nukertou's body; there were a few bones and some hair, but the hungry dogs, during the previous winter, had broken into the snow-tomb and eaten away all her flesh.

On November 23d the Innuits began to build their igloos, or winter habitations, in the place of their summer tents. On the 25th a great many of the natives came on board to pass the evening with our foremast hands. They spent some time in singing and dancing to whistling and the music of an instrument called the "keeloun."* The sport served an excellent purpose in keeping all in good spirits and helping to pass away the long night.

The following night, November 26th, "theatrical" performances took place on board the *George Henry*. The cabin was filled to its utmost capacity with Innuits and the ship's crew. "Jim Crow," the son of Artarkparu, occupied the centre of the cabin, and was performing on the "keeloun," while the other Innuits were seated all around, the female portion singing to the music. I made my way to the little after-cabin, and there seated myself so as to have a full view of what was going on.

The keeloun was accompanied by a tambourine made by Mr. Lamb. Another instrument was a *triangle*, a steel *square* pendent from a tow string, and struck with an iron spoon. The keeloun was played in turn by Annawa, Ooksin, Koojesse, and young Smith, *à la negro!* While Annawa was going through the "sweating" process, playing the instrument and dancing the ridiculously wild figures that are indispensable, according to

---

* The "keeloun" is an instrument made by stretching a thin deerskin, or the skin of the whale's liver, upon a wooden or whalebone hoop about thirty inches in diameter, forming something not very unlike the tambourine known in this country. It is held, however, by a handle, and the player strikes, not the skin, but the hoop, accompanying his music by an uncouth sort of dance.

Innuit ideas, his music being accompanied by a full chorus of
native female voices, there came bouncing into the very midst a

PLAYING THE 'KEELOUN.

strapping negress, setting the whole house in a roar of laughter.
It was young Smith dressed in this character. The tambourine
was passed into his hands, and he soon did full justice to the
instrument, his or *her* sable fists soon knocking a hole through
the whale's liver skin with which it was covered.

When Smith first entered some of the Innuit women were much frightened. Jennie, the angeko, was seated near me, and she tried to put as great a distance as possible between herself and the negress, believing the apparition to be an evil spirit. But all shortly became reconciled to the stranger, especially when Smith resumed his place, playing and shouting, Innuit-like, and making so much fun that all our sides ached with laughter. Even the singing women were obliged occasionally to give way and join in the merriment.

The negress was next called on to act as drummer. Ooksin held the keeloun while *she* performed "Yankee Doodle," "Hail Columbia," and other pieces, with admirable skill and effect, using two iron spoons for drum-sticks. The *finale* was a dance by two Innuit ladies and two of the ship's crew, the music being furnished by Bailey with his "viddle."

At the early hour of half-past six the performances closed, all concerned being highly pleased with the enjoyments of the evening. "A hearty laugh is as good as a feast." The number of Innuit guests exceeded fifty; many of the ladies were orna-mented in the height of fashion among the arctic aristocracy. The brightly-glittering head-bands, and the pendents of varie-gated beads which hung from each side of their hair, made the assembly look quite theatre-like. Tookoolito was present with her infant, as were many other ladies with similar organs of melody at their backs.

On the 28th of November we celebrated Thanksgiving Day to the best of our ability. It is true, we had no turkeys, roast beef, or onions; but yet we had something extra—something besides whale, salt junk, salt pork, and hard bread. It was a sea-pie of foxes. The arctic fox is a very pretty species, and is killed in considerable numbers by the Innuits for its flesh and its fine white fur.

The time wore on without many incidents especially worthy of note till the 10th of December. I must, however, mention one scene which was deeply interesting. The captain and several of the aft hands were in the main-cabin, where were also Shevikoo, Koojesse, and other Innuits. The captain had a way of his own in occasionally breaking out in strong, unmis-takable terms against that northern country. While speaking of it on the evening referred to, he said, "Koojesse, what do you have such a cold, bleak, barren, mountainous, rocky, icy, stormy, freezing country here for, unfit for a white man or any one else to live in?" It was at once noticed that the Innuit

Shevikoo was bathed in tears, and such of the other Innuits as comprehended the captain's words seemed much hurt. How true that every one likes his own country best. Shevikoo was one of the noblest of his people; he could not repress the flood of tears that burst forth on hearing his native land thus spoken of.

As soon as it was fairly decided that the *George Henry* must remain imbedded in the ice through another winter, I determined to make, as soon as possible, a sledge journey up Frobisher Bay for the purpose of effecting a complete exploration of every bay and inlet in those waters, and also of investigating still more closely the matters connected with the Countess of Warwick's Sound. Previous to this, however, it became necessary for me to make a shorter trip to Jones's Cape, in order to obtain reindeer skins by trading with the natives; these I wanted for bedding and winter dresses for myself and for Ebierbing and Tookoolito, and to bring home with me to the United States.

On Tuesday, December 10th, I went over to Ebierbing's tupic to see him about going on this excursion with me. While talking with Tookoolito I asked her to go with me to see the old Innuit whose name is *Kar-ping*, for I wanted to talk with him. Before we started there came into the tupic a young Innuit with Tookoolito's infant, its whole length stuck into the leg of a pair of tuktoo *kodlings*—breeches. The fur turned inside made a warm envelope for the body of the child, otherwise naked, except for a tuktoo cap and jacket. Tookoolito then sent the young man who brought the infant for old Karping, who soon came in. He had quite a stock of grey whiskers and mustache, and I should think he was from sixty-five to seventy years old.

Tookoolito acted as my interpreter, and I cautioned her not to assist the old man by any remarks of her own. I first asked, "Have you ever heard of a place called Kodlunarn?" He replied, "I have. It is a small island, and near Oopungnewing." "Why is it called Kodlunarn?" "Because white men lived there, and built oo-mi-ark-chu-a"—ship. "Did you see the *kodlunas* who lived on Kodlunarn and built ship there?" Raising up his eyes, with wonder pictured in them, at the question, he said "*Argi.*"

He then proceeded to say that it was a long time before he was born; he knew nothing about it but what his old father and mother told him. I asked him how the white men could build a ship in the Innuit country where trees did not grow, where there was no wood, no iron, no materials of any sort. I

told Tookoolito to say to him that it sounded very strange to
me to hear about ship-building there. Tookoolito smiled, and
did as requested. The old Innuit smiled also, and then proceeded to explain how it was, saying that the ship was built out
of material carried there by *kodlunas*. I then asked him if there
was anything on Kodlunarn now that the *kodlunas* who built
the ship left there. The old man answered:—

"Ar-me-larng, amasuadlo!" (Yes, a great many.) "What
were they?" "Little red pieces" of something; he didn't know
what they were. "Anything else?" "Yes, little black pieces,
a great many;" he didn't know what they were for. There was
nothing like them in the Innuit country; but these black things
were on Niountelik, not on Kodlunarn. I then asked if he had
seen anything else. At first he said he had not, but, on thinking
a while, he said he had seen "heavy stone"—one small one at
Tikkoon, one large one, he thought, on Oopungnewing. The
last he saw four years before, and he said the Innuits used to
try their strength in lifting it. He could lift it as high as his
knees, but no higher.

I asked him if any one could see the place where the *kodlunas*
built the ship. He replied, "Yes;" and then proceeded to show
what kind of a place it was. A snow-block was in the bottom
of the igloo, having been brought in for making snow-water.
I told Tookoolito to have him take a snow-knife, and show us
what kind of a place the ship was built in. The old man took
the snow-knife and commenced trimming the block, and then
proceeded to chip out a trench, comparatively wide, and deep at
the edge, but shallow and narrow at its termination. He then
swept his knife around the block of snow to represent the
location of the trench in the island. I asked what was the
character of the land where they dug the trench. As I asked
this question, I put my finger at the bottom of the model trench
before us. The answer astonished me, it being the very reverse
of what I expected, for I knew the bottom of the excavation of
Kodlunarn to be of stone. The old man's answer was that it
was *soft*. By this I understood him to mean that it was like
sand or loam; but to a repetition of the question, he answered,
"Soft—*very soft—same as wood all falling in pieces;* the *tarrio*
—sea—came up into the trench where the wood was."

Here was a deeply-interesting fact unexpectedly disentombed.
I had previously found at Kodlunarn several pieces of wood at
the bottom of this trench, the larger portion of it being of the
character described by this old Innuit. It was beneath stone

that had fallen from the bank, the top of the stick being dry, while the base was imbedded firmly in rocks and sand. The old Innuit said that a good deal of something soft (wood) used to be in the bottom of the trench. (Manuscript records of Frobisher's expedition now in the British Museum, but seen by me only since my return, show that quantities of timber, carried out for the purpose of building a fort, were buried at the bottom of one of his mines.)

Being questioned farther, the old man said that only three men built the ship; the others stood around "all same as captains." The Innuits did not help make the ship, but they helped the *kodlunas* get the ship down into *tarrio*.

On December 15th, the thermometer being 20° below zero, the wind light from the northwest, the weather a little cloudy, I took an early breakfast of whale-steaks and coffee, and at 5·45 A.M. was on my sledge, to which were harnessed eight dogs, the place of my destination being Jones's Cape. I had with me my Innuit dog-driver "Kooksmith" and young Smith. Shortly after starting, and upon getting into some snow saturated with sea-water, a surprising phenomenon was seen. When the dogs put their feet into the snow and water, it was like stepping into a flood of molten gold, and the phosphorescent light thus produced was not confined to the space beneath the dogs and the sledge, but spread itself around, and continued for several seconds.

In an hour and twenty minutes we crossed the bay, and reached the land on the other side; in an hour more we were at the crest of Bayard Taylor Pass, and in less than another hour had safely accomplished the steep descent, and were on the smooth ice of Lincoln Bay, an arm of the Countess of Warwick's Sound. After lunching on frozen black skin, we pursued our journey, and arrived at Oopungnewing at 1 P.M. There I made a fruitless search for the *anvil*, and in an hour resumed our trip. At 8·10 P.M. we reached Jones's Cape, having travelled thirty-five miles, and were soon greeted by the familiar voices of many Innuits we knew. Among them were Samson and his family, and I was speedily located in their hospitable abode.

That night I slept closely packed among seven of the Innuits, the little girl *Puk-e-ney-er* being on one side of me, and her uncle on the other. On rising, I took two ounces of whale-skin for my breakfast—I would gladly have eaten two pounds could I have had it—and soon afterward started for the head of Peter Force's Sound, where some more igloos of the natives were situated. Arriving there at noon, I directed my steps to the igloo of *Oo-soo-kar-loo*, whom I had seen the night before at Samson's. I was met and kindly welcomed by his wife, quickly finding myself at home. I now quote from my diary :—

"*Monday, December* 16*th*, 1861. * * * * After a few words of greeting and gladness from her, I commenced taking off my feet gear, for the object of holding my almost frozen feet over the *ikkumer*. I had just removed my *kumings* as in came a very venerable Innuit woman, whom I remembered having seen several times before, but whose name I could not call to mind ; but I passed the compliments of the day by saying, '*As-shu-e-tid-ley ?*' (Are you well ?) To which she replied, '*Ter-boy-ou-loo*' (very well). I was seated on the tuktoo bed, and commenced at once to move on one side to make room for the old lady. But she signified me to keep my seat, at the same time picking

THE HEIGHT OF HOSPITALITY.

up the snow-shovel (*pwa-kin*), which is a small pine board with handle, placing it near my feet, and seating herself on it. The old lady, seeing me engaged in extricating my feet from their gear, put forth her hands, and drew off my double set of native socks and tuktoo stockings. She did not stop here, though I assured her that would do. I had on, next my feet, civilization stockings, and intended keeping them on ; but *Pe-ta-to*—for this is the name of the warm-hearted old mother—grasped first one foot and then the other, stripping each bare ! Quick as thought she lifted up the double flaps of the front of her tuktoo jacket,

and as quickly placed my *ik-ke is-si-kars* (cold feet) flatly upon
her body, and against a breast whereon has fed as robust and
persevering a generation of Innuits as ever honoured this Northern land.

"This act of Petato's, represented in the preceding engraving,
is considered by the natives the very *beau ideal* of genuine hospitality. Knowing this to be the custom of this people, and
believing in the old saw that 'when you are in Rome you must
do as the Romans do,' my heart leaped with gratitude for this
kindly deed of good old Petato. My feet must have been like
lumps of ice, and yet she quailed not at their contact with her
calorific body.

"While warming my feet in the peculiar mode written of, I
told Smith and the Innuit Kooksmith that I wished to have a
conversation with Petato relative to Kodlunarn, Oopungnewing,
and Niountelik, and of white people, &c. &c.

"I asked Petato if she knew 'heavy stone.' Asked if she
ever 'sat down' [that is, made her home] on Kodlunarn. To
which she answered, *'Ar-me-larng'* (Yes). Then I asked, *'Shoo
Innuits pil-e-tay nu-na Innuit ar-ting-a nar-me ?'* * (Why did
not the Innuits give to that island an Innuit name?) *'Shoo
Innuits pil-e-tay kod-lu-narn ar-ting-a ?'* (Why did Innuits give
white man's name to it?) Old Petato proceeded to answer these
two questions thus :—

"*'Am-a-su-it oo-mi-ark-chu-a ki-ete wich-ou! wich-ou! wich-ou!
wich-ou! Wong-nuk ki-ete sal-e-koo oo-mi-ark-chu-a'* (A long, long,
long, long time ago, a great many ships came here. A northerly
gale prevailed, and broke—or smashed—some of the ships). That
is, then it was that the island was given the name 'Kodlunarn.'

"Following this, I asked the question, *'Ka-chin-ning oo-mi-
ark-chu-a sal-e-koo ?'* (How many ships were destroyed?) Petato
answered, *'Shev-e-ming'* (She did not know).

"When Petato was attempting to convey to me the many
years ago that a great many ships came into this bay, she was
truly eloquent. When pronouncing the word *'wich-ou,'* and
repeating it, which she did the several times indicated, she lifted

* It should be said, with reference to the Esquimaux language as introduced in the text, that, though it could be easily and perfectly comprehended by the Innuits when spoken, and though it can be understood
when read to them in its present form by the natives with me in this
country, it is nevertheless what we may call "broken," being such as a
person would naturally use whose acquaintance with the language is
imperfect, as mine necessarily was.

her hands to each side of her head, raising in them handfuls of her grey locks. At the same instant Kooksmith, standing by her side, having caught the spirit of her inspiring thought and eloquence, seized another handful of her venerable hairs, lifting them up too. Then, with increasing emphasis, Petato proceeded, pronouncing *wich-ou* at first with strong voice, then with louder and louder voice, till the final pronunciation of the word, when her whole soul seemed on fire, her face glorified by the spirit of her earnestness, and, as if attempting to measure infinity, she looked wildly to the right, to the left, then turned her head behind, while her voice burst forth as a thunderbolt, leaving the word *wich-ou* ringing in my ears still.

" The word ' *wich-ou*,' in Innuit, has two significations. For instance: suppose I say to an Innuit, '*Ki-ete wong-a*' (Come here to me). If he should not be prepared just at the moment, he would say '*Wich-ou*' (Wait a while, or I'll come in a short time). In the other signification it refers to time past. For instance: suppose I should ask an Innuit when his people were very numerous here North, he might answer '*Wich-ou*' (that is, a long time ago). In this latter sense Petato uses this word.

" Petato proceeded : ' *Kod-lu-nas ki-ete in-e-tete nu-na* make it *am-a-su-it*' (White people came and landed on the island, and put things on it in large quantities). The old lady has been much around the ships, and occasionally uses an English word when conversing with those who talk that language. It will be seen that she used to good effect the two words ' *make it*,' in her last sentence.

" She continued : ' *Wich-ou kod-lu-nas in-e-tete* make it *Kod-lu-narn*' (After a while white men sat down—made a house or houses on Kodlunarn). She described this house by placing one stone upon another, indicating by some snow placed between that some substance of white colour was between the layers of stone.

" Petato was then asked the question, ' *Kis-su kod-lu-nas in-e-tete man-er ?*' (What is now on the island that kodlunas left there ?) She answered that a great many little pieces, red (*oug**), were on the island, such as Innuits use to clean and brighten their *kar-oongs* (brass ornaments for the head).

" When Petato was asked ' who told her all about kodlunas

---

* *Oug* really means blood, but the Innuits use this word to signify any thing red when talking with a stranger not well versed in their language.

coming here, and the many ships that come in this bay,' she answered, 'My mother's grandmother's grandfather knew a good deal about it.' The inference is that Petato's mother told her about it, the grandmother of Petato's mother told *her*, and the grandfather of Petato's mother's grandmother told said grandmother of it.

"Thus Petato's knowledge is direct from the sixth generation of her family ; or, rather, the information I gained was from the sixth generation direct from the day of the aforementioned grandfather.

"I now continue the information conveyed by old Petato, giving the points as they come to mind

"Kodlunas built a ship on Kodlunarn. She described, by peculiar scooping movements of her hands, the place they dug out in the island in which they made the vessel. She said there were two places dug out in the rocks—one a little distance from where they built the ship, made to catch and hold water (fresh water) for the kodlunas. Innuits all around were kind to the white people ; brought them seals, tuktoo, &c. &c.

"They were on Kodlunarn through one winter—that is, while there, *wintered* there but once. When ice broke up, went away in the ship. After a while come back again. *Seko* (ice) brought them back. Could not get out. Very cold—great storm. Innuits built them igloos on Kodlunarn, but they all died.

"Petato was about to tell how many kodlunas built the ship and tried to go away. She first raised one hand, opened the fingers and thumb, showing *five;* thinking a moment, and looking at said fingers and thumb, she finally threw up the other hand, fingers and thumb spread out ; then she said she did not recollect whether they were *mik-u-ook-oo-loo* or *am-a-su-ad-loo* (few or many)."

After concluding this interview with Petato we returned to Jones's Cape, arriving there at 5 P.M. An hour after my entrance into his igloo, Samson returned from his trip to a *cache* of tuktoo, bringing the saddles and carcasses of two deer. As soon as he arrived these were thrown into the igloo ; the network over the *ikkumer*, placed there to receive articles of clothing which need drying, was cleared off, and the frozen masses of tuktoo placed carefully upon it, in order that the outside might lose some of its *burning* quality ; for let it be borne in mind that anything exposed to the cold of the North, if touched with the bare fingers, gives a sensation as if hot iron were handled.   Meanwhile invitations were given to the village Innuits for the tuktoo feast about to come off at Samson's igloo, and soon the guests rushed in.   The position of the ladies was, of course, upon the bed platform, and I drew off my boots and took a place among the " fair of creation ;" all others of my sex had to take standing seats wherever they could find them down on the snow floor.   Fully thirty souls were crammed into our igloo.   I was sandwiched between the wife of Koo-kin and the wife of New-wat-che, the latter being the sister to Samson's wife.

Samson was the master of the ceremonies ; he first made the ladies on the bed give way so as to clear a space whereon he might do the carving ; then he placed on this spot the table-cloth, a huge sealskin, and upon that put the carcass of a large deer ; he then took a boat hatchet, and began to carve the deer. Slabs of its side were chopped and peeled off ; chips of ice flew here and there into the very faces of the guests at each stroke of the axe.   As fast as Samson rolled off the venison other men took the pieces, and by means of a saw and seal-knives reduced them to a size adapted for handling ; then Samson distributed these bits, one to each, till every mill had grist to grind.   Thus for half an hour Samson carved ; then his hatchet handle broke off close up to the head.   Another axe was sent for, and meanwhile, with the half of a saw, the two saddles were divided into the proper number of pieces, ready for distribution ; the carcass was then once more attacked, and the shell was broken, split, and sawed into pieces.   In it was the " kernel," to which all looked with anxious eyes ; this was at last divided into as many pieces as there were pieces of saddle, and then one of each was given to every guest.   I received my share with gratitude, and with a piece in each hand began eating.   I bit off a mouthful of the saddle-piece : it was good.   I took a morsel of the other ; it was *delightful ;* its flavour was a kind of sorrel acid ; it had an *ambrosial* taste ! it fairly melted in my mouth !   When nearly through, I had the curiosity to crowd my way to a light to see what this delicious frozen food was, for where I sat I was shaded by large forms between me and the fire-light.   I looked at it, rolled it over, and looked again.   Behold, it was the contents of a reindeer's paunch !   On this discovery I stopped feasting for that night.

While the guests were arriving, I was busily writing in my note-book ; several Innuits crowded round me, interested in this curious work.   I wrote two or three of their names, pointing to the writing and pronouncing the word, as Kop-e-o, Ning-u-ar-ping, Koo-choo-ar-chu ; this pleased them much. The call was then raised for me to write my own name, which I did, also pronouncing it. Then "Hall! Hall! Hall!" rung from tongue to tongue through the igloo amid general laughter.

After securing what skins I wanted, I started on my return to the ship on December 18th with the sledge and dogs. A few minutes after passing Kodlunarn we rounded the point of Tikkoon, the place I had visited on the 23d of September. Having passed by this spot and made a short distance, less than a quarter of a mile, "Kooksmith" pointed to a bluff on the mainland, saying, "Ki-ete, oo-mi-ark-chu-a Kodlunarn"—that is, the ship came from Kodlunarn to the said place. He then proceeded to say (though I did not fairly understand his meaning at the time), that after the ship was built and launched the kodlunas towed her round to this spot in order to have a good place for raising the masts and putting them in the vessel. Kooksmith represented by the handle of his whip how they raised one end of the mast up on the bluff by the coast. At the time, as I said above, I did not fully comprehend what he wanted to say, but supposed him to mean that a mast was made there, and then taken round to Kodlunarn ; later, as will be seen shortly, the whole force of his description came out.

The most tiresome portion of our day's work was the ascent of the Bayard Taylor Pass. Our load was not heavy, but it required the combined exertions of all to push and pull the sledge up the abrupt mountain's side. We were all tired, the dogs quite so, for they had had nothing to eat since leaving the vessel. The little "camels" of the North—the Innuit dogs—are of inestimable value in that country ; when well fed up before starting on a journey, they will do hard work for many days in succession without any food.

When we reached the summit and began our descent, we found still hard and also dangerous work going down with a loaded sledge and a team of dogs. While Smith hung to the rope made fast to the hind part of the sledge, and Kooksmith kept just ahead of the dogs, whipping them back, I had hold of the fore part of the sledge, to guide it and help keep it back. Notwithstanding all our precautions, the sledge occasionally bounded away over snow-drifts, down steep pitches, now and then plunging dogs and men into one general heap. We had an exciting ride indeed going down on the Field Bay side, the dogs springing with all their might to keep ahead of the flying sledge. We reached the ship at 7·20 P.M.

The next morning, December 19th, while writing in the after-cabin, Kooksmith came in, and I made further inquiries relative to the place at Tikkoon before written of in connexion with the ship's mast. He took from the table on which I was writing, a small memorandum-book, held it just beneath the edge of the table to represent the ship, then took a pencil, one end of which rested on the book, and the other on the table, slightly inclined. The edge of the table represented the bluff at Tikkoon. Then Kooksmith raised up the pencil, which indicated the mast, and thus all was simply and effectively explained; the vessel, when launched, was taken to the bluff of Tikkoon that the masts could there be raised and set.

Soon after Kooksmith had gone I called Tweroong into the cabin, and asked her, in Innuit, if she knew the story of the white people taking the ship to Tikkoon from Kodlunarn. Tweroong comprehended my question at once. She immediately took my pen and a tobacco-pipe, then bade me hold a book down by the table's edge, and placed on the book and table, at one end of the former, the pen, and at the other the pipe, both inclining against the table's edge, just as in the illustration shown by Kooksmith. She next raised one of the mimic masts to a perpendicular position, I still holding the book and then the other. Taking up a pencil, I also raised that, and asked her if there were not *three* masts. To my question she answered *decisively* "*Argi*"—No; adding, "*Muk-ko ! muk-ko !*" meaning *Two*.

I then recalled to mind a remark made to me by Koojesse the previous winter, when we were passing Oopungnewing at a distance from that bluff: "There," said he, "the place where kodlunas make or put in masts." I thought the remark preposterous at the time, and gave but little attention to it.

Another curious point in connexion with the matter of the ship's masts was this: When conversing with some of the natives after the discoveries above narrated, I learned that the name "*Ne-pou-e-tie sup-bing*" had been given to the bluff spoken of. On making closer inquiries, I found that this was a phrase coined for the purpose of expressing a certain idea, as was the case with the word Kodlunarn. Its translation is, "To set up masts."

The significance of these discoveries with reference to Frobisher's expedition, and the bearing they had, to my mind, on more recent matters, will be seen by the following extract from my diary at the close of December 19th :—

" How long it does take to gather in all of the links of this chain three hundred years old ! I am convinced that were I on King William's Land and Boothia, and could I live there two years, I could gather facts relative to Sir John Franklin's expedition—gather facts from the Innuits—that would astonish the civilized world. How *easy* to go back a score of years or so, and get truthful history from among the Innuits, compared with what it is to plunge into the history of near three centuries, and draw out the truth ! May I live to see the day when I can visit King William's Land and Boothia, and secure the full history, as it *must* exist among the Innuits there, of that expedition ! "

CHAPTER XXXI.

Movements of the Ship's Company—Scarcity of Provisions—A Man's Feet frozen stiff—Amputation necessary—Dreadful Story of a Woman deserted—Attempt to Rescue her—The Attempt a failure—A perilous Situation—A second Effort—The Woman found Dead—Ebierbing at a Seal-hole—Innuit Perseverance—The Author's Plans.

EARLY in January of 1862 the men of the ship's company divided themselves among the Innuits, trying the native life, such a course being necessary by reason of the shortness of our provisions on board. They were not steadily absent, however, but now and then returned to the ship, finding the privations of Innuit life harder to be borne than the scarcity on board the vessel. On the 2d of January, Robert Smith went with Annawa to Lincoln's Bay, and at the same time, Mate Lamb and one of the seamen started for the reindeer plains at the head of Field Bay. A few days before, a party of the men had gone to the Countess of Warwick's Sound. On the day just mentioned they all returned, with beds, bags, and baggage. They brought sad tales of want and suffering, owing to the short supply of provisions among their Innuit friends.

Ebierbing, on hearing of their return and the cause, said laughingly, "They be all same as small boys." The Innuits are certainly a very different people from white men. They submit to deprivation of food quite philosophically; to all appearance, it is the same to them whether they are abundantly supplied, or on the brink of starvation. No murmur escapes their lips; they preserve their calmness, and persevere till success rewards their exertions.

On January 4th Sterry and "Fluker" (William Ellard) left the ship for Jones's Cape, and on the 10th Robert Smith came back, having been unable to sustain the privation he was forced to endure any longer. On the 12th an Innuit boy, called "Bone Squash," arrived from the plains, bringing to Captain B. the following letter:

"CAPTAIN—SIR: 'Shorty' (Ooksin) got one small deer to-day, and I send this to you for yourself, and hope that soon we may have the luck to send you more. They see quite a number of deer every day, but half the time their guns will not go. I hope that you are well, for I know that your mind is troubled, as I have heard that all of the men have come back to the ship. I saw three deer yesterday on the ice. We are quite hard up here now, for all the 'black skin' is gone, and I have only about ten pounds of whale meat left; but I shall not come to the ship, for I might as well die here as there, for all I know.—R. LAMB."

The above note presents in a truthful light the experiences of some of the ship's company.

On the night of the 12th January, at ten o'clock, the thermometer down to 72° below the freezing point, Fluker was brought to the ship by the Innuit Sharkey, with a sledge drawn by dogs. Fluker soon reported that he had frozen his great toe while going up to Jones's Cape, and that he thought it best to come back and have the black thing attended to. He went forward with such a light and springing step that it seemed impossible that his toe could be badly frozen. Soon after, he came down into the after-cabin, and sat down by the stove warming himself, and eating heartily. While taking his supper, he told us of the experiences of Sterry and himself. They left the ship, as was above stated, on January 4th, and were five days in getting to Jones's Cape. There they found abundant food, but he discovered that his toe was black, and he thought it best to return.

The captain caused a poultice to be prepared, and then directed Fluker to pull off his boot; the poor fellow made several ineffectual efforts to do so, when the captain said, "Hold on, Fluker; let me pull for you." With considerable difficulty the boot and double stockings were taken off, when the captain suddenly exclaimed, "*Fluker your foot is frozen now as hard as ice!*" In a moment the other foot was stripped of its gear, and *that also was found to be frozen stiff.* "Away, away with him from this fire! What are we thinking about! Ice-water and salt! I fear this man's feet are gone!" Such were the hurried exclamations of the captain, and all hands were at once engaged in endeavours to thaw and preserve the feet of the unfortunate Fluker. The sequel may be given in a word: on the 17th the captain was obliged to amputate all the poor man's toes, performing the operation skilfully with instruments improvised for the emergency; some days after it became necessary to take off another portion of his feet, and from that date the patient slowly recovered, being able after a time to resume his duties.

On January 21st two of the ship's company arrived at the vessel from Cornelius Grinnell Bay, nearly dead from hunger. They had been without food, except a mere morsel, for several days. They had left the ship four weeks before, and they said that they had not eaten on an average more than three ounces a day, so little game had been secured in that locality by the natives. Some days they had to eat sealskins, walrus-hide, reindeer sinew, blasted whale-meat, and scraps remaining after trying out the *ooksook*. One of them, after two days' fasting, received from the hands of an Innuit a piece of reindeer sinew, weighing perhaps an ounce, for his supper; but, after chewing it awhile, he gave up the attempt to eat it.

On the 20th of February Robert Smith and five of the forward hands returned to the ship from Oopungnewing, where they had been living. Shevikoo, with his dogs and sledge, brought their bags of bedding. They said that the provisions at Oopungnewing were all out, and that they had had nothing to eat for several days. They reported also a sad occurrence. When the Innuits removed from the "Plains" to Oopungnewing they abandoned one of their number, the wife of "Jim Crow," leaving her, with but a trifle of provisions, to die. The reasons given for this act were that she was sick and unable to help herself. As soon as I was informed of this, I at once proposed to raise a party and go the next morning to ascertain the fate of the deserted woman, and, if she were still living, to bring her on a sledge to the ship.

In accordance with this purpose, I set out on the next day, February 21st, accompanied by Mate Lamb and four of the ship's crew, who volunteered for the work. We had a small sledge and four dogs, and took with us a variety of articles for the comfort of the suffering woman, if she should be alive when we reached her. It was ten o'clock before we started, new harness having to be made for the dogs, and the sledge to be dug out of a heavy snow-drift. The prospect of a successful issue of the trip was doubtful at starting. As I anticipated, we found the travelling very laborious. We walked in Indian file; I led the way occasionally, as did the others in turn. The walking through the snow was terrible work, and the one who led the way had to make footsteps for the others. No one except Lamb and myself could hold out longer than five minutes at a time in making these tracks. The snow was deep, and much of the way was just hard enough to *almost* bear our weight, but at each step down we would go, knee deep, thigh deep. It is impossible to convey to any one a correct idea of the nature of the travelling we experienced on this journey. First one and then another of my companions gave up and returned, leaving only Lamb and myself to proceed. The wind had freshened to a gale, sweeping the snow directly into our faces, and cutting us like powdered glass. The cold was intense. What could we do? Persevere? Yes, while I had any hope at all of effecting the object for which we had set out.

Lamb tried hard to persevere; but finally, he too had to abandon the task as hopeless. The dogs were unable to get on, moreover, and I was at last reluctantly obliged to turn my face again toward the ship, having decided that it was my duty to return to save the living rather than to strive to reach one who might be already dead. Never had I experienced harder work than in travelling back. The condition of Lamb was such that I feared for his life if we did not soon get on board. Every few steps the snow had to be broken down to make a passage. It was of God's mercy that I had strength enough to hold up, else both of us must have perished. Occasionally I threw myself down on the ice or snow, thoroughly exhausted; then I would start up, arouse Lamb, who seemed to be verging toward that sleep which in cold regions becomes the sleep of death, and once more battle onward.

During this hard passage back to the vessel my noble dog Barbekark was like a cheering friend; as now and then I lay almost exhausted upon the snow for a moment's rest, he danced around me, kissing my face, placing himself by my side, where I could pillow my head upon his warm body. No one who knew his characteristics could fail to perceive that he realized the critical situation of Lamb and myself. He would bound toward me, raise himself on his hinder legs, place his paws upon my breast, and glance from me toward the vessel, and from the vessel to Lamb, then leap away, leading the sledge-team on a distance ahead, there to wait till we again came near, the few dogs and the soft state of the snow preventing us from riding.

I was indeed a happy man as I walked into the gangway of the *George Henry*, and learned that all my company were safely back to its shelter.

On February 25th I made another attempt to see what had become of the woman who had been abandoned, and I now take from my diary the history of that excursion:—

"This morning Ebierbing and I were up early. While my Innuit friend (who was to be my companion and auxiliary in my renewed attempt to rescue the one at the plains) was engaged in icing* the sledge and harnessing the dogs, I was busy bagging blankets, pemmican, oil, &c.—the same articles I provided myself with on Friday last, with the object of making the woman comfortable before starting to bring her back. On getting the dogs together, Ebierbing found two missing. As it was essential to have a full team, we spared no exertions to find them. After searching all around the ship and the boats which are out on the ice, and not finding them, Ebierbing indicated that they might be over on the island at the deserted snow-houses of the Innuits. The two harnesses in hand, I offered to go and make a trial in getting them. I directed my steps to that part of the island where the abandoned igloos of Ebierbing and Koodloo are.

"Arriving there after severe struggling through the deep snow, I found dog-tracks leading to the openings into the two igloos, the said openings being through the dome, where the seal-entrail windows had been. Looking down through these openings, and searching around, I could see nothing of the dogs. I then made my way laboriously along, over to the village proper, on the farther side of Fresh-water Pond, and was unsuccessful here also. As I was making my return, I determined to visit again the igloos where I had first searched for the dogs, and on turning to them I saw one of the animals in the distance. On calling to him the other soon made its appearance; but, as I was a stranger to them, I had a difficulty in capturing them. They broke past me and ran into the broken-down passage-way leading into Ebierbing's deserted igloo. The drift, as well as the falling in of the dome, had so completely shut up this passage that I was a long time in enlarging the fox-hole sufficiently to admit my contracted size. By perseverance I kicked a way before me, being prostrate, and pushing along feet foremost; but on getting the length of the passage leading to the main igloo, and making a turn so that I could not look ahead, my dilemma was far from enviable, for there the dogs were, beyond a possibility of my reaching them, the dome of the igloo having stooped, as it were, to kiss its foundation. By using dog-persuasive talk, I at length induced one of them to come out of the wolf-like den and approach me. Here it played "catch-me-if-you-can," coming just without my reach, and dodging back into its lair. After fifteen minutes' coaxing the dog was tempted to hold out its paw, but as often as I attempted to meet it with mine it was tormentingly

* See chapter xxxvii.

withdrawn.   The paw was finally fast within my hold, and quickly I had the dog in harness, dragging him after me, and of course his companion followed after.   When back to the vessel I was covered with perspiration, though the thermometer was 62° below the freezing point.

"At fifteen minutes past 10 A.M. Ebierbing and I started, with little expectation of being back to-night.   We took along the pair of snow-shoes of Ebierbing's (of Esquimaux style and make), to be used alternately by each of us if the occasion required it, and added to our traps a snow-knife, with which to make us a snow-house on the way if we needed it.

"The team of dogs was an excellent one, tractable, strong, and of great speed wherever and whenever the travelling would admit of it.   The number was not what we could wish, being only *seven*, but it was as great as we could have.   Had my four 'Greenlanders' been here, their help would have been ample for almost any emergency.

"The leader of Ebierbing's team proved to be of no ordinary quality.   Though, for much of the way to the point where I was obliged to turn back on Friday last in order to save my remaining companion (Lamb), the tracks we had made were obliterated, yet this leader, with admirable instinct, kept us in the desired course.   We had not proceeded far from the vessel before I found, to my joy, that the travelling had greatly improved since Friday.   The snow, in many places, had become firmly packed— much of the way sufficiently firm to hold up the dogs and the broad shoe of the sledge with both Ebierbing and me on it.

"We had other work than travelling to do.   We worked desperately to keep our faces and feet from freezing.   The wind was blowing a smart breeze all the way up the bay, directly from ahead, at a temperature of 62° below the freezing mark. The air calm, with a temperature of 100° below the freezing point of water, would be much more endurable than with such a wind charged with the temperature it was.   We took turns in trotting along beside the sledge, more for the object of keeping ourselves from freezing than with the view of easing the dogs of our additional weight.   By the aid of these seven dogs, and the broad runners of this sledge of Ebierbing's, we were enabled in two hours to reach the ultimatum of our attempt on Friday. After getting half a mile beyond said point we really found good passable travelling, and, by keeping close inshore, as far as our course would admit of it, we found much fair ice, the tide having overflowed the snow and changed it to ice.

" As we came within the distance of half a mile of the plains, I kept a constant look-out to see if I could discover some human figure out watching our approach. I may here remark, as an incident of this journey, that so cutting was the cold wind that it froze the water of the eyes, locking them up in ice, so that it was only by vigilance and effort that I could keep myself in seeing order. Many a lump of ice that I was forced to withdraw from my eyes showed specimens of eyelashes embalmed in crystal. As I said, I kept as good a look-out as I could, hoping that our approach might be welcomed by the one we sought to snatch from her desolate imprisonment. The ascent from the sea-ice to the plains was so gradual that I knew not when we were on the one or the other. I was also in doubt about our having made the correct landing, for the snow had covered up all former sledge and dog markings; but, on watching the motions of our noble, vigilant leader, I felt satisfied that his instinct was proving true—that he was leading us, by marks imperceptible to human eye, to the point we so impatiently sought to reach. This confidence we soon found not misplaced, for ahead of us we perceived various articles left by the Innuits who were recently living there sticking up above the snow. The dogs increased their speed, as is usual with them on nearing an inhabited place, and soon placed us alongside where the igloos had been. But where were the three igloos that I had visited Thursday, January 30th, a little less than four weeks ago ? Not one to be seen ! I took my snow-knife from the sledge, and, after my companion had finished his work of whipping down the dogs to a prostrate position, I bade him follow me.

" Around and around we walked, searching for the igloos. Sure was I that we were at the point I had struggled to reach. Could it be possible that the deep snow had covered them up ? My Innuit friend told me that such was probably the case. No footprints save our own could I discover. Were we travelling heedlessly over the grave of her whom we were fighting to save? This was a question that rushed into my brain. Then the thought came to me, Perhaps she still lives in some tomb beneath our feet. List ! list ! methought I heard a sound as if muffled ! All was as still as a charnel-house. Ebierbing's accustomed eye was not long in discerning a spot that satisfied him that, by cutting down through the snow, it would lead to the dome of an igloo.

" Knowing it to be repugnant to his feelings to touch anything belonging to an igloo covering the dead, I spared him all

pain on that score by digging down unassisted. A few moments
sufficed to satisfy me that Ebierbing had indicated to me the
precise spot leading to an igloo, for a few cuts with my snow
knife brought me down to the dome of one, and a few more
through it. After cutting a hole of sufficient size to let in light
and my head, I knelt down, and, with throbbing heart, surveyed
within. The igloo was vacated of everything save a large lump
of blubber back upon the dais or platform—the bed-place and
seat of the Innuits—and a few bones, the remains of some of
the tuktoo that had been killed by the Innuits on the plains.
A brief search revealed the apex of another igloo. Through

SEEKING THE LOST VILLAGE.

the dome of this I cut a hole, but found the interior still more
vacant; not a thing was in it, if I except a drift of snow that
completely filled the front of the igloo, closing up the place
that had been used as the entrance. This made two igloos that
I had searched without finding the object of my sympathy and
pursuit. Where was the third? That was now the question,
beyond the probability of being immediately answered. We
sought here and there, but unsuccessfully for a while. Ebierbing took an *oo-nar* (seal-spear)—which was among the articles
I indicated as pointing up through the snow which we saw as
we made our approach—and 'sounded,' striking it down through
the deep snow in one place after another, till he hit what told
him the third igloo was there. He called to me and pointed to
the spot, withdrawing himself a little distance off, where he
awaited my opening up whatever might be below. Stroke after

stroke with my long knife loosened the hard pure snow-drift. I lifted the blocks up out of their bed, casting them aside. This was the final search. My feelings, as I delved away at this heart-tearing work, may be better conceived than described. The dome of the igloo was reached. The heat that had been generated within from the fire-light had turned the snow of which it was made into solid ice, and I had difficulty in getting a hole through this. All this time we were exposed to the wind, blowing its cold, freezing blast from the north west. My snow-knife gave way in cutting this icy dome, and I was obliged to take in its place the seal-spear. With this I quickly penetrated the wall under me, thus revealing the fact that a lining, or second envelope, was yet to be cut through before I could determine my success in finding her whom I sought. It is a custom quite prevalent with the Innuits to line their snow-houses with sealskins, or such sail-cloth as they occasionally obtain from the whalers, for the object of shedding the droppings from the melting dome of the igloo, which follow when a large fire-light is kept burning, or when the weather becomes very moderate.

"This igloo I found to be lined with both sealskins and sail-cloth sewed together. With the knife I made an opening through this material. Throwing back its folds, and peering down into the interior, I there beheld her whom my soul aspired to help and to save. But she moved not, she answered not to my call. Could she be slumbering so soundly, so sweetly, that the ordinary tone of the human voice could not arouse her? There she was, her face turned to the wall at her right, reclining in her couch, fully enveloped in bed-covering. Enlarging the opening I had already made for the purpose of descending into this igloo, I called first to my Innuit friend to come near me. With cautious steps he approached. I told him the discovery I had made, and that I wished him to assist me as I descended, and to remain by while I determined whether the woman breathed or not. As the opening was directly over the ikkumer, I had considerable difficulty in getting down into the igloo, but at last I was within. In breathless silence I approached the object before me. I unmittened my right hand, and placed it on her forehead. *It was frosted marble!* She is dead! she is dead! were my uttered words to my friend, who stood on the snow roof looking down, and watching intently for the momentous result. Her whom we thought to rescue, *God Himself had rescued.* He found her here, lonely and hopeless, imprisoned in a clay tabernacle, and *this* entombed in ice walls and snow—deserted, abandoned by her people, when at *His* bidding an angel with white wing—whiter than the pure, radiant snow

"SHE MOVED NOT, SHE ANSWERED NOT TO MY CALL.

around—took the jewel from its broken casket, and bore it away to its home.

"I turn to the simple record of my investigations of whatever might lead to a conjecture of the time of this woman's death, and other incidents relating thereto.

" At the immediate entrance to the igloo—within the igloo—was a drift of snow reaching from the base to the dome. This snow had found its way in by a crevice not larger than my finger. On digging the drift away, I found a portion of a snow block that had been a snow door. As it had become but a fragment of insufficient size to seal up the entrance from the *took-soo*, or passage-way, into the main igloo, slabs of 'black skin' had been piled up, to make up the deficiency of the snow block. Whether this was done by the deserted woman or not I cannot decide. There is a probability that the Innuits, who so cruelly abandoned her to her fate, nearly filled up the entrance, then withdrew, turned round, and, by means of their arms and hands, reaching within through the small opening, completed the sealing up, the last act being to place a block of snow in the small remaining crevice.

" The woman, I doubt not, was so helpless as to be unable to get off the bed-platform from the time the Innuits left till her death. On the network over the fireplace was a single article—a *pau-loo* (mitten). Over the instrument used by the Innuits to contain their fire-light was hung a long iron pan in which to make snow-water. This contained ice, leaving the evidence that the woman's fire had ceased to burn, that the water had become frozen, and that, in order to quench her burning thirst, she had chipped ice from the pan (which hung close by her head as she lay in bed) by means of her *oodloo* (woman's knife). A tobacco-pipe was near her head also, apparently having been used just before she died. By her side—between her and the wall of the igloo—was a four-gallon tin can, containing articles of the character and variety possessed by every Innuit woman—needles, reindeer sinews (for thread), oodloo, beads, &c. &c. There was abundance of whale skin within the igloo, and so of ooksook with which to continue a fire ; but all of it was down on the floor of the igloo, without the reach of the woman, if she were unable to get from her bed, which I presume was the case when the Innuits left her. The bedding was extremely scanty. Over her limbs was nought but an old sealskin jacket, over her body and shoulders the shreds of a tuktoo skin and piece of an old blanket. As I turned back the covering from her shoulders, I saw that she was reduced to 'skin and bones.' As I looked upon her tattooed face, it was youthful and fair; even a smile was there, as if the King of Cold had fastened upon her at the very moment when her spirit welcomed the white-winged angel from heaven.

"I know not how long I tarried in this that had been her living tomb, and was now the tomb of that only which is earthly. But at last I raised myself through the opening in the dome by which I had made my entrance, and, with the assistance of my Innuit friend, proceeded to cut out snow-blocks and place them over the excavated place in the igloo. Having secured it as well as we could, thus reburying, as it were, the dead, we turned our faces to the sledge and dogs, and were soon on our way to the ship."

On Saturday, March 1st, news arrived by Koodloo of the ill success attending him and Ebierbing on their seal-hunts at Too-koo-li-to Inlet, and of the starving condition of their families. I thereupon determined to return with Koodloo and carry food to relieve them, and also to effect arrangements to have Koodloo and Ebierbing, with their families, removed to Field Bay. We started with eight dogs attached to our sledge, but the deep yielding snow made our progress at first very slow. Our course for the first four miles was nearly due north, when we struck the land on the east side of Grinnell Mount; thence, for a distance of fifteen miles, our journey was inland, first traversing a chain of lakelets embosomed amid mountains. When about three miles inland on our way, we came across an igloo nearly buried in snow; it was one that had been made a half-way house by Ebierbing and his party in going up. After this our way wound in and out among the mountains, up and down the steep sides, the sledge often nearly running over the dogs, till we came to Tookoolito Inlet, where we expected to find Ebierbing, his wife, and Koodloo's family.

"Isaiah," the little son of Koodloo, was seen coming out to meet us, and soon afterward we reached the igloos. Tookoolito gladly welcomed us, her husband being out over a seal-hole. The next day, March 3d, finding that Ebierbing had not yet come in, Koodloo and I went in search of him with dogs and sledge. When within three cables' distance of where he was still seated beside the seal-hole, having been there since the previous morning, he signified to us not to approach nearer, lest we should frighten the seal, as it had come up and given a puff. We then returned to the igloo, and remained another night. On the morning of March 4th, Ebierbing had not returned, and I went once more to look for him, but soon discovered him approaching. He had been *two and a half days and two nights*

EBIERBING WAITING A SEAL'S "BLOW."

at that seal-hole, patiently sitting over it *without food or drink!* and he had not caught the seal either. On returning to the igloo some soup and other food was given him, and he then expressed a determination to go and try again.

On the evening of March 5th I was again at the ship, Ebierbing, his wife, and infant having accompanied me. I left a supply of my pemmican for Koodloo and his family, until Ebierbing should return with the dogs and sledge for them.

The last half of the month of March I was chiefly occupied with preparations for the sledge journey which I proposed making up Frobisher Bay, and to which I have before referred.

CIVILIZATION SLEDGE. (See Appendix, No. V.)

CHAPTER XXXII.

On Tuesday, the 1st of April, 1862, I started on my proposed
exploring trip up Frobisher Bay. Some of the officers and crew
of the *George Henry* were proceeding to Oopungnewing with a
whale-boat and whaling apparatus lashed to a sledge drawn by
dogs, and I took the opportunity of transporting my material
over the Bayard Taylor Pass, proposing to go on from Oopungnewing with the ship's sledge.

The party consisted of nine persons, four belonging to the
ship's company, four Innuits, and myself, and at 7 A.M. we
started from the ship. Our team of dogs was a good one,
numbering nineteen, all in excellent order, and in two hours we
made the land, commencing the journey across the Pass. Tookoolito, who had been of great assistance to me in making my
preparations for this journey, had promised to see me in the
morning, and bid me good-bye ; but she over-slept herself, and I
was disappointed of seeing her. After making three quarters of
a mile, on looking back, I saw an Innuit far behind, but supposed it to be one of our party whom our quick movement had
left in the rear. Presently one of the ship's company called my
attention to the fact that Tookoolito was hastening after us. I
knew at once that the noble-hearted woman was anxious to see
me, in accordance with her expressed purpose of the previous
evening. Turning back, I met her laboriously working her way
along the hummocky ice, quite exhausted with her exertions.
As soon as she could speak, she said, " I wanted to see you before you left, to bid you good-bye." I thanked her, expressed
my regret for the trouble she had taken, and asked where her
babe was. She rolled down her hood, and there, nestled at her

back, was the sweetly-sleeping Tuk-e-lik-e-ta. Taking Tookoo-lito by the hand, I thanked her for all her kindness to me, and assured her that Captain B. would attend to her and Ebierbing's wants while I was absent, seeing that they did not suffer for lack of food. I then sent her back with two of the crew who had accompanied us thus far, but were now returning.

The descent of the Pass was for a portion of the way dangerous, and at all times exciting; the passage was down three declivities, one of which was at an angle of 45°. To guard against accident, the Innuits placed straps made of walrus hide over the forward part of each runner, allowing the same to sweep back under the runners; this acted as a drag by digging deep into the snow. To the stern of the sledge was fastened a line twenty fathoms long, to which Lamb, Morgan, and myself clung for the purpose of holding back. The dog-driver was directly in front of his team, whipping them back, so that they might not give to the sledge any swifter motion than it would have from its own impetus. Thus the descent was safely accomplished.

We arrived at Oopungnewing at 4 P.M. having been on the way but nine hours, and were kindly welcomed by the Innuits, large and small, as we drove up to their igloos on the south-east end of the island. Several of the ship's crew were also there, living with them, and apparently enjoying perfect health.

Soon after our arrival I proceeded to the igloo of Artarkparu, to learn the precise spot where he had last seen the "anvil." Annawa was with the old man; and from the conversation that followed, I soon found that *Ar-lood-loong*, the wife of Artark-paru, who was seated at her usual place before the ikkumer, was better acquainted with the particulars than any other one of the party. I immediately promised her beads and tobacco if she would accompany me to the spot where the relic could be found. With alacrity she drew on her *kodlings*, and bounded out like a deer, proceeding over the rocks westward, while I exchanged a few more words with the two old men. They informed me that when this "anvil" was last seen it was within ten fathoms of where we then were, but that it had tumbled off the rocks into the sea. At very low water it could be seen; and they told me that the ice would go away from the place before the ship sailed, and that they would help me get it then.

I then joined Arloodloong, who had waited for me upon the rocks, and she directed my attention to a certain level spot of land not far off, where the natives sometimes build their igloos or erect tupics. She said that, when she had a *nu-tar-ung* (babe) yet unborn, the "heavy stone" (anvil) was there, and was used as a seat by herself and many Innuits who at that time had their igloos on the spot. On inquiring which of her sons was the nutarung to which she referred, she replied *Kod-la-ar-ling*, a young man I supposed to be about twenty-five years of age. Her mother had also seen it there ; but, after a time, her people had brought it away to the locality indicated by Artarkparu, and had finally tumbled it into the sea.

In the evening Koojesse came home, drawing into his igloo three seals and a fox. One seal, I should think, weighed 200 pounds. The two others were young ones, of but two or three days old, both as white as snow. He caught the mother and one of the young ones in a seal's igloo, which was on the ice and over a seal-hole.

Just before sundown I took a walk to the top of the hill at Oopungnewing, and saw Jones's Cape, and many other places where I had previously been. Kingaite's rampart of mountains also stood up in grandeur before me. The Bay of Frobisher was filled with fragments of ice, sending forth thundering noises as the swift tides dashed piece after piece upon each other. I was delighted to see on the north side an unbroken pathway along the coast upward.

That evening a great seal-feast took place in Koojesse's igloo, old Artarkparu and his family being present. Of course I joined in it, and participated in eating the raw, warm-blooded seal, taking it in Innuit fashion—that is, disposing of several pounds of raw meat at one sitting. The young seal (which I tasted at supper on the following day) was tender and fine, eating like a spring chicken.

Owing to various causes, I had to stay at Oopungnewing for several days, and during that time I occupied myself with writing and making observations. On April 5th, Koojesse, with several others of the natives, went out on a walrus hunt, and in the afternoon I spent some time watching them in their operations. They were about four miles out, walking in Indian file, making their way on drifting, broken ice. Soon after, one of the Innuits, looking at the party, said they had killed a walrus, and the dogs were at once harnessed to the sledge, and sent out on the ice-floe, to the edge of it, to wait there till the Innuits should get the walrus cut up. At about ten o'clock at night it was announced that they were returning ; then the cry of the dogs was heard, and soon Koojesse entered, dragging after him

LEIGHTON, BROS.

HARPOONING A WALRUS.

a huge cut of walrus. The news he communicated was cheering. He had struck and secured one, and Annawa another. Five had been struck through the day, though only two had been secured. Ooksin struck one, but his iron " drew ;" Kooksmith lost one by the breaking of his " gig." A considerable portion of the next day was consumed in bringing in the meat. The walrus struck by Annawa was of good size, weighing not far from 1,500 pounds ; that of Koojesse was not so large.

The manner of taking the walrus is as follows : The hunter has a peculiar spear, to which is attached a long line made of walrus hide ; this line is coiled, and hung about his neck ; thus prepared, he hides himself among the broken drifting ice, and awaits the moment for striking his game. The spear is then thrown (as shown in the accompanying engraving), and the hunter at once slips the coil of line off his head, fastens the end to the ice by driving a spear through a loop in it, and waits till the walrus comes to the surface of the water, into which he has plunged on feeling the stroke of the harpoon ; then the animal is quickly despatched by the use of a long lance. The recklessness and cool daring of the Innuit is forcibly shown in this operation, for if he should fail to free his neck of the coil at just the right moment, he would inevitably be drawn headlong beneath the ice.

At length, on the morning of April 7th, I resumed my trip. Ebierbing had come over with the sledge on the previous day, and I made an exchange with him, taking his, and giving him that belonging to the ship. My company consisted of Koojesse, his wife Tunukderlien, *Kar-nei-ung* (" Sharkey "), his wife *Noudlarng* (" Jennie "), and young Henry Smith. We proceeded on the sea-ice, nearly north-west, for Chapel's Point, at the west side of the entrance of Wiswell's Inlet. Our sledge was heavily laden, especially with *kow* (walrus hide) for dog food, and walrus beef for our own eating ; but the travelling was good, and we made better progress than I had expected, arriving at the place named at about 4 P.M.

Then Sharkey and Koojesse proceeded to build an igloo in the regular manner, which may be described thus : They first sounded or " prospected " the snow with their seal-spears to find the most suitable for that purpose. Then one commenced sawing out snow blocks, using a hand-saw, an implement now in great demand among the Innuits for this purpose ; the blocks having been cut from the space the igloo was to occupy, the other Innuit proceeded to lay the foundation tier, which consisted of seventeen blocks, each three feet long, eighteen inches wide, and six inches thick. Then commenced the "spiraling," allowing each tier to fall in, dome-shaped, till the whole was completed, and the key-stone of the dome or arch dropped into its place, the builders being within during the operation. When the igloo was finished the two Innuits were walled in; then a square hole was cut at the rear of the dwelling, and through this Smith and I passed some snow blocks which we had sawed out. These Sharkey and Koojesse chipped or "minced" with their snow knives, while Tunukderlien and Jennie trod the fragments into a hard bed of snow, forming the couch or dais of the igloo. This done, the women quickly erected on the right and left the fire-stands, and soon had fires blazing, and snow melting with which to slake our thirst. Then the usual shrubs, kept for that purpose, were evenly spread on the snow of the bed-place; over that was laid the canvas of my tent, and over all were spread tuktoo furs, forming the bed. When the work had been thus far advanced, the main door was cut out of the crystal white wall, and the walrus meat and other things were passed in. Then both openings were sealed up, and all within were made happy in the enjoyment of comforts that would hardly be dreamed of by those at home.

I must here mention an incident which shows that the Innuits are equal to any emergency which may arise in their own country. For my supper I had some pemmican soup, but, on tasting it, it was too fresh, and we had no salt. What could we do? In a moment that was decided. Sharkey, on hearing what was wanted, took his knife and cut down into the snow floor of the igloo, in less than a minute coming to salt water.

This astonished me, and I asked how it was that salt water had thus got above the main ice. They replied that the great depth of snow on the ice pressed it down.

During that day's trip I found that two puppies formed part of our company. Their mother was an excellent sledge-dog of our team. The pups were carried in the legs of a pair of fur breeches, and they rode on the sledge when travelling. Every time we made a stop they were taken out of their warm quarters and given to the mother for nursing. When we arrived at our encampment above referred to, Sharkey built up a small snow hut for the parent dog and her offspring. The Innuits take as much care of their young dogs as they do of their children, and sometimes even more.

The following day, April 8th, I found that some of my Greenland dogs were missing. This consequently delayed me. All I could do was to wait patiently until they were recovered from Oopungnewing, to which place they had returned. Koojesse and Sharkey went out after young seals, and came back with one, its coat white and like wool. In the evening we had our supper from a portion of this seal, and never did I eat more tender meat. It were a "dainty dish to set before a king." But the great delicacy we enjoyed was *milk*. Every young seal has usually in its stomach from a pint to a quart of its mother's milk. The Innuits consider this a luxury, either raw or boiled, and so do I. I partook of this milk, eating some of it first raw, and afterward some of it boiled. It had the taste of cocoa-nut milk, and was white like that of a cow.

The next two days, April 9th and 10th, were spent at the same encampment, though on the former day I explored Wiswell Inlet to its northernmost limit. On the morning of the 11th we proceeded on our journey. As we neared Peter Force Sound, a sledge party of Innuits met us, and it was soon found that we were mutual friends. They were stopping on an island close by Nouyarn, and intended to go up the bay; I therefore expected to meet them again. We arrived at a place on the ice near Brewster's Point, on the western side of Peter Force Sound, and the two male Innuits immediately began to erect an igloo. The two women started off, each with dog and hook, to hunt for seal igloos, and in five minutes Jennie's loud voice announced that Tunukderlien had captured a young seal. Instantly Koojesse and Sharkey dropped their snow-knife and saw, leaped the walls of their partly-erected igloo, and hastened with all speed to the women. Henry and I had preceded them; but, after we had all started, I remembered that we had left our walrus meat and other provision exposed to the dogs; I therefore directed Henry to return and look out for them.

On reaching the place of capture, we found that Tunukderlien had beneath her feet a young seal alive and kicking. Koojesse immediately made a line fast to one of its hind flippers, and allowed the seal to re-enter the igloo where it had been caught. As this was something new and interesting to me, I intently watched what followed. The seal was perhaps two or three weeks old, and, like all young seals, was white, though not as white as untainted snow. While Koojesse kept hold of the line, four or five fathoms long, the seal worked itself hastily back into the igloo, its birthplace, and there made a plunge down the seal-hole into the sea. Koojesse allowed it the whole play of his line, crawling into the igloo, taking the seal-hook with him, and waiting patiently for the parent seal to come up. I was close by him, there being just sufficient room through the opening made when the young seal was caught for me to push myself in. There, lying flat down, we both carefully watched. In three or four minutes the young seal returned, popping up its round, shining head, and blowing or puffing like a whale, though on a reduced scale, its large eyes glistening like lights from twinkling stars. It came directly to its bed-place where we reclined. As it attempted to crawl up, Koojesse gave it a stroke on the head, signifying "Go away—dive down—show to your mother that you, the darling of her affections, are in trouble, and when she comes to your aid I'll hook her too." The two women were now close by us, each with a seal-dog, and while thus waiting I had a good opportunity for inspecting a seal's igloo. It was a model of those which the Innuits make for themselves, and was completely dome-shaped. It was five feet or so in diameter, and two and a half feet high, with a depth of snow above it of some five feet. The platform of sea-ice was where the parent seal gave birth to its young and afterward nursed it. On one side was the seal-hole, filled with sea-water, which was within two inches of the top of the platform.

After waiting for some time, and finding that the old seal would not show itself, the young one was withdrawn and placed on the snow. Then Koojesse put his foot upon its back, between the fore-arms or flippers, and pressed with all his weight, the object being to kill the seal by stopping its breath. Innuits adopt this mode in preference to using knife or spear. It prevents the loss of what is to them the precious portion— the blood.

On returning to our encampment, we found that the dogs had made sad havoc with our walrus meat and blubber, and other things in general. However, as it could not now be helped, we put up with it. Our supper that night was blessed cold water, chunks of cold pemmican, and raw frozen walrus meat.

The following day, April 12th, while Sharkey and Koojesse were engaged in the locality of my third encampment hunting young seal, I started, accompanied by my attendant, Henry Smith, to explore another bay which appeared to run up some distance beyond Peter Force Sound. I expected to be able to go and return in one day, and therefore made no preparations beyond taking half a pound of pemmican and a quarter of a pound of Borden's meat-biscuit, intended for our lunch. As I wished to keep a careful account of the distance travelled, I took the line used by me when on the Greenland coast, near Holsteinborg, in drawing out of the great deep many a cod and halibut, and measured off with tape-line seventy-five feet; my log then consisted of a cold chisel used by me in cutting out my rock pemmican.

It should be said, however, that previous to this time, and on all subsequent occasions when my whole company were with me, and all our provision was to be carried, no one could ride on the sledge, the dogs having difficulty even in dragging their necessary load. Consequently, at such times, all my measurements between my astronomically-determined points had to be made by pacing—a tolerably accurate, but, withal, a very tiresome method of working.

I found many apparent heads to the bay during my passage up, and at each turn it seemed as if we had reached the termination; but, on making the several points of land, others were found beyond.

After some hours of travel the dogs became very tired, the snow allowing them to sink to their bodies at every step. It was growing late; a snow-storm was coming on; to return was impossible; we therefore set about making ourselves as comfortable as circumstances would allow. We had no snow-knife, but an impromptu igloo was planned which we built of the sledge and snow, getting out the blocks of the latter in the best way possible, that is to say, with a broken sledge-beam.

When the igloo was finished, and before the door was sealed up, we took in the dogs, and were soon really comfortable. The storm came down fearfully, but we were well protected; the beating snow sought an entrance, but could find none. Fortunately, we had saved a piece of the pemmican from our lunch, and this served to give us just a mouthful for supper; some fragments of the meat-biscuit also remained; and after this frugal repast and some pipes of tobacco, we retired to our snow bed. I had one dog for my feet-warmer, another for my pillow, while a third was arched at my back. Henry was also comfortably provided for. My diary for that day, written in the igloo of a white man's invention, concludes as follows :—

" Now within a few minutes of midnight. Hark! a singular noise strikes the ear. Perhaps it is a polar bear! We listen. Again the same alarming noise. Another sound, and we determine its source. It is the snoring of one of the dogs! So good night to all the sleeping world. Heaven bless all those who need it; none needs it more than myself."

The next morning, April 13th, I arose from my snowy couch at five o'clock, knocked my head against the snow door, made my way over its ruins on all-fours, then stood erect and looked around. The heavens seemed to indicate the dawn of a beautiful day. I called up Henry, and soon the dogs were harnessed, when we proceeded toward the head of this narrow bay—Newton's Fiord* as I named it—which we reached at 7 A.M. The termination I found to consist of a broken narrow plain, walled by a line of mountains on either side.

THE RETURN FROM NEWTON'S FIORD.

Before we reached this spot, the snow commenced falling, though the fall was accompanied by no wind, and the weather was very thick. Soon after seven we started on our return journey to our encampment, and at nine o'clock we were abreast of the place where we had passed the previous night. At that time the wind was freshening, and it was snowing hard. Our passage thence to the place of our encampment was very difficult. Not only had we to encounter a severe northwest gale, charged with cold at 32° below the freezing point, accompanied by drift-snow filling the air so thickly that often no object at three

---

* Named after O. E. Newton, M.D. of Cincinnati, Ohio. The termination of Newton's Fiord is in lat. 63° 22′ N. long. 66° 05′ W.

fathoms' distance could be seen, but the dogs became perfectly exhausted from being overworked, and from going long without food. On making inquiries of Henry Smith, I learned that Sharkey and Koojesse had been feeding their own dogs and neglecting my " Greenlanders," which were now just upon the point of giving out. Two of them were so knocked up before reaching home that they could not pull a pound; one was so fatigued that he repeatedly fell down. I was obliged to lead the way for several miles by the compass, it being impossible to see the land, though the fiord was only from half a mile to two miles wide.

During the afternoon the sun shone down through the storm that seemed only hugging the earth. For the last nine miles which I made along the west side of the fiord and Peter Force Sound, the mountains would every few minutes show a shaded contour—a ghost-like faintness—by which I was enabled to make my course without the compass. When within two miles of the igloos I came upon our sledge-tracks of the day before, and these I followed carefully while they were visible; but, with all my care, the track was soon lost; and as the land was again closed from view, we should have been in grievous difficulty had not the compass guided me. The risk was great indeed; for in such a storm we might easily have gone out to sea, or the ice of the bay on which we were travelling might have broken up and carried us away.

Providentially, we reached the encampment—my fifth, as I called it, which was the same as the third—at 5·10 P.M. finding Sharkey on the look-out, anxiously awaiting us, while Koojesse was out in search of me. The Innuits, all through the previous night, had kept my lantern suspended to a pole by the igloo as a beacon light. Hot suppers were quickly prepared for us by the women, and we soon retired to rest.

CHAPTER XXXIII.

DURING the day, April 14th, 1862, I remained quiet in the igloo, engaged in writing and working up observations. On the 15th I made a trip up the east arm of Peter Force Sound ; and on the 16th we left the fifth (same as third) encampment, and proceeded on up Frobisher Bay. We made but slow progress on account of sealing, there being a necessity for obtaining all the food that could be found. Six of us, beside the dogs, required a large quantity. After journeying seven miles, we made our next encampment on the ice a few paces from a point of land forming the west cape of a pretty little bay, which, on the boat voyage in the previous fall, I had called Beauty Bay. That night we had a different kind of dwelling from the one ordinarily occupied by us. The weather was now occasionally warm enough to admit of half igloo and half tupic, which was made by omitting the dome, and placing tent-poles, covered with canvas, on the snow walls.

An exciting scene occurred while the igloo wall was being erected. Koojesse and Sharkey were at work on the building, while Henry and I removed everything from the sledge. We being at some little distance, the dogs suddenly sprung in a pack upon the sledge, and each snatched a piece of the meat and blubber still remaining upon it. With a club in my hand, and seal-spear in Henry's, we belaboured them lustily, but they were so hungry that it really seemed as if they cared nothing for blows. As a piece of meat was rescued from the jaws of one, another, and perhaps two others, as quickly had it. Blow followed blow ; dogs flew this way and that, all acting like devils, determined to conquer or die in their devouring work. It was quite five minutes before the battle was through, and not then till Koojesse leaped the walls of the igloo, and came to our assistance. During this *mêlée*, Henry unfortunately broke the wood portion of Koojesse's *oo-nar* (seal-spear), and this enraged the Innuit to a degree not easily to be described, for no instrument is constructed by the natives with more care than this.

WE MUST CONQUER OR STARVE.

The following day, April 17th, I made an exploring trip up Beauty Bay, and on my return found that our igloo had fallen in. The sun was now becoming so powerful that the upper tier of the snow wall melted, and brought down the top and poles upon the two women who were within, and were consequently overwhelmed in the ruins.

Next morning, April 18th, at 9 A.M. we again started, taking a course direct for Gabriel's Island of Frobisher, in the main bay, called by the Innuits *Ki-ki-tuk-ju-a*. Our progress was slow, owing to the heavy load and the poor condition of the dogs; and at noon, symptoms of a gale coming on, it was deemed advisable to make for shelter. Before we could obtain it, the gale had burst upon us, filling the air with the "white dust" of the country. Presently we saw an Innuit in the distance approaching, and, after winding in and out among numerous small islands, we met him. It proved to be Ninguar-ping, son of Kokerjabin, out seal-hunting. He said there were other Innuits not far off, among them Miner and Kooperneung, with their families, and we quickly made towards them. I was glad to learn that these Innuits were so near; for I thought I would take my dogs and sledge, and run up from my next encampment to see my good friend Tweroong. I should have been sadly disappointed had I done so, as will soon appear. Ninguarping then accompanied us to the spot selected for our encampment, and assisted in building an igloo. Soon a sledge of Innuits, with a team of fourteen dogs, came bounding wildly towards us. They were quickly alongside, proving to be our friends "Jack" and "Bill," on their way to an island not far off for a load of walrus beef which was deposited there. They invited us to go to their village. This we did, abandoning our half-completed igloo.

We arrived about 4 P.M. and found a village of five igloos, all inhabited by Innuit families, composed of my old friends and acquaintances. Old *Too-loo-ka-ah* was one of the first whom I saw, and he invited me to his capacious igloo, where his wife, Koo-muk, quickly gave me water to drink and food to eat, the latter being portions of frozen walrus entrails. To say that I enjoyed this food would only be to repeat what I have said before, though, no doubt, many will feel surprised at my being able to eat, as I so frequently did, raw meat, contents of tuktoo paunch, entrails of seals and walrus, whale skin and krang, besides drinking train-oil and blood.

In the previous December, when on my trip to Jones's Cape after skins, I saw Toolookaah and his wife, and was both sur-prised and gratified to learn that she had an infant; it was a girl of only two weeks, and had been named *Ek-ker-loon.* Toolookaah was at this time, as I thought, sixty years old, and his wife not less than fifty-five years. When I now saw the parents again on this journey of which I am writing, I inquired for the child, and received the mournfully sad reply, "*Tuk-a-woke*," meaning, it is dead.

I should add to this record the news I received at the same time of the death of my never-to-be forgotten friend Tweroong.

Oo-soo-kar-lo, son of old Petato, told me that she had died several weeks before. Some days later I obtained the details of her death, and they were truly heart-rending. When her husband "Miner," and her son, "Charley" removed from Oopungnewing, a few weeks before this time, Tweroong was unable to walk, and had to be carried on a sledge. After going a few miles up Frobisher Bay, an igloo was built for her, when she was placed in it, without any food, and with no means of making a fire-light, and then abandoned to die alone. A few days after some Innuits visited the igloo and found her dead.

The next day, April 19th, in the afternoon, I received an invitation from old Petato to come into her igloo and partake of a seal-feast. Taking Henry Smith along with me, I accompanied Oosookarlo to the place indicated. We found Petato seated on her dais, with an immense stone pot hanging over the full blazing ikkumer; the pot was filled with smoking-hot seal and seal-soup; Sharkey, Kopeo, his wife and infant, and several young Innuits were there, awaiting the "good time coming." Petato, the presiding genius, took out a piece of the seal with her hands and gave it to me, doing the same by the others. Before I had half-finished mine, the old lady handed me another and a larger piece; but, without difficulty, I did ample justice to all of it. Henry declared he never partook of a meal he relished more. The second course was seal soup, of which Petato gave me a huge bowl full; that is the nectar of a seal-feast. After I was supplied, another bowl, of a capacity equivalent to four quarts, was placed on the floor for the dog to wash with his pliant tongue; when he had lapped it clean, outside as well as within, it was filled with the luscious soup, which the Innuits at once disposed of, taking turns at the bowl.

Later in the evening, as I was seated in my own igloo surrounded by my company, I heard a loud Innuit shout just outside. As quick as thought, Koojesse, Sharkey, Tunuk-derlien, and Jennie sprang for the long knives lying around, and hid them wherever they could find places. My first thought was that a company of warlike Innuits were upon us, and I asked Koojesse the meaning of all this. He replied "Angeko! angeko!" Immediately there came crawling into the low entrance to the igloo an Innuit with long hair completely covering his face and eyes. He remained on his knees on the floor of the igloo, feeling round like a blind man at each side of the entrance, back of the fire-light, the place where meat is usually kept, and where knives may generally be found. Not finding any, the angeko slowly withdrew. I asked Koojesse what would have been the consequence if the angeko had found a knife; he replied that he—the angeko—would have stabbed himself in the breast.

On April 22d we broke up our encampment, all the Innuits with the exception of Toolookaah's family, being about removing up Frobisher Bay. Two families, including Petato, Kopeo, Oosookarlo, with the wives and children of the two men, were to go with me one day's journey at least. Old Toolookaah, who was to remain behind, wore a sorrowful face on account of my departure. I find in my diary the following record: " This noble free-hearted Innuit loves me, I do believe; I know that I love him. We have now been acquainted more than a year; have voyaged together, have shared perils of storms and the glory of sunshine, have feasted together, slept beneath the same tupic, have been, as it were, father and son. Successful be his sealing, his tuktoo hunts, and his conflicts with the polar bear—the lion of the North; and, at last, peace and glory to his noble soul. When all were ready for a start this morning, this old Innuit accompanied me from this island some distance on the ice. At last we locked hands, and, with prolonged 'terboueties,' tears started in his eyes, and rolling down his iron-ribbed face, we parted, probably never to meet again on earth."

Throughout our day's journey there was a continuous gale, with snow-drift, closing all from our view; but we finally reached our next encampment, on a small island, above Kikitukjua, at 4·30 P.M. having gone nearly nine miles.

The following day we parted with Petato and my other Innuit friends, and proceeded some five or six miles direct toward Kingaite coast, making our ninth encampment * on the main ice clear of land.

We were obliged to remain here encamped for ten days, the desperate struggle being to get enough to sustain life. My hunters and sealers, Sharkey and Koojesse, went down every fair day a distance of five miles to the open water, where were white whales, seals, and ducks in abundance, but they were then all so shy that it was impossible to approach them within killing distance. That they might be successful was our earnest wish,

* The ninth encampment was in lat. 62° 51′ N. long. 66° 40′ W. due east of Gabriel's Island, and midway of it and Kingaite coast. (See Chart.)

for we were living mostly on dog food—*kow*—that is, walrus hide with hair on. Besides, we had no oil for the lamp, and without the lamp we were unable to obtain fresh water.

One day they came home successful, having caught a seal, the first of the season, and no happier beings could exist than we were for the time at the feast of raw seal that followed. In the evening of the next day, April 28th, Koojesse and Sharkey drove up with two seals, one of about 200 pounds' weight, and the other weighing 100 pounds. This was success indeed, and it enabled them to feed the dogs as well as ourselves. By this time the weather had become so warm that we could not keep our igloo dry, and it was resolved to erect a tupic or tent. This finished, we moved into it; and a few minutes after we had vacated our old home, down fell the igloo a mass of ruins.

On May 1st, 1862, I started from this encampment on a trip to Kingaite coast. While Henry was engaged harnessing up the dogs, I put together my instruments, a little bag of rock pemmican, and some Borden meat-biscuit, of which I had saved merely a trifle for use on excursions of this kind. Sharkey, with sledge and dogs, was ready, and, after a good hot breakfast, we started, at 7·40 A.M. for the point I had selected—near the President's Seat—viz. that where an ascent could probably be made of the glacier which I had seen on my voyage up the bay the previous fall.

My course across the bay to Kingaite coast was south 4° east, true. The number of dogs in the team was ten, but as they were in poor condition, we made but three and a half to four and a half miles per hour. In crossing the bay we found abundance of hummocky ice, and the snow-wreaths were numerous, abrupt, and high. A few minutes before noon we drew into a small bay that extended on toward the point I sought to reach. With great solicitude, I watched that part of the heavens in which the sun was, but, to my deep regret, the thick clouds were as a veil between my eyes and it. I had my instruments in readiness in case the sun should show itself for a few moments. If I could have got two solar observations, keeping correct account of the time elapsing between, by which to obtain accurately the "hour angle," I should have done so, for thus I could have determined my actual latitude; but the clouds were too thick for the sun's rays to penetrate them. I kept, however, a careful account of my course and of the distance made, by which I determined the latitude of Kingaite coast where I struck it.

As the dogs turned up the narrow bay leading to the point of land we were making, I was delighted to see the face of an abutting glacier, which fully proved the truth of my anticipations that there were iceberg discharges on Kingaite side. At noon our progress was arrested by the glacier, which seemed to smile a defiance—"thus far, and no farther."

Here, by this crystal wall, I stood, in admiration and awe beholding its beauty and grandeur. My Innuit companion seemed satisfied and gratified in witnessing the effect it had upon me. I turned and took a look seaward. A few degrees of opening between the points of land leading into the harbour in which we were gave a view bounded only by the sea horizon. My quickened thoughts almost made me exclaim, "Tell us, time-aged crystal mount, have you locked in your mirror chambers any images of white man's ships, that sailed up these waters near three centuries ago?" This train of fancy-painting was soon dissipated by the substantial reality of a lunch on cold rock pemmican and gold dust (Borden's pulverized meat-biscuit), washed down with chips from the glacier, after which we were prepared for an attempt to scale the ice mountain. This could be done only by ascending one of the rock ridges flanking the abutting arm of the glacier, and thence striking up its steep side.

For the first quarter of a mile it was very abrupt, and difficult to climb. The most laborious and dangerous part of the ascent was accomplished by following the footsteps of a polar bear. My "illustrious predecessor" had evidently ascended the glacier some time previous, just after a fresh fall of snow, impacting it by his great weight into such hard steps that the gales had no effect in destroying them. These polar bear steps made it feasible for us to ascend where we did. After the first quarter of a mile the inclination of the glacier was gradual, then for a quarter of a mile farther it became greater, but it did not so continue. Each side of this arm of the glacier was walled in by mountains, the east side by the group I called the President's Seat.

On making two miles—S. 16° E. true—we arrived where the glacier opens to a *sea of ice*. At this time and point the glacier was covered with snow, with a cropping out here and there of the clear, crystal blue ice, giving relief to the view of an apparently illimitable sea of white around. My Innuit companion, being well experienced in all the coast from Karmowong, a place on the north side of Hudson's Straits, to Resolution

ARM OF THE GRINNELL GLACIER BY MOUNT "PRESIDENT'S SEAT."

Island, and all about Frobisher Bay, said that this great glacier extended far, far below where we then were, and also continued on northwest a great way, reaching over also nearly to Hudson's Straits.   From the information I had previously gained, and the data furnished me by my Innuit companion, I estimated the Grinnell glacier to be fully 100 miles long.   At various points on the north side of Frobisher Bay, between Bear Sound and the Countess of Warwick's Sound, I made observations by sextant, by which I determined that over fifty miles of the glacier was in view from the southeast of the President's Seat. A few miles above that point the glacier recedes from the coast, and is lost to view by the Everett chain * of mountains ; and, as Sharkey said, the *ou-u-e-too* (ice that never melts) extends on *wes-se-too-ad-loo* (far, very far off).   He added that there were places along the coast below what I called the President's Seat, where this great glacier discharges itself into the sea, some of it large icebergs.

From the sea of ice down to the point where the abutting glacier arrested my advance with sledge and dogs, the ice-river or arm of the glacier was quite uniform in its rounding up, presenting the appearance—though in a frozen state—of a mighty rushing torrent.   The height of the discharging face of the glacier was 100 feet above the sea.

Without doubt, the best time of the year to travel over glacier mountains is just before the snows have begun to melt.   The winter snows are then well impacted on the glacier surface, and all the dangerous cracks and water-ditches are filled up.   Storms and gales do good work with snow-flakes once within their fingers. Grinnell Glacier,† a limited portion of which was visited, would, in three and a half or four months' time, present quite a different appearance.   Now it was robed in white ; then, below the line of eternal snow, it would be naked,—clear, bright, flashing cerulean blue meeting the eye of the observer.   This contrast I have seen. When on my boat-voyage up the bay in the previous fall, this great glacier of Kingaite heaved heavenward its hoary head, supported by a body of crystal blue : on my return the same was covered with its winter dress.   Before the cold weather sets in, all the crevices in the glacier are charged with water, which, congealing, is caused to expand ; and the ice explodes with a sound

_____

* Named after Edward Everett.   For location of " Everett Chain," see Chart.

† This great glacier I named after Henry Grinnell.   Its height, in the vicinity of President's Seat, is 3,500 feet.

like loud thunder, rending the mountains and shooting off ice-bergs and smaller fragments at the various points where the glacier has its arms reaching down to the sea.

After some time spent on the glacier, of which my view was not so extensive or protracted as it would have been but for the clouds that capped the heights where we were, my companion and myself returned to the sledge. I then walked to the shore and obtained a few geological specimens, and we started on our way back to the ninth encampment. Two or three miles from the glacier we came to a small island. I took several bearings of distant objects and sextant angles for elevation of the mountain heights; but the wind began to freshen almost to a gale, and caused considerable risk in crossing the bay. There was a probability of the floe cracking off and drifting us to seaward; the open water was within a mile of our course, and the floe, giving way, would have been swept rapidly to the southeast. My driver was constantly urging the dogs to their greatest speed while making passage over the most dangerous part of the way. Fortunately no mishap occurred, and we arrived at the tupic in the evening.

CHAPTER XXXIV.

On leaving our ninth encampment on Saturday, May 3d, 1862, we proceeded toward some islands nearly due east of us, and, after a journey of ten miles, came to M'Lean Island,* where we found two igloos occupied by the Innuits Koo-kin and "Bill," with their families. We were hospitably received, and made our tenth encampment† there.

I was now living wholly on Innuit food, to which I had become so accustomed as to eat it without difficulty. Were I to mention in detail what took place, and what was eaten at our meals, it would doubtless appear disgusting to most of my readers ; but there is no alternative in the matter of eating with Innuits. One has to make up his mind, if he would live among that people, to submit to their customs, and to be entirely one of them. When a white man for the first time enters one of their tupics or igloos, he is nauseated with everything he sees and smells —even disgusted with the looks of the innocent natives, who extend to him the best hospitality their means afford. Take, for instance, the igloo in which I had an excellent dinner on the day last mentioned. Any one fresh from civilization, if entering this igloo with me, would see a company of what he would call a dirty set of human beings, mixed up among masses of nasty, uneatable flesh, skins, blood, and bones, scattered all about the igloo. He would see, hanging over a long, low flame, the *oo-koo-sin* (stone kettle), black with soot and oil of great age, and filled to its utmost capacity with black meat, swimming in a thick, dark, smoking fluid, as if made by boiling down the

---

* Named after the late Judge John M'Lean. It is an island in the midst of Frobisher Bay, near to and due west of Gabriel's Island.

† Our tenth encampment was near the southern extreme of M'Lean Island, and was in lat. 62° 52′ N. long. 66° 28′ W.

dirty scrapings of a butcher's stall. He would see men, women, and children—my humble self included—engaged in devouring the contents of that kettle, and he would pity the human beings who could be reduced to such necessity as to eat the horrid stuff. The dishes out of which the soup is taken would turn his stomach, especially when he should see dogs wash them out with their long pliant tongues previous to our using them. But I will not multiply particulars.

Sharkey this day saw a rabbit when out on the island hunting partridges, but could not get a shot at it. If " Jennie," or any other female songster, had been with him, he would probably have secured it. Innuits, when they go after rabbits, generally have such a vocalist with them. While she sings "*charmingly*," the sportsman is enabled to have a fair shot. The rabbit delights in listening to the music of a female Innuit voice, and will stop, sit up, and be shot under its charms.

The scarcity of provisions, combined with the troubles I encountered with the evil-disposed Innuits, Koojesse and Jennie, had been so great, that I had determined to abandon my journey farther up the bay, and return at once to the Countess of Warwick's Sound; but we now found ourselves so abundantly supplied that I concluded to take Sharkey, and, leaving the rest of my company at the place of the tenth encampment, to make a flying trip up the bay with sledge and dogs. Sharkey at first cheerfully assented to my proposition, but on May 6th he signified to me his desire to take Jennie with him. I declined to accede to this request, and he acquiesced in my decision, but Jennie flew into a rage. She put on her kodlings and dodged out of the igloo, attempting to run away; Sharkey darted after her, and in about an hour they returned, on apparently amicable terms.

The next morning, May 7th, I went on with my preparations for departure; the movements of Jennie showed plainly that she intended to go. When the sledge was nearly loaded I went to Koojesse and asked him if Jennie was really going with us; he answered affirmatively, and therefore I called Sharkey into the igloo and talked with him. He acted nobly, telling Jennie she must remain with Koojesse and Tunukderlien till our return. He had previously bound her jacket and tuktoo bed upon the sledge, but at once threw them off, though I could see that he had a mountain of trouble within. After much delay we started.

When we were out on the sea-ice we kept a sharp watch of Jennie's movements. She was out on the rocks with her head turned to a bluff, and bellowing like an angeko while engaged in some of his incantations. In about half an hour she was discovered following us ; Sharkey closely examined her movements through the glass, and declared that she was indeed after us, and that she would travel all day and all night till she reached us. I at once decided to await her coming up, for my heart was moved for the poor fellow, who so fondly loved her, though she was unworthy of his affection.

When we paused for her to come up, Sharkey took the water-bag and the tin cup, and set out for an island at our left, distant a quarter of a mile, for water. His course was taken so that he intercepted Jennie when he was returning with his water to the sledge. She, however, paid no attention to him, but kept on, turning neither to the right hand nor to the left. Sharkey called to her, but she turned not, still continuing her rapid gait, and proudly striking into her open hand a loose mitten she carried in the other. Sharkey quickened his pace to catch up to her, repeatedly calling to her, but she walked stoically on. At length he overtook her, and tried to arrest her in her course. She threw him aside as if he were a viper, and walked on. Then Sharkey once more approached, and threw his arm around her caressingly. She gave no heed. Finally, in despair, he gave up, stooped down, buried his face in his hands, and poured out his weeping soul in a flood of tears. Then, rising up, he swung his arms about, and gave vent to his feelings in loud and broken cries, returning to the sledge, while the stubborn idol of his affections, with apparent indifference, pursued her way.

I addressed him sympathizingly, my heart overflowing with love for my wounded friend. He pointed to his wife, who still trudged on, crying "Jennie ! Jennie !" putting his hand on his heart and weeping. Under the circumstances, I decided to return to our encampment. As soon as we reached it, Sharkey started out with the dogs, ostensibly for the purpose of sealing. I knew, however, that his purpose was to go in pursuit of his wife. Some hours later he returned with Jennie, both apparently contented

I now at first thought I might as well give up this trip, and commence my return down the bay. Then I determined to take Henry as my dog-driver, and proceeded to explore the bay alluded to on page 347, some fifty miles to the N.W. by W. of our tenth encampment. I had before believed that Koojesse was at the bottom of Jennie's evil actions, and I now became thoroughly convinced of the fact; for, when he heard of my latest plan, he seemed determined to put as many blocks in my way as possible. He consented, for a consideration, to let me have the use of his dogs, but refused to allow me to take my own tupic. Then I hinted at returning at once to the ship; but this did not suit him; he wanted to stop where we were several days; and he declared that, if he was compelled to start the next day, the distance made would be "smalley." At last I offered him my rifle, which he wanted very much, if he would accompany me and do as he should on the trip I wished to make. His whole conduct changed immediately from that of a bitter enemy to that of a cheerful friend. The arrangement was made that Koojesse and Sharkey were to go, while Jennie and Tunuk-derlien were to remain with Henry, the Innuits Kooking and "Bill" having agreed with me to supply them with food. My conviction that Koojesse was the instigator of Jennie's freaks prior to this received confirmation from the perfect acquiescence of the woman in this plan after hearing a few words from him.

So, after much trouble, with Koojesse and Sharkey as my companions for the trip, I again started at 9 A.M. of the 8th of May. Our progress on the firm ice was fair, our course northerly and westerly. In and out among numerous islands, and with a few stoppages to take bearings and make observations, we passed on for several miles, seeing places on the mainland familiar to me, and finally, after twelve hours' travel, making a distance of twenty-three miles, encamped on Field's Island,* at the entrance of Waddell Bay. The following day, May 9th, we were at the entrance to the bay—A. H. Ward's Inlet,† as I named it—which I had so long desired to explore; but, on the next, owing to bad weather and soft snow, we could proceed only a short distance. On the 11th, however, we made rapid progress, passing on the east side of a long island, the scenery magnificent, and, going through a place where the mountains almost meet, and which I call "The Narrows," finally arriving at the head of this truly romantic and beautiful inlet at about 2 P.M.

Just before passing up through the Narrows, we saw that the ice ahead was completely riddled with seal-holes, and that seals in immense numbers were lying by them basking. Sharkey laid himself down, and proceeded with his gun to make the

---

* Named after Dudley Field, of New York City.
† Named after Augustus H. Ward, of New York City.

usual Innuit approaches, as already described, toward a place where some seals were close together. At last he shot one, having been one hour and twenty-five minutes crawling up to within six fathoms of his prey. A raw and blood-warm seal-feast immediately followed, for this was the first thing secured for four days. Never did I enjoy anything with a better relish.

On the right of the extreme termination there is a bold mountain, with a ravine between it and the opposite side, which is gradually sloping. The bay or harbour between the Narrows

TERMINATION OF WARD'S INLET—THE NARROWS AND ANN MARIA PORT.

and the termination of the inlet is indeed magnificent. After staying here as long as my time would permit, and having determined that no "*strait*" or passage exists in this direction, I started on my return, and soon again arrived at the Narrows. Here the view below was one of the most interesting I had beheld since arriving North. From the Narrows, which is from one-sixth to one-third of a mile wide, to the termination of this arm of Ward's Inlet, is a distance of four miles. This beautiful sheet of water I have named Anna Maria Port.* As we made our way through the narrows on our return, the view, on looking down the inlet, was truly magnificent. The long line

* Named after the wife of Augustus H. Ward. The head or termination is in lat. 63° 44′ N. long. 67° 48′ W. *Vide* Chart.

of black, jagged, buttress-like mountains on either side of the pure white pathway before us presented a scene that I shall not soon forget.

As we returned down this inlet, going at a slower rate than usual, a seal was seen ahead. In an instant the dogs, which were very hungry, bounded off at a rate of not less than twelve miles an hour. The seal, frightened, made a plunge down into its hole; the dogs, flying onward so furiously, passed it, but the wind, carrying the smell of the seal to their noses, made them turn sharply round in a second. The consequence was that the sledge-runner caught in the snow-crust, and sent me heels over head off the sledge, to which my Innuit companions clung with all their might. The runners of this sledge were twelve feet long, and the left one was split from stem to stern; but, though this was a serious disaster, yet no considerable regret was manifested on the part of the natives. Koojesse and Sharkey immediately set to work with their seal-spears, and succeeded in mortising three holes in the lower half of the runner in the short space of time that it took me to write the pencil notes recording the incident. It was not long before the runner was strapped together, and we were again on our way down on the western side of the large island which we passed in the morning, I hoping not to see another seal that day. It was 10 P.M. when we arrived at the south end of the Kikitukjua— Augustus Island, as I called it—and made our fourteenth encampment. We had travelled forty miles that day after leaving the thirteenth encampment, which was on a small island not far from the east side of Augustus Island. We slept soundly, though our couch was the bare rock. On the morning of the 12th, when we awoke, we found ourselves beneath a snow-drift —that is to say, some eight or ten inches of snow had fallen during the night, giving us a clean, warm coverlet. The weather being unpropitious for travelling, we remained at the same place during the day. The following day, May 13th, at 10 A.M. we resumed our journey, passing along down by the coast of Becher Peninsula,* on the west side of the inlet, directing our course towards Mary's Island, the place of the twentieth encampment of my boat expedition the previous fall. We had not proceeded far on our way when a smart breeze from the northwest sprung up, and before we had made half the distance to Mary's Island it increased to a gale, accompanied with pelting drift. I know

* The land between Ward's Inlet and the main Bay of Frobisher I thus named after Captain A. B. Becher, R.N. of England. See Chart.

not that I ever experienced more disagreeable travelling than on this occasion. The snow flew furiously, eddying around our heads, and dropping down into our laps as we sat upon the sledge with our backs to the gale. The sun was out with thawing heat, melting the snows in our front, wetting our furs, while the temperature at our backs was 14° below the freezing mark. When we reached the point at the west side of the entrance to Ward's Inlet at 8 A.M. we were compelled to stop and go into camp.

My notes, written upon the spot, read, " Stop on account of the driving gale and drift. Sharkey proceeds to make an igloo. Koojesse is sick—knocked up completely, while I am in perfect health."

As I have said, the sun was out, notwithstanding the flying drift ; therefore I proceeded to occupy myself as usual in making observations for time, and taking a round of angles, &c.

I continue extracts from my rough and ready note-book of same date (May 13th) : " The gale abated 2 P.M. yet snow flying thick over toward Kingaite. Thought of starting, but, desirous of having good and extensive views when I cross the Bay of Frobisher to Kingaite side, I decided to hold over till to-morrow. It will take two days' good weather to get back to the place of tenth encampment — perhaps three. Koojesse and Sharkey gathered from the mountain's side a skin jacket full of Northern wood (dwarf shrub), with which we cooked a soup. The dogs have no food. To supply them and ourselves, shall have to let the Innuits seal to-morrow. Gave Koojesse pills to-night ; he is badly off.

" *Wednesday, May* 14*th.* — Up at 2 A.M. We cooked our breakfast of tuktoo and seal. Used the straw (dwarf shrub) of our beds for fuel. This morning, as a matter of trial of the pluck of my companions, I proposed to continue up to the head of Frobisher Bay. The Innuits expressed a willingness to go. I have no idea of doing this, but now intend to cross Frobisher Bay to-day from Noo-ook-too-ad-loo, a small island close by Rae's Point, direct to Kingaite, and thence pass down by the coast to near where I had my ninth encampment, and then recross the bay to place of tenth encampment. The weather is thick this morning, but there is a bright streak along the horizon in the east. The dogs are very hungry. Last night they ate up the whip-lash, which was thirty feet long. They are *voracious.* I witnessed a sight some days since of a hungry dog swallowing down a piece of *kow* (walrus hide and blubber) one inch and a half square and six feet long in seven seconds ! The act I timed by chronometer."

At 5 A.M. we left the place of sixteenth encampment, directing our course to the westward, and in two hours arrived at the island Noo-ook-too-ad-loo, which Sharkey and myself ascended. Here we saw some partridges and many rabbit tracks. One of the former Sharkey shot. While on this island I took a round of angles, sighting various important points necessary toward completing my chart of the bay. Thence we departed at 9 A.M. striking nearly due west to cross the Bay of Frobisher. We found the ice very rough, and consequently our progress was slow. A few minutes before twelve, meridian, as we were about to enter among the numerous islands that lie across the bay, beginning at " Frobisher's Farthest," we stopped, when I proceeded to make observations for latitude, solar bearings, &c. When I found my position was such that various capes, promontories, islands, and inlets that I had visited were in sight, and knowing I could then better determine their relative geographical position, I was delighted, and especially so when I had the President's Seat dancing and circling round in the mirror of my sextant, till it finally rested on the mountain heights of Frobisher's Farthest, on the exact spot where I had made astronomical observations on the 22d of August, 1861, the previous year. Thence we proceeded among many islands, and came to a channel where we found a space of open water abounding in ducks and other aquatic birds, and seals. Here the tide was rushing furiously through like a mill-race, and this prevented us from securing more than half of our game, for as the ducks and seals were shot they were liable to be carried rapidly away beneath the ice. Sharkey, however, shot and secured one seal which weighed about three hundred pounds, and also killed several brace of ducks.

While the hunters were engaged at this work I took my instruments and went upon the hill of an island to have a look around and to triangulate. When at the summit and quietly taking a survey, I heard a deep tiger-like growl. I listened, and glanced quickly in the direction whence it came. I saw nothing, and soon raised my sextant to my eye, when another and another growl assailed my ear. Again I looked around, but could see nothing, though I concluded it must be either a polar bear or a wolf. Therefore, considering my unarmed state, and the distance I had climbed up the mount, away from all assistance, I thought the better part of valour in such a case was to beat a hasty retreat. The distance to the sea-ice was one mile, and thence to where my companions were, another mile. I shall not soon forget that day's adventure. I awaited the fourth growl, and when that came I quickly packed up instruments and started on a run, turning every few moments to see whether I was ahead. In my course was a long drift of snow, and as I was making a rapid transit of this, a spot in it proved treacherously soft, which gave me a fall, and heels over head I went to the bottom of the hill. Fortunately it was the quickest and most direct passage I could make, and, as it happened, no bone or anything else was broken. When I arrived back and told my companions what I had heard, they declared I had had a narrow

THE HUNGRY WOLVES.

escape from either hungry wolves or a polar bear. It was 4·30 P.M. when we resumed our way across Frobisher Bay. Having got fairly through the passage between the islands on the ice-foot, we turned southerly. We soon saw ahead immense numbers of seals out on the ice. They extended over a large area, and were so numerous that with my glass I could not count them.

Just as we were turning off the ice to an island—J. K. Smith Island, as I named it—on which we had proposed to make our seventeenth encampment, three wolves appeared in sight, coming swiftly on our track, and presently on came a fourth—all most ferocious-looking brutes. They were bold, approaching quite near, watching our movements, and now and then opening and snapping their teeth, and smacking their chaps, as if already feasting on human steaks and blood. We prepared for the fray by arming with rifle, gun, and spear, each ready to defend himself as best he could. Between the wolves and us was much hummocky ice. Behind this ice we placed ourselves, each seeking to get a good shot. Sharkey led in the attack, levelling his gun on the instant that one of these savage foes began to make its approach. The result was that the hungry wolf turned tail, and went off limping, minus a man-supper, his companions following him.

After the excitement of this affair was partially over, Koojesse informed me that he had known many instances in which Innuits had been attacked, killed, and devoured by hungry wolves. When once so attacked, it was generally sure death to the Innuit. It was, indeed, with thankful heart that I retired to my snowy couch that night, as I thought of my narrow escape from the very midst of that hungry pack, unarmed as I was, and far away from all help save that of Him who is ever mighty to save.

The following morning, May 15th, we were about to resume our journey, when, the wind having increased to a gale, accompanied with drift, and Koojesse being quite ill, we were obliged to hold over, and keep in the igloo all day. Our fare that day was raw seal and raw ducks. The ducks were very fat, the fat being like butter both in appearance and taste.

In the morning of Friday, the 16th, the weather was thick, and at times spitting snow. We were up at 3 A.M. intending to start early, and complete the crossing of Frobisher Bay to Kingaite coast ; but the shore-ice by the island of our encampment was in such an impassable condition from ebb tide that we had to wait for the flood. At 7·30 we were under way, passing to the westward and northward for some time along the coast of Resor Island * on our left, over the rough ice, and among the thousand and one islands of that part of Frobisher Bay. At 11 A.M. we arrived at White Island, which I had seen on my boat-voyage in the previous fall, and then thought very remarkable. On this occasion I landed to examine it and procure geological specimens.

Thirty minutes after meridian we arrived close to a point of Kingaite coast, whence I could see what the natives call *Sharko* (low land), where I had my eighteenth encampment of the boat-voyage in the fall of 1861. Having reached the point—Turn Point,† as I called it—where my survey of the Kingaite coast

* Named after William Resor, of Cincinnati, Ohio. The centre of this island is in lat. 63° 16′ N. long. 67° 55′ W.

† Turn Point is in lat. 63° 19′ N. long. 68° 09′ W.

terminated when on that voyage, I turned about and resumed the survey, passing rapidly down a beautiful channel—Cincinnati Press Channel, as I named it, in honour of the Associated Press of the Queen City—between Kingaite and Pugh Island.*

A BEAR-HUNT.

At 3 P.M. while we pursued our journey down the channel, an exciting scene occurred. A polar bear, with its cub, was observed on the ice near the base of a bold high mountain. Immediately the dogs were stopped and the guns loaded. Koojesse forgot that he was lame and sick, and prepared to join us in the hunt. I, with spy-glass in hand, watched the bear's movements, and when all was ready, the dogs were again started. They soon caught sight of the prey, and bounded forward. While drawing us with great speed, and when within 200 fathoms, the draught-

* Named after George E. Pugh, of Cincinnati, Ohio. This island is ten miles long, the centre being in lat. 63° 16′ N. long. 68° W.

line of the leader was cut, and away he flew toward the bear. Then another, and then another of the running dogs was cut loose and sent in chase, until all were free from the sledge and in pursuit.

The bear, with her cub following, made her way over the broken ice between the main ice and the shore, direct for the mountain steep, which they at once began to ascend. One of the dogs had now neared them, and constantly attacked the cub until it became separated from its mother. Then another dog sprang at the hinder part of the old bear, which turned and made a plunge at the dog, causing both to tumble headlong down the declivity, which was so steep that I wondered how the bear could have ascended it.

The fight now became earnest, and the dog yelped with pain, as the bear's paw came heavily upon him. Presently Bruin was obliged to turn again, and, with head swinging to and fro, and roaring plaintively on hearing the cries of her cub, she reascended the mountain where it was impossible for dog or man to follow. The eleven dogs finally all took after the cub, which was part way up the mountain side, and, as one seized it, over rolled cub and dog together, and so came tumbling down. While Koojesse and Sharkey sought to get a shot at the old one, I went forward simply to see the fray between young polar and the dogs. On making my way from the main ice to the shore, the cub made a rush at me with jaws widely distended. I instantly placed myself in position, prepared to receive the threatened shock. I received young polar on the point of my spear, having directed it well toward the neck, and pierced it through. The dogs at once flew to my aid, and soon the savage beast was flat over on its back. Withdrawing the spear, a stream of hot blood immediately poured forth ; and then, with heavy blows on the head, I broke in its skull, and thus killed it. I took it that my Innuit friends would rejoice on learning my success, but I soon found how mistaken I was in this idea. On showing them what I had done, they shrugged their shoulders and—said nothing. Of course I was surprised, and knew not what to make of such conduct, it being the reverse of what I had expected. It was not long before I learned the *mistake* I had made in killing the young bear. This I ascertained in the following way : While Koojesse and Sharkey were engaged skinning *ar-tuk-ta* (young polar bear), I proposed to them to go into camp where we were. They objected to this. I then told them how desirous I was to remain in that locality for a day or so. My great and earnest object was to ascend the high land close by, and connect together some of the points of my past and prospective visitation. I found that nothing whatever would induce them to stop and make encampment there. They said that the old bear would return in the night, and, smelling the blood of her young, she would be

YOUNG POLAR COMING TO THE POINT.

enraged to madness, and kill all of us. Furthermore, they said that their people always avoided killing the young of a Ninoo till the old one was dead, from the very fact that the previous death of the offspring made the mother a hundredfold more terrible than she otherwise would be. The result of this matter was no camp there or about there that night.

My companions, having completed their work of skinning the bear, buried in snow the liver and head, which Innuits never eat, nor allow their dogs to eat, if they can help it. However, one of my dogs, Barbekark, got loose from the sledge and found the liver, when the whole pack bolted away and pitched in for a share. The carcass of the bear was placed on the sledge, when (5 P.M.) we started on our way down the channel. In half an hour we arrived at open water—a tide-opening one-third of a mile long and thirty fathoms wide. Sharkey had told me about this open water while we were at the seventeenth encampment, on occasion of my proposing to strike from thence to Kingaite, and continue down the coast. Sharkey said it was altogether doubtful whether we should be able to do so, on account of the *ou-kun-nier* (an extended opening in the ice caused by the tides). It seems that, during the coldest weather, these open places between the numerous islands in this part of Frobisher Bay never freeze over on account of the swiftly-running tides. However, we experienced no great trouble in making our way over an ice-belt that led past this *ou-kun-nier*. This space of water abounded in seals. In the course of a few minutes Sharkey fired two shots, the last being successful, killing a fine large seal, which we soon had fast to the sledge. We now had a Ninoo and a seal—enough for a feast for both men and dogs.

When at the tide-opening we were only one mile and a half from where we had killed the bear. This distance would not satisfy my friends by several miles for making encampment, therefore, at 6 P.M. we resumed our journey. A few minutes brought us to where the channel opened out to a beautiful bay, which I named Eggleston Bay.* Our course then was over a smooth field of ice. After making a distance of some six miles from where the bear was killed, and as we were making good progress homeward directly down the bay, all at once the dogs were turned by the driver sharply to the left, nearly but not quite half round, and directed toward the south termination of Pugh Island, where we made our eighteenth encampment. Before we retired for the night the sledge was stuck up on end in an ice-crack, and the guns and spears were put in order, at the head of our couch, for immediate use, if occasion should require it. As I needed an explanation of some of these movements of my Innuit companions, so my readers may require one

* Named after Benjamin Eggleston, of Cincinnati, Ohio. The centre of this bay is in lat. 63° 13′ N. long. 68° W. See Chart.

of me. I thus give it : The reason of going to such a distance from the scene of the bear-hunt before making our encampment has already been given. The sharp turn—nearly reversing our course—was designed, as the Esquimaux explained it, for a safeguard against pursuit by the enraged old bear. If she should attempt to pursue on our sledge-track, her movements would be rapid ; and, finding the track nearly in a straight line for so long a distance, she would become somewhat confident, "thinking" that the same undeviating course had been kept to the end ; therefore, on her reaching the place of the sharp turn, it might be unnoticed and unscented, and she would continue her course some time longer before discovering her mistake. But, in case she should track us to our igloo (our sixteenth, seventeenth, and eighteenth encampments were igloos or snow-houses), then the first thing she would do would be to throw down the sledge (one of many things that polar bears do not like to see standing), and thus we should be awakened, and put on our guard against the ferocious beast. But, happily, no enraged "she bear" made her appearance. The trick of the sharp turn may have saved us.

The bladder of the young Ninoo was kept hung up, at whatever place we happened to be, for three days, according to custom ; and that night we had an excellent supper off my prize, the flesh appearing and tasting like veal.

On the morning of Saturday, May 17th, having first ascended the heights of the island of our encampment, and made the necessary observations for continuing my survey, we resumed our journey down the bay, passing rapidly, on our right, Cape Poillon and Newell's Sound, and at our left Pike's Island, our course being along near the Kingaite coast and direct for Cape Vanderbilt, which point we reached at 3·40 P.M. On arriving there, I found it a capital point for connecting together much of my previous work by a round of angles. Unfortunately, before I could accomplish much work in that line, a thick fog closed distant objects from view. As I did not like to leave such a favourable point without additional sights, I proposed to my company to remain there till the next day. To this Koojesse, who was quite ill and peevish, obstinately objected. I therefore concluded to strike across the bay at once for the place of tenth encampment, our starting point on this flying trip, which we had left on the 8th instant. At 5·17 P.M. we left Cape Vanderbilt, purposing to travel all night. Our course was almost in line with Cape Hill, which is the south termination of Chase Island.

Never shall I forget that night. It was very cold, and we sat on the sledge well clothed in furs, while the dogs flew merrily and at their most rapid rate. Occupying a place in the rear of all the rest, where all was clear for action, with the box chronometer under my eye, I threw the log every ten minutes, holding the reel up in my right hand.* We all felt the cold severely, and had recourse to various contrivances to keep some warmth in our limbs. No doubt I presented rather a grotesque appearance as I sat with native stockings on my hands now and then instead of outside mittens. Toward midnight we felt the want of shelter and rest ; but, in my own case, all sense of discomfort which was banished by the beauty Nature placed before me. The grandeur of Kingaite's grotto mountains that we were leaving behind us, with their contrasts of light and shade, as viewed in the night, and watched as light increased with advancing day, filled my soul with inexpressible delight. It was like beholding a mighty city of cathedrals, monuments, palaces, and castles overthrown by an earthquake, the ruins resting amid mountain drifts of snow.

At 3 A.M. of the 18th, when near the islands which diversify Frobisher Bay in the locality between M'Lean Island and Chase Island, the sun began to peer out from behind the dark clouds, when we stopped the dogs, threw ourselves flat on the bare snow, and slept soundly for one hour and thirty-five minutes.

At 8 A.M. we arrived at the eighteenth encampment (which was the same as the tenth), whence we had started on the 8th instant, making an absence while on this journey of just ten days. The number of miles travelled was 176 nautical, or 203 English miles, this distance having been made in exactly fifty-four hours and thirty-one minutes travelling time.†

* See accompanying engraving, and also type on larger scale of sledge-log, line and reel, on page 510, drawn to one-sixth of the size of the original. This contrivance was made while encamped on the ice in the middle of Frobisher Bay (ninth encampment). The reel was wood, the line a codfish line, the log a relic of the wrecked *Rescue* — a ring-bolt, weighing just two pounds, which answered admirably the purpose for which I desired it.

† Taking my departure from the tenth encampment on May 8, 1862, and sledging 176 miles (nautical), now, on my return to same place, my "*dead reckoning*"—which has been kept independent of all the astronomical observations taken during the trip—makes the same place differ in latitude $2\frac{83}{100}$ miles, and in longitude less than half a geographical mile, an approximation I little expected to make.

HALL AND HIS EXPEDITION CROSSING FROBISHER BAY.

I found Henry very sick, and it was necessary that I should get him to the vessel as soon as possible. Tunukderlien and Jennie were well, the latter as evil-disposed as ever. Sharkey, however, had to receive sad news. By his former wife he had a child, which had been given in care to another Innuit. This child would occasionally, by various acts as are common to young children, annoy its guardian, who accordingly conveyed it to the top of a lonely and rocky mountain, sewed it up in a seal-skin, and threw it down a deep cleft, leaving it there to be frozen to death, and there its little corpse was afterwards discovered by some Innuits.

We found plenty of food among the people here, and blubber, the commercial value of which would have been some hundreds of dollars, and yet all soon to be wasted. One ookgook which they had captured must have weighed quite 1,500 pounds, and its blubber was two inches thick.

The following day, May 19th, finding that Koojesse was too sick to accompany me farther, and that Sharkey had to remain with his wife, I made arrangements with the Innuit "Bill," who agreed to take Henry and myself, with my dogs, to Oopungnewing. After farewells with my Innuit friends, away we went, all six of us (Bill would have his wife and two children along too), down the bay ; but in the evening a heavy snow-storm came on, and, though we tried to breast it for some time, we were at length obliged to give in, and encamp, after midnight, on Clarke's Island, which is between Jones's Cape and Chapel's Point.

The next morning, the 20th, we again proceeded, the travelling, in consequence of rough ice, being very bad, and, on arriving at a point near Twerpukjua, we were obliged to make our course over a narrow neck of land, called the Pass of *Ee-too-nop-pin*, which leads directly to the Countess of Warwick's Sound. The channel between Niountelik and Oopungnewing was also much broken up, and it was only with great difficulty we reached the latter-named place in the afternoon. Here I found numerous Innuit families, and also heard that Captain B. had visited the place, but had gone down to Cape True fifteen days before. " Bill," my sledge-driver, was so stricken with snow-blindness that I had to make arrangements with Innuit " Charley " to carry me back to the ship. This was speedily effected, and in an hour's time we again started.

We proceeded rapidly across the sound to Lincoln Bay, and thence, taking Bayard Taylor Pass, arrived at Field Bay. While on the descent of the land pass, Field Bay side, the sledge capsized and broke down, and one of the runners split from stem to stern.

At first we thought that it was a complete wreck, and that nothing could be done except to walk the remaining distance; but "Charley" at once proceeded to unload the sledge and make repairs. With a seal-knife he bored three holes through the two-inch plank runner, bound the shattered parts together, made all secure, reloaded the sledge, and then, when we had taken something to eat and drink, declared that all was once more ready to proceed. The dexterity with which "Charley" did this was remarkable. In fifty minutes from the time the sledge was broken he had it all in order again.

It was nearly two o'clock in the morning of Tuesday, May 21st, when we arrived at the ship, where I found on board only the steward and "Fluker."

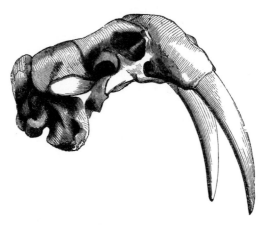

WALRUS SKULL AND TUSKS.

CHAPTER XXXV.

For a week after my return to the ship nothing especially worthy of note occurred. An extract from my diary of May 25th, 1862, will show that I was reasonably certain of having Innuit companions on my return to the United States : " Ebierbing and his nuliana, Tookoolito, will return here in season to accompany me to America. I am to take them for the purpose of having them accompany me on a future expedition to King William's Land. I hope, after what I have done here in the North in the way of explorations, in discovering relics of Frobisher's expeditions of near three centuries ago, and in determining the probable fate of the five of his company that were kidnapped here, I shall have no insurmountable obstacle to overcome in preparing for that voyage which I still have at heart — the voyage to King William's Land and Boothia—to investigate all the facts relative to Sir John Franklin's expedition while in the vicinity of the places named. That the Innuits are still living who know all about the mysterious termination of that expedition *I have not the shadow of a doubt.* What is requisite is to visit those regions, get acquainted with and establish friendly relations among the Innuits there, become familiar with their language, and then learn of them the history of that expedition."

On the 3d of June I was fortunate in obtaining two more relics of the Frobisher expedition. Ooksin, an Innuit whom I had known before, came on board from Oopungnewing, and gave me, as a present from Annawa's wife, Noodlooyong, a piece of brick, or rather of tile, about two inches long, one inch thick, and one and a half inches wide, and also a musket-ball, both found on Kodlunarn many years ago, and before guns were used by the natives. The piece of tile was similar to those used by the native women in that locality for polishing their brass ornaments. It afforded evidence enough, in dirt and grease, that it must have been in Innuit hands a long time. The ball had the appearance of having been carefully preserved since first found. It had several small indentations upon its surface, and the whole of it was covered with a white coat (oxide of lead), in consequence of long exposure. It is $\frac{11}{20}$ths of an inch in diameter. Ooksin said the ball was found on Kodlunarn, under one of the embankments by the "ship's trench," before Innuits knew anything of guns, and when they used only bows and arrows.

A day or two after this, on June 7th, I started on a sledge-exploring trip to Cornelius Grinnell Bay, being accompanied by Ebierbing as dog-driver, but after proceeding down the bay, coasting along by Clement's Land,* rounding Farrington's Cape,† and making some distance to the north, we were obliged, on account of the deep, soft snow upon the sea-ice, to return on the 10th of June without accomplishing my object.

While on this trip, however, I met with old Ookijoxy Ninoo —who, with Ebierbing, Koodloo, and their families, was living near Farrington's Cape, on a spot called by the natives *Twer-puk-ju-a-chune*, which means a place with many small stones—and had an interesting conversation with her concerning matters pertaining to Frobisher's expedition, being fortunate enough to find her in a communicative mood. She was in her tupic, sometimes sitting, sometimes reclining, and, as usual with her (being old and infirm, and mostly confined to her bed), was quite naked, with the exception of a tuktoo coverlet over her shoulders. When she reclined she rested her chin in her hands, which were propped up by her elbows. Beside her lay her sick grandchild, a one-eyed boy of nine years, at whose illness she greatly grieved. Near at hand was Ookoodlear, Ookijoxy Ninoo's granddaughter, who was almost constantly employed in attending to the calls of the old lady; she was now engaged in dressing a tuktoo skin and tending the infant of Tookoolito, who acted as my interpreter.

The old lady then, in answer to questions put by me through Tookoolito, repeated to me, though in a somewhat different form, what I had learned in previous conversations with her, namely, that ships with white men came to those regions; that the *kodlunas* who were left behind, built a ship, attempted to escape

* For Clement's Land, see Chart.
† This cape is in lat. 62° 50′. N long. 64° 33′ W.

from the country, failed in the attempt, and finally froze to death. She also gave me two names, which show how accurately the traditions of the Innuits are handed down; one was the name of a native who was particularly kind to the white men, and who was called "*E-loud-ju-arng;*" he was a Pim-ma-in, a great man or chief among the Innuits, as Tookoolito, translating the old lady's words, said, "All same as king." When the white men were about to set out with their ship for home, this Eloud-juarng had a song made wishing the kodlunas a quick passage and much joy, and he caused his people, who were then very numerous, to sing it. The other name handed down is that of one native who saw the kodlunas, "*Man-nu.*"

Ookijoxy Ninoo gave me, moreover, an entirely new fact. She said that the kodlunas in the ships who first came to the country went up the bay called by the Innuits *Ker-nuk-too-joo-a,* and by me Newton's Fiord, and there, a little distance inland, erected a monument. Some time later, Tookoolito brought me a sketch of the monument, made by the old lady herself, and the accompanying illustration presents a *fac-simile* of this sketch. The monument itself is not on very high land. The Innuits for a very long time, and down even to the present day, have been in the habit of going there; and wishing success in hunting, they would give it presents of young tuktoo meat, bows and arrows, beads, &c. hanging the same on it or placing them close about it. It was on all occasions treated with the greatest respect, the belief being that he who gave much to the monument would kill much game. Ebierbing, on seeing the sketch, said that he had frequently given arrows in a similar way.

At one point in her narrative old Ookijoxy Ninoo seized an oodloo—a knife shaped like the chopping-knife in use among us (see page 240)—and severed a lock of her hair, which she gave into my hands with the request that I would take it to America, and show it to many people as that of the oldest Innuit inhabitant. She said that there was no one living in her country who was a child when she was. Her hair was nearly all black, there being only now and then a white or grey hair on her head. I doubt not Ookijoxy Ninoo was fully 100 years old. Finding the old lady becoming exhausted, I took my leave and returned to the sledge.

On the 14th of June I left the ship on a visit to the whaling depôt at Cape True. As no other sledge was at hand I took a small one which I had previously made of such material as I found on board, and with *two* dogs started on my journey alone.

I was not expert at driving, and at first made slow progress, but finally succeeded in getting my team into good working order.

AC-SIMILE SKETCH BY OOKIJOXY NINOO, who represents herself performing her devotions to the *kok-kon-e-tu-arng*, the ancient monument of the *kod-lu-nas* (white men). The rude sketch in the lower part of this illustration represents a fresh-water lake, which is near the monument. The pending lines around the top of the monument are strings to which the natives hang their presents.

Barbekark was my leader, and, by dint of hard blows, I managed to keep him in a right position. On my way I called at the tupics of Ebierbing and Koodloo, at Farrington Cape. Here I had a pleasant conversation with Tookoolito, and, soon after, Ugarng arrived from Allen's Island, in Cornelius Grinnell Bay. I stopped here for the night, and the next morning departed for Cape True, my company being increased by seven souls, with two large dog-teams and two sledges. We arrived at the whaling depôt without mishap, and found the captain and his men, and several Innuits—among them my faithful attendant "Sharkey"—all well, fat, and healthy.

I remained a short time at this place, and then—June 18th —returned to the ship, whence I expected to depart in a few days for Cornelius Grinnell Bay, for the purpose of making a survey of it.

At 7·23 on the morning of the 25th, Ebierbing and myself left the ship, taking our course directly down the Bay for Farrington Cape. Thence we turned and travelled northwardly and eastwardly for Cape Haven,* a mountain island at the eastern extreme of Williams's Peninsula.† Cape Haven was the place of my first encampment on this trip, and distant by sledge route from George Henry Harbour fifteen miles. On ascending its heights I found the view that it commanded to be very extensive.

On the following day I held over at the place of my first encampment till 11 A.M. hoping the sun would make its appearance from behind the clouds, so that I might make observations for time, latitude, and solar bearings.

Having no prospect of sun, we started on, striking along to the north on the ice of Davis's Strait, our course leading us not far from the coast of Williams's Peninsula. Before leaving Cape Haven, however, we discerned from its summit the state of the ice over which we expected to travel that day, and found it rent here and there with wide and diversified fissures. The prospect before us was certainly not very flattering, still we determined on doing the best we could in making a trial. This trial we made, but with what success will now appear. In passing almost direct for Rogers's Island, we found the ice of a very dangerous character. It was groaning and cracking to an alarming extent. The open water was only some three miles off, and the heaving sea beneath us threw up the frozen mass

---

* Cape Haven is in lat. 62° 54′ N. long. 64° 23′ W.

† The Esquimaux name of the land which I called Williams's Peninsula is *Sing-ey-er*.

upon which we travelled in a way that made it doubtful if we could proceed. Wide fissures and numerous tide-holes were met, and frequently my companion Ebierbing and myself had to move along the edge of these fissures for some distance before we could find any passage across. On one occasion the dogs were trotting along by the side of an ice-fissure, while I was intent upon examining the land we were passing, and Ebierbing was looking after a seal; they suddenly drew the sledge almost into the yawning chasm; but, on my raising a cry of warning, Ebierbing, by a word, turned the team off from the dangerous spot, and thus saved us. We arrived at Rogers's Island at 7 P.M. and made our second encampment, having made the distance of just twenty miles from Cape Haven on a course N. by W. true.

We were detained on Rogers's Island one full day and two nights by a terrific gale and snow-storm which occurred on the 24th. It was an anxious time with us, for there was every probability that the gale would make disastrous work with the ice over which I intended to make my return to the ship. In case it did so, we should not be able to reach the vessel in less than two or three weeks, as we should have been obliged to make our way as best we could to the land on the opposite side of the bay, and thence, abandoning everything, to have gone on foot over mountains of rock and snow to Field Bay.

Fortunately, we were preserved from this peril, and on the 25th of June we reached Allen's Island in safety; but, although I had originally intended to go to the extreme of this bay, the advanced season had made ice-travelling so precarious that I was forced to confine my labours to the survey of that part of the bay south of Allen's Island, and I commenced a renewed examination of the place. A short distance from where we had our third encampment, which was on the south end of Allen's Island, I saw the ruins of an old Innuit village, which showed a custom of the people in former times of building their winter houses or huts underground. Circles of earth and stones, and skeleton bones of huge whales were to be seen, as also subterranean passages. There were, moreover, bones of seals and other animals beneath sods and moss, indicative of their great age. I discovered with my glass two monuments at the distance of about a mile inland, and thither I directed my steps. They were seven or eight feet high, four feet square at the base, and about three fathoms distant from each other. The top of one had been torn or blown down. The stones of which they were composed were covered with black moss. They were erected by the Innuits evidently ages ago.

My record of the succeeding day commences thus:—

"*Thursday, June 26th,* 1862.—I much desired to continue my trip up to the extreme of this bay, but, on consulting freely with my Innuit companion, I found that my better policy was to give up the idea of doing so. It would take some three or four days to go up and return, allowing the loss of one or

MONUMENTAL ISLAND OF SIR JOHN FRANKLIN.

two days bad weather, as Ebierbing said, and in that time the probability of losing our chance to return on the ice with our sledge and instruments; besides, Ebierbing said that Ugarng had told him that there would be great risks to run in going up th echannel on either side of Allen's Island on account of thin ice and tide-holes."

On the morning of the above day we commenced our return to the vessel. I omitted nothing on my way back that I could do in the way of making observations for completing my chart.

Our fourth encampment was near the north end of Williams's Peninsula.

On Friday, the 27th of June, 11 A.M. we were back again at Cape Haven, the place of our first encampment. As I was desirous of spending a day at this place in making numerous observations, it being a favourable look-out point, I therefore chose it for my fifth encampment.

One could scarcely have more joyous feelings than I had at the prospect that was before me of doing some excellent work, and of doing a large amount of it. The day was fine—that is, I had a bright clear sun, while there was a light breeze from the northwest which was just warm enough, or, rather, just *cold* enough for my comfort.

While I was engaged at my work on the heights of this cape, Ebierbing proceeded far out on the ice of Davis's Straits and employed himself in sealing. Many, very many places that had now become familiar to me even as friends, were in view; in truth, I was nearly encircled by them, though the most were far off. Prominent among these were the Monumental Island of Sir John Franklin,* twenty miles distant, bearing E.S.E. (true), and Lady Franklin Island, nearly due east, while far away to the north were Cape Murchison, Brevoort Island, Robinson Sound † Beekman's Peninsula,‡ Archibald Promontory,§ and Cape Arnoux.‖ A channel or strait, which I named Anderson Channel,¶ leading from Robinson Sound up toward

---

* I so named this island as my tribute to the memory of Sir John Franklin. The Innuit name of it is *Oo-mi-en-wa*, from its resemblance to an inverted oo-mi-en (a woman or family boat). Its geographical position I determined by triangulation, which was done repeatedly and carefully, that I might have confidence in recommending this as a desirable and reliable point by which navigators, who might desire it, could regulate their chronometers. The centre of the Monumental Island of Sir John Franklin I found to be in lat. 62° 45′ 45″ N. and long. 63° 41′ 07″ west of Greenwich. See Chart.

† This extensive sound I have named after Captain Henry Robinson, of Newburg, N. Y. It is between Beekman's Peninsula and Brevoort Island. See Chart.

‡ Named by me after James W. Beekman, of New York. Beekman Peninsula is bounded on the east by Robinson Sound and Anderson Channel, and on the west by Cornelius Grinnell Bay.

§ Named after E. M. Archibald, H. B. M. consul at New York. This promontory is on the west side, at the entrance of Robinson Sound.

‖ Named after William Henry Arnoux, of New York. Cape Arnoux is on the east side, at the entrance to Cornelius Grinnell Bay.

¶ This channel I named after Captain Anderson, of the steam-ship *China*.

Northumberland Inlet, was lost to my view by the high land of Beekman's Peninsula. The observations I made at this point were quite numerous and important. On the following day (27th) we continued our return, and at 5 P.M. arrived at the ship, where Captain B. with four of the crew had arrived the day previous from Cape True.

On the 30th of June I started on a sledge trip to Cape True, where most of the officers and crew of the *George Henry* were yet staying. There I remained for several days, trying to form a company of natives to go with me by boat to Countess of Warwick's Sound. I succeeded in obtaining a company of eleven, consisting of Miner and his new wife " Suzhi "—my old boat companion on my voyage up Frobisher Bay—·Kooperneung and his two wives—for he had recently married a second—Sharkey and his Jennie, young " Captain," " Bone Squash," and two Innuit children—a girl and a boy.

We left Cape True at 9·45 A.M. on the morning of July 13th, and at 3 P.M. reached a small island near Oopungnewing, named by me Ookijoxy Ninoo; thence, after a short stop, we went on to Oopungnewing. My purpose in visiting this island was to hunt for the "anvil," which, as I have already stated, had been thrown from the south end into the water. It was just after the full moon, and therefore the tides were rising and falling to their extreme limits, near thirty feet; at low water a wide shore was left perfectly exposed, and nothing could have escaped my eye. I sought carefully and with anxiety for the relic I so much desired to obtain, but in vain; it was not there. It was clear that the " thick-ribbed ice " had embraced it, as it evidently had every loose stone and heavy rock in that locality, and had carried it away from the land in its grasp.

On the following day, July 14th, we started for Kodlunarn, where we remained till the 17th, during which time I occupied myself in making researches for relics, investigating all that I could which had a bearing upon the subject, besides making a complete survey of the island. These days of hard work resulted in the discovery of additional relics, confirming me in the opinions I had previously formed, and which I have elsewhere in this work expressed. In addition to what I had done before, I found very clear evidences of the existence of a blacksmith's forge or a furnace. I must not omit to say here that the Esquimaux women and children, and occasionally the men, aided me greatly while on Kodlunarn, searching for and securing relics.

The men were obliged to be off, most of the time, sealing and hunting tuktoo for our subsistence.

Our tupics were close by the place that we called the "ship's trench" (see Plan No. 1 on Chart Sheet), and occasionally, as I have said, all hands were engaged with me in gathering Frobisher relics. One may get a good idea of our appearance when so engaged from the accompanying engraving.

THE AUTHOR AND HIS INNUIT COMPANY on Kodlunarn, or White Man's Island, gathering Frobisher Relics, July 14–17, 1862.

The following list is an extract from the catalogue that accompanied the Frobisher relics which I sent to the British government, through the Royal Geographical Society of London, shortly after my return to the States, and embraces twenty articles that were inclosed in a small black-velvet-lined box, lettered J, which, with all that I sent, have been deposited by the British government in the Greenwich Hospital Museum, the same institution in which the Franklin relics are to be seen. The unabridged list comprised 136 separate parcels.

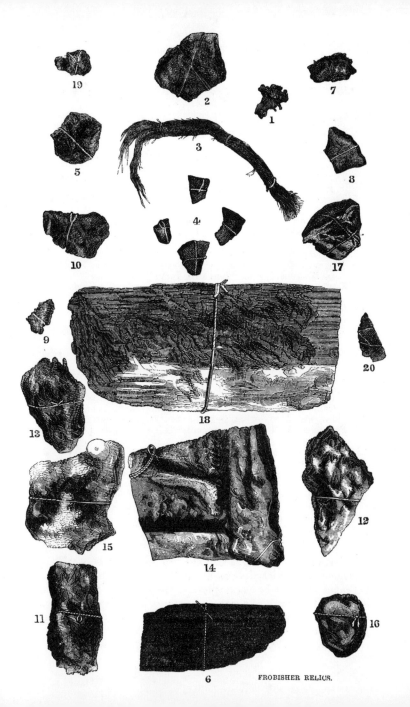

FROBISHER RELICS.

LIST OF ARTICLES ILLUSTRATED IN THE PRECEDING
ENGRAVING.

" 1. Fragment of tile and 4 gravel-stones, united by the moss of ages.
  2. Fragment of Pottery, found near " Best's Bulwark." E.   See Chart,
     Plan No. 1.
  3. Small pieces of cord (apparently of hair), found deeply imbedded in
     coal-deposite of Ekkelezhun.
  4. Four fragments of glass (apparently of a jar or bottle), found on the
     ground near the ship's way.   The exact spot, I.
  5. Piece of oxyd of iron, with the moss of ages upon it, found near the
     ship's trench.   AA.
  6. Piece of wood dug up at the foot or base of the ship's trench.   AA.
  7. Sea-coal, with the moss of ages upon it, found near " Best's Bul-
     wark."   E.
  8. Piece of pottery, found near " Best's Bulwark."   E.
  9. Fragment of white pottery (?) black glazing outside and inside, found
     on Kodlunarn, near " Best's Bulwark."   E.
10. *Choice* specimen of tile, covered with the moss of ages, from Kod-
     lunarn.
11. Sea-coal, covered with the moss of ages, from coal-deposite, Ekkele-
     zhun.
12. Stone, covered with the moss of ages, from the top of one of the
     ship's embankments.   GG.
13. Flint-stone, covered with the moss of ages, found near the head of
     the ship's way.   AA.
14. Fragment of tile (glazed), apparently a portion of a human figure
     represented upon it—leg and foot in *relievo*.   Largest piece of
     tile found ; dug from beneath one of the ship's embankments.
     GG.
15. Stone, with lime cement, from the ruins of stone house.   B.
16. Probably one of the ears or knob-handles of an earthen jar, from
     near " Best's Bulwark."   E.
17. Flint-stone with the moss of ages upon it.
18. Chip found deeply imbedded in coal-deposite, Ekkelezhun.
19. Burnt flint-stone, with lime cement, from the ruins of stone house.
     B.
20. Charcoal of coarse-grained wood, apparently of thrifty growth, found
     under stones and sods by the ruins of the blacksmith's shop.
     The grain of this charcoal indicates it to be of the same kind
     of wood as that found at the base of the ship's trench. A A.
     Vide box D, 1."

The reader may observe that the capital letters here and there
appended to the descriptions in the list refer to spots of ground
indicated by those letters respectively in Plan No. 1 of the Chart
Sheet.   The form and general appearance of each of the twenty
articles are exhibited in the preceding engraving, taken from a
photograph.   Of course they are reduced in size.

On the 18th, after coasting by Tikkoon, visiting the bluff

Ne-pou-e-tie Sup-bing, crossing the Countess of Warwick's Sound, and entering Victoria Bay, I landed at Ekkelezhun, where I had found the heap of coal in the previous fall. Here I again carefully examined the place, and on the next day commenced my return, encamping at night near a bay or inlet—Sabine Bay*— on the east side of Sharko. While exploring this inlet, I was led to the discovery of a monument, built within the previous five or six years, on the top of a mountain in the rear of our encampment, and which I learned from the Esquimaux had been erected by an English whaling-captain named Brown. From this monument I took numerous compass bearings and sextant angles, and then, returning to the boat, started back for Cape True, where we arrived in the evening. Without delay I proceeded up, along the coast, one mile, and renewed my observations to connect with those made at Brown's Monument, and thus—as far as lay in my power with the instruments I possessed —completed the link of bearings and sextant angles, that now extended all round Frobisher Bay. I now wanted to make another trip to the "southeast extreme"—the Hall's Island of Frobisher. On my mentioning my desire to the natives, all of them, at first, refused to accompany me, owing to their dread of the place; but at length Sharkey, the bold Innuit who was of my company in the late sledge-journey up Frobisher Bay, consented to go, if I would allow his wife to be of the party. Mate Lamb and four of the ship's crew also went with me, as the ship's company were doing nothing, except now and then capturing a walrus and eating it, simply living at Cape True until the ice in Field Bay should break up and free the ship. They remained at Cape True to be near the walrus grounds. Our only means of subsistence consisted of such products as the country afforded. About 100 pounds of raw walrus meat was placed in the bottom of the boat, and, besides that, every man had enough of the same food, cooked, to last two days.

We left the whaling depôt at 3 A.M. of the 21st of July, and proceeded through Bear Sound and Lupton Channel to Sylvia Island, where we arrived at five o'clock. I landed and went to the summit, where I could obtain a good view, and, to my vexation, found that Field Bay was still heavily covered with ice. I had purposed making my outward trip along the north side of Lok's Land, and return coasting along its south shore, thus making a complete circuit of the island; but the presence

* Named by me after Edward Sabine, of London. The entrance to Sabine Bay is in lat. 62° 39' N. long. 65° 05' W.

of the ice convinced me that this could not be done by boat, and consequently I had to try the southern, or Frobisher Bay side. After spending an hour there, taking a round of angles, and doing other work in the way of confirming my survey, we therefore returned down Bear Sound, passing directly under the beetling cliffs of Matlack's Island,* which is near the centre of the Sound. About meridian we were among the islands at the entrance of Bear Sound, visiting one after another for egg and duck hunting, which proved to be quite successful. A short time after we rounded Cape Chapel,† and made our course nearly due east, coasting along under oars. We had not proceeded far before we were passing the mouth of a beautiful bay—Bigler Bay,‡ as I named it—which made up some two miles into Lok's Land. Then we entered a long narrow channel—New York Press Channel §—having low land on either side, that at our right being what I called Harper Brothers' Island.‖ After several hours' hard pulling at the oars we arrived at the termination of this channel, and made our first encampment on Lok's Land, opposite the east end of Harper Brothers' Island. We had boiled ducks and eggs for supper, and our sleeping accommodation for the men was made of the boat's sails, while that for Mr. Lamb and myself was merely a shawl to cover us.

At 7 A.M. next day, July 22d, we again started, and, as we passed along Lok's Land, I noticed a monument of stone standing near the edge of the shore. Sharkey told me that this was erected by himself and some Innuit companions on reaching this spot a few years ago, after having been drifted out to sea when the ice broke away, at a time they were out on a walrus hunt from Toongwine (Jones's Cape). It was in the winter, and the weather was so severe while they were thus adrift that their dogs all died. The Innuits escaped by the tide setting the ice inshore. They managed to return to their families by crossing the island, and thence reached the main land by traversing the ice-pack. Before they got back every one had considered them lost, and their return was an occasion of joy to their friends, as if the dead had come to life.

* Named after B. Matlack, of Cincinnati, Ohio.
† Named after Captain Edward A. Chapel, of Hudson, New York. This cape is on the east side, at the entrance to Bear Sound of Frobisher.
‡ Named after James Bigler, of Newburg, New York.
§ Named after the Associated Press of New York City.
‖ Named after "Harper Brothers" of New York. The centre of Harper Brothers' Island is in lat. 62° 20′ 30″ N. long. 64° 30′ W.

More monuments were seen, and I was informed that they indicated the land dreaded by all Innuits, and that they told of a time long ago (already mentioned), when many of the native people lived there, who ultimately were all lost; since when, no Innuit dares dwell upon the island.

In the course of the day I visited Bear Island—the place where, one year before, while on my sledge-trip, Ebierbing, with Koodloo, had killed a bear—and at 2 P.M. we reached its eastern end. Here we found the pack-ice setting in with the tide too heavily for risking the boat, and we again had to encamp. Next morning, however, we succeeded in crossing the entrance to Osbon's Bay,* and getting to Hall's Island of Frobisher—the Extreme Land—and, as soon as possible, I was on my way to the summit of Mount Warwick, which I had ascended in the previous year. It was a laborious task on this occasion, with the sun's hot rays pouring down upon our backs; but, finally, I reached the spot where, on my former visit heavy fog-banks had shut out all distant objects from my sight. Now I was more fortunate. A meridian observation of the sun was made, and two solar bearings obtained, which enabled me to connect many important places by sextant angles. In recognising distant lands I received much assistance from Sharkey, who is well acquainted with the coast from Northumberland Inlet down to Resolution Island, and also up Hudson's Strait to Karmowong.

The view from the point where I stood was a very extensive one, and probably there is no place in the whole country equal to it. Certainly no place which I visited while North affords such a commanding view as this from Mount Warwick. I could see far away to the north, even to the high land near the entrance of Northumberland Inlet, and thence, sweeping round by the west, away to Resolution Island south. Seaward, as far as my eye could reach from an elevation of 1,200 feet, was pack-ice. Field Bay, except the entrance, was also full of last winter's ice, as was also as much of Frobisher Bay as I could observe.

Our return was made, though not without danger and some difficulty.

Leaving Hall's Island of Frobisher at 6. P.M. we arrived at the place of our first encampment at 9·30, night, where we made our second and last. Next morning, at 4·25, we started, continuing our return voyage. Before we got through New York Press

* Named by me after B. S. Osbon, of New York. Osbon's Bay is at the east end of Lok's Land. The entrance to it is on the south side of Hall's Island of Frobisher and Hudson's Island.

Channel the wind had freshened to a gale from the northeast, but on and on our boat bounded like a thing of life. The gale continued, if anything increased, till we were athwart Bear Sound, when it burst into fury, madly hurling the foaming breakers in upon us and the unnumbered islands that lay in our course. To add to our dangers, a thick fog was upon us; yet our little craft, though with half sail, and all the time nearly upon her beam-ends, flew full fifteen knots an hour. Speedily and safely, but wet as "drowned rats," we arrived at 8·15 A.M. though in our passage across Bear Sound we had but just escaped destruction.

I may here state that the whole party at Cape True were in no want of food while I was there. Walrus was abundant, and was, indeed, almost exclusively our diet. We had walrus brains for supper; stewed walrus, or walrus boiled, for dinner; but always walrus, and *no bread*.

MY SLEDGE-LOG, LINE, AND REEL.

CHAPTER XXXVI.

I WILL here give a few brief extracts from my journal, written while stopping at Cape True, commencing with—

"*Thursday, July* 31*st*, 1862.—One year ago to-day the *George Henry* broke out of her ice-prison. This morning, Mates Rogers, Gardiner, and Lamb, with their three boats and crews, went out in the Bay—Frobisher Bay—after walrus. A short time after they left a thick fog set in, and the tide carried them up opposite Countess of Warwick's Sound before they were aware of it. After the lighting up of the fog a little, they fell in with a shoal of walrus, of which they harpooned three large ones. This walrus party returned at 3 P.M. with three tons of fresh meat. There is no place in the world where a "living" is obtained with less work than here. These three walruses added make the whole number forty that have been taken since the *George Henry's* company first came here this season, not including some two or three young ones.

"*Friday, August* 1*st*.—And still, as we learn, the *George Henry* is fast in the ice. Anxious are all of us to depart for the States, but King Ice will not yet let us go. A good 'nor'wester' would drive away the pack which presses so closely and so unrelentingly the west side of Davis's Strait, and allow the ice which holds dominion over the *George Henry's* pathway to the sea to give way. It may be the pack will keep us here another year; but I hope not. I trust in two weeks more we shall be on our way home, there to prepare for the voyage I have so much at heart. God grant an early deliverance from our ice-foe.

"*August* 2*d*.—This afternoon, learning that the Innuits here were about to remove up into Field Bay as far as the open water would allow them, I at once set my wits to work to devise some plan to secure some of them to accompany me again to Countess of Warwick's Sound, and to be of such service to me in the boat that I shall be able to keep good dead reckoning. I first conversed with Mate Rogers. He agreed to accompany me, with two of his men not otherwise engaged. The Innuits ' Miner ' and ' Charley ' signified a willingness to accompany me with their wives and kias. I hope now to complete my survey of the Countess of Warwick's Sound, and to be enabled to keep a correct account of distances and courses made. Arrangements are now complete to start to-morrow, with the expectation of being absent two or three days. By that time I hope that we shall have word to vacate this place (Cape True), and make for the ship, to depart for the States. This will probably be my last research voyage before leaving for home. I wish the time would admit of my proceeding up to Ker-nuk-too-ju-a (Newton's Fiord), near which is that monument (see page 498) which the natives say was erected by kodlunas long, long time ago, which I have been so very anxious to visit since old Ookijoxy Ninoo first told me about it."

At 8 A.M. of August 3d, with an increasing breeze, we left the whaling depôt, my whole company being in one boat, except Charley and Miner, who were each in his kia. Our progress was good, and we got on without any mishap over half way; but when near Cape Cracroft, at the entrance to the sound we wished to enter, the storm which had been threatening for some time broke upon us all at once, tearing up the sea in its wildest fury, so that several times we were in great danger. The heavy squalls from off the high land at our right caused us to exercise the greatest caution in managing the little sail we were able to carry; the rain was pouring down, and the white-caps tumbled into our boat, making it necessary to keep incessantly baling; but finally, after much skilful management on the part of Mate Rogers as boat-steerer, we effected a safe landing at Cape Ood-loo-ong.

Directly after landing I ascended Harris Highlands,* to examine the Countess of Warwick's Sound, when, to my vexation, I found that between us and Hazard's Land,† Oopungnewing,

* The mountainous land between Lincoln Bay and Victoria Bay I named Harris Highlands, after J. N. Harris, of New London, Connecticut.

† The land on the north of the Countess of Warwick's Sound, and east of Wiswell's Inlet, I named Hazard's Land, after A. G. Hazard, of Enfield, Connecticut.

Niountelik, and Kodlunarn, all was packed ice, and in such a state that no boat could be forced through it. The presence of this ice is accounted for in this way: the heavy, incessant gale of July 24th and 25th had driven the pack hard on to the west side of Davis's Strait, and when, on August 2d, another gale prevailed, coming from the southeast, it drove the rattling pack up into Frobisher Bay, filling it almost solid, except close inshore between Bear Sound and Victoria Bay. My hopes, therefore, to accomplish what I designed in making this final trip were doomed to be disappointed; but, while an opportunity remained for doing anything, I determined to thoroughly examine the remarkable bay in which we then were—Victoria Bay—and its surroundings. This I did on the following day. The weather, however, was very bad, and it was with difficulty I could accomplish anything at all. Then, too, we had to guard against being shut up in the pack; and our critical situation became so evident that, on the morning of the 5th, we saw that to delay our return a moment longer would be sheer presumption. Accordingly, at an early hour we started, the whole company in the boat (the two kias were left at Cape Ood-loo-ong); but we had not gone far before we met the pack drifting in with the tide, and blocking up our way. And now began the usual work of hauling the boat over ice, tracking her through narrow channels, turning now to the right, then to the left, going forward awhile, then back to another opening, and cutting away obstructions.

Several hours of heavy labour were consumed in lifting, pushing, and pulling our boat over several miles of driving, drifting, whirling, crashing, thundering ice. Occasionally, while my company—both men and women—would be getting the boat upon an ice-floe, and dragging it along, the dogs and children accompanying, I would be busily engaged with my instruments taking my "last sights" of the principal places in and around the ever memorable "Countess of Warwick's Sound," which had been lost to the world for near three hundred years, but now was found. At last we got clear, arriving at open water, when we at once launched the boat and pushed off. From thence it was not long that we were on our way to Cape True, where we arrived in perfect safety, though, within two hours after our arrival, the pack *ribbed* the whole coast, and we thus narrowly escaped being closed in the second time.

Two days after our return, on Friday, August 8th, we were agreeably surprised, in the early morning, by the arrival of Captain B. in a boat direct from George Henry Harbour, in the

upper part of Field Bay.   He announced that the ship was
nearly free, and that the ice of Field Bay was all broken up,
and much of it had drifted out to sea.   His orders were for all
hands to proceed immediately on board.

This news caused immense joy.   All was excitement.   Tents
were quickly struck, boats were made ready, and stowed with
such of the material as we intended carrying on board, and in a
very short time we were ready for a start.   As for myself, I had
to regret the loss of some of my geological specimens, which I

ESCAPE OVER DRIFTING PACK.—MY " LAST SIGHTS."

was obliged to abandon here on account of their weight in the
already overloaded boat.

At 4 A.M. we took our final leave of Cape True, after a friendly
adieu to the people in that locality, with whom we had become
so familiar.   We struck direct for Hubbel's Point,* and soon
after were passing up Bear Sound.   The day was calm and clear,
and the boats had to be pulled nearly the whole way; but no
fatigue was felt while anticipating a speedy arrival on board the
ship.   At seven o'clock we were through Bear Sound, where the
tide, as usual, was running very swiftly and strong, though it
was in our favour.   Many well-known spots were quickly passed,

* This point, on the west side at the entrance of Bear Sound, I have
named after Charles C. Hubbel, of Hudson, New York.

receiving our farewell, and we were soon through Lupton Channel, when we turned into Field Bay, which was seen to be nearly full of drift-ice moving out and in with the tide. French Head, the scene of poor John Brown's death, was gazed upon with some saddening memories; but the brightness of the day, and the hope before us of soon being under way for home, forbade much lingering on painful recollections. At 1 P.M. we passed Parker's Bay, and in an hour and a half more arrived at the ship, glad again to tread her decks, but more especially rejoiced to find her once more free.

I went on shore immediately after to take some observations; and then, upon my return on board, and after a supper of hard bread and salt junk, I started with a boat's crew down the north side of the bay to Farrington Cape, to bring off Ebierbing and Tookoolito, with their child. I had previously asked them several times about accompanying me to the United States, and they had expressed a desire to do so. Now, however, the time for preparation was so short, and the event, withal, so sudden to them, that I feared they would not like to come; but on my arrival at their encampment, some seven miles down, I was agreeably surprised, after some conversation, to find them prepared to make the venture. In less than an hour these children of the icy North had packed up their effects, and, together with their child and their fine seal-dog "Ratty," were with us in the boat, ready to proceed on a voyage to a strange and distant land. My faithful dog Barbekark could not be forgotten nor left behind; he was already aboard. The arrangement we had made was, that they should accompany me to the States, and then on my voyage to King William's Land; and that, if the ice would admit of it, on leaving the States and getting near their country, I would stop with them to see their friends. The only objection they made was, that they were fearful they should lose their infant boy while on board the ship.*

At the same time, Ugarng, "John Bull," Koodloo, and their wives, came along with us in their boats; and many other Innuit families, from various places near the ship, with whom we had been acquainted, did the same. It was near midnight when we got on board, and I found everything in readiness for the vessel's departure on the following morning.

Saturday, the 9th of August, commenced with calm and clear weather. All were full of excitement. Every man felt equal to

---

* *Tuk-e-lik-e-ta*, the infant child of Ebierbing and Tookoolito, died in New York City of pneumonia, on February 28th, 1863.

and ready for any amount of work. Eagerly was the word of
command waited for. The ice had cleared away; the ship was
swinging lazily to her anchors, and all now required was to weigh
them and spread sail. But there was no wind. This, for a time,
made us hold on, until at length the captain, finding it useless to
wait longer for a breeze, gave the signal, and away went the
windlass round to the mirthful notes of joyous men, as they
hove in chain and lifted anchor once more. Soon the ship was
clear, and then, with lines out, all the boats were manned to tow
her down the bay.

" *Ter-bou-e-tie, In-nu-it* "—(Farewell, Innuits).

As we left the anchorage all our Innuit friends surrounded us,
and with many words of kind regret again and again bade us
" *ter-bou-e-tie* " (farewell). There were not a few among us who
felt this parting. We had received much and constant kindness
at their hands, and the final adieu was not without those softer
shades of feeling which generally characterize partings at home.

But now it is over. The vessel moves on her way. The kias
and oomiens, with their occupants, gradually recede from our

view, and with a last wave of the hands, a parting look, we turn our glances seaward, and allow our thoughts to be occupied only with home.

During the morning we were compelled to use the boats in towing, but in the afternoon made sail, though with a light, baffling breeze. In the evening, however, a fog came up, and at 11 P.M. we had to make fast to a floe. The weather continued the same next day until midnight; then, with a fresher breeze, we made all sail, and kept working through the ice for twenty-four hours, when at length we got clear, and were once more fairly at sea.

It was a strange feeling I had when again experiencing the peculiar motion of a ship on the heaving, ever-restless bosom of the ocean. After being so long imprisoned in that ice-locked region, the sensation now was similar to what had come over me when taking my departure from home. But a few days soon put me to rights, and as the vessel made good way, my spirits rose buoyant over the temporary attack of sea-sickness, and I was myself again.

On the 17th we were all delighted by the sight of four vessels, the first signs of civilization we had seen for twenty months. As we neared one of them bearing the English flag, an officer, with a boat's crew, was sent from our ship on board, to try to obtain some provisions, as we were living on very short allowance—three-fifths of a pound of sea-biscuit per man per day, with a little salt junk and salt pork. Unfortunately we could get none, as the supercargo of the ship stated that they had no more than enough for themselves. Another ship was tried. She proved to be a Spanish vessel; but a small quantity was obtained from her, and this was most acceptable.

On the 21st we neared St. John's, Newfoundland, and it was considered advisable that we should visit that port to obtain supplies, as all of us were nearly half-starved. Of course, we made all the preparations we could in regard to our persons and our dress, for we were once more to mix with civilized beings. At 6 A.M. on the 23d, a pilot came on board, and, as soon as he had passed the gangway, I put the question, which is generally the first from an American's lips on such occasions, " Who is President of the United States?" But so little did our affairs trouble this Newfoundlander that he could give us no information. I put the leading names to him, but still without effect. He " did not know." This was mortifying, for I was naturally anxious to learn who had the ruling power in my native land; but, seeing I could get no satisfactory reply, I turned aside, while the pilot conversed with Captain B. Presently the latter came to me and said,—

"So there's war, then, in reality, among us at home. The North and the South are fighting against each other."

"What!" I exclaimed, in utter amazement; "what—*war? War in the United States, and among ourselves?*"

"True enough," was the response; "at least so says our pilot."

A few words with the pilot assured me of the main fact, though without informing me of any particulars, for he could give none. But the news was so astounding that I did not for awhile recover from the shock. Bitter was the feeling that came over me on receipt of the intelligence, and I tried hard to doubt it, until doubt became impossible, especially when I landed and heard all the facts from our consul. This first news from home created a general gloom among us on board, and much of the joy which we should naturally have felt on reaching a civilized port was lost by reflecting upon the fact that so serious a calamity had fallen upon our beloved land.

As we approached the harbour of St. John's the excitement among us was intense. The head became somewhat confused as it turned from one object to another in the vast and noisy assemblage around us. But when the ship had dropped anchor and I had landed, the overpowering sensations that followed were more than I can describe. I was in a constant whirl. It seemed to me as if I were just coming from death into life, and it was with difficulty I could manage to control myself in the society of the many kind and warm-hearted friends to whom I was soon introduced.

The news of our arrival soon spread through the town, and many persons flocked round the ship to see us, all expressing much surprise at our robust and healthy appearance. My Innuit companions, Ebierbing and Tookoolito, with their infant, also attracted much attention. Everywhere on shore we were most hospitably received, and I shall never forget the names of those in St. John's who so warmly welcomed me.

On first landing I immediately telegraphed my arrival to Mr. Grinnell and to my own home, and received replies in a few hours.

We stayed at St. John's until the 26th, when we made sail for New London, where we arrived on Saturday morning, September 13, 1862; and thus ended my voyage and explorations of two years and three and a half months in and about the arctic seas.

CHAPTER XXXVII.

INNUIT OR ESQUIMAUX CHARACTER, CUSTOMS, ETC.

The Innuit Name—Character of the People—Their Domestic Life—Peculiar Customs concerning Women—Social and Political Life—Theological Ideas—Belief in a God—The Angekos—Mingumailo and his two Wives—His Rage against Koojesse—Superstitious Customs of the Innuits—Customs connected with Hunting—Innuit Christmas and New Year—Innuit Language—Innuit Costume—Native Sagacity in studying Natural History—Anecdotes of the Seal—Of the Polar Bear—Conclusion.

THE race of people whom we denominate *Esquimaux* are, in their own language, called *In-nu-it*—that is, "the people." *In-nu*, in the singular number, signifies "man;" in the plural, *In-nu-it*, "people," "the people;" or (as they understand it) "our people," as distinguished from foreigners. The name *Esquimaux* is entirely foreign, and not to be interpreted from any elements hitherto found in their language. In illustration of its origin, a friend, who is philologically devoted, has favoured the author with the following suggestions:—

The appellation "*Esquimaux*"—of which the traders' term "*Husky*" is a mere corruption—is obviously derived from some Algic dialect, doubtless from the Chippeway or the Cree. The Cree language is very nearly the same as the Chippeway, the difference being merely dialectic.

In the Chippeway, *ush-ke* signifies "raw." In the same language, *um-wau* signifies "he eats." From these elements we readily form the word *ush-ke-um-wau*, "raw he eats." And a noun derived from this verb, as a national denomination, must be some such form as *Aish-ke-um-oog*, "raw-flesh-eaters;" the double *o* being long, like *oa* in *boat*. Use has softened this name into Es-ke-moog (pronounced *Es-ke-moag*); the *sh* of the Chippeway becoming simple *s*, it would seem, in the Cree. All that remains is the consideration that the French traders, of course, used the French orthography.

According to Innuit mythology, the *first* man was a failure—that is, was imperfect, though made by the Great Being; therefore he was cast aside and called *kob-lu-na*, or *kod-lu-na*, as pronounced by the modern Innuits, which means white man. A second attempt of the Great Being resulted in the formation of a perfect man, and *he* was called *In-nu*.

As a general statement, it may be said that the Innuits, among themselves, are strictly honest. The same may be said as between them and strangers—that is, whites, though with some modification. The Innuits have an impression that the *kodlunas* (white people) possess plenty; that is, plenty of iron, wood, beads, knives, needles, &c. which is the reason why the Innuits, whenever they meet with whites, always cry "*pil-e-tay! pil-e-tay!*" ("give! give!") And the word *kodlunas*, in fact, signifies not only "*white people*," but the people who always have plenty. I have no hesitation in saying that, as respects honesty, these unsophisticated people, the Innuits, do not suffer by a comparison with civilized nations.

While with the Innuits, I saw enough to convince me that they are a kind, generous people. As between themselves, there can be no people exceeding them in this virtue—kindness of heart. Take, for instance, times of great scarcity of food. If one family happens to have any provisions on hand, these are shared with all their neighbours. If one man is successful in capturing a seal, though his family may need it all to save them from the pangs of hunger, yet the whole of his people about, including the poor, the widow, the fatherless, are at once invited to a seal-feast.

Though there is occasionally to be found among this people an evil person, yet, taken as a whole, they are worthy of great credit. They despise and shun one who will *shag-la-voo* ("tell a lie"). Hence they are rarely troubled by any of this class.

Children are sometimes betrothed by their parents in infancy. As Tookoolito says, "The young people have nothing to do with it." The old men make the marriage entirely. When the betrothal is made, the couple can live together at any time, usually decided by the ability of the man to support the woman. In other cases, when a young man thinks well of a young woman, he proposes to take her for his wife. If both are agreed, and the parents of the girl consent, they become one. There is no wedding ceremony at all, nor are there any rejoicings or festivities. The parties simply come together, and live in their own tupic or igloo. It sometimes happens that two who are intended for each other live together as companions for a term of probation, always without consummating their marriage.

It may happen, in such a case, that the trial develops a want of congeniality, or what is called in a higher state of civilization "an incompatibility of temper." Then the two separate, and the woman returns to her parents. In all cases, love—if it come at all—comes after the marriage.

There generally exists between husband and wife a steady, but not very demonstrative affection, though the woman is frequently subjected to violent usage by reason of some sudden outbreak of temper on the man's part, and though, when she is near her death, he leaves her alone to die.

When a child is born, the mother is attended by one or more of her own sex; even the husband is not allowed to be present. If it is a first child, the birth takes place in the usual tupic or igloo;* if it is a second, or any other than the first, a separate tupic or igloo is built for the mother's use, and to that she must remove. Male children are desired in preference to females, but no difference is made in their treatment, and there are always rejoicings and congratulatory visits when an infant is born. Immediately after the birth, the infant's head must be firmly squeezed side to side with the hands, and a little skin cap placed tightly over the compressed head, which is to be kept there for one year. This custom prevails throughout the region of Frobisher Bay, Field Bay, C. Grinnell Bay, Northumberland Inlet, and all places known to me and my Innuit informants. The infants are nursed until three or four years of age. The children, when old enough, find their amusement in playing with toys made of bone and ivory in the forms of various animals. When older, the boys are educated in rowing, hunting, and sealing; the girls are taught to trim the fire-light and keep it burning, to cook, dress leather, sew, help row the *oomiens*, and to do various other kinds of work.

The women are not prolific. I believe they consider children troublesome. The race is fast dying out. Not many years more and the "Innuit" will be extinct.

The affection of the parents for their children is very great, and disobedience on the part of the latter is rare. The parents never inflict physical chastisement upon the children. If a child does wrong—for instance, if he becomes enraged, the mother says nothing to it until it becomes calm. Then she talks to it, and with good effect.

---

* There is an occasional exception to this rule, as in the case of Tookoolito. She was obliged to have a separate tupic. This was so ordered by the angeko, because of Ebierbing's sickness.

On Saturday, February 28th, 1863, the infant son of Ebierbing and Tookoolito died in New York, aged eighteen months. The loss was great to both of them, but to the mother it was a terrible blow. For several days after its death she was unconscious, and for a part of the time delirious. When she began to recover from this state she expressed a longing desire to die, and be with her lost *Tuk-e-lik-e-ta*. The child was greatly beloved by both of the parents. In truth—I must be allowed to diverge here for a moment—there was cause for their great affection, and reason for peculiar grief on the part of the bereaved mother. I never saw a more animated, sweet-tempered, bright-looking child. Its imitativeness was largely developed, and was most engaging. Tukeliketa was a child to be remembered by all who ever saw him.

For a certain length of time after a child is born the mother must remain in her own home, visiting no other tupic or igloo. The period for which this limitation holds good varies, sometimes reaching to the length of two months. At the expiration of the time she makes a round of calls at all the dwellings about, having first changed all her clothing. She never touches again that which she throws off on this occasion, and which she has worn since the birth of the child. Another custom forbids the mother to eat by herself for a year after the birth of the child. When asked the reason of this, Tookoolito only said, " The first Innuits did so." In respect to Innuit customs in general, it may be observed that they are often adhered to from fear of ill report among their people. The only reason that can be given for some of the present customs is that "the old Innuits did so, and therefore they must."

Another custom in relation to their females is this :—

At certain periods separation igloos are built for them. The woman must live secluded for so many days, and it would be a great offence for her to enter into any other tupic or igloo during this time. On one occasion, while on my sledge-journey in the middle of Frobisher Bay, and at the place of the tenth and nineteenth encampments, I met Samson, his wife, and family proceeding to another encampment. While I was talking with them the wife asked me for something to eat. I was surprised at this, for I knew Samson's family were generally well provided with food. But an explanation followed. I was told that the Innuit custom is for females, at certain times, not to partake of certain kinds of Innuit food. In this case, Samson's wife had been nearly a week without eating, and was very hungry. I gave her what little I had of pemmican. She insisted on my taking something for it, thrusting into my hands twelve miniature ducks and other sea-birds, carved in walrus ivory. These I retain as mementoes of the occasion.

The women, generally, are tattooed on the forehead, cheeks, and chin. This is usually a mark of the married women, though unmarried ones are sometimes seen thus ornamented. This tattooing is done from principle, the theory being that the lines thus made will be regarded in the next world as a sign of goodness. The manner of the operation is simple. A piece of reindeer-sinew thread is blackened with soot, and is then drawn under and through the skin by means of a needle. The thread is only used as a means of introducing the colour or pigment under the epidermis.

The longevity of this people, on the whole, in latter years is not great. The average duration of life among them is much less than formerly. The time was, and that not long ago, when there were many, very many old people, but now they are very few. Old Ookijoxy Ninoo, as I have already mentioned, once observed to me that there were no Innuits now living who were young when she was. She was, as I believe, over 100 years old when I saw her. She died a few months after my departure for the States. I learned this last fall (1863) by one of the American whalers, who saw her son Ugarng at Northumberland Inlet two months previous.

The Innuit social life is simple and cheerful. They have a variety of games of their own. In one of these they use a number of bits of ivory, made in the form of ducks, &c. such as Samson's wife gave me, as just mentioned. In another, a simple string is used in a variety of intricate ways, now representing a tuktoo, now a whale, now a walrus, now a seal, being arranged upon the fingers in a way bearing a general resemblance to the game known among us as "cat's cradle." The people were very quick in learning of me to play chess, checkers, and dominoes.

If an Innuit stranger come among them, an effort is made to conform as closely as possible to the manners of the section from which he comes, for it should be observed that there exists a great diversity of manners and habits among the people of different regions not very far separated from each other.

Though in old times there were chiefs among the Innuits, there are none now. There is absolutely no political organization among them. In every community, with them as with all the rest of the world, there is some one who, in consideration of his age, shrewdness, or personal prowess is looked up to, and whose opinions are received with more than usual deference; but he has no authority whatever, and an Innuit is subject to no man's control. The people are not naturally quarrelsome, and theft and murder are almost unknown. When a quarrel arises, the two parties keep aloof from each other, sometimes for a long time. Sometimes, however, a mutual and elderly friend arranges the matter, and then a quiet talk often shows that the quarrel—with them as with us—was the result of an entire misunderstanding of words reported by gossiping tongues. If a murder is committed, it appears, from what the Innuits say, that the nearest relative or most intimate friend of the slain has a right to kill the murderer; but this crime is very rare.

Innuit opinions upon theological questions are not easily obtained in an intelligible form. Their belief on some points may thus be very generally stated: There is one Supreme Being, called by them *Ang-u-ta*, who created the earth, sea, and heavenly bodies. There is also a secondary divinity, a woman, the daughter of Anguta, who is called *Sid-ne*. She is supposed to have created all things having life, animal and vegetable. She is regarded also as the protecting divinity of the Innuit people. To her their supplications are addressed; to her their offerings are made; while most of their religious rites and superstitious observances have reference to her.

The Innuits believe in a heaven and a hell, though their notions as to what is to constitute their happiness or misery hereafter are varied as one meets with different communities. Tookoolito says:—

"My people think this way: *Kood-le-par-mi-ung* (heaven) is upward. Everybody happy there. All the time light; no snow, no ice, no storms; always pleasant; no trouble; never tired; sing and play all the time—all this to continue without end.

"*Ad-le-par-me-un* (hell) is downward. Always dark there. No sun; trouble there continually; snow flying all the time; terrible storms; cold, very cold; and a great deal of ice there. All who go there must always remain.

"All Innuits who have been good go to Koodleparmiung; that is, who have been kind to the poor and hungry—all who have been happy while living on this earth. Any one who has been killed by accident, or who has committed suicide, certainly goes to the happy place.

"All Innuits who have been bad — that is, unkind one to

another—all who have been unhappy while on this earth, will go to Adleparmeun. If an Innuit kill another because he is mad at him, he will certainly go to Adleparmeun."

They have a tradition of a deluge, which they attribute to an *unusually high tide*. On one occasion, when I was speaking with Tookoolito concerning her people, she said, "Innuits all think this earth once covered with water." I asked her why they thought so. She answered, "Did you never see little stones, like clams and such things as live in the sea, away up on the mountains?"

The subject of the religious ideas and observances of the Innuits is nearly connected with that of their angekos, who have a great influence among these people, and exercise the only authority to which they in any degree submit. With regard to these angekos, it appeared to me that man or woman could become such if shrewd enough to obtain a mental ascendancy over others.

The angeko's business is twofold : he ministers in behalf of the sick, and in behalf of the community in general. If a person falls ill the angeko is sent for. He comes, and, before proceeding to his peculiar work, demands payment for his services, stating his price, usually some article to which he has taken a liking. Whatever he demands must be given at once, otherwise the expected good result of the ministration would not follow.

When the preliminary arrangements have been satisfactorily disposed of, the family of the sick person sit around the couch of the patient, and with earnestness and gravity join in the ceremonies. The angeko commences a talking and singing, the nature of which it is impossible to state more precisely than to say that it seems to be a kind of incantation or prolonged supplication, perhaps mingled with formulas which are supposed to charm away the disease. At intervals during this performance the family respond, frequently uttering a word corresponding to our *amen*. As to medicine, none is ever prescribed, nor do the Innuits ever take any.

The duties of the angeko, with reference to the community, consist in ankooting for success in whaling, walrusing, sealing, and in hunting certain animals ; for the disappearance of ice, and for the public good in various particulars. These more public ministrations are accompanied by what sounds to a stranger's ear like howling, but is doubtless a *formula*, either handed down by tradition, or composed on the spot by the angeko, varying according to the talent of the operator. Some descriptions of ankooting have been given in the body of this work.

Even Tookoolito was not exempt from the general belief in the efficacy of the angeko's ministrations, One day, when visiting her, I found that she had parted with her cooking-pan, which she had always considered indispensable and of great value. On inquiry, I learned that she had given it to "Jennie," a female angeko, in payment for her attendance upon Ebierbing when sick ; and, moreover, she had in like manner given nearly all her valuable things, even to some of her garments. I was hardly astonished, for I knew that the Innuits considered that in proportion to the value of what they give for an angeko's services, so are the benefits conferred upon the sick. "Make poor pay, and the help is poor; good pay, and the benefit is great."

On one occasion (it was at the time we were about to start for the States, but were suddenly frozen in at the commencement of the second winter), having seen the angeko very busy ankooting on the hills, I asked Ebierbing and Tookoolito what it was for. They replied, "To try and get the pack-ice out of the bay." It may be remarked here that this attempt to get the ice out of the bay was caused by the desire of the Innuits to have the *George Henry* leave the country, they having become tired of the presence of the sailors, and being, perhaps, somewhat jealous of them. On the occasion referred to, the angeko had told the people that on a certain day they were not to do any work. Then, in the evening, he commenced his incantations ; and on that day it had been noticed by the ship's company that the Innuits went on board the vessel in their best attire, though no one then knew the cause.

The general deference to the wishes of the angeko has some exceptions, though they are rare. One such exception was this : One day in the month of July, 1861, the angeko Mingumailo, who had two wives, sent from his tupic among the mountains to Koojesse, who was then staying at Cape True, with an order for the exchange of wives. Now Koojesse's wife, Tunukderlien— "Isabel," as we sometimes called her—was something of a belle, and, though Koojesse had been a good disciple of the angeko, he would not now yield to his demands. He refused to exchange his Tunukderlien for either of the two wives sent for his choice, and the latter returned to their husband. Thereupon the angeko became so enraged that he immediately came from the mountains, and entered the village of tupics like a demon. He first tried to negotiate a peaceable exchange, and then attempted by threats to effect what he wanted. With a loaded musket and a large knife, he prowled all night long around Koojesse's tupic, trying to take his life; but Koojesse had been warned, and finally took up his abode in one of the white men's tents near by. The next day Mate Rogers arrived, and the angeko, fearing him, fled away to his haunt in the mountains.

Another instance of inattention to the angeko's advice I will relate here. One of the former husbands of Suzhi was sick. The angeko said Kokerjabin, who was at that time the wife of Samson, must live with the invalid husband for two or three months, or he would die before spring. All the Innuits thought the angeko should be obeyed, but Kokerjabin refused to comply, declaring that she did not believe what the angeko said. Before spring, Suzhi's husband died as the angeko predicted, and therefore all the people despised Kokerjabin.

I will now mention various customs which have relation to the religious belief of the Innuits, though many of them can be explained only by the broad phrase, " The first Innuits did so." When they kill a reindeer, and have skinned it, they cut off bits of different parts of the animal, and bury them under a sod, or some moss, or a stone, at the exact spot where the animal was killed. When an Innuit passes the place where a relative has died, he pauses and deposits a piece of meat near by. On one occasion, when travelling with Sharkey, I saw him place a bit of seal under the snow near an island which we were passing. When I questioned him, he said that it was done out of respect for the memory of an uncle who had died there.

When a child dies, everything it has used, either as a plaything or in any work it did, is placed in or upon its grave. When Tukeliketa, Tookoolito's boy, died, some weeks after the mother collected all his playthings and put them upon his grave.* Visiting the spot some time after, she found that one article, a gaily-painted little tin pail, had been taken away, and her grief was severe at the discovery. In March, 1862, while I was in the Northern country, the wife of Annawa found beneath the tuktoo bed of their recently-deceased child a toy game-bag. A consultation among the Innuits who were then there was held, and the bag, together with all the articles that had been presented to the child by the ship's hands from time to time,

---

* The remains of Tukeliketa rest in Groton, Connecticut, in the burial-ground near the residence of Captain Budington.

consisting of powder, shot, caps, tobacco, and a pistol, was deposited at the grave of their beloved boy.

There exists also among the Innuits many curious customs connected with hunting. They cannot go out to take walrus until they have done working upon tuktoo clothing; and after beginning the walrus hunt, no one is allowed to work on reindeer skins. One day in March, I wanted Tookoolito and Koodloo's wife to make me a sleeping-bag of tuktoo skin; but nothing could persuade them to do it, as it was then walrus season. They " would both die, and no more walrus could be caught."

When a walrus is caught, the captor must remain at home, doing no work, for one day; if a bear is killed, he must remain quiet, in like manner, for three days; after the taking of a whale, two days. If, however, he is on a hunt and game is plentiful, the Innuit frequently keeps on at the sport, making up all his resting days at the end of the hunt.

When a seal is captured, a few drops of water are sprinkled on its head before it is cut up. If there is no water to be had, the man holds snow in his hands, till he squeezes out a single drop, the application of which answers every purpose.

Women are not allowed to eat of the first seal of the season, and this rule is so strictly enforced that they do not feel at liberty even to chew the blubber for the sake of expressing the oil. When Tunukderlien and Jennie were with me on my sledge-journey up Frobisher Bay, the first seal of the season was caught, and Henry was obliged to pound the blubber to obtain the oil we needed, because the women were not allowed to do it.

There is a regular order for cutting up a walrus. The first man who arrives at the captured animal cuts off the right arm or flipper; the second, the left arm; the third, the right leg or flipper; the fourth, the left leg; the fifth, a portion of the body, beginning at the neck, and so on till the whole is disposed of.

One very curious custom among the Innuits is this: At a time of the year apparently answering to our Christmas, they have a general meeting in a large igloo on a certain evening. There the angeko prays on behalf of the people for the public prosperity through the subsequent year. Then follows something like a feast. The next day all go out into the open air and form in a circle; in the centre is placed a vessel of water, and each member of the company brings a piece of meat, the kind being immaterial. The circle being formed, each person eats his or her meat in silence, thinking of Sidne, and wishing for good things. Then one in the circle takes a cup, dips up some of the water, all the time thinking of Sidne, and drinks it; and then, before passing the cup to another, states audibly the time and the place of his or her birth. This ceremony is performed by all in succession. Finally, presents of various articles are thrown from one to another, with the idea that each will receive of Sidne good things in proportion to the liberality here shown.

Soon after this occasion, at a time which answers to our New Year's day, two men start out, one of them being dressed to represent a woman, and go to every igloo in the village, blowing out the light in each. The lights are afterward rekindled from a fresh fire. When Tookoolito was asked the meaning of this, she replied, " New sun—new light," implying a belief that the sun was at that time renewed for the year.

When one of these meetings and outdoor ceremonies took place, I was absent from the village where most of my Innuit friends were living. Koojesse, Sharkey, and others wished to have me sent for, thinking I would like to be present; but old Artarkparu objected, fearing that I should grow weary before the ceremony was complete, and, retiring from the circle, break the charm. So I was not sent for, but was obliged to gain my information from the natives.

The language of this people is peculiar to themselves. They have nothing written, and all that they can tell is derived from oral tradition, handed down from parent to child for many generations. The pronunciation of the same words by Esquimaux living a considerable distance apart, and having little intercourse, is so different that they can hardly understand each other on coming together. It was with the greatest difficulty that the Innuits who came to Field Bay from Seko-selar, or any other place on the northern shores of Hudson's Strait, could make themselves understood by Innuits residing north of them. Sometimes Innuits arrive from Igloolik (which is at the entrance to the Strait of Fury and Hecla), at Northumberland Inlet, and it takes a long time for the two parties to understand each other. Still more difficult is it for a Greenland native to be understood by those on the west side of Davis's Strait. The Innuits with whom I was acquainted could count only ten, as follows :—

At-tou-sen,	one.	Ok-bin-er-poon,	six.
Muk-ko,	two.	Mok-ke-nik,	seven.
Ping-a-su-it,	three.	Ping-a-su-nik,	eight.
Tes-sa-men,	four.	Tes-sa-men-ik,	nine.
Ted-la-men,	five.	Kood-lin,	ten.

However, there was this exception: Kooõulearng (Suzhi), whose native place was on the north side of Hudson's Strait, could count to twenty. She said that all the people of her country—meaning *Kar-mo-wong*, which is on the north side of the strait—could do the same. By signs—that is, by throwing open the fingers, Innuits everywhere can and do count much larger numbers.

The dress of the Innuits is made of the skins of reindeer and of seals; the former for winter, the latter for summer. The jacket is round, with no opening in front or behind, but is slipped on and off over the head. It is close-fitting, but not tight. It comes as low as the hips, and has sleeves reaching to the wrists. The women have a long tail to their coat reaching nearly to the ground. These jackets are often very elaborately ornamented. In one of my visits to Samson, I noticed that his wife's jacket was trimmed thus: Across the neck of the jacket was a fringe of beads—eighty pendents of red, blue, black, and white glass-beads, forty beads on each string. Bowls of Britannia metal, tea-spoons, and table-spoons were on the flap hanging in front. A row of *elongated lead shot* ran around the border of the tail. Six pairs of Federal copper cents, of various dates, were pendent down the middle of the tail; and a huge brass bell, from an old-fashioned clock, was at the top of the row of cents.

On another occasion, Tweroong, the wife of Miner, came on board with a dress made of the fur of very young deer, with a spencer of reindeer hair cut off short, and so evenly that I could not well understand how it was done. I made her a present of a lady's hand dressing-glass, which sent her into ecstasies, especially when she found it would enable her better to arrange her hair.

All the jackets have a hood made at the back for carrying their children or covering their heads in cold weather. In winter they wear two jackets: the exterior one with the hair outside, the inner one with the hair next to the body. Before the men enter into the main igloo they take off the outer part of their jackets, and place the same in a recess made in the snow wall of the passage-way.

Their breeches reach below the knee, and are fastened with a string drawn tightly around the lower part of the waist. Those worn by the women are put on in three pieces, each leg and the body forming separate parts.

The full winter dress for the feet consists of, 1st. Long

stockings of reindeer fur, with the hair next the person; 2d. Socks of the eider-duck skins, with the feathers on and inside; 3d. Socks of sealskin, with the hair outside; 4th. Kumings [native boots], with legs of tuktoo, the fur outside, and the soles of ookgook.

All wear mittens, though the women generally wear only one, and that on the right hand; the left is drawn within the sleeve.

NO. 1, SECTIONAL VIEW OF SEAL HOLE AND SEAL IGLOO.

Finger-rings and head-bands of polished brass also form part of the female costume.

The Innuits show a remarkable sagacity in studying the habits of their animals, and gaining therefrom lessons of value for their own guidance. They observe how the seal constructs its igloo or snow hut, and their own winter dwelling is formed upon this model. The above illustration gives a sectional

view of a seal's hole and igloo,* with the young one lying
within, and the mother coming up to visit it. By the time the
sun melts off the covering snow, exposing and destroying the

NO. 2, SECTIONAL VIEW OF SEAL HOLE.

* The horizontal lines extending across the lower part of the engraving
represent the sea-water, as do the short lines running in the same direction
within the seal hole which is through the ice. The ice is represented by
the perpendicular lines on either side of the seal hole. Resting on the ice
are a young seal and the igloo, the latter shown by the dark half circle.
On either side and above the igloo is the snow covering the sea-ice. Before
the igloo is made, the prospective mother, to get herself upon the ice,
scratches away the inverted tunnel-like-shaped ice, as seen in the second
engraving. The igloo is then made by the seal scratching an excavation from the snow with the sharp, lady-like nails with which its fore
flippers are *armed*, the excavated snow being taken down beneath the
thick ice from time to time by the seal. Soon after this house is prepared
a little seal is born. Seal igloos are made about the 1st of April, the time
when the "pupping" season commences. None but very sharp-scented

dome of the igloo, the young seal is ready to take care of itself. The second engraving represents a seal that has just come up through the water to its breathing-hole, which is covered by snow. Above it sits an Innuit, who has pierced the snow with his spear just over the seal's hole in the ice, and who watches till he hears the animal puff, then quickly and almost unerringly strikes.*

From the polar bear, too, the Innuits learn much. The manner of approaching the seal which is on the ice by its hole basking in the sunshine is from him. The bear lies down and crawls by hitches toward the seal, "talking" to it, as the Innuits say, till he is within striking distance, then he pounces upon it with a single jump. The natives say that if they could "talk" as well as the bear, they could catch many more seals.

The procedure of the bear is as follows : He proceeds very cautiously toward the black speck far off on the ice, which he knows to be a seal. When still a long way from it, he throws himself down on his side, and hitches himself along toward his

animals can find these igloos, and they are the seal's worst enemies. These animals are the polar bear, the fox, and the seal-dog. The latter, however, simply scent out the igloo, leaving the master to catch the game, while the bear and fox not only find, but capture it. When the dog has led his master to the secret seal lodge beneath the snow, the man retreats from fifteen to twenty paces, and then runs forward swiftly, leaping high and far on concluding his race. As he comes down he crushes in the dome, and quickly thrusts his seal-hook this way and that around in the igloo, till he has the young seal quivering in the agonies of death.

* The water, ice, and snow of the second engraving are represented in like manner as in the preceding one. The appearance of the seal hole, and the bed of snow above, as they are during the winter season till about the 1st of April, is well represented. The sealer is awaiting the seal's blow. It is time he was up and ready to strike, for as soon as a seal has its nose out of the water, as the one here represented, its puffing noise is heard. When the sealer, by the aid of his dog, has found the seal hole, he has sometimes to watch there two or three days and nights. The dog has indicated the precise point within a circle of about ten inches in diameter. The sealer, therefore, thrusts the spindle of his seal-spear down through the hard snow, seeking to find the breathing-hole, which is not more than one or two inches in diameter. After perhaps a dozen attempts, he finally strikes the hole. Now he carefully withdraws his spear, and marks with his eye the hole, which leads down through perhaps eighteen to twenty-four inches depth of snow. When now he hears the seal, he raises his spear, and strikes unerringly through the snow to the seal's head. The animal at once dives, and runs out the full length of the line, one end of which is fast in the hand of the sealer. He proceeds to cut away the deep snow, and to chisel the ice so as to enlarge the top of the seal hole, from which he soon draws forth his prize.

game. The seal meanwhile is taking its naps of about ten seconds each, ultimately raising its head and surveying the entire horizon before composing itself again to brief slumber. As soon as it raises its head the bear " talks," keeping perfectly still. The seal, if it sees anything, sees but the head, which it takes for that of another seal. It sleeps again. Again the bear hitches himself along, and once more the seal looks around, only to be " talked " to again, and again deceived. Thus the pursuit goes on till the seal is caught, or till it makes its escape, which it seldom does.

In Chapter XXXII. there occurs a description of the manner in which a young seal is often used to lure the mother within striking distance of the hunter. This is copied by the Innuits from the habits of the polar bear. This animal finds by his keen scent where a seal's igloo has been built under the snow. He then goes back a little distance, runs and jumps with all his weight upon the dome, breaks it down, and immediately thrusts in his paw and seizes the young seal. Then, holding it by one of its hind flippers, he scoops away all the snow from the seal hole leading up through the ice into the igloo, and afterward allows the young one to flounder about in the water. When the old seal comes up, the bear draws the young one slily on toward him, till the anxious mother gets within reach, when he seizes her with his other paw.

The natives tell many most interesting anecdotes of the bear, showing that they are accustomed to watch his movements closely. He has a very ingenious way of killing the walrus, which is represented in the accompanying engraving.

In August, every fine day, the walrus makes its way to the shore, draws his huge body up on the rocks, and basks in the sun. If this happen near the base of a cliff, the ever-watchful bear takes advantage of the circumstance to attack this formidable game in this way : The bear mounts the cliff, and throws down upon the animal's head a large rock, calculating the distance and the curve with astonishing accuracy, and thus crushing the thick bullet-proof skull.

If the walrus is not instantly killed—simply stunned—the bear rushes down to it, seizes the rock, and hammers away at the head till the skull is broken. A *fat* feast follows. Unless the bear is very hungry, it eats only the blubber of the walrus, seal, and whale.

The bear can catch a seal in the water. He sees it, drops his body beneath the surface, allowing only his head to be visible,

that having the appearance of a piece of ice. While the seal
has its head above water, and is looking around, the bear sinks,
swims under it, and clutches it from beneath.

When the sea-ice begins to make, we will say about the middle
of October to the 1st of November, the female bear captures and
kills several seals, which she hides away among the hummocks.

BEAR KILLING WALRUS.

Then she retires to the land and eats moss, the object being
to produce an internal mechanical obstruction called "tappen."
After this she goes to her deposits of meat, and feasts upon seal-
blubber to her utmost limit of expansion. She is now ready
for retiring to her winter's home, which is generally an excavation she has "chiselled out" of a glacier. Some time after entering she brings forth her young, which sometimes number one,
more frequently two, and sometimes three. In this crystal nursery
she continues exercising her progeny daily by walking them to

and fro till about the 1st of April, at which time seals begin to
bring forth their young. The bear family then walks forth, the
matron snuffing the air. Perhaps it is charged with seal-scent.
She then follows up the scent till it brings her to a seal igloo.
When she is satisfied that all is right below, she prepares herself,
gives a fearful leap—high and far—striking forcibly with her
paws upon the roof, crushing it in, and seizing the young occupant of the house, soon making of it a dainty feast for the young
polars.

It is a custom among the Innuits, dating from time immemorial, that whoever first sees a Ninoo is entitled to the skin, no
matter whether the fortunate person be man, woman, or child.
If the captured bear be a male, his bladder, with certain instruments belonging to the men, must be placed for three days on
the top of the igloo or tupic. If the bear be a female, her
bladder, with one of the women's brass head-ornaments and some
beads, must be hung in like manner.

The Innuits show a remarkable degree of ingenuity in all the
operations of life, and an astonishing readiness in emergencies.
They thoroughly know their waters and coasts. An illustration
of this is shown in the accompanying *facsimile* of a chart made
by Kooperneung, which I have in my possession.

When travelling with a sledge they are accustomed to coat the
bottom of the runners with ice, thus making a shoe which is
smoother than anything else that could be invented. The manner of performing this operation is curious. The sledge is turned
bottom up, and the Innuit fills his mouth with water in which
has been mingled a little seal's blood, in order to give it tenacity.
He then sends it out in a fine, well-directed, and evenly-applied
stream upon the runner, where it at once congeals. When, after
some hours' travel, the coating is worn away, it is renewed in the
same manner. But the question naturally arises, How can the
water be carried without freezing? The Innuit does this by
filling a bag of sealskin or ookgook bladder, and slipping it
down between his shoulders, under his clothing, the warmth of
his body keeping it liquid.

Once, while I was on a sledge-journey with Koojesse, I was
suffering from thirst, and we had no water. Koojesse turned
aside, and went off with his seal-spear upon a little fresh-water
pond. I knew that the ice there would naturally be ten feet
thick at that season, and therefore wondered how he expected to
find water. After looking about carefully for some time, he selected a place where the snow seemed to be very deep, and there,

ESQUIMAUX CHART, No. II.

DRAWN BY KOOPERNEUNG (CHARLEY) WHILE WE WERE AT CAPE TRUE, AUGUST, 1862.

A. Frobisher Bay.
B. Countess of Warwick's Sound.
C. Lupton Channel, which leads down to Bear Sound.   On the
    right is Lok's Land ; on the left Bache's Peninsula.
D. Cyrus W. Field Bay.
E. Cornelius Grinnell Bay.
F. Robinson Sound.
G. Resolution Isles.
H. Hudson's Strait.
X. Cape True, on Blunt's Peninsula.

after clearing it away, he struck with his spear upon the ice, and very soon made a hole through which he obtained water. When I inquired about it, I learned that a heavy body of snow falling upon the ice would press it down, allowing the water to come up and collect above it. The surface of this collected water would freeze, forming a comparatively thin coating of ice, but leaving a reservoir of water inclosed, which could be easily reached, as I found to my relief.

On another occasion, while travelling in a bitter cold day, facing a cutting breeze, I found great difficulty in keeping the lower parts of my body from freezing. The Innuits saw me trying to shield myself and gain additional warmth by adjusting a thickly-folded scarf; this they took from me, made it into a girdle, and tied it tightly round my body just above the hips. This restored warmth to me at once, and warded off the danger of freezing.

APPENDIX.

I.

The Wreck of the "George Henry."—Page 123.

The following account of the wreck of the *George Henry* appeared in a New London journal, shortly after the occurrence of the disaster to which it relates :—

"Captain Christopher B. Chapell, of Norwich Town, has arrived in the bark *Monticello*, from Hudson's Bay, together with the mate and part of the crew of the bark *George Henry*, of New London, which has been wrecked upon the Lower Savage Islands. She was forced upon the rocks the 16th of July, by strong tides in calm weather, heavily beset by large floes of ice, which, for the lack of wind, rendered the vessel unmanageable, and she became a total wreck. After saving a great quantity of provisions, stores, and other valuable property, Captain Chapell left the island, with his whole crew and officers, in five boats, to make the best of their way toward St. John's, Newfoundland. Leaving the island on the 26th of July, they crossed down to Resolution Island 28th, when a stress of weather, and much ice, caused them to land on the rocks, where they were detained for four days, at the end of which time they launched toward Button Island, on the opposite side of the Straits, distant fifty miles ; but, owing to calms and head-winds, were thrown back near Resolution Island, and surrounded by a pack of ice. This closed together so quick upon their boats that they had but just time enough to haul them up on the ice, and save them from being crushed to pieces. Three of them were slightly stove. They remained on the ice three hours, before it got so still that they could launch with safety, and make for the shore, which the last two boats reached in time to shun a gale which came on suddenly. Here the boats were detained for ten days, both ice and wind bound, and the rain scarcely ceased during the time, making their situation very uncomfortable. On the 10th of August they launched again, and proceeded on the voyage. Owing to lack of wind, they had to toil with oars for twelve hours, when with a breeze came fog and rain, that soon wet and chilled all hands. They then sailed among ice, making a course as well as they could toward Button Island, which they were unable to reach for ice. On the night of the 11th two of the boats got separated in thick, dark weather, and on the morning of the 12th a gale of wind came on, which, together with a high sea, discomfited the boats not a little. Consulting one another how best to proceed for safety, it was decided to run for land, which was distant twenty-five miles. On running toward the land, they came to a heavy pack of ice, through which it was necessary to go, if possible, to reach the land, it being their only way of safety. They sailed on, and fortunately found the ice so slack that the boats could run among it—still heading for the land, which now appeared only about six miles, though it was much farther off, and presented nothing but perpendicular cliffs, up which it would be impossible for man to climb, and no prospect of saving the boats, without which there would be no chance of escape from the barren island, where they might have been delivered from the jaws of the ocean only to starve. So they held another consultation. In all eyes their hope seemed forlorn, and their hearts sank within them as the gale increased and the sea arose. Then all were ready to give up in despair, when, lo! a sail appeared—a tiny sail—and they rejoiced that the lost boats were still afloat. With the aid of a glass they made out a schooner, for which they steered with joyful hearts, and, after a long time, were discovered by her captain and kindly received. It was then found that, two hours before, she had picked up the missing boats. Thus all were providentially drawn together, and delivered out of much danger."

II.

Frobisher's Expeditions.—Page 247.

Frobisher left England on the 15th of June, 1576, with three vessels—the *Gabriel*, a bark of twenty-five tons; the *Michael*, a bark of twenty tons; and a pinnace, of ten tons. On the 11th of July "he had sight of an high and ragged land," which was the southern part of Greenland; but he was kept from landing by ice and fogs. Not far from that point his pinnace, with four men, was lost. "Also the other barke, named the Michael, mistrusting the matter, conveyed themselves privily away from him, and returned home, with great report that he was cast away." Frobisher, nevertheless, went on alone with the *Gabriel*, and after encountering much severe weather, entered the water which he called "Frobisher Strait," now to be known by the name of Frobisher Bay. He shortly after had interviews with the natives, several of whom came on board his vessel. The mariners, trusting them, began to hold open intercourse with the people, and a party of five went on shore in a boat; these were captured by the natives, and the captain could get no intelligence of them during the remainder of the time he spent there. Frobisher then turned his attention to obtaining some tokens of his voyage to carry back with him to England. He lured one of the native men on board, and took him off with him. "Whereupon," says Hakluyt, "when he found himself in captivity, for very choler and disdaine he bit his tongue in twaine within his mouth; notwithstanding, he died not thereof, but lived till he came in England, and then he died of cold which he had taken at sea."

Frobisher reached England, on his return, early in October of that year. Among the relics and tokens he brought home with him was one piece of black stone, of great weight, "much like to a sea cole in colour." This, being accidentally put in the fire, presented an appearance something like gold. Certain refiners of London expressed the opinion that the specimen submitted to them contained gold, and a second expedition was quickly set on foot. This expedition was, as Hakluyt says, "for the searching more of this golde ore than for the searching any further discovery of the passage."

On the 31st of May, 1577, Frobisher set sail on his second voyage, having three vessels—the *Hyde*, of two hundred tons; the *Gabriel*, and the *Michael*—and in due time again entered Frobisher Bay. On the 19th of July he went ashore with a large company of his officers and men, and ascended a high hill, which, with much ceremony, he named Mount Warwick. Two of the Englishmen then had an interview with two of the natives, a great crowd of whom had collected to view the strange spectacle exhibited before them. This interview resulted in trading to a considerable extent. Shortly afterward, Frobisher went with the master of his vessel to hold an interview with two others of the natives, meaning to seize them and carry them on board his vessel, intending to dismiss one with many presents, and to retain the other as an interpreter. They made the attempt at capture as agreed upon, but their feet slipped on the snow, and the natives escaped from their grasp; thereupon turning and attacking the two Englishmen, slightly wounding Frobisher. Some of the ship's company, coming to the others' assistance, captured one of the natives and carried him on board.

On the 26th of July, what was thought to be a very rich mine of ore was discovered in the Countess of Warwick's Sound, and twenty tons of it were got together. On one of the islands in Bear Sound a tomb was found with a white man's bones in it. The captive native, being interrogated by signs, declared that the man had not been killed by the Innuits, but by wolves. In the latter part of July, various portions of the clothing of the missing five men of the first expedition were found in York Sound. The finding of the clothes gave hope that the men were yet alive, and a note was written and left where the relics were discovered. These things having been reported to the others, an expedition was made to the point indicated. When the place was reached, however, all vestiges had disappeared, having clearly been taken away by the natives. The expedition penetrated farther from the shore, and soon came upon a village of tents, the inhabitants of which, to the number of sixteen or eighteen, put to sea in a boat. Being then hardly pressed, the natives went again on shore on a point in York Sound, where they were attacked by the English. In the fight which ensued, five or six of the natives were killed, most of the rest escaping. The party thereupon returned to the ships, carrying with them one of their own men dangerously hurt by an arrow, and a native woman who had been captured.

Then all the vessels returned to the Countess of Warwick's Sound. Not long after, the natives came to treat for the return of the captive woman. Frobisher intimated to them that he demanded first the release and delivery of his five men. The captive man, who acted as interpreter, was at first so much affected at sight once more of his people, that he "fell so out into tears that he could not speake a word in a great space." Then he conferred with them, and afterward assured Frobisher that the men were alive, and should be delivered up; calling on him, moreover, to send them a letter. Therefore a letter was written, and on the 7th of August the natives took it, signifying that in three days they would return. At the appointed time they indeed returned, and showed themselves in small numbers, but yet brought no letter or word from the missing men. Moreover, it was observed that many of them were concealed behind the rocks, and it seemed clear that some treachery was meditated; whereupon the

English prudently kept away from the trap. By the 21st of August, the work of loading the ships with two hundred tons of the ore was finished, and on the 23d sail was made for England.

The show of ore which Frobisher took back to England excited so much enthusiasm for another expedition, that a fleet of fifteen vessels was ready to sail in May, 1578. It was proposed to establish a colony of one hundred persons, who should live through the year on an island in the Countess of Warwick's Sound. This colony was to consist of miners, mariners, soldiers, gold-refiners, bakers, carpenters, &c. A "strong fort or house of timber, artificially framed and cunningly devised by a notable learned man," was to be carried out in the ships, and put up on the island. On the way out, however, one of the barks was sunk, and part of the house was lost.

On the 1st of August the order was given from Frobisher, who had reached the Countess of Warwick's Sound, to disembark from the vessels all the men and stores, and land them on the Countess of Warwick's Island, and to prepare at once for mining. "Then," says Hakluyt, "whilst the Mariners plyed their worke, the Captaines sought out new mynes, the goldfiners made tryall of the Ore," &c. On the 9th, a consultation on the house was held. It was discovered that only the east side and the south side of the building had come safely to hand, the other parts having been either lost or used in repairing the ships, which had been much beaten by storms in the passage. It was then thought, seeing there was not timber enough for a house to accommodate one hundred people, that a house for sixty should be set up. The carpenters, being consulted, declared that they should want five or six weeks to do the work, whereas there remained but twenty-three days before the ships must leave the country; consequently it was determined not to put up the house that year.

On the 30th of August, as Hakluyt says, "the Masons finished a house which Captaine Fenton caused to be made of lyme and stone upon the Countess of Warwick's Island, to the end we might prove, against the next yeere, whether the snow could overwhelme it, the frost break it up, or the people dismember the same." Again: "We buried the timber of our pretended [intended] fort."

The fact that this expedition carried a large quantity of coal is shown by the following extract from Hakluyt, concerning the leakage of water on board the fleet: "The great cause of this leakage and wasting was for that the great timber and sea cole, which lay so weighty upon the barrels, brake, bruised, and rotted the hoopes asunder."

On the last day of August the fleet set sail on its return to England.

The following, upon the same subject, is from the *Gentleman's Magazine* for 1754, vol. xxiv. p. 46:—

"*Philadelphia, Nov. 15.*—Sunday last arrived here the schooner *Argo*, Captain *Charles Swaine*, who sailed from this port last spring on the discovery of the N.W. passage. She fell in with the ice off *Farewell;* left the eastern ice, and fell in with the western ice, in lat. 58, and cruized to the northward to lat. 63 to clear it, but could not, it then extending to the eastward. On her return to the southward, she met with two *Danish* ships bound to *Bull* river and *Discoe,* up *Davis's* streights, who had been in the ice fourteen days, off *Farewell,* and had then stood to westward; and assured the commander that the ice was fast to the shore all above *Hudson's* streights to the distance of 40 leagues out; and that there had not been such a severe winter as the last these 24 years that they had used that trade ; they had been nine weeks from *Copenhagen*. The *Argo*, finding she could not get round the ice, pressed through it, and got into the streight's mouth the 26th of *June* [sic], and made the island Resolution ; but was forced out by vast quantities of driving ice, and got into a clear sea the 1st of *July* [sic]. On the 14th, cruising the ice for an opening to get in again, she met four sail of *Hudson's Bay* ships endeavouring to get in, and continued with them till the 19th, when they parted in thick weather, in lat. 62 and a half, which thick weather coniinued to the 7th of *August ;* the *Hudson's Bay* men supposed themselves 40 leagues from the western land. The *Argo* ran down the ice from 63 to 57.30, and after repeated attempts to enter the streights in vain, as the season for discovery on the western side of the Bay was over, she went in with the *Labrador* coast, and discover'd it perfectly from 56 to 65 ; finding no less than six inlets, to the heads of all which they went, and of which they have made a very good chart, and have a better account of the country, its soil, produce, &c. than has hitherto been publish'd. The captain says 'tis much like *Norway ;* and that there is no communication with *Hudson's Bay* through *Labrador*, where one has been imagined ; a high ridge of mountains running N. and S. about 51 leagues within the coast. In one of the harbours they found a deserted wooden house with a brick chimney, which had been built by some *English*, as appeared by sundry things they left behind ; and afterwards, in another harbour, they met with captain *Goff*, in a snow from *London*, who inform'd [sic] that the same snow had been there last year, and landed some of the *Moravian* brethren, who had built the house ; but the natives having decoyed the then captain of the snow, and five or six of his hands, in their boat, round a point of land at a distance from the snow, under pretence of trade, carried them all off (they having gone imprudently without arms) ; the snow, after waiting sixteen days without hearing of them, went home, and was obliged to take the *Moravians* to help to work the vessel. Part of her business this year was to inquire after those men. Captain *Swaine* discovered a fine fishing-bank, which lies but six leagues off the coast, and extends from lat. 57 to 54, supposed to be the same hinted at in Captain *Davis's* second voyage."

P. 577, [under date] *"Tuesday, 31st Dec.* 1754. * * * The schooner *Argo*, Captain *Swaine*, is arrived at *Philadelphia*, after a second unsuccessful attempt to discover a northwest passage. (*See an account of the first voyage*, p. 46. *See also* p. 542.) "

[On that page, 542, there is merely a list of all voyages to discover a northwest passage, &c. previous to that of the *Argo*.—Hall.)

Macpherson ("The Annals of Commerce, Manufactures, Fisheries, and Navigation," in 4 vols. London, 1805, vol. iii.) says :—

"This summer [Sept. 1722.—H.] some gentlemen in Virginia subscribed for the equipment of a vessel to be sent upon an attempt for a northwest passage. Under their auspices, Captain Wilder sailed in the brig *Diligence* to the lat. 69° 11′, in a large bay which he supposed hitherto unknown. He reported that, from the course of the tides, he thought it very probable that there is a passage, but that it is seldom free of ice, and therefore impassable.* But an *impassable passage* (if such language may be allowed)

---

* This Virginia voyage of discovery had escaped the diligence of Dr. Forster, the historian of voyages and discoveries in the North.

is no passage for ships. But the impossibility of finding such a passage, in any navigable sea, was, at the same time, further demonstrated by the return in this summer of Mr. Hearne, a naval officer then in the service of the Hudson Bay Company," &c. &c.

[Following this is matter that refers to the information the Indians gave Hearne.—Hall.]

III.

The Loss of the Bark "Kitty."—Page 263.

The Bark *Kitty*, of Newcastle, England, sailed from London for Hudson's Bay, on the 21st of June, 1859, and was wrecked on the ice, September 5th in the same year. The wife of the captain, writing to an arctic voyager, with the hope that he might procure some tidings of her husband, thus states the material facts, as reported by the survivors who had returned to England. After mentioning the date of the shipwreck, she continues as follows :—

"The crew, having sufficient time to provide themselves with every necessary they thought prudent to take into their boats, *landed on Saddleback Island*, and remained there four days, during which time they met several natives. They agreed to separate themselves into two boats, and to proceed up the straits in hope of meeting the Company's ships coming down. My husband, Captain Ellis, with ten men in the long-boat, and Mr. Armstrong, chief mate, with four in the skiff, left Saddleback Island on the morning of September 10th, and at night, either from a snow-storm or in the dark, the boats lost sight of each other. The skiff, inshore the next morning, could see nothing of the long-boat. They then proceeded down the straits again, and sailed for the coast of Labrador. After sailing sixty-one days, they were picked up by the Esquimaux and taken to a Moravian missionary settlement. Finally, they arrived at North Shields on the 28th of August, 1860, and since then there has never been any tidings of the missing long-boat and her crew."

The following, on the same subject, is from the *London Times* of Nov. 17th, 1862 :—

"MURDER OF BRITISH SEAMEN.—In September, 1859, the *Kitty*, of Newcastle, was lost in Hudson's Straits by being nipped in the ice. Five of her crew, who got into a small boat, after enduring great suffering by exposure to the cold, succeeded in reaching a Moravian missionary station, where they were hospitably entertained, and three of them sent to their homes in England next summer. But of the fate of the master of this vessel, Mr. Ellis, and the remainder of the crew, who left the ship in a long-boat, nothing has been heard until the arrival of the vessels from the Hudson's Bay stations this autumn, when the sad intelligence has been brought that the eleven poor fellows fell into the hands of unfriendly Esquimaux, and were murdered for the sake of their blankets. The missionaries at Okak, writing to the widow of the master of the vessel in August last, say, 'It is with grief, madam, we must inform you that it is, alas! only too true that the long-boat, with her master and crew, arrived at Ungava Bay, but that none of the men survive. Last winter, Esquimaux from Ungava Bay visited our northernmost settlement, Hebron, who related that in the winter of 1859-60, several Europeans in a boat landed at the island called Apatok, in Ungava Bay. They lived with the Esquimaux until about January, upon what the latter could provide for them ; but then, most likely when their provisions became short, the Esquimaux attacked them when they were asleep and killed them, stabbing them with their knives. There is no doubt of these really being the men from the *Kitty*, because the Esquimaux knew there had been another boat, with five men belonging to them, whom they deemed lost. They said one man of the murdered company had very frostbitten feet, and him the Esquimaux would not kill by stabbing, but showed him a kind of heathen mercy, as they put him in the open air until he was dead by severe cold.' It seems that these unfortunate men had been murdered for the sake of the blankets they had with them. It would appear that one of the Esquimaux wanted to save the three Europeans who lodged with him, but they met the same fate as their companions. The tribe who have committed this murder do not appear to have been brought in contact with the European missions ; and the friendly tribe who brought the information into Hebron further informed the Moravian missionaries at that place that a little farther north from Ungava Bay, a whole crew, consisting in all of about forty men, were enticed on shore and then killed by the Esquimaux."

IV.

Mineralogical and Geological Specimens.—Page 367.

The following is from *Silliman's Journal* of March, 1863 : —

"*Report on the Geological and Mineralogical Specimens collected by* Mr. C. F. Hall *in Frobisher Bay.*

"To the New York Lyceum of Natural History :—

" One of your Committee, appointed to examine the collection of minerals and fossils made by Mr. Charles F. Hall in his late Arctic Exploring Expedition, begs leave to report that he found the collection of fossils small in number of individual specimens, and limited in the range of its species, but possessing great interest to the student of arctic geology.

"The specimens are as follows :—

"*Maclurea magna* (Lesueur).	No. of specimens		7
Casts of lower surface.	,,	,,	3
Endoceras proteiforme? (Hall).	,,	,,	1
Orthoceras (badly worn specimens).	,,	,,	3
Heliolites (new species).	,,	,,	2
Heliopora ,, ,,	,,	,,	1
Halysites catenulata (Fischer).	,,	,,	1
Receptaculites (new species).	,,	,,	1

" This collection was made at the head of Frobisher Bay, lat. 63° 44′ N. and long. 68° 56′ W. from Greenwich, at a point which, Mr. Hall says, is ' a mountain of fossils,' similar to the limestone bluff at Cincinnati, with which he is familiar. This limestone rests upon mica schist, specimens of which he also brought from the same locality. Whether the limestone was conformable to the schist or not, Mr. Hall did not determine. It is much to be regretted that this interesting point was not examined by him, as it is doubtful whether this locality may ever be visited by any future explorer.

"The fossils, without doubt, are all Lower Silurian. The *Maclurea magna* would place the limestone containing it on the horizon of the Chazy limestone of New York. The *Halysites catenulata* has been found in Canada in the Trenton beds, but in New York not lower than the Niagara limestone. The *Endoceras proteiforme* belongs to the Trenton limestone. The *Receptaculites* is unlike the several species of the Galena limestone of the West, or the *R. occidentalis* of Canada. Mr. Salter speaks of one found in the northern part of the American continent. This may be that species, or it may be a new one; which it was we have no means of determining. The *Orthocerata* were but fragments, and so badly water-worn that the species could not be identified.

"The specimens of corals were very perfect and beautiful, and unlike any figured by Professor Hall in the Palæontology of New York. The *Heliolites* and *Heliopora* belong to the Niagara group in New York, but in Canada they have been found in the Lower Silurian. For the identification of strata, corals are not always reliable. Whether these species are similar or identical with any in the Canadian collection, it was out of my power to determine. They are unlike any figured by Mr. I. W. Salter.

"R. P. STEVENS.

"One of the Committee appointed to examine the mineral specimens brought from Frobisher Bay by Mr. Hall, reports that the specimens, though quite numerous, were mostly of the same general character. The rocks were nearly all mica schist. Some of the specimens were taken from boulders; some from the ruins of houses, and had the mortar still attached; and some were from the rock in its natural position. There was nothing peculiar in the rock, it presenting the usual variations in composition. The other specimens were an argillaceous limestone, determined by its fossils to be Lower Silurian; a single specimen of quartz, crystallized, and presenting, besides the usual six-sided termination, another pyramid whose angle was much more obtuse; magnetic iron, some of which was found *in situ*, and other specimens which were evidently boulders, and had undergone for some time the action of salt-water; a few pieces of iron pyrites, bituminous coal, and nodules of flint or jasper. . . . . .

"[The part of this report omitted gives reasons for believing the coal and siliceous nodules to have been brought from England by Frobisher, who, it is well known, took out large supplies and many miners, expecting to mine and smelt ores. Some 'blooms' of iron which Mr. Hall found may have been the result of their operations with the magnetic iron.— EDS.]

". . . . This theory is supported by the tradition of the natives, who say that the coal was brought there by the foreigners,[*] as well as by the entire absence of any indications of geological strata so high up in the series as the Carboniferous formation. The siliceous pebbles seem to have served as gravel for the mortar used in building the houses for carrying on the various objects for which the expedition was sent out. No trace of any mineral containing silver existed in the collections. The sands sup-

---

[*] Everything that seems to them peculiar they refer to this source.

posed by Mr. Hall to be those in which Frobisher found gold have not yet been assayed. A small bead detached from an ornament worn by the natives was found to be lead.

" Thos. Egleston."

V.

Arctic Sledge.—Page 455.

The sledge which I had made in Cincinnati, and took with me on my expedition to the North, was made after the sledge "Faith," the favourite sledge of Dr. Kane on his last expedition. The only difference between his and my sledge was as follows :—Dr. Kane's was 3 feet 8 inches wide, while mine was only 2 feet 6 inches. The shoeing of Dr. Kane's was three-sixteenths-inch steel, while the shoeing of mine, on arriving at the North, was slabs of the jawbone of the whale (the article used by the natives), 1 inch thick and $3\frac{1}{2}$ inches wide.

The dimensions of the "Faith" (of Dr. Kane's) were as follows :—

	ft.	in.
Length of runner	13	0
Height of ditto	0	8
Horizontal width of rail	0	$2\frac{3}{4}$
,, ,, base of runner	0	$3\frac{1}{4}$
,, ,, other parts	0	2
Thickness of all parts	0	$1\frac{1}{4}$
Length, resting on a plain surface	6	0
Cross-bars, five in number, making a width of	3	8

THE END.